Lecture Notes in Artificial Intelligence 3673

Edited by J. G. Carbonell and J. Siekmann

Subseries of Lecture Notes in Computer Science

T0181966

Stefania Bandini   Sara Manzoni (Eds.)

AI*IA 2005:
Advances in
Artificial Intelligence

9th Congress of the
Italian Association for Artificial Intelligence
Milan, Italy, September 21-23, 2005
Proceedings

 Springer

Series Editors

Jaime G. Carbonell, Carnegie Mellon University, Pittsburgh, PA, USA
Jörg Siekmann, University of Saarland, Saarbrücken, Germany

Volume Editors

Stefania Bandini
Sara Manzoni
University of Milano-Bicocca
Department of Computer Science, Systems and Communication (DISCo)
Via Bicocca degli Arcimboldi, 8, 20126 Milano, Italy
E-mail: {bandini, manzoni}@disco.unimib.it

Library of Congress Control Number: 2005932554

CR Subject Classification (1998): I.2, F.1, F.4.1

ISSN   0302-9743
ISBN-10   3-540-29041-9 Springer Berlin Heidelberg New York
ISBN-13   978-3-540-29041-4 Springer Berlin Heidelberg New York

Springer is a part of Springer Science+Business Media

springeronline.com

© Springer-Verlag Berlin Heidelberg 2005
Printed in Germany

Typesetting: Camera-ready by author, data conversion by Scientific Publishing Services, Chennai, India
Printed on acid-free paper   SPIN: 11558590   06/3142   5 4 3 2 1 0

Preface

This volume collects the papers selected for presentation at the IX Congress of the Italian Association for Artificial Intelligence (AI*IA), held in Milan at the University of Milano–Bicocca (September 21–23, 2005). On the one hand this congress continues the tradition of AI*IA in organizing its biannual scientific meeting from 1989; on the other hand, this edition is a landmark in the involvement of the international community of artificial intelligence (AI), directly involving a broad number of experts from several countries in the Program Committee. Moreover, the peculiar nature of scientific research in artificial intelligence (which is intrinsically international) and several consolidated international collaborations in projects and mobility programs allowed the collection and selection of papers from many different countries, all around the world, enlarging the visibility of the Italian contribution within this research field.

Artificial intelligence is today a growing complex set of conceptual, theoretical, methodological, and technological frameworks, offering innovative computational solutions in the design and development of computer-based systems. Within this perspective, researchers working in this area must tackle a broad range of knowledge about methods, results, and solutions coming from different classical areas of this discipline. The congress was designed as a forum allowing researchers to present and discuss specialized results as general contributions to AI growth.

In order to give a novel perspective in which both theoretical and application aspects of AI contribute to the growth of the area, this book mirrors the structure of the congress, grouping the papers into four main categories: (1) Theoretical Research: Results and Proposals; (2) Theoretical Research: Improvements and Consolidations; (3) Applications: Systems and Prototypes; (4) Applications: Case Studies and Proposals. Within this classification some of the main classical topics of artificial intelligence are presented (agents, knowledge representation, machine learning, planning, robotics, natural language, . . .), but here the emphasis is on the ability of AI computational approaches to face challenging problems and to propose innovative solutions.

The book contains 46 full papers (6 for the first category, 18 for the second, 15 for the third, and 7 for the fourth) and 16 short papers (for the four categories, respectively 3, 6, 4, and 3).

Many people contributed to the success of the congress and the creation of this volume, from the initial idea to its implementation. My first acknowledgement is to the General Board of AI*IA which offered me the opportunity to chair this congress. Then I thank the President of the Association (Marco Gori) for starting suggestions, all the scientists who submitted their work, and all Program Committee members and reviewers for their collaboration. A special thanks to Luigia Carlucci Aiello for her indispensable, kind, friendly and continuous consultation on the most heterogeneous aspects I met during the path. Finally, a special thanks also to the University of Milano–Bicocca for hospitality and its generous contribution in the realization of this volume.

A particular acknowledgement to all the people of the Artificial Intelligence Lab (L.INT.AR.) of the University of Milano–Bicocca, and to the "official" Local Organization Committee (Fabio Zanzotto, Federica Sartori, Fabio Sartori, Mizar Luca Federici, Alessandro Mosca, Matteo Palmonari, Davide Ungari) whose work was the fundamental contribution to the actual success of the event. Moreover, I want to thank the Department of Computer Science, Systems and Communication of my university, and those companies that financially supported the congress: AISoftware (F. Gardin), Akhela (P. Ravasio), Aletheia (F. Rebuffo), Gruppo Fabbri (F. Fabbri, A. Caruso), illycaffè (E. Illy, F. Suggi Liverani).

Finally, my gratitude for the constant, indispensable, and precious support in all the development steps of the congress to Sara Manzoni, the co-editor of this volume.

July 2005   Stefania Bandini
                               Director, Artificial Intelligence Lab (L.INT.AR.)
                                       Dept. of Computer Science, Systems
                                          and Communication (DISCo)
                                          University of Milano–Bicocca

Organization

AI*IA 2005 was organized by the Artificial Intelligence Lab (L.INT.AR.) of the Department of Computer Science, Systems and Communication (DISCo) of the University of Milano–Bicocca, in cooperation with the Italian Association for Artificial Intelligence (AI*IA).

Congress Organization

Congress Chair	Stefania Bandini
Local Organization	Fabio Zanzotto (Chair), Fabio Sartori, Federica Sartori, Mizar Luca Federici, Sara Manzoni, Alessandro Mosca, Matteo Palmonari, Davide Ungari
Workshop	Fabio Sartori (Chair), Matteo Palmonari

Program Committee

Stefania Bandini	University of Milano–Bicocca (Italy)
Luigia Carlucci Aiello	University of Rome "La Sapienza" (Italy)
Jean-Francois Boulicaut	INSA — Lyon (France)
Ernesto Burattini	University of Napoles (Italy)
Marie-Odile Cordier	University of Rennes (France)
Floriana Esposito	University of Bari (Italy)
Lee Giles	Pennsylvania State University (USA)
Martin Golumbic	University of Haifa (Israel)
Marco Gori	University of Siena (Italy)
Owen Holland	University of Essex (UK)
Lawrence Hunter	University of Colorado (USA)
Joost Kok	Leiden University (The Netherlands)
Sara Manzoni	University of Milano–Bicocca (Italy)
Giancarlo Mauri	University of Milano–Bicocca (Italy)
Peter McBurney	University of Liverpool (UK)
Andrea Omicini	University of Bologna (Italy)
Maria Teresa Pazienza	University of Rome "Tor Vergata" (Italy)
Paolo Petta	Austrian Research Institute for AI (Austria)
Erik Sandewall	Linköping University (Sweden)
Flavio Soares da Silva	University of Sao Paulo (Brazil)
Giovanni Soda	University of Florence (Italy)
Steffen Staab	University of Koblenz-Landau (Germany)

Oliviero Stock   IRST — Trento (Italy)
Furio Suggi Liverani   illycaffè — Trieste (Italy)
Pietro Torasso   University of Turin (Italy)
Franco Turini   University of Pisa (Italy)
Achille Varzi   Columbia University (USA)

Referees

Luigia Carlucci Aiello   Claudio Giuliano   Rene Quiniou
Maurizio Atzori   Martin Golumbic   Christoph Ringelstein
Stefania Bandini   Marco Gori   Carsten Saathoff
Miriam Baglion   Giorgio Grisetti   Erik Sandewall
Roberto Bisiani   Owen Holland   Matteo Santoro
Jean-Francois Boulicaut   Lawrence Hunter   Marco Schaerf
Roberto Brunelli   Luca Iocchi   Raimondo Schettini
Ernesto Burattini   Joost Kok   Dino Seppi
Marco Cadoli   Milen Kouylekov   Flavio Soares da Silva
Alessio Ceroni   Riccardo Leone   Giovanni Soda
Amedeo Cesta   Francesca A. Lisi   Steffen Staab
Ettore Colombo   Sara Manzoni   Armando Stellato
Paolo Coraggio   Giancarlo Mauri   Oliviero Stock
Marie-Odile Cordier   Peter McBurney   Carlo Strapparava
Fabrizio Costa   Alessandro Mosca   Bernhard Tausch
Stefania Costantini   Matteo Negri   Pietro Torasso
Claudia D'Amato   Andrea Omicini   Franco Turini
Nicola Di Mauro   Matteo Palmonari   Alexandre Vautier
Floriana Esposito   Andrea Passerini   Giuseppe Vizzari
Daniele Falavigna   Maria Teresa Pazienza   Fabio Zanzotto
Nicola Fanizzi   Giovanna Petrone
Alessandro Farinelli   Paolo Petta
Stefano Ferilli   Silvana Quaglini

Sponsors

AISoftware S.p.A., Milano
Akhela s.r.l., Cagliari
Aletheia s.r.l., Milano
Department of Computer Science, Systems and Communication (DISCo),
    University of Milano–Bicocca, Milan
Gruppo Fabbri S.p.A., Vignola (MO)
illycaffè, Trieste

Table of Contents

Theoretical Research: Results and Proposals

Theoretical Research: Improvements and Consolidations

Applications: Systems and Prototypes

Applications: Case Studies and Proposals

The Complexity of Action Redundancy

Andrea Ferrara, Paolo Liberatore, and Marco Schaerf

Dipartimento di Informatica e Sistemistica, Università di Roma "La Sapienza",
Roma, Italy
{ferrara, liberato, schaerf}@dis.uniroma1.it,

Abstract. An action is redundant in a planning domain if it is not
needed to reach the goal. In this paper, we study the computational
complexity of some problems related to the redundancy of actions: checking whether a domain contains a redundant action, what is the minimal
number of actions needed to make the goal reachable, checking whether
the removal of an action does not increase the minimal plan length, etc.

1 Introduction

Most problems in planning, like plan existence and plan generation, are problems
on a fixed planning domain: the initial states, goal, and possible actions are
assumed fixed and cannot be modified. This assumption is not always necessary:
there are cases in which the domain can be—to some extent—modified. In this
paper, we study some problems about the removal of actions from the domain.
For example, the problem of whether an action is necessary to reach the goal
makes sense whenever there is some gain in not performing an action at all.

It is important to remark that we are not checking whether an action can
be removed from a single plan [1,2,3], a problem that arises naturally in the
context of plan abstraction [4,5]. Rather, we are checking whether an action
can be removed at all from the domain. Such a problem makes sense in several
situations:

Design: if the planning instance is the formalization of a system that is yet to
   be built, it makes sense to consider whether some actions can be removed,
   as this may correspond to the simplification of the design;
Reliability: in some system, operation must be warranted regardless of faults;
   since the effect of faults on a planning instance is to make some actions non-
   executable, then all actions should be redundant to ensure that the system
   will work properly in all cases;
Solving: the cost of solving a planning instance is often related to the number
   of possible actions; knowing that a specific action is not really needed may
   simplify the planning generation problem (this is the motivation behind the
   work of Nebel, Dimopolous, and Koehler [6].)

It is important to note that solving the problem of action redundancy is done
before the plan is generated. We are not considering the problem of removing an

S. Bandini and S. Manzoni (Eds.): AI*IA 2005, LNAI 3673, pp. 1–12, 2005.

action from a plan after that the plan has been found, which has already been studied [1,2]; rather, we are considering the problem of the possible removal of an action before any plan is generated. In other words, the problem is not to establish the redundancy of an action in a plan, but the redundancy of an action in a planning domain. There are scenarios in which the problem of redundancy in a plan makes sense, and others in which redundancy in a domain is relevant.

Various problems are considered. First, we consider problems related to actions only: given a set of actions, is there any action that can be simulated by the other ones? In other words, is there any action that is redundant? In this case, we are not (yet) considering a specific initial state nor a specific goal. This question is therefore of interest whenever either we do not have yet an initial state or goal, or we want to study the problem for all possible initial states or goals. We call these problems Absolute Action Redundancy.

We also consider some problems about planning domains in which the initial states and goal are fixed. Actually, **the most relevant case is that in which the initial states and the goals are only partially known; however, the complexity results for the case of full knowledge carry on to the case of partial knowledge of the initial state and the goal.** The problems considered for this case are: is a specific action redundant (Single Specific Action Redundancy)? is there any action that can be removed (Single Action Redundancy)? and problems related to finding a minimal set of actions.

In this paper, we study the computational complexity of these problem. An assumption we make is that all actions have the same cost, so that minimality is considered in terms of the number of actions. Another implicit assumption is that all actions are independent, in the sense that it is possible to remove a single one of them from the domain. These assumptions are not always realistic: for example, it may be that two actions are both executed by the same part of a system: the relevant problem is whether this part is necessary, which is equivalent to the redundancy of both actions. These extensions of the problems considered in this paper are under investigation.

The paper is organized as follows. In the next section, we introduce the notion of redundancy and define the problems we study. We assume that notions of computational complexity and planning are known. In the third section we give some preliminary results that will be used in the complexity analysis. In the fourth section we show the complexity of problems related to redundancy. We conclude the paper by comparing with work in the literature.

2   Definitions

In this paper, we consider propositional STRIPS instances [7]. Its many extensions are not considered in this paper, but are under investigation. A STRIPS instance is a quadruple $\langle P, O, I, G \rangle$ where P is a set of conditions (a.k.a. facts, fluents, or variables), O is a set of operators (a.k.a. actions), I is the initial state, and G is the goal. A state is a subset of P: the state of the domain at some point is represented by the set of conditions that are true. An action is composed of four parts: the positive and negative preconditions and the positive and negative postconditions. These are simply the conditions that must be true or false to make the action executable, and the conditions that are made true or false by the execution of the action. The initial state is a state (the initial state is therefore fully known), while the goal is represented by a set of conditions that must be made true and a set that must be made false.

A plan is a sequence of actions that are executable in sequence from the initial state and lead to a state satisfying the goal. We use the following notation: $\mathcal{P}(\langle P, O, I, G \rangle)$ is the set of plans of the instance $\langle P, O, I, G \rangle$. Clearly, this set can be empty. Given a plan p, we denote by p_i its i-th action. In some cases, we are also interested into the minimal plan length, i.e., the length of the shortest plans. Redundancy is defined as follows.

Definition 1 (Redundant Action). *An action is redundant for a planning instance $\langle P, O, I, G \rangle$ iff there is a plan not containing it.*

In other words, a is redundant if $\langle P, O \backslash \{a\}, I, G \rangle$ has plans. Necessary actions are actions that cannot be removed from the planning instance if one wants goal to still exist.

Definition 2 (Necessary Action). *An action is necessary for $\langle P, O, I, G \rangle$ iff it is contained in all of plans of $\langle P, O, I, G \rangle$.*

Redundant actions are actions that can be removed while some plans still exist. In other words, for an action to be redundant we only require the action not to be in some plans. A stronger notion is that of useless action: actions that are not contained in any plan.

Definition 3 (Useless Action). *An action is useless for a planning instance $\langle P, O, I, G \rangle$ iff it is not part of any plan.*

We now describe the problem we consider. In the following, we assume that the initial state and the goal are either fully specified or not specified at all. Clearly, the most interesting problems are those in which these two parts of the domain are only partially specified. The reason for not considering this case is simply that all hardness proofs extend from the fully specified to the partially specified case, and that the membership proofs are easy to extend because non-deterministic polynomial space is equal to polynomial space. In other words, the restriction to the fully specified case is done only for the sake of simplicity, but all results carry on the more interesting case of partial specification.

First we consider the problems about the redundancy of actions in an instance.

Single Specific Action Redundancy. Given a planning instance $\langle P, O, I, G \rangle$ and an action $a \in O$, is a redundant in $\langle P, O, I, G \rangle$?

Single Action Redundancy. Given a planning instance $\langle P, O, I, G \rangle$, is there a redundant action in O?

The latter problem is similar to the former, but we are not checking whether a specific action is redundant but whether there is a redundant action in O.

While the two above problems are about the redundancy of actions for a given initial state and goal, we also consider the redundancy of actions when neither the initial state nor the goal are specified.

Absolute Specific Action Redundancy
Given: $\langle P, O \rangle$ and an action $a \in O$
Question: is a redundant? In other words, is it true that $\langle P, O, I, G \rangle$ has plans if and only if $\langle P, O \backslash \{a\}, I, G \rangle$ has plans for every I and G?

Absolute Action Redundancy
Given: $\langle P, O \rangle$
Question: is there any redundant action in O?

The following problems are related to minimizing the number of actions.

Minimal Number of Actions
Given: a planning instance $\langle P, O, I, G \rangle$ and an integer k with $k < |O|$
Question: do $O_k \subset O$, where $|O_k| = k$, exist s.t. $\langle P, O_k, I, G \rangle$ has plans?

Minimal Set of Actions
Given: a planning instance $\langle P, O, I, G \rangle$ and $O' \subset O$
Question: is O' minimal? (minimal = does not contain any redundant action)

Specific Action of a Minimal Set
Given: a planning instance $y = \langle P, O, I, G \rangle$ and $a \in O$
Question: is a in a minimal subset of $O' \subset O$ such that $\langle P, O', I, G \rangle$ has plans?

Finally, we consider four problems related to the length of plans.

Plan Length for a Specific Action Subset
Given: a planning instance $y = \langle P, O, I, G \rangle$ and $O' \subset O$
Question: does $y' = \langle P, O', I, G \rangle$ have a plan of the same length of the shortest plans for y?

Plan Length for an Action Subset
Given: a planning instance $y = \langle P, O, I, G \rangle$
Question: does $O' \subset O$ exist s.t. $y' = \langle P, O', I, G \rangle$ has a plan of the same length of the shortest plans for y?

Plan Length Increase for a Specific Action Subset
Given: a planning instance $y = \langle P, O, I, G \rangle$, $O' \subset O$, and an integer $c > 0$
Question: does $y' = \langle P, O', I, G \rangle$ have a plan of length $l + c$ where l is the length of the shortest plans for y?

Plan Length Increase for an Action Subset
Given: a planning instance $y = \langle P, O, I, G \rangle$ and an integer $c > 0$
Question: does $O' \subset O$ exist s.t. $y' = \langle P, O', I, G \rangle$ has a plan of length $l + c$ where l is the length of the shortest plans for y?

3   General Results

Some results that are used in more than one proof are reported here. The first of these results is that two planning instances can be combined in such a way the plans of the resulting instance are related to the plans of the two original ones.

Formally, we are given two planning instances built on disjoint sets of conditions and operators. The disjunction of these two planning instances is defined as follows.

Definition 4. *The disjunction of $\langle P_1, O_1, I_1, G_1 \rangle$ and $\langle P_2, O_2, I_2, G_2 \rangle$ is $\langle P, O, I, G \rangle$, where:*

$$P = P_1 \cup P_2 \cup \{x\}$$
$$O = O_1 \cup O_2 \cup \{o_1, o_2\}$$
$$I = I_1 \cup I_2$$
$$G = \langle \{x\}, \emptyset \rangle$$

where $\{x\}$ is a new condition and $\{o_1, o_2\}$ are new operators; o_1 has G_1 as precondition and x as a positive postcondition, while o_2 has G_2 as precondition and x as a positive postcondition.

The plans of $\langle P, O, I, G \rangle$ are the plans of $\langle P_1, O_1, I_1, G_1 \rangle$ with o_1 added at the end, the plans of $\langle P_2, O_2, I_2, G_2 \rangle$ with o_2 at the end, plus any other sequence that is obtained by interleaving other actions to these plans. In a way, the new planning instance is a "disjunction" of the original instances, as it has all plans of both. The minimal plans of the disjunction are exactly the shortest of the plans of the two instances.

The second result we prove is that a planning instance can be modified in such a way the resulting instance always have plans composed of all operators, in addition to the plans of the original one.

Definition 5. *The maximized versions of a STRIPS instance $\langle P, O, I, G \rangle$ is the instance $\langle P \cup Y \cup Z \cup \{w\}, B \cup C \cup \{d\}, I, G' \rangle$, where Y and Z are sets of new variables of the same cardinality of O, w is a new variable, B and C are sets of new actions of the same cardinality of O, and d is a new action. The goal G' is similar to G, but it also requires w to be false. The effects of the actions are: c_i is the same as a_i, but also makes y_i true; b_i has no precondition, but makes z_i, w, and the preconditions of c_i true. Finally, d is only applicable if all variables $Y \cup Z$ are true and makes the goal satisfied.*

This instance has plans: the sequence $[b_1, c_1, \ldots, b_m, c_m]$ makes all variables $Y \cup Z$ true; the application of d therefore makes the goal reached. In order for this plan to work, no action can be removed from it: removing d leads to having w true in the final state; on the other hand, d is only applicable if all variables $Y \cup Z$ are true, which can be accomplished only if all actions $B \cup C$ have been applied at least once.

On the other hand, if the original instance is satisfiable, then the plans of the original instance can be mapped into plans of this new one just be replacing each a_i with the corresponding c_i. No other sequence of actions is a plan: if a sequence contains any of the b_i, then it has to contain d as well, as b_i makes w true and d is the only action that makes it false, as required by the goal. In turn, d is applicable only if all variables in $Y \cup Z$ are true, which means that all actions $B \cup C$ must been applied beforehand.

Some of the proofs use a planning instance whose minimal plans are of exponential length. Such instances are known. We do not report how these instances are made because of the lack of space.

4   Complexity of Action Redundancy

In this section, we characterize the complexity of the problems we have introduced. Most of these problems are easy to be proved in PSPACE, as they can be solved by solving a number of regular planning problems, such as plan existence of planning size, that are known to be in PSPACE. The difficult part of their complexity characterization, indeed, is the hardness part.

The first problem we consider is the Single Specific Action Redundancy. The redundancy of a single specific action has been called *complete irrelevance* by Nebel, Dimopolous, and Koehler [6], who proved the following theorem.

Theorem 1 ([6]). *Single Specific Action Redundancy is* PSPACE-*complete.*

Proof. Nebel, Dimopolous, and Koehler [6] proved this theorem in the general form. We can however prove the hardness part even if the instance is guaranteed to have plans.

*M*embership. The problem amounts to remove the specific action under consideration and check the resulting domain for plan existence. Since the latter problem is in PSPACE, the problem can be solved in polynomial space.

*H*ardness. We reduce the problem of planning to the one under consideration. Given a planning instance $\langle P, O, I, G \rangle$, we reduce it to $\langle P, O \cup \{a\}, I, G \rangle$, where a is a new action that has no preconditions and makes the goal satisfied as postcondition. Checking the redundancy of a in this new instance is the same as checking whether the original instance has a plan or not. As a result, the problem is PSPACE-hard.   □

A related question is: given a planning instance for which we *know* a plan, does the removal of a cause the domain not to have plans any more? This problem is still PSPACE-complete.

The following result is about the existence of a redundant action in a plan.

Theorem 2. *Single Action Redundancy is* PSPACE-*complete.*

Proof. Membership. This is the problem of checking whether a planning instance contains an action that can be removed. In other words, it is equivalent to solve the Single Specific Action Redundancy for all actions. Since solving each of these problems is in PSPACE, the problem of Single Action Redundancy is in PSPACE as well.

Hardness. Proved by reduction from the problem of plan existence. Given a STRIPS instance for which we want to establish the plan existence, we build its maximized version. This maximized version is an instance that has the same plans of the original instance plus some plans composed of all actions. If the original instance does not have plans, the maximized version has only the plans composed of all actions; as a result, no action is redundant. If the original instance has some plans, even if they contains all actions, the maximized version has the same plans, which however do not contain the action d because this action is not present in the original instance. As a result, the modified instance contains a redundant action if and only if the original instance has plans.   □

Let us now consider the problems of absolute redundancy. These are the problems of checking redundancy of actions when neither the initial state nor the goal are known. As for the case of (non-absolute) redundancy, we consider first the redundancy of a single specific action and then the presence of a redundant action.

Theorem 3. *Absolute Specific Action Redundancy is PSPACE-complete.*

Proof. Membership. We are given a set of actions O, and want to check whether an action $a \in O$ is not necessary for whatever initial state and goal. In other words, for any possible I and G, we have to check whether the existence of plans $\langle P, O, I, G \rangle$ implies the existence of plans in $\langle P, O \backslash \{a\}, I, G \rangle$. The problem can be therefore solved by nondeterministically guessing I and G and then solving a problem in PSPACE. The problem is therefore in PSPACE.

Hardness. We show a polynomial reduction from the problem of checking the existence of a plan for the instance $\langle P, O, I, G \rangle$. We build the Absolute Specific Action Redundancy instance $\langle P, O \cup a \rangle$ where a is a new action that is only executable in the state I and has postcondition G. Clearly, this action a is redundant if and only if the goal can be reached from the initial state.   □

Theorem 4. *Absolute Action Redundancy is PSPACE-Complete.*

Proof. Membership. We solve the Absolute Specific Action Redundancy problem for each of the actions in O. Since we solve a polynomial number of problems that can all be solved in polynomial space, the problem is in PSPACE.

Hardness. We show a polynomial reduction from Absolute Specific Action Redundancy. Let the instance of this problem be $\langle P, O \rangle$ where $O = \{a_1, .., a_n, a\}$ and a is the "candidate" redundant action. The idea of the reduction is to make all actions but a irredundant. To this aim, we consider an action a'_i for each a_i: this action has the same preconditions and postconditions of a_i plus a new postcondition y_i. The instance we build is $\langle P \cup \{y_1, .., y_n\}, O' \rangle$ where $O' = \{a'_1, .., a'_n, a\}$. None of the actions a'_i is redundant, as a'_i is the only action that makes y_i true. As a result, a is redundant for $\langle P, O \rangle$ iff $\langle P \cup \{y_1, .., y_n\}, O' \rangle$ contains a redundant action.   □

Let us now consider the problems related to minimality. The first one is that of checking the existence of a group of k actions that are sufficient for building a plan. It is easy to see that this problem is not the same as checking the existence of a plan of length k, as an action may occur more than once in a plan. In other words, we are checking the plans of a minimal number of actions, not the plans of minimal length.

Theorem 5. *Minimal Number of Actions is* PSPACE-*Complete.*

Proof. Membership. Guess a subset of $O' \subseteq O$ composed of k actions, and check the existence of plans for the instance in which there are only actions O'. Since the problem can be solved by a nondeterministic guessing followed by the solution of a PSPACE problem, the problem is in NPSPACE and is therefore in PSPACE.

Hardness. We show a polynomial reduction from Single Action Redundancy. The instance $\langle P, O, I, G \rangle$ contains a redundant action if and only if there exists a set of $k = |O| - 1$ that are sufficient to make the goal reachable. $\square$

Checking whether a set of actions is minimal is the complementary problem of Single Action Redundancy: a set of actions is minimal if and only if it does not contain any redundant action.

Corollary 1. *Minimal Set of Actions is* PSPACE-*complete.*

We now consider the problem of checking whether an action is in some minimal set of actions.

Theorem 6. *Specific Action of a Minimal Set is* PSPACE-*complete.*

Proof. Hardness. For each $O' \subseteq O$, we check whether this set of actions is sufficient for the existence of a plan; if it is, we check it for minimality; if it is minimal, we check whether $a \in O'$. This algorithm requires only a polynomial amount of space.

Hardness. We show a reduction from the problem of plan existence. Given a STRIPS instance, we build its maximized version, and check whether d is in some minimal set of actions. The plans of the maximized version are composed of all actions plus any plan of the original instance. As a result, if the original instance has no plans, then no action is redundant. On the other hand, if the original instance has plans, then the goal is reachable even if the action d is removed. As a result, d is not in any minimal set of actions. $\square$

The problem of redundancy considered so far are about whether actions can be removed from a domain while preserving the plan existence. We now consider the problem of whether the removal of actions increases the length of the minimal plans.

Theorem 7. *Plan Length for a Specific Action Subset is* PSPACE-*Complete.*

Proof. Membership. Find the minimal plan length for both the original instance and the instance without the actions to remove. Both problems can be solved in polynomial space.

Hardness. Given an instance $\langle P, O, I, G \rangle$ with n conditions, we build the composition of this instance with a planning instance that is known to have plans longer than 2^n. The resulting instance has plans that are made of plans of $\langle P, O, I, G \rangle$ followed by the action o_1 plus plans of the exponential-plan instance followed by o_2 (plus other plans that are obtained by interleaving these plans with other actions.)

We can now exploit the fact that $\langle P, O, I, G \rangle$ has plans if and only if it has plans of length bounded by 2^n. As a result, the minimal plans of the composed instances are those of $\langle P, O, I, G \rangle$ followed by o_1 if this instance is satisfiable, or the plans of the second instance followed by o_2 otherwise. As a result, removing o_1 leads to an increase of the minimal plan length if and only if the instance $\langle P, O, I, G \rangle$ has plans. □

The following theorem is about the similar problem in which there is no specific set of actions to remove: we are only checking whether some actions can be removed without increasing the minimal plan length.

Theorem 8. *Plan Length for an Action Subset is* PSPACE-*Complete.*

Proof. Membership. Check the minimal plan length for the original instance and for all instances obtained from it by removing some actions. All these problems can be solved in polynomial space.

Hardness. Proved by reduction from plan existence. We modify the planning instance in such a way a plan composed of all actions always exists. We then create the translation of this instance on a new alphabet, with the only exception that d is replaced by two actions a and b, which have the same effect when executed in sequence. Finally, we compose the two planning instances, making sure that the actions o_1 and o_2 are duplicated.

This instance is built in such a way that every action can be removed without increasing the plan length. There is however an exception: if all minimal plans contain d, then the removal of d can only be compensated by the two actions a and b, which means that the minimal plan length is increased. In turns, this is only possible if the original instance has no plan. □

The problems with the similar formulation but where the minimal plan length is allowed to increase of a given number k are clearly as hard as the ones above, where $k = 0$. The membership of these problems to PSPACE can be proved by modifying the proofs for the case $k = 0$.

Corollary 2. *Plan Length Increase for a Specific Action Subset and Plan Length Increase for a Action Subset are* PSPACE-*Complete.*

Finally, we note that all hardness results about a specific instance $\langle P, O, I, G \rangle$ extend to the case where this instance is not fully specified. More precisely, if a problem about instances $\langle P, O, I, G \rangle$ is extended to the case where only a part of I and G is given, then hardness results maintain their validity. For example, the problem of a specific action redundancy, which consists in checking whether an action $a \in O$ can be removed from $\langle P, O, I, G \rangle$, can be extended to the case of partial knowledge of I and G by assuming that some of the conditions are not (yet) known in the initial state, and some conditions are not known whether they will be part of the goal. This is exactly what we expect when the domain is fixed but the initial state and goal are not completely known. In this case, an action is redundant if it so for any possible initial state and goal. Since the case of full specification is simply a particular case, the hardness proof holds for the general case as well. Moreover, the general problem can be formalized as: for any I and G that extends the known parts of the initial state and goal, solve the problem of action redundancy for the case of full specification. Since the latter problem is in PSPACE, cycling over all possible I and G does not increase complexity, and the problem therefore remains in PSPACE. In summary, **the complexity of all problems that are stated with a fixed I and G extends to the case of partially specified initial state and goal.**

5   Related Work

The problem of checking the redundancy of actions in a domain is clearly related to the problem of checking the existence of a plan, and to the problem of finding such a plan. These are the two most studied problems in planning, and a large number of papers on this topic are in the literature. Just to cite some that are related to complexity, we mention the work by Bylander [8], Nebel [6,9,10], and Bäckström [11,12,13,14].

The paper that is the most close to the present one is the paper by Nebel, Dimopolus, and Koehler [6] where they analyze the problem of checking the redundancy of STRIPS instances. More precisely, the problem they have considered is whether a specific action or a specific fact (condition) is really needed to achieve the goal. They also considered the problem of whether an action or a fact is needed by *some* of the plans of the domain. Their paper is mainly focused on finding irrelevant actions of facts to the aim of simplifying the plan search. Most of their work is therefore devoted to developing heuristics, and only one complexity result is given (checking whether a fact or action is redundant is PSPACE-complete.) In a sense, the present paper extends Nebel, Dimopolus, and Koehler's by giving a more complete complexity characterization of redundancy in planning.

A concept related to checking redundancy of an action in a domain is that of redundancy of an action in a specific plan. Removing redundant actions in a plan is a problem that has been investigated in the context of planning by abstraction [4,3,5], where a plan is called *justified* if it does not contain actions that can be removed. This idea has been formalized in a number of different ways by Fink and Yang [1,2] Given the similarity with the work reported in the present paper, it is important to clarify the differences:

1. In the work on justified planning, a plan is given, and the goal is to remove actions from it; on the other hand, in action redundancy, the work has to be done on the domain, not on a specific plan;

2. A plan is justified if it does not contain actions that can be removed; on the other hand, it may be that a plan contains two times the same action, and only one of them can be removed; in other words, justification is not the irredunancy of actions, but rather the irredundancy of *action occurrences* in a plan; on the contrary, if an action is redundant then it can be removed altogether from the domain.

Clearly, whether justification or redundancy is of interest depends on the stage of planning: if the system on which planning is needed can be modified, then action redundancy is of interest; once the domain is fixed, and a plan has been found, the aim of reducing the plan length is of interest.

The problem of checking the redundancy of actions in a specific plan is also of interest in the context of plan recognition. It is indeed clear that not all actions may be directed toward a single goal; for example, it has been observed that "operators of control system, when not otherwise occupied, often glance at the current value of process variables" [15]. These "checking" actions are often redundant to the plan, and not taking this fact into account may produce a wrong plan identification.

The problems studied in this paper are about planning domains where actions can be removed. A similar assumption that has been considered by several authors [16,17,18,19] is that the initial state and the goal may change. The aim of plan modification or plan adaptation is to change an already known plan to take into account the different initial state or goal.

In spite of a name homonymy, redundancy in partially ordered planning search spaces [20] is not really related to redundancy as intended in this paper. Roughly speaking, redundancy in a search space is the presence of solutions that are not really necessary to visit. Clearly, this kind of redundancy is about plans, and is about searching for plans, while action redundancy is about a domain and is not directly related to a particular planning algorithm.

6   Conclusions

While the results of this paper are about the redundancy of actions in a domain, several other problems can be considered if we remove the assumption that the planning domain cannot be modified. For example, actions can be associated to costs, and the aim of the redundancy elimination would be to reduce the overall cost of the actions. If actions consume resources, one can consider whether the cost associated to an action is useful to reduce (for example, we may replace a part of a system with a more efficient one.)

A restriction we have (implicitely) assumed in this paper is that actions can be eliminated one-by-one. This is however not always true, as the removal of an action is only effective if all actions that require a part of a system are removed. In such cases, we are no more interested in removing a single action, but rather into removing groups of actions. These extensions are currently under investigation by the authors of this paper.

References

1. Fink, E., Yang, Q.: Formalizing plan justifications. In: Proceedings of the Ninth Conference of the Canadian Society for Computational Studies of Intelligence. (1992) 9–14
2. Fink, E., Yang, Q.: A spectrum of plan justifications. In: Proceedings of the AAAI 1993 Spring Symposium. (1993) 29–33
3. Knoblock, C., Tenenberg, J., Yang, Q.: Characterizing abstraction hierarchies for planning. In: Proc. of AAAI'91. (1991) 692–697
4. Yang, Q., Tenenberg, J.: ABTWEAK: Abstracting a nonlinear, least commitment planner. In: Proc. of AAAI'90. (1990) 204–209
5. Bacchus, F., Yang, Q.: The downward refinement property. In: Proc. of IJCAI'91. (1991) 286–293
6. Nebel, B., Dimopoulos, Y., Koehler, J.: Ignoring irrelevant facts and operators in plan generation. In: Proc. of ECP'97. (1997) 338–350
7. Fikes, R., Nilsson, N.: STRIPS: a new approach to the application of theorem proving to problem solving. Artificial Intelligence 2 (1971) 189–208
8. Bylander, T.: Complexity results for planning. In: Proc. of IJCAI'91. (1991) 274–279
9. Nebel, B., Bäckström, C.: On the computational complexity of temporal projection, planning, and plan validation. Artificial Intelligence 66 (1994) 125–160
10. Bäckström, C., Nebel, B.: Complexity results for SAS+ planning. Computational Intelligence 11 (1995) 625–656
11. Bäckström, C.: Equivalence and tractability results for SAS+ planning. In: Proc. of KR'92. (1992) 126–137
12. Bäckström, C., Nebel, B.: On the computational complexity of planning and story understanding. In: Proc. of ECAI'92. (1992) 349–353
13. Bäckström, C., Nebel, B.: Complexity results for SAS+ planning. In: Proc. of IJCAI'93. (1993) 1430–1435
14. Bäckström, C., Jonsson, P.: Planning with abstraction hierarchies can be exponentially less efficient. In: Proc. of IJCAI'95. (1995) 1599–1605
15. Goldman, R., Geib, C., Miller, C.: A new model of plan recognition. In: Proceedings of the Fifteenth Conference on Uncertainty in Artificial Intelligence (UAI'99). (1999) 245–254
16. Kambhampati, S., Hendler, J.: A validation-structure-based theory of plan modification and reuse. Artificial Intelligence 55 (1992) 193–258
17. Hanks, S., Weld, D.: A domain-independent algorithm for plan adaptation. J. of Artificial Intelligence Research 2 (1995) 319–360
18. Nebel, B., Koehler, J.: Plan reuse versus plan generation: A theoretical and empirical analysis. Artificial Intelligence 76 (1995) 427–454
19. Liberatore, P.: On non-conservative plan modification. In: Proc. of ECAI'98. (1998) 518–519
20. Kambhampati, S.: On the utility of systematicity: Understanding tradeoffs between redundancy and commitment in partial-ordering planning. In: Proc. of IJCAI'93. (1993) 1380–1387

On the Impact of Small-World on Local Search

Andrea Roli

Dipartimento di Scienze,
Università degli Studi "G. D'Annunzio",
Chieti–Pescara (Italia)
a.roli@unich.it

Abstract. The impact of problem structure on search is a relevant issue in artificial intelligence and related areas. Among the possible approaches to analyze problem structure, the one referring to constraint graph enables to relate graph parameters and characteristics with search algorithm behavior. In this work, we investigate the behavior of local search applied to SAT instances associated to graphs with small-world topology. Small-world graphs, such as friendship networks, have low characteristic path length and high clustering. In this work, we first present a procedure to generate SAT instances characterized by an interaction graph with a small-world topology. Then we show experimental results concerning the behavior of local search algorithms applied to this benchmark.

1   Introduction

The impact of problem structure on search is a relevant issue in artificial intelligence and related areas. In order to design and tune effective and efficient algorithms for constraint satisfaction problems (CSPs) and constrained optimization problems (COPs), the relations between structural problem instance features and algorithm performance have to be investigated. These relations have been studied from different perspectives. In particular, search algorithm behavior w.r.t. graph properties of some constraint satisfaction problems and constrained optimization problems has been discussed in [22,21,15,18]. The definition of structure emerging from the literature on CSPs and COPs is usually based on the informal notion of a property enjoyed by non-random problems. Thus, *structured* is used to indicate that the instance is derived from a real-world problem or it is an instance generated with some similarity with a real-world problem. Commonly, we attribute the characteristic of structured to a problem that shows, at a given level of abstraction, regularities such as well defined subproblems, patterns or correlations among problem variables. In this work, we focus on one among the possible ways of characterizing the structure of a problem instance: We analyze the structure of links among its components, i.e., the network that connects the components. Some problems suggest a natural structural description, since they have a representation that can be directly used for structure analysis. A classical example are problems defined on graphs, such as the Graph Coloring Problem and the k-Cardinality Tree Problem. For CSPs, an interaction graph can be defined [11], in which nodes correspond to variables and edges connect two variables if there exists a constraint involving them. Hence, the structure of any CSP can be characterized by a graph. Relevant features of a graph that

S. Bandini and S. Manzoni (Eds.): AI*IA 2005, LNAI 3673, pp. 13–24, 2005.

can affect search behavior are, for example, the *average node degree* and its frequency, the *path length* and the *clustering*. The impact of node degree frequency on search has been studied in [22,12,17,13]. In this work, we investigate the relations between the *small-world* property and search algorithm performance. Small-world graphs [23,24] are characterized by the simultaneous presence of two properties: the average number of hops connecting any pair of nodes is low and the clustering is high. Social networks defined on the basis of friendship relationships are a typical example of graphs with a small-world topology. The impact of small-world topology on search problems (e.g., Graph Coloring Problem) has been discussed in [21], where it is shown that many CSPs and COPs have a small-world topology and the search cost can be characterized by a heavy-tail distribution [4].

In this work, we report experimental results concerning the behavior of local search applied to instances of the Satisfiability Problem (SAT) with an interaction graph characterized by a small-world topology. The aim of these experiments is to address the question whether small-world SAT instances are harder to solve than others and if this behavior is common across different local search algorithms.

The contribution of this work is twofold. First, we define a procedure to construct SAT instances with a lattice structure, along with a method to generate small-world SAT instances. Then, we test three different local search algorithms on the generated benchmark. Results show that the behavior strongly differentiates across the algorithms. In some cases, results show that many harder instances have a small-world structure. This empirical analysis shows that, even if local search can be affected by instance structure, an important role is played by the actual search space exploration strategy.

This paper is structured as follows. Sec.2 introduces the basic concepts of small-world graphs and graphs associated to SAT instances. In Sec.3, we describe the properties of the instances composing the testbed and the procedure used to generate them. Sec.4 presents experimental results obtained by applying three different local search algorithms, namely WalkSAT, GSAT and Iterated local search. We conclude by briefly discussing the results obtained and outlining future work.

2   Preliminaries

In this section, we succinctly introduce small-world graphs and the graph associated to SAT instances.

Given a graph $G = (V, E)$, where V is the set of nodes and E the set of edges, the *characteristic path length* $L(G)$ of G is formally defined as the median of the means of the shortest paths connecting each node $v \in V$ to all other nodes. The *clustering* coefficient is defined on the basis of the notion of neighborhood. The neighborhood Γ_v of a node $v \in V$ is the subgraph consisting of the nodes adjacent to v (not including v itself). The clustering of a neighborhood is defined as $\gamma_v = |E(\Gamma_v)| / \binom{k_v}{2}$, where $|E(\Gamma_v)|$ is the number of edges in Γ_v and k_v is the number of neighbors of v. Therefore, γ_v is the ratio between the number of edges of the neighborhood and the maximum number of edges it can have. The clustering coefficient γ of a graph G is defined as the average of the clustering values γ_v for all $v \in V$. For example, we compute L and γ for the graph depicted in Fig.1. The characteristic path length is the median of the average

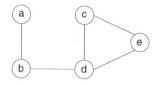

Fig. 1. Constraint graph associated to the SAT instance $(a \vee \neg b) \wedge (b \vee d) \wedge (c \vee \neg d \vee \neg e)$

path lengths related to the nodes a, b, c, d and e, i.e., $L = \text{median}\{\frac{9}{4}, \frac{6}{4}, \frac{7}{4}, \frac{5}{4}, \frac{7}{4}\} = \frac{7}{4} = 1.75$. The clustering γ is the average of the neighborhood clustering values, i.e., $\gamma = \frac{1}{5}(0/\binom{1}{2} + 0/\binom{2}{2} + 1/\binom{2}{2} + 1/\binom{3}{2} + 1/\binom{2}{2}) \approx 0.467$.

Typically, random graphs are characterized by low characteristic path length and low clustering, whilst regular graphs (such as lattices) have high values for L and γ. Conversely, small-world graphs are characterized by low L and high γ.

In this paper, we apply the notion of small-world to a graph associated to SAT instances. SAT belongs to the class of NP-complete problems [9] and can be stated as follows: given a set of clauses, each of which is the logical disjunction of $k > 2$ *literals* (a literal is a variable or its negation), we ask whether an assignment to the variables exists that satisfies all the clauses. The graph we associate to a SAT instance is called the *interaction graph* [11] and it is defined as an undirected graph $G = (V, A)$, where each node $v_i \in V$ corresponds to a variable and edge $(v_i, v_j) \in A$ $(i \neq j)$ if and only if variables v_i and v_j appear in a same clause (see Fig.1). Observe that the same graph corresponds to more than one formula, since nodes are connected by one arc even if the corresponding variables belong to more than one clause. Having a set of clauses associated to the same graph, makes this representation quite rough. Nevertheless, in the following, it will be shown that some properties of this graph can strongly affect the behavior of local search.

3   Small-World SAT Instances

In order to explore the behavior of search algorithms on small-world SAT instances, we generated a benchmark by morphing between instances constructed on lattice graphs and random instances. The core idea of the morphing procedure is derived from [3], wherein a method that enables to generate instances gradually morphing from a source to a destination instance is presented. This procedure is also quite similar to the one used in [24] to generate small-world graphs by interpolating between lattice and random graphs (see Fig.2). Starting from a lattice graph, links are randomly removed and rewired. Small-world graphs can be obtained by randomly rewiring just a few links between nodes.

SAT instances with a small-world graph topology can be obtained by morphing between a SAT instance associated to a lattice graph and a random SAT instance. Therefore, we have first to define a procedure to construct SAT instances associated to a lattice graph. Instead of starting from a SAT formula, expressed as a conjunction of clauses, we start from a graph with the desired topology and we use it as a skeleton for

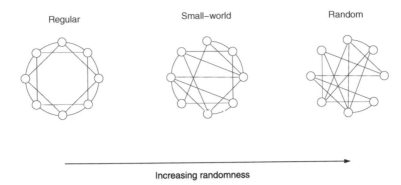

Fig. 2. Morphing between a lattice graph and a random graph. Small-world graphs can be obtained by randomly rewiring just a few links between nodes.

generating a SAT formula. The starting graph is a *lattice graph*. Lattice graphs have a very regular topology and every node is connected to a fixed (usually quite small) number of neighbors. Examples of lattice graphs are ring lattices (also called cycles) with adjunctive links connecting neighbors and hypercubes. Once obtained the graph with the given topology, we have to assign variables to nodes and to generate the clauses of the formula. The first step can be completed very easily by assigning variables in order: variable x_i is assigned to node i, for $i = 1, \ldots, n$. The generation of clauses, i.e., of a formula that can be mapped into the given lattice graph, is a bit more complex. First of all, we remind that the graph associated to a SAT instance, as previously defined, corresponds to a set of SAT instances. Therefore, it is important to define a given structure for the formula. Our choice is to follow the usual experimental settings for random generated SAT instances: 3-SAT formulas with controlled ratio m/n, where n is the number of variables and m the number of clauses.

In the following, we describe the algorithm to generate 3-SAT instances with given ratio m/n on a lattice graph. The generalization of the algorithm to k-SAT instances is straightforward. The high level algorithm is described in Alg.1. The algorithm is structured in two phases. In the first phase, a minimal set of clauses is generated to obtain a formula that can be represented by the given lattice graph. In the second phase, the additional required number of clauses is generated by adding clauses randomly chosen from the first set and by randomly changing the sign of literals.

In the first phase, clauses of three literals are constructed, by taking in turn each variable as a *pivot* and adding two subsequent variables (see Fig.3 and Fig.4). In order to avoid repetitions of clauses, for every variable x_i only subsequent variables $x_j, j > i$ (modulo n) are considered. Indeed, given the symmetry of the graph, the clauses involving the symmetric part of neighbors will be generated by using those neighbors as pivot (see Fig.5 and Fig.6). The instances composing the benchmark are generated by morphing between a lattice SAT instance and a random one. Each instance is obtained by taking from the lattice SAT instance all the clauses except for a prefixed number which are randomly chosen from a random SAT instance with the same number of variables and clauses. This procedure is indeed very similar to the morphing procedure described in [3], but in this case we control the exact number of clauses taken from the destination

---

Algorithm 1 Generation of a 3-SAT instance on a lattice graph

---

INPUT: n, m, λ {λ is the number of neighbors, supposed even}
OUTPUT: 3-SAT formula $\Phi = \{C_1,\ldots,C_m\}$ with n variables and m clauses associated to a lattice graph with n nodes with λ neighbors each.

Build a lattice graph $G(n,\lambda)$ (on a circle) with n nodes with λ neighbors each;
Assign variables (clockwise) to nodes;
$\Phi \leftarrow \emptyset$
for $i-1$ to $n-1$ **do**
    The neighbors of x_i are $\mathcal{N}^+ = \{x_{i+1},\ldots,x_{i+\lambda/2}\}$ (mod n) and $\mathcal{N}^- = \{x_{i-1},\ldots,x_{i-\lambda/2}\}$ (mod n);
    for each pair x_j, x_{j+1} in $\mathcal{N}^+$ **do**
        Construct the clause $C = x_i \vee x_j \vee x_{j+1}$
        Negate each variable in C with probability 0.5;
        $\Phi \leftarrow \Phi \cup C$
    end for
end for
{Now the number of clauses is $|\Phi| = n(\lambda/2 - 1)$ }
while $|\Phi| < m$ **do**
    repeat
        Pick randomly a clause C' in Φ;
        Negate each variable in C' with probability 0.5;
    until a new clause C' is generated
    $\Phi \leftarrow \Phi \cup C'$
end while

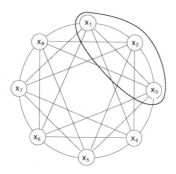

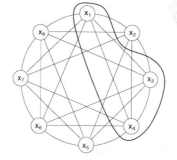

Fig. 3. Construction of the first clause involving variable x_1

Fig. 4. Construction of the second clause involving variable x_1

instance. In this way it is possible to smoothly interpolate from lattice to random and observe the arising of small-world properties in SAT instances.

In order to have a quantitative measure of the small-world characteristic, we introduce the *proximity ratio* μ [21], defined as the ratio between clustering and characteristic path length, normalized with the same ratio corresponding to a random graph, i.e., $\mu = (\gamma/L)/(\gamma_{rand}/L_{rand})$. In Fig.7, the clustering and the characteristic path length of SAT instances gradually interpolating from lattice to random are plotted (in semi-log scale). We observe that L drops very rapidly with the introduction of clauses from the

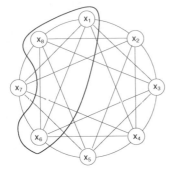
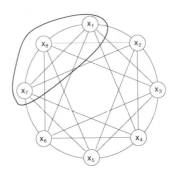

Fig. 5. Construction of the third clause involving variable x_1. The pivot is variable x_6.

Fig. 6. Construction of the fourth clause involving variable x_1. The pivot is variable x_7.

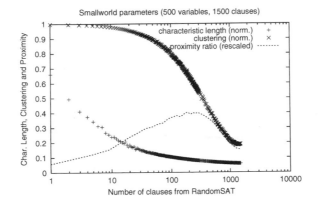

Fig. 7. Characteristic path length L, clustering γ and proximity ratio μ for instances generated by morphing from a lattice SAT instance to a random SAT instance of 500 variables and 1500 clauses

random instance. Conversely, γ maintains a relatively high value for a larger amount of perturbation. The instances with low length and high clustering are characterized by the small-world property. This is also indicated by the proximity ratio curve, which approximately assumes its maximum in that region.

We generated four sets of instances (respectively with 100, 200, 500 and 800 variables), each obtained by morphing between a lattice 3-SAT and a random 3-SAT with same number of variables and clauses. All the generated instances are satisfiable (unsatisfiable instances have been filtered by means of a complete solver). The ratio between the number of clauses and the number of variables is 3, lower than the so-called critical ratio (which is close to 4.3 for 3-SAT instances [1,8,5]). This is due to the structure of lattice SAT instances which turned out to be almost all unsatisfiable at the critical ratio. In Fig.8, the proximity ratio of the instances composing the benchmark is plotted. The value μ ranges approximately from 0.5 to 10. We can observe the typical behavior of instances interpolating between regular and random instances. In the next section we

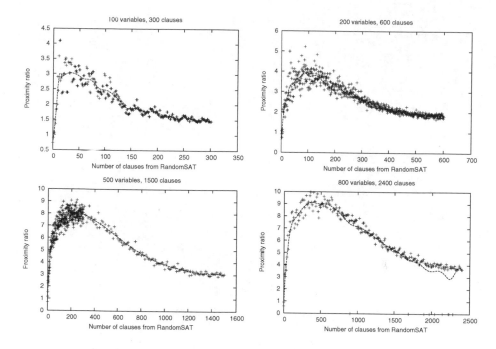

Fig. 8. Proximity ratio of the instances composing the benchmark

present experimental results on the behavior of local search algorithms on the benchmark defined.

4 Experimental Results

Some constraint satisfaction problems and constrained optimization problems with small-world topology have been found to require a higher computational search cost with respect to "non small-world" ones [21,22]. Since those results only concern complete algorithms, we question whether this behavior could also be observed in the case of approximate algorithms, namely local search.

We performed a series of experiments aimed at checking whether small-world SAT instances are harder to solve than both regular (lattice) and random ones. In the following, we will use the notion of *hardness* referred to the algorithm at hand. We estimate the hardness by means of the search cost, namely the number of iterations required for the algorithm to find a satisfying assignment. Since the algorithms we deal with are stochastic, we run each of them 1000 times on the same instance and we took the median value. We emphasize that we use the concept of hardness referring to a given algorithm $\mathcal{A}$ and we say that an instance I_1 is harder than I_2 if the search cost (as defined above) for solving I_1 via $\mathcal{A}$ is higher than that of I_2. Even if this definition of hardness is grounded to the algorithm used, in general it is possible to observe that a class of instances is harder than another class for a set of algorithms. This case reveals that there is a characteristic of the class that makes the instances difficult for all the considered algorithms.

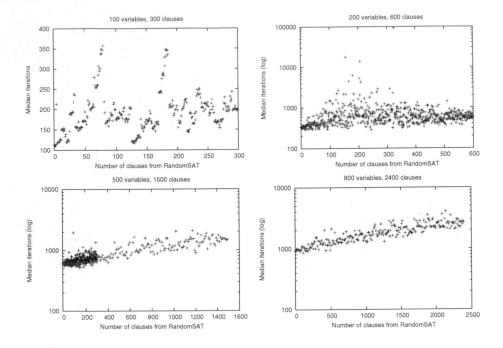

Fig. 9. Search cost of WalkSAT across the instances, from lattice to random structure. Points represent median iterations over 1000 runs. Log-scale on the y-axis has been used when necessary.

We applied three different local search procedures, that are based on different heuristic strategies. The algorithms we considered are WalkSAT [19], GSAT [20] and Iterated local search (ILS, [7,14]). GSAT was the first effective local search algorithm proposed for SAT. It applies a greedy strategy, by flipping the variable that, if flipped, leads to the greatest gradient in the number of satisfied clauses. GSAT suffers from being frequently trapped in confined areas of the search space, therefore its performance is often not satisfactory for large instances. WalkSAT is based on the principle of repair: It randomly chooses one unsatisfied clause and flips one variable within it. There are some different heuristics for the choice of the variable to flip [6]. In our implementation, we applied a GSAT-like heuristic, i.e., the variable that produces the largest increment in the number of satisfied clauses is flipped (no random walk is performed). WalkSAT has usually a far better performance than GSAT. Nevertheless, both algorithms lack a global strategy that could guide them during the exploration of the search space. Algorithms equipped with such a strategy are commonly called metaheuristics [2]. In order to extend the diversity of the techniques compared, we applied also an ILS designed to attack SAT and MAXSAT problems [14,15]. In essence, this metaheuristic is a tabu search-based WalkSAT guided by a strategy that tunes both the tabu tenure and the intensification/diversification balance by using the search history.

Before describing the results concerning local search, it is important to point out that in [15,16] a complete algorithm has been applied to this benchmark and results strikingly show that small-world SAT instances are the hardest (i.e., the search cost,

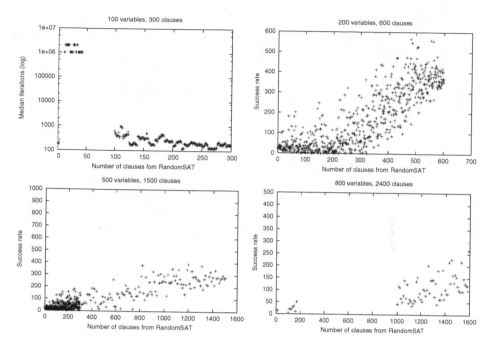

Fig. 10. Search cost of GSAT across the instances, from lattice to random structure. In the uppermost left plot, points represent median iterations over 1000 runs. The remaining plots report an estimation of the search cost in terms of success ratio, i.e., the number of instances solved – given a termination condition defined as the maximum number of non-improving moves.

evaluated as number of variable assignments performed by the algorithm before solving the instance, is the highest).

Results are shown in Figs. 9, 10 and 11. In the plots, we reported for each algorithm the median iterations (over 1000 runs) on every instance. The algorithms run until a feasible solution was found[1]. Results are very interesting and show the complexity of empirical analysis of local search behavior. First of all, we note that the behavior across the three algorithms is very different. In the first two plots of Fig.9, we observe that some of the hardest instances for WalkSAT are located in the small-world area. Nevertheless, for the instances of size 500 and 800, the search cost regularly increases –linearly in semi-log scale– while morphing from lattice to random. This peculiar behavior requires a deeper investigation and from these preliminary results we can only conjecture that size scaling amplifies a characteristic of the instances such that the closer the instance to a lattice, the easier for WalkSAT.[2] GSAT and ILS show a mild tendency of requiring higher search cost in the vicinity of the small-world area, as shown in Fig.10 and Fig.11,

---

[1] In the case of GSAT, due to the extremely high execution time, we stopped the algorithm at a maximum number of non-improving moves and we reported the success ratio, i.e., the number of successful runs out of 1000. Thus, in this case, the lower the value, the harder the instance.

[2] For example, the regular *chaining* pattern of clauses in lattice instances could make the repair process easier.

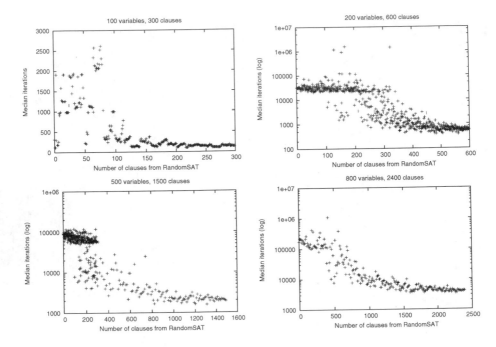

Fig. 11. Search cost of ILS across the instances, from lattice to random structure. Points represent median iterations over 1000 runs. Log-scale on the y-axis has been used when necessary.

respectively. The hardest instances for GSAT and ILS are the ones located in the first part of the plots, i.e., the instances with strong lattice/small-world topologies[3]. In some plots, we also observe that the instances corresponding to the maximal proximity ratio are the hardest on average[4]. Nevertheless, this behavior is not regular nor clear and the statistical correlation between search cost and proximity ratio is quite low.

The peculiar behavior observed is a clear signal that different factors other than small-world topology affect algorithm behavior. Among the main factors, we consider the search landscape characteristics induced by the SAT instance and the actual search process performed by the algorithm on the landscape. In fact, the landscape characteristics and the strategy used to explore it are the main elements that affect local search behavior. The relations between instance structure and search landscape are an extremely important research issue, that is subject of ongoing work (see, for instance, [10]).

5   Conclusion and Future Work

In this work, we have presented a procedure to generate SAT instances associated to an interaction graph with small-world topology. Small-world SAT instances are constructed by introducing clauses from random instances into lattice based ones.

---

[3] The 800-2400 instances are indeed not solved by GSAT in the range corresponding to small-world.

[4] This observation is also confirmed by evaluating a moving window average.

We tackled the benchmark instances with three different local search algorithms and observed their behavior across the whole spectrum, from regular lattice to random topologies. Our aim was to check whether there is a positive correlation between search cost and small-world topology of SAT instances, as observed in the case of complete solvers. Results showed primarily that the behavior of local search algorithms is fairly different. In some cases, we observed that most of the hardest instances are concentrated in the lattice/small-world area. Nevertheless, this result is not as clear as in the case of complete solvers and further investigations are required. If the conjecture on the positive correlation between instance hardness and proximity ratio is true, then the phenomenon may be explained considering the locality of decisions taken by the heuristics, as supposed in [21]: a locally good decision taken w.r.t. the clustering properties might be wrong with respect to the whole graph.

The study of relations between structure and local search behavior is still a partially unexplored area. First of all, in this work we have just considered one of the possible ways of characterizing structure. Other definitions for graphs are possible (such as weighted graphs), to capture different problem features and to extend our results to problems other than SAT. Moreover, concerning local search algorithms, we believe that the core issue to explain the algorithm behavior is the investigation of the relations between problem structure and search landscape, and, in turn, search landscape and the actual strategy used to explore it.

References

1. D. Achlioptas and C. Moore. The asymptotic order of the random k-SAT threshold. In *Proc. of FOCS02*, pages 779–788, 2002.
2. C. Blum and A. Roli. Metaheuristics in combinatorial optimization: Overview and conceptual comparison. *ACM Computing Surveys*, 35(3):268–308, 2003.
3. I. P. Gent, H. H. Hoos, P. Prosser, and T. Walsh. Morphing: Combining structure and randomness. In *Proc. of AAAI99*, pages 654–660, 1999.
4. C.P. Gomes, B. Selman, N. Crato, and H. Kautz. Heavy-Tayled phenomena in Satisfiability and Constraint Satisfaction Prpblems. *Journal of Automated Reasoning*, 24:67–100, 2000.
5. T. Hogg, B. A. Huberman, and C. P. Williams. Phase transitions and the search problems. *Artificial Intelligence*, 81(1–2), 1996.
6. H. H. Hoos and T. Stützle. Towards a characterisation of the behaviour of stochastic local search algorithms for SAT. *Artificial Intelligence*, 112:213–232, 1999.
7. H. R. Lourenço, O. Martin, and T. Stützle. Iterated local search. In F. Glover and G. Kochenberger, editors, *Handbook of Metaheuristics*, volume 57, pages 321–353. Kluwer Academic Publishers, Norwell, MA, 2002.
8. D. G. Mitchell, B. Selman, and H. J. Levesque. Hard and easy distributions of SAT problems. In *Proc. of AAAI92*, pages 459–465. AAAI Press/MIT Press, July 1992.
9. M.R.Garey and D.S.Johnson. *Computers and intractability; a guide to the theory of NP-completeness*. W.H. Freeman, 1979.
10. S. Prestwich and A. Roli. Symmetry breaking and local search spaces. In *Proceedings of CPAIOR 2005*, volume 3524 of *Lecture Notes in Computer Science*. Springer–Verlag, 2005.
11. I. Rish and R. Dechter. Resolution versus search: Two strategies for SAT. *J. Automated Reasoning*, 24:225–275, 2000.
12. A. Roli. Criticality and parallelism in GSAT. *Electronic Notes in Discrete Mathematics*, 9, 2001.

13. A. Roli. Criticality and parallelism in structured SAT instances. In P. Van Henteryck, editor, *Proc. of CP02*, volume 2470 of *Lecture Notes in Computer Science*, pages 714–719. Springer-Verlag, 2002.
14. A. Roli. Design of a new metaheuristic for MAXSAT problems (extended abstract). In P. Van Henteryck, editor, *Proceedings of CP02*, volume 2470 of *Lecture Notes in Computer Science*, page 767. Springer-Verlag, 2002.
15. A. Roli. Metaheuristics and structure in satisfiability problems. Technical Report DEIS-LIA-03-005, University of Bologna (Italy), May 2003. PhD Thesis - LIA Series no. 66.
16. A. Roli. Problem structure and search: Empirical results and open questions. In *Proceedings of CPAIOR03*, Montreal (Canada), 2003.
17. A. Roli and C. Blum. Critical Parallelization of Local Search for MAX–SAT. In F. Esposito, editor, *AI*IA2001: Advances in Artificial Intelligence*, volume 2175 of *Lecture Notes in Artificial Intelligence*, pages 147–158. Springer-Verlag, 2001.
18. A. Roli. Links between complex networks and combinatorial optimization. In *Proc. of Workshop on Experimental Analysis of Algorithms for Artificial Intelligence – AI*IA* working group on Knowledge Representation and Reasoning, Università di Ferrara, Italy, June 10 2005.
19. B. Selman, H.A. Kautz, and B. Cohen. Noise strategies for local search. In *Proc. of AAAI-94*, pages 337–343, 1994.
20. B. Selman, H. J. Levesque, and D. Mitchell. A new method for solving hard satisfiability problems. In *Proc. of AAAI92*, pages 440–446, Menlo Park, California, 1992. AAAI Press.
21. T. Walsh. Search in a small world. In *Proc. of IJCAI99*, pages 1172–1177, 1999.
22. T. Walsh. Search on high degree graphs. In *Proc. of IJCAI01*, 2001.
23. D.J. Watts. *Small Worlds: The Dynamics of Networks between Order and Randomness.* Princeton University Press, 1999.
24. D.J. Watts and S.H. Strogatz. Collective dynamics of 'small-world' networks. *Nature*, 393:440–442, 1998.

A Hybrid Logic for Commonsense Spatial Reasoning

Stefania Bandini, Alessandro Mosca, and Matteo Palmonari

Department of Computer Science, Systems and Communication (DISCo),
University of Milan - Bicocca,
via Bicocca degli Arcimboldi,
820126 - Milan (Italy)
Tel: +39 02 64487857; Fax: +39 02 64487839
{bandini, alessandro.mosca, matteo.palmonari}@disco.unimib.it

Abstract. The current technological trend depicts a scenario in which space, and more generally the environment in which the computation takes place, represents a key aspect that must be considered in order to improve systems' context awareness, even if the kind of information processed is not only of spatial nature. This paper focuses on the notions of "place" and "conceptual spatial relation" to present a formal model of space supporting Commonsense Spatial Reasoning. The model can be viewed as the semantic specification for a Hybrid Logic, whose formulas represent spatially qualified information. Interesting classes of Commonsense Spatial Models are identified according to the properties of their characteristic relations and an axiomatization of the associated hybrid language is given; a sound and complete tableau based calculus for these classes of models is provided.

1 Introduction

Thanks to the improvement and growing availability of technology such as sensors, personal devices, and so on, computational power can be embedded almost in every object populating the environment [1]. This new kind of systems is characterized by different, possibly mobile, distributed components and are devoted to collect, process and manage information in order to support users in different kind of activities (e.g. from monitoring and control [2] to the management of personal data [3]). In this scenario, there is an increasing need of relating computation with the spatial context in which it takes place, and models managing spatially related information are necessary to correlate local information, to coordinate devices and to supply context aware services.

This kind of activities involves a form of spatial reasoning that seems quite different from existing approaches developed in the Artificial Intelligence area so far, and, in particular, in Knowledge Representation. Usually, spatial reasoning consists is conceived as reasoning about the morphology of the objects present in the space, e.g. relations among spatial entities and properties of them are taken into account in order to infer other relations and properties not immediately identifiable. Objects are analyzed by means of abstract mathematical concepts in such a way that certain inferences are made possible according to different goals (e.g. if two topological regions share a point of their boundaries, then they can be inferred to be tangent). Research on spatial reasoning

S. Bandini and S. Manzoni (Eds.): AI*IA 2005, LNAI 3673, pp. 25–37, 2005.

presented several mathematical formalisms based on topology, or affine, metric and vector spaces (as shown in [4]). In particular, focusing on the kind of qualitative topological relationships among objects, it has been possible to model and implement different spatial reasoners (e.g. for computer vision) whose formal languages include suitable sets of part-whole relations, topological relations and topological properties of individual regions (the topological route maps [5,6] and [7], are just a few examples). Moreover, it is known that topology can provide the semantics for different logical languages of increasing expressive power and complexity (the Region Connection Calculus first order axiomatization [8] and the modal languages [9] are two examples).

However, as far as pervasive systems are concerned, there is little interest in applying reasoning to obtain a deeper knowledge of the spatial environment as for its morphological aspects, mainly because those aspects are partly known by design and partly computable by means of technological tools (e.g. the position of mobile devices by a GPS). Spatial information is often available (although possibly incomplete), but it needs to be integrated with *other domain theories* to carry out specific tasks, such as a theory about the formation of traffic anomalies in traffic monitoring and control [10].

The model that supports this integration must necessarily include the system itself (with its components) and the relevant elements of the environment in which it habits. All these elements can be considered as "interesting places" and different "common-sense spatial relations" can hold among them. Nevertheless, three classes of common-sense relations (i.e. Orientation, Proximity and Containment) can be identified as fundamental relations holding among interesting places according to some representational issues that will be discussed in the paper. Such a model will be called a "Commonsense Spatial Model" in order to distinguish it from other spatial models and calculi based on strong mathematical theories such as trigonometry, topology, vector spaces, and so on. A commonsense spatial model of space supporting reasoning about the environment emerges as a topology whose nodes are identified by interesting places and whose relations are commonsense spatial relations (CSR) arising from an abstraction of the spatial disposition of these places. A place is a conceptual entity completely identified by the aggregation of its properties, which may concern the type of place (e.g. a place can be a sensor or a room), the internal status of the place (e.g. "is_faulty", "is_working"), its functional role (e.g. a kitchen or a living room), and so on. The three classes of relations can be characterized according to thier formal properties.

The framework described can supports logical reasoning in a very natural way, since the commonsense spatial model - formally a relational structure - can be viewed as the semantic specification for a *hybrid modal* language [11]. Hybrid Modal Logics are a family of modal logics, whose language provides names for states of the model and allow expressing, in the language itself, sentences about the satisfiability of formulas [12]. This extra power gives the opportunity to refer to specific places in the environment, which is an essential feature in the context of pervasive Computing.

In particular, this approach has been presented in [13] to address the problem of Context Awareness in Pervasive Computing. Spatial aspects of the environment are in fact key elements of the context, which need to be represented and exploited to enable some awareness of what is true at a given moment in the environment. The commonsense spatial model has been presented as a joint representation of the spatial environment in which a pervasive system is located and of the components of the system themselves. By means of Hybrid Logic formulas it is possible to represent information about the environment and Hybrid Reasoning enable inference capabilities according to specific domain theories about information correlation.

This paper is organized as follows: the notions of Commonsense Spatial Model (CSM) and Standard CSM are discussed in the following section. Section 3 gives an overview of the fundamental notions of Hybrid Logic, while Section 4 shows how Hybrid Logic can be exploited to perform commonsense spatial reasoning; after some remarks on the definability of Standard CSMs, it is shown that for this class of models a sound and complete tableau based calculus can always be defined. Section 5 introduces the Basic Standard Commonsense Spatial Logic according to the observations about pervasive systems from which we started. Concluding remarks end the paper.

2 CSM, A Model for Commonsense Spatial Reasoning

A general commonsense spatial model is thus defined as follows:

Definition 1. *A Commonsense Spatial Model* $CSM = \langle P, R_S \rangle$ *is a relational structure, where* $P = \{p_1, ..., p_k\}$ *is a finite set of places, and* $R = \{R_1, ..., R_n\}$ *is a finite non-empty set of binary conceptual spatial relations labeled by a set of labels* $L \subset \mathbb{N}$, *and where, for each* $i \in L$, $R_i \subseteq P \times P$.

A place can be any entity identifiable by a set of properties as argued in the previous section. As for the set R, from a conceptual point of view R can be any arbitrary set of binary CSRs, although some classes of relations significant for a wide reasoning domains will be analytically and formally characterized in the following paragraphs. This lack of constraints on what can be taken as a CSR, may be seen as a weakness of the model, but is related to the main principles guiding this approach. In fact, in comparison with other well known topological models (e.g. RCC calculus in [8], and spatial modal logic of [9]) and since a morphological account of spatial relations is not the first object of our commonsense model of space, it must be observed that it is not possible (nor useful) to identify a minimal set of primitive relations (as for the RCC calculus). Indeed, this approach is not aimed at providing a mathematical model of space, but rather at defining the basic elements for the specification of axioms characterizing relevant properties of specific environments.

Nevertheless, as already mentioned, there are some significant classes of relations that play a special role in the definition of a commonsense model of space. In particular, a place can be "oriente" with respect to another (distinct) place, or it can be "contained i" or can be "proximal to" another place. The concepts of *orientation*, *proximity* and *containment* identify three classes of relations, which, in their various declination, seem to be somehow archetypical in commonsense spatial reasoning and can be discussed according to the formal properties of the relations they group together.

Proximity. A first basic relation useful to define space concerns the possibility of reaching one place from another (in both physical and metaphorical sense). Two places are said to be proximal, in this sense, if it is possible to go from one to the other one without passing through another place. A *proximity* relation R_P is a *reflexive* and *symmetric* relation that is said to hold between two places p and q when the place q is directly reachable from place p. However, different criteria of reachability can be adopted to define an adjacency proximity relation. Another example of proximity relation could be networking among devices in distributed systems.

Containment. Since places are arbitrary entities possibly with different shapes, dimensions and nature (e.g. a room and a printer are both places), a physical inclusion relation R_{IN} over places is needed in order to relate different types of places: an object may be in a room that may be in a building (where the object, the room and the building are interesting place of the same commonsense spatial model). The relation $R_{IN}(p, q)$ is interpreted as stating that the place q is *contained* in the place p; R_{IN} is a typical mereological relation (a partial order, that is, a *reflexive*, *antisymmetric* and *transitive* relation). Note that stronger antisymmetry allows to infer identity between two places for which it is said that one is in another and vice versa.

Orientation. Finally, we need some relations to ensure *orientation* in space giving an account of entities' disposition: assuming reference points is a fundamental way to start orienting into space. Assuming specific reference points consists in ordering entities with respect to these particular points, that is in such a way that every entity is put in relation with the reference point directly or indirectly (if related to another entity related to that point). Whatever the contingent choice of the reference point, what is really important is the notion of *order* coming from the existence of the reference point. Anyway a natural choice into a 2D space can be to exploit the four cardinal points North, East, South, West, introducing relation such as R_N, R_E, R_S, and R_W among the places (where a relation $R_N(p, q)$ holds *iff* q is *north of* p). The class of orientation relations consists of *strict partial orders* on the set of places that is, they are *irreflexive*, *asymmetric* and *transitive* relations; the order is "partial" because two places might be incomparable, and has always a greatest element, that is, a top element (e.g. the North for R_N). Some relations can be defined as the converse of other ones (e.g. R_S of R_N), and other non-primitive relations such as *north-east of* (R_{NE}), can eventually be defined by means of usual set theoretic operators from the previous ones, e.g. $R_{NE} = R_N \cap R_E$ (notice that so far more than one orientation relation may hold between two places).

These three relation classes play a fundamental role in commonsense spatial reasoning because, as far as a qualitative account of the things arrangement into space is concerned, the joint assumption of relations of the three classes above, although not provably exhaustive, provides a characterization of the environment, yet qualitative and rough, but which meets at least the following representational requirements:

- the definition of a basic graph relating places according to their reachability by means of proximity relations. This responds to the answer "where can I go from here?";
- a rough (qualitative) ordering of places into a 2Dd or 3D space by means of orientation relations (3D if a up-down order is added): this is important to someway reflect the idea of disposition of places and objects in space. Neither a grid nor a Cartesian reference system are necessarily exploited here, but the notion of disposition is traced back to the concept of *order*, and more precisely, to the projection of various orders on the place domains;

- the possibility of taking into account places of various types and size, representing different layers of abstraction by means of containment relations (a desk into a room, a room into a building).

Since those three classes are so important in the definition of a Commonsense Model of space, according to the previous observations, we want to define a class of *standard CSM* as the set of CSMs where all the relations are of the categories discussed above (proximity, containment and orientation) and there is at least one relation for each category. Moreover, since the orientation relations are always defined with respect to a reference point, that is, the *top* of the respective order, the set of places must include a place for every orientation relation to be taken as the *top* element. Let proximity, containment and orientation be three classes of relations for which the formal properties discussed above hold, formally a Standard Commonsense Spatial Model can be defined as follows:

Definition 2. *Let assume that* $\{R_1^p, ..., R_k^p\}$ *is a set of* proximity *relations,* $\{R_1^c, ..., R_m^c\}$ *is a set of* containment *relations, and* $\{R_1^o, ..., R_n^o\}$ *is a set of* orientation *relations each one with its top element* top_i. *A Standard Commonsense Spatial Model* $SCSM$ *is a* CSM *with* $R = \{R_1^p, ..., R_k^p, R_1^c, ..., R_m^c, R_1^o, ..., R_n^o\}$ *and* $\{top_1, ..., top_n\} \subseteq P$.

Notice only that if a relation R_i^o, where $1 < i < n$, belongs to the '"orientation"' class, each place must be R_i^o-oriented with respect to the top_i place, that is, for all $p \in P - \{top_i\}$, $R_i^o(p, top_i)$ must hold; indeed, the proof of this property is given in Example 1 for the Hybrid Logic that will be introduced later on.

The considerations above about orientation, containment and proximity relations refer to the nature of each relation of those three types. Nevertheless, besides the properties of each type of relation there are *cross properties* of the model that concern the relations among different CSRs and their interdependencies. Something has been said for orientation relations such as R_S and R_N, since the last has been defined as the inverse of the first (the same holds for Up/Down relations), but much more can be done, for example if we want to exploit the inheritance of orientation relations through the containment relation (i.e. if a place p_0 is at west of a place p_1, every place contained in p_0 is at west of p_1). Extensionally those relations are contained in the relational structure, but it will be shown in the next section that hybrid languages allow to specify those cross properties.

3 Reasoning into Space: An Hybrid Logic Approach

Now, since the commonsense spatial model just introduced is a relational structure, it is natural to view it as the semantic specification for a modal logical language. Modal languages already proved to be very useful to reason about relational structures, and have been exploited for temporal and spatial logics, for logic of necessity and possibility and many others ([11]). Hybrid languages are modal languages that, improving expressiveness and power of modal logic, allow to express (in the language itself) sentences about satisfiability of formulas, that is to assert that a certain formula is satisfiable at a certain state (i.e. at a certain place in our framework). In other words, its syntactic side is a formidable tool to reason about what is going on at a particular place and to reason about place equality (i.e. reasoning tasks that are not provided by basic modal logic).

To give an idea of how Hybrid Logic works let us say that the way in which this extra power is achieved is by the introduction of a specific set of formulas, called *nominals*. Nominals are formulas that partly behave like normal formulas - they are atomic formulas and can be used to build other arbitrarily complex ones -, but since they are evaluated to be true at a single state of the model, they allow us to refer to the specific state at which they are true. Another facility that can be embedded in Hybrid Logic is quantification over states, with imaginable repercussions on the complexity side, but since non-quantified formulas will be proved to be sufficient for our goals, in this paper we refer to Hybrid Logic as to non-quantified Hybrid Logic.

We will briefly recall some formal definitions for Hybrid Logic starting from the multimodal hybrid language.

Definition 3. *(Hybrid multimodal language) Let be* $PROP = \{p_0, ..., p_n\}$ *a set of propositional symbols,* $MOD = \{\pi_0, ..., \pi_n\}$ *a set of modality labels and* $NOM = i_0, ..., i_n$ *a nonempty set of propositional symbols disjoint from* $PROP$. *A hybrid multimodal language is defined as the set of well formed formulas given as follows:*

$$WFF := p|i|\neg\varphi|\varphi \wedge \psi|\varphi \vee \psi|\varphi \rightarrow \psi| \langle \pi \rangle | [\pi] |@_i\varphi$$

For any nominal i, *the symbol sequence* $@_i$ *is called a satisfaction operator. As standard, we will typically refer to nominals with symbols such as* i, j *and* k *and we will use* p *and* q *for other propositional variables.*

Semantics for basic Hybrid Modal Logic is given by means of Kripke models, as usual for modal logics, adding the clauses relative to nominals and satisfaction operators.

Definition 4. *(Hybrid models, satisfaction and validity) A hybrid model is a triple* $(W, \{R_\pi | \pi \in MOD\}, V)$ *where* $(W, \{R_\pi | \pi \in MOD\})$ *is a frame and* V *is a hybrid valuation. A hybrid valuation is a function with domain* $PROP \cup NOM$ *and range* $\wp(W)$ *such that for every nominal* i, $V(i)$ *is a singleton subset of* W. *If* $V(i) = w$, w *is called the denotation of* i. *Hybrid languages are interpreted on hybrid models as usual for modal logic (see [12]), but introducing the following clauses:*

$$M, w \vDash i \qquad iff \qquad w \in V(i), \text{ where } i \in NOM$$
$$M, w \vDash @_i\varphi \qquad iff \qquad M, w' \vDash \varphi, \text{ where } w' \text{ is the denotation of } i.$$

If $M, w \vDash \varphi$, φ *is said to be satisfied in* M *at* w. *If* φ *is satisfied in all states in all models based on a frame* F, φ *is said to be valid on* F *(in notation* $F \vDash \varphi$). *If* φ *is valid on all frames, then* φ *is said to be valid and we will write simply* $\vDash \varphi$.

A very intuitive way to formalize hybrid reasoning is by means of tableaux as presented in various works about different Hybrid Logics and their extensions (e.g. [12,14]). The Blackburn's tableau system is given in Table 1. We want to stress at least two peculiarities of tableau based calculi for Hybrid Logic that will turn out to be very important for commonsense spatial reasoning.

Table 1. Tableaux for Hybrid Logic. Here s and t are metavariables over nominals and a is a metavariable over nominals not used so far in the proof. Rules for $\vee$ and $\rightarrow$ can be taken as variants of the rules for $\wedge$.

$$\frac{@_s \neg\varphi}{\neg@_s\varphi}\ [\neg] \qquad \frac{\neg@_s\neg\varphi}{@_s\varphi}\ [\neg\neg] \qquad \frac{@_s(\varphi \wedge \psi)}{@_s\varphi \atop @_s\psi}\ [\wedge] \qquad \frac{\neg@_s(\varphi \wedge \psi)}{\neg@_s\varphi \mid \neg@_s\psi}\ [\neg\wedge]$$

$$\frac{@_s@_t\varphi}{@_t\varphi}\ [@] \qquad \frac{\neg@_s@_t\varphi}{\neg@_t\varphi}\ [\neg@] \qquad \frac{@_s\langle\pi\rangle\varphi}{@_s\langle\pi\rangle a \atop @_a\varphi}\ [\langle\pi\rangle] \qquad \frac{\neg@_s[\pi]\varphi}{@_s\langle\pi\rangle a \atop \neg@_a\varphi}\ [\neg[\pi]]$$

$$\frac{\neg@_s\langle\pi\rangle\varphi \quad \neg@_s\langle\pi\rangle t}{\neg@_t\varphi}\ [\neg\langle\pi\rangle] \qquad\qquad \frac{@_s[\pi]\varphi \quad @_s\langle\pi\rangle t}{@_t\varphi}\ [[\pi]]$$

$$\frac{[s \text{ on branch}]}{@_s s}\ [\text{Ref}] \qquad \frac{@_t s}{@_s t}\ [\text{Sym}] \qquad \frac{@_s t \quad @_t\varphi}{@_s\varphi}\ [\text{Nom}] \qquad \frac{@_s\langle\pi\rangle t \quad @_t t'}{@_s\langle\pi\rangle t'}\ [\text{Bridge}]$$

– First, Hybrid Logic's pure formulas, that is, formulas that do not contain propositional variables, make the definition of frame classes very easy and powerful. In fact, since pure formulas refer directly to the states of the model, it is easy to exploit them to define well known properties (e.g. transitivity) and usual classes of frames (s5, s4 and so on); furthermore, since pure formulas allow defining more properties than normal modal formulas, Hybrid Logic allow defining a much larger class of frames than plain modal logic. We will refer to this issue as *"frame definability"*.

– Secondly, Hybrid Logic allows us to fully exploit *frame definability* for reasoning purposes. In fact, consider that the tableau rules given by Blackburn provide a sound and complete calculus for Hybrid Logic in this sense: a formula φ is tableau provable *iff* it is valid, that is, *iff* it is true in every frame. This seems to be not very helpful when, as in our case, we are interested in reasoning in specific frame classes. Nevertheless, it has been proved that it is sufficient to add a set of pure formulas defining the desired frame to the tableaux to obtain a sound and complete calculus with respect to that frame. We will refer to this property as to *"modularity"*.

4 Spatial Reasoning with Hybrid Logic

Coming back to the notion of Commonsense Spatial Model (CSM) introduced in Section 2, the relational structure in which it consists can be exploited to specify the semantics of a Hybrid Logic, and this should easily enable logical reasoning over CSMs. Nevertheless, this connection must be specified better and in a more formal way. To do this, we exploit the notion of Standard Commonsense Spatial Model that is by far more precise and somewhat paradigmatic for our approach and, giving a complete axiomatization according to the classes of relations for SCSMs, we provide a sound and complete calculus for this class of models. Then, we show how the introduction of the Hybrid Logic makes it easier to characterize those *cross properties* of the model (interdependencies among single relations) that the previous definition left someway obscure. Finally, we show how easy it is, with the new formalization, to extend a SCSM to a richer CSM exploiting the *frame definability* property of Hybrid Logic.

First of all, bridging the definition of Section 2 with standard modal logic notions, observe that each CSM (including the place selection and an extensional definition of the relations) *is* a frame, whose accessibility relations are precisely the chosen CSRs; therefore, *classes of CSMs* characterized by constraints on relations or their properties identify *classes of frames*. On the reasoning side, since we are interested in providing reasoning procedures independently of a specific choice of places, we want to know if it is possible to define a complete calculus with respect to those classes of frames. Standard CSMs have been defined formally enough to answer this question, and the answer will be shown to be positive.

The first step consists in the definition of the properties of the CSRs, that is, the accessibility relations of the frame classes corresponding to SCSMs. Classes of relations have been grouped according to their formal properties, so that it will be sufficient to show how the properties characterizing orientation, containment and proximity relations can be defined by means of pure hybrid formulas. Table 2 addresses this issue and needs no further explanation since all the reported correspondences have been largely discussed in the literature (e.g., again in [12]).

Instead, some problems arise when we want to define the *top* element of the orientation relations. The top element has the following properties: there is one and only one top_n element for every orientation relation R_n^o and every node is referred to it, with the exception of itself (the relation is irreflexive). A top element is an end point for the respective relation and we can define this property with $\neg\Diamond\top$, where $\top$ is a pure formula always true. Thus, consider these two formulas:

$$@_i\Box\Diamond\top \leftrightarrow \neg\Diamond\top \qquad\qquad (ex)$$
$$@i\neg\Diamond\top \to @j\neg\Diamond\top \to @_ij \qquad\qquad (uni)$$

It is easy to see that the second one says that if there are two end points, they must be the same state. In order to clarify the first one, consider the equivalent formula $@_i\Diamond\top \leftrightarrow \Diamond\neg\Diamond\top$: this says that if from a state i it is possible to access a node, say k, then it is possible to reach also the end point defined by $\neg\Diamond\top$; in other terms, since from any non-top element the top element is accessible and the relation is irreflexive, $\Diamond\top$ is not true for every state accessible from it. What is still missing is the condition of existence

Table 2. SCSM properties definability

	Property	CSR class	Definition
(ref)	*reflexivity*	P,C	$@_i\Diamond i$
(irref)	*irreflexivity*	O	$@_i\neg\Diamond i$
(sym)	*symmetry*	P	$@_i\Diamond\Diamond i$
(asym)	*asymmetry*	O	$@_i\neg\Diamond\Diamond i$
(antisym)	*antisymmetry*	C	$@_i\Box\,(\Diamond i \to i)$
(trans)	*transitivity*	C,O	$\Diamond\Diamond i \to \Diamond i$

of a top element; allowing quantification, this could be achieved by adding a very simple formula such as $\exists x \neg \Diamond \top$: unfortunately, this is not a formula of our language but a formula of Quantified Hybrid Logic. Nevertheless, for every finite frame (SCSM is finite) such an existence statement is not necessary: suppose the two formulas are true, the relation is irreflexive, asymmetric and transitive, and the frame is finite. If there were not places i for which $@_i \neg \Diamond \top$ is true, then $\Diamond \top$ would be true for every j (for uni), so the order would not have any upper bound, but this contradicts the fact that every finite partial order (strict or not strict) has some upper bound (here there is only one, as granted by ex). Therefore:

Lemma 1. *For every SCSM S there exists a finite frame F^S that corresponds to it and is definable by a set of pure hybrid formulas Φ. If Φ^S is such a set of formulas, S is said to be defined by it.*

Proof. The constructive proof is trivial since it exploits well known results in correspondence theory for Hybrid Logic and what has been shown in the above paragraph for the top elements of orientation relations. Given a SCSM $S = \{R, P\}$, take each $R_i \in R$ as an accessibility relation of F^S. F^S is defined by the set of pure formulas Φ^S obtained as follows: for each proximity relation add ref and sym; for each containment relation add ref, $antisym$, $trans$; for each orientation relation add $irref$, $asym$, $trans$, and (ex) and (uni) for defining top elements.

Now, according to Blackburn's Theorem 5.4 in [12], taken the tableau H of Table 1, a finite or countably infinite set of pure satisfaction statements A and a class of frames F defined by A, then $H + A$ is complete with respect to F. Hence, it is easy to see that a complete calculus can be given for any SCSM, as stated by the theorem below.

Theorem 1. *For every SCSM S there exists a tableau based calculus sound and complete with respect to the corresponding class of frames F^s.*

The proof of the theorem is straightforward from Blackburn's Theorem and Lemma 1 (remember that any SCSM is finite). Anyway, the proof is constructive and therefore a complete tableau based calculus for a SCSM S is given by $T = H + \Phi^S$, where Φ^S is the set of formulas that defines S.

Example 1. An illustration of what we can prove in our system can be given by the proof of a fundamental property of orientation relation that was not made explicit by the couple of uni and ex axioms. We want to be able to infer that if a place is not the end point of the orientation relation, it is oriented with respect to the top element. This can be shown proving the formula $@_j \neg \Diamond \top \rightarrow @_i (\neg j \rightarrow \Diamond j)$, as shown in Table 3.

Now that we have a good tool to talk about SCSMs, as promised, we can specify SCSMs even better by means of pure Hybrid Modal formulas, characterizing interdependencies and interdefinitions among different CSRs. In fact, thanks to the expressiveness of the hybrid language, several interesting *cross properties* governing the relationships between modal operators can be introduced. Assume to have four orientation relations interpreted over classic cardinal-point based relations. Interdependencies between East/West and North/South are a relevant property of the environment model.

Table 3. Proof for $@_j \neg \Diamond \mathrm{T} \rightarrow @_i(\neg j \rightarrow \Diamond j)$ in Example 1

1	$\neg @_s(@_j \neg \Diamond \mathrm{T} \rightarrow @_i(\neg j \rightarrow \Diamond j))$		
2	$@_s @_j \neg \Diamond \mathrm{T}$		$[1,\neg \rightarrow]$
2'	$\neg @_s @_i(\neg j \rightarrow \Diamond j)$		*ditto*
3	$@_j \neg \Diamond \mathrm{T}$		$[2,@]$
4	$\neg @_i(\neg j \rightarrow \Diamond j)$		$[2',\neg @]$
5	$@_i \neg j$		$[4,\neg \rightarrow]$
5'	$\neg @_i \Diamond j$		*ditto*
6	$@_i(\Diamond \mathrm{T} \rightarrow \Diamond \neg \Diamond \mathrm{T})$		$[\mathbf{Ex}]$
7	$@_i \neg \Diamond \mathrm{T}$ $\vert$	$@_i \Diamond \neg \Diamond \mathrm{T}$	$[6,\rightarrow]$
8 [3,7,**Uni**]	$@_{ij}$	$@_i \Diamond a$	$[7,\Diamond]$
8'	$\maltese\ 8,5\ \maltese$	$@_a \neg \Diamond \mathrm{T}$	$[ditto]$
9		$@_a j$	$[3,8',\mathbf{Uni}]$
10		$@_i \Diamond j$	$[8,9,\mathrm{Bridge}]$
11		$\maltese\ 5',10\ \maltese$	

Consider that the following definitions are valid principles: (1') $\forall xy(x R_N y \leftrightarrow y R_S x)$; (2') $\forall xy(x R_E y \leftrightarrow y R_W x)$. The formulas

$$@_i \Box_N \Diamond_S i \wedge @_i \Box_S \Diamond_N i \tag{1}$$

$$@_i \Box_E \Diamond_W i \wedge @_i \Box_W \Diamond_E i \tag{2}$$

establish the *mutual conversion* of the relations R_N and R_S, and of R_E and R_W, respectively (in other words, these two conjunctions precisely define those frames in which R_N and R_S, and R_E and R_W, are mutually converse). Another interesting cross-property regards the relationship among the orientation and containment modal operators that is, the following formula is assumed to be valid:

$$\Diamond_\star i \rightarrow \Box_{IN} \Diamond_\star i \tag{3}$$

where $\star = \{N, S, E, W\}$. The Formula (3) ensures that if a place has a specific orientation with respect to another place (e.g. when we say that the place t is *north of* a place s), then every place contained in it inherits such an orientation (e.g. if s' is *contained in* s, then the place t is *north of* s'). In other words, from the truth of $@_s \Diamond_N t$ and $@_s \Diamond_{IN} s'$, it follows the truth of $@_{s'} \Diamond_N t$.

A last issue that need to be developed in this section concerns general CSMs (possibly richer than Standard CSMs) and what we called the "*modularity*" property. At the beginning Commonsense Spatial Models have been defined as open models and it has been argued that there is not much interest in the identification of a specific set of modal operators, or CSRs from a semantic point of view, which are expected to work in every context. Rather, the problem of choosing the right set of relations concerns an ontological research over the domain. Although a basic Hybrid Logic to reason about SCSMs will be introduced later on, now we want to remark why Hybrid Logic is so suitable for our approach to Commonsense Spatial Reasoning with respect to "*modularity*". Thanks to the Blackburn's Theorem reported above, in fact, it is sufficient to add a set of formulas defining a frame to the tableau H (see Table 1) to obtain a sound and complete calculus with respect to that frame classes. Some classes have been characterized here

with respect to SCSMs, but formulas defining other frames can often be found in literature, and Hybrid Logic showed to be very powerful for such a task. Modifying some of
the relations specified for SCMS or adding a new one it is not very hard given a good
domain analysis.

For example in an ubiquitous computing environment, *networking* among different
devices can be viewed as a *proximity* relation. Anyway, if more complex access policy
need to be taken into account, the relation may loose symmetry property. To introduce
the respective modal operator, it is sufficient to cut out the *sym* axiom for that relation
from the set Φ^S.

5   A Hybrid Logic for Commonsense Spatial Reasoning

The class of SCSMs has been defined in the previous section. Now it is time to see
an instance of it introducing a specific Hybrid Language with its proper set of modal
operators. The choice of this specific language is related to the observation about pervasive systems from which we started, for our definition of Commonsense Spatial Model
(see also [13]). We want to grant flat orientation in space, adjacency among places (it
is possible to reach a place from another one) and to model containment among places;
with respect to the latter, in order to simplify reasoning, we introduce two containment
relations defining the second one as the inverse of the other one, so that it will be easy
to reason along both directions of the $\leq$ relation. We call the following Basic Standard
Commonsense Spatial Logic.

Definition 5. *Basic Standard Commonsense Spatial Logic* $(SCSL^{basic})$.
 Language. $\mathcal{L}^b$ is a Hybrid Language containing the modal operators $\Diamond_N$, $\Diamond_E$, $\Diamond_S$,
$\Diamond_W$, $\Diamond_{IN}$, $\Diamond_{NI}$ and $\Diamond_A$, the respective boxes ($\Box_N$, and so on), and where
$\{north, east, south, west\} \in NOM$.
 Semantics. Formulas of $\mathcal{L}^b$ are interpreted over a $SCSM$: $\Diamond_{IN}$, $\Diamond_{NI}$ are interpreted over containment *accessibility relations*, $\Diamond_A$ over a proximity *relation, and* $\Diamond_N$,
$\Diamond_E$, $\Diamond_S$, $\Diamond_W$ over orientation *relations, whose top elements are respectively the denotation of "north", "east", "south", "west".*
 Calculus. *A sound and complete calculus for* $SCMS^{basic}$ *is given by* $H + \Phi^S + X^S$
where:

 – H *is as defined in Section 4*
 – Φ^S *consists of the following combination of pure formulas:*

$$\begin{array}{ll} \Diamond_A & \textit{ref, sym} \\ \Diamond_{IN}, \Diamond_{NI} & \textit{ref, antisym, trans} \\ \Diamond_N, \Diamond_E, \Diamond_S, \Diamond_W & \textit{irref, asym, trans, ex, uni} \end{array}$$

 – X^S *is given by the following cross-property formulas:*

$$@_i (\Box_N \Diamond_S i \wedge \Box_S \Diamond_N i)$$
$$@_i (\Box_E \Diamond_W i \wedge \Box_W \Diamond_E i)$$
$$@_i (\Box_{IN} \Diamond_{NI} i \wedge \Box_{NI} \Diamond_{IN} i)$$
$$\Diamond_\star i \rightarrow \Box_{IN} \Diamond_\star i \quad \textit{where } \star = (N|E|S|W)$$

Finally, the interpretation of "north" is bound by the formula $@_{north}\neg\Diamond_N i$, and analogous formulas are introduced for the other top elements.

To see the logical calculus in action we can take a simple example from the domain we started from, that is, alarm correlation in pervasive computing environments. This example is the formalized version of an example intuitively presented in [13].

Example 2. Often a single alarm signal is not sufficient to infer that in a wider zone where it has been sensed, there is a dangerous situation. So, in order to reduce the false alarm rate, it can be required that at least two different devices must return alarm signals. In the Basic Standard Commonsense Language, this can be modeled introducing the axiom $@_i(al \wedge \Diamond_{NI}k) \rightarrow (@_j(al \wedge \Diamond_{NI}k \wedge \neg i) \rightarrow @_k al)$, which states that, if an alarm has been detected in two different places i and j both contained in another place k, it should be inferred that in k there is an alarm as well. Now, the following proof shows that, if s_1 and s_2 are two sensors that detected an alarm ("al", here below), since they are contained in the *kitchen* ("kit" below), in the kitchen *alarm* is inferred. We prove it assuming premises (2,3,4,5,6) and refuting $\neg@_{kit}al$ (1):

1   $\neg@_{kit}al$
2   $\neg@_{s_1}s_2$
3   $@_{s_1}al$
4   $@_{s_2}al$
5   $@_{s_1}\Diamond_{NI}kit$
6   $@_{s_2}\Diamond_{NI}kit$
7   $@_{kit}(@_{s_1}(al \wedge \Diamond_{NI}kit) \rightarrow @_{s_2}(al \wedge \Diamond_{NI}kit \wedge \neg s_1) \rightarrow @_{kit}al)$
8   $\neg@_{kit}(@_{s_1}(al \wedge \Diamond_{NI}kit)$ | $@_{kit}(@_{s_2}(al \wedge \Diamond_{NI}kit \wedge \neg s_1) \rightarrow @_{kit}al)$
9   $\neg@_{s_1}(al \wedge \Diamond_{NI}kit)$ $\neg@_{s_2}(al \wedge \Diamond_{NI}kit \wedge \neg s_1)$ | $@_{kit}al$
10 $\neg@_{s_1}al$ | $\neg@_{s_1}\Diamond_{NI}kit$ $\neg@_{s_2}al$ | $\neg@_{s_2}\Diamond_{NI}kit$ | $\neg@_{s_2}\neg s_1$ ✠ 1,9 ✠
11 ✠ 3, 10 ✠   ✠ 5, 10 ✠   ✠ 4, 10 ✠   ✠ 6, 10 ✠   ✠ 2, 10 ✠

6   Concluding Remarks

In this paper we presented a commonsense spatial model of space particularly suitable for supporting correlation of information coming from distributed sources, which does not assume a strong mathematical ontology, but focuses on the commonsense concepts of place and spatial conceptual relation. We have shown that the proposed model can suitably provide a formal semantics for a hybrid modal language, and a sound and complete tableaux calculus has been introduced for reasoning with formulas that represent contextual information. Notice that a CSM is not a closed model, in the sense that, although some basic conceptual spatial relations have been formally characterized (as in Section 4), the definition of new arbitrary relations is left open, still preserving the basic model definition (Def. 1).

A still open issue concerns the complexity and decidabilty of the $SCSL^{basic}$; however, as a preliminary observation, it can be stated that the logic is not enough expressive to talk about grid-like frames and thus it is not possible to encode the tiling problem [15] into $SCSL^{basic}$ in order to derive undecidability. In fact, this is not a multidimensional modal logic and the East/West, and the North/South relations are not orthogonal. Moreover, any grid-like frame would be inconsistent with respect to the characterization of end points given by the *uni* and *ex* axioms for orientation relations.

Finally, there are many domains in which dynamic aspects of the environment should be taken into account explicitly. In particular this concerns the ability to reason along the time dimension or about changes in the model. These issues concerning dynamical aspects of spatial reasoning open interesting research scenarios that it is our intention to address in future works.

References

1. Zambonelli, F., Parunak, H.: Signs of a revolution in computer science and software engineering. In: Proceedings of Engineering Societies in the Agents World III (ESAW2002). Volume 2577., Springer-Verlag (2002) 13–28
2. Bandini, S., Bogni, D., Manzoni, S.: Alarm correlation in traffic monitoring and control systems: a knowledge-based approach. In van Harmelen, F., ed.: Proceedings of the 15th European Conference on Artificial Intelligence, July 21-26 2002, Lyon (F), Amsterdam, IOS Press (2002) 638–642
3. Joshi, A., Finin, T., Yelsha, Y.: Me-services: A framework for secure & personailzed discovery, composition and management of services in pervasive environments. LNCS **2512** (2002) 248–259
4. Davis, E.: Representations of commonsense knowledge. Morgan Kaufmann Publishers (1990)
5. Leisler, D., Zilbershatz, A.: The traveller: A computational model of spatial network learning. Environment and Behaviour **21** (1989) 435–463
6. Kuipers, B.: Modelling spatial knowledge. Cognitive Science **2** (1978) 129–154
7. Gopal, S., Klatzky, R., Smith, T.: Navigator: A psychologically based model of environmental learning through navigation. Journal of Environmental Psychology **9** (1989) 309–331
8. Randell, D.A., Cui, Z., Cohn, A.G.: A spatial logic based on regions and connection. In: Proc. 3rd Int. Conf. on Knowledge Representation and Reasoning, San Mateo, CA, Morgan Kaufmann (1992) 165–176
9. Aiello, M., van Benthem, J.: Logical patterns in space. In D. Barker-Plummer, D. Beaver, J.v.B., di Luzio, P.S., eds.: Words, Proofs, and Diagrams, CSLI (2002) 5–25
10. Bandini, S., Mosca, A., Palmonari, M., Sartori, F.: A conceptual framework for monitoring and control system development. In: Ubiquitous Mobile Information and Collaboration Systems (UMICS'04). Volume 3272., Springer-Verlag (2004)
11. Blackburn, P., de Rijke, M., Venema, Y.: Modal Logic. Cambridge University Press (2000)
12. Blackburn, P.: Representation, reasoning and realtional structures: a hybrid logic manifesto. Logic Journal of the IGPL **8** (2000) 339–365
13. S. Bandini, A.M., Palmonari, M.: Commonsense spatial reasoning for context–aware pervasive systems. In: Location- and Context-Awareness, First International Workshop, LoCA 2005. Volume 3479., Springer-Verlag (2005) 180–188
14. Blackburn, P., Marx, M.: Tableaux for quantified hybrid logic. In Egly, C., Fernmller, C., eds.: HAutomated Reasoning with Analytic Tableaux and Related Methods, International Conference, Copenhagen, Denmark (2002) 38–52
15. Harel, D.: Recurring dominoes: making the highly undecidable highly understandable. In: Selected papers of the international conference on "foundations of computation theory" on Topics in the theory of computation, New York, NY, USA, Elsevier North-Holland, Inc. (1985) 51–71

Using a Theorem Prover for Reasoning on Constraint Problems

Marco Cadoli and Toni Mancini

Dipartimento di Informatica e Sistemistica,
Università di Roma "La Sapienza",
Via Salaria 113, I-00198 Roma, Italy
{cadoli, tmancini}@dis.uniroma1.it

Abstract. Specifications of constraint problems can be considered logical formulae. As a consequence, it is possible to infer their properties by means of automated reasoning tools, with the goal of automatically synthesizing transformations that can make the solving process more efficient. The purpose of this paper is to link two important technologies: automated theorem proving and constraint programming. We report the results on using ATP technology for checking existence of symmetries, checking whether a given formula breaks a symmetry, and checking existence of functional dependencies in a specification. The output of the reasoning phase is a transformed constraint program, consisting in a reformulated specification and, possibly a search strategy. We show our techniques on problems such as Graph coloring, Sailco inventory and Protein folding.

1 Introduction

The efficiency of current systems for constraint programming (CP), e.g., OPL [18], GAMS [5], DLV [10], and NP-SPEC [4], depends on the choices that users have to make in order handle instances of realistic size. This may degrade the declarativeness of the CP approach. The main user choices that greatly influence performances are about:

- The model for the given problem. In fact, different, but equivalent formulations for the same problem usually exist, and choosing one of them can make the difference. To this end, many techniques have been proposed, in order to modify the given constraint problem into an equivalent one, with the goal of reducing the solving time (e.g., symmetry-breaking, addition of implied constraints, or the opposite strategy of constraint abstraction).
- The search strategy to be applied, and the heuristic to be used to order variables and domain values. To this end, even if some systems, e.g., OPL [18], use a default strategy if the user-defined one is missing, there are many situations in which a smart reasoning on the problem specification is needed in order to infer good ones. An example is given by specifications in which functionally dependent predicates exist, either because of a precise modelling

S. Bandini and S. Manzoni (Eds.): AI*IA 2005, LNAI 3673, pp. 38–49, 2005.

choice (e.g., redundant modelling), or because of intrinsic properties of the modelled problem. In [3] (and in forthcoming Section 4) we show how a suitable search strategy that exploits dependencies can be synthesized.

Although much research has been done on these aspects, all techniques proposed in the literature in order to optimize the solving process either apply at the instance level, or are reformulations of a specific constraint problem, obtained as the output of a human process. In particular, the use of automated tools for preprocessing and reformulating arbitrary constraint problems has been limited, to the best of our knowledge, to the *instance* level (cf., e.g., [15,9,11]).

On the other hand, current systems for CP exhibit a neat separation between problem *specifications* and *instances*, and, in many cases, the structure of the problem, and not the instance at hand, exhibits properties amenable to be optimized. Hence, reasoning at the symbolic level can be more natural and effective than making these "structural" aspects emerge after instantiation, when the structure of the problem has been hidden. This makes specification-level reasoning very attractive from a methodological point of view, also for *validation purposes*, since the presence or lack of a property (e.g., a dependence) may reveal a bug in the problem model.

Our research explicitly focuses on the specification level, and aims to transform the constraint model given by the user into an equivalent one (possibly integrated with additional information about the search strategy to be used), which is more efficiently evaluable by the solver at hand. We note that focusing on the specification does not rule out the possibility of applying all existing optimization techniques at the instance level, to handle also those aspects that arise from the instance considered.

In previous work, we studied how to highlight constraints that can be ignored in a first step (the so called "safe-delay constraints") [2], how to detect and break symmetries [1,12], and how to recognize and exploit functional dependencies in a specification [3], showing how the original problem model can be appropriately reformulated. Experimental analysis shows how these approaches are effective in practice, for different classes of solvers. In this paper, we tackle the following question: *is it possible to check the above mentioned properties, and possibly other ones, automatically?* The main result is that, even if the underlying problems have been proven to be not decidable (cf. previously cited works), in practical circumstances the answer is often positive. In particular, we show how automated theorem proving (ATP) technology can be effectively used to perform the required forms of reasoning.

We report the results on using theorem provers and finite model finders for reasoning on specifications of constraint problems, represented as existential second order logic (ESO) formulae. We focus on two forms of reasoning:

- Checking existence of *value symmetries*; on top of that, we check whether a given formula breaks such symmetries or not;
- Checking existence of *functional dependencies*, i.e., properties that force values of some guessed predicates to depend on the value of other ones.

The rest of the paper is organized as follows: in Section 2 we give some preliminaries on modelling combinatorial problems as formulae in ESO. Sections 3 and 4 are devoted to the description of experiments in checking symmetries and dependencies, respectively. In Section 5 we conclude the paper, and present current research.

2   Preliminaries

In this paper, we use *existential second-order logic* (ESO) for the formal specification of problems, which allows to represent all search problems in the complexity class NP [7]. For motivations about the use of ESO as a modelling language, cf. our previous work [1,3,2]. Here, we recall that ESO can be regarded as the formal basis of virtually all languages for constraint modelling, as long as only finite domains are considered. Additionally, many reasoning tasks on problem specifications written in ESO reduce to check semantic properties of first-order formulae. Finally, our results are a basis for transforming specifications written in higher-level languages.

An ESO specification describing a search problem π is a formula ψ_π:

$$\exists \boldsymbol{S} \; \phi(\boldsymbol{S}, \boldsymbol{R}), \tag{1}$$

where $\boldsymbol{R} = \{R_1, \ldots, R_k\}$ is the *relational schema* for every input instance, and ϕ is a quantified first-order formula on the relational vocabulary $\boldsymbol{S} \cup \boldsymbol{R} \cup \{=\}$ ("=" is always interpreted as identity). An instance $\boldsymbol{I}$ of the problem is given as a relational database (coherently with all state-of-the-art systems) over the schema $\boldsymbol{R}$. Predicates (of given arities) in the set $\boldsymbol{S} = \{S_1, \ldots, S_n\}$ are called *guessed*, and their possible extensions over the Herbrand universe encode points in the search space for problem π. Formula ψ_π correctly encodes problem π if, for every input instance $\boldsymbol{I}$, a bijective mapping exists between solutions to π and extensions of predicates in $\boldsymbol{S}$ which verify $\phi(\boldsymbol{S}, \boldsymbol{I})$. It is worthwhile to note that, when a specification is instantiated against an input database, a CSP in the sense of [6] is obtained.

Example 1 (Graph 3-coloring [8]). Given a graph, the question is whether it is possible to give each of its nodes one out of three colors (red, green, and blue), in such a way that adjacent nodes (not including self-loops) are never colored the same way. The question can be easily specified as an ESO formula ψ on the input schema $\boldsymbol{R} = \{edge(\cdot, \cdot)\}$:

$$
\begin{aligned}
\exists RGB \quad & \forall X \quad R(X) \vee G(X) \vee B(X) \; \wedge & (2)\\
& \forall X \quad R(X) \rightarrow \neg G(X) \; \wedge & (3)\\
& \forall X \quad R(X) \rightarrow \neg B(X) \; \wedge & (4)\\
& \forall X \quad B(X) \rightarrow \neg G(X) \; \wedge & (5)\\
& \forall XY \; X \neq Y \wedge R(X) \wedge R(Y) \rightarrow \neg edge(X,Y) \; \wedge & (6)\\
& \forall XY \; X \neq Y \wedge G(X) \wedge G(Y) \rightarrow \neg edge(X,Y) \; \wedge & (7)\\
& \forall XY \; X \neq Y \wedge B(X) \wedge B(Y) \rightarrow \neg edge(X,Y). & (8)
\end{aligned}
$$

Clauses (2) and (3-5) force every node to be assigned exactly one color (covering and disjointness constraints), while (6-8) force nodes linked by an edge to be assigned different colors (good coloring constraints).   □

3 Detecting and Breaking Uniform Value Symmetries

In this section we face the problem of automatically detecting and breaking some symmetries in problem specifications. In Subsection 3.1 we give preliminary definitions of problem transformation and symmetry taken from [1], and show how the symmetry-detection problem can be reduced to checking semantic properties of first-order formulae. We limit our attention to specifications with monadic guessed predicates only, and to transformations and symmetries on values. Motivations for these limitations are given in [1]; here, we just recall that non-monadic guessed predicates can be transformed in monadic ones by unfolding and by exploiting the finiteness of the input database. We refer to [1] also for considerations on benefits of the technique on the efficiency of problem solving, in particular on the Graph coloring, Not-all-equal Sat, and Social golfer problems. In Subsection 3.2 we then show how a theorem prover can be used to automatically detect and break symmetries.

3.1 Definitions

Definition 1 (Uniform value transformation (UVT) of a specification).
Given a problem specification $\psi \doteq \exists \boldsymbol{S} \ \phi(\boldsymbol{S}, \boldsymbol{R})$, *with* $\boldsymbol{S} = \{S_1, \ldots S_n\}$, S_i *monadic for every* $i \in [1, n]$, *and input schema* $\boldsymbol{R}$, *a* uniform value transformation (UVT) *for* ψ *is a mapping* $\sigma : \boldsymbol{S} \to \boldsymbol{S}$, *which is total and onto, i.e., defines a permutation of guessed predicates in* $\boldsymbol{S}$.

The term "uniform value" transformation in Definition 1 is used because swapping monadic guessed predicates is conceptually the same as uniformly exchanging domain values in a CSP. Referring to Example 1, the domains values are the colors, i.e., red, green, and blue. We now define when a UVT is a symmetry for a given specification.

Definition 2 (Uniform value symmetry (UVS) of a specification). *Let* $\psi \doteq \exists \boldsymbol{S} \ \phi(\boldsymbol{S}, \boldsymbol{R})$, *be a specification, with* $\boldsymbol{S} = \{S_1, \ldots S_n\}$, S_i *monadic for every* $i \in [1, n]$, *and input schema* $\boldsymbol{R}$, *and let* σ *be a UVT for* ψ. *Transformation* σ *is a* uniform value symmetry (UVS) *for* ψ *if every extension for* $\boldsymbol{S}$ *which satisfies* ϕ, *satisfies also* ϕ^σ, *defined as* $\phi[S_1/\sigma(S_1), \ldots, S_n/\sigma(S_n)]$ *and vice versa, regardless of the input instance, i.e., for every extension of the input schema* $\boldsymbol{R}$.

Note that every CSP obtained by instantiating a specification with UVS σ has at least the corresponding uniform value symmetry.

In [1], it is shown that checking whether a UVT is a UVS reduces to checking equivalence of two first-order formulae:

Proposition 1. *Let ψ be a problem specification of the kind (1), with only monadic guessed predicates, and σ a UVT for ψ. Transformation σ is a UVS for ψ if and only if $\phi \equiv \phi^{\sigma}$.*

Once symmetries of a specification have been detected, additional constraints can be added in order to *break* them, i.e., to transform the specification in order to wipe out from the solution space (some of) the symmetrical points. These kind of constraints are called *symmetry-breaking formulae*:

Definition 3 (Symmetry-breaking formula). *A symmetry-breaking formula for $\psi \doteq \exists \boldsymbol{S}\ \phi(\boldsymbol{S}, \boldsymbol{R})$ with respect to UVS σ is a closed (except for $\boldsymbol{S}$) formula $\beta(\boldsymbol{S})$ such that the following two conditions hold:*

1. *Transformation σ is no longer a symmetry for $\exists \boldsymbol{S}\ \phi(\boldsymbol{S}, \boldsymbol{R}) \wedge \beta(\boldsymbol{S})$:*

$$(\phi(\boldsymbol{S}, \boldsymbol{R}) \wedge \beta(\boldsymbol{S})) \not\equiv (\phi(\boldsymbol{S}, \boldsymbol{R}) \wedge \beta(\boldsymbol{S}))^{\sigma}\ ; \tag{9}$$

2. *Every model of $\phi(\boldsymbol{S}, \boldsymbol{R})$ can be obtained by those of $\phi(\boldsymbol{S}, \boldsymbol{R}) \wedge \beta(\boldsymbol{S})$ by applying symmetry σ:*

$$\phi(\boldsymbol{S}, \boldsymbol{R}) \models \bigvee_{\boldsymbol{\sigma} \in \sigma^{*}} (\phi(\boldsymbol{S}, \boldsymbol{R}) \wedge \beta(\boldsymbol{S}))^{\boldsymbol{\sigma}}\ ; \tag{10}$$

where $\boldsymbol{\sigma}$ is a sequence (of finite length ≥ 0) over σ, and, given a first-order formula $\gamma(\boldsymbol{S})$, $\gamma(\boldsymbol{S})^{\boldsymbol{\sigma}}$ denotes $(\cdots(\gamma(\boldsymbol{S})^{\sigma})\cdots)^{\sigma}$, i.e., σ is applied $|\boldsymbol{\sigma}|$ times (if $\boldsymbol{\sigma} = \langle\rangle$, then $\gamma(\boldsymbol{S})^{\boldsymbol{\sigma}}$ is $\gamma(\boldsymbol{S})$ itself).

If $\beta(\boldsymbol{S})$ matches the above definition, then we are entitled to solve the problem $\exists \boldsymbol{S}\ \phi(\boldsymbol{S}, \boldsymbol{R}) \wedge \beta(\boldsymbol{S})$ instead of the original one $\exists \boldsymbol{S}\ \phi(\boldsymbol{S}, \boldsymbol{R})$. It is worthwhile noting that, even if in formula (10) $\boldsymbol{\sigma}$ ranges over the (infinite) set of finite-length sequences of 0 or more applications of σ, this actually reduces to sequences of length at most $n!$, since this is the maximum number of successive applications of σ that can lead to all different permutations. Finally, we note that the inverse logical implication in formula (10) always holds, because σ is a UVS, and so $\phi(\boldsymbol{S}, \boldsymbol{R})^{\sigma} \equiv \phi(\boldsymbol{S}, \boldsymbol{R})$.

3.2   Experiments with the Theorem Prover

Proposition 1 suggests that the problem of detecting UVSs of a specification ψ of the kind (1) can in principle be performed in the following way:

1. Selecting a UVT σ, i.e., a permutation of guessed predicates in ψ (if ψ has n guessed predicates, there are $n!$ such UVTs $-n$ is usually very small);
2. Checking whether σ is a UVS, i.e., deciding whether $\phi \equiv \phi^{\sigma}$.

The above procedure suggests that a first-order theorem prover can be used to perform automatically point 2. Even if we proved in [1] that this problem is not decidable, we show how a theorem prover usually performs well on this kind of formulae. As for the symmetry-breaking problem, from conditions of Definition 3 it follows that also the problem of checking whether a formula breaks a given UVS for a specification clearly reduces to semantic properties of logical formulae.

In this section we give some details about the experimentation done using automated tools. First of all we note that, obviously, all the above mentioned conditions can be checked by using a refutation theorem prover. It is interesting to note that, for some of them, we can use a finite model finder. In particular, we can use such a tool for checking statements (such as condition (9) of Definition 3 or the negation of the condition of Proposition 1) which are syntactically a non-equivalence. As a matter of facts, it is enough to look for a finite model of the negation of the statement, i.e., the equivalence. If we find such a model, then we are sure that the non-equivalence holds, and we are done. The tools we used are OTTER [14], and MACE [13], respectively, in full-automatic mode.

Detecting Symmetries. The examples we worked on are the following.

Example 2 (Graph 3-coloring: Example 1 continued). The mapping $\sigma^{R,G} : \boldsymbol{S} \to \boldsymbol{S}$ such that $\sigma^{R,G}(R) = G$, $\sigma^{R,G}(G) = R$, $\sigma^{R,G}(B) = B$ is a UVT for it. It is easy to observe that formula $\phi^{\sigma^{R,G}}$ is equivalent to ϕ. This implies, by Proposition 1, that $\sigma^{R,G}$ is also a UVS for this problem. The same happens also for $\sigma^{R,B}$ and $\sigma^{G,B}$ that swap B with, respectively, R and G. □

Example 3 (Not-all-equal Sat [8]). Given a propositional formula in CNF, the question is whether it is possible to assign a truth value to all the variables in such a way that the input formula is satisfied, and every clause contains at least one literal which is false. An ESO specification for this problem (cf. [1]) has two monadic guessed predicates $T(\cdot)$ and $F(\cdot)$, representing variables whose truth value is true and false, respectively. It is easy to prove that the UVT $\sigma^{T,F}$, defined as $\sigma^{T,F}(T) = F$ and $\sigma^{T,F}(F) = T$, is a UVS, since $\phi^{\sigma^{T,F}}$ is equivalent to ϕ. □

Example 4 (Social golfer (cf. www.csplib.org)). Given a set of players, a set of groups, and a set of weeks, encoded in monadic relations $player(\cdot)$, $group(\cdot)$, and $week(\cdot)$ respectively, this problem amounts to decide whether there is a way to arrange a scheduling for all weeks in relation $week$, such that: *(i)* For every week, players are divided into equal sized groups; and *(ii)* Two different players don't play in the same group more than once. A specification for this problem (assuming the ratio $|player|/|group|$, i.e., the group size, integral) has a single guessed predicate $Play(P, W, G)$ stating that player P plays in group G on week W (cf. [1]). In order to highlight UVSs according to Definition 2, we need to substitute the ternary guessed predicate $Play$ by means of, e.g., $|week| \times |group|$ monadic predicates $Play_{W,G}(\cdot)$ (each one listing players playing in group G on week W). UVTs $\sigma_W^{G,G'}$, swapping $Play_{W,G}$ and $Play_{W,G'}$, i.e., given a week W, and two groups G and G', assign to group G' on week W all players assigned to group G on week W, and vice versa, are symmetries for the (unfolded) Social golfer problem (because group renamings have no effect). It is worth noting that unfolding non-monadic predicates is just a formal step in order to apply the definitions of [1], and has not to be performed in practice. □

Table 1. Performance of OTTER for proving that a UVT is a UVS

Spec	Symmetry	CPU time (sec)
3-coloring	$\sigma^{R,G}$	0.27
Not-all-equal Sat	$\sigma^{T,F}$	0.22
Not-all-equal 3-Sat	$\sigma^{T,F}$	4.71
Social golfer (unfolded)	$\sigma_W^{G,G'}$	0.96

The results we obtained with OTTER are shown in Table 1. The third row refers to the version of the Not-all-equal Sat problem in which all clauses have three literals, the input is encoded using a ternary relation $clause(\cdot, \cdot, \cdot)$, and the specification varies accordingly. It is interesting to see that the time needed by OTTER is often very low. As for the fourth row, it refers to the unfolded specification of the Social golfer problem with 2 weeks and 2 groups of size 2. Unfortunately, OTTER does not terminate for a larger number of weeks or groups (cf. Section 5).

A note on the encoding is in order. Initially, we gave the input to OTTER exactly in the format specified by Proposition 1, but the performance was quite poor: for 3-coloring the tool did not even succeed in transforming the formula in clausal form, and symmetry was proven only for very simplified versions of the problem, e.g., 2-coloring, omitting constraint (2). Results of Table 1 have been obtained by introducing new propositional variables defining single constraints. As an example, constraint (2) is represented as

```
covRGB <-> (all x (R(x) | G(x) | B(x))).,
```

where `covRGB` is a fresh propositional variable. Obviously, we wrote a first-order logic formula encoding condition of Proposition 1, and gave its negation to OTTER in order to find a refutation.

As for proving non-existence of symmetries, we used the following example.

Example 5 (Graph 3-coloring with red self-loops). We consider a modification of the problem of Example 1, and show that only one of the UVTs in Example 2 is indeed a UVS for the new problem. Here, the question is whether it is possible to 3-color the input graph in such a way that every self loop insists on a red node. In ESO, one more clause must be added to (2–8): $\forall X \; edge(X, X) \rightarrow R(X)$.

UVT $\sigma^{G,B}$ is a UVS also of the new problem, because of the same argument of Example 2. However, for what concerns $\sigma^{R,G}$, in this case $\phi^{\sigma^{R,G}}$ is not equivalent to ϕ: as an example, for the input instance $edge = \{(v,v)\}$, the color assignment $\overline{R}, \overline{G}, \overline{B}$ such that $\overline{R} = \{v\}, \overline{G} = \overline{B} = \emptyset$ is a model for the original problem, i.e., $\overline{R}, \overline{G}, \overline{B} \models \phi(R, G, B, edge)$. It is however easy to observe that $\overline{R}, \overline{G}, \overline{B} \not\models \phi^{\sigma^{R,G}}(R, G, B, edge)$, because $\phi^{\sigma^{R,G}}$ is verified only by color assignments for which $\overline{G}(v)$ holds. This implies, by Proposition 1, that $\sigma^{R,G}$ is not a UVS. For the same reason, also $\sigma^{R,B}$ is not a UVS for the new problem.   □

We wrote a first-order logic formula encoding condition of Proposition 1 for $\sigma^{R,G}$ on the above example and gave its negation to MACE in order to find a model of the non-equivalence. MACE was able to find the model described in Example 5 in few hundreds of a second.

Breaking symmetries. We worked on the 3-coloring specification given in Example 1 and the UVS $\sigma^{R,G}$ defined in Example 2. This UVS can be broken by, e.g., the following formulae:

$$\beta_{sel}^{R,G}(R,G,B) \doteq R(\overline{v}) \vee B(\overline{v}), \tag{11}$$

that forces a selected node, say $\overline{v}$, not to be colored in green;

$$\beta_{least}^{R,G}(R,G,B) \doteq \forall w \ G(w) \rightarrow \exists v \ R(v) \wedge v < w, \tag{12}$$

where "$<$" is a (possibly pre-interpreted) total ordering on the graph nodes, hence forcing the least green node to be greater than the least red one (the so-called *lowest index ordering* on red and green nodes);

$$\beta_{card}^{R,G}(R,G,B) \doteq |R| \leq |G|, \tag{13}$$

that forces green nodes to be at least as many as the red ones. It is easy to prove that formulae (11), (12) and (13) respect both conditions of Definition 3. As for condition (10), σ can be limited to sequences of length at most 2, since $\sigma^{R,G}$ swaps only two guessed predicates.

For what concerns formula (13), some considerations are in order, since this example highlights some difficulties that can arise when using first-order ATPs. In fact, formula (13) can be written in ESO (it evaluates to true if and only if a total injective function from tuples in R to those in G exists). Therefore, conditions in Definition 3 are second-order (non-)equivalences, and the use of a first-order theorem prover may in general not suffice. However, in some circumstances, it is possible to write first-order conditions that can be used to infer the truth value of those of Definition 3. One such case is that of formulae in ESO (details omitted for lack of space).

Table 2. Performance of OTTER for proving that a formula $\beta(\mathcal{S})$ is symmetry-breaking for a given symmetry. "–" means that a timeout of 1 hour occurred, while "?" that OTTER terminated without a proof.

Spec	Symmetry	$\beta(\mathcal{S})$	CPU time (sec)	
			Cond. (9) (MACE)	Cond. (10) (OTTER)
3-coloring	$\sigma^{R,G}$	$\beta_{sel}^{R,G}(R,G,B)$	1.47	1.89
	$\sigma^{R,G}$	$\beta_{least}^{R,G}(R,G,B)$	2.67	?
	$\sigma^{R,G}$	$\beta_{card}^{R,G}(R,G,B)$	0.25	–
Social golfer	$\sigma_W^{G,G'}$	$\beta_{least\ W}^{G,G'}(\cdots)$	0.04	?

We used MACE and OTTER in order to prove that the formulae described above are symmetry-breaking for 3-coloring with respect to $\sigma^{R,G}$, by checking conditions of Definition 3. As Table 2 shows, results are always good when checking the first condition, while may become worse when OTTER is used to prove the second one (the third row of Table 2 refers to the overall time needed to check whether formula (13) satisfies the first condition of Definition 3). However, these poor performances do not make the approach meaningless. In fact, it is often possible to have candidate symmetry-breaking formulae, e.g., (13) and its generalizations, that respect the second condition of Definition 3 *by design*. In these cases, checking the first condition with MACE suffices.

4   Recognizing and Exploiting Dependent Predicates

In this section we tackle the problem of recognizing guessed predicates that functionally depend on others in a given specification. This means that, for every solution of any instance, the extension of a dependent guessed predicate is determined by the extensions of the others.

In [3] we showed how dependent predicates arise very often in declarative problem specifications, especially when auxiliary information or partial computations must be maintained. We recall in Subsection 4.1 the formal definition of dependent predicate in a specification, taken from [3], as well as some results. Then, in Subsection 4.2 we show how a first-order theorem prover can be effectively used to automatically recognize functional dependencies.

4.1   Definitions

Definition 4 (Functional dependence of a set of predicates). *Given a problem specification* $\psi \doteq \exists \mathcal{S} \mathcal{P} \ \phi(\mathcal{S}, \mathcal{P}, \mathcal{R})$, *with input schema* $\mathcal{R}$, *set* $\mathcal{P}$ *functionally depends on set* $\mathcal{S}$ *if, for each instance* $\mathcal{I}$ *of* $\mathcal{R}$ *and for each pair of interpretations* M, N *of* $(\mathcal{S}, \mathcal{P})$ *it holds that, if* (i) $M \neq N$, (ii) $M, \mathcal{I} \models \phi$, *and* (iii) $N, \mathcal{I} \models \phi$, *then* $M_{|\mathcal{S}} \neq N_{|\mathcal{S}}$, *where* $\cdot_{|\mathcal{S}}$ *denotes the restriction of an interpretation to predicates in* $\mathcal{S}$.

As an example, in Graph 3-coloring (cf. Example 1), one of the three guessed predicates (e.g., B) is dependent on R and G, since $\forall X \ B(X) \leftrightarrow \neg(R(X) \vee G(X))$. Also, in Not-all-equal Sat (cf. Example 3), predicate T is dependent on F or vice versa.

The problem of checking functional dependencies reduces to semantic properties of a first-order formula, as the following result of [3] shows:

Proposition 2. *Let* $\psi \doteq \exists \mathcal{S} \mathcal{P} \ \phi(\mathcal{S}, \mathcal{P}, \mathcal{R})$ *be a problem specification with input schema* $\mathcal{R}$. $\mathcal{P}$ *functionally depends on* $\mathcal{S}$ *iff the following formula is valid:*

$$[\phi(\mathcal{S}, \mathcal{P}, \mathcal{R}) \wedge \phi(\mathcal{S}', \mathcal{P}', \mathcal{R}) \wedge \neg(\mathcal{S}\mathcal{P} \equiv \mathcal{S}'\mathcal{P}')] \rightarrow \neg(\mathcal{S} \equiv \mathcal{S}'). \qquad (14)$$

To simplify notations, given two sets of predicates T and T' of the same arities, we write $T \equiv T'$ as a shorthand for $\bigwedge_{T \in T} \forall X \ T(X) \equiv T'(X)$.

Unfortunately, in [3], the problem of checking whether the set of predicates in $\mathcal{P}$ is functionally dependent on the set $\mathcal{S}$ is proven to be not decidable. Nonetheless, as shown in the next section, an ATP can perform very well in deciding whether formulae of the kind of (14) are valid or not.

4.2   Experiments with the Theorem Prover

Using Proposition 2 it is easy to write a first-order formula that is valid if and only if a given dependence holds. We used OTTER for proving the existence of dependencies among guessed predicates of different problem specifications:

- Graph 3-coloring (cf. Example 1), where one among the guessed predicates R, G, B is dependent on the others.
- Not-all-equal Sat (cf. Example 3), where one between the guessed predicates T and F is dependent on the other.

For each of the above specifications, we wrote a first-order encoding of formula (14), and gave its negation to OTTER in order to find a refutation. For the purpose of testing effectiveness of the proposed technique in the context of more complex specifications, we considered also the *Sailco inventory*, and the *HP 2D-Protein folding* problems (description of the latter problem is omitted for lack of space, and can be found in [3]).

Example 6 (The Sailco inventory problem [18, Section 9.4, Statement 9.17]). This problem specification, part of the OPLSTUDIO distribution package (as file `sailco.mod`), models a simple inventory application, in which the question is to decide how many sailboats the Sailco company has to produce over a given number of time periods, in order to satisfy the demand and to minimize production costs. The **demand** for the periods is known and, in addition, an inventory **inv** of boats is available initially. In each period, Sailco can produce a maximum number of boats at a given unitary cost. Additional boats (**extraBoats**) can be produced, but at higher cost. Storing boats in the inventory also has a cost per period.

The following relationship among the variables holds: `inv[t] = regulBoat[t] + extraBoat[t] - demand[t] + inv[t-1]`. Of course, the same relationship holds in the equivalent ESO specification (omitted for brevity), making guessed predicate $inv(\cdot, \cdot)$ functionally dependent on $regulBoat(\cdot, \cdot)$ and $extraBoat(\cdot, \cdot)$. (The arity of such predicates is 2, since functions must be modelled in ESO as relations, plus additional constraints.)

We opted for an OTTER encoding that uses function symbols: as an example, the `inv[]` array is translated to a function symbol $inv(\cdot)$ rather than to a binary predicate. More precisely, according to Proposition 2, a pair of function symbols $inv(\cdot)$ and $inv'(\cdot)$ is introduced. The same happens for `regulBoat[]` and `extraBoat[]`. Moreover, we included in the OTTER formula additional constraints in order to make the system able to correctly handle expressions of interest (in particular, arithmetic constraints). Notably, the following formulae allow to infer $\forall t\ inv(t) = inv'(t)$ from equality of inv and inv' at the initial time period and equivalence of increments in all time intervals of length 1.

```
equalDiscrete <-> (inv(0) = inv_prime(0) &
                  (all t (t > 0 -> (inv(t) - inv(t-1)) =
                                   (inv_prime(t) - inv_prime(t-1)))))).
induction <-> (equalDiscrete -> (all t (inv(t) = inv_prime(t)))).
```

Table 3. Performance of OTTER for proving that the set $\mathcal{P}$ of guessed predicates is functionally dependent on the set $\mathcal{S}$

Spec	$\mathcal{S}$	$\mathcal{P}$	CPU time (sec)
3-coloring	R, G	B	0.25
Not-all-equal 3-Sat	T	F	0.38
Sailco	$regulBoat,$ $extraBoat$	inv	0.21
HP 2D-Prot. fold. (simpl.)	$Move$	X, Y	569.55

Results of the experiments to check that dependencies for all the aforementioned problems hold are shown in Table 3. As it can be observed, for almost all of them the time needed by OTTER is very small. Actually, as for HP 2D-Protein folding, OTTER was able to solve only a simplified version of the problem (in which dependence of guessed predicate *Hits* is not checked, cf. [3]). To this end, we are investigating the use of other theorem provers (cf. Section 5).

When functional dependencies have been recognized in a problem specification, they can be exploited in several ways, in order to improve the solver efficiency. In [3] we show how simple search strategies can be automatically synthesized in order to avoid branches on dependent predicates. Despite their simplicity, such strategies are very effective in practice. As an example, speed-ups of about 99% have been observed for Protein folding and Blocks world [3].

5   Conclusions and Current Research

The use of automated tools for preprocessing CSPs has been limited, to the best of our knowledge, to the instance level. In this paper we proved that current ATP technology is able to perform significant forms of reasoning on specifications of constraint problems. We focused on two forms of reasoning: symmetry detection and breaking, and functional dependence checking. Reasoning has been done for various problems, including the ESO encodings of graph 3-coloring and Not-all-equal Sat, and the OPL encoding of an inventory problem, and 2D HP-Protein folding. In the latter examples, arithmetic constraints exist, and we have shown how they can be handled. In many cases, reasoning is done very efficiently by the ATP, although effectiveness depends on the format of the input, and auxiliary propositional variables seem to be necessary. There are indeed some tasks which OTTER –in the automatic mode– was unable to do. Hence, we plan to investigate other provers, e.g., VAMPIRE [17]. We note that the wide availability of constraint problem specifications, both in computer languages, cf., e.g., [18], and in natural language, cf., e.g., [8], the CSP-Library[1], and the OR-Library[2], offers a brand new set of benchmarks for ATP systems, which is not represented in large repositories, such as TPTP[3].

Currently, the generation of formulae that are given to the theorem prover is performed by hand. Nonetheless, we claim that, as it can be observed from

---

[1] www.csplib.org
[2] www.ms.ic.ac.uk/info.html
[3] www.tptp.org

the various examples, this task can in principle be performed automatically, starting from an implemented language such as OPL. This is possible because the OPL syntax for expressing constraints is similar to first-order logic. We plan to investigate this topic in future research.

References

1. M. Cadoli and T. Mancini. Detecting and breaking symmetries on specifications. In *Proc. of SymCon, in conj. with CP 2003*, 2003.
2. M. Cadoli and T. Mancini. Automated reformulation of specifications by safe delay of constraints. In *Proc. of KR 2004*, 2004. AAAI Press/The MIT Press.
3. M. Cadoli and T. Mancini. Exploiting functional dependencies in declarative problem specifications. In *Proc. of JELIA 2004*, 2004. Springer.
4. M. Cadoli and A. Schaerf. Compiling problem specifications into SAT. *Artif. Intell.*, 162:89–120, 2005.
5. E. Castillo, A. J. Conejo, P. Pedregal, R. Garcia, and N. Alguacil. *Building and Solving Mathematical Programming Models in Engineering and Science*. John Wiley & Sons, 2001.
6. R. Dechter. *Constraint Networks (Survey)*. John Wiley & Sons, 1992.
7. R. Fagin. Generalized first-order spectra and polynomial-time recognizable sets. In R. M. Karp, ed., *Complexity of Computation*, pages 43–74. Amer. Math. Soc., 1974.
8. M. R. Garey and D. S. Johnson. *Computers and Intractability: A Guide to the Theory of NP-Completeness*. W.H. Freeman and Co., 1979.
9. E. Giunchiglia and R. Sebastiani. Applying the Davis-Putnam procedure to non-clausal formulas. In *Proc. of AI*IA'99*, 2000. Springer.
10. N. Leone, G. Pfeifer, W. Faber, T. Eiter, G. Gottlob, S. Perri, and F. Scarcello. The DLV System for Knowledge Representation and Reasoning. *ACM Trans. on Comp. Logic*. To appear.
11. C. M. Li. Integrating equivalency reasoning into Davis-Putnam procedure. In *Proc. of AAAI 2000*, 2000. AAAI Press/The MIT Press.
12. T. Mancini and M. Cadoli. Detecting and breaking symmetries by reasoning on problem specifications. In *Proc. of SARA 2005*, 2005. Springer.
13. W. McCune. MACE 2.0 reference manual and guide. Tech. Rep. ANL/MCS-TM-249, Argonne Nat. Lab., Math. and Comp. Sci. Div., 2001. Available at `http://www-unix.mcs.anl.gov/AR/mace/`.
14. W. McCune. Otter 3.3 reference manual. Tech. Rep. ANL/MCS-TM-263, Argonne Nat. Lab., Math. and Comp. Sci. Div., 2003. Available at `http://www-unix.mcs.anl.gov/AR/otter/`.
15. B. D. McKay. *Nauty* user's guide (version 2.2). Available at `http://cs.anu.edu.au/~bdm/nauty/nug.pdf`, 2003.
16. P. Meseguer and C. Torras. Solving strategies for highly symmetric CSPs. In *Proc. of IJCAI'99*, 1999. Morgan Kaufmann.
17. A. Riazanov and A. Voronkov. Vampire. In *Proc. of CADE'99*, 1999. Springer.
18. P. Van Hentenryck. *The OPL Optimization Programming Language*. The MIT Press, 1999.

Good and Bad Practices in Propositionalisation

Nicolas Lachiche

LSIIT, Pôle API, Bd Brant, F-67400 Illkirch, France
lachiche@lsiit.u-strasbg.fr

Abstract. Data is mainly available in relational formats, so relational data mining receives a lot of interest. Propositionalisation consists in changing the representation of relational data in order to apply usual attribute-value learning systems. Data mining practitioners are not necessarily aware of existing works and try to propositionalise by hand. Unfortunately there exists some tempting pitfalls. This article aims at bridging the gap between data mining practitioners and relational data, pointing out the most usual traps and proposing correct approaches to propositionalisation. Similar situations with sequential data and the multiple-instance problem are also covered. Finally the strengths and weaknesses of propositionalisation are listed.

1 Introduction

Most of the available data involves some relations between different entities. Relational databases are the most common databases, e.g. customers and their orders, flights and passengers, warehouses and their products, and so on. Therefore data mining is more and more concerned with relational data. Several recent data mining challenges addressed relational datasets, e.g. bank accounts and their transactions (PKDD'99), patients and their examinations (PKDD'01-04).

While relational learning systems are available [5, 11], an alternative consists in turning the relational representation into a propositional representation – this change of representation is called propositionalisation –, then applying any of the numerous available propositional (a.k.a. attribute-value) learners. Propositionalisation has been a very active research area for years and several approaches have been proposed [8]. However they are not yet familiar to the whole data mining community, and, unfortunately, there exists several attractive, often intuitive, but incorrect, approaches. We have regularly encountered data mining practitioners, from students to colleagues, who fell in those traps and did not necessarily notice it. Fortunately it is usually corrected, but not always in particular in more complex contexts, e.g. [14] makes a bad use of join by associating the risk label of a patient to its controls, or [2] makes a bad use of the concatenation of columns by refering to the control absolute number. Therefore we feel that it is urgent not only to show the good practices of propositionalisation, but also to point out bad practices, explaining why they lead to meaningless results. Existing publications on propositionalisation propose new approaches, e.g. [6, 7, 1], relate successful applications [12, 4], review the state-of-the-art [8]

S. Bandini and S. Manzoni (Eds.): AI*IA 2005, LNAI 3673, pp. 50–61, 2005.

and compare some approaches [9], but none of them points out incorrect approaches. In this paper we take a broader view, and not only remind what can be done of propositionalisation – when propositionalisation is useful –, and what can be done in propositionalisation – how propositionalisation can be correctly performed –, but also explain what should not be done in propositionalisation – what incorrect propositionalisations are –.

So this paper is intended to newcomers to propositionalisation. Section 2 provides a minimum package to deal with relational data, namely a running example and the notations used in the paper. Section 3 lists common traps, i.e. incorrect approaches in propositionalisation. Section 4 presents correct approaches. Related issues are discussed in section 5, in particular close data formats such as multiple-instance problems and sequential data. The strengths and weaknesses of propositionalisation are also emphasized. Section 6 concludes.

2 Relational Data

This section presents the mutagenicity domain that will serve as a running example. It also introduces our notations.

2.1 Running Example

The mutagenicity problem [13] aims at predicting whether a molecule is mutagenic. In this paper we will use a simplified representation, to get a simple example of a relational domain involving several one-to-many relationships, namely a molecule is made of several atoms, and an atom is involved in at least one and possibly several bonds.[1] The property of the molecule is its class only. Atoms are described by their element (e.g. carbon, oxygen) and their electric charge. Bonds are characterized by their kind (e.g. single, double). Figure 1 presents an Entity-Relationship model. Figure 2 gives a partial view of the relations of the corresponding relational data. The `molid atomid` and `bondid` fields are the respective primary keys of molecules, atoms and bonds.

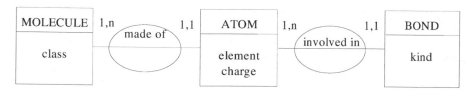

Fig. 1. Simplified Entity-Relationship model of the mutagenicity domain

---

[1] This is not a correct representation of a molecule, in particular a bond involves several atoms.

Molecules

Atoms

Bonds

molid	class
d1	mutagenic
d10	mutagenic
d100	non-mutagenic
⋮	⋮

atomid	element	charge	molid
d1_1	c	-0.117	d1
⋮	⋮	⋮	⋮
d1_26	o	-0.388	d1
d10_1	c	-0.119	d10
⋮	⋮	⋮	⋮

bondid	kind	atomid
d1_1_1	7	d1_1
d1_1_2	1	d1_1
d1_1_3	7	d1_1
⋮	⋮	⋮
d1_26_1	2	d1_26
⋮	⋮	⋮
d10_1_1	1	d10_1
⋮	⋮	⋮

(188 molecules)   (4893 atoms)   (10486 bonds)

Fig. 2. Partial view of the mutagenicity relational data

2.2 Notations

In this paper we will refer to ISP (Individual, Structural predicates and Property) declarations and to first-order features [6, 10]. Briefly an ISP declaration is similar to a relational datamodel where individuals denote the primary keys, e.g. `molid`, `atomid`, and `bondid` in our example, structural predicates are the foreign keys, denoted `molecule2atom` and `atom2bond`, and properties are the remaining attributes, i.e. `class`, `element`, `charge` and `kind`. A learning task normally focuses on one type of individual who will be called the individual, e.g. the molecule, and the other types of individuals will be called objects, i.e. the atoms and bonds of a molecule. A first-order feature represents a property of the individual, e.g. "the number of atoms of the molecule" or "whether the molecule contains a carbon atom involved in a double bond". It is the minimal conjunction of structural predicates and properties to relate properties of the objects to the main individual. An elementary first-order feature makes use of a single property.

In the following sections the presentation of every approach, be it correct or incorrect, will follow the same schema. We will give its principle, show the resulting table in the mutagenicity domain. Then we will run the same propositional algorithm and show its results. The flaws of the results and of the approach will be discussed for incorrect approaches. In all experiments, we aim at illustrating each propositionalisation approach rather than providing useful results on the mutagenicity domain [13], comparing propositional learning algorithms, or even comparing propositionalisation approaches. We refer to [9] for the last issue.

3 Common Traps

This section deals with frequent incorrect approaches to propositionalisation. We will use italic and conditional sentences to present flawed approaches and we will use normal style and more directive sentences (e.g. using "should" or "must") to propose corrections.

bondid	kind	atomid	element	charge	molid	class
d1_1_1	7	d1_1	c	-0.117	d1	mutagenic
d1_1_2	1	d1_1	c	-0.117	d1	mutagenic
d1_1_3	7	d1_1	c	-0.117	d1	mutagenic
d1_26_1	2	d1_26	o	-0.388	d1	mutagenic
⋮	⋮	⋮	⋮	⋮	⋮	⋮
d10_1_1	1	d10_1	c	-0.119	d10	mutagenic
⋮	⋮	⋮	⋮	⋮	⋮	⋮

(7 columns, 10486 lines)

Fig. 3. Universal join in the mutagenicity domain

3.1 Universal Join

From a database expert's point of view, the only way to turn several linked tables into a single table relies on a universal join, where a join is performed between all tables. Figure 3 illustrates the universal join in the mutagenicity domain.

Given such a table, a data miner *can* easily perform a 10-fold cross-validation using his favorite data mining tool, e.g. Weka [15]. We ran Part, a rule learning algorithm implemented in Weka that extract rules from a decision tree, and got *83.9%* accuracy, which is comparable to usual results on that dataset. It is even *possible* to generate a model for the whole training set. For instance, the first rule generated by Part is: if `charge > -0.123 and charge <= -0.108` then `mutagenic`. Finally it is also *possible* to misunderstand that rule and *interpret* it as: *"if the molecule contains an atom whose charge is between -0.123 and -0.108 then it is mutagenic"*, and *use* the resulting decision list to classify new molecules. So, it is *possible* to get *likely* results from a universal join. However those results are incorrect: the rules learned so far apply to bonds, not to molecules. Indeed, in attribute-value learning, each line corresponds to one example, and vice-versa. The accuracy corresponds to 83.9% of the 10486 bonds, i.e. 8802 bonds, that have been *correctly* classified, not at all to 83.9% of the 188 molecules in the training set. And the rule should be read as: "if the bond belongs to an atom whose charge is between -0.123 and -0.108 then the bond belongs to a mutagenic molecule". If a new molecule has to be classified, such rules should only be used to classify its bonds, then some operation (e.g. a majority vote among the bonds) should be performed to transfer the knowledge learned on the bonds to the molecule.

A necessary condition to apply a standard attribute-value learner, right out of the box, is that each line corresponds to exactly one example. A universal join satisfy this constraint only if it is performed following the foreign keys in a deterministic way. In our example, it could only be applied to classify the kind of a bond given the properties of its atom and its molecule.

3.2 Concatenation of Columns

Given that each molecule must be represented by a single line, it is very tempting to concatenate the properties of the atoms as properties of the molecule.

molid	class	atomid1	elt1	ch1	...	atomid26	elt26	ch26	atomid27	elt27	ch27	...
d1	mutagenic	d1_1	c	-0.117	...	d1_26	o	-0.388	?	?	?	...
d10	mutagenic	d10_1	c	-0.119	...	d10_26	h	0.061	d10_27	h	0.061	...
⋮	⋮	⋮	⋮	⋮		⋮	⋮	⋮	⋮	⋮	⋮	⋮

(188 lines, 122 columns, i.e. 2 + 3 * the maximum number of atoms)

Fig. 4. Concatenation of the properties of atoms in the mutagenicity domain

Figure 4 presents the concatenation of properties of the atoms to the properties of the molecule.

This approach *looks* more natural in domains where instances' labels follow an *apparent* ordering, e.g. the numbering of atoms in the mutagenicity domain. Of course the molecules do not necessarily have the same numbers of atoms, so *remaining* columns are filled in with *missing* values. Again an attribute-value learner *can* be used. We ran Part, and got *73.9%* accuracy. The first rule is: ``if element2 = c and charge2 <= 0.208 and element1 = c and element3 = c and charge2 > -0.128 and element18 = c then mutagenic''. It means: *"if the first three and 18th atoms are carbon atoms and the charge of the second atom is between -0.128 and 0.208 then it is mutagenic"*. Those results are incorrect. Indeed there is no predefinite orderings of atoms, at least in that domain, so the atoms are arbitrarily numbered. The atoms of a given molecule could be numbered differently, leading to different rules if the molecule belongs to the training set, or to a different predicted class if the molecule belongs to the test set! It makes no sense to use atom numbers to name columns. Resulting columns are not uniquely defined for the molecule.

A necessary condition to apply a standard attribute-value learner, right out of the box, is that each line corresponds to exactly one example and that each column is meaningful and uniquely defined for each example. A concatenation of columns can satisfy this constraint only if each column is a determinate function of the example. In this case it means that the domain could naturally have been represented by a single table and that the relational representation came from an unnecessary and artificial splitting of that single table.

While a meaningless concatenation of columns is fairly common with two tables, it is unlikely to happen with more tables since the ad-hoc concatenation (and numbering!) of columns quickly looks less attractive. For instance, figure 5 shows the concatenation of the properties of atoms and bonds.

molid	class	atomid1	elt1	ch1	bondid1_1	kind1_1	bondid1_2	kind1_2	...
d1	mutagenic	d1_1	c	-0.117	d1_1_1	7	d1_1_2	1	...
d10	mutagenic	d10_1	c	-0.119	d10_1_1	1	?	?	...
⋮	⋮	⋮	⋮	⋮	⋮	⋮	⋮	⋮	⋮

(188 lines, the number of columns depends on the maximum number of bonds for each atom and on the maximum number of atoms)

Fig. 5. Concatenation of the properties of atoms and bonds in the mutagenicity domain

3.3   Concatenation of Values

In order to get one line per example and no problem of numbering the properties, it is possible to gather the values of the properties. Figure 6 shows the gathering of properties of the atoms.

Let us notice that part of the structural information has been lost. In such a representation, it is impossible to relate the element of an atom to one of its bonds, e.g. to learn a rule such as: "if the molecule has an oxygen atom involved in a single bond..."

Moreover a standard attribute-value learner cannot deal with sets as values. It is *possible* to *solve* this difficulty by concatenating the values into a single value. Figure 7 shows the concatenation of properties of atoms. Obviously a concatenation of numeric values is no longer numeric and missing values are also concatenated. So all new columns take on categorical values. The number of possible values for each new column is the combination of values from the original column, filled in with concatenated missing values (missing values are encoded with the question mark in Weka). Due to the combinatorial number of values, Part gets a *66.5%* accuracy and outputs a single rule: "it is always mutagenic", corresponding to the majority class. This approach is clearly incorrect. It drops missing values and numeric values on its way. Moreover it is also sensitive to the ordering of the atoms, which is arbitrary.

molid	class	atomids	elements	charges
d1	mutagenic	{d1_1,d1_2,...}	{c,c,...}	{-0.117,-0.117,...}
d10	mutagenic	{d10_1,d10_2,...}	{c,c,...}	{-0.119,-0.119,...}
⋮	⋮	⋮	⋮	⋮

(188 lines, 5 columns)

Fig. 6. Gathering the properties of atoms in the mutagenicity domain

molid	class	atomids	elements	charges
d1	mutagenic	d1_1:d1_2:...	c:c:...	-0.117:-0.117:...
d10	mutagenic	d10_1:d10_2:...	c:c:...	-0.119:-0.119:...
⋮	⋮	⋮	⋮	⋮

(188 lines, 5 columns)

Fig. 7. Concatenation of the properties of atoms in the mutagenicity domain

molid	class	atomids	elements	charges	bondids	kinds
d1	mutagenic	d1_1:d1_2:...	c:c:...	-0.117:-0.117:...	d1_1_1:d1_1_2:...	7:1:...
d10	mutagenic	d10_1:d10_2:...	c:c:...	-0.119:-0.119:...	d10_1_1:d10_1_2:...	1:7:...
⋮	⋮	⋮	⋮	⋮	⋮	⋮

(188 lines, 7 columns)

Fig. 8. Concatenation of the properties of atoms and bonds in the mutagenicity domain

If more than two tables have to be merged, the resulting table becomes worse. Figure 8 illustrates the concatenation of properties of atoms and bonds.

4   Correct Approaches

This section presents sound approaches of propositionalisation. While the presented approaches roughly cover the state-of-the-art in propositionalisation, our aim is rather to give directions along which sound propositionalisation can be performed. We refer to [8, 9] for details about implemented approaches.

Normally propositionalisation consists in building a single table where each line corresponds to exactly to one example, and each column is meaningful for each example, and takes on a determinate, but perhaps unknown, value for each example. The following subsections list several ways of building up such tables.

4.1   Existential First-Order Features

A first approach consists in generating existential first-order features. Examples of such features are:

- does the molecule contain a carbon atom? an oxygen atom? ...
- does the molecule contain an atom involved in a single bond? a double bond? ...
- does the molecule contain a carbon atom involved in a single bond? a carbon atom involved in a double bond? ... an oxygen atom involved in a single bond? ...
- does the molecule contain a carbon atom and an oxygen atom? ...
- ...

The number of possible existential features is large, often infinite. Usually some minimality requirements are added, e.g. removing subsumed features. For instance, we will only consider elementary first-order features. While the first-order feature "does the molecule contains a carbon atom involved in a single bond?" is subsumed by the following two elementary first-order features "does the molecule contains a carbon atom?" and "does the molecule contains an atom involved in a single bond?", let us emphasize that it is not equivalent to their conjunction. Elementary first-order features in the mutagenicity domains are illustrated in figure 9.

molid	class	element=c	element=o	...	kind=1	kind=2	...
d1	mutagenic	yes	yes	...	yes	yes	...
d10	mutagenic	yes	yes	...	yes	yes	...
⋮	⋮	⋮	⋮	⋮	⋮	⋮	⋮

(188 lines, 26 columns if the charge is discretised into 10 intervals)

Fig. 9. Existential elementary first-order features in the mutagenicity domain

For the experiments, the charge was discretised into 10 equal bins, i.e. intervals containing the same number of instances. We ran Part and got a 78.2% accuracy. The first rule is: "if charge3=yes then mutagenic", meaning "if the molecule has an atom whose charge is between -0.118 and -0.112 then it is mutagenic".

4.2 Cardinalities

An extension of existential first-order features consists in considering cardinalities, roughly how many objects in the individual satisfy some property instead of whether there exists one. Features become:

- how many carbon atoms does the molecule contain? oxygen atoms? ...
- how many single bonds does the molecule contain? double bonds? ...
- how many pairs of atoms and bonds such that a carbon atom is involved in a single bond does the molecule contain? a carbon atom is involved in a double bond? ... an oxygen atom is involved in a single bond? ...
- how many pairs of a carbon atom and an oxygen atom does the molecule contain?...
- ...

Given a minimal conjunction of structural predicates and properties, let us denote I the variable referring to the individual and X the tuple of remaining variables referring to the other objects than the individual, e.g. in mol2atom(M,A), element(A,carbon), atom2bond(A,B) bond(B,1) the variable M refers to the individual, and (A,B) refers to a pair of an atom and a bond (actually one of the bonds the atom is involved in). Given an individual i, existential first-order features consider whether there exists a substitution x of X satisfying the conjunction and cardinalities consider how many such substitutions there are. Figure 10 shows cardinalities corresponding to the elementary first-order features.

molid	class	element=c	element=o	...	kind=1	kind=2	...
d1	mutagenic	14	2	...	20	4	...
d10	mutagenic	14	2	...	32	4	...
:	:	:	:	:	:	:	:

(188 lines, 26 columns if the charge is discretised into 10 intervals)

Fig. 10. Cardinalities in the mutagenicity domain

For the experiments, the charge was discretised into 10 equal bins, i.e. intervals containing the same number of instances. We ran Part and got a 85.6% accuracy. The first rule is: "if carbon > 11 and charge1 <= 8 and kind7 > 24 then mutagenic", meaning "if the molecule has more than 11 carbon atoms, at most 8 atoms whose charge is between -0.383 and -0.126, and more than 24 bonds of kind 7 then it is mutagenic".

molid	class	elements	avg_charge	min_charge	max_charge	sum_charge	kinds
d1	mutagenic	4	0	-0.388	0.812	0	3
d10	mutagenic	4	0	-0.388	0.812	0	3
⋮	⋮	⋮	⋮	⋮	⋮	⋮	⋮

(188 lines, 8 columns)

Fig. 11. Aggregation in the mutagenicity domain

4.3   Aggregation

Cardinalities are a special case of aggregation functions. All aggregation functions can be used in propositionalisation, but they are applied to the values rather than on the objects, e.g. counting how many different elements of atoms there are in a molecule, rather than counting how many carbon atoms there are. Typically the average, minimum, maximum and sum are computed for numeric attributes, and the number of different values is used for nominal values. Figure 11 shows the application of those aggregation functions to properties of atoms and bonds in the mutagenicity domain.

We ran Part and got a 73.9% accuracy. The first rule is: "if min_charge > -0.392 and elements <= 4 then mutagenic", meaning "if the molecule has atoms of at most 4 elements and all atoms' charge is at least -0.392 then it is mutagenic".

5   Discussion

This section first deals with propositionalisation in related frameworks, namely in multiple-instance problems and with sequential data. Then it highlights the strengths and weaknesses of propositionalisation.

5.1   Multiple-Instance Problems

A multiple-instance problem [3] is a problem where each individual is described by several lines of a single table: each individual is a set of elements, each element is described by one line, an individual is labelled positive if at least one of its elements satisfies a target property. A typical example concerns molecules: a molecule is active if and only if at least one of its conformation matches the target receptor.

Such a problems looks like a relational problem with only two tables: one for the individuals, and one for the elements. Indeed some propositionalisation approaches, mainly based on existential first-order features, can be used to solve those problems with usual attribute-value learners.

However neither all propositionalisation approaches make sense in multiple-instance problems, nor multiple-instance learners can solve all two tables relational problems. Multiple-instance learners assume that the solution can be expressed by "there exists an element such that...". They are not intended to learn any relational hypothesis such as "there exists an element 1 and an element 2 such that...". The expressiveness of most propositionalisation approaches should therefore be reduced to the appropriate search space. Aggregation approaches, that aggregates properties over the element, are typically useless in multiple-instance problems.

5.2 Sequential Data

In sequential data a label is associated to a sequence of observations. It can be represented by two tables: one for the individual – containing the properties of the sequence itself, at least its class – and a second table for the observations, assuming that one line describes one observation. Either relational learners or propositionalisation approaches can be used on such data, but they are usually not able to make use of the temporal aspect, such as "if a property 1 is observed 10 seconds after the occurrence of property 2..." or "if the variation of property 1...". Aggregation approaches could be designed for the latter kind of hypotheses.

Sequential data can easily lead to an incorrect concatenation of columns. Let us consider the example of the stulong dataset studied in the last PKDD challenges: patients had an examination every year, those examinations are numbered. Concatenating the properties of the examinations is very tempting: all patients have a first control, a second one, and so on. Though it is incorrect: while the related ordering of examinations (denoting the temporal difference) is meaningful, the absolute number of an examination is useless. Let us imagine that patient 10009 entered in the study 3 years later, then its new first control would correspond to his old fourth control, and so on. First the attribute-value representation would change, i.e. attributes are no longer function of the given individual. Secondly his classification based on the absolute numbering of the examinations could change! Propositionalisation should be used with care with every kind of data.

5.3 Strengths and Weaknesses

In this subsection we discuss the strengths and weaknesses of propositionalisation compared to relational learners. The obvious advantage of propositionalisation is that it allows the data miner to make use of his favorite attribute-value learners. Propositionalisation has also proven to outperform relational learners on some applications [12, 4]. The feature construction being decoupled of the model construction, the data miner can first focus on relevant hypotheses, before using the most appropriate propositional learner. Propositionalisation provides more flexibility, and a wider choice of features and ready-to-use algorithms.

On the other hand, propositionalisation requires an exhaustive generation of features before any model construction. No pruning of uninteresting parts of the hypotheses space can be performed as in relational learners where the feature construction is guided by the learning process. Therefore a large number of features has to be generated, requiring a lot of time and a lot of space. A large number of irrelevant features prevents the use of most distance-based learners, either supervised like k-nearest neighbors or unsupervised like k-means.

Moreover the results of some relational learning algorithms cannot be obtained through propositionalisation. For instance, 1BC2's probabilities [10] cannot be easily obtained from a propositionalised table, unless 1BC2 itself be considered as an aggregation operator, recursively estimating the probabilities of objects, and the resulting columns being the conditional probabilities only. Finally another advantage of relational learners compared to propositionalisation is that their expressiveness naturally fits to relational data, so they prevent incorrect propositionalisation approaches.

6   Conclusion

This paper complements existing publications about propositionalisation by pointing out incorrect approaches, giving general guidelines of correct approaches, and discussing related domains and limitations of propositionalisation. It is intended as a guide to propositionalisation for new relational data miners. It does not pretend to list all incorrect and correct approaches exhaustively, but try to teach how to avoid mistakes and show good directions. More generally it invites the data mining practitioner to take as much care as possible of the data representation and of its influence on the learning results.

References

[1] A. Braud and C. Vrain. A genetic algorithm for propositionalization. In Céline Rouveirol and Michèle Sebag, editors, *Proceedings of the Eleventh International Conference on Inductive Logic Programming*, volume 2157 of *Lecture Notes in Artificial Intelligence*, pages 27–40. Springer-Verlag, September 2001.

[2] M. Collard. how to deal with temporal data for association rules. Meeting of the French work group on the stulong challenge, 2004. http://users.info.unicaen.fr/~bruno/asdisco/index.php?Choix=290304.

[3] T. G. Dietterich, R. H. Lathrop, and T. Lozano-Pérez. Solving the multiple-instance problem with axis-parallel rectangles. *Artificial Intelligence*, 89(1–2):31–71, 1997.

[4] S. Džeroski, H. Blockeel, B. Kompare, S. Kramer, B. Pfahringer, and W. Van Laer. Experiments in predicting biodegradability. In S. Džeroski and P. Flach, editors, *Proc. of the Ninth International Workshop on Inductive Logic Programming*, volume 1634 of *LNCS*, pages 80–91. Springer, 1999.

[5] S. Džeroski and N. Lavrač, editors. *Relational Data Mining*. Springer, 2001.

[6] P. Flach and N. Lachiche. 1BC: a first-order bayesian classifier. In S. Džeroski and P. Flach, editors, *Proc. of the Ninth International Workshop on Inductive Logic Programming*, volume 1634 of *LNCS*, pages 92–103. Springer, 1999.

[7] A. J. Knobbe, M. de Haas, and A. Siebes. Propositionalisation and aggregates. In *Proceedings of the Sixth European Conference on Principles of Data Mining and Knowledge Discovery*, volume 2168 of *Lecture Notes in Artificial Intelligence*, pages 277–288. Springer-Verlag, September 2001.

[8] S. Kramer, N. Lavrač, and P. Flach. Propositionalization approaches to relational data mining. In Džeroski and Lavrač [5], chapter 11, pages 262–291.

[9] M.-A. Krogel, S. Rawles, F. Železný, P. A. Flach, N. Lavrač, and S. Wrobel. Comparative evaluation of approaches to propositionalization. In T. Horváth and A. Yamamoto, editors, *Proceedings of the Thirteenth International Conference on Inductive Logic Programming*, volume 2835 of *Lecture Notes in Artificial Intelligence*, pages 197–214. Springer-Verlag, 2003.

[10] N. Lachiche and P. A. Flach. 1BC2: a true first-order bayesian classifier. In S. Matwin and C. Sammut, editors, *Proc. of the Twelfth International Conference on Inductive Logic Programming*, volume 2583 of *LNAI*, pages 133–148. Springer-Verlag, 2003.

[11] N. Lavrač and S. Džeroski. *Inductive Logic Programming: Techniques and Applications*. Ellis Horwood, New York, 1994. Freely available at http://www-ai.ijs.si/SasoDzeroski/ILPBook/.

[12] A. Srinivasan, R. D. King, and D. W. Bristol. An assessment of submissions made to the predictive toxicology evaluation challenge. In *Proceedings of the Sixteenth International Joint Conference on Artificial Intelligence*, pages 270–275. Morgan Kaufmann, 1999.

[13] A. Srinivasan, S. Muggleton, R. D. King, and M. Stenberg. Theories for mutagenicity: a study of first-order and feature based induction. *Artificial Intelligence*, 85(1–2):277–299, 1996.

[14] J. C. Werner and T. Kalganova. Risk evaluation using evolvable discriminate function. In *Proceedings of the ECML/PKDD 2003 Discovery Challenge*, 2003. http://lisp.vse.cz/challenge/ecmlpkdd2003/program.htm.

[15] I. Witten and E. Frank. *Data Mining: Practical Machine Learning Tools and Techniques with Java Implementations*. Morgan Kaufmann, 1999. http://www.cs.waikato.ac.nz/~ml/weka/.

Periodicity-Based Temporal Constraints

Paolo Terenziani[1], Luca Anselma[2], and Stefania Montani[1]

[1] DI, Univ. Piemonte Orientale "A. Avogadro", Spalto Marengo 33, Alessandria, Italy
{terenz, stefania}@mfn.unipmn.it
[2] DI, Università di Torino, Corso Svizzera 185, 10149 Torino, Italy
anselma@di.unito.it

Abstract. We propose a framework for performing extensional and intensional temporal reasoning about qualitative and quantitative "periodicity-dependent" temporal constraints between repeated events, also considering user-defined periodicities.

1 Introduction

Recently, several specialized approaches to deal with different kinds of temporal constraints have been developed [9]. Some of these approaches work on "periodicity-based" temporal constraints, in which qualitative constraints (e.g., *"before"* [6]) or durations [3] between periodic events depend on the specific periodicity in which such events occur. Independently, since the use of a periodicity or calendar depends on the cultural, legal, and even business orientation of the users (see e.g., [5]), several approaches have been devised to model user-defined periodicities (consider, e.g., the survey in [8]). The goal of this paper is to propose a comprehensive framework taking into account both the above phenomena, as needed in many application areas, ranging, e.g., from scheduling to office automation. To the best of our knowledge, our work represents the first effort in this direction in the AI literature.

2 Representing Periodicity-Based Constraints

In our approach, a (binary) periodicity-based constraint is modelled by a triple *<Ev, Per, Con>*, where *Ev* denotes a pair of events, *Per* a user-defined periodicity, and *Con* the temporal constraints[1]. The (intuitive) semantics of periodicity-based constraints $<<ev_1, ev_2>, P, C>$ is the following:

ev_1 and ev_2 are two periodic events. For *each* occurrence (*instance*) p_i of the periodicity P:

    (i)   there is exactly one instance $e1_i$ of ev_1 taking place in p_i;

    (ii) there is exactly one instance $e2_i$ of ev_2 taking place in p_i;

    (iii) $C(e1_i, e2_i)$ holds.

Since our main goal is that of devising a comprehensive framework, in the current version we have chosen to rely on widely known and used AI approaches: the

---

[1] Durations are a degenerate case, in which the *Ev* component only consists of one event, and the *Con* component of the distance between its endpoints.

S. Bandini and S. Manzoni (Eds.): AI*IA 2005, LNAI 3673, pp. 62–65, 2005.

collection formalism [2] as regards user-defined periodicities, and *STP* (Simple Temporal Problem [1]) as regards temporal constraints. In particular, in the STP framework different types of qualitative and quantitative constraints between endpoints of events can be modeled as shown in [4].

For example, the constraint *"On Monday, Tom starts to work before Mary, and finishes between 10 and 30 minutes before her"* can be represented in our formalism as follows (given the definition of *Mondays* in Leban et al.'s language and expressing temporal constraints as minimal and maximal distance between endpoints (<*start/start, start/end, end/start, end/end*>)):

$$(\alpha) \ \ <<TW, MW>, \text{Mondays}, <(0,+\infty), (10,+\infty), (-\infty,+\infty), [10,30]>>.$$

3   Extensional and Intensional Calculi

Given a KB of periodicity-based temporal constraints, we provide two constraint-propagation-based forms of temporal reasoning to amalgamate them and to check their consistency.

Our *extensional* algorithm "expands" each periodicity over a time span of interest (or, in the most general case, on the "least common multiple" of the period of each periodicity in the KB), explicitly generating all the repetitions (instances) of the events over such time span, and imposes all the input temporal constraints on the generated instances. This results into an set of STP constraints on which we apply Floyd-Warshall's constraint-propagation algorithm.

Property. Our extensional approach is complete and cubic in the number of "expanded" events.

However, the extensional approach has two main drawbacks:

(i)   in most cases, too many instances of events need to be taken into account (e.g., the least common multiple of "week" and "month" is 28-year long);

(ii) the output of constraint propagation is neither user-friendly nor perspicuous (e.g., train schedules do not report departure times for every day of the year).

Therefore, we also introduce an *intensional* calculus, which, although not complete, performs part of the inferences providing a perspicuous (i.e., intensional) output. To this aim, we use a standard algorithm for transitive closure, applying a cubic (in the number of "intensional" events) number of times the operations of intersection $\cap$ and composition @. The basic idea is that of developing the calculus in a modular fashion, so that intersection and composition are separately computed on the constraints and on the periodicities.

Constraints. The definition of intersection and composition between STP constraints (the *Con* component) is the standard one [1].

Periodicities. Several problems need to be faced in order to provide an intensional definition of intersection and composition between user-defined periodicities (the *Per* component). Specifically, operating at the intensional level means taking into account only one "prototypical" repetition, i.e., the repetition in a *"typical" common period, represented in an intensional way*. This means that:

(1) a one-to-one correspondence between the instances of periodicities must be singled out;
(2) the *collection* formalism [2] must be extended to intensionally express the common period;
(3) rules must be devised to compute the common period on the basis of two periodicities.

We have therefore extended the *collection* language with the operators of pairwise intersection $\cap^P$ and pairwise restricted union $\cup^P$. Both operators are defined only in case there is a one-to-one correspondence between events (see point (1) above), and take into account corresponding pairs of events. Additionally, union is restricted to provide a non-empty result only in case the corresponding pairs intersect in time (so that only convex time intervals are coped with).

To provide "perspicuous" results, the intensional operations must perform at least two types of simplifications:

(i) **redundancy elimination**; e.g., the output of the intersection of "Working-Days" (i.e., days from Monday to Friday) and "Mondays" should be just "Mondays" and not the symbolic formula "Working-Days $\cap^P$ Mondays";
(ii) **empty periodicity detection**; for instance, the output of the intersection of "Mondays" and "Wednesdays" should be empty and not "Mondays $\cap^P$ Wednesdays".

Since periodicities are user-defined, it is not possible to define a priori all the intersections and compositions between all pairs of periodicities. Thus, we have pointed out a set of five relations between two user-defined periodicities which are exhaustive and mutually exclusive, and we have defined intersection and composition on these bases. For example, the inclusion relation $\subseteq^P$ holds between two periodicities P_1 and P_2 if and only if there is a one-to-one correspondence between the instances of P_1 and P_2 and temporal inclusion holds between each corresponding pair of instances. We also provide sets of rules in order to compute the relation holding between two *basic* periodicities (i.e., without the use of $\cap^P$ and $\cup^P$ as in Leban et al.'s language,) on the basis of their definition.

Intersection and composition about *basic* periodicities are thus defined as a conditional *simplification* rule of the form: "If Relation Then P_1 OP^P P_2 = formula", where OP^P is either intersection $\cap^P$ or composition $@^P$ between periodicities. For example, if $P_1 \subseteq^P P_2$, then $P_1 \cap^P P_2 = P_1$ and $P_1 @^P P_2 = P_2$.

From the operational standpoint, simplification rules are more complex in the case of *composite* periodicities (i.e. periodicities that have been defined resorting to $\cap^P$ and $\cup^P$). In particular, it is difficult to find rules to determine which one of the five relations holds between two composite periodicities. Therefore, we devise a compositional and modular calculus, in which operations between composite periodicities are decomposed by considering pairwise the basic periodicities composing them. Unfortunately, since certain simplifications can only be captured considering composite periodicities as a whole, such a compositional approach cannot be simplification-complete. Therefore, we proved the following.

Property. *Our simplification rules are correct and complete as regards basic periodicities, and correct but not complete as regards composite periodicities.*

Corollary. *Our intensional calculus is correct, but not simplification-complete.*

Example. Since Mondays $\subseteq^P$ Working-Days, their intersection is "Mondays" and their composition is "Working-Days"; thus, intensional reasoning on the constraints (α), (β) and (γ) gives as a result – among the others – (δ) and (ϵ):

(β) <<TW>,Working-Days,<[480,480]>>;

(γ) <<TW,AW>,Working-Days,<[10,20],(10,+∞),(-∞,+∞),[10,30]>>;

(δ) <<AW>,Mondays,<[470,500]>>;

(ϵ) <<MW, AW>, Working-Days, < (-500,20), (-20,510), (-500,-470), (-20,20)>>.

Our intensional calculus is also non-complete as regards consistency checking. In our approach such kind of completeness is obtained through the extensional reasoning.

A more detailed description of our approach can be found in [7].

4 Conclusions and Comparisons

In this paper, we have described a comprehensive approach dealing with both (i) *qualitative* and (ii) *quantitative* periodicity-based temporal constraints, and considering also (iii) *user-defined* periodicities. Dealing with these issues and with the interplay between them required to devise a novel approach that integrates and extends the STP framework [1] and the Leban's formalism [2]. In particular, we have: (1) proposed a formalism to represent periodicity-based temporal constraints; (2) extended Leban's formalism to represent composite periodicities; (3) singled out five relations between periodicities and used them to (4) define the operations of intersection and composition among both basic and composite periodicity-based temporal constraints; (5) described an *intensional* approach, which is correct and provides perspicuous (intensional) output, but is not complete, and (6) an *extensional* approach, which can be used to check consistency, and which is correct and complete.

References

[1] R. Dechter, I. Meiri, J. Pearl, "Temporal Constraint Networks", AIJ, 49:61-95, 1991.

[2] B. Leban, D.D. McDonald, D.R. Forster, A representation for collections of temporal intervals, in Proc. AAAI'86, pp. 367-371, 1986.

[3] R. Loganantharaj, S. Gimbrone, "Representation of, and Reasoning with, Near-Periodic Recurrent Events", In 9th IJCAI Workshop on Spatial and Temporal Reasoning, 1995.

[4] I. Meiri, "Combining Qualitative and Quantitative Constraints in Temporal Reasoning", in Proc. AAAI'91, pp. 260-267, 1991.

[5] M. Soo, R. Snodgrass, Multiple Calendar Support for Conventional Database Management Systems, Proc. ITDB'93, 1993.

[6] P. Terenziani, "Integrating calendar-dates and qualitative temporal constraints in the treatment of periodic events", IEEE TKDE 9(5):763-783, 1997.

[7] P. Terenziani, L. Anselma, S. Montani, "Periodicity-based temporal constraints", Dip. di Informatica, Università di Torino, Technical Report 89/05, 2005.

[8] A. Tuzhilin and J. Clifford, "On Periodicity in Temporal Databases", Information Systems, 20(8):619-639, 1995.

[9] L. Vila. "A Survey on Temporal Reasoning in Artificial Intelligence", AI Comm., 7(1):4-28, 1994.

A Survey of Problem Difficulty in Genetic Programming

Leonardo Vanneschi[1], Marco Tomassini[2],
Philippe Collard[3], and Manuel Clergue[3]

[1] Dipartimento di Informatica, Sistemistica e Comunicazione (D.I.S.Co.),
University of Milano-Bicocca, Milan, Italy
[2] Computer Systems Department, University of Lausanne, Lausanne, Switzerland
[3] I3S Laboratory, University of Nice, Sophia Antipolis, France

Abstract. This paper presents a study of fitness distance correlation and negative slope coefficient as measures of problem hardness for genetic programming. Advantages and drawbacks of both these measures are presented both from a theoretical and empirical point of view. Experiments have been performed on a set of well-known hand-tailored problems and "real-life-like" GP benchmarks.

1 Introduction

This work represents a short survey of our main outcomes on fitness distance correlation (fdc) and negative slope coefficient (nsc) as measures of problem difficulty for tree-based Genetic Programming (GP). Paper's structure is the following: the next section gives a short description of the genotypic distance used to calculate fdc, followed by the definition of two basic mutation operators that go hand-in-hand with it. Section 3 presents a series of experimental results obtained using two kinds of GP process: GP with standard Koza's crossover as the only genetic operator and GP using only these two new mutation operators. The test problems that we have chosen include multimodal trap functions. This is the first attempt to quantify the difficulty of problems with multiple optima by the fdc in EAs. In section 4 we show a counterexample for fdc in GP. Finally, section 7 gives our conclusions and hints to future work.

2 Fitness Distance Correlation

Fitness distance correlation has previously been studied for Genetic Algorithms (GAs) in [5] and for GP in [12,11,13,14,2]. It is defined as follows: given a sample $F = \{f_1, f_2, ..., f_n\}$ of n individual fitnesses and a corresponding sample $D = \{d_1, d_2, ..., d_n\}$ of the n distances to the nearest global optimum, fdc is defined as: $fdc = \frac{C_{FD}}{\sigma_F \sigma_D}$, where: $C_{FD} = \frac{1}{n} \sum_{i=1}^{n} (f_i - \overline{f})(d_i - \overline{d})$ is the covariance of F and D and σ_F, σ_D, $\overline{f}$ and $\overline{d}$ are the standard deviations and means of F and D. As shown in [5], GAs problems can be classified in three classes, depending on

S. Bandini and S. Manzoni (Eds.): AI*IA 2005, LNAI 3673, pp. 66–77, 2005.

the value of the *fdc* coefficient: **misleading** ($fdc \geq 0.15$), **unknown** ($-0.15 <$ $fdc < 0.15$) and **straightforward** ($fdc \leq -0.15$). The second class corresponds to problems for which the difficulty can't be estimated because there is virtually no correlation between fitness and distance. In this paper, we show that this problem classification also holds for GP.

2.1 Structural Tree Distance

The distance metric used to calculate the *fdc* should be defined with regard to the neighborhood produced by the genetic operators, so to assure the conservation of the genetic material between neighbors. In this paper the well known structural distance (see [4]) is used. This distance is the most suitable between the different definitions found in literature and the tranformations on which this distance is based allow to define two new genetic operators in a very simple way. The new resulting evolutionary process will be called *structural mutation genetic programming* (SMGP), to distinguish it from GP based on the standard Koza's crossover (that will be referred to as standard GP).

According to structural distance, given the sets $\mathcal{F}$ and $\mathcal{T}$ of functions and terminal symbols, a coding function c must be defined such that $c : \{\mathcal{T} \cup \mathcal{F}\} \to \mathbb{N}$. The distance of two trees T_1 and T_2 with roots R_1 and R_2 is defined as follows:

$$d(T_1, T_2) = \overline{d}(R_1, R_2) + k \sum_{i=1}^{m} d(child_i(R_1), child_i(R_2)) \qquad (1)$$

where: $\overline{d}(R_1, R_2) = (|c(R_1) - c(R_2)|)^z$, $z \in \mathbb{N}$, $child_i(Y)$ is the ith of the m possible children of a generical node Y, if $i \leq m$, or the empty tree otherwise, and c evaluated on the root of an empty tree is 0. Constant k is used to give different weights to nodes belonging to different levels. In most of this paper, except the MAX function, individuals will be coded using the same syntax as in [2] and [9], i.e. considering a set of functions A, B, C, etc. with increasing arity (i.e. $arity(A) = 1$, $arity(B) = 2$, and so on) and a single terminal X (i.e. $arity(X) = 0$) as follows: $\mathcal{F} = \{A, B, C, D, \ldots\}, \mathcal{T} = \{X\}$ The c function, for this particular language, will be defined as follows: $\forall x \in \{\mathcal{F} \cup \mathcal{T}\}$ $c(x) = arity(x) + 1$. In our experiments we will always pose $k = \frac{1}{2}$ and $z = 2$.

2.2 Structural Mutations

Given the sets $\mathcal{F}$ and $\mathcal{T}$ and the coding function c defined in section 2.1, we define c_{max} (resp. c_{min}) as the maximum (resp. the minimum) value assumed by c on the domain $\{\mathcal{F} \cup \mathcal{T}\}$. Moreover, given a symbol n (resp. m) such that $n \in \{\mathcal{F} \cup \mathcal{T}\}$ (resp. $m \in \{\mathcal{F} \cup \mathcal{T}\}$) and $c(n) < c_{max}$ (resp. $c(m) > c_{min}$), we define: $succ(n)$ (resp. $pred(m)$) as a node such that $c(succ(n)) = c(n) + 1$ (resp. $c(pred(m)) = c(m) - 1$). Then we can define the following operators on a generic tree T: (1) **inflate mutation**: a node labelled with a symbol n such that $c(n) < c_{max}$ is selected in T and replaced by $succ(n)$. A new random terminal node is added to this new node in a random position (i.e. the new terminal becomes the ith son of $succ(n)$, where i is comprised between 0 and $arity(n)$).

(2) **deflate mutation**: a node labelled with a symbol m such that $c(m) > c_{min}$, and such that at least one of his sons is a leaf, is selected in T and replaced by $pred(m)$. A random leaf, between the sons of this node, is deleted from T.
Given these definitions, the following property holds:

Property 1. Distance/Operator Consistency. Let's consider the sets $\mathcal{F}$ and $\mathcal{T}$ and the coding function c defined in section 2.1. Let T_1 and T_2 be two trees composed by symbols belonging to $\{\mathcal{F} \cup \mathcal{T}\}$ and let's consider the k and z constants of definition (1) to be both equal to 1. If $d(T_1, T_2) = D$, then T_2 can be obtained from T_1 by a sequence of $\frac{D}{2}$ editing operations, where an editing operation can be a inflate mutation or a deflate mutation. (this property has been formally proven in [12,15]).

From this property, we conclude that the operators of inflate mutation and deflate mutation are coherent with the notion of structural distance: an application of these operators enable to move on the search space from a tree to its neighbors according to that distance.

3   Experimental Results on *fdc*

In all experiments, *fdc* has been calculated via a sampling of 40000 randomly chosen individuals without repetitions. The total population size is 100, tournament selection of size 10 is used and the GP process has been stopped either when a perfect solution has been found (global optimum) or when 500 generations have been executed. All experiments have been performed 100 times.

3.1   Unimodal Trap Functions

A function $f : distance \rightarrow fitness$ is a unimodal trap function if it is defined in the following way:

$$
f(d) = \begin{cases} 1 - \dfrac{d}{B} & \text{if } d \leq B \\[2mm] \dfrac{R \cdot (d - B)}{1 - B} & \text{otherwise} \end{cases}
$$

where d is the distance of the current individual from the *unique* global optimum, opportunely normalized so to belong to the set $[0, 1]$, and B and R are constants belonging to $[0, 1]$. By construction, the difficulty of trap functions decreases as the value of B increases, while it increases as the value of R decreases. For a more detailed explanation of trap functions see [2]. Figure 1 shows values of the performance p (defined as the proportion of the executions for which the global optimum has been found in less than 500 generations over 100 runs) and of *fdc* for various trap functions obtained by changing the values of the constants B and R and keeping E as maximum arity node. In these experiments the tree represented in figure 1(c) was the global optimum. The same experiments have been performed using as global optimum the trees shown in figure 1(e, f, g) and the results (not shown here for reasons of space) are qualitatively analogous. In all cases *fdc* is confirmed to be a reasonable measure to quantify problem difficulty both for SMGP and standard GP for unimodal trap functions.

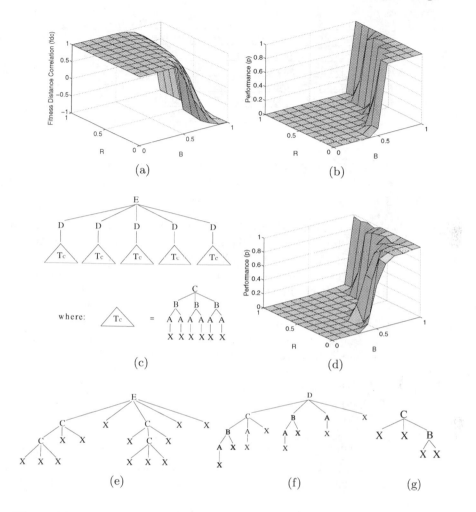

Fig. 1. (a): *fdc* values for some trap functions obtained by changing the values of the constants B and R. (b): Performance values of SMGP for traps. (d): Performance values of standard GP for traps. (c): Stucture of the tree used as optimum in the experiments reported in (a), (b) and (d). (e), (f), (g): Trees used as optima in analogous experiments.

3.2 Royal Trees

Royal trees (proposed by Punch *et al.* [9]) are a set of functions using the same coding language as in section 2.1, but a different algorithm to calculate fitness (see [9] or [2] for a description of this algorithm). They have been defined in such a way that the difficulty should increase as the maximum arity allowed for the trees increases. We have performed different experiments, considering different nodes as the node with maximum arity allowed. Results are shown in figure 2, where the first column contains the node with maximum arity. Predictions made by *fdc* are always correct.

root	fdc	fdc prediction	p (SMGP)	p (stGP)
B	-0.31	straightf.	1	1
C	-0.25	straightf.	1	1
D	-0.20	straightf.	0.76	0.70
E	0.059	unknown	0	0.12
F	0.44	misleading	0	0
G	0.73	misleading	0	0

Fig. 2. Results of *fdc* for the royal trees using SMGP and standard GP

3.3 "MAX" Problem

The task of the MAX problem, studied in [7], is "to find the program which returns the largest value for a given terminal and function set with a depth limit d, where the root node counts as depth 0". We set d equal to 8 and we use the set of functions $\mathcal{F} = \{+\}$ and the set of terminals $\mathcal{T}_1 = \{1\}$ or $\mathcal{T}_2 = \{1, 2\}$. When using $\mathcal{T}_1$, we specify the coding function c as: $c(1) = 1$, $c(+) = 2$, when using $\mathcal{T}_2$, we pose: $c(1) = 1$, $c(2) = 2$, $c(+) = 3$. The study of standard GP for these MAX functions comports no particular problem, while for the case of SMGP, the definitions of the operators of inflate and deflate mutation given in section 2.2 must be slightly modified, since we are considering a different coding language. The new definitions can be found in [15]. Figure 3 shows the *fdc* and p values for these test cases. Both problems are correctly classified as straightforward by *fdc*, both for SMGP and standard GP.

max problem	fdc	fdc prediction	p (SMGP)	p (stGP)
{+} {1}	-0.87	straightf.	1	1
{+} {1,2}	-0.86	straightf.	1	1

Fig. 3. Results of *fdc* for the MAX problem using SMGP and standard GP. The first column shows the sets of functions and terminals used in the experiments.

4   Counterexample

An hand-tailored problem, built to contradict the *fdc* conjecture, is presented in this section. This problem is based on the royal trees and is inspired by the technique used in [10] to build a counterexample for *fdc* in GAs. The technique basically consists in assigning to all the trees of the search space the same fitness as for the royal tree problem, except all the trees containing only the nodes A and X. To these trees, a fitness equal to the optimal royal tree's fitness times its own depth is assigned. It is clear that the optimal royal tree is now a local optimum, while the global optimum is the tree containing only A and X symbols having the maximum possible depth. Moreover, it is clear that a very specific "path" $\{A(X), A(A(X)), A(A(A(X))), A(A(A(A(X)))), ...\}$ has been defined. Each tree belonging to this path has a fitness greater or equal to the optimal royal tree, while all the trees that don't belong to this path have a fitness smaller or equal to the optimal royal tree. The value of fdc for this function is 0.88. Thus, according to fdc this function should be difficult to solve. By the way, over 100 independent runs, the global optimum has been found 100 times before generation 500 (i.e. $p = 1$) both by standard GP and by SMGP. These results, obviously contradict the fdc conjecture.

5   Negative Slope Coefficient

In the previous sections, fdc has been shown a reliable, though not infallible, measure for problem difficulty in tree-based GP. In view of a counterexample, it is suitable to look for an alternative measure of difficulty in GP which should, hopefully, be calculable without prior knowledge of the global optima, thus eliminating the strongest limitation of fdc. The measure we present here, nsc is based on the concept of fitness cloud, that we introduce in the following.

5.1   Fitness Clouds

Evolvability is a feature that is intuitively related, although not exactly identical, to problem difficulty. It has been defined as the capability of genetic operators to improve fitness quality [1]. The most natural way to study evolvability is to plot the fitness values of individuals against the fitness values of their neighbors, where a neighbor is obtained by applying one step of a genetic operator to the individual. Such a plot has been first introduced for binary landscapes by Vérel and coworkers [16] and called by them *fitness cloud*. In this paper, the genetic operator used to generate fitness clouds is standard subtree mutation [6], i.e. mutation obtained by replacing a subtree of the selected individual with a randomly generated tree. Formally, let: $\Gamma = \{\gamma_1, \gamma_2, \ldots, \gamma_n\}$ be the whole search space of a GP problem. The following set is defined: $V = V(\gamma_1) \cup V(\gamma_2) \cup \ldots \cup V(\gamma_n)$, where: $V(\gamma_j) = \{v_1^j, v_2^j, \ldots, v_m^j\}$ is the set of all the neighbors of individual $\gamma_j, \forall j \in [1, n]$. Now let f be the fitness function of the problem at hand. The following set of points on a bidimensional plane can be defined: $S = \{(f(\gamma_j), f(v_k^j)), \ \forall j \in [1, n], \ \forall k \in [1, m]\}$. The graphical representation of S, or fitness cloud, is the scatterplot of the fitness of all the individuals belonging to the search space against the fitness of all their neighbors.

5.2   Sampling Methodology

In general, the size of the search space and the size of the neighborhood of each individuals are huge. Thus, samples are needed. Uniform random sampling has the merit of being simple and algorithm-independent (only random search is implied), but it gives the same weight to all the sampled points. However, as it happens, many of those points are not really significant from the problem space point of view. For example, points belonging to the same plateau of fitness may be repeatedly sampled, which may be wasted effort. Analogously, many points with bad fitness value and thus likely to disappear under the effect of selection pressure may be sampled. For this reason, in this paper the search spaces will be sampled according to a distribution that gives more weight to "important" values, for instance those at a higher fitness level, via the well-known *Metropolis-Hastings* technique [8,12]. In the same way, neighborhhods will be sampled by applying k-tournament selection algorithm [6]. The terminology of section 5.1 is thus updated as follows: from now on, Γ represents a sample of individuals obtained with the Metropolis-Hastings technique and, for each γ_j belonging to Γ, $V(\gamma_j)$ is a subset of its neighbors, obtained by the application of the tournament selection mechanism.

5.3   Definition of the *nsc*

Let $\{I_1, I_2, \ldots, I_m\}$ be a partition into m segments of a fitness cloud. Analogously, a partition of the ordinates $\{J_1, J_2, \ldots, J_m\}$ can be done, where each segment J_i contains all the ordinates corresponding to the abscissas contained in I_i. Let $M_1, M_2, \ldots, M_m$ be the averages of the abscissa values contained inside the segments $I_1, I_2, \ldots, I_m$ and let $N_1, N_2, \ldots, N_m$ be the averages of the ordinate values in $J_1, J_2, \ldots, J_m$. Then, the set of segments $\{S_1, S_2, \ldots, S_{m-1}\}$ can be defined, where each S_i connects the point (M_i, N_i) to the point (M_{i+1}, N_{i+1}). For each one of these segments S_i, the *slope* P_i can be calculated as follows: $P_i = (N_{i+1} - N_i)/(M_{i+1} - M_i)$ Finally, the negative slope coefficient is defined as:

$$nsc = \sum_{i=1}^{m-1} c_i$$

where:

$$\forall i \in [1, m) \quad c_i = min\,(0, P_i)$$

The hypothesis is that *ncs* should classify problems in the following way: if $nsc = 0$, the problem is easy, if $nsc < 0$ the problem is difficult and the value of nsc quantifies this difficulty: the smaller its value, the more difficult the problem. In other words, according to this hypothesis, a problem is difficult if at least one of the segments $S_1, S_2, \ldots, S_{m-1}$ has a negative slope and the sum of all the negative slopes quantifies problem hardness. The idea behind this hypothesis is that the presence of a segment with negative slope indicates a bad evolvability for individuals having fitness values contained in that segment (see [12] for a detailed discussion on this issue). In the following, a technique called *hybrid bisection* has been used to partition the fitness cloud into bins. The starting point of this algorithm is the partition of the fitness cloud into two segments, each of which contains the same number of points. After that, the segment with larger (abscissa) size is further partitioned. Partition is done, once again, by bisection, i.e. the segment is partitioned into two bins, each one containing the same number of points. The algorithm is iterated until one of the two following conditions becomes true: either a segment contains a smaller number of points than a prefixed threshold, or a segment has become smaller than a prefixed minimum size. In this paper, as a first approximation, 50 has been chosen as a threshold for the number of points belonging to a bin, and the 5% of the distance between the leftmost and the rightmost points in the fitness cloud has been chosen as the minimum distance between abscissas of the extremes of a segment.

6 Experimental Results on nsc

6.1 The Binomial-3 Problem

This benchmark (first introduced by Daida *et al.* in [3]) is an instance of the well known symbolic regression problem. The function to be approximated is $f(x) = 1 + 3x + 3x^2 + x^3$. Fitness cases are 50 equidistant points over the range $[-1, 0)$. Fitness is the sum of absolute errors over all fitness cases. A hit is defined as being within 0.01 in ordinate for each one of the 50 fitness cases. The function set is $\mathcal{F} = \{+, -, *, //\}$, where $//$ is the protected division, i.e. it returns 1 if the denominator is 0. The terminal set is $\mathcal{T} = \{x, \mathcal{R}\}$, where x is the symbolic variable and $\mathcal{R}$ is the set of ephemeral random constants (ERCs). ERCs are uniformly distributed over a specified interval of the form $[-a_{\mathcal{R}}, a_{\mathcal{R}}]$, they are generated once at population initialization and they are not changed in value during the course of a GP run. According to Daida and coworkers, difficulty tuning is achieved by varying the value of $a_{\mathcal{R}}$.

Figure 4 shows the scatterplots and the set of segments $\{S_1, S_2, \ldots, S_m\}$ as defined in section 5.3 (with $m = 10$) for the binomial-3 problem with $a_{\mathcal{R}} = 1$ (figure 4(a)), $a_{\mathcal{R}} = 10$ (figure 4(b)), $a_{\mathcal{R}} = 100$ (figure 4(c)) and $a_{\mathcal{R}} = 1000$ (figure 4(d)). Parameters used are as follows: maximum tree depth $= 26$, $|\Gamma| = 40000$, i.e. a sample of 40000 individuals has been used, obtained with the Metropolis-Hastings sampling, $\forall j \in [1, 40000]$ $|V(\gamma_j)| = 1$, i.e. for each sampled individual, only one neighbor has been considered. It has been obtained by one step of tournament selection and standard subtree mutation has been used as operator to generate the neighborhood. Table 1 shows some data about these experiments. Column one of table 1 represents the corresponding scatterplot in figure 4. Column two contains the $a_{\mathcal{R}}$ value. Column three contains performance. Columns four contains the value of the nsc.

These results show that nsc values get smaller as the problem becomes harder, and it is zero when the problem is easy ($a_{\mathcal{R}} = 1$). Moreover, the points in the scatterplots seem to cluster around good (i.e. small) fitness values as the problem gets easier.

Table 1. Binomial-3 problem. Some data related to scatterplots of figure 4.

scatterplot	$a_{\mathcal{R}}$	p	nsc
fig. 4(a)	1	0.89	0
fig. 4(b)	10	0.42	-0.53
fig. 4(c)	100	0.35	-1.01
fig. 4(d)	1000	0.29	-3.39

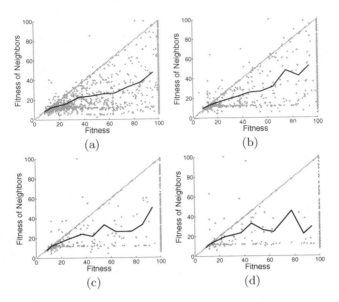

Fig. 4. Binomial-3 results. (a): $a_\mathcal{R} = 1$. (b): $a_\mathcal{R} = 10$. (c): $a_\mathcal{R} = 100$. (d): $a_\mathcal{R} = 1000$.

6.2   The Even Parity k Problem

The boolean even parity k function [6] of k boolean arguments returns *true* if an even number of its boolean arguments evaluates to true, otherwise it returns *false*. The number of fitness cases to be checked is 2^k. Fitness is computed as 2^k minus the number of hits over the 2^k cases. Thus a perfect individual has fitness 0, while the worst individual has fitness 2^k. The set of functions we employed is $\mathcal{F} = \{NAND, NOR\}$. The terminal set is composed of k different boolean variables. Difficulty tuning is achieved by varying the value of k.

Figure 5 shows the scatterplots and the set of segments for the even parity 3, even parity 5, even parity 7 and even parity 9 problems. Parameters used are as follows: maximum tree depth $= 10$, $|\Gamma| = 40000$ obtained with the Metropolis-Hastings sampling, $\forall j \in [1, 40000]$ $|V(\gamma_j)| = 1$. Tournament has been used as a selection mechanism and standard subtree mutation as the operator for generating the neighborhood. Table 2 shows some data about these experiments with the same notation and meaning as in table 1, except that column two now refers to the problem rank.

Table 2. Even parity. Indicators related to scatterplots of figure 5.

scatterplot	problem	p	nsc
fig. 5(a)	even parity 3	0.98	0
fig. 5(b)	even parity 5	0.01	-0.11
fig. 5(c)	even parity 7	0	-0.49
fig. 5(d)	even parity 9	0	-0.55

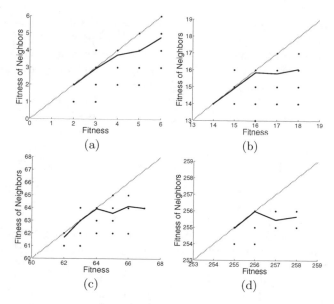

Fig. 5. Results for the even parity k problem. (a): Even parity 3. (b): Even parity 5. (c): Even parity 7. (d): Even parity 9.

Analogously to what happens for the binomial-3 problem, nsc values get smaller as the problem becomes harder, they are always negative for hard problems, and zero for easy ones.

7   Conclusions and Future Work

Two indicators of problem hardness for GP, called fitness distance correlation (fdc) and negative slope coefficient (nsc), are proposed in this work. The fdc is shown a suitable hardness indicator on a large set of test functions, including a large set of multimodal trap functions (results not shown here for lack of space). Nevertheless, the fdc presents some limitations, among which the existence of couterexamples and the fact that it is not a predictive measure. The nsc has been defined to overcome these limitations. It is based on the concept of fitness cloud, which visualizes on a plane the relationship between the fitness values of a sample of individuals and the fitness of some of their neighbors. The nsc can be used to quantify difficulty of standard GP benchmarks, where the cardinality and shape of global optima is not known *a priori*. Studies over some well-known GP benchmarks have been presented, confirming the suitability of nsc as measure of problem hardness. Other experiments on these benchmarks using a different sampling technique (standard Metropolis) and on other classes of tunably difficult problems (like trap functions and royal trees) have been done. Fitness clouds using more than one neighbor for each sampled individual have been analysed. Moreover, fitness clouds obtained by applying more than once the mutation operator at each sampled individual have been studied. Finally, a less disruptive mutation operator (structural mutation introduced in [15]) has been used. Finally, the *nsc* has been tested on other well known GP problems, such as the artificial ant on the Santa Fe trail, the multiplexer and the intertwined spirals problem. All these results (not shown here for lack of space) confirm the suitability of *nsc* as an indicator of problem hardness.

Future work includes a more exhaustive study of *nsc* and other measures based on fitness clouds over a wider set of GP benchmarks and the use of more sophisticated sampling techniques. Since we don't believe *nsc* to be infallible, as any statistic based on samples, these studies should also lead to the discovery of some drawbacks of this measure that should inspire future extensions.

References

1. L. Altenberg. The evolution of evolvability in genetic programming. In K. Kinnear, editor, *Advances in Genetic Programming*, pages 47–74, Cambridge, MA, 1994. The MIT Press.
2. M. Clergue, P. Collard, M. Tomassini, and L. Vanneschi. Fitness distance correlation and problem difficulty for genetic programming. In *et al.* W. B. Langdon, editor, *Proceedings of the Genetic and Evolutionary Computation Conference, GECCO'02*, pages 724–732, New York City, USA, 2002. Morgan Kaufmann, San Francisco, CA. *Best Conference Paper Award Nomination*.
3. J. M. Daida, R. Bertram, S. Stanhope, J. Khoo, S. Chaudhary, and O. Chaudhary. What makes a problem GP-hard? analysis of a tunably difficult problem in genetic programming. *Genetic Programming and Evolvable Machines*, 2:165–191, 2001.
4. A. Ekárt and S. Z. Németh. Maintaining the diversity of genetic programs. In J. A. Foster, E. Lutton, J. Miller, C. Ryan, and A. G. B. Tettamanzi, editors, *Genetic Programming, Proceedings of the 5th European Conference, EuroGP 2002*, volume 2278 of *LNCS*, pages 162–171, Kinsale, Ireland, 3-5 April 2002. Springer-Verlag.
5. T. Jones. *Evolutionary Algorithms, Fitness Landscapes and Search*. PhD thesis, University of New Mexico, Albuquerque, 1995.
6. J. R. Koza. *Genetic Programming*. The MIT Press, Cambridge, Massachusetts, 1992.
7. W. B. Langdon and R. Poli. An analysis of the max problem in genetic programming. In J. R. Koza, K. Deb, M. Dorigo, D. B. Fogel, M. Garzon, H. Iba, and R. L. Riolo, editors, *Genetic Programming 1997: Proceedings of the Second Annual Conference on Genetic Programming*, pages 222–230, San Francisco, CA, 1997. Morgan Kaufmann.
8. N. Madras. *Lectures on Monte Carlo Methods*. American Mathematical Society, Providence, Rhode Island, 2002.
9. B. Punch, D. Zongker, and E. Goodman. The royal tree problem, a benchmark for single and multiple population genetic programming. In P. Angeline and K. Kinnear, editors, *Advances in Genetic Programming 2*, pages 299–316, Cambridge, MA, 1996. The MIT Press.
10. R.J. Quick, V.J. Rayward-Smith, and G.D. Smith. Fitness distance correlation and ridge functions. In *Fifth Conference on Parallel Problems Solving from Nature (PPSN'98)*, pages 77–86. Springer-Verlag, Heidelberg, 1998.
11. M. Tomassini, L. Vanneschi, P. Collard, and M. Clergue. A study of fitness distance correlation as a difficulty measure in genetic programming. *Evolutionary Computation*, 2004. (to appear).

12. L. Vanneschi. *Theory and Practice for Efficient Genetic Programming.* Ph.D. thesis, Faculty of Science, University of Lausanne, Switzerland, 2004. Downloadable version at: http://www.disco.unimib.it/vanneschi. *Honored with the Excellence Award by the Science Faculty of the University of Lausanne.*

13. L. Vanneschi, M. Tomassini, M. Clergue, and P. Collard. Difficulty of unimodal and multimodal landscapes in genetic programming. In Cantú-Paz, E., *et al.*, editor, *Proceedings of the Genetic and Evolutionary Computation Conference, GECCO'03*, LNCS, pages 1788–1799, Chicago, Illinois, USA, 2003. Springer-Verlag. *Best Conference Paper Award Nomination.*

14. L. Vanneschi, M. Tomassini, P. Collard, and M. Clergue. Fitness distance correlation in genetic programming: a constructive counterexample. In *Congress on Evolutionary Computation (CEC'03)*, pages 289–296, Canberra, Australia, 2003. IEEE Press, Piscataway, NJ.

15. L. Vanneschi, M. Tomassini, P. Collard, and M. Clergue. Fitness distance correlation in structural mutation genetic programming. In Ryan, C., *et al.*, editor, *Genetic Programming, 6th European Conference, EuroGP2003*, Lecture Notes in Computer Science, pages 455–464. Springer-Verlag, Heidelberg, 2003.

16. S. Vérel, P. Collard, and M. Clergue. Where are bottleneck in nk-fitness landscapes? In *CEC 2003: IEEE International Congress on Evolutionary Computation. Canberra, Australia*, pages 273–280. IEEE Press, Piscataway, NJ, 2003.

Intelligent Information Access by Learning WordNet-Based User Profiles

M. Degemmis, P. Lops, and G. Semeraro

Dipartimento di Informatica,
Università di Bari,
Via E. Orabona, 4 - 70125 Bari, Italia
{degemmis, lops, semeraro}@di.uniba.it

Abstract. The central argument of this paper the induction user profiles by *supervised machine learning* techniques for Intelligent Information Access. The access must be highly *personalized* by user profiles, in which representations of the users' interests are maintained. Moreover, users want to retrieve information on the basis of *conceptual content*, but individual words provide unreliable evidence about the content of documents. A possible solution is the adoption of WordNet as a lexical resource to induce *semantic user profiles*.

1 Introduction

Machine learning algorithms are used for the induction, from labeled text documents, of a structured model of a user's interests, referred to as *user profile*, exploited for *personalized information access*. Keywords are rarely an appropriate way of locating the information in which a user is interested into because of *polysemy* and *synonymy*. The result is that, due to synonymy, relevant information can be missed if the profile does not contain the exact keywords occurring in the documents and, due to polysemy, wrong documents could be deemed as relevant. These problems call for methods able to learn *semantic* profiles that capture concepts representing users' interests from relevant documents. This paper shows how user profiles based on WordNet [1] can be inferred from documents represented by features generated using a novel indexing method. In Section 2 we propose a strategy to represent documents using WordNet synsets. Section 3 describes a method able to learn user profiles from the documents disambiguated using WordNet, while Section 4 describes some experiments.

2 Documents Representation

In the classical *bag of words* (BOW) representation, each feature corresponds to a single word in the training set. We propose a model, called *bag of synsets* (BOS), in which the senses corresponding to the words in the documents are considered as features. The adopted sense repository is WordNet (version 1.7.1) [1], a large lexical database for English. In WordNet, nouns, verbs, adjectives and adverbs

S. Bandini and S. Manzoni (Eds.): AI*IA 2005, LNAI 3673, pp. 78–81, 2005.

are organized into *synsets* (*synonym sets*), each representing one underlying lexical concept. Synsets are and organized in hierarchies. The problem of word sense disambiguation (WSD) has to be solved. The task consists in determining which of the senses of an ambiguous word is invoked in a particular use of the word [2]. We propose a WSD strategy based on the idea that semantic similarity between synsets a and b is inversely proportional to the distance between them in the WordNet IS-A hierarchy, measured by the number of nodes in the path from a to b. The path length similarity, computed by the function SINSIM(A,B) is used to associate the proper synset to a polysemous word w. SINSIM(A,B)$=$ $-log(N_p/2D)$, where N_p is the number of nodes in path p from a to b, D is the maximum depth of the taxonomy (in WordNet 1.7.1 $D = 16$) [1]. Let S be the set of all candidate synsets for w and C the context of w, that is the window of all words that surround w with a fixed radius. The strategy first builds T, the set of all synsets of the word forms in C with the same part-of-speech as w, and then computes the semantic similarity $score_{ih}$ between each synset s_i in S and each synset s_h in T. The synset s associated to w is the s_i with the highest similarity $score_{ih}$. A document is mapped into a list of WordNet synsets according to the following three rules: *a)* each monosemous word w in a slot of a document d is mapped into the corresponding WordNet synset; *b)* for each couple of words $\langle noun, noun \rangle$ or $\langle adjective, noun \rangle$, a search in WordNet is made in order to verify if at least one synset exists for the bigram $\langle w_1, w_2 \rangle$. In the positive case, the WSD strategy is applied on the bigram, otherwise it is applied separately on w_1 and w_2, using all words in the slot as the context C of w; *c)* each polysemous unigram w is disambiguated using all words in the slot as the context C of w. The WSD strategy has been used to process documents in the EachMovie dataset, a collection of movie descriptions. Each movie is represented by a set of 5 *slots*; each slot is a textual field corresponding to a specific feature of the movie: *title*, *cast*, *director*, *summary* and *keywords*. The text in each slot is represented using the *BOS* model. The representation of a document consists of a list of synsets recognized from the words in the document.

3   Learning WordNet-Based User Profiles

We consider the problem of learning user profiles as a binary text categorization task: each document has to be classified as interesting or not with respect to the user profile. The set of classes is restricted to c_+ (user-likes), and c_- (user-dislikes). In the Rocchio algorithm [3], learning is achieved by combining document vectors of positive and negative examples into a prototype vector $\vec{c}$ for each class in the set of classes C. Items within a certain distance from the prototype are considered as interesting. Two control parameters (β and γ) are used to set the relative importance of all positive and negative examples. In order to assign a class $\tilde{c}$ to a document d_j, the similarity between each prototype vector $\vec{c_i}$ and the document vector $\vec{d_j}$ is computed and $\tilde{c}$ will be the c_i with the highest value of similarity. Our version of this method is able to manage documents represented using different slots and represented by the concatenation of the five bag of synsets: $d_j = \langle w_{1j}^m, \ldots, w_{|T_m|j}^m \rangle$, where $|T_m|$ is the cardinality of the vocabulary (the set of all different synsets found in the training set) for the slot s_m and w_{ij}^m is the weight of the synset t_i in the document d_j, in the slot s_m. The strategy used to assign weights w_{ij}^m to synsets is based on the *Max Term Frequency-Square Page Frequency* measure adopted in [4], that we modified in order to obtain a measure called *Weighted Max Synset Frequency-Page Frequency* (weighted MAXSF-PF-ICF), that exploits ratings given by users to weight the occurrences of synsets. The score of a synset t_k that appears in the slot s_m of a document d_j belonging to class c_i is given by the product of a synset frequency-inverse document frequency score, computed as in the classical TFIDF word weighting scheme [3] by counting synsets occurrences instead of word occurrences, and the (weighted MAXSF-PF-ICF) score. Given the training document d_j, belonging to class c_i, for each synset t_k in the slot s_m, the frequency $\text{SF}(t_k, d_j, s_m)$ of the synset in the document is computed. Then, the following statistics are computed:

- MAXSF(t_k, c_i, s_m), the weighted maximum value of SF(t_k, d, s_m) on all training documents d of class c_i;
- $PF(t_k, c_i, s_m)$, the weighted page frequency, that is weighted the percentage of documents of class c_i in which the synset t_k occurs in the slot s_m;
- $ICF(t_k, c_i, s_m)$ - the *weighted* inverse category frequency, computed as:

$$ICF(t_k, c_i, s_m) = \frac{1}{1 + \sum_{j \neq i} PF(t_k, c_j, s_m)} \tag{1}$$

The weighted MAXSF-PF-ICF score is given by the product of MAXSF, PF and ICF. Given a user u and a set of rated movies in a specific category of interest, the goal is to learn a profile able to recognize movies liked by the user in that category. The learning process consists in inducing a prototype vector for *each slot*: these five vectors will represent the user profile. The algorithm separately exploits the training examples: it learns two different profiles $\vec{p_i} = \langle w_{1i}^m, \ldots, w_{|T|i}^m \rangle$ (T is the cardinality of the vocabulary), for a user u and a category c_i by taking into account the ratings given by the user on documents in that category. One profile is learned using the positive examples, while the other one is learned from negative examples. The rating $r_{u,j}$ on the document d_j is a discrete judgment ranging from 0 to 5. It is used in order to compute the coordinates of the vectors in the positive and in the negative user profile. A coordinate w_{ki}^m of the positive profile is computed as in equation (2), while a coordinate w_{ki}^m of the negative profile is computed as in equation (3):

$$w_{ki}^m = \sum_{\{d_j \in POS_i\}} \frac{w_{kj}^m \cdot r_{u,j}'}{|POS_i|} \tag{2} \qquad w_{ki}^m = \sum_{\{d_j \in NEG_i\}} \frac{w_{kj}^m \cdot r_{u,j}'}{|NEG_i|} \tag{3}$$

where $r_{u,j}'$ is the normalized value of $r_{u,j}$ ranging between 0 and 1 (respectively corresponding to $r_{u,j} = 0$ and 5), $POS_i = \{d_j \in T_r | r_{u,j} > 2\}$, $NEG_i = \{d_j \in T_r | r_{u,j} \leq 2\}$, and w_{kj}^m is the weight of the synset t_k in the document d_j in the slot s_m computed as previously described. Equations (2) and (3) differ from the classical Rocchio formula in the fact that the parameters β and γ are substituted by the ratings $r'_{u,j}$ that allow to give a different weight to each document in the training set. As regards the computation of the similarity between a profile $\overrightarrow{p_i}$ and a movie $\overrightarrow{d_j}$, five partial similarity values are computed between each pair of corresponding vectors in $\overrightarrow{p_i}$ and $\overrightarrow{d_j}$. A weighted average of the values is computed, by assigning to the similarity for the slots *summary* and *keywords* an heavier weight than the ones assigned to the others. Since the user profile is composed by the positive and the negative profiles, we compute one similarity values for each profile. Document d_j is considered as interesting only if the similarity value of the positive profile is higher than the similarity of the negative one.

4   Experimental Results

The experimental work has been carried out on the EachMovie dataset, a collection of 1628 descriptions of movies rated by real users on a 6-point scale (from 1 to 6, mapped linearly to the interval [0,1]). Movies are subdivided into 10 different genres. For each genre, a set of 100 users was randomly selected among users that rated n items, $30 \leq n \leq 100$ in that movie category. For each category, a dataset of at least 3000 triples (user,movie,rating) was obtained. A movie is considered as *relevant* by a user if the rating is greater or equal than 3. The profiling algorithm classifies an item as relevant if the similarity score of the class *likes* is greater than the one for the class *dislikes*. Classification effectiveness is measured by *precision, recall* and *F-measure* [3]. We also adopted NDPM [5] to measure the distance between the ranking imposed on items by the user ratings and the ranking predicted by the system. Values range from 0 (agreement) to 1 (disagreement). For each 'genre' dataset, we run n experiments, where n is the number of users in the dataset: the triples (user,movie,rating) of each specific user and the content of the rated movies have been used for learning the user profile and measuring its predictive accuracy. By analyzing the results, obtained by a 10-fold cross-validation, we observed a slight improvement in precision (BOS=76%, BOW=74%, +2%), recall (BOS=84%, BOW=82%, +2%) and F-measure (BOS=78%, BOW=76%, +2%). NDPM remains acceptable. More detailed results and comments are not reported here due to space limitations.

References

1. Fellbaum, C.: WordNet: An Electronic Lexical Database. MIT Press (1998)
2. Manning, C.D., Schutze, H.: Foundations of Statistical Natural Language Processing. The MIT Press, Cambridge, US (1984)
3. Salton, G., McGill, M.: Introduction to Modern Information Retrieval. McGraw-Hill, New York (1983)
4. Ceci, M., Malerba, D.: Hierarchical classification of HTML documents with WebClassII. In Sebastiani, F., ed.: Proc. of ECIR-03, Springer Verlag (2003) 57–72
5. Yao, Y.Y.: Measuring retrieval effectiveness based on user preference of documents. Journal of the American Society for Information Science **46** (1995) 133–145

Refined Approximation of Concepts in Ontology*

Dazhou Kang, Baowen Xu, Jianjiang Lu, Yanhui Li, and Peng Wang

Dep.of Computer Science and Engineering, Southeast University,
Nanjing 210096, China
Jiangsu Institute of Software Quality, Nanjing 210096, China
bwxu@seu.edu.cn

Abstract. Finding approximations of concepts in other ontologies is the key problem in approximate query rewriting, an approach of querying in heterogeneous ontologies. The data-driven method suffers from the extremely overlarge expressions of approximations. The paper defines multielement least upper bounds and multielement greatest lower bounds of concept to get refined approximations. They are proved having the same answer sets as the approximations from data-driven method, but are in simplified expressions. The effective algorithms to find the multielement bounds are also provided.

1 Introduction

Information retrieval is one of the most basic and important services on the Web [1]. Ontology-based information systems [2] can greatly increase the precision and recall of queries. They classify information items with respect to an ontology O. A query with respect to O is a Boolean expression on the set of concepts in O. Then the system can answer the query. For any information system S, let $Q^{\mathcal{I}(S)}$ means the set of all answers in S to query Q .

Let the ontology of the user and the system be $\mathcal{O}_1$ and $\mathcal{O}_2$. Generally, the system is only able to answer queries with respect to $\mathcal{O}_2$ and cannot answer the users' queries with respect to $\mathcal{O}_1$. This paper focuses on the approximate query rewriting approaches to solve the problem[3]. And the key problem is how to find approximations with respect to $\mathcal{O}_2$ for each concept C in $\mathcal{O}_1$ [4].

The method in [2] can find the closest approximations of concept based on learning all the objects in the answer set of a concept. Let information source S be the training set, K be a nonempty set of objects in S. They define two sets of non-negative queries with respect to O_2: $K^+ = \{Q|K \subseteq Q^{\mathcal{I}(S)}\}$ and $K^- = \{Q|Q^{\mathcal{I}(S)} \subseteq K\}$. Then an upper and a lower name of K can be computed: $\mathrm{name}^+(K) = \bigwedge_{Q \in K^+} Q$, $\mathrm{name}^-(K) = \bigvee_{Q \in K^-} Q$. A function mapping an object o to conjunction of concepts is introduced: $\mathrm{D_I}(o) = \bigwedge\{D_i \in T|o \in D_i^{\mathcal{I}(S)}\}$, where

---

* This work was supported in part by the NSFC (60373066, 60425206, 90412003, 60403016), National Grand Fundamental Research 973 Program of China (2002CB312000), National Research Foundation for the Doctoral Program of Higher Education of China (20020286004), Advanced Armament Research Project(51406020105JB8103).

S. Bandini and S. Manzoni (Eds.): AI*IA 2005, LNAI 3673, pp. 82–85, 2005.

T is the set of concepts in O_2. Then it can be proved (see Theorem 5.1 and 5.2 in [2]) that: $\bigvee_{o \in K} D_I(o) \sim \mathrm{name}^+(K)$ and $\bigvee\{D_I(o)|o \in K, (D_I(o))^{\mathcal{I}(\mathcal{S})} \subseteq K\} \sim \mathrm{name}^-(K)$. If C is a concept in O_1, and $K = C^{\mathcal{I}(\mathcal{S})}$, then $\mathrm{name}^+(K)$ and $\mathrm{name}^-(K)$ are the closest approximations of C with respect to O_2.

But the method has several lacks. Firstly, it needs to traverse all objects to compute the approximations. The expressions of the approximations are often full of too many small concepts. Secondly, their approximations are regardless of the semantic relations. This paper defines multielement bounds of concepts, and uses them to compute refined approximations of concepts to overcome the above lacks.

2   Refined Approximations

Our refined approximations are defined in terms of query subsumption [5]. Query subsumption is a transitive and reflexive relation. Let Q, R be concept queries, R subsumes Q ($Q \sqsubseteq R$) if $Q^{\mathcal{I}(\mathcal{S})} \subseteq R^{\mathcal{I}(\mathcal{S})}$ in any information source $\mathcal{S}$. Q and R are equivalent queries ($Q \equiv R$) if $R \sqsubseteq Q$ and $Q \sqsubseteq R$; R properly subsumes Q ($Q \sqsubset R$) if $Q \sqsubseteq R$ but not $R \sqsubseteq Q$; $Q \sqsubseteq \bot$ if $Q^{\mathcal{I}(\mathcal{S})} = \emptyset$ in any $\mathcal{S}$. Let C be a concept in $\mathcal{O}_1$, T be the set of all concepts in $\mathcal{O}_2$. If $E = \{D_1, \ldots, D_i\}$ is a set of concepts in T, then E is called a i-concept-set in T, and $|E| = i$. We define $\check{E}$ be the disjunction of all concepts in E called i-concept-disjunction in T; $\hat{E}$ be the conjunction of all concepts in E called i-concept-conjunction.

Definition 1 (Multielement least upper bounds). *The multielement least upper bounds of C with respect to T is a set of concept-disjunctions in T, notated as* $\mathrm{mlub}^T(C)$, *if the following assertions hold:*

$$\forall \check{E} \in \mathrm{mlub}^T(C) \to C \sqsubseteq \check{E} \; ; \tag{1}$$

$$\forall F \subseteq T, C \sqsubseteq \check{F} \to \exists \check{E} \in \mathrm{mlub}^T(C), \check{E} \sqsubseteq \check{F} \; . \tag{2}$$

$$\forall \check{E} \in \mathrm{mlub}^T(C) \to \begin{cases} \neg \exists F \subseteq T, C \sqsubseteq \check{F} \sqsubset \check{E} \; ; \\ \neg \exists \check{F} \in \mathrm{mlub}^T(C), \check{F} \equiv \check{E} \; ; \\ \neg \exists F \subseteq T, (\check{F} \equiv \check{E}) \wedge (|F| < |E|) \; . \end{cases} \tag{3}$$

Definition 2 (Multielement greatest lower bounds). *The multielement greatest lower bounds of C with respect to T is a set of concept-conjunctions in T, notated as* $\mathrm{mglb}^T(C)$, *if the following assertions hold:*

$$\forall \hat{E} \in \mathrm{mglb}^T(C) \to \hat{E} \sqsubseteq C \; ; \tag{4}$$

$$\forall F \subseteq T, \hat{F} \sqsubseteq C \to \exists \hat{E} \in \mathrm{mglb}^T(C), \hat{F} \sqsubseteq \hat{E} \; . \tag{5}$$

$$\forall \hat{E} \in \mathrm{mglb}^T(C) \to \begin{cases} \neg \exists F \subseteq T, \hat{E} \sqsubset \hat{F} \sqsubseteq C \; ; \\ \neg \exists \hat{F} \in \mathrm{mlub}^T(C), \hat{F} \equiv \hat{E} \; ; \\ \neg \exists F \subseteq T, (\hat{F} \equiv \hat{E}) \wedge (|F| < |E|) \; . \end{cases} \tag{6}$$

In each definition, the first two assertions are necessary conditions, and the last assertion simplifies the bounds to have the least number of necessary members. Then two refined approximations of concept can be defined:

$$\mathrm{MA}^{T+}(C) = \bigwedge_{\check{E}_i \in \mathrm{mlub}^T(C)} \check{E}_i \; ; \quad \mathrm{MA}^{T-}(C) = \bigvee_{\hat{E}_i \in \mathrm{mglb}^T(C)} \hat{E}_i \; .$$

Theorem 1. *If for any queries* Q, R, $Q^{\mathcal{I}(\mathcal{S})} \subseteq R^{\mathcal{I}(\mathcal{S})} \iff Q \sqsubseteq R$, *and* $K = C^{\mathcal{I}(\mathcal{S})}$, *then* $\mathrm{name}^+(K)^{\mathcal{I}(\mathcal{S})} = \mathrm{MA}^{T+}(C)^{\mathcal{I}(\mathcal{S})}$ *and* $\mathrm{name}^-(K)^{\mathcal{I}(\mathcal{S})} = \mathrm{MA}^{T-}(C)^{\mathcal{I}(\mathcal{S})}$.

Proof. A premiss of the proof is that any query can be transformed to an equivalent *CNF* or *DNF* [6]. The proof can be divided into four parts:

1. $\mathrm{MA}^{T+}(C)^{\mathcal{I}(\mathcal{S})} \subseteq \mathrm{name}^+(K)^{\mathcal{I}(\mathcal{S})}$. Let Q be the equivalent *CNF* of $\mathrm{name}^+(K)$, $\mathrm{name}^+(K) \equiv Q = \bigwedge_{i=1}^n \check{F}_i$, where $F_i \subseteq T$. Since $K = C^{\mathcal{I}(\mathcal{S})}$, so $C \sqsubseteq Q$, and then it has $C \sqsubseteq \check{F}_i$ for any $\check{F}_i$. Then from Eq.2, for any $\check{F}_i$, there exists $\check{E}_i \in \mathrm{mlub}^T(C)$ that $\check{E}_i \sqsubseteq \check{F}_i$. Therefore, we can get that $\mathrm{MA}^{T+}(C) = \bigwedge_{\check{E}_i \in \mathrm{mlub}^T(C)} \check{E}_i \sqsubseteq \bigwedge_{i=1}^n \check{F}_i \equiv \mathrm{name}^+(K)$.
   The next three parts can be analogously proved.
2. $\mathrm{name}^+(K)^{\mathcal{I}(\mathcal{S})} \subseteq \mathrm{MA}^{T+}(C)^{\mathcal{I}(\mathcal{S})}$.
3. $\mathrm{MA}^{T-}(C)^{\mathcal{I}(\mathcal{S})} \subseteq \mathrm{name}^-(K)^{\mathcal{I}(\mathcal{S})}$.
4. $\mathrm{name}^-(K)^{\mathcal{I}(\mathcal{S})} \subseteq \mathrm{MA}^{T-}(C)^{\mathcal{I}(\mathcal{S})}$.

From the above theorem, the refined approximations have the same answer sets as the approximations from the data-driven method. So they are also the closest approximations of the concept. But the multielement bounds are simplified and have the least number of necessary members. So they can greatly reduce the size of approximations and increase query efficiency. Furthermore, the refined approximations are independent of the method to find query subsumption, so the existing semantic relations between ontologies can be used.

3 Algorithms of Finding the Multielement Bounds

This subsection gives an algorithm of finding the multielement least upper bounds, which is called Algorithm 1. The combinatorial explosion problem may occur, so one of the main objectives is to reduce the searching space.

Here are the notations used in Algorithm 1. Let $ps = \{\check{E} | \check{E}$ is a member of the multielement least upper bounds$\}$; $ns = \{\check{E} | \forall F \subseteq T, F \supset E \to \check{F} \notin ps\}$. We only deal with disjunctions of i concepts in step i. Let c_i be the set of candidate disjunctions which need be tested in step i. At the end of the step, let a set of all potential members of ps in c_i be v_i, and the set of residual members be r_i.

We introduce the processes in Algorithm 1 in detail:

1. Finding v_1 and r_1 from c_1. In step 1, initiatively $c_1 = T$.
   - Firstly we deal with equivalent concepts: if there are several equivalent concepts in c_1, then only one of them has to remain. If there is $A \in c_1$ such that $C \equiv A$, then let $ps = \{A\}$, and end the algorithm.

- Secondly we can find v_1 by $v_1 = \{A \in c_1 | (C \sqsubset A) \wedge (\neg \exists B \in c_1, C \sqsubset B \sqsubset A)\}$, which is obviously a super set of $ps \cap c_1$.
- Then we find members of ns in c_1: for any $A \in c_1$, if $C \wedge A \equiv \bot$, or $C \sqsubset A$, or $\exists B \in c_1$ such that $A \sqsubset B \sqsubset C$, then $A \in ns$ and will be deleted. Lastly the residual members form r_1. Let $i = 2$.

2. Generate c_i from r_{i-1}. Assume we have got r_{i-1}, we can generate c_i by $c_i = \{\breve{E} | (|E| = i) \wedge (\forall F \subset E, |F| = i - 1 \to \breve{F} \in r_{i-1})\}$. Especially, when generate c_2 from r_1, for any $A, B \in r_1$, if $A \subset B$, then $A \vee B$ is not in c_2.

3. Finding v_i and r_i from c_i.
   - In step i, firstly, if there is $\breve{E} \in c_i$ such that $C \equiv A$, then let $ps = \{\breve{E}\}$, and end the algorithm.
   - Secondly we find v_i by $v_i = \{\breve{E} \in c_i | (C \sqsubset \breve{E}) \wedge (\neg \exists \breve{F} \in c_i, C \sqsubset \breve{F} \sqsubset \breve{E})\}$.
   - Then we find members of ns in c_i: for any $\breve{E} \in c_i$, if $C \sqsubset \breve{E}$, then $\breve{E} \in ns$ and will be deleted. Lastly the residual members form r_i.

4. Let $i = i + 1$, repeat processes 2 and 3 until r_{i-1} is empty.

5. Validate process. Let $v = v_1 \cup v_2 \cup \ldots \cup v_n$. For any different $\breve{E}, \breve{F} \in v$, if $\breve{E} \sqsubset \breve{F}$, then delete $\breve{F}$; if $\breve{E} \equiv \breve{F}$ and $|E| \leq |G|$, then delete $\breve{F}$. This process removes the redundancy, and returns ps.

The results can be proved both complete and correct. And the searching space has been greatly reduced. So Algorithm 1 is efficiently for finding the simplified multielement least upper bounds. The algorithm of finding the simplified multielement greatest lower bounds is similar to Algorithm 1.

4   Conclusion

This paper presents new defined multielement least upper bounds and multielement greatest lower bounds for computing refined approximations of concept. The refined approximations have the same answer sets as the approximations from the data-driven method. But they are in simplified expressions and can improve the query effectiveness. The effective algorithms to find the multielement bounds are also provided.

References

1. Shah, U., Finin, T., Joshi, A., Cost, R.S., Mayfield, J.: Information Retrieval on the Semantic Web. In: the 10th International Conference on Information and Knowledge Management. McLean: ACM Press (2002) 461–468
2. Tzitzikas, Y.: Collaborative Ontology-based Information Indexing and Retrieval. Doctoral Dissertation, Heraklion (2002)
3. Chang, C., Garcia-Molina, H.: Approximate query mapping: Accounting for translation closeness. The VLDB Journal, **10(2-3)** (2001) 155–181
4. Stuckenschmidt, H.: Ontology-Based Information Sharing in Weakly Structured Environments. PhD thesis, AI Department, Vrije Universiteit Amsterdam (2002)
5. Goasdoué, F., Rousset, M.C.: Answering Queries using Views: a KRDB Perspective for the Semantic Web. ACM Transactions on Internet Technology, **4(3)** (2004) 255–288
6. A. Galton, *Logic for Information Technology*, John Wiley & Sons (1990)

Argumentation for Access Control

Guido Boella[1], Joris Hulstijn[2], and Leendert van der Torre[3]

[1] Universitá di Torino
[2] Vrije Universiteit, Amsterdam
[3] CWI Amsterdam and Delft University of Technology

Abstract. In this paper we are interested in argument based reasoning for access control, for example in the context of agents negotiating access to resources or web services in virtual organizations. We use a logical framework which contains agents with objectives concerning access to a resource or provision of a service, including security objectives. The access control mechanism is described by a set of policy rules, that specify that access to a resource or service requires a specific set of credentials. Our contribution is a formalization of the reasoning about access control using a planning theory formalized in Dung's abstract argumentation framework. We build on Amgoud's argumentation framework for plan arguments, which is based on an adaptation of Dung's notion of defence. Our formal argumentation framework allows arguments about the backward derivation of plans from objectives and policy rules (abduction), as well as arguments about the forward derivation of goals from general objectives. We show that reasoning about the feasibility of goals requires mixed goal-plan arguments, and we show how to formalize the plan arguments in Dung's framework without adapting the notion of defence.

1 Introduction

Traditionally, access control mechanisms are centered around the certification of identities, as for example in the X.509 protocol. When managing access control becomes more complex, and agents want to reason about access control, a *declarative approach* to the specification and verification of access control policies becomes necessary [3]. Declarative policy rules state which signed credentials are needed for actions. Moreover, with the advent of web services and virtual organizations, access control becomes not only based on the identity of a client, but on the credentials needed to access the service. Since the required credentials are not always known to the client, the process of accessing a resource becomes an interaction between client and server, discussing modalities until they reach an agreement. Thus, based on declarative policies, Koshutanski and Massacci [7,8] developed *interactive access control*. A similar approach is advocated by Bonatti and Samarati [4].

In interactive access control approaches, a so called trust management system is introduced, which contains a logical reasoning engine to make it easier to reason about the details of an access request, and about the context in which access requests are evaluated. The application that makes the access request does not have to guess beforehand which credentials may be needed. Credentials are provided by the applicant and verified, using deduction. If the credentials are insufficient to satisfy the access control

S. Bandini and S. Manzoni (Eds.): AI*IA 2005, LNAI 3673, pp. 86–97, 2005.

policy, abduction is used to work out which (minimal) set of credentials is missing. The server will then request the applicant to provide these missing credentials. This process is repeated until the access is granted or the applicant runs out of credentials. This explains the term interactive access control.

We are interested in the case in which parties negotiate to find an agreement about which policy to apply, because there may be more than one way to achieve a security objective. Parties use arguments to support their case until one wins the dispute. Moreover, during this negotiation process, further security objectives can arise. For example, once an agent has gained access to a resource, requests for another resource may have to be denied, to avoid potential conflicts of interest.

To model this situation we suggest the following conceptualization. The search for credentials can be modeled as a planning process, where presentation of the credentials corresponds to actions. A declarative access control policy corresponds to a skeleton plan. It consists of the combinations of credentials that are required to achieve some overall security objective. Thus different alternative combinations of credentials may exist to achieve the same objective. The set of objectives need not remain stable; as the environment changes, or as the underlying security preferences change, new objectives may be triggered. Thus we distinguish between two processes: *plan generation*, the derivation of combinations of credentials that will achieve those objectives, and *goal generation*, the derivation of security objectives on the basis of the state variables and basic security principles. This conceptualization is based on an analogy with non-classical planning, where goals are derived on the basis of more basic desires and beliefs about the current situation [15].

A formal framework for negotiation about access control needs (i) a formal representation of the content, in this case arguments about access control, and (ii) a formal representation of the possible moves (request, grant, challenge, defend, etc.) and a interaction protocol to specify what sequences of moves are well formed. In this paper we address only the former of these two issues: the the formalization of arguments about interactive and declarative access control situations. This breaks down into two sub-questions:

1. Which kind of arguments can be distinguished in interactive access control?
2. What is a logical framework for arguments about interactive access control?

We define arguments as trees that represent a line of reasoning. To distinguish the arguments in this theory, we distinguish goal and plan arguments for two relevant kinds of reasoning. Goal generation needs forward reasoning from the current state of affairs to preferable objectives (deduction). In case several sets of mutually compatible objectives are derived, so called options, a selection has to be made on the basis of some priority principle. Plan generation on the other hand, needs backward or "means-ends" reasoning from objectives to required and missing credentials (abduction). Moreover, we define mixed goal-plan arguments for the interaction between goal and plan generation. Goal generation and the subsequent process of selecting objectives partly depend on plan generation, because potential goals are required to be feasible. A goal or objective is called feasible when some policy exists that is likely to achieve it. In the context of agent planning Rao and Georgeff [11] call an agent that only generates feasible goals *strongly realistic*. It is waste of resources to consider infeasible goals. The feasibility restriction requires that plan generation can somehow constrain goal generation.

For the logical framework we apply techniques from formal argumentation theory, which allow us to cope with both the interaction and the planning aspects of interactive access control, and which also offers the advantages of non-monotonic reasoning. Formal argumentation theory originates from theories of dialogue and natural language, but it has become popular in artificial intelligence as a formal framework for default reasoning. Dung's [5] abstract framework characterizes many instances of non-monotonic reasoning, such as Reiter's default logic, autoepistemic logic, logic programming, and circumscription, as instances of argumentation. Amgoud's version of Dung's argumentation framework allows reasoning about conflicting plans [1,2]. The central analogy is the following. An objective that has several possible plans, i.e. policies or combinations of credentials, can be modeled just like an argument which consists of a claim with the supporting argumentations. The attack relation defined over the set of arguments can serve as a criterium to deal with possible conflicts among policies, and to select a set of compatible policies that achieves a set of objectives. However, Amgoud argues that the framework must be adapted, because conflicts between plans are fundamentally different from the kinds of conflicts studied in non-monotonic reasoning, such as defaults. This alteration is discussed in depth.

To illustrate the use of arguments for interactive access control, we present a running example throughout this paper.

The paper is structured as follows. In Section 2 we introduce the running example and explain formal arguments of policies and objectives. In Section 3 we show how to reason about these arguments in an argumentation framework. Related work and concluding remarks end the paper.

2   Arguments for Policies and Objectives

In interactive access control situations we consider the possibility that clients and servers have their own preferences and principles concerning which credential to disclose or require. Hence, parties may be said to argue about the outcome of an access request. We introduce a running example to illustrate this possibility. The following dialogue between a client A and a library clerk B could take place in a traditional library, but it is easy to imagine a similar exchange – formalized – at some automated online article repository. This example illustrates two aspects. First, different sets of credentials can be used to access a service. In our example, a pass, credit and a signed order are applied in turn. Secondly, during the interaction process new objectives can pop up. In our example the requirement to let successful applicants participate in a survey leads the librarian to request the applicant to fill in a questionnaire.

A: I would like to retrieve an article.
B: Yes, but you have to buy a subscription to the library
A: I am a University employee.
B: Please show me your pass.
A: < showing pass >

B: You have to pay for the copy of the paper anyway.
A: Ok, I will use my credit.
B: Your credit has already depleted.
A: I will use a signed order from my boss, instead.
B: < checking order > Ok.
A: This is the article I would like to retrieve.
B: Here it is. Could you please fill out this questionnaire about the article?
B: Ok.

To formalize the example we need to introduce quite some notation. We need to represent credentials and facts about the world. More importantly, we need policy rules that indicate what credentials are needed to grant some access or service request. And finally, we need rules that indicate how additional objectives can be derived. In the logical language, we distinguish among credentials (C) and state variables (S).

Definition 1. Let C and S be two disjoint sets of credentials and state variables respectively. Let L be a propositional language built from $C \cup S$. A literal l is an element of C or S, or its negation. A rule is an ordered nonempty finite list of literals: $l_1 \wedge l_2 \wedge \ldots \wedge l_{n-1} \rightarrow l_n$. We call $l_1 \wedge l_2 \wedge \ldots \wedge l_{n-1}$ the body of the rule, and l_n the head. If $n = 1$ the body is empty and we write l_n. The *closure* of a set of rules R over a set of literals V, is defined by $Cl(R, V) = \bigcup_{i=0}^{i=\infty} S^i$ with $S^0 = V$ and $S^{i+1} = S^i \cup \{l \mid l_1 \wedge \ldots \wedge l_n \rightarrow l \in R, \{l_1...l_n\} \subseteq S^i\}$.

A so called *objective-policy description* consists of a set of conditional objectives (O), a set of policy rules (P), and a set of integrity constraints (K), representing general knowledge. A conditional objective $l_1 \wedge \ldots \wedge l_{n-1} \rightarrow l_n$ in O means that l_n is required in the context $l_1 \wedge \ldots \wedge l_{n-1}$; a policy rule means that l_n is achieved if $l_1 \wedge \ldots \wedge l_{n-1}$ is achieved, and an integrity constraint represents that l_n is true when $l_1 \wedge \ldots \wedge l_{n-1}$ are true. Since a credential needs no further policy rules, we require that the head of a policy rule is not a credential. In general, an objective is something which should be true but is not true yet, a policy rule explains how objectives can be achieved, and integrity constraints contain all other relevant rules. These rules behave as production rules. For explanatory reasons, we restrict the language here to conjunction and a syntactic form of negation. The general idea is to use these rules to generate extensions. An extension is a set of arguments or 'policies', depending on how you look at it, that are mutually compatible. Ideally, an extension will contain policies to fulfill all objectives, while no integrity constraints are violated. More elaborate logics exist in the literature on logic programming. Some of those are mentioned in section 4.

Definition 2. Let C, S and L be as defined in Definition 1. An *objective-policy description* is a tuple $\langle O, P, K \rangle$ with O, P and K sets of rules from L, such that the heads of rules in P are built from a variable in S.

We illustrate the three kinds of rules in an objective-policy description of our running example.

Example 1 (Access Control). Suppose you want to get an electronic copy of an article from the digital library. To do so you have to be authorized to use the library and you have to comply with the digital rights. Authorization is only given after paying a subscription to the library with your e-money, or after showing a university employee pass. To comply with the digital rights you have to pay with your e-money or present a signed order of your employer. Moreover, if you want to get an mp3 file, you also have to pay with e-money. Since you have a limited budget, using your e-money in this way prevents you from paying the rights for the paper. So these objectives conflict.

Granting access to an article is relevant only when there is a request by an applicant. Once the applicant gets the paper, the system wants to collect a survey, and to do so the applicant has to fill in and send a questionnaire. Moreover, if the system receives a request for an mp3 file, it will let the applicant access it if it complies with the policy. Once the applicant has access to the mp3 file, the system will want to improve its bandwidth. This objective is achieved when the applicant decreases the downloading speed or shares the file.

Let $C = \{es, sp, el, sr, em, ra, f, rm, ds, sm\}$ and $S = \{a, al, cr, m, cs, ib\}$, where

a	access article from digital library		
al	authorized to access library	ra	request article
es	subscribe to library with e-money	cs	collect survey
sp	send university employee pass	f	fill in questionnaire
cr	comply with digital rights	rm	request mp3 file
el	pay library with e-money	ib	improve bandwidth
sr	signed order by employer	ds	decrease download speed
m	access mp3 file	sm	share downloaded mp3 file
em	pay mp3 file with e-money		

Consider the following objective-policy description:

$O = \{ra \rightarrow a, a \rightarrow cs, rm \rightarrow m, m \rightarrow ib\}$

$P = \{al \wedge cr \rightarrow a, sp \rightarrow al, es \rightarrow al, sr \rightarrow cr, el \rightarrow cr, f \rightarrow cs, em \rightarrow m, sm \rightarrow ib,$
    $ds \rightarrow ib\}$

$K = \{ra, rm, em \rightarrow \neg es, em \rightarrow \neg el\}$

The system has the objective to grant access to an article or mp3 file, when requested ($ra \rightarrow a, rm \rightarrow m$). There are several ways to achieve both objectives, but if we add $em \rightarrow \neg sr$ as a rule to K, there is no way to achieve both.

The applicant requests an article or an mp3 file. When the system sends an article, it further requires to collect a survey, and when it sends an mp3 file it further requires to improve the bandwidth. There are several ways in which the applicant can comply with these objectives of the system. E.g., to participate in the survey, the applicant can fill in a questionnaire and send it to the system, and to improve bandwidth the applicant can reduce the downloading speed or share the file it just downloaded.

We now define our first kind of arguments about interactive access control, involving the derivation of security objectives on the basis of the state variables and basic security principles. We define arguments for a *goal set*. A goal set is an option that is selected to be enforced, and which is derived from a set of *related* objectives, such that we can find mutually compatible policies that can realize them. A goal argument is simply a sequence (linear tree) that represents a derivation of a goal set. Using goal arguments, we say that a conditional objective *depends* on another conditional objective, if the former can only be applied on the basis of the latter.

There is one technical complication which has to do with the minimality of arguments, sometimes these are called minimal arguments. In our argumentation theory where an argument involves the derivation of a set of formulas (goal set) from another set of formulas (objectives), we can consider a minimality restriction on either the goal set or on the variables that occur in the tree. We define our notion of minimality using the intermediate notion of a candidate goal tree for potential goal sets, which contains all conditional objectives which can be applied, based on application of earlier conditional objectives. Intuitively, a candidate goal argument is a goal argument, if its goal set cannot be split into a set of goal sets.

Definition 3. Let $\langle O, P, K \rangle$ be an objective-policy description.

- A *goal set* G is a set of literals.
- A *candidate goal argument* for *goal set* G, written $c(G)$, is a finite linear tree consisting of pairs of sets of literals with its unique leave (B, G) or any B, such that for each node (B, H) there exists a conditional objective $l_1 \wedge \ldots \wedge l_n \rightarrow l \in O$ such that:
  (a) $B = \{l_1, ..., l_n\} \subseteq Cl(K, U)$, where U is the union of all literals occurring in the ancestors of (B, H).
  (b) if (B, H) is the root, then $H = \{l\}$, otherwise $H = \{l\} \cup H'$ when the unique parent of (B, H) is (B', H') for some B'.
- A *goal argument* for *goal set* G, written $g(G)$, is a candidate goal argument $c(G)$ such that there is no set of goal sets $\{G_1, ..., G_n\}$ with each $G_i \neq G$ and $G = G_1 \cup ... \cup G_n$. A *maximal goal set* is a goal set which has a goal argument and which is maximal with respect to set inclusion.
- We say that two goal arguments *conflict* if they contain nodes $\langle B_1, H_1 \rangle$ and $\langle B_2, H_2 \rangle$ such that $Cl(K \cup B1 \cup H_1 \cup B2 \cup H_2, \emptyset) \vdash \bot$, where $\bot$ stands for any contradiction.

The running example illustrates that a goal set is derived from a set of related objectives.

Example 2 (Continued). The goal sets are $\{a\}$, $\{a, cs\}$, $\{m\}$ and $\{m, ib\}$. The set $\{a, cs, m, ib\}$ is not a proper goal set, because it can be split in $\{a, cs\}$ and $\{m, ib\}$. The latter two are the maximal goal sets. Here, a and cs are related, because the objective to collect a survey (cs) is conditional on granting access (a). Likewise, (m) and (ib) are related, because the objective to improve bandwidth (ib) is conditional on access to an mp3 file (m).

The following proposition illustrates that constructing a goal argument is analogous to deductively applying inference rules in classical logic, together with the minimality constraint. Note that this is a recursive definition, but since the goal set decreases and its finiteness, the definition is well founded.

Proposition 1 (Goal Set with goal argument). We write $H(R)$ for the set of heads of rules in R. Given an objective-policy description $\langle O, P, K \rangle$, a finite set of literals G is a *goal set* with a goal argument iff there exists a subset O' of O such that:

$$\langle a, \{al, cr\}\rangle \qquad \langle a, \{al, cr\}\rangle \qquad \langle a, \{al, cr\}\rangle \qquad \langle a, \{al, cr\}\rangle$$

$$\nearrow \quad \searrow \qquad \nearrow \quad \searrow \qquad \nearrow \quad \searrow \qquad \nearrow \quad \searrow \qquad \langle m, \{em\}\rangle$$

$$\langle al, \{sp\}\rangle \; \langle cr, \{sr\}\rangle \quad \langle al, \{sp\}\rangle \; \langle cr, \{el\}\rangle \quad \langle al, \{es\}\rangle \; \langle cr, \{el\}\rangle \quad \langle al, \{es\}\rangle \; \langle cr, \{sr\}\rangle \qquad \uparrow$$

$$\uparrow \qquad \uparrow \qquad \uparrow \qquad \uparrow \qquad \uparrow \qquad \uparrow \qquad \uparrow \qquad \uparrow \qquad \langle em, \emptyset\rangle$$

$$\langle sp, \emptyset\rangle \quad \langle sr, \emptyset\rangle \quad \langle sp, \emptyset\rangle \quad \langle el, \emptyset\rangle \quad \langle es, \emptyset\rangle \quad \langle el, \emptyset\rangle \quad \langle es, \emptyset\rangle \quad \langle sr, \emptyset\rangle$$

$$t_1 \qquad\qquad t_2 \qquad\qquad t_3 \qquad\qquad t_4 \qquad\qquad t_5$$

Fig. 1. The plan arguments for Example 1

- $G = Cl(O' \cup K, \emptyset) \cap H(O')$;
- $Cl(O' \cup K, \emptyset)$ is consistent, i.e., does not contain l and $\neg l$;
- There is no set of goal sets with goal arguments $\{G_1, ..., G_n\}$ with each $G_i \neq G$ and $G = G_1 \cup ... \cup G_n$.

The second type of argument we consider are plan arguments constructed from policies, which serve as a way to represent and reason with policies and their motivating objectives. Each node of the tree represents a pair of a literals and a set of literals. Note that this is distinct rom the nodes in a goal arguments, where nodes are pairs of sets of literals. These nodes are interpreted as atomic plans to be executed for having access, are defined as tuples $\langle h, H\rangle$ analogous to a claim for h with support H [1,5]. The leaves of the tree are credentials.

Definition 4. A *plan argument* for $\langle O, P, K\rangle$ for a goal in a goal set $g \in G$, written $t(g)$, is a finite tree whose nodes are pairs of a literal and a set of literals, either $\langle h, \emptyset\rangle$ for any $h \in C$, called a credential; or $\langle h, \{l_1, ..., l_n\}\rangle$ for any rule $l_1 \wedge ... \wedge l_n \rightarrow h \in P \cup K$, such that

- $\langle g, H\rangle$ is the root of the tree, for some H;
- $\langle h, \{l_1, ..., l_n\}\rangle$ has exactly n children $\langle l_1, H_1\rangle, ..., \langle l_n, H_n\rangle$;
- The leaves of the tree are credentials.

We say that two plan arguments conflict if they contain nodes $\langle h_1, H_1\rangle$ and $\langle h_2, H_2\rangle$ such that $Cl(K \cup H_1 \cup H_2, \{h_1, h_2\}) \vdash \bot$.

The plan arguments generated by Example 1 are shown in Figure 1. We visualize plan arguments with arrows directed from the leaves to the root.

Example 3 (Continued). There are five plan arguments, four for the objective a, and one for the objective m. We call the plan arguments for a t_1, t_2, t_3 and t_4, based on respectively $\{sp, sr\}$, $\{sp, el\}$, $\{es, el\}$ and $\{es, sr\}$. The plan argument for m is called t_5, and is based on $\{em\}$.

The third type of argument we consider is called *goal-plan argument* and combines a goal argument with plan arguments for each of the goals in the goal set. Because a goal argument is a linear tree, there is only one leaf, which contains the goal set. A goal set represents a cluster of objectives that belong together. The policy generation process produces plan arguments, i.e. combinations of policies, for each of the objectives in the goal set.

$$\langle\{ra\},\{a\}\rangle \qquad\qquad \langle\{rm\},\{m\}\rangle$$
$$\downarrow \qquad\qquad\qquad \downarrow$$
$$\langle\{a\},\{cs,a\}\rangle \qquad\qquad \langle\{m\},\{ib,m\}\rangle$$
$$\nearrow\quad\nwarrow \qquad\qquad \nearrow\quad\nwarrow$$
$$\langle a,\{al,cr\}\rangle\ \langle cs,\{f\}\rangle \quad \langle ib,\{sm\}\rangle\ \langle m,\{em\}\rangle$$
$$\nearrow\quad\nwarrow\qquad \uparrow \qquad\qquad \uparrow\qquad\qquad \uparrow$$
$$\langle al,\{sp\}\rangle\ \langle cr,\{sr\}\rangle\{\}\rangle \quad \langle sm,\{\}\rangle \quad \langle em,\{\}\rangle$$
$$\uparrow\qquad\quad \uparrow$$
$$\langle sp,\{\}\rangle\ \ \langle sr,\{\}\rangle$$

Fig. 2. Two goal-plan arguments

Definition 5. Given an objective-policy description $\langle O, P, K \rangle$, a *goal-plan argument* is a goal argument $g(G)$, which is linked to a plan argument $t(l)$ for each literal $l \in G$.

Figure 2 shows two goal-plan arguments for Example 1. The goal generation steps are visualized with downward arrows.

In principle more complex arguments can be constructed, in which plan arguments are connected again to goal arguments. Such complex arguments are more difficult to handle, and therefore left for further research. We now turn to the argumentation theory to deal with these kinds of arguments.

3 Argumentation Theory for Interactive Access Control

In this section we develop a formal argumentation theory for our arguments for interactive access control. We use Dung's abstract framework, in which an argumentation framework is defined as a set of arguments with a binary relation that represents which arguments attack which other arguments [5]. In general, the attack relation is the parameter that covers domain dependent aspects of argumentation. In our case, the arguments are goal-plan arguments, and the attack relation has to be derived from conflicts between arguments [1].

Definition 6. An argumentation framework is a tuple $\langle T, Attack \rangle$ such that T is a set of arguments and $Attack$ is a binary relation over T.

At this point, it may seem that we can simply define the attack relation among goal-plan arguments by saying that argument 1 attacks argument 2 when argument 1 and 2 are conflicting. However, Amgoud [1] shows that such a symmetric attack relation leads to counterintuitive results. In her theory of plan arguments the semantics of a plan argument is a complete plan to achieve an objective. The aim is to achieve a maximum of objectives. If a given objective o_1 can be achieved with a plan p_1 then if another plan p_2 for the same objective attacks a plan p_3 of another objective o_2, we will accept p_3 to enable the agent to achieve its two objectives. In the running example in Figure 1, read $o_1 = a$, $p_1 = t_4$, $p_2 = t_1$, $o_2 = m$, and $p_3 = t_5$. Therefore, Amgoud proposes to alter the definition of defend since there is a difference between conflicts among the usual kinds of arguments, i.e., defaults or beliefs, and conflicts among plans.

We consider a different notion of attack. The basic idea is as follows. We want to achieve a maximal number of objectives, and consequently an extension contains a maximal number of goal-plan arguments. However, considering different policies for the same objective may burden the client with requests for unnecessary credentials, which it could prefer not to disclose for privacy reasons. We therefore exclude the possibility that an extension contains two goal-plan arguments for the same objective. In a sense, this is the opposite of Amgoud's approach. Under her definition a basic extension, for example, may contain several plan arguments for the same objective.

There is one complication due to our introduction of goal arguments. With only plan arguments, each argument is for a single goal literal. However, with goal arguments, arguments can be for a *goal set*, and such sets may overlap. For example, consider three goal-plan arguments for goal sets $\{p, q\}$, $\{q, r\}$ and $\{r, p\}$. In that case we only want to include two of the three goal-plan arguments in an extension. We deal with this issue by two ideas. First we define an argument as a pair of a goal-plan argument and a literal in the goal set of the goal-plan argument. Secondly, we say that an argument attacks another argument when either there are complementary literals in the goal-plan trees, or the objective literal of the latter occurs in the goal set of the former.

Our approach can be motivated as follows. We model the deliberation process of an access control manager. During goal generation, alternative policies for an objective are considered, to test the feasibility of the objective. Objectives may conflict, which is why we use argumentation theory: to reason with multiple extensions. In our view, an extension corresponds to a maximally consistent subset of objectives, along with their policies. Thus an extension models a potential set of related objectives: an option. Ultimately, an access control manager must select one option to be enforced. Therefore it does not make sense to also consider alternative options within an extension. Keeping alternative options open requires additional deliberation effort. Moreover, policies may compete for resources and thus be incompatible.

The definitions of attack free, defend, preferred extension and basic extension are taken from Dung's framework.

Definition 7. An argumentation framework $\langle T, Attack \rangle$ for a objective-policy description $\langle O, P, K \rangle$ is an argumentation framework in which T contains all pairs $\langle t(G), l \rangle$ such that $t(G)$ is a goal-plan argument and $l \in G$. Let $S \subseteq T$ and $t, t_1, t_2 \in T$ be (sets of) such pairs.

- $\langle t_1(G_1), l_1 \rangle$ attacks $\langle t_2(G_2), l_2 \rangle$, iff either
    1. there exist two nodes p_1 and p_2 in the goal-plan arguments of t_1 and t_2 respectively, such that p_1 and p_2 conflict, or
    2. $t_1 \neq t_2$ and $l_2 \in G_1$: the literal of t_2 occurs in t_1's goal-plan tree.
- S is attack free iff there are no $t_1, t_2 \in S$ such that t_1 attacks t_2.
- S defends t iff for all $t_1 \in G$ such that t_1 attacks t, there is an alternative $t_2 \in S$ such that t_2 attacks t_1.
- S is a preferred extension iff S is maximal w.r.t. set inclusion among the subsets of G that are attack free and that defend all their elements.
- S is a basic extension iff it is a least fixpoint of function $F(S) = \{t \mid t \text{ defended by } S\}$

Our running example shows that, unfortunately, the basic extension no longer contains t_1 and t_5.

Example 4 (Continued). Under the new definition, the plan arguments t_1, t_2, t_3, t_4 for objective a attack each other. There are four preferred extensions: $S_1 = \{t_2\}$, $S_2 = \{t_3\}$, $S_3 = \{t_4\}$, $S_4 = \{t_1, t_5\}$. The basic extension is $\emptyset$.

The reason that the basic extension no longer works as desired, is that multiple policies for the same objective attack each other. In such cases the basic extension does not contain any of these. This is a consequence of the fact that basic extensions are always unique. There are various ways to repair this. One approach is to define a notion of extension* which is constructive, like a basic extension, but which splits in case of multiple policies for the same objective. The following definition adds all arguments which are defended, and non-deterministically adds one argument that is only attacked by alternative plans for the same objective.

Definition 8. Let $C(S) = \{t(o) \in T\backslash S \mid \forall t'(o') \in T \text{ if } t' \text{ defend } t \text{ then } o = o'\}$ and let F be as in Definition 7.

– S is a basic extension* iff it is a least fixpoint of the non-deterministic function
$$F'(S) = \begin{cases} F(S), & \text{if } C(S) = \emptyset, \\ F(S) \cup \{t\}, & t \in C(S) \text{ otherwise.} \end{cases}$$

There is always at least one basic extension*. In the running example, the basic extension* comes out as desired.

Example 5 (Continued). The unique basic extension* is $\{t_1, t_5\}$.

4 Related Research

Despite the analogy between arguments and plans, we know of few other researchers apart from Amgoud, that have combined planning and argumentation theory.

There has been relevant research on the differences of deduction and abduction in knowledge representation and reasoning. Often deduction is associated with prediction, whereas abduction is associated with explanation [14]. A combination of deduction and abduction has been applied to agent-architectures before [9,12]. In that case, deduction is used for reasoning with integrity constraints; abduction finds those actions or subgoals, that are required to achieve some goal.

A combination of abduction and deduction can also be applied to agent interaction. Hindriks et al. [6] use abduction to generate responses to queries, and Sadri et al. [13] use it in the deliberation cycle for agents in a dialogue.

Our application of goal generation and planning to interactive access control owes much to Koshutanski and Massacci [7,8]. They too apply both deduction and abduction. Deduction is used to verify that a set of credentials would satisfy a request for access control, given a set of policy rules. Similar to planning, abduction is used to find the missing credentials to satisfy some request r. Suppose C_P is the set of current credentials, expressed as literals, and P_A is the set of policy rules, expressed as a logic program. Now use abduction to find a minimal set of missing credentials C_M, such that both $P_A \cup C_P \cup C_M \models r$ and $P_A \cup C_P \cup C_M \not\models \bot$. If no such set exists, access is denied. Otherwise the set C_M is sent as a response to the client, after which the process is repeated. Our contribution to this line of work, apart from the application of argumentation theory, is that we allow derivation of additional objectives on the basis of an earlier set of objectives. As the access control process becomes interactive and even argumentative, handling such additional requirements becomes necessary.

5 Concluding Remarks

In this paper we address the formalization of interaction and argumentation about access control and service provision. Interactive argumentation about access control requires on the one hand a representation of the moves and the interaction protocol, and on the other hand a representation of the content: a logical framework to express argumentations about access control. We develop a logical framework for access control in which policies are described by sets of credentials, and two kinds of rules: conditional objectives that tell us when new objectives are created, and policy rules that tell us which credentials are needed to achieve these objectives.

In this logical framework we define arguments for access control as complex trees that relate credentials to objectives. Putting these arguments in Dung's abstract argumentation framework, we can use the attack relation derived from conflicts between basic policies and credentials, to derive extensions. The traditional ways of comparing extensions, e.g. preferred extensions, can now be reapplied. An extension corresponds to a set of related objectives along with the mutually compatible policies that realize them. In this way, a trust management system that must choose between different possibly conflicting security objectives, can now do so using the standard techniques of argumentation theory.

A subject of further research is a more detailed conflict resolution for policy conflicts. In selection of objectives, the application of a priority order is difficult. The easiest solution is to define a local priority order over rules. However, single rules often have undesired consequences. Rules should therefore be compared by their outcomes, using a utility value for example. Other research makes use of maximally consistent sets of rules to represent a set of related objectives. This has some drawbacks, both practical and conceptual. The sets themselves become large, and their consistency becomes difficult to check and maintain.

References

1. L. Amgoud. A formal framework for handling conflicting desires. In *Procs. of ECSQARU'03*, LNCS 2711, pages 552–563. Springer, 2003.
2. L. Amgoud and C. Cayrol. On the use of an ATMS for handling conflicting desires. In *Procs of KR'04*. AAAI, 2004.
3. M. Blaze, J. Feigenbaum, and J. Lacy. Decentralized trust management. In *IEEE Symposium on Security and Privacy*, pages 164–173. IEEE, 1996.
4. P. Bonatti and P. Samarati. A uniform framework for regulating service access and information release on the web. *Journal of Computer Security*, 10(3):242–272, 2002.
5. P. M. Dung. On the acceptability of arguments and its fundamental role in non-monotonic reasoning, logic programming and n-person games. *Artificial Intelligence*, 77:321–357, 1995.

6. K.V. Hindriks, F.S. de Boer, W. van der Hoek, and J.-J.Ch. Meyer. Semantics of communicating agents based on deduction and abduction. In *Issues in Agent Communication*, LNAI 1916, pages 63–79. Springer Verlag, 2000.
7. H. Koshutanski and F. Massacci. Interactive trust management and negotiation scheme. In *Procs.of FAST'04 Workshop*, pages 139–152. Kluwer, 2004.
8. H. Koshutanski and F. Massacci. A system for interactive authorization for business processes for web services. In *Procs. of ICWE04*, LNCS 3140, pages 521–525. Springer Verlag, 2004.
9. Robert A. Kowalski and Fariba Sadri. From logic programming towards multi-agent systems. *Annals of Mathematics and Artificial Intelligence*, 25(3-4):391–419, 1999.
10. Kraus, S., Sycara, K., and Evenchik, A. Reaching agreements through argumentation: A logical model and implementation. *Artificial Intelligence*, 104(1-2):169, 1998.
11. A. S. Rao and M. P. Georgeff. Decision procedures for BDI logics. *Journal of Logic and Computation*, 8(3):293–343, 1998.
12. Fariba Sadri and Francesca Toni. Abduction with negation as failure for active and reactive rules. In *Procs. of AI*IA'99*, volume LNCS 1792, pages 49–60. Springer Verlag, 2000.
13. Fariba Sadri, Francesca Toni, and Paolo Torroni. An abductive logic programming architecture for negotiating agents. In *Procs. of JELIA'02*, LNAI 2424, pages 419 – 431. Springer Verlag, 2002.
14. Murray Shanahan. Prediction is deduction but explanation is abduction. In *Procs. IJCAI'89*, pages 1055–1060. Morgan Kaufmann, 1989.
15. R. Thomason. Desires and defaults: A framework for planning with inferred goals. In *Procs. of KR'00*, pages 702–713, 2000.

Determining Preferences
Through Argumentation

Sylvie Doutre*, Trevor Bench-Capon, and Paul E. Dunne

Department of Computer Science, University of Liverpool, UK
{sd, tbc, ped}@csc.liv.ac.uk

Abstract. Arguments concerning what an agent should do cannot be considered in isolation: they occur in the context of debates where arguments attacking and defending each other are advanced. This is recognised by the use of argumentation frameworks which determine the status of an argument by reference to its presence in a coherent position: a subset of the arguments advanced which is collectively able to defend itself against all attackers. Where the position concerns practical reasoning, defence may be made by making a choice justified in terms of the values of an agent. Participants in the debate, however, are typically not neutral in their attitude towards the arguments: there will be arguments they wish to accept and others they wish to reject. In this paper we model how a participant in a debate can develop a position which is coherent both with respect to the attack relations between arguments and any value choices made. We define a framework for representing a set of arguments constituting the debate, and describe how a position including the desired arguments can be developed through a dialogue with an opponent. A key contribution is that the value choices are made as part of the argumentation process, and need not be determined in advance.

1   Introduction

In this paper we will be concerned with *practical reasoning* - reasoning about the action to perform in a given situation. We will begin by drawing attention to a number of features of such reasoning which any account must respect.

First, arguments justifying actions must be considered in the context of other related arguments. Arguments justifying actions are typically presumptive in nature [19], [2], as there are always alternatives, and often reasons to refrain from the action as well as reasons to perform it. Even a universal and deep seated norm such as *thou shalt not kill* is acknowledged to admit exceptions in circumstances of self-defence and war. Such presumptive justifications can only be accepted if due consideration to arguments attacking and defending them is given. In a set of arguments relating to an issue - which we call a *debate* - the acceptability of an argument relies on it forming part of a coherent subset of such arguments able to defend itself against attacking arguments in the debate. We call such a coherent

---

* Supported by the ASPIC project of the European Commission (IST-FP6-002307).

S. Bandini and S. Manzoni (Eds.): AI*IA 2005, LNAI 3673, pp. 98–109, 2005.
© Springer-Verlag Berlin Heidelberg 2005

subset a *position*. The notion of the acceptability of an argument deriving from its membership of a defensible position in a debate has been explored in AI through the use of argumentation frameworks, e.g. [9,4]. These debates can also be seen as representing the relevant presumptive arguments and the critical questions [19] that may be posed against them. Such reasoning is naturally modelled as dialectical and can be explored through the use of a dialogue in which a claim is attacked and defended. Dialogues to identify positions in debates represented as argumentation frameworks have been explored in [7], [11] and [3].

Second, debates about which action is best to perform must permit rational disagreement. Whereas the truth of facts may be demonstrated and compel rational acceptance, with regard to actions there is an element of choice: we cannot choose what is the case, but we can choose what we attempt to bring about, and different people may rationally make different choices. This is well summarised by Searle in [17]:

> Assume universally valid and accepted standards of rationality, assume perfectly rational agents operating with perfect information, and you will find that rational disagreement will still occur; because, for example, the rational agents are likely to have different and inconsistent values and interests, each of which may be rationally acceptable.

Such differences in values and interests mean that arguments will have different *audiences*, to use the terminology of [16][1] and what is acceptable to one audience may be unacceptable to another. Disagreements are represented in argumentation frameworks such as that of Dung [9] by the presence within a debate of multiple acceptable positions. In [4], Bench-Capon advances an extended argumentation framework which explicitly relates arguments to values and explicitly represents audiences in terms of their preferences over values.

While a framework such as that of [4] can be used to explain disagreements between different audiences in terms of their different ranking of values, it does not explain how these value rankings are formed. A third feature of practical reasoning (as indicated by Searle in [17]) is that we cannot presuppose that people bring to a debate a knowledge of their value preferences. It means that the value preferences should emerge from the construction of a position instead of being taken as an input.

Finally, practical reasoners may not be equally open to all arguments: they may have certain arguments that they wish to include in their position, certain arguments that they wish to exclude, and they may be indifferent to the status of the remainder. For example a politician forming a political programme may recognise that raising taxation is electorally inexpedient and so must exclude any arguments with the conclusion that taxes should be raised from the manifesto, while ensuring that arguments justifying actions bringing about core objectives are present: other arguments are acceptable if they enable this. Such

---

[1] The term "audience" is also used in Hunter [14], although he distinguishes between audiences only in terms of beliefs, whereas [4] distinguishes them in terms of values, while also accommodating differences in beliefs.

a distinction between arguments has been taken into account in the construction of positions for Dung's framework [9] by [6]. This treatment, however, does not relate arguments to values, and so cannot use these reasons for action in order to explain choices. Moreover, it is in consequence not possible to require these choices to show a consistent motivation: in order to do this we need to use an extension of [9] such as provided by [4].

Providing an account of how we can explain disagreements in terms of a consistent ranking of values is the objective of our work. In particular, we provide a means for explaining how the ordering of values emerges from the construction of a position.

Section 2 recapitulates the argumentation frameworks which provide our formal starting point, Section 3 describes the dialogical framework introduced in [8] for developing a position and Section 4 points to some related work, draws some conclusions and identifies directions for further exploration.

2   Value-Based Argumentation Framework

We start with a review of Dung's argument system [9] upon which the value-based argumentation framework proposed by Bench-Capon in [3,4] relies.

Definition 1. *[9] An argument system is a pair $\mathcal{H} = \langle \mathcal{X}, \mathcal{A} \rangle$, in which $\mathcal{X}$ is a finite set of arguments and $\mathcal{A} \subseteq \mathcal{X} \times \mathcal{X}$ is the attack relationship for $\mathcal{H}$. A pair $\langle x, y \rangle \in \mathcal{A}$ is referred to as 'y is attacked by x' or 'x attacks y'. A set $S \subseteq \mathcal{X}$ is conflict-free if no argument in S attacks an argument in S.*

Definition 2. *[4] A value-based argumentation framework (VAF) is defined as $\langle \mathcal{X}, \mathcal{A}, \mathcal{V}, \eta \rangle$, where $\langle \mathcal{X}, \mathcal{A} \rangle$ is an argument system, $\mathcal{V} = \{v_1, v_2, \ldots, v_k\}$ is a set of k values, and $\eta : \mathcal{X} \to \mathcal{V}$ is a mapping that associates a value $\eta(x) \in \mathcal{V}$ with each argument $x \in \mathcal{X}$.*

Definition 3. *An audience ϑ for a VAF $\langle \mathcal{X}, \mathcal{A}, \mathcal{V}, \eta \rangle$ is a binary relation on $\mathcal{V}$, such that (i) there is no $v \in \mathcal{V}$ such that $\langle v, v \rangle \in \vartheta$ (ϑ is irreflexive) and (ii) for any v_1, v_2, and v_3 in $\mathcal{V}$, if $\langle v_1, v_2 \rangle \in \vartheta$ and $\langle v_2, v_3 \rangle \in \vartheta$, then $\langle v_1, v_3 \rangle \in \vartheta$ (ϑ is transitive). A pair $\langle v_i, v_j \rangle$ in ϑ is referred to as 'v_i is preferred to v_j' with respect to ϑ.*

A specific audience α is an audience such that all the values are comparable with respect to it, i.e. for two distinct values v_1 and v_2 in $\mathcal{V}$, either $\langle v_1, v_2 \rangle \in \alpha$ or $\langle v_2, v_1 \rangle \in \alpha$.

An audience is an ordering of values that does not need to be total. In [3,4], an audience corresponds to what we call here a 'specific audience'. The following definitions are slightly adapted versions of those from [3,4].

Definition 4. *Let $\langle \mathcal{X}, \mathcal{A}, \mathcal{V}, \eta \rangle$ be a VAF, ϑ be an audience, and x and y be two arguments of $\mathcal{X}$. x successfully attacks y with respect to ϑ if: $\langle x, y \rangle \in \mathcal{A}$ and $\langle \eta(y), \eta(x) \rangle \notin \vartheta$. x definitely attacks y with respect to ϑ if: $\langle x, y \rangle \in \mathcal{A}$, and $\eta(x) = \eta(y)$ or $\langle \eta(x), \eta(y) \rangle \in \vartheta$. The arguments x and y are in conflict with* *respect to ϑ if x successfully attacks y with respect to ϑ or y successfully attacks x with respect to ϑ. S is* conflict-free with respect to ϑ *if there are no arguments in S in conflict with respect to ϑ. The argument y is a* defender *of x with respect to ϑ if and only if there is a finite sequence $a_0, \ldots, a_{2n}$ such that $x = a_0$, $y = a_{2n}$, and $\forall i, 0 \leq i \leq (2n-1)$, a_{i+1} successfully attacks a_i w.r.t. ϑ.*

For $S \subseteq \mathcal{X}$, x is acceptable *to S with respect to ϑ if: for every $y \in \mathcal{X}$ that successfully attacks x with respect to ϑ, there is some $z \in S$ that successfully attacks y with respect to ϑ; S is* admissible with respect to ϑ *if: S is conflict-free with respect to ϑ and every $x \in S$ is acceptable to S with respect to ϑ.*

Motivating examples showing the advantages of VAFs are given in [3,12].

To accomodate the fourth feature of practical reasoning, that is, to take into account that reasoners may have certain arguments they wish to include in a position, others they wish to exclude and that they are indifferent to the rest, we extend the definition of a VAF as follows:

Definition 5. *A VAF $\langle \mathcal{X}, \mathcal{A}, \mathcal{V}, \eta \rangle$ is* DOR-partitioned *if $\mathcal{X} = D \cup O \cup R$ for disjoint sets D, O and R, which denote respectively a set of* desired *arguments, a set of* optional *arguments and a set of* rejected *arguments. We use $\mathrm{Des}(\mathcal{X})$ to denote D, $\mathrm{Opt}(\mathcal{X})$ to denote O and $\mathrm{Rej}(\mathcal{X})$ to denote R. A* DOR-*partitioned VAF is called a* DOR-VAF.

An admissible set which can be adopted as a position in a DOR-VAF, is a set that contains the desired arguments and possibly some optional arguments, whose role is to help a desired argument to be acceptable to the position. We formally define this new notion of a position via:

Definition 6. *Given a* DOR-*VAF $\langle \mathcal{X}, \mathcal{A}, \mathcal{V}, \eta \rangle$, a set $S = \mathrm{Des}(\mathcal{X}) \cup Y$ where $Y \subseteq \mathrm{Opt}(\mathcal{X})$, is a* position *if and only if there exists at least one audience ϑ w.r.t. which S is admissible and $\forall y \in Y$, $\exists x \in \mathrm{Des}(\mathcal{X})$ such that y is a defender of x. An audience w.r.t. which S is a position is said to be a* corresponding audience *of S.*

This new notion of a position accomodates the third feature of practical reasoning: the preferences between values are not given as an input on the basis of which the position is constructed, but are a result of constructing the position.

3   Development of a Position

In order to build a position, one may start by considering the set of desired arguments. This set must be first tested to demonstrate that there is at least one audience w.r.t. which it is conflict-free. It may be that this condition can only be satisfied by imposing some value preferences. If we can satisfy this test we must next ensure that any defeated argument in the set has a defender in the set w.r.t. at least one audience. To this end, some optional arguments may be added to the set as defenders of defeated arguments and/or some additional constraints on the ordering of values may be imposed. We would like such extensions of the position under development to be kept to a minimum. If the process succeeds, then the set developed is a position and the set of constraints determined by the construction can be extended into a corresponding audience of this position, by taking its transitive closure. Otherwise, the user has to reconsider the partition of the set of arguments; such issues are the subject of ongoing research.

This construction can be presented in the form of a *dialogue* between two players. One, the *opponent*, outlines why the set under development is not yet a position by identifying arguments which defeat members of the set. The other, the *proponent*, tries to make the set under development a position by extending it with some optional arguments and/or some constraints between values. If the opponent has been left with no legal move available then the set of arguments played by the proponent is a position and the set of constraints advanced can be extended into a corresponding audience. If the proponent has no legal move available the set of desired arguments cannot be extended into a position.

This presentation in a dialogue form has the main advantage of making clear why some constraints between values must be imposed and why some optional arguments must belong to the position. Moreover, it is highly appropriate to the dialectical nature of practical reasoning identified above.

In Section 3.1, we present a formal dialogue framework that we instantiate in Section 3.2 in order to check if a set of desired arguments is conflict-free for at least one audience. We instantiate the dialogue framework in Section 3.3 to check if a conflict-free set of desired arguments can be made acceptable. Finally, in Section 3.4 we combine these two instantiations to construct positions and we give an example of such a construction.

3.1 Dialogue Framework

A dialogue framework to prove the acceptability of arguments in Dung's argument system has been developed by [15] and refined in [7]. We extend this last framework to deal with the development of positions in a DOR-VAF.

Informally, a dialogue framework provides a definition of the players, the moves, the rules and conditions under which the dialogue terminates, i.e. those situations wherein the current player has no legal move in the dialogue. In order to capture the construction of positions, the dialogue framework we define comprises two players, PRO and OPP. The rules are expressed in a so-called 'legal-move function'. Regarding the definition of a move, since playing an argument may be possible only if some preferences between values hold, a move must comprise an argument and a set of value preferences. In particular, a player may propose some ordering of values, i.e without any specific argument being involved (for example, when he wants to make a set of desired arguments conflict-free for at least one audience). To this end, it is convenient to extend the arguments of a DOR-VAF $\langle \mathcal{X}, \mathcal{A}, \mathcal{V}, \eta \rangle$ with an 'empty argument' denoted $\_$. This argument can be used if the proponent's move is only to advance a value ordering. We denote by $\mathcal{X}^-$ the set $\mathcal{X} \cup \{\_\}$.

Definition 7. *Let* $\langle \mathcal{X}^-, \mathcal{A}, \mathcal{V}, \eta \rangle$ *be a DOR-VAF. A move in* $\mathcal{X}^-$ *is described via a pair* $[P, \langle X, V \rangle]$ *where* $P \in \{\text{PRO}, \text{OPP}\}$, $X \in \mathcal{X}^-$, *and* $V \subseteq \mathcal{V} \times \mathcal{V}$. PRO *denotes the* proponent *and* OPP *denotes the* opponent.

For a move $\mu = [P, \langle X, V \rangle]$, *we use* $\text{pl}(\mu)$ *to denote* P, $\text{arg}(\mu)$ *to denote* X, *and* $\text{val}(\mu)$ *to denote* V. *The set of moves is denoted by* $\mathcal{M}$ *with* $\mathcal{M}^*$ *being the set of finite sequences of moves.*

Let $\phi : \mathcal{M}^* \to 2^{\mathcal{X}^- \times 2^{\mathcal{V} \times \mathcal{V}}}$ *be a legal-move function. A dialogue (or ϕ-dialogue)* d *about* $S = \{a_1, a_2, \ldots, a_n\} \subseteq \mathcal{X}$ *is a countable sequence* $\mu_{0_1} \mu_{0_2} \cdots \mu_{0_n} \mu_1 \mu_2 \cdots$ *of moves in* $\mathcal{X}^-$ *such that the following conditions hold:*

1. $\text{pl}(\mu_{0_k}) = \text{PRO}$, $\text{arg}(\mu_{0_k}) = a_k$, *and* $\text{val}(\mu_{0_k}) = \emptyset$ *for* $1 \le k \le n$
2. $\text{pl}(\mu_1) = \text{OPP}$ *and* $\text{pl}(\mu_i) \ne \text{pl}(\mu_{i+1})$, *for* $i \ge 1$
3. $\langle \text{arg}(\mu_{i+1}), \text{val}(\mu_{i+1}) \rangle \in \phi(\mu_{0_1} \mu_{0_2} \cdots \mu_{0_n} \mu_1 \cdots \mu_i)$.

In a dialogue about a set of arguments, the first n moves are played by PRO to put forward the elements of the set, without any constraint on the value of these arguments (*1.*). Subsequent moves are played alternately by OPP and PRO (*2.*). The legal-move function defines at every step what moves can be used to continue the dialogue (*3.*). We do not require $\text{arg}(\mu_{i+1})$ to attack $\text{arg}(\mu_i)$, because we want a dialogue to be sequential, so we need to let OPP try all possible answers to any of PRO's arguments, but only one at a time.

Let $\langle \mathcal{X}^-, \mathcal{A}, \mathcal{V}, \eta \rangle$ be a DOR-VAF, $S \subseteq \mathcal{X}$ and $d = \mu_{0_1} \cdots \mu_{0_n} \mu_1 \mu_2 \cdots \mu_i$ be a finite ϕ-dialogue about S. We denote μ_i by $\text{last}(d)$ and write $\phi(d)$ for $\phi(\mu_{0_1} \cdots \mu_{0_n} \mu_1 \mu_2 \cdots \mu_i)$. In addition, $\text{argPRO}(d)$ (resp. $\text{valPRO}(d)$) will denote the set of arguments (resp. values) played by PRO in d.

Now that we have a way to define a dialogue and the rules of a dialogue, let us define when a dialogue terminates (i.e. cannot be continued).

Definition 8. *Let* $\langle \mathcal{X}^-, \mathcal{A}, \mathcal{V}, \eta \rangle$ *be a DOR-VAF,* ϕ *be a legal-move function, and* d *be a finite ϕ-dialogue.* d *cannot be continued if* $\phi(d) = \emptyset$. d *is said to be won by PRO if and only if* d *cannot be continued, and* $\text{pl}(\text{last}(d)) = \text{PRO}$.

We introduce additional notation to instantiate the dialogue framework to develop positions. Given a DOR-VAF $\langle \mathcal{X}^-, \mathcal{A}, \mathcal{V}, \eta \rangle$ and a set $V \subseteq \mathcal{V} \times \mathcal{V}$, $\text{TC}(V)$ denotes the transitive closure of V. Given an audience ϑ and $x \in \mathcal{X}^-$, we use,
- $\mathcal{A}_\vartheta^+(x)$ for the set of arguments successfully attacked by x,
- $\mathcal{A}_\vartheta^{++}(x)$ for the set of arguments definitely attacked by x,
- $\mathcal{A}_\vartheta^-(x)$ for the set of arguments that successfully attack x,
- $\mathcal{A}_\vartheta^{--}(x)$ for the set of arguments that definitely attack x,
- $\mathcal{A}_\vartheta^\pm(x)$ for the set $\mathcal{A}_\vartheta^+(x) \cup \mathcal{A}_\vartheta^-(x)$.

Note that $\mathcal{A}_\vartheta^+(\_) = \mathcal{A}_\vartheta^-(\_) = \mathcal{A}_\vartheta^{--}(\_) = \mathcal{A}_\vartheta^{++}(\_) = \emptyset$. Moreover, given a set $S \subseteq \mathcal{X}$ and $\varepsilon \in \{+, -, \pm, ++, --\}$, $\mathcal{A}_\vartheta^\varepsilon(S) = \bigcup_{x \in S} \mathcal{A}_\vartheta^\varepsilon(x)$.

3.2 Checking Conflict-Freeness

Let $\langle \mathcal{X}^-, \mathcal{A}, \mathcal{V}, \eta \rangle$ be a DOR-VAF and ϑ be an audience. $\text{Des}(\mathcal{X})$ is not conflict-free w.r.t. ϑ if there are two desired arguments x and y such that y successfully attacks x, that is, $\langle y, x \rangle \in \mathcal{A}$ and $\langle \eta(x), \eta(y) \rangle \notin \vartheta$. In order to make $\mathrm{Des}(\mathcal{X})$ conflict-free, the value of x should be made preferred to the value of y, that is, $\langle \eta(x), \eta(y) \rangle$ added to ϑ. This is possible only if under the new set of constraints the transitive closure of $\vartheta \cup \{ \langle \eta(x), \eta(y) \rangle \}$ remains an audience.

Consider a dialogue d about $\mathrm{Des}(\mathcal{X})$, based on a legal-move function where OPP plays moves using arguments such as y and the value ordering is empty, and where PRO only exhibits constraints on the value of these arguments. Then the set of arguments played by PRO in d (i.e. argPRO(d)) is $\mathrm{Des}(\mathcal{X})$, possibly along with $\{\_\}$. The transitive closure of the value orderings played by PRO in d (i.e. TC(valPRO(d))) must be the audience w.r.t. which moves are made. Formally:

Definition 9. *Let* $\langle \mathcal{X}^-, \mathcal{A}, \mathcal{V}, \eta \rangle$ *be a DOR-VAF,* d *be a dialogue about* $\mathrm{Des}(\mathcal{X})$, *and* $\vartheta = \mathrm{TC}(\mathrm{valPRO}(d))$. $\phi_1 : \mathcal{M}^* \to 2^{\mathcal{X}^- \times 2^{\mathcal{V} \times \mathcal{V}}}$ *is defined by:*

- *if the last move of* d *is by* PRO *(next move is by* OPP*),*

$$\phi_1(d) = \bigcup_{y \in \mathcal{A}_\vartheta^- (\mathrm{argPRO}(d)) \cap \mathrm{argPRO}(d)} \{ \langle y, \emptyset \rangle \};$$

- *if the last move of* d *is by* OPP *(next move is by* PRO*), let* $y = \arg(\mathrm{last}(d))$, $V = \bigcup_{x \in \mathcal{A}_\vartheta^+(y) \cap \mathrm{argPRO}(d)} \{ \langle \eta(x), \eta(y) \rangle \}$,

$$\phi_1(d) = \begin{cases} \{ \langle \_ , V \rangle \} & \text{if } \mathrm{TC}(\mathrm{valPRO}(d) \cup V) \text{ is an audience,} \\ \emptyset & \text{otherwise.} \end{cases}$$

The dialogue framework instantiated with the legal-move function ϕ_1, is correct and complete w.r.t. the determination of an audience w.r.t. which the set of desired arguments is conflict-free:

Property 1. Let $\langle \mathcal{X}, \mathcal{A}, \mathcal{V}, \eta \rangle$ *be a DOR-VAF. If* d *is a* ϕ_1*-dialogue about* $\mathrm{Des}(\mathcal{X})$ *won by* PRO, *then* $\mathrm{Des}(\mathcal{X})$ *is conflict-free w.r.t. the audience* $\mathrm{TC}(\mathrm{valPRO}(d))$. *If* $\mathrm{Des}(\mathcal{X}) \neq \emptyset$ *is conflict-free w.r.t. at least one audience, then there exists a* ϕ_1*-dialogue about* $\mathrm{Des}(\mathcal{X})$ *won by* PRO.

3.3   Making the Arguments Acceptable

Given a DOR-VAF $\langle \mathcal{X}, \mathcal{A}, \mathcal{V}, \eta \rangle$, let us assume that the set $\mathrm{Des}(\mathcal{X})$ is conflict-free in the most restricted sense, i.e. there are no arguments x and y in $\mathrm{Des}(\mathcal{X})$ such that $\langle x, y \rangle \in \mathcal{A}$. For an audience, ϑ, we call the set containing the desired arguments which aims at being a position the '*position under development*'. The reason why the position under development would not be admissible w.r.t. ϑ is that some arguments in it would not be acceptable to it w.r.t. ϑ, i.e. there is (at least one) argument x in the position under development such that some argument y successfully attacks x w.r.t. ϑ and no argument z in the position successfully attacks y w.r.t. ϑ.

Let us consider a dialogue d about the conflict-free set $\mathrm{Des}(\mathcal{X})$, based on a legal-move function where OPP plays moves involving some argument y and the value ordering is empty, and where PRO uses one of (W1)–(W4) below. The arguments in the position under development are those played by PRO. The transitive closure of the value orderings played by PRO (i.e. TC(valPRO(d))) must be the audience w.r.t. which the moves are made.

We identify four ways to make an argument x acceptable to the position under development:

(W1) Add to the position under development an optional argument z which definitely attacks y and which is not in conflict with any argument of the position under development.

(W2) Make the value of the arguments successfully but not definitely attacked by y preferred to the value of y, if the addition of these preferences to the current audience ϑ can be extended into an audience.

(W3) Add to the position under development an optional argument z which successfully but not definitely attacks y and which is not in conflict with any argument of the position under development.

(W4) Add to the position under development an optional argument z which successfully attacks y, and which might be successfully but not definitely attacked by the position under development or which might successfully but not definitely attack the position under development; the addition of value preferences to the current audience in order for the addition of z to the position to be correct must form an audience.

Our next definition gives formal translations of (W1) through (W3) as dialogue moves. We omit the rather lengthier specification (W4) for space reasons.

Definition 10. *Let* $\langle \mathcal{X}^-, \mathcal{A}, \mathcal{V}, \eta \rangle$ *be a* DOR-VAF, *d be a dialogue about* $\mathrm{Des}(\mathcal{X})$, *$\vartheta = \mathrm{TC}(\mathrm{valPRO}(d))$. $\phi_2 : \mathcal{M}^* \to 2^{\mathcal{X}^- \times 2^{\mathcal{V} \times \mathcal{V}}}$ is defined by:*

- *if* $\mathrm{pl}(\mathrm{last}(d)) = \mathrm{PRO}$ *(next move is by OPP), let* $Y = \mathcal{A}_\vartheta^-(\mathrm{argPRO}(d)) \setminus \mathcal{A}_\vartheta^+(\mathrm{argPRO}(d))$,

$$\phi_2(d) = \bigcup_{y \in Y} \{\langle y, \emptyset \rangle\};$$

- *if* $\mathrm{pl}(\mathrm{last}(d)) = \mathrm{OPP}$ *(next move is by PRO), let* $y = \mathrm{arg}(\mathrm{last}(d))$, *and:*
(W1) *let* $Z_1 = (\mathrm{Opt}(\mathcal{X}) \cap \mathcal{A}_\vartheta^{--}(y)) \setminus \mathcal{A}_\vartheta^\pm(\mathrm{argPRO}(d))$; *if* $Z_1 \neq \emptyset$, *then*

$$\phi_2(d) = \bigcup_{z \in Z_1} \{\langle z, \emptyset \rangle\}$$

(W2) *else, let* $Z_2 = \mathrm{argPRO}(d) \cap (\mathcal{A}_\vartheta^+(y) \setminus \mathcal{A}_\vartheta^{++}(y))$; *if* $Z_2 \neq \emptyset$ *then*

$$\phi_2(d) = \langle \_ , \bigcup_{x \in Z_2} \{\langle \eta(x), \eta(y) \rangle\} \rangle$$

(W3) *else, let* $Z_3 = (\mathrm{Opt}(\mathcal{X}) \cap \mathcal{A}_\vartheta^-(y)) \setminus \mathcal{A}_\vartheta^\pm(\mathrm{argPRO}(d))$; *if* $Z_3 \neq \emptyset$, *then*

$$\phi_2(d) = \bigcup_{z \in Z_3} \{\langle z, \{\langle \eta(z), \eta(y) \rangle\} \rangle\}$$

else if (W4) is played $\phi_2(d)$ *contains the corresponding moves; else* $\phi_2(d) = \emptyset$.

Each of these four ways would be tried in turn. In responding to an attack, the proponent will wish to maintain as much flexibility to respond to further attacks as possible. The order in which the four ways are tried is thus determined by the desire to make the least committal move at any stage. Flexibility is limited in two ways. If the position is extended by including an additional argument, as in W1, W3 and W4, the set of potential attackers of the position is increased since this argument must now also be defended by the position. If a commitment to a value ordering is made, as in W2, W3 and W4, this must be subsequently respected, which restricts the scope to make such moves in future responses. We regard this second line of defence as more committal that the first. Therefore W1 is tried first since it imposes no constraints on the audience, although it does extend the position. W2 is selected next because, although it does constrain the audience to adopt certain value preferences, it does not introduce any additional arguments to the position, and so does not give rise to any additional attackers. If W3 is resorted to, both the position is extended and a value ordering commitment is made, but the argument introduced is compatible with the existing position. W4 is the final resort because it extends the position, constrains the audience, and requires further constraints to be imposed to enable it to cohere with the existing position.

The dialogue framework instantiated with the legal-move function ϕ_2 is correct and complete w.r.t. the determination of an audience for which the conflict-free set of desired arguments is admissible for at least one audience:

Property 2. Let $\langle \mathcal{X}^-, \mathcal{A}, \mathcal{V}, \eta \rangle$ be a DOR-*VAF*. Assume that $\mathrm{Des}(\mathcal{X})$ is conflict-free. If d is a ϕ_2-dialogue about $\mathrm{Des}(\mathcal{X})$ won by PRO, then $\mathrm{argPRO}(d) \setminus \{\_\}$ is a position such that $\mathrm{TC}(\mathrm{valPRO}(d))$ is a corresponding audience. If $\mathrm{Des}(\mathcal{X}) \neq \emptyset$ is contained in a position, then a ϕ_2-dialogue about $\mathrm{Des}(\mathcal{X})$ won by PRO exists.

3.4   Development of Positions

Let us consider the following legal-move function:

Definition 11. *Let* $\langle \mathcal{X}^-, \mathcal{A}, \mathcal{V}, \eta \rangle$ *be a* DOR-*VAF, d be a dialogue about* $\mathrm{Des}(\mathcal{X})$, *and* $\vartheta = \mathrm{TC}(\mathrm{valPRO}(d))$. $\phi_3 : \mathcal{M}^* \rightarrow 2^{\mathcal{X}^- \times 2^{\mathcal{V} \times \mathcal{V}}}$ *is defined by:*
   - *if* $\mathrm{pl}(\mathrm{last}(d)) = \mathrm{PRO}$ *(next move is by OPP: if* $\phi_1(d) \neq \emptyset$ *then* $\phi_3(d) = \phi_1(d)$ *else* $\phi_3(d) = \phi_2(d)$;
   - *if* $\mathrm{pl}(\mathrm{last}(d)) = \mathrm{OPP}$ *(next move is by PRO): if* $\mathrm{arg}(\mathrm{last}(d)) \in \mathrm{Des}(\mathcal{X})$ *then* $\phi_3(d) = \phi_1(d)$ *else* $\phi_3(d) = \phi_2(d)$.

Property 3. Let $\langle \mathcal{X}, \mathcal{A}, \mathcal{V}, \eta \rangle$ be a DOR-VAF. If d is a ϕ_3-dialogue about $\mathrm{Des}(\mathcal{X})$ won by PRO, then $\mathrm{argPRO}(d) \setminus \{\_\}$ is a position such that $\mathrm{TC}(\mathrm{valPRO}(d))$ is a corresponding audience. If $\mathrm{Des}(\mathcal{X}) \neq \emptyset$ is contained in a position, then there exists a ϕ_3-dialogue about $\mathrm{Des}(\mathcal{X})$ won by PRO.

Example Consider the following VAF $\langle \mathcal{X}, \mathcal{A}, \mathcal{V}, \eta \rangle$:

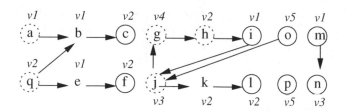

The arguments are the vertices of the graph and the edges represent the elements of the attack relation. The set of values is $\mathcal{V} = \{v1, v2, v3, v4, v5\}$. The value associated to an argument is indicated just below or just above the argument. The desired arguments are plain-circled, the optional arguments are dot-circled, and the rejected arguments are not circled. Let us develop a position. We start a ϕ_3-dialogue d about $\mathrm{Des}(\mathcal{X})$. The first moves of d contain the desired arguments, i.e. $\mu_{0_1} \mu_{0_2} \mu_{0_3} \mu_{0_4} \mu_{0_5} \mu_{0_6} \mu_{0_7} \mu_{0_8} = [\mathrm{PRO}, \langle c, \emptyset \rangle][\mathrm{PRO}, \langle f, \emptyset \rangle][\mathrm{PRO}, \langle i, \emptyset \rangle]$ $[\mathrm{PRO}, \langle l, \emptyset \rangle][\mathrm{PRO}, \langle m, \emptyset \rangle][\mathrm{PRO}, \langle n, \emptyset \rangle][\mathrm{PRO}, \langle o, \emptyset \rangle][\mathrm{PRO}, \langle p, \emptyset \rangle]$. Then, to ensure the conflict-freeness of $\mathrm{Des}(\mathcal{X})$ w.r.t. one audience:

$\mu_1 = [\mathrm{OPP}, \langle m, \emptyset \rangle]$
$\mu_2 = [\mathrm{PRO}, \langle \_, \{\langle v3, v1 \rangle\} \rangle]$

Now, to make the arguments of $\mathrm{Des}(\mathcal{X})$ acceptable:

$\mu_3 = [\mathrm{OPP}, \langle b, \emptyset \rangle]$
$\mu_4 = [\mathrm{PRO}, \langle a, \emptyset \rangle]$ **(W1)**
$\mu_5 = [\mathrm{OPP}, \langle e, \emptyset \rangle]$
$\mu_6 = [\mathrm{PRO}, \langle \_, \{\langle v2, v1 \rangle\} \rangle]$ **(W2)**
$\mu_7 = [\mathrm{OPP}, \langle h, \emptyset \rangle]$
$\mu_8 = [\mathrm{PRO}, \langle g, \{\langle v4, v2 \rangle\} \rangle]$ **(W3)**
$\mu_9 = [\mathrm{OPP}, \langle j, \emptyset \rangle]$
$\mu_{10} = [\mathrm{PRO}, \langle \_, \{\langle v4, v3 \rangle\} \rangle]$ **(W2)**
$\mu_{11} = [\mathrm{OPP}, \langle k, \emptyset \rangle]$
$\mu_{12} = [\mathrm{PRO}, \langle j, \{\langle v3, v2 \rangle, \langle v3, v5 \rangle\} \rangle]$ **(W4)**

$d = \mu_{0_1} \dots \mu_{0_8} \mu_1 \mu_2 \mu_3 \mu_4 \mu_5 \mu_6 \mu_7 \mu_8 \mu_9 \mu_{10} \mu_{11} \mu_{12}$ is a ϕ_3-dialogue won by PRO. The set $\mathrm{argPRO}(d) = \mathrm{Des}(\mathcal{X}) \cup \{a, g, j\}$ is a position, and the transitive closure of $\mathrm{valPRO}(d) = \{\langle v4, v3 \rangle, \langle v3, v2 \rangle, \langle v4, v2 \rangle, \langle v2, v1 \rangle, \langle v3, v1 \rangle, \langle v3, v5 \rangle\}$ is one of its corresponding audiences.

At certain points we may be presented with a choice of arguments to use with W1-4. For example b may be attacked by a or, if $v1$ is not preferred to $v2$, q. Similarly there are choices when we declare value preferences: in the example we can either prevent the attack of j on g succeeding, or choose preferences which lead to i or o defeating j. Such choices may, if badly made, lead to backtracking. Some heuristics seem possible to guide choices: it is better to attack an undesired argument with an argument of its own value where possible, as with a and b above, as this attack will succeed even if the value order changes. Also, when a value preference is required, a choice which keeps an optional argument available is better than one which defeats it, as the argument may be required to defeat a future attack, as in the example where j is required to defeat k. For a discussion of how preferences over values emerge in a particular domain, see [5], which gives an account of how the decisions made in a body of case law reveal the social priorities of the jurisdiction in which they are made.

4   Related Work and Conclusion

The basis for our consideration of positions within sets of arguments is the abstract framework of [9]. This, however, does not distinguish between an attack and an attack which succeeds. Refining the concept of "successful attack" together with the computational problems associated with Dung's schema[2] has motivated approaches in addition to the VAF formalism [3] underpinning the present work. Thus, [1] introduce "preference-based argument" wherein the attack $\langle x, y \rangle$ is a *successful attack* by x on y in the event that the *argument* y is "not preferred" to x. A comparison of the preference and value-based approaches may be found in [12, pp. 368–69].

The dialogue mechanism for position construction uses the expressive formalism presented in [15] which also forms the basis of schemes described in [1,7]. Use is made of a partitioned argumentation framework to introduce restricted notions of admissibility to Dung's framework in [6]. A related approach – the TPI-dispute protocol introduced in [18] – has been analysed extensively in [11] with respect to its computational efficiency. In view of the intractability of deciding whether a position exists (cf. [12]), it would be interesting to obtain a characterisation of rules W1-4 as a proof-theoretic technique as was done in [11] for TPI-disputes w.r.t. the CUT-free Sequent calculus.

In this paper we have described an approach to practical reasoning which respects four important phenomena of such reasoning. It addresses the need to consider arguments in context, so that alternatives are properly considered, and so that actions are chosen with reference to what else must be done: it is a position comprising a set of actions rather than a single argument that is adopted. It permits of a dialogical construction which corresponds to the presumption and critique structure of practical reasoning. It accommodates different value preferences to explain rational disagreement as to the proper course of action. Finally, and this is a key contribution of this paper, it permits the ordering of value preferences to emerge from the debate rather than requiring the unrealistic assumption that agents are able fully to determine their rankings in advance. We believe that this approach will have significant application in the analysis and modelling of argumentation in areas where choice in terms of the values of the audience is important such as case law in and political debate as in [13]. Both of these areas are receiving increasing attention as the notion of e-democracy becomes widespread.

---

[2] See e.g. [10, pp. 188-89] for a discussion of these.

References

1. L. Amgoud and C. Cayrol. A reasoning model based on the production of acceptable arguments. *Annals of Math. and Artificial Intelligence*, 34:197–215, 2002.
2. K. Atkinson, T. J. M. Bench-Capon, and P. McBurney. Justifying practical reasoning. ECAI Workshop CMNA'04, 2004.
3. T. J. M. Bench-Capon. Agreeing to differ: modelling persuasive dialogue between parties with different values. *Informal Logic*, 22(3):231–245, 2002.
4. T. J. M. Bench-Capon. Persuasion in practical argument using value-based argumentation frameworks. *Journal of Logic and Computation*, 13(3):429–448, 2003.
5. T. J. M. Bench-Capon and G. Sartor. A model of legal reasoning with cases incorporating theories and values. *Artificial Intelligence*, 150(1–2):97–143, 2003.
6. C. Cayrol, S. Doutre, M.-Ch. Lagasquie-Schiex, and J. Mengin. "Minimal defence": a refinement of the preferred semantics for argumentation frameworks. In *Proc. NMR'2002*, pages 408–415, 2002.
7. C. Cayrol, S. Doutre, and J. Mengin. On decision problems related to the preferred semantics for argumentation frameworks. *Journal of Logic and Computation*, 13(3):377–403, 2003.
8. S. Doutre, T. J. M. Bench-Capon, and P. E. Dunne. Explaining preferences with argument positions. In *Proc. IJCAI-05 (to appear)*, 2005.
9. P. M. Dung. On the acceptability of arguments and its fundamental role in non-monotonic reasoning, logic programming and n-person games. *Artificial Intelligence*, 77:321–357, 1995.
10. P. E. Dunne and T. J. M. Bench-Capon. Coherence in finite argument systems. *Artificial Intelligence*, 141:187–203, 2002.
11. P. E. Dunne and T. J. M. Bench-Capon. Two party immediate response disputes: properties and efficiency. *Artificial Intelligence*, 149:221–250, 2003.
12. P. E. Dunne and T. J. M. Bench-Capon. Complexity in value-based argument systems. In *Proc. 9th JELIA*, volume 3229 of *LNAI*, pages 360–371. Springer-Verlag, 2004.
13. P. E. Dunne and T. J. M. Bench-Capon. Identifying audience preferences in legal and social domains. In *Proc. DEXA'04*, volume 3180 of *LNCS*, pages 518–527. Springer-Verlag, 2004.
14. A. Hunter. Making argumentation more believable. In *Proc. of the 19th American National Conference on Artificial Intelligence (AAAI'2004)*, pages 269–274. MIT Press, 2004.
15. H. Jakobovits and D. Vermeir. Dialectic semantics for argumentation frameworks. In *Proc. ICAIL-99*, pages 53–62, 1999.
16. C. Perelman and L. Olbrechts-Tyteca. *The New Rhetoric: A Treatise on Argumentation*. Univ. of Notre-Dame Press, 1969.
17. J. R. Searle. *Rationality in Action*. MIT Press, 2001.
18. G. Vreeswijk and H. Prakken. Credulous and sceptical argument games for preferred semantics. In *Proc. 7th JELIA*, volume 1919 of *LNAI*, pages 224–238. Springer-Verlag, 2000.
19. D. N. Walton. *Argument Schemes for Presumptive Reasoning*. Lawrence Erlbaum Associates, 1996.

Avoiding Order Effects in Incremental Learning

Nicola Di Mauro, Floriana Esposito, Stefano Ferilli, and Teresa M.A. Basile

Department of Computer Science, University of Bari, Italy
{ndm, esposito, ferilli, basile}@di.uniba.it

Abstract. This paper addresses the problem of mitigating the order effects in incremental learning, a phenomenon observed when different ordered sequences of observations lead to different results. A modification of an ILP incremental learning system, with the aim of making it order-independent, is presented. A backtracking strategy on theories is incorporated in its refinement operators, which causes a change of its refinement strategy and reflects the human behavior during the learning process. A modality to restore a previous theory, in order to backtrack on a previous knowledge level, is presented. Experiments validate the approach in terms of computational cost and predictive accuracy.

1 Introduction

In many situations, intelligent systems are bound to work in environments that change over time. In these cases, their learning component, if any, must take into account that the available knowledge about the world is provided over time. For instance, a learning system should revise its learned knowledge when new observations are available, while still being able to provide at any stage of the learning process such a knowledge in order to carry out some task. This kind of learning is often named *Incremental Learning*.

As pointed out in [1], the three most important assumptions characterizing an incremental learning system are: a) "it must be able to use the learned knowledge at any step of the learning"; b) "the incorporation of experience into memory during learning should be computationally efficient" (theory revision must be efficient in fitting new incoming observations); and, c) "the learning process should not make unreasonable space demands, so that memory requirements increase as a tractable function of experience" (memory requirements must not depend on the training size).

It is clear that, in the incremental learning setting, the shape of the learned theories can be strongly influenced by the order in which the examples are provided to the system and taken into account by it. This paper carries on the work reported in [2], facing the problem of making a learning system insensitive to examples ordering. While the aim of that work was a preliminary check of the performance of the proposed technique (and hence it focused on a specific feature of the system, namely the generalization operator), here the research is extended to take into account the general case, in which positive and negative examples, and consequently generalization and specialization operations, can be interleaved. As reported in [1], we can define incremental learning as follows:

S. Bandini and S. Manzoni (Eds.): AI*IA 2005, LNAI 3673, pp. 110–121, 2005.
© Springer-Verlag Berlin Heidelberg 2005

Definition 1 (Incremental Learning). *A learner L is incremental if L inputs one training experience at time, does not re-process any previous experience, and retains only one knowledge structure in memory.*

The first condition, *"L inputs one training experience at time"*, avoids to consider as incremental the learning algorithms exploited by *batch* learning systems, that process many instances at at time, by simply storing the instances observed so far and running the method on all of them. The second condition, *"does not re-process any previous experience"*, places a constraint on the learning mechanism itself, by ruling out those systems that process new data together with old data in order to come up with a new model. in that it can process each experience only once. The important idea is that *the time taken to process each experience must remain constant* or nearly so with increasing numbers, in order to guarantee efficient learning of the sort seen in humans. Finally, the third condition, *"retains only one knowledge structure in memory"*, leaves out algorithms like CE [3], since it requires to memorize exactly one definition for each concept. CE processes instances one at a time and does not need to reprocess them. However, it retains in memory a set of competing hypotheses summarizing the data, that can grow exponentially with the number of training items, and it reprocesses these hypotheses upon incorporating each training case.

Systems whose behaviour falls in Definition 1 can be seen as incremental hill climbing approaches to learning, affected by the training instances ordering. The cause of such a phenomenon can be discovered by looking at the learning process as a search in the space of knowledge structures. In this perspective, an incremental learner chooses which path to follow from a set of possibilities (generated by new incoming instances and constrained by the previous ones) but there is no warranty that future instances will agree with this choice.

Definition 2 (Order Sensitivity). *A learner L is order sensitive if there exists a training set T on which L exhibits an order effect.*

Since robustness is a primary issue for any machine learning system, mitigating the phenomenon of order sensitivity is very desirable. The approach to decreasing order sensitivity in incremental learning systems, proposed in this paper, is based on a backtracking strategy. It aims at being able to preserve the incremental nature of the learner, as stated in Definition 1, and to offer a strategy that alleviates the order sensitivity while preserving efficiency of the learning process. Indeed, a generic learner is not required to provide an exact definition of the target concept but, rather, to identify a good approximation of the concept itself that makes it able to behave efficiently on future incoming instances.

As pointed out in [1], there exist at least three different levels at which order effects can occur: at the level of attributes of the instances, at the level of instances, and at the level of concepts. The last two are more interesting for a deep analysis of the order effect phenomenon. This paper focuses on the second level, where the task is to learn a concept definition from instances. In particular, we investigate the approach in the Inductive Logic Programming (ILP) framework, in which the concept definition is made up of clauses and the instances are a set of positive and negative examples describing the target concept. The problem of order effects at the level of concepts requires further analysis and represents a future work issue.

2   Related Works

It is widely known in the Machine Learning literature that incremental learning suffers from instance order effects and that, under some orderings, extremely *poor* theories might be obtained. However, when the purpose of a machine learning system is to work in a robust manner, it is very desirable for it to be not order sensitive. Thus, a lot of approaches in order to decrease/overcome the order effect phenomenon in an incremental learner have been proposed.

The simplest way proposed to alleviate the problem is to retain all possible alternatives for a revision point, or more than one description in memory. Unfortunately, this method results very expensive from the computational complexity point of view, in both time and space. An alternative is to make strong assumptions about the nature of the target concept. The disadvantage of this method concerns the validity of such assumptions, since checking these representational restrictions could be computationally heavy. A more interesting approach consists in imposing constraints on the learning process by means of a background knowledge. A formal analysis of the conditions under which background knowledge reduces order effects is reported in [4]. The Author identifies the causes of the order effect in the system's incapacity to focus on an optimal hypothesis (when it has to choose among the current potential ones) and to keep enough information not to forget potential hypotheses. These characteristics correspond to a local preference bias that heuristically selects the most promising hypotheses. Such a bias can be viewed as a prior knowledge built into the system and can be obtained by means of additional instances provided to an order-independent system. Hence, the Author reduces the problem of the correct instances ordering to the problem of adding such instances (representing the prior knowledge) to an order-independent system. In this way it is proved that there are strong contingencies for an incremental learner to be order independent on some collection of instances.

Other specific strategies have been proposed to overcome the order effect problem in incremental clustering. The NOT-YET strategy [5] exploited in COB-WEB [6] tries to overcome the problem by means of a buffering strategy. The instances that cannot be added to the current cluster are stored into a buffer for future elaborations. The size of the buffer (i.e., the number of instances that can be "remembered") is a user-defined parameter. During the learning process, when the size of the buffer exceeds the user defined-size, the strategy elaborates the buffered instances up to this moment in order to include them in the existing clusters. Experimental results reported in [5] show that, in such an approach, there can be cases in which to induce a good cluster an high number of instances must be "bufferized" in order to be reconsidered later, and in some cases this number may amount to even 90% of the dataset. Another approach is represented by the ID5R algorithm [7], an incremental version of the ID3 batch algorithm, that builds a decision tree incrementally. The tree is revised as needed, achieving a tree equivalent to the one that the basic ID3 algorithm would construct, given the same set of training instances. In ID5R the information needed to revise the tree is maintained at each test node. This information consists of the counts of positive and negative instances for every possible value of every attribute coming from the training instances. The tree is revised changing the *position* of some (or all) test nodes according to a measure calculated on all the information (positive and negative instances) regarding such a node. Hence, the algorithm does not forget any information contained in the input data and, when it makes a choice between alternative hypotheses, it keeps enough information in order to compose all potential competing models and, thus, to select the best one at any moment.

3   The Backtracking Strategy

The goal of a machine learning system is to simulate the human learning process, hence it is necessary to understand how to replicate in an automatic way some human behaviors. We think that there is a strict relation between incremental learning and the human learning process, since human learners receive information in an incremental fashion, as confirmed in learning naive physics experiments [8]. Our approach to mitigate order effects in incremental learning can be explained by making a parallel with the identification of the exit path in a maze. In a maze, arriving to a choice point, a decision about which direction to follow has to be taken. If a dead end is reached then it is necessary to go back to the last decision point and choose another direction. This process is repeated until the way out is found. In other words, the system must be provided with the ability to hypothesize the existence of another path, better than the current one, that leads to the correct solution.

From the machine learning point of view, when a learner is not able to revise the theory to fit new incoming observations, due to specific *constraints* it must fulfill, it should assume that probably it had previously chosen a wrong path. In particular, an incremental learning system explores the hypotheses space with an hill-climbing approach, and this kind of myopia could be avoided providing the learner with a mechanism for backtracking over previous hypotheses. In order to do this, it is necessary to define some criteria, or constraints, indicating when the system must backtrack, such as *completeness, consistency*, and *theory minimality*. Thus, when the learner achieves a point in which it is not able to revise the current theory with respect to a new incoming instance, fulfilling the completeness and consistency criteria, then it could try to revise a previous one.

Furthermore, in order to backtrack on a previous theory, the system must remember at what moments it revised the theory and how it was revised. In particular, during the learning process, if at time t the system revised the theory T in T', then it should memorize that "T' *was obtained from* T *at time* t". In order to perform this task, the learner memorizes a list of revisions, where each element R_t indicates that at the time t there was a revision of the theory due to incorrectness with respect to an example e_t. Furthermore, each element in this list contains the previous theory, the instance that fired the revision, and the new revised theory. Note that it is not necessary to memorize the whole theories in each element, but only the specific modification made to the theory. In an ILP setting, this means that not all the clauses composing the theory are memorized but just the revised clause(s). It is important to note that this does not mean rembering/memorizing all the possible refinements for a revision point, but only that at the specific time t the theory T was revised in T' in order to fit the example e_t. This list represents a chronological trace of the knowledge changes and it is a powerful information for a theory revision system.

After having introduced the main idea of the backtracking approach to avoid order effects, and how to make it effective by memorizing a chronology of the knowledge revisions, let us now show how the learner should reason. As already pointed out, the backtracking process is activated at time t if any constraint is violated. The learner hypothesizes that *"the current theory was obtained by choosing a wrong path"*. In order to check if this hypothesis is correct the learner restores a previous theory (say the one at time $t-k$), by using the list of revisions, and performs another revision. At this point there are two alternatives: 1) re-processing all the instances arrived from time $t - k + 1$ up to the time t; or, 2) choosing a revision that does not violate the constraints on the instances arrived from time $t - k + 1$ up to time t. Since the first alternative violates the assumption of incremental learning, the system tries to find a revision that fits all the examples seen up to the moment of the backtracking step.

At least three different situations can arise dealing with incremental concept learning in ILP. The first corresponds to the case in which the concept to be learnt is represented by a definition made up of only one clause. The second situation concerns the concepts with more than one clause in their definition. Finally, the third case corresponds to multi-conceptual learning. In this paper we give a general strategy for order effect in incremental learning, and a possible implementation dealing with the first situation above reported. Furthermore, we provide an analysis of the problems that arise when we consider the order effect in the second situation.

3.1   One Target Concept Made Up of a Single Clause

When the system has to learn a target concept C whose definition is made up of only one clause, we can make some assumptions about its behavior. Specifically, when the current theory (clause) is incomplete (resp. inconsistent) with respect to a new incoming positive (resp. negative) example, and it is not possible to revise it, then we are sure that it is always possible to backtrack and find a new theory (clause) complete and consistent with respect to all known examples.

3.2   One Target Concept Made Up of More Than One Clause

When the target concept is defined by two or more clauses the problem of order effects becomes more difficult to handle. Given the concept C to be learnt made up of the clauses $C_1, C_2, \ldots, C_n$, and a set of examples $\{e_{11}, \ldots, e_{1m_1}, e_{21}, \ldots,$

$e_{2m_2}, \ldots, e_{n1}, \ldots, e_{nm_n}\}$ such that C_i explains all e_{ik}'s $(1 \leq i \leq n \wedge 1 \leq k \leq m_i)$, and C_i does not explain any e_{jh} $(j \neq i \wedge 1 \leq h \leq m_j)$. Obviously, if the learner takes as input the examples in this ordering then it should be able to learn the concept $\mathcal{C}$ expressed exactly as the disjunction of the clauses $C_1, C_2, \ldots, C_n$. Suppose that we have another random ordering of the examples, and that at time t the system learned a theory made up of only one clause C'. Furthermore, suppose that at time $t + 1$ the system takes as input a new positive example e not covered by the theory and it is not able to generalize the clause C' to fit e. Hence, it is necessary to add to the theory a new clause covering the example e to make the theory complete. The problem in this situation is that the clause C' is a generalization of a set of examples that are not all, in principle, in charge of the same clause C_i. For instance, suppose that the example e belongs to the concept "black" and that the clause C' generalizes 3 examples for the concept "black" and 2 examples for the concept "white". The system is not able to generalize the clause C' with respect to the example e because C' is forced to cover also some examples for the concept "white".

A possible solution is to go back on a previous revision point by choosing another clause (revision) and to re-consider (i.e., use to revise it, if needed) all the examples acquired after this revision point. Another solution could be to define a similarity measure to extract from the set of examples covered by the clause C' a subset E of examples closer to the example e and generalize them into a new clause. In this way the clause C' is no longer forced to cover the examples of the set E, and a future generalization of C' could be possible. This second solution can be viewed as an *incremental clustering in first-order logic*. But all these solutions contrast with the main idea that a learning system is not required to learn exactly the correct definition. Indeed, the goal is to achieve a good approximation of the target concept evaluated, for instance, by the completeness and consistency errors on new unseen examples. Let us now analyze whether the backtracking strategy is a good solution to mitigate the order effects at least on the base cases and then to extend it to more complicated problems.

4   Implementation in INTHELEX

INTHELEX (INcremental THeory Learner from EXamples) is a fully incremental, multi-conceptual learning system for the induction of hierarchical theories from examples [9]. In particular, *full incrementality* avoids the need of a previous theory to be available, so that learning can start from an empty theory and from the first example; *multi-conceptual* means that it can learn simultaneosly various concepts, possibly related to each other. Moreover, it is a *closed loop system*, hence the learned theory is checked to be valid on any new example available, and in case of failure a revision process is activated upon it, in order to restore the *completeness* and *consistency* properties. INTHELEX learns theories, expressed as sets of Datalog^{OI} clauses, from positive and negative examples. Datalog^{OI} is a logic language, based on the notion of *Object Identity* ("*Within a clause, terms denoted with different symbols must be distinct")*, that has the same expressive power as Datalog [10].

In a logical framework for the inductive synthesis of Datalog theories, a fundamental problem is the definition of *ideal* refinement operators. Unfortunately, when full Horn clause logic is chosen as representation language and either θ-subsumption or implication is adopted as generalization model, there exist no ideal refinement operators [11]. On the contrary, they exist under the weaker, but more mechanizable and manageable ordering induced by θ_{OI}-subsumption, as proved in [12]. Note that, like θ_{OI}-subsumption, θ_{OI}-subsumption induces a quasi-ordering upon the space of Datalog clauses, but this space is not a lattice when ordered by θ_{OI}-subsumption, while it is when ordered by θ-subsumption.

INTHELEX adopts a *full memory* storage strategy, i.e., it memorizes all the examples. When our knowledge is inconsistent with new observations, we may ignore the inconsistency, hoping that it is insignificant or accidental, and retain our knowledge unaltered, or we may use the *evolutionary* approach[1], defined in [13], by making incremental modifications to the appropriate part of our knowledge. The strength of an incremental *full memory* method lies in its ability to use all the original facts for guiding the process of modifying and generalizing knowledge structures, and selecting alternative solutions, and to guarantee the *completeness* and *consistency* of the modified knowledge with all the examples. This is not in contrast with Definition 1, since original examples are only used to guarantee the completeness and consistency requirements of ILP systems.

INTHELEX incorporates two inductive refinement operators, one for generalizing hypotheses that reject positive examples, and the other for specializing hypotheses that explain negative examples. When a new incoming positive example is not covered, a generalization of the theory is needed. The system chooses a clause defining the wrong concept to be generalized and tries to compute the least general generalization under object identity (lgg_{OI}) of this clause and the example. If one of the computed generalizations is consistent with all the past negative examples, then it replaces the chosen clause in the theory, or else a new clause (if it exists) is chosen to compute the lgg_{OI}. If no clause can be generalized, the system checks if the example itself, with the constants properly turned into variables, is consistent with the past negative examples. Such a clause is added to the theory, or else the example itself is added as an exception to the theory. When a negative example is covered, a specialization of the theory must be performed. Among the program clauses occurring in the SLD-derivation of the example, INTHELEX tries to specialize one at the lowest possible level, in order to refine the concepts that are used in the definitions of other concepts, by adding to it one or more positive literals, which can discriminate all the past positive examples from the current negative one. In case of failure, it tries to add the negation of a literal, which discriminates the negative example from all the past positive ones, to the first clause of the SLD-derivation (related to the concept of which the example is an istance). If none of the clauses obtained

---

[1] That is opposite opposite to the *revolutionary* approach to throw away this piece of knowledge altogether and develop another one from scratch.

makes the theory consistent, then INTHELEX adds the negative example to the theory as an exception.

Naturally, like other incremental machine learning systems, INTHELEX is order sensitive. As already pointed out, the hypothesis space ordered by the θ_{OI}-subsumption relation is not a lattice as for θ-subsumption, and hence, for any two clauses many mutually uncomparable minimal refinements might exist. When the system tries to generalize a clause, if it has more than one path to choose it cannot decide in advance which is the correct one, because it does not know future examples. For the specialization INTHELEX uses a non-minimal specialization operator by appending additional premises to the clause. Also in this case, if the system has many ways to specialize the clause it cannot choose the correct one.

INTHELEX$_{back}$, the improvement of INTHELEX that reduces the order effects, embeds a backtracking strategy into the two inductive refinement operators. The constraint imposed by INTHELEX$_{back}$ during learning is to have a minimal theory, and the violation of this constraint starts the backtracking revision process. In particular, as reported in Algorithm 1, when the generalization operator fails in finding a lgg$_{OI}$ of a clause, it tries to revise a previous theory. If this second step fails, the system continues in the usual way by adding a new clause to the theory. On the other hand, the specialization operator tries to revise a previous theory only if it is not able to specialize, by adding positive literals, the clause that covers the negative example. The choice to revise a previous theory after step 'a1' is justified by the theory minimality constraints; conversely, in the other case, after step 'a2', we preferred to have a theory obtained without negative literals since once added they cannot be ever removed.

Algorithm 1 INTHELEX$_{back}$ algorithm

Given: a theory T and a source of examples
acquire the next example e
if e is positive and not covered by T **then**
  a1) try to find the lgg$_{OI}$ of a clause in T; otherwise, b1) *try to revise a previous theory*; otherwise, c1) try to add a new clause to T; otherwise, d1) add a positive exception to T
if e is negative and covered by T **then**
  a2) try to specialize a clause of T by adding positive literal(s); otherwise, b2) *try to revise a previous version of T*; otherwise, c2) try to specialize a clause of T by adding negative literal(s); otherwise, d2) add a negative exception to T

In order to be able to restore a previous version of the theory to be revised, INTHELEX$_{back}$ memorizes all the theory revisions. Futhermore, it memorizes also the type of the revision and at what time it happened. Given a set of concepts $C_1, C_2, \ldots C_n$ to be learnt, INTHELEX$_{back}$ maintains a stack of revisions for each clause of each concept C_i. In particular, when the system performs a theory revision, this revision is "pushed" in the correspondig stack of the revised clause.

In this way, the system is able to perform backtracking on previous versions of a single clause. The following is the detailed description of a generic element in the stack: (Type, OldClause, NewClause, ExampleID), where Type can be: 1) "adding a new clause", 2) "lgg of a clause", 3) "adding a positive exception", 4) "specialization with positive literal(s)", 5) "specialization with negative literal", or 6) "adding negative exception"; OldClause is the clause revised while NewClause is the new clause obtained by generalization or specialization; finally, ExampleID represents the number of the example that caused the revision (i.e., the time at which the revision happened).

For a new incoming example, if the system decides to backtrack on a previous theory, then it chooses a clause C belonging to the concept to be revised. While there are items in the revisions' stack S_C of C, the system "pops" a revision $R = (T_R, OC_R, NC_R, EID_R)$ from S_C and restores the previous theory by just replacing the clause NC_R with OC_R in the theory. According to the type T_R of the revision R, the system performs one of the following tasks:

a) if T_R was a lgg then it tries to find another lgg of the clause OC_R that is consistent with all negative examples older than the example EID_R, and consistent and complete with all examples newer than EID_R;
b) if T_R was a specialization by adding literals then it tries to find another specialization of the clause OC_R that is complete with respect to all positive examples older than the example EID_R, and consistent and complete with all examples newer than EID_R;
c) if T_R was addition of an exception then the system does not perform any task and "pops" another revision;
d) when T_R was addition of a new clause this means that it is not possible to revise a previous version of this clause, and hence the backtracking revision process on this clause fails.

When a backtracking process fails on a clause, and there are no other clauses for that concept to be revised, then INTHELEX$_{back}$ is forced to violate the constraint of theory minimality by adding a new clause or an exception.

5   Experiments

The relevance of the new proposed strategy was evaluated by comparing the learning behaviour of INTHELEX$_{back}$ to that of INTHELEX, in which it was embedded. In the particular context of this work, experiments are based on a purposely designed artificial dataset. The main reason for excluding real-world datasets is that we want to evaluate the effectiveness of the proposed strategy in avoiding ordering-effect, rather than the goodness of the learning system itself. Furthermore, the results obtained by INTHELEX$_{back}$ depend on the performance of INTHELEX and hence we may expect that possible improvements obtained on artificial datasets, could be confirmed on real-world problems too. Last but not least, we needed a dataset for a concept whose definiton was made of only one clause, since there is not still a well defined approach to solve the case of a concept expressed by many clauses.

5.1 The Problem Domain

In order to investigate the ability of INTHELEX$_{back}$ in learning the correct target concept without being order sensitive, the following learning problems P_1 and P_2 were defined. Both regard a target concept represented by a clause made up of 3 variables and 4 predicate symbols:

$$C : h(A) \leftarrow p_1(A, D, C), p_2(A, B, C), p_3(A, D, B), p_4(A, B, C).$$

Note that variable A is used just for linkedness purposes, since the theories learned by INTHELEX are made up of linked clauses only, thus all predicates can be considered as binary. Then, for each problem, 100 positive and 100 negative examples were generated at random. Specifically, each example contains 4 literals for each predicate symbol p_1, p_2, p_3, p_4, whose arguments are selected, uniformly and without replacement (so that the same literal cannot occur twice), from the set of all possible pairs of 4 constants for problem P_1, and 6 constants for problem P_2. Each example was considered as positive if it is covered by clause C, negative otherwise. Specifically, the probability that a generated example is positive is equal to $497/597 = 0.83$ for problem P_1, while it is equal to $100/1070 = 0.09$ for problem P_2. Thus, for problem P_1 it was necessary to generate 497 positive examples in order to generate 100 negative ones, while for problem P_2 970 negative examples had to be generated to reach 100 positive examples. Hence, in P_2 we expect a number of specializations higher than in P_1.

INTHELEX$_{back}$ has been evaluated along the same parameters as INTHELEX i.e. complexity (how many clauses the theory contains) and correctness (whether the theory contains the correct target clause) of the learned theory, and cost (time complexity and number of theory revisions) spent to learn it. To highlight the order sensitivity of INTHELEX and the improvements of the new approach, independent orderings of the examples were generated from the training set.

5.2 Experimental Results

In the first experiment INTHELEX was run on 100 different orderings of the training set. Table 1 reports the averaged results. For each problem, P_1 and P_2, the row labeled *Correct* refers to the cases in which INTHELEX learnt a theory containing the target clause, the row labeled *Wrong* reports the cases in which it was not able to learn a correct theory, while the row labeled *All* represents all cases. For problem P_2 only "All" is reported, since in only one case INTHELEX was unable to learn a correct theory. The columns indicate, respectively: the runtime (expressed in milliseconds), the number of clauses composing the theory, the number of lgg$_{OI}$ performed, the number of specializations (positive + negative), and the number of exceptions (positive + negative), all averaged on the number of orderings, reported in the last column. Whenever the learned theory contains other clauses in addition to the correct one, this means that the correct clause was learnt at the end of learning process. In this case, a 'cleaning' process that eliminates all the clauses subsumed by the correct one can be used.

For problem P_1, INTHELEX is able to find the correct solution in 55 cases out of 100. The high values in the row "Wrong" indicate the difficulty of the

Table 1. INTHELEX performance

Problem	Time	Clauses	Lgg	Specializat.	Excepti.	Run
(All)	44160.5	4.93	16.95	4.39 + 1.54	0 + 19.01	100
P_1 (Correct)	23961.64	4.07	14.78	4.4 + 1.33	0 + 9.47	55
(Wrong)	68848	5.98	19.6	4.38 + 1.8	0 + 30.67	45
P_2 (All)	19128.9	5.98	11.54	5.37 + 6.14	0 + 2.39	100

Table 2. INTHELEX$_{back}$ performance

	Time	Clauses	Lgg	Pos.Spec.	Backtracking	Push	Pop
P1	13376.3	1	6.47	0.29	2.29	7.76	4.04
P2	2718.8	1	4.25	0.44	1.87	5.69	2.95

system to learn when the ordering of examples is bad. Table 2 witnesses the performance improvement obtained by using the modified system INTHELEX$_{back}$ on the same set of orderings. Results reveal that it always learns the correct clause spending on average less time than INTHELEX. The fourth column indicates the number of backtrackings needed by the system during the learning process, that corresponds to the number of mistakes it made. Specifically, the number of revisions corresponds to the number of "push" operations. Conversely, the number of "pop" operations corresponds to the wrong refinements that were withdrawn by the system for each backtracking. It is interesting to note that the number of withdrawn refinements is on average 1.76 (= 4.04/2.29) on a total of about 7 (6.47 + 0.29) refinements performed in problem P_1 (1.58 (= 2.95/1.87) on about 5 (4.25 + 0.44) refinements for problem P_2, respectively), indicating that backtracking does not retract too many choices, which is important since going too deep into the refinements stack could cause an increase in computational time.

Running INTHELEX$_{back}$ on the 100 orderings we found that it always learns the correct target concept for problem P_1 (respectively P_2) after 20.11 (respectively 13.61) examples on average, with minimum of 8 (respectively 6) and a maximum of 37 (respectively 37). These results show the capability of the system to converge rapidly to the target concept. Note that using higher values of the parameters (number of constants, variables, predicates and literals) to generate the examples, than in this experimental setting, has not proved to affect effectiveness of the system, but only its efficiency (more time, revisions and backtraking). For instance, increasing the number of constants and/or literals changes the probability that the clause C covers the examples, while increasing the number of variables and/or predicates causes a growing of the search space. What one expects is a greater effort in finding the correct concept, and not that in these conditions the system does not find it.

6 Conclusions and Future Works

This paper presented a backtracking strategy for mitigating order effects in incremental learning, that was implemented in INTHELEX$_{back}$, a modification of

the first-order learning system INTHELEXExperimental results on a purposely
designed dataset show that the system, modified with the new approach, achieves
better performance with respect to the basic version in all metris. Future work
will concern an investigation on how to manage the case of learning a concept
whose definition is made up of more than one clause, and the more difficult case
of a multiple concept learning task.

References

1. Langley, P.: Order effects in incremental learning. In Reimann, P., Spada, H., eds.: Learning in humans and machines: Towards an Interdisciplinary Learning Science. Elsevier (1995)
2. Di Mauro, N., Esposito, F., Ferilli, S., Basile, T.A.: A backtracking strategy for order-independent incremental learning. In de Mantaras, R.L., ed.: Proceedings of ECAI04, IOS Press (2004)
3. Mitchell, T.: Generalization as search. Artificial Intelligence **18** (1982) 203–226
4. Cornuéjols, A.: Getting order independence in incremental learning. In Brazdil, P., ed.: Proceedings of ECML93. Volume 667 of LNAI., Springer (1993) 196–212
5. Talavera, L., Roure, J.: A buffering strategy to avoid ordering effects in clustering. In: Proceedings of ECML98. (1998) 316–321
6. Fisher, D.H.: Knowledge acquisition via incremental conceptual clustering. Machine Learning **2** (1987) 139–172
7. Utgoff, P.E.: Incremental induction of decision trees. Machine Learning **4** (1989) 161–186
8. Esposito, F., Semeraro, G., Fanizzi, N., Ferilli, S.: Conceptual change in learning naive physics: The computational model as a theory revision process. In Lamma, E., Mello, P., eds.: Advances in Artificial Intelligence (AI*IA99). LNAI, Springer (1999) 214–225
9. Esposito, F., Ferilli, S., Fanizzi, N., Basile, T., Di Mauro, N.: Incremental multistrategy learning for document processing. Applied Artificial Intelligence Journal **17** (2003) 859–883
10. Semeraro, G., Esposito, F., Malerba, D., Fanizzi, N., S.Ferilli: A logic framework for the incremental inductive synthesis of datalog theories. In Fuchs, N., ed.: Proceedings of LOPSRT97. Volume 1463 of LNCS., Springer (1998) 300–321
11. Nienhuys-Cheng, S.H., de Wolf, R.: Foundations of Inductive Logic Programming. Volume 1228 of LNAI. Springer (1997)
12. Esposito, F., Laterza, A., Malerba, D., Semeraro, G.: Locally finite, proper and complete operators for refining datalog programs. In Rás, Z., Michalewicz, M., eds.: Proceedings of ISMIS96. Volume 1079 of LNAI., Springer (1996) 468–478
13. Michalski, R.S.: Knowledge repair mechanisms: Evolution vs. revolution. In: Proceedings of ICML85, Skytop, PA (1985) 116–119

Evaluating Search Strategies and Heuristics for Efficient Answer Set Programming

Enrico Giunchiglia and Marco Maratea

STAR-Lab, DIST, University of Genova,
viale Francesco Causa, 13, 16145 Genova, Italy
{enrico, marco}@dist.unige.it

Abstract. Answer Set Programming (ASP) and propositional satisfiability (SAT) are closely related. In some recent work we have shown that, on a wide set of logic programs called "tight", the main search procedures used by ASP and SAT systems are equivalent, i.e., that they explore search trees with the same branching nodes. In this paper, we focus on the experimental evaluation of different search strategies, heuristics and their combinations that have been shown to be effective in the SAT community, in ASP systems. Our results show that, despite the strong link between ASP and SAT, it is not always the case that search strategies, heuristics and/or their combinations that currently dominate in SAT are also bound to dominate in ASP. We provide a detailed experimental evaluation for this phenomenon and we shed light on future development of efficient Answer Set solvers.

1 Introduction

Answer Set Programming [MT99, Nie99] (ASP) and propositional satisfiability (SAT) are closely related. If a logic program Π is "tight"[Fag94] there exists a 1 to 1 correspondence between the solutions (Answer Sets) of the logic program (under the answer set semantics [GL88]) and the propositional formula given by its Clarke's completion [Cla78] $Comp(\Pi)$. In some recent work [GM05], we have shown that, on the wide set of tight logic programs, the relation goes up to the point that the main search ASP and SAT procedures are equivalent, i.e., that they explore search trees with the same branching nodes, when running on Π and $Comp(\Pi)$ respectively. Given the above result, state-of-the-art ASP systems like SMODELS,[1] CMODELS2[2] and ASSAT[3] are equivalent because they are based on the main search procedures for ASP and SAT: SMODELS is a native procedure working directly on a logic program, while CMODELS2 and ASSAT are based on the Davis-Logemann-Loveland (DLL) procedure.

In this paper we focus on the experimental evaluation of different search strategies, heuristics and their combinations that have been shown to be effective in the SAT community, in ASP systems. The analysis is performed used

---

[1] http://www.tcs.hut.fi/Software/smodels
[2] http://www.cs.utexas.edu/users/tag/cmodels.html
[3] http://assat.cs.ust.hk

S. Bandini and S. Manzoni (Eds.): AI*IA 2005, LNAI 3673, pp. 122–134, 2005.

CMODELS2 as a common platform: CMODELS2 is an AS solver based on SAT, strengthening in this way the relationship, and already incorporates most state-of-the-art SAT techniques and heuristics. Given the equivalence on search procedures, the results obtained for CMODELS2 extend to ASSAT and SMODELS if enhanced with corresponding techniques. For the search strategies, we evaluate both look-ahead strategies (used while descending the search tree) and look-back strategies (used for recovering from a failure in the search tree). In particular we analyze

- Look-ahead: basic unit-propagation, based on lazy data structures;
- Look-ahead: unit-propagation+failed-literal detection.
- Look-back: basic backtracking;
- Look-back: backtracking+backjumping+learning.

In SAT, failed-literal detection [Fre95] has been shown to be effective on randomly generated benchmarks, while optimized look-back techniques like backjumping [Pro93] and learning [SS96, BS97] have been shown to be effective on propositional formulas arising from real-world applications (such as planning and model checking). Among the SAT heuristics, we analyze

- Static: based on the order induced by the appearance in the SAT formula.
- VSIDS (Variable State Independent Decaying Sum): based on the information extracted from the optimized look-back phase of the search.
- Unit: based on the information extracted from the failed-literal detection technique.
- Unit with pool: Unit heuristic restricted to a subset of the open (not yet assigned) atoms.

The static heuristic is used for evaluating the contribution of individual look-ahead and look-back strategies *independently* from the heuristic. VSIDS [MMZ$^+$01] heuristic has been shown to be very effective on real-world benchmarks, while unit and unit with pool heuristics [LA97] have been shown effective on randomly generated benchmarks.

Finally, we also evaluate several combinations of look-head, look-back strategies and heuristics. There are 16 (2x2x4 for look-ahead, look-back and heuristics respectively) possible combinations of techniques we have presented, but only 10 among them make sense. This is because

- VSIDS heuristic makes sense only if learning is enabled
- Unit-based heuristics make sense only if failed-literal is enabled

The analysis has been performed by means of the following methodology: First, we fixed the heuristic (static) and analyzed the 4 remaining possible combinations (all the combinations between look-ahead and look-back strategies). The goal here is to understand the impact of each single strategy independently from (the interaction with) the heuristics. Second, we added the remaining heuristics where possible. The goal here is to evaluate how "real" ASP solvers perform on different benchmarks. We have used both randomly generated logic programs and logic programs arising from real-world applications. Besides tight logic programs, we have taken into account also non-tight logic programs. They are interesting because most of the state-of-the-art ASP systems, such as CMODELS2, ASSAT, SMODELS and DLV[4], can also solve non-tight logic programs.

The results of our experimental analysis point out that

1. on "small but relatively hard", randomly generated logic programs, failed-literal detection is very effective, especially in conjunction with unit-based heuristics. This result reflects what happens in SAT.
2. on "big but relatively easy", real-world logic programs of "medium" size (in the number of atoms in the logic programs), learning is very effective. A combination of learning, failed-literal and unit (with pool) heuristic is the best combination on these benchmarks. This is very different to what happens in SAT.
3. on real-world logic programs of large size, e.g. with more than about 15000 atoms, learning is again very effective, but now it leads to the best results in combination with simple unit-propagation and VSIDS heuristic.

The division in two categories, random and real-world, follow from the literature, in particular from SAT [LS05]. Here we have introduced a further division in the real-world category, related to the size, i.e. the number of atoms, of the logic programs. This further (sub)division is useful for isolating and underlying different behaviors in the real-world benchmarks.

This is the first paper that we know of, in which a variety of look-ahead, look-ahead strategies and heuristics are evaluated and combined in the ASP community. Previous works (such as [FLP01]) mostly considered and evaluated only one technique (the heuristic in the paper cited). The evaluation of a single technique is often not sufficient, because it is well-known that for the performances of systems what is crucial is the *combination* of techniques: For example, VSIDS heuristic is effective on real-world problems in conjunction with unit-propagation and learning, but becomes ineffective when failed-literal is added and does not make even sense with basic backtracking. Moreover, it is important to remark that a significant analysis ought to be performed on a *unique* platform, otherwise the results can be biased by implementation issues.

2   Answer Set Programming

A *rule* is an expression of the form

$$A_0 \leftarrow A_1, \ldots, A_m, not\ A_{m+1}, \ldots, not\ A_n \qquad (1)$$

where A_0 is an atom or the symbol $\perp$ (standing for false), and $A_1, \ldots, A_n$ are atoms ($0 \leq m \leq n$). A_0 is the *head* of the rule, $A_1, \ldots, A_m, not\ A_{m+1}, \ldots, not\ A_n$ is the *body*. A *(non disjunctive) logic program* is a finite set of rules.

---

[4] http://www.dbai.tuwien.ac.at/proj/dlv

CMODELS2(Γ, S)
  if $\Gamma = \emptyset$ **then return** $test(S, \Pi)$;
  if $\emptyset \in \Gamma$ **then return** *False*;
  if $\{l\} \in \Gamma$ **then return** CMODELS2$(assign(l, \Gamma), S \cup \{l\})$;
  $A :=$ an atom occurring in Γ;
  CMODELS2$(assign(A, \Gamma), S \cup \{A\})$;
  CMODELS2$(assign(\neg A, \Gamma), S \cup \{\neg A\})$.

Fig. 1. The ASP-SAT procedure

In order to give the definition of an answer set, we consider first the special case in which the program Π does not contain negation as failure (*not*) (i.e., such that for each rule (1) in Π, $n = m$). Let Π be such program, and let X be a consistent set of atoms. We say that X is *closed* under Π if, for every rule (1) in Π, $A_0 \in X$ whenever $\{A_1, \ldots, A_m\} \subseteq X$. We say that X is an *answer set* for Π if X is the smallest set closed under Π.

To extend this definition to programs with negation as failure, take any program Π, and let X be a consistent set of atoms. The *reduct* Π^X of Π relative to X is the set of rules

$$A_0 \leftarrow A_1, \ldots, A_m$$

for all rules (1) in Π such that X does not contain any of $A_{m+1}, \ldots, A_n$. Thus Π^X is a program without negation as failure. We say that X is an *answer set* for Π if X is an answer set for Π^X.

Now we want to introduce the relation between the answer sets of a program Π and the models of the completion of Π. In the following, we represent an interpretation (in the sense of propositional logic) as the set of atoms true in it. With this convention, a set of atoms X can denote both an answer set and an interpretation. Consider a program Π.

If A_0 is an atom or the symbol $\bot$, the *completion of* Π *relative to* A_0 is the formula

$$A_0 \equiv \bigvee (A_1 \wedge \cdots \wedge A_m \wedge \neg A_{m+1} \wedge \cdots \wedge \neg A_n)$$

where the disjunction extends over all rules (1) in Π with head A_0. The *completion* $Comp(\Pi)$ of Π consists of one formula $Comp(\Pi, A_0)$ for each atom A_0 and the symbol $\bot$.

For the wide set of tight logic programs, if X is an answer set of Π, then X satisfies $Comp(\Pi)$, and the converse is also true. In the following, we say that a program Π is *tight* if there exists a function λ from atoms to ordinals such that, for every rule (1) in Π whose head is not $\bot$, $\lambda(A_0) > \lambda(A_i)$ for each $i = 1, \ldots, m$.

2.1   cmodels2 and assat: SAT-Based Answer Set Programming

In this section we review the SAT-based approach to ASP. We present CMODELS2's algorithm, and then we say how it extends to the algorithm of ASSAT. There are various versions of CMODELS, all of them with the same behavior on tight programs. Here we consider the one proposed in [GML04], represented in Figure 1, in which l denotes a literal (a literal is an atom or its negation);

SMODELS(Π,S)
$\langle \Pi, S \rangle := simplify(\Pi, S)$;
if $(\{l, not\ l\} \subseteq S)$ **return** *False*;
if $(\{A : A \in A_\Pi, \{A, not\ A\} \cap S \neq \emptyset\} = A_\Pi)$ exit with *True*;
A := an atom occurring in Γ;
SMODELS(A-$assign(A, \Pi)), S \cup \{A\}$);
SMODELS(A-$assign(not\ A, \Pi)), S \cup \{not\ A\}$);

Fig. 2. A recursive version of the algorithm of SMODELS for tight logic programs

Γ a set of clauses; S an *assignment*, i.e., a consistent set of literals. Given an atom A, $assign(A, \Gamma)$ is the set of clauses obtained from Γ by removing the clauses to which A belongs, and by removing $\neg A$ from the other clauses in Γ. $assign(\neg A, \Gamma)$ is defined similarly. In the initial call, $\Gamma = Comp(\Pi)$ and S is the empty set. Here we consider $Comp(\Pi)$ after clausification. We assume that (i) $Comp(\Pi)$ signature extends the signature A_Π of Π, and (ii) for each set X of atoms in $Comp(\Pi)$ signature, X satisfies $Comp(\Pi)$ iff $X \cap A_\Pi$ satisfies $Comp(\Pi)$ before clausification. Standard clausification methods satisfy such conditions.

The algorithm of CMODELS2 is very similar to the well-known DLL decision procedure for SAT [DLL62]. The only difference is in the basic case when $\Gamma = \emptyset$, where "exit with *True*" is substituted with "return $test(S, \Pi)$", a new function which has to return

- *True*, and exit the procedure, if the set of atoms in S is an answer set of Π, and
- *False*, otherwise.

CMODELS2($Comp(\Pi), \emptyset$) returns *True* if and only if Π has an answer set.

ASSAT has the same behavior on tight logic programs, while on non-tight logic programs the approaches are different. Moreover, CMODELS2 has a number of advantages in comparison with ASSAT. For more details, see [GML04].

2.2 Relation with smodels

Consider now Fig. 2. This is a recursive version of the algorithm of SMODELS. In the Figure, Π is a program, initially set to the program of which we want to determine the existence of answer sets; S is an assignment, initially set to $\{\top\}$; A denotes an atom, r a rule, and l a literal. A-$assign(l, \Pi)$ returns the program obtained from Π by (i) deleting the rules r such that $not\ l \in body(r)$; and (ii) deleting l from the body of the other rules in Π. If $l_1, \ldots, l_n$ are the literals in a set S', A-$assign(S', \Pi)$ is A-$assign(l_1, \ldots, A$-$assign(l_n, \Pi) \ldots)$.

In the paper [GM05], has been formally proved that, for tight logic programs, the algorithm of CMODELS2 and SMODELS are equivalent: They explore search trees with the same branching nodes (considering the heuristics return the same atom). What it is interesting to say, is that in the mentioned paper the rules considered in Fig. 2 to extend the assignment S in function *simplify* are exactly the same used in SMODELS (procedure *expand*, see [Sim00] pagg. 17, 32-37).

3   Experimental Analysis

Due to the strong link between the solving procedures of state-of-the-art ASP solvers, the experimental results are independent from the chosen solver (at least on tight programs). We have used our solver, CMODELS2, also because

- its front-end is LPARSE [Sim00], a widely used grounder for logic programs;
- its back-end solver already incorporates lazy data structures for fast unit propagation as well as some state-of-the-art strategies and heuristics evaluated in the paper; and
- can be also run on non-tight programs.

There is no other publicly available AS system having the above features, and that we know of. SMODELS does not contain lazy data structures, and adding them to SMODELS would basically boil down to re-implement the entire solver.

The experimental results we present (at least the ones on tight programs) extend to ASSAT and SMODELS if enhanced with reasoning strategies corresponding to the ones that we considered.

The analysis is focused on tight logic programs, but we also run non-tight logic programs in order to understand (at least on the experimental side) if the results on the tight domain can be extended to the non-tight domain. We considered several domains of publicly available, currently challenges for ASP solvers, benchmarks for our investigation; in particular

- Randomly generated logic programs: The tight programs are (modular) translation from classical random 3SAT instances; the non-tight are randomly generated according to the methodology proposed in [LZ03].
- tight blocks-worlds, queens and 4-coloring problems[5]; tight bounded model checking (BMC) problems.[6]
- non-tight blocks-world problems and non-tight Hamiltonian Circuit on complete graphs.[7]

In the introduction, we already introduced the various strategies and heuristics used in the experimental evaluation. In more details

- "U" (unit-propagation), assigns repeatedly open literals in unit clauses until either (i) there are no more unit clauses, or (ii) a contradiction is found. It is based on two-literal watching, an efficient lazy data structure for propagate unit clauses [MMZ$^+$01];
- "F" (unit-propagation+failed-literal detection), failed-literal detection is applied if unit-propagation has not reached a contradiction. For each unassigned atom A, A is assigned to *True* and then unit-propagation is called again: If a contradiction is found (and A is said to be a *failed literal*), $\neg A$ can be safely assigned. Otherwise, $\neg A$ is checked. If both branches fail, backtracking occurs;

---

[5] Publicly available at http://www.tcs.hut.fi/Software/smodels/tests/.

[6] Available at http://www.tcs.hut.fi/~kepa/tools/boundsmodels/.

[7] Encoding due to Esra Erdem [Esr02] and Ilkka Niemela [Nie99] respectively.

- "B" (basic backtracking), performs chronological backtracking;
- "L" backtracking+backjumping+learning, when a contradiction is found, a clause (called *reason*) is created. The reason is a clause, unsatisfied under the current assignment, that contains only the literals "responsible" for the conflict. Instead of just backtrack chronologically, the atoms not in the reason are skipped until we encounter an atom in the reason that was chosen by the heuristic. Reasons are updated during backtracking via resolution with the clauses that caused the atoms to be assigned. The idea here is to avoid the visit of useless parts of the search tree. Learning adds,[8] under given conditions, some of the reasons in order to avoid the repetition of the same mistakes in other parts of the search tree. CMODELS2 implements 1-UIP learning [ZMMM01].

For the heuristics

- "S" (static), is based on the order induced by the appearance in the SAT formula: The first an atom is in the formula, the sooner is selected;
- "V" (VSIDS), is the acronym for Variable State Independent Decaying Sum. It is based on the information extracted from learning. Each literals has a weight associated with it. The weight is initialized with the occurrences of the literal in the formula and incremented if the literal appears in a learned clause. Periodically, the score is divided by a constant (2 in our case): The rational here is to take into closer consideration the atoms involved in recent conflicts;
- "U" (Unit), is based on the failed-literal detection technique. Given an unassigned atom A, while doing failed-literal on A we count the number $u(A)$ of unit-propagation caused, and then we select the atom with maximum $1024 \times u(A) \times u(\neg A) + u(A) + u(\neg A)$;
- "P" (Unit with pool), unit heuristic restricted to a subset of the unassigned atoms. It is similar to "U" except that (i) we first select a pool of 10 "most watched" atoms, and (ii) we perform failed-literal and score accordingly only with the atoms in the pool. Our simple pooling criteria is motivated by the fact that we are using a solver with lazy data structures. State of the art SAT solvers (e.g. SATZ) that implements failed-literal detection use much more sophisticated criteria. Because of this, results using the pool should be considered significant only if they are positive: Negative results could be biased by the simplicity of our criteria.

We will refer to the actual combination of search strategies and heuristics using an acronym where the first, second and third letter denote the look-ahead, look-back and heuristic respectively, used in the combination. For example, ulv is a standard look-back, "CHAFF"-like, solver similar to CMODELS2. fbu is a standard look-ahead solver. flv and flu have both a powerful look-ahead and look-back but different heuristic. All the tests were run on a Pentium IV PC,

---

[8] A policy to delete reasons when they became useless is also needed in order to maintain in polynomial space the procedure.

Table 1. Performances for uls, ubs, fls and fbs on tight programs. Problems (1-3), are randomly generated; (4-6) are blocks-world; (7-9) are queens; (10-14) are bounded model checking; (15-17) are 4-colorability.

	PB	# VAR	uls	ubs	fls	fbs
1	4	300	TIME	TIME	230.86	338.05
2	5.5	300	TIME	TIME	478.46	TIME
3	6	300	371.28	TIME	120.02	84.16
4	bw-large.d9	9956	0.9	2497.02	2.68	2.62
5	bw-large.e9	12260	1.11	1928.43	1.95	1.9
6	bw-large.e10	13482	1.61	TIME	5.28	19.52
7	queens21	925	0.20	0.23	0.36	0.38
8	queens24	1201	0.46	1.14	0.67	0.74
9	queens50	5101	3.67	TIME	12.41	TIME
10	dp-12.fsa-i-b9	1186	12.51	2651.28	20.30	TIME
11	key-2-i-b29	3199	157.29	TIME	111.61	293.37
12	mmgt-3.fsa-i-b10	1933	TIME	TIME	1570.27	3241.45
13	mmgt-4.fsa-s-b8	1586	1004.36	TIME	1054.06	TIME
14	q-1.fsa-i-b17	2201	165.07	TIME	301.16	TIME
15	p1000	14955	7.69	TIME	377.02	TIME
16	p3000	44961	178.26	TIME	TIME	TIME
17	p6000	89951	1275.62	TIME	TIME	TIME

with 2.8GHz processor, 1024MB RAM, running Linux. The timeout has been set to 600 seconds of CPU time for random problems, and 3600 for real-world problems.

We present results using CPU time (remember that we performed the experiments on a unique platform: Our results are not biased by implementation issues).

We have considered far more benchmarks for each category than the ones we show. In the Tables are only shown the bigger benchmarks we run for each category when significant (i.e., when at least one of the combinations in each table does not reach the time limit, denoted with TIME). In the Tables, the second column is the ratio between number of rules and number of atoms for random problems, and the name of the benchmarks for real-world problems. The third columns contain the number of atoms after grounding.

3.1 Tight Logic Programs

In Table 1 the results about the CMODELS2's versions with plain heuristic S on tight programs are shown. Randomly generated tight programs are modular translation of classical random 3SAT benchmarks with 300 atoms, 10 instances per point. Here we have not taken into account ratios 4.5 and 5 because all the medians are in timeout. For these problems (1-3), we immediately see that failed-literal is very effective, being much faster than the versions using only unit-

Table 2. Performances for ulv, flv, flu, fbu, ulp and ubp on tight programs. The problems presented are the same as in Table 1.

	PB	# VAR	ulv	flv	flu	fbu	ulp	ubp
18	4	300	0.41	0.52	0.85	0.66	21.79	3.01
19	4.5	300	TIME	TIME	81.92	22.53	TIME	54.7
20	5	300	448.21	485.36	8.27	4.72	452.75	14.35
21	bw-large.d9	9956	1.02	5.84	2.69	2.75	1.01	TIME
22	bw-large.e9	12260	0.98	1.91	1.92	1.93	1.03	1.54
23	bw-large.e10	13482	1.29	7.51	5.03	4.95	1.55	TIME
24	queens21	925	786.14	1864.49	384.87	47.33	0.24	0.24
25	queens24	1201	TIME	TIME	TIME	368.76	0.28	0.29
26	queens50	5101	TIME	TIME	TIME	TIME	347.98	43.16
27	dp-12.fsa-i-b9	1186	223.93	383.66	353.53	TIME	2910.96	1051.17
28	key-2-i-b29	3199	415.54	204.87	44.14	589.45	1329.53	TIME
29	mmgt-3.fsa-i-b10	1933	16.23	32.23	26.71	16.55	6.19	372.54
30	mmgt-4.fsa-s-b8	1586	17.02	27.59	421.30	327.55	13.79	2492.62
31	q-1.fsa-i-b17	2201	1539.96	505.15	259.05	816.26	TIME	TIME
32	p1000	14955	0.48	37.86	15.41	15.23	3.69	TIME
33	p3000	44961	8.86	369.27	144.12	142.83	223.62	TIME
34	p6000	89951	99.50	TIME	583.55	578.98	2549.50	TIME

propagation. fls is slightly better than fbs because, with a static heuristic, L can help to escape from unsatisfied portion of the search tree where the uninformed static heuristic could be trapped. These results are in according to those from the SAT community. Lines (4-17) show the results for real-world problems. From the comparison between the 4th and 5th columns, and the 6th and 7th columns, we can conclude that L is of fundamental importance on real-world problems, being often faster by orders of magnitude w.r.t. the same combination but using B. Also this result reflects what happens in the SAT community. The effects of adding failed-literal follow from the comparison between 4th and 6th, and 5th and 7th columns. When L is enabled, adding failed-literal does not help (except for two BMC problems) in improving the performances. This phenomenon was already partly encountered in the SAT community in [GMT03]. Otherwise, when using simple backtracking failed-literal helps in general in improving performances, avoiding (with a forward reasoning) the visit of useless parts of the search tree that otherwise (due to the absence of L) the solver would explore (the results are confirmed by some smaller experiments on 4-coloring problems not shown here).

In Table 2, there are the results on tight programs when using CMODELS2 with a non-static heuristic. For randomly generated logic programs (18-20), using a non-static heuristic in general helps for increasing the performances. It is also clear that using failed-literal in combination with a look-head based heuristic is the best choice. In particular fbu is the best, but flu and ubp are not far. Here, using L is not effective in conjunction with failed-literal: The positive effects it had with the static heuristic are shadowed by the unit-based heuristics. Even more, now it leads to negative results, with a huge difference when using heuristic "P". Rows (21-34) in Table 2 are results for tight real-world logic programs. The situation here is far less similar w.r.t. the SAT case. Indeed, combinations based on look-back (in particular ulv) perform quite well on a wide variety of benchmarks, but not as well as one would expect. In particular, the performances on the BMC instances (problems (27-31)) of ulv (resp. the version using failed-literal) are worse (resp. better) than expected: In SAT, BMC instances are the benchmarks where look-back solvers (resp. solvers with powerful look-ahead) give their best (resp. their worst). ulp is often very competitive with ulv. This is indeed explained if we look at the number of variables "# VAR" of these instances, which is in the order of a few thousands. Indeed, for such "# VAR" it still makes sense to perform an aggressive look-ahead at each branching node. On the other hand, as "# VAR" increases this is no longer the case, as the results on the 4 colorability instances (lines 32-34) show.

Summing up about the experimental analysis for tight programs

- on randomly generated logic programs, failed-literal is very effective, especially in conjunction with unit-based heuristics;
- on real-world logic programs, learning is usually very effective;
- on real-world logic programs of "medium" size, a combination of powerful look-ahead and powerful look-back like ulp is very competitive even if not the overall most effective alternative;
- on real-world logic programs of "large" size, e.g. with more than 15000 atoms, a look-back based solver like ulv becomes the most effective combination.

3.2   Non-Tight Logic Programs

Besides the analysis on tight logic programs, we also analyzed non-tight logic programs. The analysis is aimed at trying to understand if the results obtained on the tight domain can be extended to the non-tight domain (at least from the experimental point of view).

In Table 3 and 4 the results for non-tight logic programs using plain heuristic "s" and non-static heuristics respectively. Problems (35-37) and (44-46) are randomly generated logic programs with 300 atoms, 10 instances per point. The instances were generated using the method proposed in [LZ03]. The ratios from 3.5 to 7 have not been shown in Table 3 because all the medians are in time-out. Lines (38-43) and (47-52) contain the results for blocks-world and complete graphs problems.

Summing up, on the non-tight domain

- results obtained in the tight domain extend to the non-tight for CMODELS2; but
- it can be the case that results on non-tight benchmarks do not extend to other solvers

Table 3. Performances for uls, ubs, fls and fbs on non-tight programs. Problems (35-37), are randomly generated; (38-40) are blocks-world; (41-43) are Hamiltonian Circuit on complete graphs.

	PB	# VAR	uls	ubs	fls	fbs
35	3	300	9.75	31.63	4.69	4.4
36	7.5	300	TIME	TIME	TIME	567.78
37	8	300	544.83	TIME	199.05	178.98
38	bw-basic-P4-i	5301	2.08	43.19	4.07	6.91
39	bw-basic-P4-i-1	4760	1.73	15.55	2.54	2.57
40	bw-basic-P4-i+1	5842	2.29	47.09	5.04	8.17
41	np60c	10742	6.8	TIME	125.83	TIME
42	np70c	14632	12.34	TIME	326.34	TIME
43	np80c	19122	19.89	TIME	745.26	TIME

Table 4. Performances for ulv, flv, flu, fbu, ulp and ubp on non-tight programs. The problems presented are the same as in Table 3.

	PB	# VAR	ulv	flv	flu	fbu	ulp	ubp
44	4	300	265.43	218.48	41.97	31.05	77.41	123.31
45	5	300	TIME	TIME	136.67	99.75	439.71	323.15
46	6	300	TIME	TIME	107.34	65.83	591.3	337.45
47	bw-basic-P4-i	5301	2.16	15.54	6.07	5.79	2.54	79.64
48	bw-basic-P4-i-1	4760	1.64	4.92	2.47	2.44	1.86	13.44
49	bw-basic-P4-i+1	5842	2.49	24.27	22.01	19.71	2.41	11.60
50	np60c	10742	2.83	1611.32	44.12	44.12	4.77	597.82
51	np70c	14632	4.69	TIME	97.44	97.89	5.91	TIME
52	np80c	19122	6.91	TIME	192.29	196.32	12.88	TIME

4   Conclusions

In this paper, motivated by the strong existing link between ASP and SAT, we have investigated several search strategies, heuristics and their combinations that have been shown to be effective for SAT, in ASP systems. Our results have shown that on randomly generated problems look-ahead solvers dominate, like in SAT, while on logic programs arising from real-world applications, despite the strong link, a combination of powerful look-ahead and look-back is currently what dominate in ASP systems.

Given the relatively low number of variables in most currently challenging instances in ASP, we believe that if the goal is to develop a general purpose ASP solver, an ulp-based solver is, at the moment, the way to go. We have also shed light on future development: As soon as the number of variables in the challenges benchmarks will increase, for real-world problems we expect that ulv-based solvers, leaders in the SAT community, become leaders also in ASP.

Finally, we believe that this paper is a major step in the direction of closing the gap between ASP and SAT.

References

[BS97]   Roberto J. Bayardo, Jr. and Robert C. Schrag. Using CSP look-back techniques to solve real-world SAT instances. In *Proceedings of AAAI-97*, pages 203–208, Menlo Park, July 27–31 1997. AAAI Press.

[Cla78]   Keith Clark. Negation as failure. In Herve Gallaire and Jack Minker, editors, *Logic and Data Bases*, pages 293–322. Plenum Press, 1978.

[DLL62]   M. Davis, G. Logemann, and D. Loveland. A machine program for theorem proving. *Journal of the ACM*, 5(7), 1962.

[Esr02]   Erdem Esra. *Theory and applications of answer set programming*. PhD thesis, University of Texas at Austin, 2002. PhD thesis.

[Fag94]   François Fages. Consistency of Clark's completion and existence of stable models. *Journal of Methods of Logic in Computer Science*, 1:51–60, 1994.

[FLP01]   W. Faber, N. Lcone, and G. Pfeifer. Experimenting with heuristics for asp. In *Proc. IJCAI*, 2001.

[Fre95]   Jon W. Freeman. *Improvements to propositional satisfiability search algorithms*. PhD thesis, University of Pennsylvania, 1995.

[GL88]   Michael Gelfond and Vladimir Lifschitz. The stable model semantics for logic programming. In Robert Kowalski and Kenneth Bowen, editors, *Logic Programming: Proc. Fifth Int'l Conf. and Symp.*, pages 1070–1080, 1988.

[GM05]   E. Giunchiglia and M. Maratea. On the relation between sat and asp procedures. Submitted to AAAI 2005, 2005.

[GML04]   E. Giunchiglia, M. Maratea, and Y. Lierler. SAT-based answer set programming. In *American Association for Artificial Intelligence*, 2004.

[GMT03]   E. Giunchiglia, M. Maratea, and A. Tacchella. (In)Effectiveness of lookahead techniques in a modern SAT solver. In *9th International Conference on Principles and Practice of Constraint Programming (CP-03)*, pages 842–846, 2003.

[LA97]   Chu Min Li and Anbulagan. Heuristics based on unit propagation for satisfiability problems. In *Proceedings of the 15th International Joint Conference on Artificial Intelligence (IJCAI-97)*, pages 366–371, San Francisco, August 23–29 1997. Morgan Kaufmann Publishers.

[LS05]   D. LeBerre and L. Simon. Fifty-five solvers in vancouver: The sat 2004 competition. In *8th International Conference on Theory an Applications of Satisfiability Testing. Selected Revised Papers.*, Lecture Notes in Computer Science. Springer Verlag, 2005. To appear.

[LZ03]   F. Lin and Y. Zhao. Asp phase transition: A study on randomly generated programs. In *Proc. ICLP-03*, 2003.

[MMZ+01]   Matthew W. Moskewicz, Conor F. Madigan, Ying Zhao, Lintao Zhang, and Sharad Malik. Chaff: Engineering an Efficient SAT Solver. In *Proceedings of the 38th Design Automation Conference (DAC'01)*, June 2001.

[MT99]   Victor Marek and Miroslaw Truszczynski. Stable models as an alternative programming paradigm. In *The Logic Programming Paradigm: a 25.Years perspective*, Lecture Notes in Computer Science. Springer Verlag, 1999.

[Nie99]   I. Niemelä. Logic programs with stable model semantics as a constraint programming paradigm. *Annals of Mathematics and Artificial Intelligence*, 25:241–273, 1999.

[Pro93]   Patrick Prosser. Hybrid algorithms for the constraint satisfaction problem. *Computational Intelligence*, 9(3):268–299, 1993.

[Sim00]   Patrick Simons. *Extending and implementing the stable model semantics.* PhD thesis, Helsinky University, 2000. PhD thesis.

[SS96]   João P. Marques Silva and Karem A. Sakallah. GRASP - a new search algorithm for satisfiability. Technical report, University of Michigan, 1996.

[ZMMM01]   L. Zhang, C. F. Madigan, M. H. Moskewicz, and S. Malik. Efficient conflict driven learning in a boolean satisfiability solver. In *ICCAD*, 2001.

The $\mathcal{S}$CIFF Abductive Proof-Procedure

Marco Alberti[1], Marco Gavanelli[1], Evelina Lamma[1],
Paola Mello[2], and Paolo Torroni[2]

[1] ENDIF, Università di Ferrara
{m alberti,m gavanelli,elam ma}@ing.unife.it
[2] DEIS, Università di Bologna
{pm ello,p torroni}@deis.unibo.it

Abstract. We propose an operational framework which builds on the classical understanding of abductive reasoning in logic programming, and extends it in several directions. The new features include the ability to reason with a dynamic knowledge base, where new facts can be added anytime, the ability to generate expectations about such new facts occurring in the future (forecasting), and the process of confirmation/disconfirmation of such expectations.

1 Introduction

Often, automated reasoning paradigms in AI mimic human reasoning, providing a formalisation of the human basic inferences. Abductive Logic Programming (ALP) is one such paradigm, and it can be seen as a formalisation of abductive reasoning and hypotheses making. Hypotheses make up for lack of information, and they can be put forward to support the explanation of some observation. For instance, an explanation could assume that some unknown events have happened, or that some not directly measurable conditions hold.

Borrowing an example from the medical domain, we can think of observations as symptoms, of conditions as diseases, which are not directly measurable, and of unknown events as the subject of questions that a doctor may ask to a patient, or as new symptoms that may occur in the future.

ALP [1] is an extension of logic programming, in which the knowledge base may contain special atoms that can be *assumed* to be true, even if they are not defined, or cannot be proven. These atoms are called *abducibles*. Starting from a goal G, an abductive derivation tries to verify G, by using deductive inference steps as in logic programming, but also by possibly assuming that some abducibles are true. In order to have this process converging to a meaningful explanation, an abductive theory normally comes together with a set of *integrity constraints IC*, and it is required that hypotheses be consistent with *IC*. In its classical understanding, an abductive logic program is defined as a triple, $\langle P, IC, \mathcal{A} \rangle$, where the set $\mathcal{A}$ specifies which atoms are abducibles.

In this way, classical ALP formalises and in some cases operationalises hypothetical reasoning, through a number of proof-procedures [2,3,4,5,6,7,8]. The distinction that is always made is a dichotomy, between facts, *known* to be true

S. Bandini and S. Manzoni (Eds.): AI*IA 2005, LNAI 3673, pp. 135–147, 2005.

or false, defined within a static theory, and *potentially true*, abducible atoms, which are not necessarily verified but only hypothesised.

But in a broader understanding, information is not static, and hypothetical reasoning is not only about making hypotheses. As in the previous example, it includes *adapting* the assumptions made to upcoming events, such as new symptoms occurring, or new clinical evidence becoming available, and *foreseeing* the occurrence of new events, which may or may not occur indeed, such as a potential course of illness.

In order to support hypothetical reasoning about events, we extend the concepts of abduction and abductive proof procedure. We distinguish between two classes of abducibles: *hypotheses*, as classically understood in abductive reasoning, and *expectations* about events, which can be (dis)confirmed as new facts (called *events*) become known. With this aim, we cater for the dynamic detection of such facts, which may indeed impact on the abductive reasoning process, by generating new expectations or modifying the current hypotheses. Therefore, we propose a new abductive framework, where hypothesis making and reasoning with expectations and upcoming events are seamlessly integrated with each other. We propose a language, able to state required properties of the events supporting the hypotheses and their combination with hypotheses and expectations. Expectations are also modelled as abducible literals, like hypotheses, and they can be "positive" (to be confirmed by certain events occurring), or "negative" (to be confirmed by certain events not occurring). Note that we do not blur the concept of abduced literal and event: in our framework the declarative knowledge does not express explicit changes to the history. Our aim is a *reasoning system*, which, of course, does not generate events, but takes events as facts that must be accepted as they are, and explained. A pure reasoning system can only generate expectations about events, that are indeed of a different nature with respect to actual events. Events are generated in the external world, and the abductive system just checks that the history is consistent with expectations.

Drawing inspiration from the IFF proof procedure [5], we use integrity constraints written in our new extended language to generate both hypotheses and expectations. We define a declarative semantics, and a proof-procedure, called $\mathcal{S}$CIFF, of which we can prove a soundness result under reasonable assumptions. Moreover, we introduce *variables* and *constraints* on variables occurring in hypotheses and expectations. Our proof-procedure extends the IFF by using a constraint solver, by being able to reason upon dynamically upcoming events and to generate positive and negative expectations besides making hypotheses, and by implementing the concepts of confirmation and disconfirmation of expectations. We are able to generate expectations with constraints, which can be used, for example, to reason about deadlines, by imposing a constraint over a variable which represents time. We are also able to express and handle expectations involving universal quantification: this is typically more useful with negative expectations ("The patient is expected *not* to show symptom Q *at all times*"), where the variable representing the time is universally quantified.

Such an expressive kind of quantification is, to the best of our knowledge, to be hardly found in most existing operational abductive frameworks. The $\mathcal{S}$CIFF proof-procedure has been implemented in Constraint Handling Rules [9] and integrated in a Java-based system for hypothetical reasoning [10].

In next section we introduce our framework's knowledge representation. We then proceed to Sect. 3 and 4, which provide its declarative and operational semantics, and a soundness result. Before concluding, we discuss related work in Sect. 5. Additional details about the syntax of the $\mathcal{S}$CIFF language and allowedness criteria for proving soundness are in [11].

2   Knowledge Representation

The $\mathcal{S}$CIFF abstract framework is strongly related to classical abductive frameworks, but it takes the dynamic happening of events into account, so supporting a more dynamic style of hypothetical reasoning. We first recall the classical definition of ALP, then we extend it for the dynamic case.

An Abductive Logic Program [1] is a tuple $\langle KB, IC, \mathcal{A} \rangle$ where KB is a logic program, (i.e., a set of clauses), $\mathcal{A}$ is a set of predicates that are not defined in KB and that are called *abducibles*, IC is a set of formulae called *Integrity Constraints*. An abductive explanation for a goal G is a set $\Delta \subseteq \mathcal{A}$ such that $KB \cup \Delta \models G$ and $KB \cup \Delta \models IC$, for some notion of entailment $\models$.

We extend the concept of ALP to get more dynamics. New events may dynamically arrive and are encoded into atoms $\mathbf{H}(D[, T])$ where D is a ground term representing the event and T is an integer representing the time at which the event happened. Such events are recorded in a history $\mathbf{HAP}$ (a set containing $\mathbf{H}$ atoms) that defines a predicate $\mathbf{H}$. The history dynamically grows during the computation, as new events happen. We do not model the source of events, but it can be imagined as a queue of received events that arrive in the same temporal order in which they happen. Our system does not *generate* events, but only accepts them as input. A Dynamic Abductive Logic Program (DALP) is a sequence of ALPs, each grounded on a given history. Formally, it can be considered as a function $DALP : 2^{\mathcal{H}|_{\mathbf{H}}} \mapsto ALP$ (where with $\mathcal{H}|_{\mathbf{H}}$ we mean the Herbrand universe restricted to predicate $\mathbf{H}$) that given a set $\mathbf{HAP} \subseteq \mathcal{H}|_{\mathbf{H}}$ provides the ALP: $\langle KB \cup \mathbf{HAP}, IC, \mathcal{A} \rangle$. We write $DALP_{\mathbf{HAP}}$ to indicate the abductive logic program obtained by grounding the DALP with the history $\mathbf{HAP}$.

An instance $DALP_{\mathbf{HAP}}$ of this framework is queried with a *goal* G. The goal may contain both predicates defined in KB and abducibles. The abductive computation produces a set Δ of hypotheses, which is partitioned in a set ΔA of general hypotheses and a set $\mathbf{EXP}$ of *expectations*. Expectations represent events that are expected to (but might not) happen (*positive* expectations, of the form $\mathbf{E}(D[, T])$) and events that are expected *not* to (but might) happen (*negative* expectations, of the form $\mathbf{EN}(D[, T])$). Typically, expectations will contain variables, over which CLP [12] constraints can be imposed. Variables in $\mathbf{E}$ expectations will be existentially quantified, while in $\mathbf{EN}$ will be universally (if they do not appear elsewhere), accordingly with the default negation implicit in **EN**. Explicit negation can be applied to expectations[1], coherently with the idea that there could be positive/negative expectations about the happening of an event, or no expectation at all about that event.

Constraints on universally quantified variables are considered as *quantifier restrictions* [13]. For instance, $\mathbf{EN}(p(X))$, $X > 0$ has the semantics $\forall_{X>0}\,\mathbf{EN}(p(X))$. To the best of our knowledge, this is the first abductive proof-procedure with such an expressivity.

For the full syntax of the language, the reader can refer to previous publications [14,11]. We conclude this section with a simple example in the medical domain, where abduction is used to diagnose diseases starting from symptom observation. The aim of this example is to show the main improvements of the $\mathcal{S}$CIFF from previous work: the dynamic detection of new facts, the confirmation of hypotheses by events, and the possible universal quantification of variables. Of course, this is only an example; a real expert system would need to take into account probabilities or preferences.

Example 1. The following KB expresses that a symptom s can be explained by one of three diseases. Each of the clauses in the KB defines a possible explanation.

$symptom(s, T_1) \leftarrow \mathbf{disease}(d_1, T_1) \wedge not\ \mathbf{disease}(d_3, T_1)$
$\quad \wedge \mathbf{EN}(temperature(T), T_1) \wedge T < 37.$
$symptom(s, T_1) \leftarrow \mathbf{disease}(d_2, T_1) \wedge \mathbf{E}(red\_spots, T_2) \wedge T_1 < T_2 \leq T_1 + 4.$
$symptom(s, T_1) \leftarrow \mathbf{disease}(d_3, T_1) \wedge \mathbf{E}(exam(r, +), T_1).$

The first clause explains the symptom with the first desease ($\mathbf{disease}(d_1, T_1)$) if the patient does not also have the third disease (*not* $\mathbf{disease}(d_3, T_1)$), and in this case the patient cannot have a temperature less than 37 Celsius degrees ($\mathbf{EN}(temperature(T), T_1) \wedge T < 37$; note that the T variable's quantification is universal and restricted by $T < 37$, which expresses the negative expectations over *all* the temperatures lesser than 37). The symptom s can also be explained by disease d_2 ($\mathbf{disease}(d_2, T_1)$), and in this case red spots are supposed to appear on the patient's skin within 4 days ($\mathbf{E}(red\_spots, T_2) \wedge T_1 < T_2 \leq T_1 + 4$; T_2's quantification is existential, and the constraints on it are used to impose the deadline). Finally, disease d_3 can explain s ($\mathbf{disease}(d_3, T_1)$) provided that an exam r gives a positive result ($\mathbf{E}(exam(r, +), T_1)$).

We have two types of abducibles: classical ones (**disease** in the example) and *expectations* that will corroborate the explanations provided that they match with actual events. Notice the twofold use of expectations: both in the second and third clause, the expectation defines a further event that can support the diagnosis. But while $\mathbf{E}(red\_spots, T_2)$ simply defines the expected course of illness (in order for the diagnosis to be corroborated), $\mathbf{E}(exam(r, +), T_1)$ can also be intended as a *suggestion* to the physician for a further exam to be done, or as a *request* of further information.

---

[1] For each abducible predicate $A \in \{\mathbf{E}, \mathbf{EN}\}$, we have also the abducible $\neg A$ for the negation of A together with the integrity constraint $(\forall X)\neg A(X), A(X) \rightarrow false$.

The combinations of abducible literals can be refined by means of ICs. In our language, they are implications that can involve literals defined in the KB, abducible literals (in particular, expectations in **EXP**), and events in **HAP**. For example, an IC could state that if the result of some exam r is positive, then we can hypothesise that the patient is not affected by disease d_1:

$$\mathbf{H}(exam(r, +), T_1) \rightarrow not \ \mathbf{disease}(d_1, T_1) \tag{1}$$

Let us see how the dynamic occurrence of new events can drive the generation and selection of abductive explanations.

If the query is $symptom(s, 1)$, there can be three alternative explanations (i.e., sets of abducibles): $\{\mathbf{disease}(d_1, 1), \ \forall_{T>37} \ \mathbf{EN}(temperature(T), 1)\}$, $\{\mathbf{disease}(d_2, 1), \exists_{1 < T_2 \leq 5} \mathbf{E}(red\_spots, T_2)\}$, and $\{\mathbf{disease}(d_3, 1), \mathbf{E}(exam(r, +), 1)\}$. If the event $\mathbf{H}(temperature(36), 1)$ happens, the first set contains a disconfirmed expectation: $\forall_{T>37} \ \mathbf{EN}(temperature(T), 1)$, so it can be ruled out. If, within the deadline $T_2 \leq 5$, the event red_spots does not happen, the second set is excluded as well, and only the third remains acceptable.

Notice the difference between **EN** and $\neg\mathbf{E}$ (both in our syntax):

$$\mathbf{H}(coma) \rightarrow \neg\mathbf{E}(wake)$$

If the patient is in coma, assuming he will wake up is not realistic. It can happen, indeed, but we should not rely on this assumption for further diagnosis. The IC

$$\mathbf{H}(coma) \rightarrow \mathbf{EN}(wake)$$

instead, would express the (pessimistic) viewpoint that he will never wake up.

Finally, integrity constraints could suggest, through expectations, possible cures, and even warn about the consequences of not taking the prescribed drugs:

$$\mathbf{disease}(d_3, T_1) \rightarrow \mathbf{E}(aspirin, T_1)$$
$$\vee \mathbf{E}(temperature(T), T_2) \wedge T > 40 \wedge T_2 < T_1 + 2.$$

3   Declarative Semantics

We give now the abductive semantics for $DALP_{\mathbf{HAP}}$, depending on the events in the history **HAP**. Throughout this section, as usual when defining declarative semantics, we always consider the ground version of the knowledge base and integrity constraints, and consider CLP-like constraints as defined predicates.

Since an instance $DALP_{\mathbf{HAP}}$ is an abductive logic program, an abductive explanation should entail the goal and satisfy the integrity constraints:

$$Comp(KB \cup \Delta A \cup \mathbf{EXP} \cup \mathbf{HAP}) \models G \tag{2}$$
$$Comp(KB \cup \Delta A \cup \mathbf{EXP} \cup \mathbf{HAP}) \models IC \tag{3}$$

where, as in the IFF proof procedure, we use three-valued completion.

Among the sets of expectations of an instance $DALP_{\mathbf{HAP}}$, we select the ones that are consistent with respect to expectations (i.e., we do not want the same event to be both expected to happen and expected not to happen); moreover, we require the set of expectations to be *confirmed*:

Definition 1. *A set* **EXP** *is* E-consistent *iff for each (ground) term p:*

$$\{\mathbf{E}(p), \mathbf{EN}(p)\} \not\subseteq \mathbf{EXP}. \tag{4}$$

Given a history **HAP**, *a set of expectations* **EXP** *is* confirmed *if and only if for each (ground) term p:*

$$Comp(\mathbf{HAP} \cup \mathbf{EXP}) \cup \{\mathbf{E}(p) \rightarrow \mathbf{H}(p)\} \cup \{\mathbf{EN}(p) \rightarrow \neg\mathbf{H}(p)\} \not\models false, \tag{5}$$

We write $DALP_{\mathbf{HAP}} \models_{\Delta A \cup \mathbf{EXP}} G$ if equations (2-5) hold.

4   Operational Semantics

The $\mathcal{S}$CIFF syntax extends that of the IFF. Quite naturally, our operational semantics also extends that of the IFF. Beside the need for interpreting a richer language, the needed additional features are: (*i*) detect new events as they happen, (*ii*) produce a (disjunction of) set of expectations, (*iii*) detect confirmation of expectations, (*iv*) detect disconfirmation as soon as possible. Following Fung and Kowalski's approach, we describe $\mathcal{S}$CIFF as a transition system. Due to space limitations, we will focus on the new transitions.

4.1   Data Structures

Each state of the $\mathcal{S}$CIFF proof-procedure is defined by a tuple

$$T \equiv \langle R, CS, PSIC, \Delta A, \Delta \mathbf{P}, \mathbf{HAP}, \Delta \mathbf{C}, \Delta \mathbf{D} \rangle$$

we partition the set of expectations **EXP** into the confirmed ($\Delta\mathbf{C}$), disconfirmed ($\Delta\mathbf{D}$), and pending ($\Delta\mathbf{P}$) expectations. The other elements are: the resolvent (R), the set of abduced literals that are not expectations (ΔA), the constraint store (CS), a set of implications, inherited from the IFF, that we call *partially solved integrity constraints* ($PSIC$), and the history of happened events (**HAP**).

Variable Quantification. In the IFF proof procedure, all variables occurring in the resolvent or in abduced literals are existentially quantified, while the others (appearing only in "$\rightarrow$" implications) are universally quantified. $\mathcal{S}$CIFF has to deal with universally quantified variables in the abducibles and in the resolvent.

For this reason, in the operational semantics we leave the variable quantification explicit. The scope of the variables that occur only in an implication is the implication itself; the scope of the other variables is the whole tuple T.

Initial Node and Success. A derivation D is a sequence of nodes $T_0 \rightarrow T_1 \rightarrow \ldots \rightarrow T_n$. Given a goal G, an initial history **HAP**^{i} (which can be empty) and a set of integrity constraints IC, the first node is:

$$T_0 \equiv \langle \{G\}, \emptyset, IC, \emptyset, \emptyset, \mathbf{HAP}^i, \emptyset, \emptyset \rangle \tag{6}$$

i.e., the resolvent is initially the query ($R_0 = \{G\}$) and the set $PSIC$ contains the integrity constraints ($PSIC_0 = IC$).

The other nodes $T_j, j > 0$, are obtained by applying the transitions defined in the next section, until no transition can be applied anymore (quiescence).

Definition 2. *Starting with an instance $DALP_{\mathbf{HAP}^i}$ there exists a successful derivation for a goal G iff the proof tree with root node of Eq. (6) has at least one leaf node $\langle \emptyset, CS, PSIC, \Delta A, \Delta \mathbf{P}, \mathbf{HAP}^f, \Delta C, \emptyset \rangle$ where CS is consistent (i.e., there exists a ground variable assignment such that all the constraints are satisfied). In that case, we write: $DALP_{\mathbf{HAP}^i} \hspace{-0.3em}\mid\hspace{-0.9em}\sim^{\mathbf{HAP}^f}_{\Delta A \cup \Delta \mathbf{P} \cup \Delta \mathbf{C}} G$*

Notice that, coherently with the declarative semantics, a success node cannot contain disconfirmed hypotheses ($\Delta \mathbf{D} = \emptyset$). However, in some applications, all the alternative sets may contain disconfirmed expectations and the goal could be finding a set of expectations with a minimal set of disconfirmed ones. We map explicitly the set $\Delta \mathbf{D}$, instead of generating a simple *fail* node, paving the way for future extensions. Answers can be extracted in a very similar way to the IFF.

Definition 3. *Let N be a non-failure node, Δ_N the set of abduced atoms in N. Let σ' be a substitution replacing all variables not universally quantified by ground terms, and such that σ' satisfies all the constraints in CS_N. Let $\sigma = \sigma'|_{vars(G)}$ be the restriction of σ' to the variables occurring in the initial goal G. Let $D = [\Delta_N]\sigma'$. The pair (D, σ) is the* abductive answer *obtained from N.*

Consistency. Besides the usual IC of explicit negation, we require consistency of expectations, i.e., we add $\mathbf{E}(T) \wedge \mathbf{EN}(T) \to false$.

4.2 Transitions

The transitions are those of the IFF proof procedure, enlarged with those of CLP [12], and with specific transitions accommodating the concepts of confirmation of hypotheses, and dynamically growing history. A complete description of all the transitions is given in [11], and is not given here due to space limitations.

IFF-Like Transitions. We borrow the transitions of the IFF, given shortly as:

Unfolding[1]. $p(s) \Rightarrow (s = t_1 \wedge B_1) \vee \ldots \vee (s = t_j \wedge B_j)$
Unfolding[2]. $[p(s) \wedge B \to H] \Rightarrow [s = t_1 \wedge B_1 \wedge B \to H], \ldots, [s = t_j \wedge B_1 \wedge B \to H]$
Propagation. $[\mathbf{a}(s) \wedge B \to H] \wedge \mathbf{a}(t) \wedge R \Rightarrow [s = t \wedge B \to H] \wedge \mathbf{a}(t) \wedge R$
Case analysis. $[c \wedge B \to H] \Rightarrow c \wedge [B \to H] \vee \neg c$
Equality rewriting. integrated in the CLP solver
Logical equivalence. $true \to L \Rightarrow L, L \wedge false \Rightarrow false, L \wedge true \Rightarrow L, \ldots$

where $\mathbf{a}$ is an abducible literal in $\Delta A_k \cup \mathbf{EXP}_k$, p is a predicate defined by clauses $p(t_1) \leftarrow B_1, \ldots, p(t_j) \leftarrow B_j$, and c is a constraint.

IFF transitions have been extended for dealing with CLP constraints (unification, in particular, is dealt with by the constraint solver), and for dealing with universally quantified variables in the abducibles, by duplicating atoms with universally quantified variables before *propagation*.

Dynamically Growing History. The happening of events is dealt with by a transition *Happening*, that takes an event $\mathbf{H}(Event)$ from the external queue and puts it in the history $\mathbf{HAP}$. Transition *Happening* is applicable only if an *Event* such that $\mathbf{H}(Event) \notin \mathbf{HAP}$ is in the external queue.

Formally, from a node N_k transition *Happening* produces a single successor $\mathbf{HAP}_{k+1} = \mathbf{HAP}_k \cup \{\mathbf{H}(Event)\}$.

Confirmation and Disconfirmation.

Disconfirmation $\mathbf{EN}$. Given a node N such that:

$$\Delta\mathbf{P}_k = \Delta\mathbf{P}' \cup \{\mathbf{EN}(E_1)\}, \ \ \mathbf{HAP}_k = \mathbf{HAP}' \cup \{\mathbf{H}(E_2)\}$$

Disconfirmation $\mathbf{EN}$ produces two nodes N^1 and N^2:

N^1	N^2
$\Delta\mathbf{P}^1_{k+1} = \Delta\mathbf{P}'$	$\Delta\mathbf{P}^2_{k+1} = \Delta\mathbf{P}_k$
$\Delta\mathbf{D}^1_{k+1} = \Delta\mathbf{D}_k \cup \{\mathbf{EN}(E_1)\}$	$\Delta\mathbf{D}^2_{k+1} = \Delta\mathbf{D}_k$
$CS^1_{k+1} = CS_k \cup \{E_1 = E_2\}$	$CS^2_{k+1} = CS_k \cup \{E_1 \neq E_2\}$

Remember that N^1 is a failure node, as in success nodes $\Delta\mathbf{D} = \emptyset$ (see Sect. 3). In Example 1, the disconfirmation of the expectation $\mathbf{EN}(temperature(T), T_1)$ made unacceptable the first diagnosis.

Example 2. Suppose that $\mathbf{HAP}_k = \{\mathbf{H}(p(1,2))\}, \exists X \forall Y \, \Delta\mathbf{P}_k = \{\mathbf{EN}(p(X,Y))\}$. Disconfirmation $\mathbf{EN}$ will produce the two following nodes:
$\exists X \forall Y \, \Delta\mathbf{P}_k = \{\mathbf{EN}(p(X,Y))\} \ \mathbf{HAP}_k = \{\mathbf{H}(p(1,2))\}$

$CS^1_{k+1} = \{X = 1 \wedge Y = 2\} \ \ CS^2_{k+1} = \{X \neq 1 \vee Y \neq 2\}$
$\Delta\mathbf{D}^1_{k+1} = \{\mathbf{EN}(p(1,2))\}$
$\qquad\qquad\qquad\qquad CS_{k+2} = \{X \neq 1\}$

where the last simplification in the right branch is due to the rules of the constraint solver (see Section CLP and [11]).

Confirmation $\mathbf{E}$ is applicable to a node N as follows:

$$\Delta\mathbf{P}_k = \Delta\mathbf{P}' \cup \{\mathbf{E}(E_1)\}, \ \ \mathbf{HAP}_k = \mathbf{HAP}' \cup \{\mathbf{H}(E_2)\}$$

and generates two nodes, N^1 and N^2; in node N^1 we assume that the expectation and the happened event unify, and in N^2 we hypothesise the opposite:

N^1	N^2
$\Delta\mathbf{P}^1_{k+1} = \Delta\mathbf{P}'$	$\Delta\mathbf{P}^2_{k+1} = \Delta\mathbf{P}_k$
$\Delta\mathbf{C}^1_{k+1} = \Delta\mathbf{C}_k \cup \{\mathbf{E}(E_1)\}$	$\Delta\mathbf{C}^2_{k+1} = \Delta\mathbf{C}_k$
$CS^1_{k+1} = CS_k \cup \{E_1 = E_2\}$	$CS^2_{k+1} = CS_k \cup \{E_1 \neq E_2\}$

N^2 is not a failure node, as $\mathbf{E}(E_1)$ might be confirmed by other events.

Disconfirmation of **E** expectations can be proved only if no event will ever match with the expected one. We assume that the events arrive in temporal order, and infer the current time from happened event; i.e., the current time cannot be less than the time of any happened event. In this way, we can state that an expectation for which the deadline is passed, is disconfirmed. Given a node:

1. $\Delta \mathbf{P}_k = \{\mathbf{E}(X, T)\} \cup \Delta \mathbf{P}'$
2. $\mathbf{HAP}_k = \{\mathbf{H}(Y, T_c)\} \cup \mathbf{HAP}'$
3. $\forall E_2, T_2 : \mathbf{H}(E_2, T_2) \in \mathbf{HAP}_k, CS_k \cup \{(E_2, T_2) = (X, T)\} \models false$
4. $CS_k \models T < T_c$

transition Disconfirmation **E** is applicable and creates a node

$$\Delta \mathbf{P}_{k+1} = \Delta \mathbf{P}', \Delta \mathbf{D}_{k+1} = \Delta \mathbf{D}_k \cup \{\mathbf{E}(X, T)\}.$$

Operationally, one can avoid checking condition 3 (i.e., (X, T) does not unify with every event in the history) by choosing a preferred order of application of the transitions. By applying Disconfirmation **E** only if no other transition is applicable, the check can be safely avoided, as the test of confirmation is already performed by *Confirmation* **E**.

Symmetrically to Disconfirmation **E**, we also have transition *Confirmation* **EN**, not reported for lack of space.

Note that the entailment of constraints from a constraint store is, in general, not easy to verify. However, in the particular case of condition 4, the check is not computationally expensive, and also makes $SCIFF$ able to benefit from the power of modern constraint solvers. In fact, the constraint $T < T_c$ is unary (T_c is ground), thus a CLP(FD) solver can verify very easily the entailment if the propagation is complete[2]: it is enough to check the maximum value in the domain of T. Also, even if the solver is not complete, the transition will not compromise the soundness/completeness of the proof procedure, but will only influence efficiency. If the solver performs powerful propagation (including pruning, in CLP(FD)), the disconfirmation will be early detected, otherwise, it will be detected later on.

CLP. We adopt the same transitions as in CLP [12]. We adopt a constraint solver on Finite Domains; moreover we delegate to the solver unification and disunification of terms: we assume that the symbols $=$ and $\neq$ are in the constraint language and we need further inference rules for coping with unification [11].

The CLP(FD) solver has been extended for dealing with universally quantified variables (considered as *quantifier restrictions* [13]). For instance, given two expectations $\forall_{X<10}\mathbf{EN}(p(X))$ and $\exists_{Y>5}\mathbf{E}(p(Y))$, the solver is able to infer $\exists_{Y \geq 10}\mathbf{E}(p(Y))$. To our knowledge, $SCIFF$ is the only proof-procedure able to abduce atoms containing universally quantified variables; moreover, it also handles constraints *à la* CLP on universally quantified variables.

---

[2] The solver is complete in various practical instances: if the constraints are all unary, or if the constraint language only contains the relational operators $<, >, =, \leq, \geq$.

4.3 Soundness

We relate the operational notion of successful derivation with the corresponding declarative notion of goal provability.

Theorem 1. *Given* $DALP_{\mathbf{HAP}^i}$ *and a ground goal* G, *if* $DALP_{\mathbf{HAP}^i} \vdash_{\Delta}^{\mathbf{HAP}} G$ *then* $ALP_{\mathbf{HAP}} \vDash_{\Delta} G$.

The proof of soundness is given for *allowed* DALPs (for a definition of allowedness see [11]). The proof is based on a correspondence drawn between SCIFF and IFF transitions, and exploits the soundness results of the IFF.

5 Related Work

Many abductive proof procedures have been proposed in the past; the reader can refer to the exhaustive survey by Kakas *et al.* [1]. This work is mostly related to the IFF [5], which it extends in several directions, as explained in the paper.

Other proof procedures deal with constraints; in particular ACLP [6] and the $\mathcal{A}$-system [7] deeply focus on efficiency issues. Both use integrity constraints in the form of denials, instead of forward rules, and both only abduce existentially quantified atoms, which makes the SCIFF in this sense more expressive.

The integration of the IFF with constraints has been explored, both theoretically [15], and in an implementation [16]. These works, however, do not deal with confirmation of hypotheses and universally quantified variables in abducibles.

Sergot [17] proposed a framework, *query-the-user*, in which some of the predicates are labelled as "askable"; the truth of askable atoms can be asked to the user. Our **E** predicates may be seen as asking information, while **H** atoms may be considered as new information provided during search. However, differently from Sergot's query-the-user, SCIFF is not intended to be used interactively, but rather to provide a means to generate and to reason upon generated expectations, be them positive or negative. Moreover, SCIFF presents expectations in the context of an abductive framework (integrating them with other abducibles).

Hypotheses confirmation was studied also by Kakas and Evans [18], where hypotheses can be corroborated or refuted by matching them with observable atoms: an explanation fails to be corroborated if some of its logical consequences are not observed. The authors suggest that their framework could be extended to take into account dynamic events, possibly, queried to the user: *"this form of reasoning might benefit from the use of a query-the-user facility"*.

In a sense, our work can be considered as a merge and extension of these works: it has confirmation of hypotheses, as in corroboration, and it provides an operational semantics for dynamically incoming events, as in query-the-user.

The dynamics of incoming events can be seen as an instance of an Evolving Logic Program [19]. In EvoLP, the knowledge base can change both because of external events or because of internal results. SCIFF does not generate new events, but only expectations about external events. Our focus is more on the expressivity of the expectations than on the evolution of the knowledge base.

Speculative Computation [20] is a propositional framework for a multi-agent setting with unreliable communication. When an agent asks a query, it also abduces a default answer; if the real answer arrives within a deadline, the hypothesis is (dis-)confirmed; otherwise the computation continues with the default. In our work, expectations can be confirmed by events, with a wider scope: they are not only questions, and they can have variables, possibly constrained.

In our framework, time is treated like other variables, in association with domains, which makes it possible to express constraints (e.g., deadlines) and to exploit an underlying constraint solver. It could be interesting to augment this framework with the Event Calculus [21], in order to explicitly reason upon properties (fluents) holding during time intervals. Among the works on abductive event calculus, we cite Shanahan [22], because his work also has a concept of expectation: a robot moves in an office, and has expectations about where it is standing, based on the values obtained by sensors. While our expectations should match with actual events, in Shanahan's work events and expectations are of the same nature, and both are abduced. Our expectations are more expressive, as they can be positive and negative. We also have a different focus: while we assume that the history is known, he proposes to abduce the events.

6 Conclusions

This paper proposed an abductive logic programming framework which extends previous work in several directions. The two main features are the possibility to account for new dynamically upcoming facts, and the possibility to have hypotheses confirmed/disconfirmed by following observations and evidence. We proposed a language, and described its declarative and operational semantics. The $\mathcal{S}$CIFF proof-procedure was initially developed for specifying and checking the compliance of agents to protocols. In the current work we also consider abduction of atoms not representing expectations. There are still some directions to explore to use $\mathcal{S}$CIFF as the basis of a more general reasoning framework. Some work has to be done towards evaluation, by grounding the framework in a large enough set of concrete examples. The medical diagnosis domain can be a possible setting. Moreover, it would be interesting to study the integration of $\mathcal{S}$CIFF with the Event Calculus, and to extend it towards pro-activity, by making it able to actually generate events, not only reason about expectations.

Acknowledgements

We would like to thank Luís M. Pereira and Marek J. Sergot for fruitful comments and the many interesting discussions. This work is partially funded by the Information Society Technologies programme of the European Commission under the IST-2001-32530 SOCS Project (http://lia.deis.unibo.it/research/socs/), and by the MIUR COFIN 2003 projects *Sviluppo e verifica di sistemi multiagente basati sulla logica* (http://www.di.unito.it/massive/), and *La Gestione e la negoziazione automatica dei diritti sulle opere dell'ingegno digitali: aspetti giuridici e informatici*.

146   M. Alberti et al.

References

1. Kakas, A.C., Kowalski, R.A., Toni, F.: The role of abduction in logic programming. In Gabbay, D.M., Hogger, C.J., Robinson, J.A., eds.: Handbook of Logic in Artificial Intelligence and Logic Programming. Volume 5., Oxford University Press (1998) 235–324
2. Console, L., Dupré, D.T., Torasso, P.: On the relationship between abduction and deduction. Journal of Logic and Computation 1 (1991) 661–690
3. Kakas, A., Mancarella, P.: On the relation between Truth Maintenance and Abduction. In Fukumura, T., ed.: Proc. PRICAI-90, Ohmsha Ltd. (1990) 438–443
4. Satoh, K., Iwayama, N.: A Query Evaluation Method for Abductive Logic Programming. In Apt, K., ed.: Proc. ICLP'92, Cambridge, MA, MIT Press (1992) 671–685
5. Fung, T.H., Kowalski, R.A.: The IFF proof procedure for abductive logic programming. Journal of Logic Programming 33 (1997) 151–165
6. Kakas, A.C., Michael, A., Mourlas, C.: ACLP: Abductive Constraint Logic Programming. Journal of Logic Programming 44 (2000) 129–177
7. Kakas, A., van Nuffelen, B., Denecker, M.: A-System: Problem solving through abduction. In Nebel, B., ed.: Proc. IJCAI'01, Morgan Kaufmann Publishers (2001) 591–596
8. Alferes, J., Pereira, L.M., Swift, T.: Abduction in well-founded semantics and generalized stable models via tabled dual programs. Theory and Practice of Logic Programming 4 (2004) 383–428
9. Frühwirth, T.: Theory and practice of constraint handling rules. Journal of Logic Programming 37 (1998) 95–138
10. Alberti, M., Chesani, F., Gavanelli, M., Lamma, E., Mello, P., Torroni, P.: Compliance verification of agent interaction: a logic-based software tool. (Applied Artificial Intelligence) To appear.
11. Alberti, M., Gavanelli, M., Lamma, E., Mello, P., Torroni, P.: Specification and verification of interaction protocols: a computational logic approach based on abduction. Technical Report CS-2003-03, Dipartimento di Ingegneria di Ferrara, Ferrara, Italy (2003) Available at http://www.ing.unife.it/informatica/tr/.
12. Jaffar, J., Maher, M.: Constraint logic programming: a survey. Journal of Logic Programming 19-20 (1994) 503–582
13. Bürckert, H.: A resolution principle for constrained logics. Artificial Intelligence 66 (1994) 235–271
14. Alberti, M., Gavanelli, M., Lamma, E., Mello, P., Torroni, P.: An Abductive Interpretation for Open Societies. In Cappelli, A., Turini, F., eds.: AI*IA 2003: Advances in Artificial Intelligence, Proceedings of the 8th Congress of the Italian Association for Artificial Intelligence, Pisa. Volume 2829 of Lecture Notes in Artificial Intelligence., Springer-Verlag (2003) 287–299
15. Kowalski, R., Toni, F., Wetzel, G.: Executing suspended logic programs. Fundamenta Informaticae 34 (1998) 203–224
16. Endriss, U., Mancarella, P., Sadri, F., Terreni, G., Toni, F.: The CIFF proof procedure for abductive logic programming with constraints. In Alferes, J., Leite, J., eds.: Proc. JELIA'04. Volume 3229 of LNAI., Springer (2004) 31–43
17. Sergot, M.J.: A query-the-user facility of logic programming. In Degano, P., Sandwell, E., eds.: Integrated Interactive Computer Systems, North Holland (1983) 27–41

18. Evans, C., Kakas, A.: Hypotheticodeductive reasoning. In: Proc. International Conference on Fifth Generation Computer Systems, Tokyo (1992) 546–554
19. Alferes, J., Brogi, A., Leite, J., Pereira, L.: Evolving logic programs. In Flesca, S., Greco, S., Leone, N., Ianni, G., eds.: Proc. JELIA'02. Volume 2424 of LNAI., Springer (2002) 50–61
20. Satoh, K., Inoue, K., Iwanuma, K., Sakama, C.: Speculative computation by abduction under incomplete communication environments. In: Proc. ICMAS'00, IEEE Press (2000) 263–270
21. Kowalski, R.A., Sergot, M.: A logic-based calculus of events. New Generation Computing 4 (1986) 67–95
22. Shanahan, M.P.: Reinventing Shakey. In Minker, J., ed.: Logic-based Artificial Intelligence. Volume 597 of Kluwer Int. Series In Engineering And Computer Science. (2000) 233–253

Scheduling with Probability and Temporal Constraints

Bassam Baki and Maroua Bouzid

GREYC, University of Caen, Bd Maréchal Juin, 14032 Caen Cedex
{bbaki, bouzid}@info.unicaen.fr

Abstract. In this paper, we present an approach of temporal probabilistic task planning. Each task has a set of temporal constraints, a set of probabilities and a set of constant costs. Tasks are connected in an acyclic AND/OR Graph. Our planner constructs a plan formed by a subset of tasks chosen to be executed in order to achieve some goals, satisfy all constraints and has a high probability of execution during a minimal total time and with a reduced cost. This approach is one of the first techniques combining probability and time in planning using an AND/OR graph.

1 Introduction

While today's planners can handle large problems with durative actions and time constraints, few researches have considered the problem concerning uncertainty and the different durations of actions. For example, IxTeT ([1], [2]) is a time-map manager that handles symbolic constraints (precedence), numeric constraints (intervals) and sharable resources. Other planners, like "C-Buridan" ([3], [4]), deal with probabilistic information-producing actions and contingent execution but they do not consider the temporal constraints or the precedence relation or the delay between tasks. Our Planner, like "C-Buridan", is sound and complete. By sound, we mean that the planner only generates correct plans which are guaranteed to succeed if some preferred assumptions bounding uncertainty are satisfied. By complete, we mean that the planner returns a correct plan whenever one exists. Otherwise, it declares failure. We are interested in finding solutions that are satisfying rather than optimal. Since finding an optimal plan is an NP-Hard problem.

Many existing works have been developed on temporal planning or probabilistic planning but little attention has been paid to the combination of these two planning techniques. In this paper, we address the problem of probabilistic planning with temporal constraints. We illustrate our problem with an AND/OR graph, where we try to find a plan of tasks that satisfies all temporal constraints and precedence relations between tasks, has a high probability of execution, a minimal cost and a reduced total time.

This problem consists in finding a set of tasks to be executed respecting all temporal constraints and precedence relations between tasks. By temporal

S. Bandini and S. Manzoni (Eds.): AI*IA 2005, LNAI 3673, pp. 148–159, 2005.

constraints we mean the start times, the end times and possible durations of tasks. By precedence relation we mean the order of execution of tasks and the delays between tasks.

Our planner uses the temporal constraint propagation technique [5] to simplify the resolution of a given problem. Practically, that can consist in withdrawing from the field of the variables of decision, the values which do not belong to any solution. This filtering avoids many attempts at resolution which are likely to fail.

In the following, we consider that an agent is concerned with achieving a set of tasks connected together in a network that forms an acyclic directed AND/OR graph. Given a set of tasks, a start time, an end time, a set of durations, a set of probabilities (a value between 0 and 1 represents the probability of successful execution of a task in a given duration time) and a set of constant costs for each task, a time delay and a precedence relation between tasks, our approach allows the agent to determine the set of tasks to be executed so that when executed, the goal will be achieved and all temporal and precedence constraints will be satisfied in order to guarantee a correct execution.

A plan leading to the achievement of the desired goals and satisfying temporal constraints would be considered as *admissible*. From all *admissible* plans, we use a filtering operator to choose the most likely one to be executed.

The paper is organized as follows: in Section 2, we describe some basic temporal concepts concerning the knowledge of an agent and tasks and the representation of a temporal precedence graph and we formulate our problem; then in Section 3, we describe a constraint propagation algorithm. Section 4 describes the probabilistic temporal planning to calculate probability of execution intervals. In Section 5 we describe methods to calculate probability, cost and time for *admissible* plans, and in Section 6 we present how we select the most likely *admissible* plan to be executed. Analysis are studied in Section 7. Finally we conclude in Section 8.

2   Background

We solve the problem of temporal probabilistic planning with durative tasks. The goal of the agent is to choose, manage and schedule a subset of executing tasks to convert some initial states into some desired goals.

2.1   Task Description

A task t, called temporal task, is an action realized by an agent throughout a duration of time. For a task t, one associates the list $< [I_t^-, I_t^+], \Delta_t, Prt, C_t >$, where :

- $[I_t^-, I_t^+]$ is the *time window* referring to absolute (global, externally defined) time during which the task can be executed; this is an interval of time $[I_t^-, I_t^+]$ so that I_t^- is the earliest start time, i.e., the earliest time at which the execution of the task can start and I_t^+ is the latest end time, i.e., the time at which the execution of the task must finish,

- $\Delta_t = \{d_t^1, d_t^2, ..., d_t^m\}$ is a set of possible durations of time such that $d_t^i \in \Re$ ($i = 1...m$), is a period of time necessary to accomplish task t,
- $Pr_t = \{pr_t^1, pr_t^2, ..., pr_t^m\}$ is a set of probabilities such that $pr_t^i \in \Re | (0 \le pr_t^i \le 1$ and $i = 1...m)$ is the probability to execute t taking duration $d_t^i \in \Delta_t$,
- finally $C_t = \{c_t^1, c_t^2, ..., c_t^m\}$ is a set of costs payed to accomplish the task t such that $c_t^i \in \Re$ ($i = 1...m$) is the cost to accomplish t taking duration $d_t^i \in \Delta_t$.

Let ST_t and ET_t be the sets of possible *start times* and *end times* of task t such that $ST_t = \{st_t^1, st_t^2, ..., st_t^m\}$ where st_t^i is a possible *start time* for the task t, and $ET_t = \{et_t^1, et_t^2, ..., et_t^m\}$ where et_t^i is a possible *end time* for the task t if it executes during $d_t^i \in \Delta_t$. We will explain the method to calculate ST_t and ET_t in section 3.

For example, if task t_1 is an initial task and has this data :
$< [2, 9], \{2, 3, 6\}, \{0.2, 0.5, 0.3\}, \{10, 19, 25\} >$, we have : $ST_{t_1} = \{2\}$ and $ET_{t_1} = \{4, 5, 8\}$.

We call $\mathcal{I}_t$ the set of all possible execution intervals of the task t. A possible execution interval is formed by a possible *start time* and a possible *end time*. $\mathcal{I}_t = \{I_t^1, I_t^2, ..., I_t^m\}$ where $I_t^i = [st_t^i, et_t^i]$ is the possible execution interval of task t if it executes during $d_t^i \in \Delta_t$.

In the above example, we have : $I_{t_1}^1 = [2, 4]$, $I_{t_1}^2 = [2, 5]$, $I_{t_1}^3 = [2, 8]$ and $\mathcal{I}_{t_1} = \{I_{t_1}^1, I_{t_1}^2, I_{t_1}^3\}$.

The Local Temporal Constraints (LTC) concerning any task t consists in satisfying the condition that the task should be executed within the given time window $([I_t^-, I_t^+])$ taking into account its duration times (Δ_t). More formally, for each $d_t^i \in \Delta_t : I_t^+ - I_t^- \ge d_t^i$ and $st_t^i + d_t^i \le I_t^+$ with its obvious interpretation.

2.2   Temporal Precedence Graph

The goal of the agent is to execute a subset of tasks linked by precedence constraints. These tasks are represented by an acyclic temporal precedence graph $G = (T, E)$ where each node in T represents a task and each arc (t_i, t_j) in E represents precedence constraints i.e. task t_j cannot start before the completion of task t_i. We distinguish between two sorts of precedence constraints :

1. **Conjunctive Precedence Constraint**: when a group of independent tasks must be executed in order to enable execution of certain other tasks. If tasks $\{t_1, t_2, ..., t_k\}$ must all be executed before attempting execution of task t_i, we call it an AND-Node.
2. **Disjunctive Precedence Constraint**: when one task of a group has to be chosen and executed before the specific task of interest can be executed. If it is enough that at least one of tasks $\{t_1, t_2, ..., t_k\}$ is executed before attempting execution of task t_i, we call it an OR-Node.

Note that, the nodes of the set T of any temporal precedence graph G can be divided into three disjoint sets $T = T_I \cup T_M \cup T_F$ of initial tasks, intermediate tasks having preceding tasks and being predecessors for other tasks and final tasks being no predecessors, appropriately.

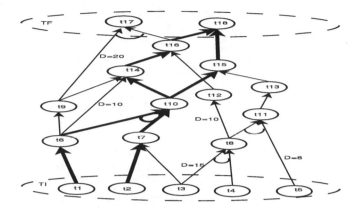

Fig. 1. A temporal precedence graph of tasks

Note also that, it is often the case that after executing the preceding task one should wait for some time before execution of the following task becomes possible. For example, after executing a transfer of money to bank account one has usually to wait until the next transaction time in order to be able to perform further operations with the money transferred. We shall call δ_{t_i,t_j} the *time delay* between tasks t_i and t_j.

Figure 1 represents a temporal precedence graph $G = (T, E)$, where $T = \{t_1, ..., t_{18}\}$ and E represents the precedence constraints between tasks. We represent the AND-nodes by arcs between the precedence constraints.

2.3   Planning Structure

The problem to be solved is to find a single plan[1] of executable tasks so that some tasks which are of interest are satisfied. In fact a plan is specified by a partial order of tasks. The plan should satisfy all constraints (AND/OR graph, precedence constraints and temporal constraints).

The solution to this problem is given by a set of tasks to be executed so that all the goals[2] can also be executed. We are interested in finding a plan that satisfies all constraints and has a high probability of execution. We use both depth-first and backwards search methods to find all *feasible* plans. We start with the goal tasks to be accomplished, and we finish when all initial tasks in T_I are accomplished. We obtain a set of all *feasible* plans.

We call P_F the set of all *feasible* plans in temporal precedence graph G and $T(P)$ the subset of T of all the tasks occurring in *feasible* plan P.

For example, consider the problem given by $T_G = \{t_{18}\}$ and $T_I = \{t_2\}$ for the graph given in Figure 1. Feasible plans, marked with a bold line, are $[\{[t_2, t_7], [t_1, t_6]\}, t_{10}, t_{14}, t_{15}, t_{18}]$ and $[\{[t_2, t_7], [t_1, t_6]\}, t_{10}, t_{16}, t_{18}]$.

---

[1] A plan is a subgraph in the initial graph that starts by a subset of initial tasks and ends by the subset of goal tasks.

[2] Goals are a subset of final tasks.

We have $P_F = \bigcup_{i=1}^{n} P_i$, where P_i is a *feasible* plan. In the next section we will use the propagation method to verify if a *feasible* plan is an *admissible* one.

3   Constraint Propagation Algorithm

Constraint propagation is a central process of constraint programming which lies in removing the values in the domains of the decision variables that cannot lead to a feasible solution with respect to a subset of the problem constraints. In the following we propose an approach allowing the propagation of temporal constraints through the graph. Our aim is to calculate for each task the set of possible execution temporal intervals.

To do that, we calculate the execution intervals for all tasks so that all of the appropriate temporal constraints are satisfied. These constraints concern the end times of all the predecessor tasks, the beginning time of the task and the set of its durations.

We can compute off-line all the possible end times of all predecessors of the task and consequently compute its possible start times. The possible intervals $\mathcal{I} = \cup I_{t_i}$ of execution, are determined with a single forward propagation of temporal constraints in the graph. This propagation organizes the graph into levels so that: l_0 is the level containing initial tasks,..., l_i contains all nodes whose predecessors include nodes at level l_{i-1} and all of whose predecessors are at level l_{i-1} or before. For each node in any given level l_i, we compute all its possible execution interval from its predecessors.

We start from the initial tasks (forward time assignment – the initial tasks are allocated first) and apply a *heuristic rule* that any task should be started as early as possible ; in our case where we have a simple precedence relation between tasks, the heuristic, defined for forward time assignment, is motivated by the idea that one should leave as much time as possible to be able to place further tasks within their time windows. This means that the possible times for starting and ending execution of task $t \in T(P)$ supposing that $\Delta_t = \{d_t^1, d_t^2, ..., d_t^m\}$ and $i = 1...m$ are defined as follows :

- Level $l_0 : t \in T_I$ (t is an initial task):
  $ST_t = \{st_t | st_t = max(I_t^-, start\_time)\}$, $ET_t = \{et_t^i | et_t^i = st_t + d_t^i$ where $i = 1...m\}$ and $\mathcal{I}_t = \{I_t^i = [st_t, et_t^i]$ where $i = 1...m\}$.
  By $start\_time$, we mean the time when the agent is activated.
  In this level, we obtain m possible execution intervals. We will analyze the number of possible execution intervals for tasks in section 7.

- Level l_i : for each node in level l_i, its possible start times are computed as all the times at which the predecessor tasks can finish. Thus we define the set of possible start and end times of each node at level l_i as follows :
  - If $t \in T_M \cup T_F$ (t is an intermediate or a final task) and t is an OR-node i.e. it has a unique predecessor t_i in the feasible plan where $ET_{t_i} = \{et_{t_i}^1, ..., et_{t_i}^n\}$ (calculated above) and suppose that $\Delta_t = \{d_t^1, d_t^2, ..., d_t^m\}$ then :

* $ST_t = \{st_t^j = max(I_t^-, et_{t_i}^j + \delta_{t_i,t})$ where $j = 1..n\}$
* $ET_t = \{et_t^{jk} = st_t^j + d_t^k$ where $j = 1..n$ and $k = 1..m\}$
* $\mathcal{I}_t = \{I_t^{jk} = [st_t^j, et_t^{jk}]$ where $j = 1..n$ and $k = 1..m\}$

- If $t \in T_M \cup T_F$ where $\Delta_t = \{d_t^1, d_t^2, ..., d_t^m\}$ and t has n tasks $\{t_1, \ldots, t_n\}$ as its immediate predecessors (the case of an AND-node) and if for each task t_i $(i = 1..n)$, $E_{t_i} = \{e_{t_i}^1, e_{t_i}^2, ..., e_{t_i}^{j_i}\}$ then :
  * $S_t = \{s_t^k = max(I_t^-, max(e_{t_i}^k + \delta_{t_i,t}))$ where $k = 1..j_i$ and $i = 1..n\}$
  * $E_t = \{e_t^{kr} = s_t^k + d_t^r$, where $k = 1..j_i, i = 1..n$ and $r = 1..m\}$
  * $\mathcal{I}_t = \{I_t^{kr} = [s_t^k, e_t^{kr}]$,where $k = 1..j_i, i = 1..n$ and $r = 1..m\}$

A *feasible* plan $\mathcal{P} \in \mathcal{P}_F$, in order to become an *admissible* one, must satisfy all the temporal constraints. More formally, for any task $t \in T(\mathcal{P})$, for each $e_t^i \in E_t$, the following condition : $e_t^i \leq I_t^+$ must hold. If a possible end time of E_t exceeds I_t^+, we consider that execution interval $I_t^i = [s_t^i, e_t^i]$ is not valid. In the other hand, if all possible end times of E_t exceed I_t^+, we consider that task t is not able to execute. Thus we consider the plan which contains such task is not admissible.

We denote by $\mathcal{P}_A$ the set of all admissible plans $\mathcal{P}$.

We have $\mathcal{P}_A = \bigcup \mathcal{P}$, where $\mathcal{P}$ is an admissible plan.

4   Probabilistic Temporal Planning

We describe in this section how we can weight each of those intervals calculated as above, with a probability. This probabilistic weight allows us to know the probability for a task to be executed during a given interval of time. For that, a probability propagation algorithm among the graph of tasks is described using for each node its execution time probability and the end-time probabilities of its predecessors.

The probability of a possible execution interval I_t^i depends on its start time (the end time of the previous tasks) and the probability of execution time pr_t^i.

Before a task t can start its execution, all its direct predecessors must be finished. The probability for the execution of t start at st_t^i is defined by :

- $p_{start}(st_t^i|et_{t'}^j)$ if t is an OR-Node, and its unique predecessor t' ends its execution at $et_{t'}^j$:
  - If $st_t^i < e_{t'}^j$ then $pr_{start}(s_t^i|e_{t'}^j) = 0$
  - If $s_t^i \geq e_{t'}^j$ then $pr_{start}(s_t^i|e_{t'}^j) = 1$
- $pr_{start}(s_t^r|e_{t_i}^k)$ if t is an AND-Node, i.e. it has several predecessors $\{t_1, t_2, \ldots, t_n\}$. Let $t_i \in \{t_1, t_2, \ldots, t_n\}$ where $E_{t_i} = \{e_{t_i}^1, e_{t_i}^2, \ldots, e_{t_i}^{j_i}\}$ such that j_i represents the number of possible end times of task t_i and let $S_t = \{s_t^1, s_t^2, ..., s_t^m\}$ be the set of possible start times of t then :
  - If $s_t^r < max\{e_{t_i}^k\}$ then $pr_{start}(s_t^r|e_{t_i}^k) = 0$
  - If $s_t^r \geq max\{e_{t_i}^k\}$ then $pr_{start}(s_t^r|e_{t_i}^k) = 1$
    where $r = 1...m$, $i = 1..n$ and $k = 1..j_i$

A special case has to be considered for the first tasks. Indeed, these initial tasks $(t \in T_I)$ have no predecessors, the probability of starting the execution of an initial task t at s^t is given by : $pr_{start}(s_t) = 1$.

Let $pr_t(d_t^i|st_t^i)$ be the probability that the execution of task t takes d_t^i units of time when it starts at st_t^i. This probability depends on the execution $start\_time$.

The probability of an execution interval I_t^i of task t on the form of OR-Node i.e. it has an only direct predecessor t', is the probability $Pr_w(I_t^i|et_{t'}^j)$ that interval $I_t^i = [st_t^i, et_t^j]$ is the interval during which a task t is executed, if the last executed task ends at $et_{t'}^j$. This probability measures the probability that a task t starts its execution at st_t^i and ends at et_t^i:

$$Pr_w(I_t^i|e_{t'}^j) = pr_{start}(s_t^i|e_{t'}^j) * pr_t(d_t^i|s_t^i)$$

where $et_{t'}^j$ is a possible end time of the last executed task.

In the case where t, such that $\Delta_t = \{d_t^1, d_t^2, ..., d_t^m\}$, is an AND-Node and has several predecessors $\{t_1, t_2, \ldots, t_n\}$ where $t_i \in \{t_1, t_2, \ldots, t_n\}$, ends its execution at $e_{t_i}^{k_{t_i}}$ ($k_{t_i} = 1..j_i$ s.t. j_i represents the number of possible execution end times of task t_i), we have :

$$Pr_w(I_t^r|e_{t_i}^{k_{t_i}}) = pr_{start}(s_t^r|e_{t_i}^{k_{t_i}}) * pr_t(d_t^r|s_t^r)$$

where $r = 1..m$.

A special case has to be considered for the first task:

$$Pr_w(I_t^r) = pr_{start}(s_t) * pr_t(d_t^r|s_t)$$

Suppose 0.7 is the probability for the execution of task t_i to take 2 units of time when it starts at 5 ($Pr_{t_i}(d_{t_i}^j = 2|st_{t_i}^j = 5) = 0.7$). We assume that the end execution of the predecessor task $t_{i'}$ is 3. We consider task t_i. The probability of the interval $[5, 7]$ is 0.7 :
$Pr_w(I_{t_i}^j = [5, 7]|et_{t_{i'}}^{j'} = 3) = 1 \times 0.7 = 0.7$
If for example task $t_{i'}$ ends at 7 : $Pr_w(I_{t_i}^j = [5, 7]|et_{t_{i'}}^{j'} = 7) = 0 \times 0.7 = 0$

5   Execution Probability, Total Cost and Total Time

As the order of searching for plans is arbitrary, the search may produce several admissible plans. In this case, it will apply further criteria (Probability, cost and time) to analyze and compare them so as to select one of them to be executed. In this section we define how we calculate the probability, the total cost and the total time for all admissible plans.

An *admissible* plan is formed by a set of scheduling $\{t_1|I_{t_1}^j, t_2|I_{t_2}^k, ..., t_n|I_{t_n}^l\}$ where each scheduling is formed by a set of tasks $t_i, ..., t_n$ executed in their execution intervals $I_{t_1}^j, ..., I_{t_n}^l$ respectively.

The probability of an *admissible* plan $P = \{t_1|I_{t_1}^j, t_2|I_{t_2}^k, ..., t_n|I_{t_n}^l\}$ is such that :

$$Pr(P) = \sum_{i=1}^{n} \prod_{j,k} Pr_w(I_{t_i}^j | et_{t_{i-1}}^k)$$

where $j = 1$ to the number of intervals of t_i and $k = 1$ to the number of intervals of t_{i-1}.

The total cost of a plan $P \in P_A$ is the sum of all costs of all tasks in P :

$$Cost(P) = \sum_{i=1}^{n} c_{t_i}^j$$

where $c_{t_i}^j$ is the cost of accomplishing task $t_i \in T(P)$ during $d_{t_i}^j$.

The total time of plan $P \in P_A$ is the maximum of the end times of goal tasks minus the smaller start time of initial tasks in P :

$$Time(P) = max(et_{t_i}^j, \ldots, et_{t_n}^k) - min(I_{t_i'}^-, \ldots, I_{t_n'}^-)$$

where $t_i, \ldots, t_n \in T(P) \cap T_G$ and $t_i', \ldots, t_n' \in T(P) \cap T_I$. This time represents the total duration time from the beginning of execution of P to its end including delay times and no execution times i.e. while waiting execution.

6   Selection of the Most Likely Admissible Plan

To select a unique plan from all *admissible* plans, we use a filtering operator for plans which is aimed at determining from an admissible plan P, and a condition C, if this plan is preferred or not. A filtering operator f is such that:

$$f(P, C) = \begin{cases} \text{P is preferred} & \text{if P satisfies C} \\ \text{rejected} & \text{otherwise} \end{cases}$$

In this paper, we are interested in finding solutions that are satisfying rather than optimal, for that we assume that condition C consists in the fact that the probability of execution $Pr(P)$ of the considered plan P is higher than the average of the probabilities of execution of all plans in P_A. Let P_{Gr} be the set of preferred plans and $(\bar{P}r)$ be the average of the probabilities of execution of all plans in P_A. We calculate the average value $(\bar{P}r)$ of the probabilities of execution of all plans in P_A as defined in section 5, and we reject those plans for which $Pr(P)$ is smaller than $(\bar{P}r)$.

Among remaining plans, we choose the one with the minimal cost, as defined in section 5, to be executed:

$$P^* = argmin_{P_i \in P_{Gr}} Cost(P_i)$$

If several plans have the same cost, we choose the one with the minimal total time as defined in section 5 : if $card(P^*) > 1$, then:

$$P^* = argmin_{P_i \in P_{Gr}} Time(P_i)$$

7 Analysis and Discussion

In this section we analyze the number of execution intervals for each task t in graph $G = (T, E)$. In the worst case, the number of execution intervals for an initial task is equal to the cardinality of its duration set. The number of execution intervals for an intermediate or final task of the form OR-Node is equal to the cardinality of its duration set multiplied by the cardinality of the set of the ends of the direct predecessor task. The number of execution intervals for an intermediate or final task of the form AND-Node is equal to the cardinality of its duration set multiplied by all the cardinalities of the sets of the ends of the direct predecessor tasks. More formally :

- If $t \in T_I$ then $|\mathcal{I}_t| = |\Delta_t|$
- If $t \in T_M \cup T_F$ is an OR-Node then $|\mathcal{I}_t| = |\Delta_t| * |E_{t'}|$ where t' is the direct precedence task for task t.
- If $t \in T_M \cup T_F$ is an AND-Node then $|\mathcal{I}_t| = |\Delta_t| * \prod_{i=1}^{n} |E_{t_i}|$ where $t_i \in \{t_1 ... t_n\}$ are the direct precedence tasks for task t.

The number of execution intervals increases exponentially with the length of the plan. But for each task we may obtain execution intervals that have the same possible start and end times with different probabilities. In this case we can assume that all identical execution intervals form a unique execution interval with its start and end times and with a probability equal to the sum of all its probabilities (demonstration in Section 7.1). For example, if for task t_i we obtain five execution intervals : $[6, 7], [6, 8], [7, 9], [6, 7]$, and $[7, 9]$ with probabilities: $0.10, 0.20, 0.09, 0.21, 0.40$ respectively, we can say that we have only three execution intervals $[6, 7], [6, 8]$ and $[7, 9]$ with probabilities $0.31, 0.20$ and 0.49 respectively. Note that the sum of all probabilities for each task is ≤ 1.

7.1 Reducing the Number of Intervals

In the following, we examine different possible cases to calculate the number of possible execution intervals for each task so as to reduce this number. We suppose there are no delays between tasks.

- Level l_0 : $t \in T_I$ (t is an initial task) such that $\Delta_t = \{d_t^1, d_t^2, ..., d_t^m\}$:
  The number of the intervals of t is equal to the number of durations that satisfy the condition : $max(start\_time, I_t^-) + d_t^i \leq I_t^+$, where $[I_t^-, I_t^+]$ is the time window of task t and $d_t^i \in \Delta_t$.
- Level l_i : $t \in T_M \cup T_F$ (t is an intermediate or a final task) :
  Let us begin by the case where t is an OR-Node and has a unique direct predecessor task t'. Suppose that the set of possible execution ends of task t' is $ET_{t'} = \{et_{t'}^1, \ldots, et_{t'}^p\}$, the time window of task t is $[I_t^-, I_t^+]$ and $\Delta_t = \{d_t^1, d_t^2, ..., d_t^m\}$. We consider the task t. We distinguish between three cases :
  1. If the maximal of end times $e_{t'}^j \in E_{t'}$ is smaller or equal to I_t^-, then the number of possible execution intervals of task t is equal to the number of its durations that satisfy the condition :
  $I_t^- + d_t^i \leq I_t^+$

2. If the minimum of end times $e_{t'}^j \in E_{t'}$ is higher than or equal to I_t^-, then the number of possible execution intervals of t is equal the cardinality of $E_{t'}$ multiplied by the number of the possible durations of task t that satisfy the condition: $e_{t'}^j + d_t^i \leq I_t^+$ where $i = 1..m$ and $j = 1..p$.

3. Otherwise, the number of possible execution intervals of task t is equal to one plus the number of intervals of t' that have different values of $et_{t'}^j$ and in which $et_{t'}^j > I_t^-$ multiplied by the number of the durations of task t that satisfy the condition :
$$max(et_{t'}^j, I_t^-) + d_t^i \leq I_t^+$$

Table 1, describes these assumptions.

Table 1. Analysis of the Number of Execution Intervals of an OR-Node

Condition	The number of execution intervals of t where t is an OR-Node ($t' \prec t$)
$max(ET_{t'}) \leq I_t^-$	$|\mathcal{I}_t| = |\{I_t^- + d_t^i|$ where $I_t^- + d_t^i \leq I_t^+$ and $i = 1..m$
$min(ET_{t'}) > I_t^-$	$|\mathcal{I}_t| = |\{e_{t'}^j + d_t^i|$ where $e_{t'}^j + d_t^i \leq I_t^+$ s.t. $i = 1..m$ and $j = 1..p$
otherwise	$|\mathcal{I}_t| = |\{s_t^j + d_t^i|$ where $s_t^j + d_t^i \leq I_t^+$ s.t. $j = 1..n$ where n is the number of possible execution start times of t and $i = 1..m$

- Now let us consider the case where t is an AND-node and has a set of direct predecessors $\{t_1, t_2, \ldots, t_n\}$. Let $t_i \in \{t_1, t_2, \ldots, t_n\}$ where $E_{t_i} = \{e_{t_i}^1, e_{t_i}^2, \ldots, e_{t_i}^p\}$ be the set of possible end times of t_i. To calculate the set of possible end times of the set of predecessor tasks of t, noted $E(t_1, \ldots, t_n)$, we make a combination between all sets E_{t_i} to choose the maximal end time from each combination. More formally :

$$E(t_1, \ldots, t_n) = \bigcup \{max_{k_{t_i}=1}^p (e_{t_1}^{k_{t_1}}, e_{t_2}^{k_{t_2}}, \ldots, e_{t_n}^{k_{t_n}})\}$$

For example, if a task t has three direct predecessors t_1, t_2 and t_3 which end their execution at $E_{t_1} = \{e_{t_1}^1, e_{t_1}^2, e_{t_1}^3\}$, $E_{t_2} = \{e_{t_2}^1, e_{t_2}^2, e_{t_2}^3\}$ and $E_{t_3} = \{e_{t_3}^1, e_{t_3}^2\}$ respectively. The set $E(t_1, t_2, t_3)$ is composed by the set of possible end times follows : $\{max(e_{t_1}^1, e_{t_2}^1, e_{t_3}^1), max(e_{t_1}^1, e_{t_2}^1, e_{t_3}^2), etc\}$.

In worst case, where all maximum of all combination are different, we have :

$$|E(t_1, \ldots, t_n)| = |E_{t_1}| * |E_{t_2}| * \ldots * |E_{t_n}|$$

After calculating the set of possible end times ($E(t_1, \ldots, t_n)$) of the set of predecessors of t, we can calculate the number of possible execution intervals of t by method described above.

In the next section, to make these analysis clearer, we give a simple example of a plan contains three tasks.

7.2   Illustrative Example

In this section, to make these analysis clearer, we will use an illustrative example. Suppose that we have three tasks t_i, t_j and t_k (Figure 2) with these temporal

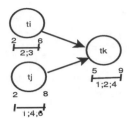

Fig. 2. An Example of a Temporal Precedence Graph of 3 Tasks

data : t_i : $([2, 6], \{2, 3\}, \{0.6, 0.4\}, \{10, 20\})$, t_j : $([2, 8], \{1, 4, 6\}, \{0.1, 0.4, 0.5\}, \{10, 30, 35\})$ and t_k : $([5, 9], \{1, 2, 4\}, \{0.1, 0.6, 0.3\}, \{15, 30, 35\})$.
We suppose there are no delays between tasks.

First, suppose that t_k is an OR-Node. Consider the plan (t_i, t_k).
Using the propagation algorithm described in section 3, we obtain : $I_{t_i}^1 = [2, 4]$
with probability equal to 0.60 and $I_{t_i}^2 = [2, 5]$ with probability equal to 0.40.
These two execution intervals satisfy the condition $et_{t_i}^m = \{4, 6\} \leq I_{t_i}^+ = 6$.
To calculate the execution intervals of task t_k we use the possible end times
of task t_i. We get six possible intervals : $[5, 6], [5, 7], [5, 9], [5, 6], [5, 7]$ and $[5, 9]$
with probabilities $0.06, 0.36, 0.18, 0.04, 0.24$ and 0.12 respectively. Note that three
execution intervals are repeated. We reduce them to a single execution interval
and we add their probabilities. We get only three execution intervals $[5, 6], [5, 7]$
and $[5, 9]$ with probabilities $0.10, 0.60$ and 0.30 respectively.

Secondly, suppose that t_k is an AND-Node. Consider the plan $([t_i, t_j], t_k)$.
Using the propagation algorithm described in section 3, we obtain : $I_{t_i}^1 = [2, 4]$
with probability equal to 0.60 and $I_{t_i}^2 = [2, 5]$ with probability equal to 0.40.
These two execution intervals satisfy the condition $et_{t_i}^m = \{4, 6\} \leq I_{t_i}^+ = 6$.
$I_{t_j}^1 = [2, 3]$ with probability equal to 0.1, $I_{t_j}^2 = [2, 6]$ with probability equal to
0.40 and $I_{t_j}^3 = [2, 8]$ with probability equal to 0.5. These execution intervals
satisfy the condition $et_{t_j}^n = \{3, 6, 8\} \leq I_{t_j}^+ = 8$. To calculate the execution
intervals of task t_k we use the possible end times of tasks t_i and t_j.

We get 18 possible intervals : $[5, 6], [5, 7], [5, 9], [6, 7], [6, 8], [6, 10], [8, 9],$
$[8, 10], [8, 12], [5, 6], [5, 7], [5, 9], [6, 7], [6, 8], [6, 10], [8, 9], [8, 10]$ and $[8, 12]$. Remark that intervals $[6, 10], [8, 10]$ and $[8, 11]$ are not valid because they do not
satisfy the condition $et_{t_k}^p = \{10, 11\} \leq I_{t_k}^+ = 9$. We eliminate scheduling that contain these intervals. Among the remaining intervals, six execution intervals are
repeated. We reduce them to a single execution interval and we add their probabilities. We get only six execution intervals $[5, 6], [5, 7], [5, 9], [6, 7], [6, 8]$ and $[8, 9]$.

8   Conclusion

The approach, described in this paper and based on simple temporal and probability propagation algorithms, allows the agent to determine the set of tasks to
execute and when to execute them by respecting all temporal and precedence
constraints.

We present an approach of temporal probabilistic task planning where we construct a plan of tasks, which have a time window validity and probabilistic execution time, that satisfies all constraints and has a high probability of execution during a minimal total time and a reduced cost.

This approach is one of the first techniques combining probability and time in planning with an AND/OR graph. We tested our planner for 50 tasks with 5 execution intervals for each one. Theoretically we obtain 250000 plans but the experiment shows that, by our approach, we get only 20569 plans.

These first experimental results consolidate our idea of the founded good of the approach. The next step in this work will be focused on other kind of experimental factors and on comparing our approach with other ones. Another issue consists of finding other heuristics to choose the most likely plan to be executed and compare them with the heuristics study in this paper, and then extend this approach to multi-agent temporal probabilistic planning systems.

References

1. M. Ghallab and H. Laruelle. Representation and Control in IxTeT, a Temporal Planner. In *Proceedings of the Second International Conference on Artificial Intelligence Planning Systems, AIPS-94*, pages 61–67, June 1994.
2. P. Laborie and M. Ghallab. Planning with Sharable Resource Constraints. In *Proceedings of the Fourteenth International Joint Conference on Artificial Intelligence, IJCAI-95*, pages 1643–1651, August 1995.
3. D. Draper, S. Hanks, and D. Weld. Probabilistic Planning with Information Gathering and Contingent Execution. In *Proceedings of the Second International Conference on AI Planning Systems, AIPS-94*, pages 31–63, June 1994.
4. N. Kushmerick, S. Hanks, and D. Weld. An Algorithm for Probabilistic Least-Commitment Planning. In *Proceedings of the Twelfth National Conference on Artificial Intelligence, AAAI-94*, pages 1073–1078, August 1994.
5. J. Bresina and R. Washington. Expected Utility Distributions for Flexible Contingent Execution. In *Proceedings of the AAAI-2000 Workshop: Representation Issues for Real-World Planning Systems*, 2000.
6. J. L. Bresina, R. Dearden, N. Meuleau, S. Ramakrishnan, D. E. Smith, and R. Washington. Planning Under Continuous Time and Resource Uncertainty: A Challenge for AI. In *AIPS Workshop on Planning for Temporal Domains*, pages 91–97, April 2002.
7. B. Baki, A. Beynier, M. Bouzid, and A.I. Mouaddib. Temporal Probabilistic Task Planning in an Emergency Service. In *Complex Systems Intelligence and Modern Technological Applications, CSIMTA-04*, pages 427–434, September 2004.
8. S. Zilberstein. The Utility of Planning. *SIGART Bulletin*, 6(1):42–47, January 1995.
9. J. C. Pemberton and L. G. Greenwald. On the Need for Dynamic Scheduling of Imagings Satellites. In *Proceedings of the American Society for Photogrammetry and Remote Sensing, ASPRS-02*, 2002.

Schedule Robustness Through Broader *Solve and Robustify* Search for Partial Order Schedules

Nicola Policella[1], Amedeo Cesta[1], Angelo Oddi[1], and Stephen F. Smith[2]

[1] ISTC-CNR, Institute for Cognitive Science and Technology,
Italian National Research Council, Rome, Italy
`name.surname@istc.cnr.it`
[2] The Robotics Institute, Carnegie Mellon University,
Pittsburgh, PA, USA
`sfs@cs.cmu.edu`

Abstract. In previous work, we have defined a two-step procedure called *Solve-and-Robustify* for generating flexible, partial order schedules. This partitioned problem solving approach — first find a viable solution and then generalize it to enhance robustness properties — has been shown to provide an effective basis for generating flexible, robust schedules while simultaneously achieving good quality with respect to optimization objectives. This paper extends prior analysis of this paradigm, by investigating the effects of using different start solutions as a baseline to generate partial order schedules. Two approaches are compared: the first constructs partial order schedules from a single fixed-time schedule, obtained by first performing an extended makespan optimization search phase; the second considers the search for fixed-time schedules and flexible schedules in a more integrated fashion, and constructs partial order schedules from a number of different fixed-time starting solutions. The paper experimentally shows how the characteristics of the fixed-time solutions may lower the robustness of the final partial order schedules and discusses the reasons for such behavior.

1 Introduction

In previous work [1,2] we have shown how a two-step procedure — first find a solution then make it robust — can provide an effective basis for generating flexible, robust schedules that also achieve good solution quality. Under this scheme, a feasible fixed-time schedule is generated in stage one (in particular an early start times solution is identified), and then, in the second stage, a procedure referred to as *chaining* is applied to transform this fixed-time schedule into a *Partial Order Schedule*, or $\mathcal{POS}$. By virtue of the fact that a $\mathcal{POS}$ retains temporal flexibility in the start times of various activities in the schedule, a $\mathcal{POS}$ provides greater robustness in the face of executional uncertainty. The common thread underlying the "chained" representation of the schedule is the characteristic that activities which require the same resource units are linked via precedence constraints into precedence chains. Given this structure, each constraint becomes more than just a simple precedence. It also represents a *producer-consumer* relation, allowing each activity to *know* the precise set of predecessors which will *supply* the units of resource it requires for execution. In this way, the resulting network of

S. Bandini and S. Manzoni (Eds.): AI*IA 2005, LNAI 3673, pp. 160–172, 2005.

chains can be interpreted as a flow of resource units through the schedule; each time an activity terminates its execution, it passes its resource unit(s) on to its successors. It is clear that this representation is robust if and only if there is temporal slack that allows chained activities to move "back and forth". Concepts similar to chaining have also been used elsewhere: for example, the Transportation Network introduced in [3], and the Resource Flow Network described in [4] are based on equivalent structural assumptions.

This paper addresses an aspect not explored in our previous work: how different start schedules influence the overall process of identifying partial order schedules. Taking a constraint-based solver and the best chaining algorithm from our previous work, we define and analyze the performance of two extended search configurations of the *Solve-and-Robustify* solution approach: the first combination schema constructs flexible schedules from a single starting point solution after an extended, iterative sampling optimization phase, while the second iterates both solve and robustify considering different fixed-time schedules as starting points and selecting the best partial order schedule found.

The paper first introduces the basic concepts of schedule robustness and Partial Order Schedules, then describes the two step approach to $\mathcal{POS}$ synthesis. The new analysis follows next. We describe each extended search procedure, present the results of an experimental evaluation and interpret these results. Finally we draw some conclusions.

2 Scheduling with Uncertainty and Partial Order Schedules

The usefulness of schedules in most practical scheduling domains is limited by their brittleness. Though a schedule offers the potential for a more optimized execution than would otherwise be obtained, it must in fact be executed as planned to achieve this potential. In practice this is generally made difficult by a dynamic execution environment, where unforeseen events quickly invalidate the schedule's predictive assumptions and bring into question the continuing validity of the schedules's prescribed actions. The lifetime of a schedule tends to be very short, and hence its optimizing advantages are generally not realized. For instance, let us consider the example in Fig. 1 that shows the allocation of three different activities on a binary resource. According to quite common practice in scheduling, a solution associates an exact start and end time to each activity.

Such solution may exhibit a high degree of brittleness, for instance, as shown in Fig. 1(b), when the first activity lasts longer than expected a conflict in

(a) Initial allocation of three activities on a binary resource   (b) Allocation after an activity lasts longer

Fig. 1. Brittleness of a fixed-time schedule

the usage of the machine is immediately generated because of the fixed start-time for the activities.

An alternative approach consists of adopting a graph formulation of the scheduling problem, wherein activities competing for the same resources are simply ordered to establish resource feasibility, and it is possible to produce schedules that retain temporal flexibility where allowed by the problem constraints. In essence, such a "flexible schedule" encapsulates a set of possible fixed-time schedules, and hence is equipped to accommodate some amount of the uncertainty at execution time.

Following this intuition we have introduced the definition of *Partial Order Schedules*, or $\mathcal{POS}$s [1,5]. A $\mathcal{POS}$ consists of a set of feasible solutions for the scheduling problem that can be represented in a compact way by a temporal graph. In a temporal graph each activity is associated to a node and temporal constraints define the order in which activities have to be executed.

To provide a more formal definition of a $\mathcal{POS}$ we use the activity on the node representation: given a problem P, this can be represented by a graph $G_P(V_P, E_P)$, where the set of nodes $V_P = V \cup \{a_0, a_{n+1}\}$ consists of the set of activities specified in P and two dummy activities representing the origin (a_0) and the horizon (a_{n+1}) of the schedule, and the set of edges E_P contains P's temporal constraints between pairs of activities. A solution of the scheduling problem can be represented as an extension of G_P, where a set E_R of simple precedence constraints, $a_i \prec a_j$, is added to remove all the possible resource conflicts. Given these concepts, a *Partial Order Schedule* is defined as follows:

Definition 1 (Partial Order Schedule). *Given a scheduling problem P and the associated graph $G_P(V_P, E_P)$ that represents P, a* Partial Order Schedule, $\mathcal{POS}$, *is a set of solutions that can be represented by a graph $G_{POS}(V_P, E_P \cup E_R)$.*

In practice a $\mathcal{POS}$ is a set of partially ordered activities such that any possible complete activity allocation that is consistent with the initial partial order is also a resource and time feasible schedule.

It is worth noting that a partial order schedule provides an immediate opportunity to reactively respond to some possible external changes by simply propagating their effects over the "graph", by using a polynomial time computation. In fact the augmented duration of an activity, as well as a greater release time, can be modeled as a new temporal constraint to post on the graph. It is also important to note that, even though the propagation process does not consider the consistency with respect the resource constraints, it is guaranteed to obtain a feasible solution by definition of $\mathcal{POS}$s. Therefore a partial order schedule provides a means to find a new solution and ensures its fast computation.

RCPSP/max. This work considers the Resource-Constrained Project Scheduling Problem with minimum and maximum time lags, RCPSP/max [6] as the reference problem. The basic entities of this problem are a set of *activities* denoted by $V = \{a_1, a_2, \dots a_n\}$. Each activity has a fixed *processing time*, or *duration*, p_i and must be scheduled without preemption.

A *schedule* is an assignment of start times to activities $a_1, a_2, \dots a_n$, i.e. a vector $S = (s_1, s_2, \dots, s_n)$ where s_i denotes the start time of activity a_i. The time at which activity a_i has been completely processed is called its *completion time* and is denoted by e_i. Since we assume that processing times are deterministic and preemption is not permitted, completion times are determined by $e_i = s_i + p_i$. Schedules are subject to both *temporal* and *resource constraints*. In their most general form temporal constraints designate arbitrary minimum and maximum time lags between the start times of any two activities, $l_{ij}^{min} \leq s_j - s_i \leq l_{ij}^{max}$ where l_{ij}^{min} and l_{ij}^{max} are the minimum and maximum time lag of activity a_j relative to a_i. A schedule $S = (s_1, s_2, \ldots, s_n)$ is *time feasible*, if all inequalities given by the activity precedences/time lags and durations hold for start times s_i. During their processing, activities require specific resource units from a set $R = \{r_1, r_2, \ldots r_m\}$ of resources. Resources are *reusable*, i.e. they are released when no longer required by an activity and are then available for use by another activity. Each activity a_i requires of the use of req_{ik} units of the resource r_k during its processing time p_i. Each resource r_k has a limited capacity of c_k units. A schedule is *resource feasible* if at each time t the demand for each resource $r_k \in R$ does not exceed its capacity c_k, i.e. $\sum_{s_i \le t < e_i} req_{ik} \le c_k$. A schedule S is called *feasible* if it is both time and resource feasible.

Metrics for Comparing Partial Order Schedules. As described before, a single $\mathcal{POS}$ represents a set of temporal solutions that are also resource feasible. This set of schedules provides a means for tolerating some amount of execution uncertainty. When an unexpected event occurs (e.g., a start time delay), the temporal propagation mechanism (a polynomial time calculation) can be applied to update the start times of all activities and, if at least one temporal solution remains viable, produces a new partial order schedule. Therefore, it is intuitive that the quality of a certain $\mathcal{POS}$ is tightly related to the set of solutions that it can represent. In fact the greater the number of solutions, the greater is the expected ability in dealing with scheduling uncertainty. Another aspect to consider in analyzing the solutions clustered into a partial order schedule is the distribution of such alternatives over all the activities. This distribution will be the result of the configuration given by the constraints present in the solution. For this reason it is necessary to introduce metrics that consider such aspects.

A first measure, $flex$, is taken from [7]. This measure counts the *number of pairs of activities in the solution which are not reciprocally related by simple precedence constraints*. This provides a first analysis of the configuration of the solution. The rationale is that when two activities are not related it is possible to move one without moving the other one. Hence, the higher the value of $flex$ the lower the degree of interaction among the activities. It is worth noting that a limitation of the $flex$ metric is that it gives only a qualitative evaluation of the solution, because it counts only existence/not-existence of a direct ordering relation. This may be sufficient for a scheduling problem with no time lag constraints like the one used in [7], but is rather limited to describe flexibility in RCPSP/max where it is necessary to integrate this flexibility measure with some factor that takes into account the quantitative aspects of the temporal problem (or solution).

A metric that satisfies this requirement is defined in [8]. It requires the presence of a fixed time horizon for the termination of all activities. In order to compare two or more $\mathcal{POS}$s we bound any partial order schedule to have a finite number of solutions. Then the metric is defined as the average width, relative to the temporal horizon, of the temporal slack associated with each pair of activities (a_i, a_j):

$$fldt = \sum_{i=1}^{n} \sum_{j=1 \wedge j \ne i}^{n} \frac{slack(a_i, a_j)}{H \times n \times (n-1)} \times 100 \tag{1}$$

where H is the temporal horizon of the problem, n is the number of activities, $slack(a_i, a_j)$ is the width of the allowed distance interval between the end time of activity a_i and the start time of activity a_j, and 100 is a scaling factor[1]. We use this metric to characterize the *fluidity* of a solution, i.e., the ability to use flexibility to absorb a temporal variation in the execution of activities. It also considers that a temporal variation concerning an activity is absorbed by the temporal flexibility of the solution instead of generating a deleterious domino effect (the higher the value of $fldt$, the less the risk, i.e., the higher the probability of localized changes).

3   Solve-and-Robustify

In [8] a two-stage approach to generating a flexible schedule is introduced as one possibility for achieving robust schedules. Under this scheme a feasible fixed-time schedule is first generated in stage one, and then, in the second stage, a procedure referred to as *chaining* is applied to obtain a robust solution. In this second step, fixed-time commitments are converted into sequences (chains) of activities to be executed by various resources.

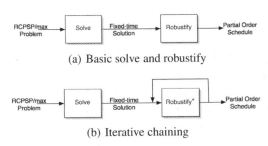

(a) Basic solve and robustify

(b) Iterative chaining

Fig. 2. Previous work

In a recent paper, [1], this approach has been generalized to RCPSP/max. These results establish the basic viability of a chaining procedure. At the same time, the procedure used in this work was developed simply to provide a means of transforming a given schedule into a $\mathcal{POS}$; no attention was given to the potential influence of the chaining procedure itself on the properties exhibited by the final, flexible solution. For these reasons, in [2] the authors examine the problem of generating $\mathcal{POS}$s from the broader perspective of producing flexible schedules with good robustness properties, and investigate the design of an informed chaining procedure that exploits knowledge of these properties to increase the robustness of the final $\mathcal{POS}$. This latter work first introduced an iterative improvement schema for a randomized chaining algorithm.

A sketchy representation of the *Solve-and-Robustify* approach can be seen in Fig. 2(a) as an open loop cascade of "solver" and "robustify" modules. The subsequent work in [2] can be represented as a first loop with respect to the simple cascade by applying an iterative improvement cycle around the robusty phase, Fig. 2(b). Iterative improvement is obtained by randomizing the basic procedure to obtain different search paths from different restarts[2].

The ESTA *Greedy Solver.* As a solver we use here the *Precedence Constraint Posting* greedy schema called ESTA described in [8,9]. This proceeds by analyzing the infinite capacity representation of a RCPSP/max problem where the temporal constraint are

---

[1] In [8] this metric was defined as robustness of a solution, RB.

[2] In the figure, a module containing a randomized procedure is labeled with a star (e.g., *Robustify**).

satisfied and the resource profiles contain violations. More precisely, a violation or *resource contention peak* consists of a set of activities that are executed at the same time and that require an amount of resource greater than the resource capacity. Then the solving process posts further precedence constraints to remove these peaks. The selection of the new constraint is accomplished by using three alternative heuristics; a first, simple strategy considers all the pairs of activities in a peak. The other two approaches use the MCS, minimal conflict sets, where an MCS is a set of resource conflicting activities such that any of its proper subset is consistent. To avoid the complexity of computing all possible MCSs two polynomial sampling approaches are used: *linear* and *quadratic*. The use of the three different heuristics gives rise to three different variants of the ESTA algorithm.

Iterative Chaining. In our current approach the robustification phase is carried out through chaining. A chaining procedure transforms a feasible fixed-time solution into a $\mathcal{POS}$ by dispatching activities to specific resource units[3]. Since choices can be made as to how to dispatch activities to resource units, it is possible to generate different $\mathcal{POS}$s from the same starting solution, and these different $\mathcal{POS}$s can be expected to have different robustness properties.

In [2] iterative sampling is used to explore this set of solutions. Randomization is added to obtain a different solution at each iteration and, in so doing, to generate a sequence of $\mathcal{POS}$s starting from the same initial schedule. The $\mathcal{POS}$s are evaluated with respect to a specific robustness measure, and the best one found is returned. Additionally, different heuristics have been explored that change the effectiveness of chaining. In this paper we use the most effective one, called MINID (*minimizing interdependencies*) in [5].

The heuristic MINID takes into account existing ordering relations with those activities already allocated in the chaining process in order to minimize possible links among pairs of chains which will degrade the flexibility of the solution. In this procedure, the allocation of an activity a_i on the chains of a multi-capacitive resource r_j proceeds according to the following steps:

(1) collect in the set P_{a_i}, the chains k belonging to r_j, for which their last element, $last_k$, is already ordered with respect to the activity a_i, i.e., $last_k \prec a_i$;

(2) if $P_{a_i} \neq \emptyset$ a chain $k \in P_{a_i}$ is randomly chosen, otherwise a chain k is randomly selected among the available ones;

(3) a constraint $a_k \prec a_i$ is posted, where $a_k = last_k$;

(4) if a_i requires more than one resource unit, then the remaining set of available chains is split into two subsets: the set of chains which has a_k as last element, C_{a_k}, and the set of chains which does not, $\bar{C}_{a_k}$;

(5) to satisfy all remaining resource requirements, a_i is allocated first to chains belonging to the first subset, $k' \in C_{a_k}$ and,

(6) in case this set is not sufficient, the remaining units of a_i are then randomly allocated to the first available chains, k'', of the second subset, $k'' \in \bar{C}_{a_k}$.

Some Properties of Chaining. Why are we interested in the use of the chaining approach? Previous works have found several interesting properties.

---

[3] Note that this procedure is required to enable schedule execution.

First, for any partial order schedule there exists a partial order schedule in chaining form that represents at least the same set of solutions [2, Theorem 1]. This result allows us to restrict attention, without loss of generality, to the set of $\mathcal{POS}$s generated by a chaining procedure.

Second, given a schedule S, the makespan of the earliest solution[4] of the partial order schedule generated through chaining, $\mathcal{POS}_S$, is not greater than the makespan of the input solution. Thus, the makespan of a solution is preserved by the chaining-based robustification phase.

Additionally, previous work has identified structural properties for the effectiveness of chaining in RCPSP/max. In particular, the analysis of solutions obtained via chaining has brought out the presence of *synchronization points* which tend to degrade solution flexibility. These stem from the presence of activities which require multiple resource units and from precedence constraints between activities allocated to different chains. In fact, each of these aspects will mutually constrain two (or more), otherwise independent processes.

Finally, an interesting aspect of the procedure is that it can be coupled with any fixed-time schedule generation procedure. Independently of the fact that we are using our own constraint-based approach to solving RCPSP/max, the robustify step can be applied to other approaches to solving this scheduling problem such as [10,11,12].

4   Generating Flexible Schedules from Different Initial Solutions

In previous work we have not investigated the effects that different fixed-time initial solutions may have on the final synthesized $\mathcal{POS}$. This complementary analysis is contributed by this paper. In particular we extend our schema as shown in Fig. 3 where dashed lines highlight the new steps: (a) understanding the influence on $\mathcal{POS}$s of a much broader search for a better makespan before the robustify

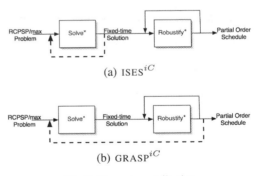

(a) ISES^{iC}

(b) GRASP^{iC}

Fig. 3. Current contribution

step; (b) considering the whole solve-and-robustify open loop within a meta-heuristic schema. For the solving phase we draw on our own CSP solvers for RCPSP/max.

The Iterative Sampling Procedure. The first approach we investigate is shown in Fig. 3(a). Instead of the simple ESTA greedy solver, we insert the ISES iterative improvement schema that is based on a randomized ESTA (hence *Solve** in the figure). The randomized version of ESTA is obtained by doing a pseudo-random selection of the decision. Conflict selection is performed not by picking the best ranked conflict but by choosing randomly within an acceptance band. This technique, introduced first in [13],

---

[4] The solution in which each activity is allocated at the earliest start time defined by the partial order schedule.

eliminates heuristic bias when the discrimination power of the estimator is low. The whole approach is called ISES^{iC} because in practice it joins the ISES optimizer with the iterative chaining that uses the MINID method.

The Grasp-Like Procedure. The second approach introduced in this paper is shown in Fig. 3(b). It follows a typical GRASP meta-heuristic schema [14]. The idea is to use the randomized ESTA to create different start schedules with the greedy solver then apply the iterative chaining exploration (hence the GRASP^{iC} name). This whole schema is iterated until a termination criterion is met. Based on a robustness metric the best $\mathcal{POS}$ found is returned.

Paths in the Search Space. In Fig. 4 we underscore graphically the different ways the iterative procedure and the GRASP-like follow through the search space. They both start from an infinite capacity solution that is not resource consistent. The ISES^{iC} performs iterative sampling for some period, then picks the best fixed-time schedule according to the makespan value, and finally calls the robustify procedure (sketched as a circle whose size is related to the number of performed iterations — see later). The GRASP^{iC} follows the different pattern of simply looking for different start schedule using the randomized ESTA then calling the robustification.

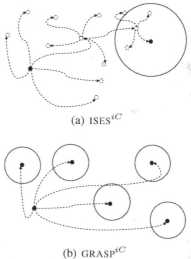

(a) ISES^{iC}

(b) GRASP^{iC}

Fig. 4. Different search paths

5 Experimental Evaluation

We apply the two approaches to two well-known RCPSP/max benchmark sets, j30 and j100. The benchmark set j30 is composed of 270 instances each of them with 30 activities and 5 resources, while the j100 is composed of 540 instances each of them with 100 activities and 4 resources.

Regarding ISES^{iC}, the ISES algorithm invoked at the first step is run using 10 restarts as its termination criterion, and the chaining procedure is run for 100 iterations at the second step to search for a $\mathcal{POS}$. For the GRASP^{iC} procedure, execution proceeds for 10 iterations of the main loop. In each iteration, an initial fixed-time schedule is computed and the chaining procedure is then applied 10 times in iterative improvement mode, generating a different $\mathcal{POS}$ at each step. Thus, in both approaches the best $\mathcal{POS}$ is selected among a set of 100 generated alternatives. We recall that in both cases the iterative chaining method is used with the MINID heuristic. In order to have a fair evaluation of the two criteria, we normalize the results according to an upper bound. For each metric $\mu()$, such bound is obtained considering the value $\mu(\mathcal{P})$, the quality of the temporal network that represents the initial structure of the problem. Any feasible schedule

Table 1. ISES^{iC} on the 30 activities benchmark

j30	$|$flex$|$	$|$fldt$|$	cpu	npc	mk
ISES^{iC}+MINID$_{flex}$	0.472	0.603	6.63	30.20	98.52
ISES^{iC}+MINID$_{flex}$ +MCS linear	0.472	0.607	8.22	30.26	98.12
ISES^{iC}+MINID$_{flex}$ +MCS quadratic	0.475	0.601	9.44	30.09	98.26
ISES^{iC}+MINID$_{fldt}$	0.451	0.627	6.63	30.64	98.44
ISES^{iC}+MINID$_{fldt}$ +MCS linear	0.446	0.631	8.22	30.64	98.10
ISES^{iC}+MINID$_{fldt}$ +MCS quadratic	0.448	0.626	9.42	30.74	98.22

Table 2. GRASP^{iC} on the 30 activities benchmark

j30	$|$flex$|$	$|$fldt$|$	cpu	npc	mk
GRASP^{iC}+MINID$_{flex}$	0.461	0.668	6.43	29.17	105.25
GRASP^{iC}+MINID$_{flex}$ +MCS linear	0.473	0.672	7.49	28.54	104.65
GRASP^{iC}+MINID$_{flex}$ +MCS quadratic	0.475	0.670	8.54	28.85	104.86
GRASP^{iC}+MINID$_{fldt}$	0.443	0.686	6.43	29.36	105.08
GRASP^{iC}+MINID$_{fldt}$ +MCS linear	0.448	0.687	7.49	28.85	104.56
GRASP^{iC}+MINID$_{fldt}$ +MCS quadratic	0.449	0.689	8.53	28.99	104.59

S is obtained by imposing further temporal constraints over the initial formulation of the problem, hence $\mu(\mathcal{P}) \geq \mu(S)$.

In the tables below, for each algorithm we report the following values: the normalized values, $|flex|$ and $|fldt|$, of the two robustness metrics, the CPU time required (in seconds), the number of posted precedence constraints, npc, and the makespan, mk.

The Set j30. Table 1 contains the results obtained using the six versions of the ISES^{iC} method[5]. An analysis of the result presented shows that the values of both metrics do not show great difference among different algorithm variants. In fact the values of $|flex|$ range from 0.472 to 0.475 and the results of $|fldt|$ from 0.626 to 0.631. Regarding the two metrics introduced above, it is possible to notice a twofold behavior. In fact the values of $flex$ are close or equal to the best value, 0.475, obtained in [2][6]. This is because in both procedures the iterative chaining method with MINID plays an important role in increasing the flexibility (in terms of $flex$) of the final partial order schedule[7]. On the contrary, the same behavior is not confirmed by the results obtained through the ISES^{iC} variants which try to optimize the $fldt$ metric. In this case, we see a decrease in quality: from 0.670 to 0.631. A different trend is observed in the case of the GRASP^{iC} variants (see Table 2). In terms of both metrics $flex$ and $fldt$, these methods are able to achieve good quality solutions. In fact in the case of $flex$, like in the case of ISES^{iC},

---

[5] These are obtained by the combination of the three heuristic with the two robustness criteria used during the iterative chaining process.

[6] This result is obtained by using ESTA^{iC}+MINID$_{flex}$ +MCS quadratic with 100 iterations.

[7] Of course there is a noticeable difference in terms of CPU time, where we have respectively 9.44 seconds for the ISES^{iC}+MINID$_{flex}$ +MCS quadratic version and 1.21 for the ESTA^{iC}+MINID.

Table 3. ISES^{iC} on the 100 activities benchmark

j100	|flex|	|fldt|	cpu	npc	mk
ISES^{iC}+MINID$_{flex}$	0.211	0.620	44.80	42.57	414.73
ISES^{iC}+MINID$_{flex}$ +MCS linear	0.211	0.619	43.63	42.22	413.67
ISES^{iC}+MINID$_{flex}$ +MCS quadratic	0.211	0.617	46.05	42.20	413.69
ISES^{iC}+MINID$_{fldt}$	0.205	0.634	44.85	42.37	414.61
ISES^{iC}+MINID$_{fldt}$ +MCS linear	0.205	0.633	43.64	42.11	413.40
ISES^{iC}+MINID$_{fldt}$ +MCS quadratic	0.205	0.632	46.00	42.17	413.47

Table 4. GRASP^{iC} on the 100 activities benchmark

j100	|flex|	|fldt|	cpu	npc	mk
GRASP^{iC}+MINID$_{flex}$	0.207	0.630	26.67	38.80	437.77
GRASP^{iC}+MINID$_{flex}$ +MCS linear	0.207	0.627	27.01	38.94	437.20
GRASP^{iC}+MINID$_{flex}$ +MCS quadratic	0.208	0.629	27.85	38.84	437.46
GRASP^{iC}+MINID$_{fldt}$	0.201	0.641	26.74	39.11	436.32
GRASP^{iC}+MINID$_{fldt}$ +MCS linear	0.201	0.641	27.01	38.79	435.72
GRASP^{iC}+MINID$_{fldt}$ +MCS quadratic	0.202	0.642	27.85	38.77	435.79

we achieved results that are close or equal to the current best (0.475). It is worth noting that in the case of $fldt$ the same results obtained in [2] are achieved. This confirm the relevance of the improvements in the chaining algorithms.

The Set j100. Table 3 and Table 4 show the results obtained in the case of the benchmark j100. In this case the difference of the two problem are smoother than in the previous benchmark. In case of $flex$ we see that the ISES^{iC} variants outperform the GRASP^{iC} (but with an improvement of only 2%). The opposite result is achieved in case of $fldt$: in this case we have 0.642 and 0.634 respectively for the best GRASP^{iC} variant and the best ISES^{iC} variant (the percentage difference is about 1%). The difference in behavior observed respectively for the j100 and j30 benchmarks underscores a distinction between these two problem sets. In fact, despite the size of each instance, the benchmark j100 presents a set of instances that are simpler with respect to the j30, both in terms of the temporal network and in the resource usage.

6   Discussion: Makespan Versus Robustness

The tradeoff between makespan and robustness highlighted above is worth a comment. We have seen before the results of the ISES^{iC} method, which is based on the use of ISES to optimize the makespan of the initial schedule as well as to increase the efficiency of the solving process. These results show that optimization of the makespan value reduces the ability to obtain robust schedules, especially if the fluidity metric is taken into account.

Figure 5 underlines possible motivations which can lead to different behaviors between flexibility and fluidity with respect to the makespan optimization factor. Fig. 5(a) presents a possible problem. This is a single resource problem in which three activities have to be scheduled. These are ordered according to the constraints in the figure, i.e., between a and b there is a simple precedence constraint[8] while between a and c the constraint specifies a time window $[1, 3]$, i.e., c cannot start more than 3 time-units after or 1 time-unit before the end of the activity a. Furthermore, the size of each activity describes both its duration (the width) and its resource need (the height). Additionally both a and b require one resource unit for two time units while c has a duration equal to three time-units and a resource requirement of 2. To complete the description of the problem, the resource capacity is equal to 2.

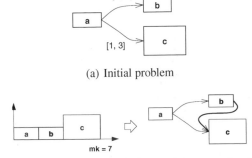

(a) Initial problem

Figure 5(b) and 5(c) show two different fixed-time schedules with the associated partial order schedule (the darker arrows represent the additional constraints necessary to obtain a flexible solution). Note that in this case for each fixed-time solution there is a unique partial order schedule: in fact any of the two proposed solutions gives a complete linearization of the activities. The two schedules have different makespan, respectively 7 and 8.

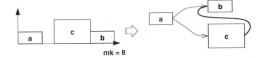

(b) Best makespan solution and its associated $\mathcal{POS}$

Let us now consider first the flexibility metric. If we look at the two partial order schedules (on the right hand side of Fig. 5(b) and 5(c)) it is possible to notice that in both cases there is the same $flex$ value. In fact in both cases the $flex$ value is zero because there is no pair of un-

(c) A sub-optimal solution and its associated $\mathcal{POS}$

Fig. 5. Dependency between makespan and robustness

ordered activities. Now we can shift the attention toward the fluidity metric. This metric considers the slack value between any pair of activities, that is, the minimum and maximum distance between them. In the figure, for the pair (a, c) we have the same value for both solutions, $dist(a, c) = [1, 3]$, which stems from the time window constraint defined between the two activities. On the other pair instead we have two different values: $dist(a, b) = [0, 1]$ in the case in Fig. 5(b) and $dist(a, b) = [4, H - 4]$ in the case in Fig. 5(c). This clearly shows that the flexibility value for the sub-optimal solution is greater than the one in Fig. 5(b). The same behavior can be found for the pair (b, c), where we have $dist(b, c) = [0, 1]$ for the case in Fig. 5(b) while for the case in Fig. 5(c) $dist(c, b) = [0, H - 8]$. The problem is that in the schedule with the optimum makespan (Fig. 5(b)) the activity b is "caged in" by the other two activities. Therefore the time window constraint defined between a and c has the effect of limiting the flexibility of activity b. Furthermore since the capacity of the resource is equal to the requirement of c, no chaining method can overcome this problem.

---

[8] Where H represents the temporal horizon of the problem.

It is possible to note that this is peculiar characteristic of the RCPSP/max problems and in particular this is due to the presence of maximum distance constraints. In fact if the maximum constraint between a and c did not exist, activity b would have the ability to move back and forth in a larger interval thus yielding in a more flexible solution.

Further Remarks. The use of a more optimized initial schedule biases the robustify phase against the construction of flexible partial order schedule. In fact the tightness (makespan) of the initial solution can preclude the achievement of good solutions. This behavior is justified from the different nature of the two metrics: $flex$ is a qualitative criterion whereas the $fldt$ is a more quantitative metric. Therefore a schedule with a better makespan value presents an allocation of the activities that is more compact, leaving fewer degrees of freedom for the iterative chaining procedure. Finally while in [2] it has been proved that the robustify step does not deteriorate the results obtained in the solve phase, we can not claim the same for the effects of some characteristics of the fixed-time solutions with regard to the final flexible schedule.

7 Conclusions

This work has considered the Solve-and-Robustify approach introduced in [1,2] and has complemented previous results by analyzing the influence of different fixed-time schedules on the final partial order schedule. In particular, two more sophisticated approaches based on Solve-and-Robustify have been defined and evaluated. The former is based on the idea of developing flexible solutions from makespan optimized solutions. The second approach instead has been obtained following the GRASP paradigm, where the robustify step can be considered as a local search procedure. The results of the experimental evaluation have shown an interesting trade-off between the makespan and the more quantitative of the robustness metrics used, $fldt$. In practice the use of more optimized initial schedule biases the robustify phase against the construction of flexible partial order schedule. In fact the tightness (makespan) of the initial solution can preclude the achievement of good flexible solutions. Therefore while the robustify step does not deteriorate the results obtained in the solve phase, some characteristics of the fixed-time solutions may lower the robustness of the final partial order schedules. The current results show from a different perspective the effectiveness of the chaining algorithms presented in [2], which obtain good quality $\mathcal{POS}$s with low CPU time with respect the new variants.

Before closing, it is worth underscoring that $\mathcal{POS}$ computation is not only useful to offer a level of robustness with respect to temporal uncertainty at execution time. In previous work, we have considered the role of such flexible representation to solve complex cumulative scheduling problems [8,1] and, additionally, we are investigating the role of $\mathcal{POS}$ in different search schema. For some results on a resource constrained scheduling problem with quality metrics see [15].

Acknowledgments. Amedeo Cesta, Angelo Oddi, and Nicola Policella's work is partially supported by MIUR (Italian Ministry for Education, University and Research) under project RoboCare. Stephen F. Smith's work is supported in part by the U.S. Air Force Research Laboratory - Rome, under contract F30602-02-2-0149, by the National Science Foundation under contract # 9900298 and by the CMU Robotics Institute.

References

1. Policella, N., Smith, S.F., Cesta, A., Oddi, A.: Generating Robust Schedules through Temporal Flexibility. In: Proceedings of the 14th International Conference on Automated Planning & Scheduling, ICAPS'04, AAAI Press (2004) 209–218
2. Policella, N., Oddi, A., Smith, S.F., Cesta, A.: Generating Robust Partial Order Schedules. In: Principles and Practice of Constraint Programming, 10th International Conference, CP 2004. Volume 3258 of Lecture Notes in Computer Science., Springer (2004) 496–511
3. Artigues, C., Roubellat, F.: A polynomial activity insertion algorithm in a multi-resource schedule with cumulative constraints and multiple modes. European Journal of Operational Research **127** (2000) 297–316
4. Leus, R., Herroelen, W.: Stability and Resource Allocation in Project Planning. IIE Transactions **36** (2004) 667–682
5. Policella, N.: Scheduling with Uncertainty: a Proactive Approach using Partial Order Schedules. PhD thesis, University of Rome "La Sapienza" (2005)
6. Bartusch, M., Mohring, R.H., Radermacher, F.J.: Scheduling project networks with resource constraints and time windows. Annals of Operations Research **16** (1988) 201–240
7. Aloulou, M.A., Portmann, M.C.: An Efficient Proactive Reactive Scheduling Approach to Hedge against Shop Floor Disturbances. In: Proceedings of 1st Multidisciplinary International Conference on Scheduling : Theory and Applications, MISTA 2003. (2003) 337–362
8. Cesta, A., Oddi, A., Smith, S.F.: Profile Based Algorithms to Solve Multiple Capacitated Metric Scheduling Problems. In: Proceedings of the 4th International Conference on Artificial Intelligence Planning Systems, AIPS-98, AAAI Press (1998) 214–223
9. Cesta, A., Oddi, A., Smith, S.F.: A Constraint-based method for Project Scheduling with Time Windows. Journal of Heuristics **8** (2002) 109–136
10. Dorndorf, U., Pesch, E., Phan-Huy, T.: A time-oriented branch-and-bound algorithm for resource-constrained project scheduling with generalised precedence constraints. Management Science **46** (2000) 1365–1384
11. Smith, T.B., Pyle, J.M.: An effective algorithm for project scheduling with arbitrary temporal constraints. In: Proceedings of the 19th National Conference on Artificial Intelligence, AAAI-04. (2004) 544–549
12. Cicirello, V.A., Smith, S.F.: Heuristic selection for stochastic search optimization: Modeling solution quality by extreme value theory. In: Principles and Practice of Constraint Programming, 10th International Conference, CP 2004. Volume 3258 of Lecture Notes in Computer Science., Springer (2004) 197–211
13. Oddi, A., Smith, S.F.: Stochastic Procedures for Generating Feasible Schedules. In: Proceedings 14th National Conference on Artificial Intelligence, AAAI-97, AAAI Press (1997) 308–314
14. Resende, M., Ribeiro, C.: Greedy Randomized Adaptive Search Procedures. In Glover, F., Kochenberger, G., eds.: Handbook of Metaheuristics. Kluwer Academic Publishers (2002) 219–249
15. Policella, N., Wang, X., Smith, S., Oddi, A.: Exploiting Temporal Flexibility to Obtain High Quality Schedules. In: Proceedings of the 20th National Conference on Artificial Intelligence, AAAI-05, AAAI Press (2005)

Optimal Scheduling with Heuristic Best First Search[*]

María R. Sierra and Ramiro Varela

Centro de Inteligencia Artificial, Departamento de Informática,
Universidad de Oviedo, Campus de Biseques, E-33271 Gijón, Spain
Tel: +34-8-5182032; Fax: +34-8-5182125
{mariasierra, ramiro}@aic.uniovi.es
http:\\www.aic.uniovi.es\Tc

Abstract. A* Nilsson´s algorithm is a systematic search paradigm that allows for exploiting domain knowledge to obtain optimal solutions. In this paper we apply A* to the Job Shop Scheduling problem. We restrict the search to the space of active schedules and exploit the Jackson' preemptive schedule to design a good heuristic function. Our objective is to study the extent to which this approach is able to solve this problem to optimality. Moreover we propose a method to obtain suboptimal solutions when no optimal ones are reached within a reasonable amount of time. We report results from an experimental study and compare with other well-known exact search paradigms such as backtracking and branch and bound.

Keywords: Job Shop Scheduling, Heuristic Search, A* Nilsson´s algorithm.

1 Introduction

The Job Shop Scheduling (JSS) requires scheduling a set of N jobs $\{J_0,...,J_{N-1}\}$ on a set of M physical resources or machines $\{R_0,...,R_{M-1}\}$. Each job Ji consists of a set of operations $\{\theta_{i0},...,\theta_{iM-1}\}$ to be sequentially scheduled from the release dates. The operation θ_{ij} requires the exclusive use of a single resource during a processing time of du_{ij} time units with no preemption. The JSS has interested to many researches and a lot of techniques have been applied to this problem. In [4], A. S. Jain and S. Meeran give an extensive review of the most outstanding approaches. Here we apply the A* Nilsson's algorithm [5] to the JSS problem. We chose the search space of active schedules and consider a heuristic strategy obtained from so called Jackson´s Preemptive Schedule (JPS) [1,2]. We compare A* against other well-known exact search paradigms such as the backtracking method proposed by N. Sadeh and M. S. Fox in [6] and the branch and bound (B&B) method proposed by P. Brucker, B. Jurisch and B. Sievers in [1].

2 The Search Space of Active Schedules

A schedule is *active* if to start earlier any operation, at least another one should be delayed. Maybe the best-known algorithm to calculate active schedules is the G&T

---

[*] This work has been supported by project FEDER-MCYT TIC2003-04153 and by FICYT under grant BP04-021.

S. Bandini and S. Manzoni (Eds.): AI*IA 2005, LNAI 3673, pp. 173–176, 2005.

algorithm proposed by B. Giffler and G. L. Thomson [3]. This is a greedy algorithm that produces an active schedule in a number of $N*M$ steps. At each step the G&T algorithm makes a non-deterministic choice. Every active schedule can be reached by taking the appropriate sequence of choices. Therefore if we consider every possible choice at each step, we have a complete search graph suitable for heuristic state space search strategies such as branch and bound, backtracking or A*. This is the approach taken, for example, by Varela and Soto in [7]. Our main contribution with respect to the later work is the use of a new heuristic and a method to calculate non-exact solutions. Figure 1 shows the expansion algorithm that generates the full search tree of active schedules when it is applied successively from the initial state.

3 The A* Algorithm

The A* Nilsson's algorithm starts from an initial state s, a set of goal nodes and a transition operator SUC such that for each node n of the search space, $SUC(n)$ provides the set of successor states of n. Each transition from n to n' has a positive cost $c(n,n')$. The algorithm searches for a solution path from s to a goal state. At any one time, there is a set of candidate nodes to be expanded which are maintained in anordered list *OPEN*. Then in each iteration, the node to be expanded is always the one in *OPEN* with the lowest value of the evaluation function f, defined as $f(n)=g(n)+h(n)$; where $g(n)$ is the minimal cost known from s to n, (of course if the search space is a tree, the value of $g(n)$ does not change, otherwise this value has to be updated as long as the search progresses) and $h(n)$ is a heuristic positive estimation of the minimal distance from n to the nearest goal. If the heuristic function underestimates the actual minimal

Algorithm *SUC(state n)*
1. *A = set containing the first unscheduled operation of each job;*
2. *Determine the operation $\theta' \in A$ with the lowest completion time if scheduled in the current state, that is $st\theta' + du\theta' \leq st\theta + du\theta,\ \forall \theta \in A$;*
3. *Let M' be the machine required by θ', and B the subset of A whose operations require to M';*
4. *Remove from B every operation that is unable to start at a time lower than $st\theta' + du\theta'$;*
5. **While** $(B \neq \varnothing)$ **do**
   6. *Select $\theta \in B$ and schedule it at its lowest possible start time to build a partial schedule corresponding to the next state n';*
   7. *Add n' to successors;*
   8. *Remove θ from A and insert in A the next operation of θ within its job sequence, if θ is not the last one;*
   endwhile;
9. *return successors;*
end.

Fig. 1. Algorithm to expand a state n. When it is successively applied from the initial state, that is an empty schedule, it generates the whole space of active schedules.

cost, $h*(n)$, from n to the goals, i.e. $h(n) \leq h*(n)$, for every node n, the algorithm is admissible, i.e. the return of an optimal solution is guaranteed. The heuristic function $h(n)$ represents knowledge about the problem domain, therefore as long as h approximates $h*$ the algorithms is more and more efficient.

For large problem instances the search for optimal solutions is impracticable even if we have the best informed heuristic. In this case the A* algorithm can be modified to obtain semi-optimal solutions at a reasonable cost. Herein we propose a method to obtain suboptimal solutions that consist on applying a greedy algorithm from a number of expanded states. To do that we use the G&T algorithm with breaking ties by means of the *JPS* value of the machine M' involved in the node expansion. In the reported experiments of section 4 we applied the greedy algorithm to only one state out of each set of 100 consecutive expanded states.

To design the heuristic we made a problem relaxation in two steps. Firstly every capacity constraint is relaxed with the exception of those of machine m. The resulting problem is known as the One Machine Sequencing (OMS) where each job is defined by its head r_i the processing time p_i over machine m, and its tail q_i. This problem is still NP-hard, hence a new relaxation is made: the non-preemption of machine m. This way an optimal solution to this problem is given by the Jackson's preemptive schedule (JPS) [3]. The the heuristic, termed as h_{JPS}, is calculated by

$$h_{JPS}(n) = MAX_{m \in Machines} \{JPS(m)\} - g(n) . \tag{1}$$

where *Machines* refers to the machines with at least one unscheduled operation in the state n, and *JPS(m)* is the *JPS* of the operations that require m and remains unscheduled in state n.

4 Experimental Results

We used an A* prototype implementation coded in C++ language and developed in Builder C++ 6.0 for Windows. In the first set of experiments we considered the set of problems proposed in [7]. This is a set of 60 problems of size 10×5 which is organized in 6 groups of 10 problems each. Each group is characterized by 2 parameters: BK (bottleneck resources) and RG (range parameter) that define some problem characteristics. Table 1 summarizes the results obtained with the h_{JPS} heuristic over the 60 problems. In [7], N. Sadeh and M. S. Fox report results from applying a backtracking algorithm guided by a variable and value ordering heuristic.

Table 1. Summary of results on the bechmark of 60 problems of size 10×5

Subset of problems	Number of problems solved	Num. of problems solved expanding 51 states	Mean number of expanded states
BK = 1, RG = 0,0	10	8	159.5
BK = 2, RG = 0,0	10	0	32120.2
BK = 1, RG = 0,1	10	6	280.5
BK = 2, RG = 0,1	10	2	45265.5
BK = 1, RG = 0,2	10	6	115.2
BK = 2, RG = 0,2	10	4	715.7

Table 2. Summary of results on the set of problems LA01-15 and problem FT20

Subset of problems	Size	A*		B&B	
		Prob. Solved	Time (sec.)	Prob. Solved	Time (sec.)
La01-05	10×5	5 of 5	46	5 of 5	< 1
La06-10	15×5	4 of 5	13.3	5 of 5	< 1
La11-15	20×5	4 of 5	285.3	5 of 5	< 1
FT20	20×5	1 of 1	30	0 of 1	> 3 days

In this study they try to reach that are not worse than about a 20 percent w.r.t. the optimal. Even within this limit the backtracking search was able to reach a feasible solution in only 52 of the 60 problem instances. Table 2 summarizes the results of exploiting A* and B&B over a set of problems taken from the OR-library. Here it is remarkable the case of the FT20 instance. In this case A* reach an optimal solution in 30 seconds, whereas B&B cannot reach an optimal solution even after 3 days of CPU time.

References

1. Brucker, P., Jurisch, B. and Sievers, B. A branch and bound algorithm for the job-shop scheduling problem. Discrete Applied Mathematics 49 , 107-127, (1994).
2. Carlier, J. and Pinson, E. Adjustment of heads and tails for the job-shop problem. European Journal of Operational Research 78, 146-161, (1994).
3. Giffler, B. Thomson, G. L. Algorithms for Solving Production Scheduling Problems. Operations Reseach 8, 487-503 (1960).
4. Jain, A. S. and Meeran, S. Deterministic job-shop scheduling: Past, present and future. European Journal of Operational Research 113, 390-434 (1999).
5. Nilsson, N., Principles of Artificial Intelligence, Tioga, Palo Alto, CA, 1980.
6. Sadeh, N., Fox, M.S., Variable and Value Ordering Heuristics for the Job Shop Scheduling Constraint Satisfaction Problem. Artificial Intelligence 86, 1-41 (1996).
7. Varela, R., and Soto, E. Scheduling as Heuristic Search with State Space Reduction. Ed. Springer, LNAI 2527, pp. 815-824 (2002).

Planning with Derived Predicates Through Rule-Action Graphs and Local Search Techniques

Alfonso Gerevini, Alessandro Saetti, Ivan Serina, and Paolo Toninelli

Dipartimento di Elettronica per l'Automazione, Università degli Studi di Brescia,
Via Branze 38, I-25123 Brescia, Italy
{gerevini, saetti, serina}@ing.unibs.it

1 Introduction

In classical domain-independent planning, derived predicates are predicates that the domain actions can only indirectly affect. Their truth in a state can be inferred by particular axioms, that enrich the typical operator description of a planning domain.

As discussed in [3,6], derived predicates are practically useful to express in a concise and natural way some indirect action effects, such as updates on the transitive closure of a relation. Moreover, compiling them away by introducing artificial actions and facts in the formalization is infeasible because, in the worst case, we have an exponential blow up of either the problem description or the plan length [6]. This suggests that is worth investigating new planning methods supporting derived predicates, rather than using existing methods with "compiled" problems.

The first version of PDDL, the language of the International Planning Competitions, supports derived predicates as particular "axioms", and the recent PDDL2.2 [3] version re-introduces them as one of the two new features for the benchmark domains of the 2004 International Planning Competition (IPC-4). Some methods for handling derived predicates have been developed and implemented in several planning systems, such as UCPOP [1] and the very recent planners DOWNWARD, SGPLAN and MARVIN [2].

In this paper, we present some techniques for planning with derived predicates, which are implemented in a new version of the LPG planner [4] called LPG-td. LPG-td took part in the fourth International Planning Competition showing good performance in many benchmark problems. For a more detailed description of our techniques, the interested reader may see [5].

2 Derived Predicates and Rule Graph

In PDDL2.2, derived predicates are particular predicates that do not appear in the effects of any domain action. The truth value of a derived predicate is determined by a set of *domain rules* of the form *if* $\Phi_{\overline{x}}$ *then* $P(\overline{x})$, where $P(\overline{x})$ is the derived predicate, $\overline{x}$ is a tuple of variables, the free variables in $\Phi_{\overline{x}}$ are exactly the variables in $\overline{x}$, and $\Phi_{\overline{x}}$ is a first-order formula such that the negated normal form of $\Phi_{\overline{x}}$ does not contain any derived predicate in negated form.

For example, "*if* $on(x, y) \vee \exists z \left(on(x, z) \wedge above(z, y) \right)$ *then* $above(x, y)$" (for each x, y) is a domain rule deriving the predicate *above* in the blocks world: a block x is *above* y if x is *on* y, or it is *on* a third block z which is *above* y.

S. Bandini and S. Manzoni (Eds.): AI*IA 2005, LNAI 3673, pp. 177–181, 2005.

A *grounded rule* is a rule where every predicate argument is a constant. Given a planning problem and a set R of rules defining the derived predicates of the domain, we can derive a logically equivalent set $\overline{R}$ of grounded rules of the form *if $\phi_{\overline{c}}$ then $P(\overline{c})$*, where $\phi_{\overline{c}}$ is a conjunction of ground literals (for a detailed description see [5]). We call a ground predicate appearing in the initial state, problem goals, or in the preconditions or effects of a domain action a *basic fact*, a ground derived predicate obtained by substituting each variable in the derived predicate of a rule with a constant a *derived fact*, the left hand side (LHS) of each rule in $\overline{R}$ the *triggering condition* of the rule, and the conjoined facts forming the LHS of the rule the *triggering facts* of the rule.

We represent the domain grounded rules $\overline{R}$ through a *Rule Graph*. The **rule graph** of a planning problem Π with derived predicates defined by a set of rules $\overline{R}$ is a directed AND-OR-graph such that:

- AND-nodes are either (i) leaf nodes labeled by basic facts of Π, or (ii) nodes labeled by derived facts of Π; OR-nodes are labeled by grounded rules in $\overline{R}$ and are not leaf nodes.
- Each AND-node p is connected to a set of OR-nodes representing the grounded rules deriving p. Each OR-node labeled r is connected to a set of AND-nodes representing the triggering condition of r.

Given a state s, and a set of domain rules R, we denote with $D(s, R)$ the set of the derived facts obtained by applying the rules in R to s with an arbitrary order until no new fact can be derived. In other words, $D(s, R)$ is the least-fixed point over all possible applications of the rules to the state where the derived facts are assumed to be false (because under the closed world assumption, they do not belong to s). An algorithm for deriving $D(s, R)$ is given in [3]. In the following, we will abbreviate $s \cup D(s, R) \models \psi$ with $s \models^R \psi$, where $\models$ is the logical entailment under the closed world assumption on s, and ψ is a (basic or derived) fact.

3   Rule-Action Graphs

We represent a (partial) plan in a domain with derived predicates through an extension of the linear action graph representation [4], which we call *Rule-Action Graph*. A **rule-action graph** (RA-graph) of a problem Π with derived predicates is a linear action graph where

- each fact level can contain two additional types of nodes: *rule nodes* and *derived nodes;*
- each rule node is labeled by a grounded rule of Π, and each *derived node* is labeled by the fact derived by a grounded rule of Π;
- each rule node labeled r at a level l is connected by incoming edges to a set of fact nodes at l representing the triggering facts of r, and by an outgoing edge to a derived node at l representing the ground predicate derived by r.

We call an action precondition node representing a derived fact a *derived precondition node*, and a node representing a triggering fact of a grounded rule *triggering node*.

The rule nodes are automatically "activated" whenever the corresponding triggering nodes are supported, i.e., a rule node is automatically inserted at a level of the graph (together with its derived fact node, if not already present) whenever its triggering nodes are all supported at that level.

In the following, $S(l)$ indicates the world state obtained (under the closed world assumption) by applying to the problem initial state the actions in the RA-graph up to level $l - 1$, ordered according to the level of their action node. A grounded rule r = (if $\varphi_1 \wedge \ldots \wedge \varphi_n$ then ψ) is **activated** at a level l of a RA-graph $\mathcal{A}$ *iff*, for each literal φ_i in r, either $S(l) \models \varphi_i$ or there exists an activated rule at l that derives φ_i.

4 Local Search Techniques for Rule-Action Graphs

An RA-graph may contain some *flaws*. A flaw at a level l of a RA-graph $\mathcal{A}$ is a precondition node of the action node at level l that is not supported in $\mathcal{A}$. A basic fact node labeled q at a level l is *supported* if there is an action node at level $l - 1$ representing an action with (positive) effect q. A derived precondition node p at a level l of a RA-graph is supported *iff* there is a rule node r at l such that p is the derived node of r. This is the case if and only if $S(l) \models^R \psi_p$, where ψ_p is the derived fact represented by p. An RA-graph with no flaw represents a valid plan.

The initial RA-graph contains the special actions a_{start} and a_{end}.[1] Each search step identifies the neighborhood $N(\mathcal{A})$ (successor states) of the current RA-graph $\mathcal{A}$ (search state), which is a set of RA-graphs obtained from $\mathcal{A}$ by adding a *helpful action node* or removing a *harmful action node* in the attempt to repair the *earliest* flawed level of $\mathcal{A}$.

The definition of helpful and harmful node relies on the notion of *Activation Fact Set*. Given an unsupported derived precondition node d at a level l of a RA-graph, an **activation fact set** for d is a set F of basic facts such that $S(l) \cup F \models^R \psi_d$, where ψ_d is the derived fact represented by d, and F is minimal with respect to set containment. Intuitively, an activation fact set is a set of basic facts activating a set of rule nodes supporting a derived precondition node. For example, let r_1= (*if* $p_1 \wedge p_2$ *then* d_1) and r_2= (*if* $p_3 \wedge d_1$ *then* d_2) be two grounded rules and $S(l) = \{p_3\}$, then $\{p_1, p_2\}$ is an activation set for d_2 at level l of the graph. Note that p_3 is not in the activation set for d_2, because at level l it is already supported.

The activation fact sets are computed by two mutually recursive algorithms which perform a backward search on the rule graph exploiting pre-computed heuristic and mutex information (for more details see [5]).

In the following, a_i denotes an action node a at level i of $\mathcal{A}$, and l_a the level of a. Given a flawed level l of $\mathcal{A}$, an action node a_i is **helpful** for l if its insertion into $\mathcal{A}$ at a level $i \leq l$ would make an unsupported fact node f at l supported, where f is a basic precondition node or it represents a fact in an activation fact set for a derived precondition node at l. a_i is **harmful** for l if its removal from $\mathcal{A}$ either (i) would remove the unsupported precondition nodes at l ($i = l$), or (ii) would make f supported.

The elements of the neighborhood are weighed according to a *heuristic evaluation function E* estimating their quality (i.e., the number of search steps required to find a

---

[1] The effect nodes of a_{start} represent the positive facts of the initial state of the planning problem Π, and the precondition nodes of a_{end} the goals of Π.

valid plan). E is an extension of the heuristic evaluation function described in [4] for handling derived predicates. An element with the lowest cost is then selected from $N(\mathcal{A})$ using a "noise parameter" randomizing the search to escape from local minima [4].

5   Experimental Results

In this section, we present some experimental results using the test problems of the IPC-4, which illustrate the effectiveness of our techniques implemented in the LPG-td planner.

Figure 1 shows the CPU-time (in logarithmic scale) of the IPC-4 planners for `Philosophers` and `PSR-Middle`. In the first domain, both LPG-td and DOWNWARD solve 48 problems, while MARVIN solves only 30 problems. LPG-td is generally faster than the other planners, except for a few problems where DOWNWARD performs better than LPG-td. In `PSR-Middle` both SGPLAN and LPG-td solve all problems, but LPG-td is generally faster.

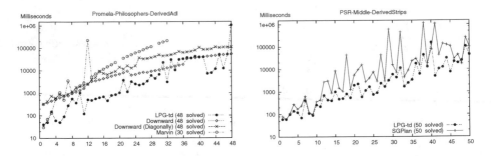

Fig. 1. Performance of LPG-td and some IPC-4 planners in three benchmark domains involving derived predicates. On the x-axis we have the problem names (abbreviated by numbers). On the y-axis, we have CPU-time (log scale).

In order to test our techniques we designed a domain that can generate many more activation fact sets than the IPC-4 domains (the number of activation fact sets can be 4 orders of magnitude larger). In this domain LPG-td and SGPLAN perform similarly, but LPG-td solves more problems, and in few cases it is significantly faster than SGPLAN. Additional results are available in [5] and in the web page of LPG (`http://lpg.ing.unibs.it`).

References

1. Barret, A., Christianson, D., Friedman, M., Kwok, C., Golden, K., Penberthy, S., Sun, Y., Weld, D. 1995. UCPOP User's Manual *T.R. 93-09-08d*, University of Washington.
2. In Edelkamp, S., Hoffmann, J., Littman, M., Younes, H. (Eds.) 2004. *In Abstract Booklet of the IPC-4 Planners (ICAPS-04)*.

3. Edelkamp, S., and Hoffmann, J. 2004. PDDL2.2: The language for the Classic Part of the 4th International Planning Competition. *T.R. no. 195*: Institut für Informatik, Freiburg, Germany.
4. Gerevini, A., Saetti, A., and Serina, I. 2003. Planning through Stochastic Local Search and Temporal Action Graphs. *Journal of Artificial Intelligence Research* 20:239–290.
5. Gerevini, A., Saetti, A., Serina, I, and Toninelli, P. Planning with Derived Predicates through Rule-Action Graphs and Relaxed-Plan Heuristics. 2005. *R.T. 2005-01-40*, University of Brescia.
6. Thièbaux, S., Hoffmann, J., and Nebel, B. 2003. In defense of PDDL Axioms. *Proc. of the Eighteenth International Joint Conference on Artificial Intelligence.*

The Architecture of a Reactive Path-Planner for Mobile Robots Based on Cellular Automata

Fabio M. Marchese

Dipartimento di Informatica, Sistemistica e Comunicazione,
Università degli Studi di Milano - Bicocca,
Via Bicocca degli Arcimboldi 8, I-20126, Milano, Italy
`fabio.marchese@disco.unimib.it`

Abstract. The aim of this paper is to describe the architecture of a Path Planner for Mobile Robots based on the paradigm of Cellular Automata. This path planner is very flexible, handling robots with quite different kinematics (omnidirectional, car-like, asymmetrical, etc.), with generic shapes (even with concavities and holes) and with generic cinematic centers locations. It can be applied to flat (Euclidean) Work Space and to natural variable terrains. Thanks to this architecture based a Potential Fields Method, it turns out to be very fast, complete and optimal, allowing to react to the world dynamics (reactive planning), generating new optimal solutions every time the obstacles positions changes.

1 Introduction

The work presented in this paper concerns Mobile Robots Path-Planning exploiting Multilayered Cellular Automata (MCA). The Path-planning problem is very important to drive mobile robots in environments avoiding collision with obstacles. In this work we introduce the architecture of a complete optimal path-planner applicable on robots with different shapes and kinematics operating in a natural world. Thanks to the use of the paradigm of Cellular Automata, the approach is distributed and very fast, even on single-processor computers. During the last twenty years, many authors have proposed different solutions to the problem (e.g. [5,6]). In the eighties, Khatib in [3] first introduced the Artificial Potential Fields Methods for the collision avoidance problem in a continuous space for a 6 DOF manipulator robot. Since then, many other authors proposed works using these methods ([1], *Distance Transform* [2], *Path Transform* [7], etc.). We used CA as a formalism for merging the Grid Model of the world (Occupancy Grid) with the $\mathcal{C}$-Space of a robot and Numerical (Artificial) Potential Field methods, with the task to find a simple and fast solution for the path-planning problem for mobile robots with different kinematics. This method uses a directional (anisotropic) propagation of distance values between adjacent automata to build a potential hypersurface embedded in 4D space. Using a constrained version of the descending gradient on the hypersurface, it is possible to find out all the admissible, equivalent and shortest (for a given metric of the discretized space) trajectories connecting two configurations of the robot $\mathcal{C}$-Space.

S. Bandini and S. Manzoni (Eds.): AI*IA 2005, LNAI 3673, pp. 182–185, 2005.

2   The Path-Planner Architecture

The planner architecture is organized in four main packages (Fig. 1). The main package is the Path-Planner itself: it coordinates the two lateral packages (Environment and Robot Models). It is worth noting that the World Model, the Robot Model and the Path-Planner use the same structure based on Cellular Automata, i.e. there is an isomorphism based on a regular decomposition structure. The CA Kernel realizes the Cellular Automata paradigm (Fig. 2.b). The architecture is organized in layers of cells depending on the underlying topological space. There are bi-dimensional spaces, such as the Work-Space, and 3D spaces (C-Space, Attraction Potential, etc.); some of them are active and are used to make calculations, others are static and are used only to represent specific information. The package makes available the basic structures to represent the information of both types of spaces and the related calculation kernel.

The Environment Model (Fig. 2.c) is subdivided in two parts: the C-Space and the Terrain Elevation Map. The first is a 3D space ($\mathbf{SE}(2)$, i.e. position and orientation) in which are represented both the $\mathcal{C}\text{-}Obstacles$ and the $\mathcal{C}_{free}\text{-}$ $Space$. The second is a regular 2D manifold representing the elevation map ($z = f(x, y)$) of the terrain on which the robot navigates. In a structured world (e.g. an office-like environment), it is simply as a flat surface ($z = 0$). There is space metric associated to the $\mathcal{C}\text{-}Space$. Formally, in a continuous space, it is a set of parameters used to define a matrix (fundamental tensor) necessary to evaluate the infinitesimal distance between two neighboring points. In our case, the space is discretized in cells (CA), and the set of parameters are slightly different, but it has the same role: the evaluation of the linear distance between two adjacent cells in the 3D $\mathcal{C}\text{-}Space$.

The robot model (Fig. 2.d) is composed by two major parts: its shape and its kinematics. The shape is defined using a 2D CA: it is a small occupancy map centered on the robot cinematic center. The robot kinematics is defined as a set of available moves. Each move allows the robot to rototranslate from the current cell to an adjacent one. The kinematics definition is completed with a robot metric. This is a set of costs associated to each robot movement, to evaluate the cost the robot has to spend to reach a new pose in terms of energy or time or path length. From this two structures is derived a secondary structure containing

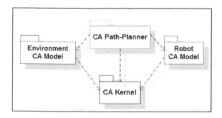

Fig. 1. Mobile Robot Path-Planner Architecture

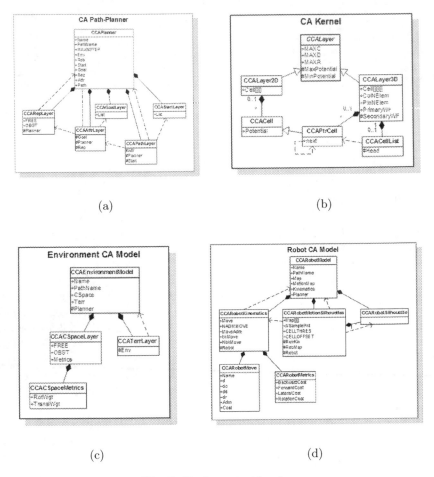

Fig. 2. Packages inside views

the Motion Silhouettes. In Regular Decomposition world models, the obstacles are decomposed in full or empty cells (Occupancy Grids) and the robot is shrunk to its cinematic center. The well-known technique of enlarging the obstacles by the maximum robot radius is then used to take into account of its real extension [5]. An anisotropic enlargement [5], i.e. a different obstacles enlargement for each robot orientation, would solve only partially the problem for asymmetric robots. We adopted a different approach to address this problem, by defining the Motion Silhouettes and evaluating cell by cell the set of admissible robot movements that avoid collisions. The Motion Silhouette is generated by sweeping the basic robot shape during a single move and marking the cells covered.

The Path-Planner of Fig. 2.a is a sort of "bridge" between the Environment Model and the Robot Model. It combines the information from both to generate a set of optimal trajectories. It is organized in two major subsystems: an Input Subsystem and an Output Subsystem. The Input Subsystem is an interface toward the outstanding environment. Its layers have to react as fast as possible to the external changes: the robot starting pose, the robot goal pose, the elevation map of the terrain and, the most important, the changes of the environment, i.e. the obstacles movements in a dynamic world. All of these changes are detected by a sensorial system not described in this work. The Output Subsystem returns the results of the planning, that is the set of complete trajectories from the *Path Extraction L.*, or a single motion step from the *Attraction L.*

3   Conclusion

In this paper we have described an architecture solution for the Path-Planning Problem for mobile robots with generic shapes (user defined) and with generic kinematics on variable (regular) terrains based on (Multilayered) Cellular Automata. An important property of this algorithm is related to the consistency of the solution found. For a given terrain surface, the solution found (if it exists) is the set of all shortest paths (for the given metric) that connect the starting cell to the goal cell. The CA evolution can be seen as a motion from one point to another point of a global state space until an optimal solution is reached. This is a convergence point for the given problem or a steady global state. If we make some perturbations, such as changing the environment (e.g. adding, deleting or moving one or more obstacles), then the point becomes unstable and the CA starts to evolve again towards a new steady state, finding a new set of optimal trajectories (*Incremental Updating*).

References

1. Barraquand J., Langlois B., Latombe J. C., Numerical Potential Field Techniques for Robot Path Planning, *IEEE Trans. on Systems, Man and Cybernetics*, Vol. 22, No. 2 (Mar 1992), 224-241
2. Jahanbin M. R., Fallside F., Path Planning Using a Wave Simulation Technique in the Configuration Space in Gero J. S., *Artificial Intelligence in Engineering: Robotics and Processes*, Computational Mechanics Publications (Southampton 1988)
3. Kathib O. Real-time Obstacle Avoidance for Manipulator and Mobile Robots, *Proc. of Int. Conf. on Robotics and Automation* (1985)
4. Kobilarov M., Sukhatme G. S., Time Optimal Path Planning on Outdoor Terrain for Mobile Robots under Dynamic Constraints, *Proc. of IEEE/RSJ Int. Conf. on Intelligent Robots and Systems* (2004)
5. Lozano-Pérez T., Wesley M. A., An Algorithm for Planning Collision-Free Paths Among Polyhedral Obstacles, *Comm. of the ACM*, Vol. **22**, No. 10, (Oct 1979), 560-570
6. Lozano-Pérez T., Spatial Planning: A Configuration Space Approach, *IEEE Trans. on Computers*, Vol. C-32, No. 2 (Feb 1983), 108-120
7. Zelinsky A., Using Path Transforms to Guide the Search for Findpath in 2D, *Int. J. of Robotics Research*, Vol. 13, No. 4 (Aug 1994), 315-325

Modal Operators with Adaptable Semantics for Multi-agent Systems

S. Borgo

LOA (ISTC-CNR), via Solteri 38, 38100 Trento, Italy
borgo@loa-cnr.it

Abstract. We look at extensions of modal logic for representation and reasoning in the area of multi-agent systems. Building on dynamic logic and Henkin quantifiers, we study an unusual type of operators that present important features for capturing concurrency, independence, collaboration, and coordination between agents. The main goal of this paper is to study the semantics of these operators and to show how it can be adapted to capture different types of agents. The formalism allows a formal comparison of a variety of multi-agent systems.

1   Introduction

For about 20 years we have witnessed an increasing interest in the formal study of *multi-agent systems* (MAS) comprising several entities which present independent and autonomous behaviors. The standard logical machinery has proven to be able to capture (although in a scattered way) many characteristics of (MAS). However, it often requires the coexistence of disparate modalities (dynamic, temporal, epistemic, deontic) in the same language. This strategy is not satisfactory because of the complexity of the logical systems obtained. Furthermore, these logics are hard to compare to the point that the uniformity of the very phenomena at stake is lost in the different formalizations. The goal of this paper is to show that the language we have developed has several natural interpretations which allow us to capture different types of agents while maintaining the very same syntax. We introduce a new type of operators that combine modality with quantification and that we dub *quantificational modal operators.*[1] Our work is not limited to a specific notion of agent (and we are not going to give one), we consider this to be an advantage of our approach. For presentation purposes, we often describe the agents as having some degree of rationality. This is not necessary but it helps in conveying the meaning of the operators. For results on some proof-theoretical aspects see [4].

Structure of the paper. In section 2 we introduce the constant modal operators and in section 3 the Henkin quantifiers. In section 4 we modify these for our purposes. Quantificational (one-column) operators are studied in section 5 and multi-column operators in 6. Section 7 presents examples while section 8 relates this formalism to other logical approaches in the literature.

---

[1] The name was suggested to us by Daniel Leivant.

S. Bandini and S. Manzoni (Eds.): AI*IA 2005, LNAI 3673, pp. 186–197, 2005.

2 Basic Modalities for MAS

Our logic is a modification of (Elementary) *Dynamic Logic* (*DL*) [6] as used in MAS. The basic operators, called *constant modal operators*, are modalities indexed by constant identifiers denoting actions (not programs). We use several constant identifiers to isolate even the simplest constant modality so to represent the concurrent activity of the agents. In a system with two agents only, say A_1 and A_2 (taken in this order), our modal operators have the shape of a $2 \times n$ matrix ($n > 0$) where the first row lists the actions performed by A_1 (in the order of their execution) and the second row lists the actions performed by A_2. For instance, $\begin{bmatrix} c_1 & c_3 \\ c_2 & c_4 \end{bmatrix}$, with c_i's action identifiers, is a modality corresponding to the transition given by the concurrent execution of action c_1 (by agent A_1) and c_2 (by agent A_2) followed by the concurrent execution of action c_3 (by agent A_1) and c_4 (by agent A_2). That is, each entry of the matrix denotes an action and the combination of these actions characterizes the meaning of the modal operator.

More generally, an operator in the shape of a $k \times n$ matrix is a modality for a system with k agents. It is always assumed that the number of rows in the operators matches the number of agents in the system (as a consequence all the operators in the language have k rows). Also, each agent is associated to the same row in all operators. We now state this more formally.

Let *PropId* be a non-empty countable set, the set of *proposition identifiers*. Let *ActId* be a disjoint non-empty countable set whose elements are called *action identifiers*. These are the individual constants of the language. Formulas are built inductively from proposition identifiers through implication ($\rightarrow$), negation ($\neg$), and the modal operators described below. As usual, we shall make use of the standard conventions for $\wedge, \vee$, and $\leftrightarrow$. Let $A_1, \ldots, A_k$ be the agents in the system.

Let $a_{ij} \in ActId$ (not necessarily distinct), then a *constant modality identifier* for k is a $k \times n$-matrix ($n \geq 1$) $M = \begin{matrix} a_{11} & a_{12} & \cdots & a_{1n} \\ a_{21} & a_{22} & \cdots & a_{2n} \\ \vdots & \vdots & & \vdots \\ a_{k1} & a_{k2} & \cdots & a_{kn} \end{matrix}$. A *constant modal operator* for k is an expression $[M]$ where M is a constant modality identifier for k.

The set of k-formulas (formulas for short) is the smallest set F satisfying:

I) *PropId* $\subseteq F$ (the elements of *PropId* are called *atomic formulas*)
II) $\neg\varphi$ and $\varphi \rightarrow \psi$ are in F if both φ and ψ are in F
III) $[M]\varphi$ is in F if $[M]$ is a constant modal operator for k and φ is in F

Given a set *Act* of actions, a k-*action* is any $k \times n$ matrix ($n \geq 1$) over *Act*.

A k-*agent Kripke Frame* is a triple $\mathcal{K} = \langle W, Act; R \rangle$ with W a non-empty set *(the set of states)*, *Act* a non-empty set *(the set of actions)*, and R a function mapping k-actions over *Act* to binary relations on W: $R\begin{pmatrix} \alpha_1 \\ \vdots \\ \alpha_k \end{pmatrix} \subseteq W \times W$.

A k-*agent Kripke Structure* is a tuple $\mathcal{M} = \langle W, Act; R, [\![\cdot]\!] \rangle$ where $\langle W, Act; R \rangle$ is a k-agent Kripke frame and $[\![\cdot]\!]$ is a function such that $[\![p]\!] \subseteq W$ for $p \in PropId$ and $[\![a]\!] \in Act$ for $a \in ActId$.

If A_1 performs the action (denoted by) a_1, A_2 the action $a_2, \ldots$, agent A_k the action a_k, we write $\begin{bmatrix} a_1 \\ a_2 \\ \vdots \\ a_k \end{bmatrix}$ for the modal operator describing the evolution of the system due to the concurrent execution of actions $[\![a_1]\!], \ldots, [\![a_k]\!]$ by, respectively, $A_1, \ldots, A_k$. That is, the interpretation of $\begin{bmatrix} a_1 \\ a_2 \\ \vdots \\ a_k \end{bmatrix}$ is the k-action $\begin{matrix} [\![a_1]\!] \\ [\![a_2]\!] \\ \vdots \\ [\![a_k]\!] \end{matrix}$.

The valuation function is extended to multi-column operators as follows: if $[A]$ is a multi-column operator obtained by juxtaposition of operators $[B]$ and $[C]$ (i.e. $[A] = [BC]$), then put $R([\![A]\!]) = R([\![B]\!]) \circ R([\![C]\!])$. In other words,

$$\begin{bmatrix} a_{11} \\ a_{21} \\ \vdots \\ a_{k1} \end{bmatrix} =_{def} \begin{matrix} [\![a_1]\!] \\ [\![a_2]\!] \\ \vdots \\ [\![a_k]\!] \end{matrix} \quad \text{and} \quad \begin{bmatrix} a_{11} & a_{12} & \cdots & a_{1n} \\ a_{21} & a_{22} & \cdots & a_{2n} \\ \vdots & \vdots & & \vdots \\ a_{k1} & a_{k2} & \cdots & a_{kn} \end{bmatrix} =_{def} \begin{bmatrix} a_{11} \\ a_{21} \\ \vdots \\ a_{k1} \end{bmatrix} \begin{bmatrix} a_{12} \\ a_{22} \\ \vdots \\ a_{k2} \end{bmatrix} \cdots \begin{bmatrix} a_{1n} \\ a_{2n} \\ \vdots \\ a_{kn} \end{bmatrix} \quad \text{extend}$$

function $[\![\cdot]\!]$ to all modality identifiers. Note that we write $[\![M]\!]$ for $[\![\,[M]\,]\!]$.

The truth-value of a formula is defined inductively:

1. Let $p \in PropId$, then $\mathcal{M}, s \models p$ if $s \in [\![p]\!]$
2. $\mathcal{M}, s \models \neg\varphi$ if $\mathcal{M}, s \not\models \varphi$
3. $\mathcal{M}, s \models \varphi \to \psi$ if $\mathcal{M}, s \not\models \varphi$ or $\mathcal{M}, s \models \psi$
4. $\mathcal{M}, s \models [M]\varphi$ if for all $t \in W$ such that $(s, t) \in R([\![M]\!])$, we have $\mathcal{M}, t \models \varphi$

A *k-agent Kripke model* for a set of formulas Σ in the language is a structure $\mathcal{M}$ for k such that all formulas $\varphi \in \Sigma$ hold in all states of $\mathcal{M}$.

This language is a modification of (Elementary) Dynamic Logic. What really changes is the general perspective. We are no longer using a single constant to describe the evolution of the whole system. Only the combination of all *concurrent actions* provides this information.

Finally, we extend the constant operators by allowing free variables to occur in them. The reason for this choice will become clear later. Let $\Im$ be an environment function from a set of variables *Var* to *Act* and let a modality identifier be any $k \times n$ matrix as before but this time with the less restrictive condition $a_{i,j} \in ActId \cup Var$ (for all relevant indices i, j). The extension of F to include these modalities is trivial. Their interpretation requires the new environment function $\Im$. For the formulas of type $[M]\varphi$ where $[M]$ contains free variables, the interpretation is given by the clause 4. above provided we extend the valuation function by defining, for all $x \in Var$, $[\![x]\!] = \Im(x)$.

3   Henkin Quantifiers

Henkin quantifiers [7,8] are matrices of quantified variables, e.g. $\left(\begin{matrix} \forall x_1 & \exists x_2 & \exists x_3 \\ \exists y_1 & \forall y_2 & \exists y_3 \end{matrix} \right)$ and were proposed by Henkin as an extension of first-order logic. Syntactically, these are unary operators as the standard quantifiers. There is no restriction on the number or positions of the quantifiers $\forall$ and $\exists$ in the matrix but no variable may occur more than once in the same operator.

Henkin furnishes a semantic interpretation in terms of game semantics and another (equivalent to the first) using Skolem functions. Let us see the latter through an example. We write $\varphi_{a_1,a_2,\ldots}^{x_1,x_2,\ldots}$ for the first-order formula φ with the free occurrences of x_i replaced by a_i. The formula

$$\begin{pmatrix} \forall x_1 \; \exists x_2 \; \exists x_3 \\ \exists y_1 \; \forall y_2 \; \exists y_3 \end{pmatrix} \varphi \tag{1}$$

is *true* in structure $(\mathcal{M}, V)$ if the formula $\forall x_1 y_2 \; \varphi_{g_1(x_1),\; g_2(x_1),\; g_3,\; g_4(y_2)}^{x_2,\; x_3,\; y_1,\; y_3}$ is true where g_1 and g_2 are obtained by Skolemization from formula $\forall x_1 \exists x_2 x_3 \varphi$, i.e. formula (1) with the second row of the Henkin quantifier erased; and analogously g_3 and g_4 are obtained from formula $\exists y_1 \forall y_2 \exists y_3 \varphi$. Note that one cannot use formula $\exists g_1, g_2, g_3, g_4 \forall x_1, y_2 \; \varphi_{g_1(x_1),\; g_2(x_1),\; g_3,\; g_4(y_2)}^{x_2,\; x_3,\; y_1,\; y_3}$ since here the choice of g_3 and g_4 is not independent from g_1 and g_2 (a similar problem arises for any permutation of the functions in the prefix $\exists g_1, g_2, g_3, g_4$).

In the game-theoretic semantics a Henkin quantifier (H) is used as the board of a game with k couples of players $(\mathbf{V}_1, \mathbf{F}_1), \ldots, (\mathbf{V}_k, \mathbf{F}_k)$ where $\mathbf{V}_i$ is the ith-*verifier* and $\mathbf{F}_i$ the ith-*falsifier*. The game consists of a set of choices (see below) and the purpose is to assign a truth-value for the formula $(H)\varphi$. For this, pair $(\mathbf{V}_i, \mathbf{F}_i)$ plays a (sub)game on row i of (H) choosing how to instantiate the variables in this row. Since the outcome of the whole game results from the choices made and since the verifiers win if $(H)\varphi$ turns out to be (always) true, the falsifiers win otherwise, we see that $\mathbf{V}_i$ and $\mathbf{F}_i$ play with opposite goals in the subgame i:

- $\mathbf{V}_i$ instantiates variables to obtain an environment in which φ is true;
- $\mathbf{F}_i$ instantiates variables to obtain an environment in which φ is false.

In practice, subgame on row i is a sequence of choices. The players proceed from left to right considering one entry at a time. $\mathbf{V}_i$ chooses whenever there is an existentially quantified variable in the entry, $\mathbf{F}_i$ in the opposite case. It is crucial to note that every move in the subgame of row i is public to $\mathbf{V}_i$ and $\mathbf{F}_i$ only. That is, these choices are *never* known to players in other rows. Finally, formula $(H)\varphi$ is true in $(\mathcal{M}, V)$ if φ is true in any $(\mathcal{M}, V')$ where V' differs from V in as much as it associate all variables occurring in row i of (H) with their values in a play of the corresponding subgame on row i. It is false, otherwise. The reader should convince himself that formula $(H)\varphi$ is true in a model $(\mathcal{M}, V)$ if and only if there exists a *strategy*[2] that guarantee the verifiers to win any play of this game.

Fix a model $(\mathcal{M}, V)$ and let $(\mathbf{V}_1, \mathbf{F}_1), (\mathbf{V}_2, \mathbf{F}_2)$ be players, we now apply game-theoretic semantics to (1). All the players are perfectly aware of the syntactic and semantic components: $\mathcal{M}$, V, the semantic clauses, formula (1). On row 1 the subgame begins with $\mathbf{F}_1$ choosing the value of x_1 (since $\forall x_1$ occurs

---

[2] Such a strategy is called a *winning strategy* for $(H)\varphi$ and consists in functions $f_1, \ldots, f_k$, called *choice-functions*, such that if we give f_i the existential variable at stake and the previous choices in row i as arguments, then it returns a value (if any) that V_i can choose to win.

first), and proceeds with $\mathbf{V}_1$ choosing the first time the value of x_2 and then the value of x_3. Note that $\mathbf{V}_1$, since moving after $\mathbf{F}_1$, knows the value of x_1 when choosing the value of x_2. Furthermore, $\mathbf{V}_1$ knows the values of both x_1 and x_2 when choosing a value for x_3. On row 2, first $\mathbf{V}_2$ chooses the value of y_1, then $\mathbf{F}_2$ chooses the value of y_2 (knowing what has been chosen for y_1). The subgame finishes with $\mathbf{V}_2$ choosing the value of y_3 (knowing the values of both y_1 and y_2). Clearly, the choices for x_1, x_2, x_3 are made without knowing the values chosen for y_1, y_2, y_3 and vice versa. Once the two subgames are over, the chosen values are used to define environment V' defined by: $V'(x) = V(x)$ for all x not in the Henkin quantifier; $V'(y) = \alpha$ for y in row i and α its value in the i subgame. Finally, the truth-value of (1) is *true* if $\mathbf{V}_1$ and $\mathbf{V}_2$ have a strategy to ensure that for all V' output of a game in (1), φ is true in $\langle \mathcal{M}, V' \rangle$. It is false otherwise.

4   Henkin Quantifiers Revisited

In the game-theoretic semantics of Henkin quantifiers two teams of players instantiate variables to determine an environment for the evaluation of the given formula. Since we are concerned with agents, we modify Henkin's interpretation by assuming that, instead of teams of players, the agents of a multi-agent system are in charge of choosing the variables' values. In other terms, we assume that each agent plays the subgame on its row by instantiating the variables there occurring. The distinction between existential and universal quantifiers is preserved assuming that the agent chooses values with *different aims at different stages*. That is, agent A_i chooses aiming at making the formula true (like $\mathbf{V}_i$ would do) wherever there is an existentially quantified variable, and aiming at making the formula false (like $\mathbf{F}_i$) wherever there is a universally quantified variable.

Unfortunately, this change alone does not do justice of the role of the agents in MAS. Indeed, here the agents can choose (in part) the environment they are in but this is not done through a notion of action. There is an obvious mismatch since the agents' decision abilities are not applied to determine their own actions.

We overcome this problem by moving to the semantics of section 2 where we can pair Henkin quantifiers and modality operators as in the following formula

$$\begin{pmatrix} \forall x_1 \ \exists x_2 \ \exists x_3 \\ \exists y_1 \ \forall y_2 \ \exists y_3 \end{pmatrix} \begin{bmatrix} x_1 & x_2 & x_3 \\ y_1 & y_2 & y_3 \end{bmatrix} p_0 \tag{2}$$

In this formula we apply Henkin quantifiers to open modal formulas to form sentences. The matching position of the quantified variable in the Henkin quantifier and the free occurrence of the same variable in the modal operator (and so the matching size of the operators) is here crucial. Note that here $\forall$ and $\exists$ range *over actions* since the goal is to instantiate the free variables in the modal operators. We now study these quantifiers in the Kripke semantics approach by taking Act as domain of quantification.

From sections 2 and 3, formula (2) is interpreted in two steps. First, we provide a game-theoretic interpretation of $\begin{pmatrix} \forall x_1 \ \exists x_2 \ \exists x_3 \\ \exists y_1 \ \forall y_2 \ \exists y_3 \end{pmatrix}$ applied to formula

$\left[\begin{smallmatrix} x_1 & x_2 & x_3 \\ y_1 & y_2 & y_3 \end{smallmatrix}\right] p_0$ by allowing the agents to independently choose from Act the values of the variables in their rows.[3] Let α be the value for z in the game and $\Im'$ be the environment defined by $\Im'(z) = \alpha$ if z occurs in the Henkin quantifier, $\Im'(z) = \Im(z)$ otherwise. The second step consists in the evaluation of formula $\left[\begin{smallmatrix} x_1 & x_2 & x_3 \\ y_1 & y_2 & y_3 \end{smallmatrix}\right] p_0$ according to the environment $\Im'$. Informally, this matches the orderly execution by the agents of the actions they have just *planned*.

5   Quantificational Modal Operators

Let *ActId*, *PropId*, and *Var* be as in section 2 with $p_0 \in PropId$. As before, we will informally write "the action a", with $a \in ActId$, to mean the action denoted by a, i.e., the action $[\![a]\!] \in Act$.

Since (2) presents two types of operators with a common structure, we can actually merge them in a unique operator without loss of information by writing formula $\left[\begin{smallmatrix} \forall x_1 & \exists x_2 & \exists x_3 \\ \exists y_1 & \forall y_2 & \exists y_3 \end{smallmatrix}\right] p_0$. The interpretation of this formula is that of (2): a first step provides instances of the quantified variables in the modality via subgames. A second step provides the evaluation of the modal operator obtained by substituting for each variable in the modality its value in the subgame.

Since we want to model also agents that are *committed to do* some action, we need to allow both action identifiers and quantified variables to occur in an operator. This brings us to the following

Definition 1. *(Quantificational identifiers and operators)*
A quantificational modality identifier for k is a $k \times n$ matrix $(n > 0)$ with each entry containing a constant, a variable, or a quantified variable. A quantificational (modal) operator for k is an expression $[M]$ where M is a quantificational modality identifier for k.
qOP stands for the set of quantificational operators for k (k fixed by the context).

The set F of k-formulas is defined as in section 2 now allowing the bigger class of quantificational operators in clause III). From our discussion, the scope of the modal operator is the formula to which it is applied and the scope of a quantifier in a modal operator is the scope of the modal operator itself.[4] As for Henkin quantifiers, a variable can occur only once in a quantificational operator.

5.1   Henkin's Isolated Agents

This section focuses on the interpretation of quantificational modal operators. Consider formula $\left[\begin{smallmatrix} \exists x \\ b \end{smallmatrix}\right] p_0$ in a system with agents A_1 and A_2.[5] This formula

---

[3] The game is a trivial modification of the game described previously. It consists of subgames (as before) where, at each entry, the agent embraces the aim indicated by the occurring quantifier. The agents have no knowledge of the choices made at other rows.

[4] Formally, a quantificational entry, say $\forall x$, stands for the quantified variable $\forall x$ as well as for a bound occurrence of x.

[5] The examples generalize easily to k agents.

holds at a state if agent A_1 can choose an action a such that $\begin{bmatrix} a \\ b \end{bmatrix} p_0$ is true at that state. Then, formula $\begin{bmatrix} \exists x \\ b \end{bmatrix} p_0$ stands for "agent A_1 can choose an action such that after the concurrent execution of it by A_1 and of b by A_2, p_0 holds". Analogously, formula $\begin{bmatrix} \forall x \\ b \end{bmatrix} p_0$ states: "no matter the action chosen by agent A_1, after A_1 has executed it and (concurrently) A_2 has executed b, p_0 holds". The intuition is that all the instances obtained by a choice of A_1 need to be considered to state the truth-value of this formula.

Building on the previous cases, the meaning of the remaining one-column operators is easily determined. The natural reading of $\begin{bmatrix} \forall x \\ \forall y \end{bmatrix} p_0$ is: "no matter which action a agent A_1 executes and which action b agent A_2 executes, p_0 holds in the reached states". Formula $\begin{bmatrix} \exists x \\ \exists y \end{bmatrix} p_0$ is true if the agents can *independently* choose actions, say a and b, such that $\begin{bmatrix} a \\ b \end{bmatrix} p_0$ is true, i.e. "for any choice a made by A_1 and any choice b made by A_2, after A_1 has executed a and A_2 has (concurrently) executed b, p_0 holds". Note that the expressions "for any choice a" and "for all a" characterize different sets of actions. Of the remaining one-column operators, consider $\begin{bmatrix} \forall x \\ \exists y \end{bmatrix} p_0$. Since the agents choose independently, i.e. not knowing each other doing, for the formula to be true the second agent has to find an action a for y such that $\begin{bmatrix} \forall x \\ a \end{bmatrix} p_0$ is true according to what said above, that is, no matter what the other agent chooses.

To capture formally this interpretation, let us assume that function g furnishes the actions chosen by the agents. The intent is that g codifies the behavior of agent A_i when taking as argument the formula to be evaluated (the modality plus its scope formula) and the variable in row i (which implicitly gives the agent's index); on this input, g returns (one or more) actions in Act which corresponds to agent A_i's choices. Then, the semantics of section 2 is extended with the following clause for quantificational *one-column* operators:[6]

5_1)   Given a formula $[X]\varphi$ where $[X]$ is a quantificational operator with variables $x_1, \ldots, x_r$ existentially quantified and $y_1, \ldots, y_s$ universally quantified; $\mathcal{M}, s.\Im \models [X]\varphi$ if for all given $\alpha_1, \ldots, \alpha_r \in Act$ such that $\alpha_i \in g([X], \varphi, x_i)$ and for all $\beta_1, \ldots, \beta_s \in Act$, if Γ is the k-action obtained by substituting, in $[X]$, $\llbracket a_h \rrbracket$ for $a_h \in ActId \cup Var$, α_i for $\exists x_i$, and β_j for $\forall y_j$ (for all relevant indices h, i, j), then for all $(s, s') \in R(\Gamma)$, $\mathcal{M}, s', \Im' \models \varphi$ with $\Im'$ defined by: $\Im'(x_i) = \alpha_i$, $\Im'(y_j) = \beta_j$, and $\Im'(z) = \Im(z)$ for the remaining cases.

We dub the agents described by this semantic clause *Henkin's isolated agents*; "Henkin's" because of the overall semantics, and "isolated" for the lack of communication among the agents (the above clause prevents the possibility of coordination plans among agents).

Formulas $\begin{bmatrix} \exists x \\ \forall y \end{bmatrix} p_0 \rightarrow \begin{bmatrix} \exists x \\ a \end{bmatrix} p_0$; $\begin{bmatrix} a \\ \forall y \end{bmatrix} p_0 \rightarrow \begin{bmatrix} \exists x \\ \forall y \end{bmatrix} p_0$ are valid in this semantics. Interestingly, and perhaps surprisingly, formulas $\begin{bmatrix} \exists x \\ \forall y \end{bmatrix} p_0 \not\rightarrow \begin{bmatrix} \exists x \\ \exists y \end{bmatrix} p_0$ and

---

[6] Clause 5_1) can be seen as a schema since varying g we capture different MAS.

$\left[\begin{smallmatrix}\exists x\\a\end{smallmatrix}\right] p_0 \nrightarrow \left[\begin{smallmatrix}\exists x\\\exists y\end{smallmatrix}\right] p_0$ fail in general. In the first case, for example, let p_0 stand for "have the cake sliced." In the case of $\left[\begin{smallmatrix}\forall x\\\exists y\end{smallmatrix}\right] p_0$, agent A_2 would do action "cut the cake" no matter what the other agent does since the latter is not committed to this goal. In the case of $\left[\begin{smallmatrix}\exists x\\\exists y\end{smallmatrix}\right] p_0$, agent A_1 (knowing agent A_2 has the same goal) may be polite and let A_2 cut. Similarly, agent A_2 may not do it to let A_1 the honor. Then, nobody cuts the cake (nobody chooses that action) and the formula turns out to be false.

5.2   Risk-Averse Coordinated Agents

So far our reading of $\forall$ and $\exists$ was driven by Henkin's work. We now investigate the interpretation one obtains when adopting the classical meaning for $\exists$ and $\forall$. Here we take formula $\left[\begin{smallmatrix}\exists x\\b\end{smallmatrix}\right] p_0$ to be true at a state s if and only if there exists an action a such that $\left[\begin{smallmatrix}a\\b\end{smallmatrix}\right] p_0$ is true at s. In this reading, the quantificational formula stands for "there exists an action such that after the concurrent execution of it by A_1 and of b by A_2, p_0 holds". Analogously, formula $\left[\begin{smallmatrix}\forall x\\b\end{smallmatrix}\right] p_0$ reads: "for any action a, after A_1 has executed it and (concurrently) A_1 has executed b, p_0 holds". It follows easily that formula $\left[\begin{smallmatrix}\exists x\\\exists y\end{smallmatrix}\right] p_0$ is true if there exist actions a and b (not necessarily distinct) such that $\left[\begin{smallmatrix}a\\b\end{smallmatrix}\right] p_0$ holds, while formula $\left[\begin{smallmatrix}\forall x\\\forall y\end{smallmatrix}\right] p_0$ is true if for all actions a and b, $\left[\begin{smallmatrix}a\\b\end{smallmatrix}\right] p_0$ is true. An interesting case is given by operators in which both quantifiers occur, for instance $\left[\begin{smallmatrix}\forall x\\\exists y\end{smallmatrix}\right] p_0$. To establish the truth value of this formula at a given state we have two choices: either we verify that a value b for y exists such that $\left[\begin{smallmatrix}\forall x\\b\end{smallmatrix}\right] p_0$ is a true formula according to our interpretation above. Or we verify that no matter which action a is substituted for x, formula $\left[\begin{smallmatrix}a\\\exists y\end{smallmatrix}\right] p_0$ is true in $\mathcal{M}$ at s.

Here we consider the first interpretation only. To capture it formally, we adopt the semantics of section 2 with the following clause for quantificational *one-column* operators:

5_2)   Given a formula $[X]\varphi$ where $[X]$ is a quantificational operator with variables $x_1, \ldots, x_r$ existentially quantified and $y_1, \ldots, y_s$ universally quantified; $\mathcal{M}, s, \Im \models [X]\varphi$ if there exist $\alpha_1, \ldots, \alpha_r \in Act$ such that for all $\beta_1, \ldots, \beta_s \in Act$, if Γ is the k-action obtained by substituting, in $[X]$, $\llbracket a_h \rrbracket$ for $a_h \in ActId \cup Var$, α_i for $\exists x_i$, and β_j for $\forall y_j$ (for all relevant indices h, i, j), then for all $(s, s') \in R(\Gamma)$, $\mathcal{M}, s', \Im' \models \varphi$ with $\Im'$ defined by: $\Im'(x_i) = \alpha_i$, $\Im'(y_j) = \beta_j$, and $\Im'(z) = \Im(z)$ in the remaining cases.

We dub the agents satisfying this clause *risk-averse coordinated agents*: "risk-averse" because they never take chances relying on other agents choices, and "coordinated" because they always agree on a combination of actions good for reaching common goals (if any).

In this semantics $\left[\begin{smallmatrix}\exists x\\\forall y\end{smallmatrix}\right] p_0 \rightarrow \left[\begin{smallmatrix}\exists x\\\exists y\end{smallmatrix}\right] p_0$ and $\left[\begin{smallmatrix}\exists x\\a\end{smallmatrix}\right] p_0 \rightarrow \left[\begin{smallmatrix}\exists x\\\exists y\end{smallmatrix}\right] p_0$ are valid.

6   Knowing the Past, Reasoning About the Future

Consider a constant two-column operator[7] $\left[\begin{smallmatrix} c_1 & c_3 \\ c_2 & c_4 \end{smallmatrix}\right]$, call it $[X]$. From clause 4. of section 2, constant operators split into simpler operators without loss of information, that is $\left[\begin{smallmatrix} c_1 & c_3 \\ c_2 & c_4 \end{smallmatrix}\right]\varphi \equiv \left[\begin{smallmatrix} c_1 \\ c_2 \end{smallmatrix}\right]\left[\begin{smallmatrix} c_3 \\ c_4 \end{smallmatrix}\right]\varphi$. This equivalence does not hold for quantificational operators though, i.e. in general

$$[M_1 M_2]\varphi \not\equiv \lfloor M_1 \rfloor \lfloor M_2 \rfloor \varphi \quad (M_1, M_2 \in qOP) \tag{3}$$

To establish the truth-value of a formula where the constant operator $[X]$ occurs, it is necessary to consider all action identifiers (and their positions) occurring in $[X]$. For instance, the information that c_1, c_3 occur in the first row in this order (i.e., knowing the actions executed by agent A_1), does not suffice in general to know which states are reachable through $[X]$.

Suppose now that we are dealing with formula $\left[\begin{smallmatrix} c_1 & \exists x \\ c_2 & c_4 \end{smallmatrix}\right] p_0$. It seems natural to read the modality in this formula as follows: "first, agent A_1 executes c_1 and (concurrently) agent A_2 executes c_2, then A_1 chooses and executes an action and (concurrently) A_2 executes c_4." In light of the previous sections, one can interpret the existential quantifier in different ways. Assume for a moment that I am agent A_1 and I am given the model $\mathcal{M}$, the state at which the formula is evaluated, and all the semantic clauses. Then, my choice for x will differ depending on what I *know* about the formula itself and in particular about operator $\left[\begin{smallmatrix} c_1 & \exists x \\ c_2 & c_4 \end{smallmatrix}\right]$. For if I am aware of the presence of c_1, c_2, c_4 and of their positions, I can use the semantic clauses to verify whether there is an action that, when executed by me after the execution of c_1, forces the system to states satisfying p_0. Assuming such an action exists, it might not be possible to identify it if I lack some information about the constant identifiers occurring in the operator.

This argument shows that to establish the truth-value of the formula, it is important to state my knowledge (or lack of) about the operator. Several options are possible. For instance, assuming perfect recall, one can assume that I am aware c_1 is in position (1,1) of the matrix since I have just chosen a value for x. If A_1 and A_2 are *isolated* agents, then we should assume that I (agent A_1) have no idea of what A_2 has done earlier, that is, I do not know what is in position (2,1) of the operator. If A_1 and A_2 are *non-communicating* but can observe each other's doings, one can assume that I know what A_2 has just done, i.e., I know that c_2 is in position (2,1). Finally, for the simple reason that A_1 and A_2 act concurrently, I might know what A_2 is going to execute as second action only if we are *coordinated* agents or if it is publicly known that agent A_2 has to execute c_4 at this point.[8]

---

[7] Our examples use mostly two-column operators. The generalization to n-column operators is generally straightforward.

[8] In the previous discussion of one-column operators we implicitly assumed that the constant identifiers are known to all the agents, they are *public knowledge*, so to speak. Here we drop this assumption as well. Indeed, one may have a commitment to do a specific action c_i at some point and prevent other agents from knowing it (an issue raised in modeling security). The semantic clauses we have introduced for one-column operators can capture these cases as well.

In this paper, we do not enter into the formalization of the semantics for multi-column operators. However, it is possible to extend clauses 5_1) and 5_2) to multi-column operators by allowing $[X]$ to be any operator in qOP. We will make use of this fact in the next section.

7 Modeling with Quantificational Operators

Our first example is in the area of planning. There are two agents, say Anthony (A_1) and Bill (A_2), and they are in charge of a project which should be turned in by a certain time. Let us say that there are 3 time-steps before the deadline (step-1, step-2, and step-3) and that Anthony cannot work at the project at step-1 since he is committed to do something else (perhaps he has to go to the bank or to meet with the company accountant). We use a for the action Anthony does at this step. Later, he is working full time on the project. Regarding Bill, the office manager already asked him to go to his office at the time corresponding to step-2 (but he did not say what the meeting is about). We represent this case in our language with the formula $\left[\begin{smallmatrix} a & \exists x & \exists z \\ \exists y & \forall u & \exists v \end{smallmatrix} \right] \varphi$, where φ stands for "the project is finished". The first row describes Anthony's attitude toward the project during this time, while the second row describes Bill's attitude. Note that the universal quantifier marks the time-step when Bill acts without regards for the project since his action at that time depends on what his office manager asks him to do. Assuming Anthony and Bill are risk-averse cooperative agents, all the actions that instantiate variables x, z, y, v should be planned together as described by clause 5_2) provided it is extended to multi-column quantificational operators as indicated earlier.

We may want to model the case where the agents have a predefine plan for the first two time-steps only. For instance, suppose they discussed a plan the day before when they knew they where going to be in different places during time-steps 1 and 2 without the possibility of sharing information. Also, let us say that later they meet, share they achievements and decide together what to do for the remaining time. This situation is described by formula $\left[\begin{smallmatrix} a & \exists x \\ \exists y & \forall u \end{smallmatrix} \right] \left[\begin{smallmatrix} \exists z \\ \exists v \end{smallmatrix} \right] \varphi$ using clause 5_2) to ensure coordination.

The second example we consider comes from robotics. Here there are two agents whose goal is to pick up an object but none of them can do it alone. If φ stands for "the object is lifted", the situation is described by formula $\left[\begin{smallmatrix} \exists x \\ \exists y \end{smallmatrix} \right] \varphi \wedge \left[\begin{smallmatrix} \forall x \\ \exists y \end{smallmatrix} \right] \neg \varphi \wedge \left[\begin{smallmatrix} \exists x \\ \forall y \end{smallmatrix} \right] \neg \varphi$. The reader can easily verify that this formula is true in 5_2).

Of course, these examples can be captured in other formalisms as well, in particular through different languages that include some type of epistemic operators [11]. However, we remark that (i) the formulas one obtains in our language are very simple and (ii) through our language agents in different systems can be compared immediately by looking at the adopted semantics.

8 Related Work and Conclusions

This paper continues the work presented in [2,3,4]. In [2] the general approach is given by focusing on the propositional case and its properties. In [3] we studied an interpretation along the lines of 5_1) exploiting fully game-theoretic framework. [4] looks at the formal properties of one of these logics. Differently from these papers, here we have looked at the variety of semantics for our operators and their relationships.

The formalism we adopted has been influenced by the notion of Henkin (branching) quantifiers and their interpretation in game-theory [7]. Nonetheless, branching quantifiers have no modal interpretation and do not allow for semantic alternatives. Furthermore, there is an ontological discrepancy between the notion of agent in MAS (agents are internal components of the system) and the formal notion of player in game-theory (players are external components that act to interpret the formalism).

Somehow related to our work is [1]. The basic features of the logic there presented (without the temporal modalities) are captured through our modal operators using an interpretation similar to 5_2). Our formalism captures *Coalition Logic* [9] as well. Other frameworks, following the *BDI* approach [10] or the *Intention Logic* [5], adopt combinations of different modalities. These are very expressive systems and differ in their motivations from our approach. We refer the reader to [11,12] for overviews of this area of research.

We have shown how to produce different interpretations for modal operators built out of action identifiers, variables, and quantified variables. Our stand is that when there is a number of practical constraints to capture, semantic pluralism should be sought. In this way, the same descriptive tool can distinguish and characterize different phenomena in a flexible way making possible the uniform description of what might seem a plethora of heterogeneous cases. Then, formal and reliable comparisons of apparently disparate phenomena become possible. Our quantificational modal operators, although limited in several ways, give a first answer to this search for semantic pluralism in the area of multi-agent systems.

Among the features of these quantificational modal operators, the followings are particularly relevant: (*a*) true concurrency is captured already at the syntactic level; (*b*) they can express independence among agents; (*c*) they are naturally associated with different semantics making possible the characterization of different agents; (*d*) they model partial knowledge and communication among agents. There are drawbacks as well. The quantificational operators inherit the restrictions of (Elementary) *DL*, in particular the rigid structure in finite steps. Extensions using constructs on action identifiers have not been studied yet. On the technical side, although adding quantificational modal operators does not make the resulting logic necessarily undecidable, this happens in many cases when equality is present. For instance, one can see that the theory in [3] is undecidable since we can embed first-order logic augmented with a binary predicate (the translation is given by: $A(x,y) \longmapsto [{}^x_y] p_0$ for some atomic p_0). For an example in the opposite sense, a slight modification of clause 5_2) gives a complete and decidable logic for the class of multi-relational Kripke frames [4].

Acknowledgments. The author has been partially supported by the Provincia Autonoma di Trento. Thanks to Daniel Leivant and Alessandra Carbone for their comments on an earlier draft of this paper.

References

1. R. Alur, T. Henzinger, and O. Kupferman. Alternating-time temporal logic. In de Roever W.-P., L. H., and P. A., editors, *Compositionality - The Significant Difference*, LNCS 1536, pages 2360. Springer-Verlag, 1999.
2. S. Borgo. Concurrency with partial information. In M. Mohammadian, editor, CIMCA *03*, pages 170181, 2003.
3. S. Borgo. A multi-agent modal language for concurrency with non-communicating agents. In CEEMAS *03*, LNAI 2691, pages 4050, 2003.
4. S. Borgo. Quantificational modal logic with sequential kripke semantics. *Journal of Applied Non-Classical Logics*, 15(2):137188, 2005.
5. P. R. Cohen and H. J. Levesque. Intention is choice with commitment. *Artificial Intelligence*, 42:213261, 1990.
6. D. Harel, D. Kozen, and J. Tiuryn. *Dynamic Logic*. MIT Press, 2000.
7. L. Henkin. Some remarks on infinitely long formulas. In *Infinitistic Methods*, pages 167183. Pergamon Press, Warsaw, 1961.
8. M. Krynicki and M. Mostowski. Henkin quantifiers. In M. Krynicki, M. Mostowski, and S. L.W., editors, *Quantifiers: Logics, Models and Computation*, pages 193262. Kluwer Academic Publishers, 1995.
9. M. Pauly. A modal logic for coalitional power in games. *J. of Logic and Computation*, 12(1):149166, 2002.
10. A. Rao and M. Georgeff. Modeling rational agents within a bdi-architecture. In J. F. Allen, R. Fikes, and E. Sandewall, editors, *Principles of Knowledge Representation and Reasoning (KR91)*, pages 473484. Morgan Kaufmann, 1991.
11. W. van der Hoek and R. Verbrugge. Epistemic logic: a survey. In L. Petrosjan and V. Mazalov, editors, *Game Theory and Applications*, pages 5394. Nova Science Publishers, 2002.
12. W. van der Hoek and M. J. Wooldridge. Towards a logic of rational agency. *L. J. of the IGPL*, 11(2):135159, 2003.

An Organisation Infrastructure for Multi-agent Systems Based on Agent Coordination Contexts

Mirko Viroli, Andrea Omicini, and Alessandro Ricci

DEIS, Alma Mater Studiorum, Università di Bologna,
Via Venezia 52, 47023 Cesena, Italy
{mirko.viroli, andrea.omicini, a.ricci}@unibo.it

Abstract. We present an organisation infrastructure for open MASs (Multi-Agent Systems) built upon a role-based access control model (RBAC) allowing agent actions toward the other entities in the MAS (agents and resources) to be enabled and controlled.

To this end, an Agent Coordination Context (ACC) is created by the infrastructure and assigned to an agent as it enters the MAS. An ACC acts as a sort of private interface for the agent toward the environment: any agent action is thereafter enabled and controlled by its own ACC, which prevents those behaviours that are incorrect with respect to the role(s) played by the agent. For this purpose, each role is assigned a policy that flexibly specifies admissible actions and perceptions over time.

Details of this infrastructure are developed formally, through a process-algebraic description of the main infrastructure entities: this is meant to serve as a formal specification of the infrastructure, as well as of the language for expressing policies.

1 Introduction

A relevant approach in the engineering of organisational aspects in complex information systems is the Role-Based Access Control (RBAC) model [1], which is used to streamline the burdensome process of articulating (system) specific organisation policies [2]. With respect to the previous approaches (discretionary and mandatory access control), RBAC models allow for a more flexible and detailed control and management of organisation. In particular, RBAC approaches make it possible to specify policies in terms of abstractions—such as roles, role permissions and inter-role relationships—that naturally occur in real-life organisations and are amenable to implementation in artificial ones.

RBAC models are gaining interest also within the MAS field for a number of good reasons. First of all, they promote conceptual integrity in MAS engineering, by framing organisation issues so that the basic bricks of the model (roles, policies, etc) can be introduced as viable concepts in MAS. Also, RBAC approaches allow organisation policies to be defined and enforced despite the typical MAS heterogeneity and openness: the same model can be applied to MASs composed by agents with heterogeneous computational models, and the model supports the openness that is typically desired

S. Bandini and S. Manzoni (Eds.): AI*IA 2005, LNAI 3673, pp. 198–211, 2005.

for MASs, in terms of dynamism of the system structure (e.g., the set of agents) and of the organisation policies as well.

Accordingly, in this paper we extend and adapt the proposed standard for the RBAC model [2] to the MAS field, and introduce the RBAC-MAS model. This model takes as key concepts agent classes, roles, sessions and policies—policies, differently from standard RBAC permissions, allow for flexibly describing dynamic access control rules, e.g. the interaction protocols to be enforced in given roles.

We discuss how to support this model in terms of a MAS infrastructure, where an organisation component (conceptually distributed in the whole MAS) stores rules and policies. The notion of Agent Coordination Context (ACC), introduced in [3] and explored in [4,5], is exploited to provide a run-time support of sessions, in particular to locally enforce the organisation policies an agent should adhere to when playing given roles in the society.

The description of the details of this infrastructure is developed formally, using a process algebraic syntax and a corresponding structural operational semantics [6]. This approach, traditional of the distributed systems field, is more and more used in the MAS context—see e.g. [7,8]—for it leads to models that specify system implementations in an abstract away, and that can be executed to simulate system behaviours and/or proving properties of interest.

2 Role-Based Access Control for Multi-agent Systems

2.1 Role-Based Access Control: An Overview

In RBAC, a *role* is a semantic construct around which an access control policy is formulated, bringing together a given collection of users and permissions in a transitory way [1]. Many different notions of role can be found in the literature, which RBAC aims at accommodating and capturing. A role can represent *competency* to do specific tasks, but also the embodiment of *authority and responsibility*: all these cases are expressed in terms of enabled/disabled operations over objects in the organisation.

RBAC makes it possible to establish relations between roles, between permissions and roles, and between users and roles. These inter-role relations can be used to enforce security policies that include e.g. *separation of duties*: for example, two roles can be established as mutually exclusive, so the same user is not allowed to take on both roles. Other than separation of duty, RBAC directly supports two well-known security principles: *least privilege*—only those permissions required for the tasks conducted by members of the role are assigned to the role—and *data abstraction*—supported by means of abstract permissions such as credit and debit for an account object, rather than low level accesses such as read and write.

RBAC is *policy-neutral*: it does not enforce itself any specific access policy, but provides means to flexibly describe the required ones. RBAC components such as role-permission, user-role and role-role relationships are dynamically configurable by system administrators, and determine whether a particular user will be allowed to access a particular piece of data or a resource in the system.

According to the reference architecture formally defined in [9], the main components of a RBAC model are depicted in Fig. 1 (left), and are defined in terms of basic

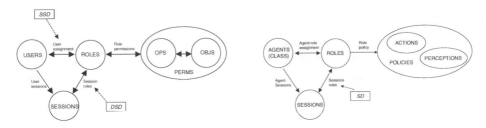

Fig. 1. RBAC (left) and RBAC-MAS (right) Reference Models

element sets (users, roles, objects, operations, permissions and sessions) and their relationships. Users are assigned to roles and permissions to roles. A *role* is understood as a job function within the context of an organisation with some associated semantics regarding the authority and responsibilities conferred to the user assigned to the role [9]. A *permission* is an approval to perform an operation on one or more protected objects—the semantics of the term *operation* and *object* depends on the specific cases. Each session is a mapping between a user and an activated subset of roles that are assigned to the users. Each session is associated with a single user and each user is associated with one or more sessions.

Organisation rules are defined in terms of relationships between the element sets. User assignment relationships define which users are assigned to a specific role, which means that they are allowed to play it inside the organisation; permission assignment defines which permissions are assigned to each role. Roles are assigned to permissions, which are subsets of the cartesian product OPS × OBJS (operations over objects). Static separation of duty properties (SSD) are obtained by enforcing constraints on the assignment of users to roles; instead, dynamic separation of duty properties (DSD) are obtained by placing constraints on the roles that can be activated within or across a user's sessions.

2.2   Moving RBAC to Multi-agent Systems

The MAS perspective introduces a new view over interaction, and therefore over organisation; as a result, RBAC has to be suitably adapted and extended to suit the nature of the agent-oriented abstractions. Accordingly, we define a new model for RBAC-like organisation of MAS called RBAC-MAS, depicted in Fig. 1 (right), featuring the following main peculiarities with respect to standard RBAC:

Agent Classes. Instead of RBAC *users*, RBAC-MAS has *agent classes*. As an agent enters a MAS it should be recognised as belonging to precisely one of these classes—most likely, after authentication. More agents can actually belong to the same class, e.g. an *anonymous* class could fit those open scenarios where not all agent identities are known a priori.

Actions and Perceptions. Operations and objects are strictly related in MAS, moreover, agent interactions are typically structured in terms of actions and perceptions. Therefore RBAC-MAS introduces the notions of *action* and *perception*, which are seen as *operations* involving a given *object*. Since we do not mean to introduce a new theory of action/perception here, but want to provide an orthogonal organisation support to MAS exploiting existing ones, we represents them in a very abstract way—their syntax will be simply expressed by terms of a first-order logic language. Then, by object we mean any entity leaving in the MAS environment which the agent can interact with: it may be another agent or a logical/software/physical resource—like a *coordination artifact* [10,7].

Policies. Instead of *permissions* (subsets of operations over objects), RBAC-MAS introduces *policies,* which are protocols (possibly infinite, concurrent, and non-deterministic) of actions and perceptions. This notion is introduced because agents typically participate in complex interaction scenarios through protocols, and different roles require an agent to act according to different protocols—e.g. an initiator and a participant in a Contract-Net scenario. Policies are first-class entities of RBAC-MAS, with their own unique identifier, and are meant to be dynamically enforced by the organisation—preventing an agent to violate the protocol. It is worth noting that a form of *obligation* that does not prevent agent autonomy is support as well: as an agent declares to play a role, he must be limited to the corresponding policy.

Roleset. RBAC-MAS does not equip agents with a default roleset. Instead, the agent initially starts a void session, and can subsequently activate roles on a step-by-step basis, according to the role activation/deactivation policies it has been assigned. The session can be left only when all its roles have been deactivated. Correspondingly, no conceptual distinction can be made any longer between SSD and DSD: in RBAC-MAS a separation of duty rule (SD) simply states whether a certain new role can be activated given the roleset currently activated.

3 Infrastructure Support and ACCs

Based on this general RBAC-MAS model, we develop an infrastructure approach to organisation in MAS. In particular, we provide concepts and design of an infrastructure that can be exploited to support at run-time all the constructs and components of RBAC-MAS, including roles, agent classes, policies, and sessions, as well as all their relationships. Notice that this infrastructure is not meant to substitute at all any existing MAS infrastructure, but is rather to be used as an additional service to be integrated with existing ones in a smooth way. For instance, an infrastructure supporting agent life-cycle and agent communication, like JADE [11], could be added a new layer with the above organisation abstractions, that is, regulating agent entrance in a MAS and enforcement of communication protocols through the appropriate policies. Similar mechanisms can be added to infrastructures providing other kinds of services to agents, such as e.g. the TuCSoN infrastructure for agent interaction through tuple centres [12], which supports the notion of coordination artifacts for MASs [10].

3.1 Sessions and ACCs

A key-notion of RBAC is that of session. An agent entering a MAS is assigned a session, which the agent uses to activate and deactivate roles, and which is used to check whether agent actions are correct with respect to the roles played. In RBAC-MAS, sessions are even more central: due to the policy-based character of access enabling/control [13], sessions should typically keep track of the current state of agent interaction, since supporting protocols calls for enabling/controlling different actions at different times—depending on earlier interactions. Thus, because sessions have a strong effect on the run-time behaviour of agents in MASs, we focus our infrastructure approach on the idea of exploiting a run-time abstraction in charge of realising an agent session. To this end, we use the Agent Coordination Context (ACC) notion [3], exploited in [4,5] as a means to enable/control agent interactions in TuCSoN.

Generally speaking, an ACC represents the conceptual boundary between the agent and the environment, encapsulating the environment *interface* to be used by the agent. Being an interface, the ACC both (i) works as a model for the agent environment, and (ii) enables and rules the interactions between the agent and the environment. Hence, the ACC abstraction is particularly fruitful to model the presence of an agent within an organisation, by defining its admissible interactions with respect to organisation resources and its admissible communications toward the other agents belonging to the organisation. Thus, an ACC is meant to enact the policies assigned to an agent—that is, to physically allow admissible agent actions/perceptions toward the environment—and to make them available for agent run-time inspection and, possibly, meta-level reasoning.

In order to give a better intuition of the ACC concept, an ACC is described as a sort of *control room* [3]. According to this metaphor, an agent entering a new environment is assigned its own control room, which is the only way it can perceive the environment, as well as the only way it can affect the environment and interact. The control room offers the agent a set of admissible inputs (perceptions) and admissible outputs (actions). The policies enforced by an ACC precisely describe how many input and output devices are available to an agents, of what sort, and for how much time.

3.2   Agent Interaction with ACCs

Two basic stages characterise the life-time of an ACC: *ACC negotiation* and *ACC use*. In order to take part actively to an organisation, to access its objects (other agents or resources), an agent must first *negotiate* an ACC with the organisation infrastructure.

In particular, through a standard welcome service of the infrastructure, an agent can authenticate its identity and therefore receive its own private ACC, representing its working session in the current MAS. Since the ACC is initially void, the negotiation phase proceeds with the agent request to the ACC to activate some role, which is granted only if the agent/role permissions allow this. If activation succeeds, the agent can start playing the role by executing actions according to the policies specified for that role. If all the policies associated to a given role are terminated, the role can be deactivated. Hence, note that the dynamics of role activation and deactivation is not fixed a priori, but varies depending on the agent needs. When no roles are activated the agent can leave the ACC, therefore leaving the whole MAS—possibly entering later again with a new authentication. Failing to deactivate a terminated role or leaving a void ACC is prevented whenever possible, or can be tracked and considered as an agent violation in other cases—e.g. involving legal consequences.

Besides these negotiation aspects, an agent typically use an ACC by executing actions (receiving perceptions) according to the currently-activated roles. In particular, any role is initially associated a number of policies, each representing a protocol of actions and perceptions. Whichever language for policies is used—in Section 4 we use a process algebraic one, shown in [5] to allow for a significant expressiveness—it should describe what are the actions/perceptions allowed at a given time, and what is the next state of policies as one action is executed or a perception occurs. So, an agent can executed any action (received a perception) allowed by any current policy of any currently activated role. Notice that the ACC prevents the agent from executing disallowed actions (or receiving unexpected perceptions).

This idea only apparently contrasts with agent autonomy: in any organisation, entities are allowed to act autonomously provided they do not violate constraints which are imposed to preserve the safety of the whole system. On the other hand, the ACC can easily provide a service to allow autonomous, intelligent agents to inspect the current state of policies, and use it to reason about which actions are to be executed to achieve a given goal—following e.g. the *operating instructions* approach [7].

4   Infrastructure Model

In this section, we formalise our conceptual framework, by using an algebraic approach to denote MASs and their evolutions. Our analysis here focuses on the interaction between agents and their ACCs, and neglects other aspects such as organisation management and inspection. Subsection 4.1 first introduce some basic notation, and discuss how the main concepts—agent, organisation, agent interaction, ACC, role—are expressed in the model. Subsequently, Subsection 4.2 formalises the semantics of RBAC-MAS through a number of transition rules defining the admissible evolutions of an RBAC-MAS system. Finally, Subsection 4.3 outlines a simple application scenario.

4.1   Notation and Syntax

Basic Notation. As a general notation convention, in the following we let Greek letters α, β, ... identify meta-variables over actions, non-capitalised letters a, b, ... over identifiers or atomic elements of different kinds, and capitalised letters A, B, ... over system components and abstractions of various sorts. Given any meta-variable x, notation $Set(x)$ stands for the set of elements over which it ranges.

Accordingly, basic items of our framework are denoted as follows: a ranges over the set of the *agent identifiers*, r ranges over *role identifiers*, p over *policy identifiers*, E over *environment configurations*, and O over *organisation configurations*. In particular, the sets $Set(a)$, $Set(r)$, and $Set(p)$ are specific to any given MAS organisation: so, no further hypothesis are made on their structure.

The set of terms $\mathcal{T}$ is equipped by a notion of *substitution*. We name substitution a total function $\sigma \in \Sigma$ from terms to terms, where $\Sigma \subseteq \mathcal{T} \mapsto \mathcal{T}$. Notation $\sigma\tau$ denotes a substitution σ applied to a term τ. As usual, this notation is often abused by allowing a substitution to be applied to elements of any syntactic category: the meaning is that any term τ occurring inside the elements gets correspondingly substituted. We say that

MAS Configurations

$$S ::= X \,||\, O \,||\, E$$
$$X ::= 0 \mid \langle a, A \rangle \mid \langle a, (C)A \rangle \mid X \,||\, X$$

Agent Interactions

$$\epsilon ::= !\tau \mid ?\tau$$
$$\nu ::= \downarrow \mid \uparrow \mid +r : R \mid -r$$
$$\alpha ::= r : p : \epsilon \mid \nu$$
$$\iota ::= a\nu$$

ACC Configurations

$$C ::= 0 \mid r : R \mid C \,||\, C$$
$$R ::= 0 \mid p : P \mid R \,||\, R$$
$$P ::= 0 \mid \pi.P \mid P + P \mid P \,||\, P \mid \mathcal{D}$$
$$\pi ::= \epsilon \mid \diamond$$

Fig. 2. Syntax

term τ is more general than τ' (and that τ' is more specific than τ) if for at least one substitution we have $\sigma\tau = \tau'$.[1]

MAS Configuration. At any given time a MAS is denoted by its *configuration*, which captures an instant of the MAS evolution over time. As summarised in Fig. 2, a MAS is conceived here as composed by three parts—*agents*, *organisation*, and *environment*. In the following, composition operator $||$ is always assumed to be commutative, associative, and to absorb the atom 0. Correspondingly, in our framework, a MAS configuration is composed by three sets:

Agent configuration. X is the *agent configuration* of a MAS, that is, at any given time, the set of the (state of) agents currently belonging to the MAS. Every agent is either an *active* or an *inert* agent. An active agent is an agent that has already entered the organisation—so, it has an ACC already assigned—, which is denoted by a term $\langle a, (C)A \rangle$, where a is the agent identifier, A the *agent state* and C its *ACC configuration*, or *context*. An inert agent is an agent that has not yet entered the organisation—so, it has no ACC assigned—, which is denoted by a term $\langle a, A \rangle$.

Organisation configuration. O is the *organisation configuration* of a MAS, that is, is the set of the organisation structures that shape the MAS at any given time. See details on their syntax and semantics in Subsection 4.2.

Environment configuration. E is the *environment configuration* of a MAS, that is the set of the elements—such as other agents, information sources, physical devices, artifacts of various kinds [5]—which altogether constitute the MAS environment. Environment configurations E will not be described in their syntax and semantics in the following, since they are peculiar to any specific MAS, and mostly orthogonal to organisation aspects.

Agent Interactions. Variable ϵ ranges over interactions of the agent toward the environment, which could be either of the kind $!\tau$ meaning execution of action represented

---

[1] The reader familiar with logics might see differences between this setting and the usual logic one. In particular, we rely on a notion of substitution instead of unification. This is because the notion of substitution is more standard for the process algebraic approach we take here.

by term τ, or $?\tau$ meaning reception of perception τ. Variable ν ranges over those actions an agent executes when negotiating an ACC structure, including entering the ACC ($\downarrow$), leaving the ACC ($\uparrow$), activating role r in the initial state R ($+r : R$), and deactivating role r ($-r$).

Interactions α globally allowed to an agent unify the two kinds of action above: other then ACC actions ν they include interactions ϵ qualified by the role and policy they refer to in the current ACC, hence they are denoted by syntax $r : p : \epsilon$. Instead, ACC actions ν have no direct effect on the environment, but should be handled and recorded globally at the infrastructure level: correspondingly, ι represents the actions for ACC negotiation or change as perceived and handled by the organisation, that is, an action ν qualified by the agent identifier a.

ACC Configuration and Policies. An ACC enforces and controls agent actions within an organisation. Every ACC is associated with an active agent, and its state, called *ACC configuration*, evolves along with the evolution of the agent behaviour. An ACC configuration is a parallel composition of roles R—for an agent possibly concurrently playing more than one role—each specified by its own role identifier r. Since it is possibly characterised by more than one policy, a role is itself a composition of policies P, each with its own policy identifier p. A possible ACC configuration is of the kind $(r_a : (p_1 : P_1 \,||\, p_2 : P_2) \,||\, r_b : p_3 : P_3)$, with role r_a with the two policies $p_1 : P_1$ and $p_2 : P_2$, and role r_b with the policy $p_3 : P_3$. As a result, an active policy is always identified by qualifying the role identifier and the policy identifier ($r : p : P$).

The syntactic category P defines a standard process algebra [6] with operators for prefix action ($\pi.P$ means action π followed by continuation P), choice ($+$) and parallel interleaved ($||$) composition, and a mechanism for calling "external" definitions of the kind $\mathcal{D} := P$—where $\mathcal{D}$ is the term denoting the invoked definition and P is the associated policy to be executed. Similarly to operator $||$, operator $+$ is assumed to be commutative, associative, and to absorb the atom 0. The policy $\pi.0$ is often abbreviated to π without the risk of ambiguity.

A policy basically describes a protocol of actions π, including not only agent interactions ϵ, but also the *escape action* $\diamond$, used to (correctly) leave a policy. [2]

4.2 Operational Semantics

The formal machinery developed so far concerns syntactic aspects of the organisation infrastructure, focussing on the relationships and interactions between an agent and its ACC. This is completed here by providing an operational semantics describing how a MAS configuration may evolve over time, describing key details about how the different kinds of interaction are managed at the organisation level. The formal framework adopted is that of labelled transition systems [6], which provide the most natural approach to define the operational semantics of process algebraic structures as defined above, serving as both a specification tool to guide correct implementations and as

---

[2] Many similarities exists between policies and operating instructions for agents [7], which in fact share the common idea of providing agents with an operational means to execute interaction protocols—see [7] for more details on the usefulness of process algebras to this end.

an abstract executable model. Given a syntactic category defined by meta-variable x representing states of a component of interest—agent state, ACC state, policy, and so on—, a labelled transition system is a triple $\langle Set(x), \rightarrow_X, Set(\lambda) \rangle$ where λ is the meta-variable over the component interactions and $\rightarrow_X \subseteq Set(x) \times Set(\lambda) \times Set(x)$ is the transition relation. Write $x' \xrightarrow{\lambda}_X x''$ for $\langle x', \lambda, x'' \rangle \in \rightarrow_X$, meaning that the component in state x' may move to state x'' by interaction λ.

Concerning internal aspects of an agent behaviour, instead of relying on some form of mental properties representation, we find it useful here to completely abstract away from agent internal machinery—deepening the relationships between agent rationality and organisational aspects is left as future work. As a result, we simply model an agent by a labelled transition system $\langle Set(A), \rightarrow_A, Set(\alpha) \cup \{\cdot\} \rangle$, denoting the evolution over time of the agent mental state as agent interactions occur or by internal changes (label "$\cdot$"). Therefore, we do not make further hypothesis on the structure of set A. Notice that all agent interactions can structurally occur only if they are enabled/controlled by the ACC, as shown in the following.

Policy. The main difference between RBAC and RBAC-MAS is grounded in the notion of policy, which actually differs from that of permission. While permissions simply define a set of allowed operations over objects, we rely on the stronger notion of protocol: a policy is an admissible protocol of actions over the environment, possibility featuring non-determinism, interleaved sub-policies, and recursive behaviours.

At any given time a policy allows for any action more specific than the one reported in the prefix action construct $\pi.P$; furthermore, the environment which the action is executed over could constrain the action to be even more specific. We tackle this aspect by allowing substitutions to make into actions. To this end, as the actions controlled / enforced by a policy are ranged over by π, we define meta-variable $\bar{\pi}$ with syntax $\bar{\pi} ::= \sigma \triangleright \pi$. An *interaction* $\sigma \triangleright \pi$ means that a further substitution σ is actually externally imposed to the allowed action π. Therefore, the transition system for policies is defined by the triple $\langle Set(P), \rightarrow_P, Set(\bar{\pi}) \rangle$, and transition relation as the smallest relation satisfying the operational rules:

$$\pi.P \xrightarrow{\sigma' \triangleright \sigma \pi}_P \sigma' \sigma P \qquad\qquad \text{[P-ACT]}$$

$$\mathcal{D} \xrightarrow{\bar{\pi}}_P P' \qquad \text{iff } (\mathcal{D} := P) \wedge (P \xrightarrow{\bar{\pi}}_P P') \text{ [P-DEF]}$$

$$P \,||\, P'' \xrightarrow{\bar{\pi}}_P P' \,||\, P'' \text{ iff } P \xrightarrow{\bar{\pi}}_P P' \qquad \text{[P-PAR]}$$

$$P + P'' \xrightarrow{\bar{\pi}}_P P' \qquad \text{iff } P \xrightarrow{\bar{\pi}}_P P' \qquad \text{[P-CHO]}$$

Besides standard rules for (exclusive) choice [P-CHO], parallel composition [P-PAR], and (recursive) definitions [P-DEF], rule [P-ACT] defines the crucial aspect of policy interactions. As action π is specified in the policy, any more specific version $\sigma\pi$ can be executed which can be further constrained by external imposition of substitution σ': in this case, the functional composition $\sigma \circ \sigma'$ is actually applied to the policy continuation P. An example of policy definition is $\mathcal{D}p := !\text{ask}(r, v_q).(?\text{fail}(r).\mathcal{D}p + ?\text{rep}(r, v_r).\diamond)$, which means that the agent should initially execute action ask (specifying a query v_q and a resource r): if the perception fail occurs the policy is iterated again, if otherwise the perception rep occurs (providing reply v_r to the query) the agent can leave the policy (and deactivate the corresponding role). As this example can act as a simple brick, the (sequential, parallel, and choice) composition constructs allow for building more complex organisation policies [7].

Agent Coordination Context. The ACC and its relationship with an agent is expressed by the two kinds of admissible agent configurations X, which can be either of the kind $\langle a, A \rangle$ (inert agent) or $\langle a, (C)A \rangle$ (active agent) according to Fig. 2. By controlling/enforcing actions of an agent through its ACC, an agent configuration X evolves by two kinds of actions: *(i)* by an action ϵ of an agent over the environment, which is amenable of substitutions (hence we define $\overline{\epsilon} ::= \sigma \triangleright \epsilon$), *(ii)* or by a negotiation action ι (a pair of an agent identifier a and an ACC action ν). Accordingly, the transition system that models the evolution of agent configurations is of the kind $\langle Set(X), \rightarrow_X, Set(\overline{\epsilon}) \cup Set(\iota) \rangle$.

The operational rule for actions ϵ (writing the side-condition on top of the rule using the standard structural operational semantics notation [6]) is as follows:

$$\frac{A \xrightarrow{r:p:\sigma\epsilon}_A A' \quad P \xrightarrow{\sigma\triangleright\epsilon}_{\mathbb{P}} P'}{\langle a, (C \| r : (R \| p : P))A \rangle \xrightarrow{\sigma\triangleright\epsilon}_X \langle a, (C \| r : (R \| p : P'))A' \rangle}$$

Structure $\langle a, (C \| r : \ldots)A \rangle$ denotes an agent playing a role r (along others occurring in C), and substructure $R \| p : P$ that in r policy identifier p is associated with policy P. One such agent can perform an interaction ϵ qualified by role r and policy p (or rather a more specific one $\sigma\epsilon$) if P allows for it ($P \xrightarrow{\sigma\triangleright\epsilon}_{\mathbb{P}} P'$). Also, this interaction makes the states of agent and policy evolve to new states A' and P'.

Substitutions of this kind are actually sufficiently expressive to model a number of scenarios. Suppose that the selected policy allows at a given time action $!f(1, v)$, for some variable v. As a first case, assume the agent intends to execute $!f(v', v'')$; the ACC allows the more specific action $!f(1, v)$, representing e.g. a query whose expected result is v—the environment could either accept it, or accept the more specific version $f(1, 2)$ by substitution $\sigma = v \mapsto 2$, where 2 stands for the reply. As a second case, assume the agent intends to execute $!f(2, 1)$, to verify whether 2 is the correct reply to the query 1; the ACC allows the action $f(2, 1)$—the environment directly accepts it with identity substitution. Similar discussion applies to perceptions.

Operational rules dealing with negotiation actions are somehow more articulated, for they alter the ACC structure. Negotiation actions ι are exposed in the transition relation $\rightarrow_X$, so that their execution can actually be controlled by the organisation and possibly affect it—e.g. activating a role may be prevented because of some organisational rules.

$$\frac{A \xrightarrow{\downarrow}_A A'}{\langle a, A \rangle \xrightarrow{a\downarrow}_X \langle a, (0)A' \rangle} \quad [NE] \qquad \frac{A \xrightarrow{\uparrow}_A A'}{\langle a, (0)A \rangle \xrightarrow{a\uparrow}_X \langle a, A' \rangle} \quad [NQ]$$

$$\frac{A \xrightarrow{+r:R}_A A'}{\langle a, (C)A \rangle \xrightarrow{a+r:R}_X \langle a, (C \| r : R)A' \rangle} \quad [NA]$$

$$\frac{\langle a, (C \| r : R)A \rangle \xrightarrow{a-r}_X \langle a, (C)A' \rangle \quad P \xrightarrow{\sigma\triangleright\diamond}_{\mathbb{P}} P'}{\langle a, (C \| r : (R \| p : P))A \rangle \xrightarrow{a-r}_X \langle a, (C)A' \rangle} \quad [ND]$$

$$\frac{A \xrightarrow{-r}_A A'}{\langle a, (C \| r : 0)A \rangle \xrightarrow{a-r}_X \langle a, (C)A' \rangle} \quad [NF]$$

Rule [NE] initially provides an agent entering an ACC with the void context, while rule [NQ] is used to let an agent in a void context leave the ACC—and the organisation as well. Rule [NA] makes an agent activate a role r with specification R—which is actually imposed/checked by the organisation as shown later. Finally, rules [ND] and [NF] (recursively) handle the deactivation of a role, policy by policy. A policy can be removed whenever it allows for the escape action $\diamond$ ([ND]); when no more policies occur for the role ($r : 0$), this can be removed from the context ([NF]).

MAS Operational Semantics. Once the evolution over time of the agent and of the ACC has been operationally defined, it is now possible to formally describe the dynamics of a MAS as a whole in our framework. The global operational semantics of a MAS is specified via an (unlabelled) transition system $\langle Set(S), \rightarrow_S, \{\}\rangle$, where MAS configurations evolve by the execution of two different actions (environment interaction and negotiation), according to the following operational rules:

$$\frac{X \xrightarrow{\sigma \triangleright \epsilon}_X X' \quad E \xrightarrow{\epsilon \triangleright \sigma}_E E'}{X \parallel E \parallel S \rightarrow_S X' \parallel E' \parallel S} \text{ [S-E]} \qquad \frac{X \xrightarrow{\iota}_X X' \quad O \xrightarrow{\iota}_O O'}{X \parallel O \parallel S \rightarrow_S X' \parallel O' \parallel S} \text{ [S-N]}$$

Rule [S-E] handles the interaction of an agent with the environment. This occurs if one of the components of the environment (E) can execute the requested action ϵ. As a result of action execution, such a component can actually enforce a substitution σ ($\epsilon \triangleright \sigma$) which is then applied to the agent configuration as previously seen. As discussed above, we do not elaborate further upon a model for the environment, as this is out of the scope of the RBAC-MAS model—correspondingly, a transition system over E is not defined here. As shown in [5], yet, the action-substitution schema adopted is sufficiently expressive to account for bi-directional communication with other agents, as well as for interaction with artifacts of various sorts. Finally, rule [S-N] describes the execution of negotiations actions ι by an agent, which are allowed only if the organisation configuration O admits this interaction.

Organisation. In order to complete the specification of the RBAC-MAS formal model, it would be sufficient to describe syntax and semantics of organisation configurations, by a labelled transition system $\langle Set(O), \rightarrow_O, Set(\iota)\rangle$. This model, which is about the representation of organisational rules (roles, permissions, classes, and their relationships) and should definitely make into a full formal model of the infrastructure, has already been developed but is here avoided for the sake of space—it will appear in an extended version of the paper.

A brief description of its main ingredients follows. Organisation configuration keeps track of the rules regulating the current organisation: (*i*) allowed agent classes, (*ii*) class-role relation, (*iii*) role-policy relation, (*iv*) policy configuration, and (*v*) separation of duty rules. Moreover, it also keeps the current state of the MAS from the organisation viewpoint, that is, (*vi*) the class of active agents and (*vii*) the corresponding activated roleset.

The four main operational rules are as follows: (*i*) an agent can enter an ACC if its class is recognised, (*ii*) an agent leaving an ACC updates the current state of active agents, (*iii*) an agent can activate a role only if not prevented by a SD constraint, and (*iv*) role deactivation updates the current agent roleset.

4.3 A Scenario

To exemplify the applicability of our approach we describe a simplified organisation scenario. Suppose an agent is willing to exploit an existing MAS to buy a good over a distributed market service. After authentication the agent activates a role called *browser*, by which it is allowed to search for the availability of the required good. This role has a number of policies, for configuring searches, placing requests, and the like: one of them is the policy for doing researches through a search engine, specified by definition $\mathcal{D}s := (!\texttt{search}(good).?\texttt{reply}(addrs).\diamond) \,\|\, \mathcal{D}$. This policy states that the agent can concurrently issue (by recursive composition through $\|$) any number of searches, and leave the policy after any reply. After a while, the agent playing this role finds that there is an auction for that good on a site s, with given identifier id. Correspondingly the agent asks its ACC for activating a new role called *bidder*—this is not mutual exclusive to *browsing* hence the agent can keep looking for other places. (The agent even tried to activate the bidder role twice, but this was rejected by the ACC due to a SD rule.) The main policy for this new role enforces the participant-side of a Contract-Net auction protocol, which the agent should now follow step-by-step—see a possible algebraic specification of it in [7]. The agent wins the auction, and by another policy contracts payment and shipment. Since all activated roles are in a state where their policies can be left, the agent leaves its ACC and quits the MAS.

5 Related Work and Conclusions

In this paper we presented the main ingredients of the design of an organisation infrastructure for MASs, developing on our previous works [5,14]. In particular, the contribution of this paper is to formally detail all the organisation details concerning negotiation aspects—e,g, role activation and deactivation. This can be the starting point for both developing a general infrastructure for MASs dealing with organisation, or for adding the described organisation services to existing infrastructures such as JADE.

In the MASs literature, computational institutions (such as e-Institutions) currently represent the most complete work (from an engineering point of view) concerning the definition and enforcement of institutional rules and norms governing MAS societies [15,16]. Typically such approaches enforce norms by introducing a middle-agent layer, which mediates the communication between the individual agent and the rest of the organisation, without considering social rules involving the state of a group of agents/roles. Instead, our approach is rooted on the notion of infrastructure, which we believe can more coherently deal with global system rules (such as role-role relationship) and norms, and with their enforcement.

The ACC notion is interesting per se, and can be considered (and exploited) as a runtime embodiment of the notion of *contract* that appeared in some work in the e-Institution and agents & law context [16], or to enforce roles as in [17].

Future work will be devoted to completing the design of the infrastructure, implementing it on top of a MAS infrastructure such as JADE, and evaluating applicability to different scenarios and integration with existing works on e-Institutions.

References

1. Sandhu, R., Coyne, E.J., Feinstein, H.L., Youman, C.E.: Role-based control models. IEEE Computer **29** (1996) 38–47
2. Ferraiolo, D., Kuhn, R.: Role-Based Access Control. In: 15th NIST–NSA National Computer Security Conference, Baltimore, MD, USA (1992) 554–563
3. Omicini, A.: Towards a notion of agent coordination context. In Marinescu, D.C., Lee, C., eds.: Process Coordination and Ubiquitous Computing. CRC Press (2002) 187–200
4. Ricci, A., Viroli, M., Omicini, A.: Agent coordination context: From theory to practice. In: Cybernetics and Systems 2004. Volume 2., Vienna, Austria, Austrian Society for Cybernetic Studies (2004) 618–623 Proceedings of 17th European Meeting on Cybernetics and Systems Research (EMCSR 2004), Vienna, Austria, 13–16 April 2004. Proceedings.
5. Omicini, A., Ricci, A., Viroli, M.: Formal specification and enactment of security policies through Agent Coordination Contexts. Electronic Notes in Theoretical Computer Science **85** (2003) 1st International Workshop "Security Issues in Coordination Models, Languages and Systems" (SecCo 2003), Eindhoven, The Netherlands, 28–29 June 2003. Proceedings.
6. Glabbeek, R.v.: The linear time – branching time spectrum I. The semantics of concrete, sequential processes. In: Handbook of Process Algebra. North-Holland (2001) 3–100
7. Viroli, M., Ricci, A.: Instructions-based semantics of agent mediated interaction. [18] 102–110
8. Kinny, D.: ViP: a visual programming language for plan execution systems. In Castelfranchi, C., Johnson, W.L., eds.: 1st International Joint Conference on Autonomous Agents and Multiagent Systems (AAMAS 2002). Volume 3., Bologna, Italy, ACM (2002) 721–728
9. Ferraiolo, D.F., Sandhu, R., Gavrila, S., Kuhn, D.R., Chandramouli, R.: Proposed NIST standard for role-based access control. ACM Transactions on Information and System Security (TISSEC) **4** (2001) 224–274
10. Omicini, A., Ricci, A., Viroli, M., Castelfranchi, C., Tummolini, L.: Coordination artifacts: Environment-based coordination for intelligent agents. [18] 286–293
11. JADE-board: Java agent development framework. http://jade.cselt.it (2000)
12. Omicini, A., Zambonelli, F.: Coordination for Internet application development. Journal of Autonomous Agents and Multi-Agent Systems **2** (1999) 251–269
13. Dulay, N., Damianou, N., Lupu, E., Sloman, M.: A policy language for the management of distributed agents. In: Agent-Oriented Software Engineering II. Volume 2222 of LNCS., Springer (2002) 84–100 2nd International Workshop (AOSE 2001), Montreal, Canada, 29 May 2001. Revised Papers and Invited Contributions.
14. Omicini, A., Ricci, A., Viroli, M.: RBAC for organisation and security in an agent coordination infrastructure. Electronic Notes in Theoretical Computer Science **128** (2005) 65–85 2nd International Workshop on Security Issues in Coordination Models, Languages and Systems (SecCo'04), 30 August 2004. Proceedings.
15. Noriega, P., Sierra, C.: Electronic institutions: Future trends and challenges. In Klusch, M., Ossowski, S., Shehory, O., eds.: Cooperative Information Agents VI. Volume 2446 of LNCS. Springer (2002) 14–17 6th International Workshop (CIA 2002), Madrid, Spain, 18–20 September 2002. Proceedings.
16. Weigand, H., Dignum, V., Meyer, J.J., Dignum, F.: Specification by refinement and agreement: Designing agent interaction using landmarks and contracts. In Petta, P., Tolksdorf, R., Zambonelli, F., eds.: Engineering Societies in the Agents World III. Volume 2577 of LNCS., Springer (2003) 257–269 3rd International Workshop (ESAW 2002), Madrid, Spain, 16–17 September 2002. Revised Papers.

17. Cabri, G., Ferrari, L., Leonardi, L.: The RoleX environment for multi-agent cooperation. In Klusch, M., Ossowski, S., Kashyap, V., Unland, R., eds.: Cooperative Information Agents VIII. Volume 3191 of LNCS., Springer (2004) 257–270 8th International Workshop (CIA 2004), Erfurt, Germany, September 27-29, 2004. Proceedings.
18. Jennings, N.R., Sierra, C., Sonenberg, L., Tambe, M., eds.: 3rd international Joint Conference on Autonomous Agents and Multiagent Systems (AAMAS 2004). ACM, New York, USA (2004)

Towards Fault-Tolerant Formal Concept Analysis

Ruggero G. Pensa and Jean-François Boulicaut

INSA Lyon, LIRIS CNRS UMR 5205,
F-69621 Villeurbanne cedex, France
{Ruggero.Pensa, Jean-Francois.Boulicaut}@insa-lyon.fr

Abstract. Given Boolean data sets which record properties of objects, Formal Concept Analysis is a well-known approach for knowledge discovery. Recent application domains, e.g., for very large data sets, have motivated new algorithms which can perform constraint-based mining of formal concepts (i.e., closed sets on both dimensions which are associated by the Galois connection and satisfy some user-defined constraints). In this paper, we consider a major limit of these approaches when considering noisy data sets. This is indeed the case of Boolean gene expression data analysis where objects denote biological experiments and attributes denote gene expression properties. In this type of intrinsically noisy data, the Galois association is so strong that the number of extracted formal concepts explodes. We formalize the computation of the so-called δ-bi-sets as an alternative for capturing strong associations between sets of objects and sets of properties. Based on a previous work on approximate condensed representations of frequent sets by means of δ-free itemsets, we get an efficient technique which can be applied on large data sets. An experimental validation on both synthetic and real data is given. It confirms the added-value of our approach w.r.t. formal concept discovery, i.e., the extraction of smaller collections of relevant associations.

1 Introduction

Formal Concept Analysis has been developed for more than two decades [1]. It supports knowledge discovery (e.g., clustering, association rule mining) in contexts where a number of Boolean properties hold or not for a collection of objects. For instance, Table 1 is a toy example data set $\mathbf{r}$ where we see that attributes p_2 and p_5 are true for object o_2. Informally, formal concepts are maximal rectangle[1] of true values. For instance, $(\{o_1, o_3\}, \{p_1, p_3, p_4\})$ is a formal concept in $\mathbf{r}$.

Among others, formal concepts can be considered as overlapping clusters which are intrinsically characterized: the reason why o_1 and o_3 are in the same cluster is that they all share properties p_1, p_3, and p_4. Such a conceptual clustering [2] is crucially needed in many application domains. For this purpose, co-clustering (also called bi-clustering) has been proposed [3,4,5,6]. The goal is to identify bi-partitions, i.e., associated partitions on both dimensions. When applied on Boolean matrices, these techniques tend to provide rectangles with

---

[1] Rectangle has to be understood modulo arbitrary permutations of lines and columns.

S. Bandini and S. Manzoni (Eds.): AI*IA 2005, LNAI 3673, pp. 212–223, 2005.

Table 1. A Boolean context **r**

	p_1	p_2	p_3	p_4	p_5
o_1	1	0	1	1	0
o_2	0	1	0	0	1
o_3	1	0	1	1	0
o_4	0	0	1	1	0
o_5	1	1	0	0	1
o_6	0	1	0	0	1
o_7	0	0	0	0	1

mainly true values. Notice however that they are based on heuristic techniques (i.e., local optimization) and that they generally compute collections of non overlapping bi-clusters. Instead, the strength of Formal Concept Analysis is that, when tractable, it is based on complete collections of formal concepts which are overlapping clusters. The state-of-the-art is that we can compute collections of formal concepts in many practical applications. First, some algorithms are dedicated to formal concept discovery (see [7] for a survey). Then, for tackling very large contexts, constraint-based mining of formal concepts has been studied (see, e.g., [8,9]). In this case, we still compute complete collections containing every formal concept which satisfies some other user-defined constraints (e.g., a minimal size for their set components).

The application domain which motivates our research is Boolean gene expression data analysis, i.e., knowledge discovery from data sets which encode gene expression properties (e.g., over-expression) in various biological situations or experiments. Given Table 1, we might say that, e.g., genes denoted by p_1, p_3, p_4 are considered over-expressed in situation o_1. Interestingly, in such a context, formal concepts can be considered as putative transcription modules, i.e., maximal sets of genes that are co-regulated associated to the maximal sets of experiments which seem to trigger this co-regulation. Notice that bi-cluster overlapping makes sense from the biological point of view (i.e., the same gene can be involved in various biological functions). Transcription module discovery is an important step towards the understanding of gene regulation and we address a severe limitation of putative transcription module discovery from formal concepts[2]. Within a formal concept, we have a maximal set of objects (i.e., a closed set) which are in relation with all the elements of a maximal set of properties and vice versa. The strength of such an association is often too strong in real-life data. Assume that, e.g., $c_1 = (\{o_1, o_3, o_4\}, \{p_1, p_3, p_4\})$ is a "valid" association in the application domain. Let us now consider that, like in **r**, we do not record that p_1 is true for o_4. As a result, we do not get c_1 but instead the two formal concepts $(\{o_1, o_3, o_4\}, \{p_3, p_4\})$ and $(\{o_1, o_3\}, \{p_1, p_3, p_4\})$. In fact, the presence of false values which have been set "by error" leads to an explosion of the number of formal concepts. We have problems with values inappropriately set to true as well. Such noisy data is quite common, e.g., in life science domains, where we can not avoid errors of measurement but also further problems with Boolean

---

[2] More generally, we consider the search for interesting bi-clusters from Boolean data.

property encoding. For instance, encoding a gene expression property, say over-expression, from typical numerical microarray data relies on the definition of a threshold whose value enables to encode true or false [10]. This intrinsically introduces noise. As a result, the number of formal concepts which hold in real-life Boolean gene expression data sets can be huge, e.g., up to several millions. Even though the extraction might remain tractable, the needed post-processing phases turn to be tedious or even impossible.

These observations have motivated a new direction of research where interesting bi-clusters are considered as dense rectangles of true values (see, e.g., [11,12,13]). Such rectangles look like formal concepts with a number of exceptions, i.e., hopefully, a bounded number of false values per line and per column. To the best of our knowledge, previous attempts are not really satisfactory for our application domain. Either they rely on very expensive algorithms (e.g., [11] which is based on formal concept merging) or they assume quite strong hypothesis on the data (e.g., [12] which assumes a built-in order on both dimensions). Instead of looking for such fault-tolerant formal concepts, we would like to revisit a previous work on the so-called δ-free itemsets, i.e., one of the few approximate condensed representations of frequent itemsets [14]. The idea was to consider specific itemsets, the δ-free ones, whose frequency have to be counted in order to infer without counting and with a bounded error the frequency of many others. We consider the bi-sets which can be built on δ-free sets of properties and their δ-closures (i.e., associated attributes which are almost always true) on one hand, on the sets of objects which support the δ-free set on the properties on another hand. As a result, δ-bi-sets contain a bounded number of exceptions per column. An example in the data set $\mathbf{r}$ is that $\{p_1\}$ is a 1-free set whose 1-closure (the properties which are almost always true with p_1, i.e., with at least 1 exception) is $\{p_3, p_4\}$. It means that the bi-set $(\{o_1, o_3, o_5\}, \{p_1, p_3, p_4\})$ is a 1-bi-set. Indeed, it has at most 1 exception per column. The extraction of δ-bi-sets can be extremely efficient thanks to δ-freeness anti-monotonicity. Such collections can be computed in many data sets, including huge ones. Our intuition is that, in real data sets, the distribution of these exceptions among the lines will be acceptable such that δ-bi-sets capture really strong associations between sets of objects and sets of properties. By considering synthetic data sets but also real-life data sets, we illustrate that formal concept extraction can be hard and/or useless in noisy data sets. We also demonstrate the added-value of the δ-bi-set extraction method in order to get an a priori interesting collections of overlapping bi-clusters.

Section 2 provides the needed definitions for the formalization and the use of the δ-bi-set mining task. Section 3 provides experimental results on synthetic or benchmark data when various levels of noise are added. Section 4 considers several experiments on real-life bio-medical data sets which are intrinsically noisy. Section 5 is a short conclusion.

2   An Alternative to Formal Concepts in Noisy Data Sets

Assume a set of objects $\mathcal{O} = \{o_1, \ldots, o_m\}$ and a set of Boolean attributes $\mathcal{P} = \{p_1, \ldots, p_n\}$. The Boolean context to be mined is $\mathbf{r} \subseteq \mathcal{O} \times \mathcal{P}$, where $r_{ij} = 1$ if the attribute p_j is true for the object o_i. In Boolean gene expression data sets, if o_i is a biological sample, p_j denotes an expression property of a gene, e.g., $r_{ij} = 1$ means that gene associated to p_j is over-expressed in o_i.

It is interesting to look for associations between sets of objects and sets of properties, i.e., bi-sets. An obvious measure which quantifies the strength of such associations is the density of true values within the bi-set. Formal concepts are maximal bi-sets with only true values. The problem is that the number of formal concepts in noisy data sets explodes and that it makes sense to relax the associated closeness constraint to capture less but relevant strong associations, i.e., some kind of fault-tolerant formal concepts.

Formally, a bi-set (T, G) is a couple of sets from $2^{\mathcal{O}} \times 2^{\mathcal{P}}$. T is called an objectset and G is called an itemset. Let us first recall the basic definition of our Galois connection (see, e.g., [1]).

Definition 1 (Galois connection). *If $T \subseteq \mathcal{O}$ and $G \subseteq \mathcal{P}$, ϕ and ψ constitute a Galois connection when $\phi(T, \mathbf{r}) = \{p \in \mathcal{P} \mid \forall o \in T, (o, p) \in \mathbf{r}\}$ and $\psi(G, \mathbf{r}) = \{o \in \mathcal{O} \mid \forall p \in G, (o, p) \in \mathbf{r}\}$. $h = \phi \circ \psi$ and $h' = \psi \circ \phi$ denote the closure operators. A set $T \subseteq \mathcal{O}$ (resp. $G \subseteq \mathcal{P}$) is said closed in $\mathbf{r}$ iff $T = h'(T, \mathbf{r})$ (resp. $G = h(G, \mathbf{r})$).*

We can now formalize some usual pattern types.

Definition 2 (1-rectangles, formal concepts, supporting sets). *A bi-set (T, G) is a 1-rectangle in $\mathbf{r}$ iff $\forall o \in T$ and $\forall p \in G$, $(o, p) \in \mathbf{r}$. A bi-set (T, G) is a formal concept in $\mathbf{r}$ iff $T = \psi(G, \mathbf{r})$ and $G = \phi(T, \mathbf{r})$. It is equivalent to $T = h'(T, \mathbf{r})$ and $G = \phi(T, \mathbf{r})$ or to $G = h(G, \mathbf{r})$ and $T = \psi(G, \mathbf{r})$. An important property is indeed that each closed set on one of the two dimensions is associated to a unique closed set on the other dimension. We say that the support of an itemset G (resp. an objectset T) in $\mathbf{r}$ is $\psi(G, \mathbf{r})$ (resp. $\phi(T, \mathbf{r})$).*

For example, $\{\{o_1, o_3\}, \{p_1, p_3\}\}$ is a 1-rectangle in $\mathbf{r}$ (see Table 1) but it is not maximal. $(\{o_1, o_3\}, \{p_1, p_3, p_4\})$, $(\{o_1, o_3, o_4\}, \{p_3, p_4\})$, and $(\{o_2, o_5, o_6\}, \{p_2, p_5\})$ are examples of formal concepts among the 8 ones which hold in $\mathbf{r}$. $\{o_1, o_3, o_5\}$ is the supporting set of $\{p_1\}$. $\{p_1, p_3, p_4\}$ is the supporting set of $\{o_1\}$.

Sections 3 and 4 illustrate on concrete examples that, even in small matrices, the number of formal concepts can be huge. In fact, the size of the collection of formal concepts in a given matrix is exponential in its smallest dimension. Formalizing the δ-bi-set mining task, we want to compute smaller collections which still capture important associations within the data. Collections are smaller because a given δ-bi-set can always be described as a merge of some formal concepts.

Let us first recall the popular association rule mining task [15] since it is needed to understand the δ-freeness property.

Definition 3 (association rule, frequency, confidence). *An association rule R in a data set $\mathbf{r}$ is an expression of the form $X \Rightarrow Y$, where $X, Y \subseteq \mathcal{P}$, $Y \neq \emptyset$ and $X \cap Y = \emptyset$. The frequency of R is $|\psi(X \cup Y, \mathbf{r})|$ and the confidence of R is $|\psi(X \cup Y, \mathbf{r})| / |\psi(X, \mathbf{r})|$.*

In an association rule $X \Rightarrow Y$ with high confidence, the properties in Y are almost always true for an object when the properties in X are true. Intuitively, the itemset $X \cup Y$ associated to the set of object $T = \psi(X, \mathbf{r})$ is then a dense bi-set. Moreover, the more the rule is frequent, the larger the bi-set will be.

We now consider our technique for computing association rules with high confidence, the so-called δ-strong rules [14].

Definition 4 (δ-strong rule). *Given an integer value δ, a δ-strong rule in a Boolean context $\mathbf{r}$ is an association rule $X \Rightarrow Y$ ($X, Y \subset \mathcal{P}$) such that $|\psi(X, \mathbf{r})| - |\psi(X \cup Y, \mathbf{r})| \leq \delta$, i.e., the rule is violated in no more than δ objects.*

Interesting collections of δ-strong rules with minimal left-hand side can be computed efficiently from the so-called δ-free-sets [14] and their δ-closures.

Definition 5 (δ-free set, δ-closure). *Let δ be an integer and an $X \subset \mathcal{P}$ be an itemset, X is a δ-free-set w.r.t. $\mathbf{r}$ if and only if there is no δ-strong rule which holds between two of its own and proper subsets. The δ-closure of X in $\mathbf{r}$, $h_\delta(X, \mathbf{r})$, is the maximal (w.r.t. set inclusion) superset Y of X s.t. for every item $p \in Y \setminus X$, $|\psi(X \cup \{p\})|$ is at least $|\psi(X, \mathbf{r})| - \delta$. In other terms, the frequency of the δ-closure of X in $\mathbf{r}$ is almost the same than the frequency of X when δ is small w.r.t. the number of objects. It means also that $\forall p \in h_\delta(X) \setminus X$, $X \Rightarrow p$ is an association rule with high confidence, more precisely a δ-strong rule.*

For example, in Table 1, the 1-free itemsets are $\{p_1\}$, $\{p_2\}$, $\{p_3\}$, $\{p_4\}$, $\{p_5\}$, $\{p_1, p_2\}$, and $\{p_1, p_5\}$. An example of 1-closure for $\{p_1\}$ is $\{p_1, p_3, p_4\}$. The association rules $\{p_1\} \Rightarrow \{p_3\}$ and $\{p_1\} \Rightarrow \{p_4\}$ have only one exception.

δ-freeness is an anti-monotonic property such that it is possible to compute δ-free sets (eventually combined with a minimal frequency constraint) in very large data sets. Notice than when $\delta = 0$, $h_0 = h$, i.e., the classical closure operator. Looking for a 0-free itemset, say X, and its 0-closure provides a closed itemset Y. When a closed set is computed by this technique, we get easily the formal concept (T, Y) by associating its supporting set of objects $T = \psi(Y, \mathbf{r})$. We can now use the properties of δ-free-sets and δ-strong rules to extract a collection of dense bi-sets with a bounded number of exceptions per column.

Definition 6 (δ-bi-set). *A δ-bi-set (T, G) in $\mathbf{r}$ is built on each δ-free-set $X \subset \mathcal{P}$ and we have $G = h_\delta(X, \mathbf{r})$ and $T = \psi(X, \mathbf{r})$.*

It is clear that for a δ-bi-set (T, G), when $\delta << |T|$, (T, G) denotes a strong association between T and G. In Table 1, itemsets $\{p_3\}$ and $\{p_5\}$ are examples of 1-free-sets. The related 1-bi-sets are $\{\{o_1, o_3, o_4\}, \{p_1, p_3, p_4\}\}$ and $\{\{o_2, o_5, o_6, o_7\}, \{p_2, p_5\}\}$. Obviously, when $\delta = 0$, each δ-bi-set is a formal concept.

An algorithm to extract δ-bi-sets. For the experimentations, we have been using a straightforward extension of the MIN-EX implementation described in [14]. Indeed, we just added the automatic generation of the supporting set for each extracted δ-free-set. MIN-EX is a typical instance of the levelwise search algorithm presented in [16]. Thanks to the antimonotonicity of the conjunction of δ-freeness and a minimal frequency constraint, it explores the itemset lattice (w.r.t. the inclusion) levelwise, starting from the empty set and stopping at the level of the largest frequent δ-free-set. More precisely, the collection of candidates is initialized with the empty set as single member (the only set of size 0) and then the algorithm iterates on candidate evaluation (i.e., checking both δ-freeness and minimal frequency) and larger candidate generation. At iteration i, it scans the data to find out which candidates of size i are frequent δ-free-sets and it computes their δ-closure as well. Then it generates candidates for the next iteration, taking every set of size $i + 1$ such that all their proper subsets are frequent δ-free-sets. The algorithm stops when there is no more candidate. The needed δ-free sets can thus be extracted by setting the frequency threshold to 1. Also, our implementation outputs each supporting set of lines for each discovered δ-free set of columns.

3   Experiments on Data Plus Noise

First, we study the relevancy of δ-bi-sets w.r.t. formal concepts when considering the addition of noise to a synthetical data set and to a benchmark data set from UCI Macine Learning Repository [17]. Let us first discuss the evaluation method.

Hereafter, **r** denotes a reference data set, i.e., a data set which is assumed to be noise-free. We use it to generate noisy data sets by adding a given quantity of uniform random noise (for a X% noise level, each value is randomly changed with a probability of X%). Then, we compare the collection of formal concepts which are "built-in" within **r** with various collections of bi-sets (i.e., formal concepts and δ-bi-sets) extracted from the noised matrices. To measure the relevancy of each extracted collection w.r.t the reference one, we look for a subset of the reference collection in each of them. Since the objectset and the itemset of each formal concept can be changed when adding noise to the data, we identify those having the largest area in common with the original ones, and we compute a measure called σ which takes into account the common area:

$$\sigma(\mathcal{C}_r, \mathcal{C}_a) = \frac{1}{N_r} \sum_{i=1}^{N_r} max_j \left(\frac{|(T_i, G_i)_r \cap (T_j, G_j)_a|}{|(T_i, G_i)_r \cup (T_j, G_j)_a|} \right)$$

where $\mathcal{C}_r$ is the collection of concepts computed on the reference **r**, $\mathcal{C}_a$ is a noised collection of bi-sets, $(T_i, G_i)_r$ and $(T_j, G_j)_a$ are bi-sets belonging to $\mathcal{C}_r$ and $\mathcal{C}_a$ respectively, and N_r is the size of the reference collection of formal concepts. When $\sigma(\mathcal{C}_r, \mathcal{C}_a) = 1$, all the bi-sets belonging to $\mathcal{C}_r$ have identical instances in the collection $\mathcal{C}_a$.

In the experiment, **r** has 30 objects and 15 properties and it contains 3 formal concepts of the same size which are pair-wise disjoints. In other terms, the formal concepts are $(\{o_1, \ldots, o_{10}\}, \{p_1, \ldots, p_5\})$, $(\{o_{11}, \ldots, o_{20}\}, \{p_6, \ldots, p_{10}\})$, and $(\{o_{21}, \ldots, o_{30}\}, \{p_{11}, \ldots, p_{15}\})$. We generated 40 different data sets by adding increasing quantities of noise (from 1% to 40% of the matrix). The idea is that a robust technique should be able to capture the three associations despite the

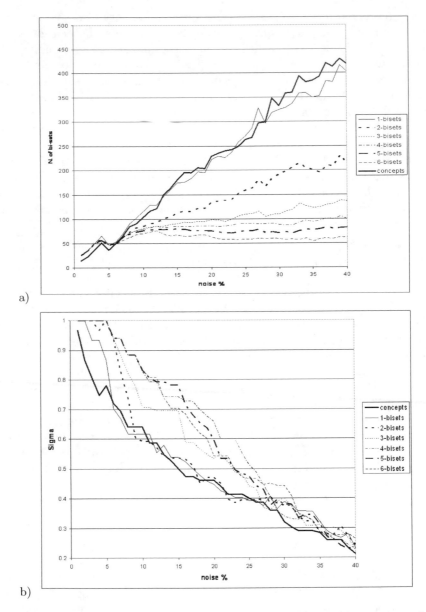

a)

b)

Fig. 1. Size of collections of bi-sets (a) and related values of σ (b) w.r.t. noise level

introduced noise. Therefore, for each data set, we have extracted a collection of formal concepts and different collections of δ-bi-sets with increasing values of δ (from 1 to 6). Then, we looked for the occurrence of the three concepts in each of these extracted collections by using our σ measure. Results are collected in Fig. 1b.

The σ measure obviously decreases when the noise level increases. Interestingly, its values for δ-bi-set collections are always greater or similar to the values for the collection of formal concepts. In particular, for $\delta = 1$, the collections of 1-bi-sets behave better than the collection of formal concepts until noise level is greater than 5%. When $\delta = 2$, this noise threshold is 10%. Finally, for higher values of δ (3,4 and 5), the noise threshold for which δ-bi-sets perform better is quite high (30%). Then, we computed the number of extracted patterns in each collection (Fig. 1a). The collections of δ-bi-sets contain always less patterns than the collection of formal concepts (for a noise level greater than 7%). For $\delta = 2$, the size is halved. For greater values of δ, noise does not influence the size of the collections of δ-bi-sets.

This experiment confirms that δ-bi-sets are more robust to noise than formal concepts. Furthermore, we can reduce significantly the size of the extracted collections and this is crucial to support the interpretation process by data owners.

We applied the same experimental methodology to the voting-records data set from UCI Machine Learning repository. We generated the reference boolean matrix by encoding each variable-modality pair (except the class variable) into a single Boolean attribute. We obtained a matrix with 435 objects and 48 properties. Then, we generated 40 data sets by adding increasing quantities of uniform random noise (from 1% to 40% of the matrix). δ-bi-sets have been extracted with three values of δ (5, 7 and 10), and with a minimal frequency constraint of 7% (i.e., the minimal δ-free-set support size is greater than 30 objects).

The collections of formal concepts have been extracted from the noised matrices with a minimal objectset size constraints set to 30 by using DMINER [9]. The reference collection is the set of all formal concepts with at least 30 objects and 10 attributes in the original matrix. This is motivated by our goal which is to look for rather large associations because too small formal concepts are not relevant in noisy data sets. Using these constraints, we obtained a collection of 4114 formal concepts.

We have computed the values of σ for the different collections of bi-sets and we obtained the results collected in Fig. 3a. The advantages of using δ-bi-sets are visible as soon as the noise level reaches about 5%. It is even more obvious when looking at another reference collection of formal concepts with a minimal itemset size constraint set to 13. In this case, we obtained 24 rather large formal concepts and the benefit of δ-bi-sets starts with a noise level of about 2%. Moreover, if we look at the number of extracted bi-sets (see Fig. 2), we see that the collection of formal concepts is huge w.r.t. any δ-bi-set collection. Notice also that starting from a noise level of 20%, all the sizes are almost the same. Again, mining dense bi-sets as δ-bi-sets enable to get a significantly smaller collection of more relevant patterns.

Until now, we added some noise to a priori noise-free data sets. We tried to identify a subset of the formal concepts which holds in these reference data sets within various collections of bi-set extracted from the matrices after noise introduction. Let us now consider a comparison between formal concepts and δ-bi-sets in three "real world" intrinsically noisy data sets. Two of them (drodophila [18] and malaria [19]) are gene expression data sets. The last one (meningitis) is a medical data set. For the gene expression data sets, the techniques used for

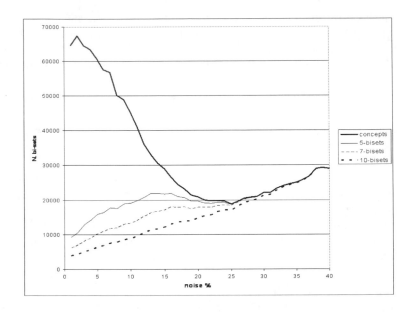

Fig. 2. Size of collections of bi-sets w.r.t. noise level in voting-record

Table 2. Sizes of different bi-set collections for three "real world" data sets

dataset	lines	columns	concepts	1-bisets	2-bisets	3-bisets
drosophila	81	3030	2,288,850	1,801,369	778,526	443,668
malaria	46	3719	3,768,135	844,245	377,739	215,821
meningitis	329	60	689,943	329,834	132,703	69,494

measuring the expression level of genes are unlikely to be fault-free. Moreover, encoding Boolean expression properties from continuous values introduces noise in the data as well. We used the encoding technique described in [10]. For the medical data set, both the discretization of continuous measures and the missing values lead to noisy data. This data set has been preprocessed and provided by Bruno Crémilleux from the University of Caen (France).

For each of these data sets, we extracted a collection of formal concepts and three collections of δ-bi-sets, with rather low values of δ (from 1 to 3), and we compared the number of extracted patterns. Results are collected in Table 2.

For the drosophila and meningitis data sets, the number of pattern is approximatively halved at each incrementation of the δ value. A quite interesting result is the important reduction of the pattern collection size when shifting from formal concept to 1-bi-set mining within malaria (see Table 2). Then, we tried to identify in this malaria data set a group of 135 genes which are known to take part in the same biological function (i.e., cytoplasmic translation machinery) in association with the group of 17 samples in which these genes are known to be active (see [19] for details). We used our σ measure, that, in this case, is

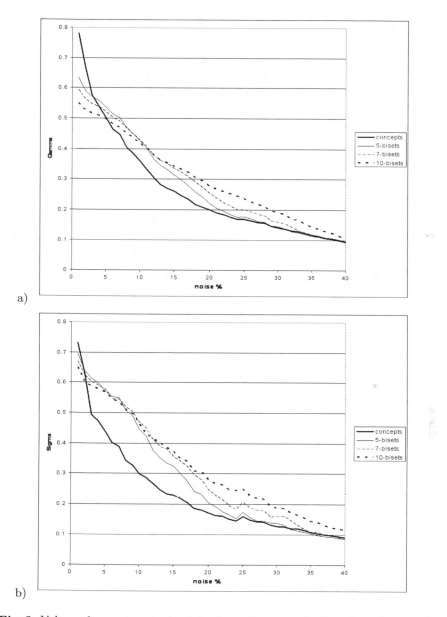

a)

b)

Fig. 3. Values of σ w.r.t. noise level for two reference collections in voting-record

equal to the normalized intersection of the previously described bi-set with the extracted bi-set which better matches it. We found that, for the collection of formal concepts, the value of σ is 0.142, while, for the 1-bi-set collection, its value is 0.146. This enforces our conviction that mining fault-tolerant formal concepts in intrinsically noisy data is a relevant method to reduce the workload for the interpretation by data owners and to provide more relevant patterns.

4   Conclusion

Looking for strong associations between sets of objects and sets of properties in eventually large and noisy Boolean data sets, we have discussed a fundamental limitation of formal concept mining. Computing fault-tolerant formal concepts, e.g., with a bounded number of exceptions on both dimensions is known to be computationally very hard. We proposed a solution based on an efficient technique for mining association rules with few exceptions. The δ-bi-set mining task has been experimentally evaluated on both noised data sets and real data sets. The results are quite promising because we get smaller collections of more relevant patterns. This is crucial for the needed post-processing phases like, e.g., the tedious process of bi-set interpretation by molecular biologists when they are looking for putative transcription modules within Boolean gene expression data sets. The relationship to other fault-tolerant formal concepts must be studied. If δ-bi-sets can indeed be extracted efficiently, it would be much more relevant to ensure a bounded number of exceptions on both lines and columns like in [11]. It means that other classes of fault-tolerant formal concepts might be more relevant than δ-bi-sets but also probably much harder to extract. Another related work in artificial intelligence concern the fuzzy concept analysis framework (see, e.g., [20]). It is an attempt to manage uncertainty and it is clearly related to noisy data analysis. Further investigation is needed in this direction. An interesting perspective on which we are currently working is to use collections of fault-tolerant formal concepts for building relevant bi-partitions from noisy data. The challenge here is to enable a user-driven control for bi-cluster overlapping and to look at the opportunities for constraint-based mining of such models.

Acknowledgements. The authors wish to thank Bruno Crémilleux who provided the data on child's meningitis. We also thanks Christophe Rigotti, Jérémy Besson and Céline Robardet for exciting discussions. This research is partially funded by ACI MD 46 (CNRS STIC 2004-2007) BINGO (Bases de Données Inductives pour la Génomique).

References

1. Wille, R.: Restructuring lattice theory: an approach based on hierarchies of concepts. In Rival, I., ed.: Ordered sets. Reidel (1982) 445–470
2. Fisher, D.H.: Knowledge acquisition via incremental conceptual clustering. Machine Learning **2** (1987) 139–172
3. Cheng, Y., Church, G.M.: Biclustering of expression data. In: Proceedings ISMB 2000, San Diego, USA, AAAI Press (2000) 93–103
4. Robardet, C., Feschet, F.: Efficient local search in conceptual clustering. In: Proceedings DS'01. Number 2226 in LNCS, Springer-Verlag (2001) 323–335
5. Dhillon, I., Mallela, S., Modha, D.: Information-theoretic co-clustering. In: Proceedings ACM SIGKDD 2003, Washington, USA, ACM Press (2003) 89–98
6. Madeira, S.C., Oliveira, A.L.: Biclustering algorithms for biological data analysis: A survey. IEEE/ACM Trans. Comput. Biol. Bioinf. **1** (2004) 24–45

7. Kuznetsov, S.O., Obiedkov, S.A.: Comparing performance of algorithms for generating concept lattices. Journal of Experimental and Theoretical Artificial Intelligence **14** (2002) 189–216
8. Stumme, G., Taouil, R., Bastide, Y., Pasqier, N., Lakhal, L.: Computing iceberg concept lattices with TITANIC. Data & Knowledge Engineering **42** (2002) 189–222
9. Besson, J., Robardet, C., Boulicaut, J.F.: Constraint-based mining of formal concepts in transactional data. In: Proceedings PaKDD'04. Volume 3056 of LNAI., Sydney (Australia), Springer-Verlag (2004) 615–624
10. Pensa, R.G., Leschi, C., Besson, J., Boulicaut, J.F.: Assessment of discretization techniques for relevant pattern discovery from gene expression data. In: Proceedings ACM BIOKDD'04, Seattle, USA (2004) 24–30
11. Besson, J., Robardet, C., Boulicaut, J.F.: Mining formal concepts with a bounded number of exceptions from transactional data. In: Proceedings KDID'04. Volume 3377 of LNCS., Springer-Verlag (2004) 33–45
12. Gionis, A., Mannila, H., Seppänen, J.K.: Geometric and combinatorial tiles in 0-1 data. In: Proceedings PKDD'04. Volume 3202 of LNAI., Pisa, Italy, Springer-Verlag (2004) 173–184
13. Geerts, F., Goethals, B., Mielikäinen, T.: Tiling databases. In: Proceedings DS'04, Padova, Italy, Springer (2004) 278–289
14. Boulicaut, J.F., Bykowski, A., Rigotti, C.: Free-sets: a condensed representation of boolean data for the approximation of frequency queries. Data Mining and Knowledge Discovery **7** (2003) 5–22
15. Agrawal, R., Imielinski, T., Swami, A.: Mining association rules between sets of items in large databases. In: Proceedings ACM SIGMOD'93, Washington, D.C., USA, ACM Press (1993) 207–216
16. Mannila, H., Toivonen, H.: Levelwise search and borders of theories in knowledge discovery. Data Mining and Knowledge Discovery **1** (1997) 241–258
17. Blake, C., Merz, C.: UCI repository of machine learning databases (1998)
18. Arbeitman, M., Furlong, E., Imam, F., Johnson, E., Null, B., Baker, B., Krasnow, M., Scott, M., Davis, R., White, K.: Gene expression during the life cycle of drosophila melanogaster. Science **297** (2002) 2270–2275
19. Bozdech, Z., Llinás, M., Pulliam, B.L., Wong, E., Zhu, J., DeRisi, J.: The transcriptome of the intraerythrocytic developmental cycle of plasmodium falciparum. PLoS Biology **1** (2003) 1–16
20. Huynh, V.N., Nakamori, Y., Ho, T.B., Resconi, G.: A context model for fuzzy concept analysis based upon modal logic. Inf. Sci. **160** (2004) 111–129

Agent-Based Management of Responsive Environments*

Flávio Soares Corrêa da Silva[1] and Wamberto W. Vasconcelos[2]

[1] Dept of Computer Science, Univ of São Paulo, 05504-090,
São Paulo, Brazil
fcs@ime.usp.br
[2] Dept of Computing Science, Univ of Aberdeen,
AB24 3UE Aberdeen, UK
wvasconcelos@acm.org

Abstract. Responsive environments are physical surroundings whose components change their behaviour to accommodate the presence of people as well as other components. We describe a means to manage such responsive environments whereby each component is dynamically assigned a software agent – these are autonomous and reactive/proactive programs that communicate via message-passing. Arbitrary functionalities can be encoded in such agents, reflecting the capabilities of the components they represent, as well as extending them. Ours is a flexible and scalable approach allowing the gradual population of an environment with physical devices and their corresponding agents.

1 Introduction

Responsive environments are those provided with ambient intelligence. Ambient intelligence was recently characterised by Gaggioli [1] as referring to digital environments that are *sensitive* and *responsive* to the presence of people. Their key features are *intelligence* and *embedding*. "Intelligence" here refers to the fact that the digital environment is able to *analyse* the *context*, adapt itself to the people and objects that reside in it, *learn* from their *behaviour*, and eventually *recognise* as well as *express emotion*. "Embedding" means that miniaturised *devices* will become *part of the invisible background* of peoples' activities, and that social interaction and functionality will move to the foreground.

We focus on the feature of *intelligence*. We concur with Ess [2] in that the development of modern computer science has followed two parallel paths, the first championed by (among others) Engelbart and his motto *augment, not automate* [3] – which led to outcomes as the whole area of human-computer interaction – and the second pioneered by (among others) McCarthy [4] – which led to outcomes as the whole research programme of Artificial Intelligence. These two paths seem, at first glance, deemed never to come to a confluence, as we could interpret that Engelbart's view embeds the proposition that computers are here

---

* Work partially sponsored by the International Exchange Programme of the Royal Society of Edinburgh, United Kingdom.

S. Bandini and S. Manzoni (Eds.): AI*IA 2005, LNAI 3673, pp. 224–236, 2005.

to enhance and extend human-centric activities, whilst the Artificial Intelligence view looks for ways to replace humans in their activities.

Ambient Intelligence is commonly aligned with the "augmentation" approach to computer science. We emphasise, nonetheless, the implicit goal in this field of research of treating environments as agents that sense and interpret events, devise plans and react based on what has been sensed. Our work is an attempt to bridge the fields of ambient intelligence and multi-agent systems. Ambient intelligence poses specific systems design challenges, especially those related to the real-time management of asynchronous, multi-purpose, concurrent systems that must be coordinated based on incomplete and partially reliable information, and which include humans as participants. Multi-agent systems, in turn, offers the possibility to incorporate sophisticated patterns of behaviour in the reactivity of environments, based on complex reasoning and interaction between devices and humans, as well as among different devices (and their software counterparts).

In this article we present some concrete scenarios in which these patterns of behaviour can be relevant, and propose a general architecture that can be used to design ambient intelligence systems for those scenarios. To make the architecture general-purpose, we abstract some specificities related to sensors and actuators. Our goal is to design a generic architecture that can be instantiated to specific cases, such that well defined devices can be easily "plugged in".

In section 2 we present a class of scenarios we aim at. In section 3 we introduce our general architecture. In section 4 we outline how the architecture could be used in the engineering of responsive environments. In section 5 we discuss related work and how other approaches differ and relate to our own proposal. Finally, in section 6 we present some conclusions and proposed future work.

2   Illustrative Scenarios

In this section we illustrate the class of problems we aim at with a scenario. Let us consider the case of a bookstore where sensors (antennae) detect the presence of customers identified by some portable device (*e.g.* a bluetooth-enabled mobile phone or PDA, or a fidelity card equipped with active RFID). In this scenario there are various sensors distributed among the shelves and sections of the bookstore which are able to detect the presence of individual customers. The bookstore can associate the identification of customers with their profiling information, such as preferences, buying patterns and so on.

With this infrastructure in place, the bookstore can provide customers with a responsive environment that would adapt to maximise their well-being with a view to increasing sales. For instance, the device playing the background music should take into account the preferences of a customer next to it. Similarly, LCD displays scattered in the store can show items based on the customer nearby, the lights on the shop's display window (showing new titles) can be rearranged to reflect a customer's preferences and interests, and so on.

In a bookstore, a customer will share the physical space with other customers. Hence, to make our scenario more realistic, the devices must detect the presence of more than one customer and adapt their behaviour to account for these different customers. For instance, the device to play background music must take into account the customers within hearing distance of itself and play music that would please most customers. Likewise, a display unit should show items that would be within the interests and preferences of most customers in its neighbourhood (assuming there is a limit on the number of items the display unit can show).

The bookstore setting is a representative of the scenarios we would like to consider. We would like to capture the most fundamental features of our aimed class of scenarios. Some of these features are:

- *A dynamic set of physical components* – the components of the physical world (*i.e.*, devices and humans) enter and leave the environment and move about.
- *Components have disparate capabilities* – a human without a personal device (PDA or mobile phone) cannot communicate directly with the environment; a communal multimedia station can output information, but may not be able to receive direct feedback from the environment.
- *Asynchronous distributed computing* – each device operates asynchronously and independently of each other; moreover there is no shared memory and information is exchanged among the devices only via message-passing.

3   A Multi-agent Architecture

We aim at a large class of systems broadly referred to as *intelligent responsive environments*. These are systems consisting of loosely coupled components such as sensors, antennae, display devices (possibly with multimedia features), digital cameras (for still and motion pictures), and so on, that perceive the presence of humans in the physical space they are immersed in and modify their behaviour to accommodate such presence. Our components may need to interact with each other and, if this is the case, they do so in an ad-hoc fashion via message exchange – no physical exclusive channels exist among the components of our systems. We explain below a means to implement the ad-hoc communication among our components via persistent tuple spaces.

In order to make our discussion more concrete, we shall employ the shopping precinct scenario described previously. Let us concentrate on the case of a department store (or shopping centre) in which customers (humans) share a physical space with devices with distinct functionalities. In Figure 1 we show the actual physical space as a rectangle (lower half of the diagram) in which humans and electronic devices coexist; the upper half of the diagram shows a "cloud" in which the software counterpart of the physical components exist. Dotted lines connect the actual components with their digital counterparts – these lines, as we explain below, stand for various forms of communication among the digital and physical components. We explain the details of both the

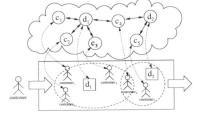

Fig. 1. World & Software Agents

digital cloud and physical space below, and also present means to (semi-) automatically connect them.

We represent actual customers (humans) inhabiting the physical space (rectangle) as "stick men"; devices also share this physical space and we represent them in a generic fashion as labelled squares. In our diagram we also represent their area of action as dotted circles – these stand for the range of the sensors or how far their behaviour or output reaches within the physical space. Humans enter, move around and leave physical spaces, interacting with devices. This interaction may take many forms: for instance, customers approach a screen that displays items they might be interested in; customers approach a sound station that plays music they might like; customers interact via terminals, mobile phones or PDAs with their agents to find out what's on offer in the shop for less than a certain amount, and so on. Devices become aware of humans through sensors (in the physical world); devices also have software agents that provide them with extensible functionalities, one of which is the management of their capabilities (e.g., devices that can only play music, multimedia devices or computers with touch screens).

The cloud above the physical world represents the computational counterpart of the physical world. Each component (human or device) has a corresponding software agent that represents its features, capabilities and interests. A useful analogy here might be to consider the digital cloud as a kind of operating system that manages and integrates existing resources. We thus regard an intelligent responsive environment as a physical space whose (electronic and human) components are managed by intelligent software agents, that is: *intelligent responsive environment = physical world + intelligent software agents*.

3.1 Formal Definitions

We need to formally define some of our concepts to enable us to carry out our discussion in a more precise manner. The definitions in this section aim at providing us with a more compact and precise notation with which we can explain and explore our scenarios. We shall first define the components of the physical world:

Definition 1. *A component is a pair $c = \langle id, cat \rangle$ where id is a unique identifier and cat is a label depicting the category of the component, according to some ontology.*

Components thus possess a unique identifier *id* which is akin to the universal resource identifiers (URIs) of the WWW [5] and that may depend on the specific physical space. The category *cat* is a concept of an associated ontology describing the component in a most specific fashion. Examples of such an ontology is FIPA's (The Foundation for Intelligent Physical Agents) Device Ontology Specification [6] and W3C's (The World Wide Web Consortium) Composite Capabilities and Preferences Profile recommendation (CC/PP) [7]. We will denote a physical space generically as the set of components $C = \{c_1, \ldots, c_n\}$.

Components have assorted computing capabilities. The simplest kind of component, say a tag that identifies its bearer to a sensor, will simply store their identifier and category; more sophisticated components, say a PC or a PDA, will possess more computing power that would enable them to carry out various tasks. We decided not to represent the components' capabilities for two reasons: *i)* these are only relevant to the component itself and not to the environment as a whole; and *ii)* a sufficiently expressive means to represent all kinds of computing capabilities (including none) goes beyond the scope of this work.

The simplest components may not have the ability to communicate with other components, that is, they may lack the capabilities to prepare and send messages to other components as well as to receive and process messages from other components. We require that *at least* one component in our environments have a communication facility with the digital "cloud" shown in Fig. 1. We elaborate on the digital cloud and such communication facility below. We shall denote a component that communicates with the digital cloud as $\widehat{c}$.

We next define the intelligent software agents, the counterparts of physical components:

Definition 2. *An intelligent software agent is represented as the triple ag = ⟨id, cat, loc⟩ where id and cat are as above and loc represents a location of the physical world.*

The location *loc* provides the position in the physical environment of the actual component the agent represents. Distinct environments render themselves differently to being broken down into regions and points of location. We are not concerned here with how accurate the positioning of components are within the environment and different scenarios may require different solutions. The actual components should provide their location to their software agents in a manner we describe below.

3.2   Connecting the Physical World with Software Agents

Our approach consists in providing an extensible and flexible software layer to manage the various components of a responsive environment. We aim at environments in which physical components can appear, move about and disappear continuously, hence our proposed solution cannot be a static one. We provide each component of a responsive environment with a software agent: a self-contained computer program that is *autonomous* and that can *communicate* with other agents [8]. Agents are automatically started, updated and terminated as their components enter, move about, and leave the environment, respectively.

We want to make our exposition as concrete as possible to allow the reproduction or adaptation of our ideas to similar scenarios. Rather than considering software agents in the abstract, we describe, hopefully with sufficient detail, a complete solution to implement them. Our architecture is built around a blackboard, implemented as a Linda *tuple space* [9] – tuple spaces have been successfully embedded in a number of programming languages (*e.g.*, Prolog [10] and Java [11]). Our solution is similar to the SPREAD approach [12] and

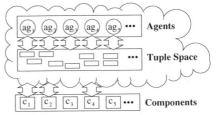

Fig. 2. Tuple Space Architecture

the LIME [13] project, in that we similarly use a tuple space to facilitate ad-hoc communication among components, thus avoiding issues concerning communication channels, point-to-point message passing, and so on. We show in Figure 2 a diagram detailing the digital cloud of Figure 1.

In Figure 2 we show components (bottom rectangle) some of which communicate with the digital cloud by writing entries on the tuple space and by reading/taking entries from it. The components that do not have communication capabilities must somehow be sensed by a component in the ambient which, on its turn, communicates with the digital cloud. Components that cannot read/take entries from the digital cloud must resort to other components to do so on their behalf. This provides an indirect form of communication that accommodates devices with disparate capabilities.

3.3   Infrastructure: Administrative Agents

We require a team of administrative agents to provide a basic infrastructure for the digital cloud. The administrative agents, among other responsibilities, continuously roam the space looking for tuples that concern them. Our architecture is bootstrapped with a team of administrative agents and an empty tuple space.

The administrative agents can be in any number, but there must be at least one of them (and its backup). If there is more than one of them, then they are exactly the same, that is, they possess the same functionalities. When a physical component $\widehat{c}$ is turned on (or alternatively, when it enters the environment) it must be assigned a software agent to represent it in the digital cloud. Its communication capabilities must allow it to write onto the space the tuple $\langle id, cat, loc \rangle$. For instance, we can have a device writing a tuple such as $\langle 4533, \texttt{antenna}, \texttt{tools\_department} \rangle$ or $\langle 843533, \texttt{VGA}, \texttt{toiletries(south)} \rangle$. The administrative agents take the entries off the space and start up an agent (and a backup for it, as above), if it has not already done so. When an agent is successfully started up, this is recorded as a tuple $\langle id, cat, \texttt{agent(on)} \rangle$. We note the absence of the loc in the tuple: the agent for the component is the only one in possession of this information.

Each administrative agent has a "dormant" backup agent: at regular intervals the backup agent sends a message checking that the active administrative agent is alive and well. We endow the active administrative agent with a thread that answers these messages. If anything has gone wrong, then the backup agent takes over the duties of the active agent becoming the new active agent. The new active agent must initially start up a backup copy of itself, thus perpetuating the active/dormant arrangement.

3.4   Software Agents for Physical Components

Once a software agent is started up by the team of administrative agents, it follows a process of sensing the environment, updating its internal model of the world and then acting upon the world, much like the usual behaviour of reactive agents [8]. However, our agents sense the environment by checking for tuples in the space – these tuples are written on the space by the physical counterpart. For instance, if a component moves about it writes a tuple $\langle$agent(id), cat, new_location(loc_{new})$\rangle$; if a sensor detects a person in its vicinity it writes the tuple $\langle$agent(id), cat, detect(person)$\rangle$, and so on. Likewise, the agents change their environment by writing tuples on the space that are aimed at their physical counterparts. For instance, an agent representing a sound station may need to send a tuple such as $\langle$component(id), cat, play(Bach)$\rangle$.

The decoupling of hardware and software capabilities has two advantages. Firstly, new devices (with arbitrary functionalities) can be added at will without requiring special software to manage them: all we need to do is to make sure their agents write adequate tuples on the space for them. Secondly, new software agents can be introduced without having to change the hardware nor its configuration. The point of contact between components and agents is the tuple space: new functionalities both in the hardware and software can be captured and harnessed by designing new kinds of tuples and an order in which they are written onto and read/taken from the space.

We can associate a different kind of software agent to each category of components expected in the physical environment. Alternatively, we can offer a generic agent that follows the process: read/take relevant tuples, process tuples and update internal state(s), write out adequate tuples. In this case, the variability stems from different ways of implementing the processing of tuples. We show in Figure 3 a generic kind of agent implemented in SICStus Prolog [10]. We chose Prolog as a programming language because of its terse syntax and precise semantics – a goal of this work, as we explain below,

```
1  main(Id,Cat,Loc):-
2      initialise(Id,Cat,Model),
3      loop([Id,Cat,Loc],Model).
4  loop([Id,Cat,Loc],Model):-
5      terminate(Id,Cat,Model).
6  loop([Id,Cat,Loc],Model):-
7      take_tuples(Id,Ts),
8      process(Id,Loc,Model,Ts,NewLoc,NewModel,OutTs),
9      write_tuples(OutTs),
10     loop([Id,Cat,NewLoc],NewModel).
```

Fig. 3. Generic Prolog Agent

is to capture the semantics of a class of computational solutions to the problem of managing responsive environments.

Predicate main/3 (lines 1–3) is called when the agent is started up – the administrative agent ensures that appropriate values for Id, Cat and Loc (obtained from the tuple space, having been written by a physical component) are passed to the predicate. The initialise/3 predicate uses Id and Cat to build the initial model Model – this predicate is responsible for, for instance, retrieving the profile of a customer or a description of the features of a PC or PDA, and using these to build an initial model for the agent to work on.

Predicate loop/2 (lines 4–10) defines the main flow of execution, continuously checking for any terminating condition (*e.g.* when a component leaves the environment or is turned off) in clause 1 (lines 4–5). The second clause (lines 6–10) checks the space for new tuples written to the agent, processes them, updating the model, and then writes out tuples. Predicate take_tuples/2 (line 7) uses the agent identification Id to take all those tuples aimed at the agent and stores them as a list in Ts. Predicate process/7 uses Id, Loc, Model and Ts and obtains a new location NewLoc (which may be the same as Loc if the component has not moved), updates the model in light of the new tuples giving rise to `NewModel` and prepares in `OutTs` a (possibly empty) list of tuples that are to be written out onto the space. Line 9 shows the predicate `write_tuples/1` that writes out the list of tuples `OutTs` onto the space. Finally, in line 10 predicate `loop/2` is recursively invoked with the appropriate new arguments.

4 Engineering Responsive Environments

We are interested in how one could engineer responsive environments. Some of the tasks for which we would like to provide support are the design, implementation, verification and analysis and deployment of software to manage a physical space. In this section we propose and justify a methodology for engineering responsive environments.

Ultimately particular devices (and their features and capabilities) will have to be considered in the design of responsive environments. However, we would like to study a complete class of solutions and thus we need to move away from manufacturers' specificities, but we still want to keep the discussion realistic. We thus employ a more abstract and flexible description of devices using ontologies.

4.1 From Physical Components to Software Agents

We propose an automatic means to provide physical components with their software counterparts. When a new component with communication capabilities enters the environment, then it writes an entry onto the space requesting its agent counterpart to the administrative agent, as explained above. Those components without communication capabilities, however, follow an indirect route to get their corresponding agents: upon being detected (and recognised, if possible) by devices with sensing features, then these sensing devices write onto the tuple space the information on the detected component. If the detected component already has an agent, then its agent will simply update its location, otherwise the administrative agent will start up an agent for the component. The sensing devices must be able to communicate with the tuple space or, alternatively, to communicate with a device that is able to communicate with the tuple space.

4.2 A Concrete Negotiation Protocol

Physical entities within the region of reach of an interactive device have corresponding software agents that exchange messages in order to reach multiple goals. Basically, the goals to be reached are individual goals of the agents, plus general goals of the organisation whose existence justifies the construction of systems like the ones we are studying. For example, in a bookstore, software agents of customers can have as goals to maximise the comfort of the customers whose interests they represent and to provide the customers with information in the most useful format, whereas the bookstore can have as goals to sell as many books as possible and to ensure that customers will come back in the future.

The reachability of goals can be ensured by means of the design of appropriate plans and message exchange protocols for the agents. These plans and protocols should be as sophisticated as necessary, in order to capture the complexity and multiplicity of behaviours of the agents that can be needed for each specific problem at hand. Our work is focused on providing systems engineers with the appropriate tools to build, calibrate and revise plans and communication protocols as easily as possible, and to implement those plans and protocols efficiently in the designed software agents.

In order to give a concrete example, we present in this section the means to implement very simple plans and a specific, also very simple, procedure for agents to exchange messages. Despite the simplicity of our plans and protocol, the overall observable behaviour of the resulting system can be surprisingly complex.

Our protocol is as follows: we assume that within the neighbourhood of an interactive device there can be agents of two sorts: *customer proxies*, named $ag_{c_1}, ag_{c_2}, ..., ag_{c_n}$ and only one *device proxy*, named ag_d. The device proxy represents the interactive device. Anytime a customer gets sufficiently close to the interactive device to be detected and identified by it, his/her corresponding proxy agent migrates to the device's region.

In our simplified scenario, the gestures of the customers are not sensed, and the amount of time each customer stays close to a device is not tracked either. The only information we take into account is the popping up of customer proxies within the range of devices, and whether they stay there for some time.

Consider a collection of attributes with corresponding numerical values which can be used to classify the contents to be presented in an interactive device. For example, we can take into account only two attributes to classify books – price range and age of customers that can have interest in a book – and classify every book in a bookstore according to these two numeric values. If a pair $\langle price, age \rangle$ is written in a public area, the agent ag_d can at any moment read this pair, select the set of books corresponding to this pair and start showing them.

Assume that each customer proxy ag_{c_i} also has a pair $\langle price_{c_i}, age_{c_i} \rangle$ that characterises the preference of the customer it represents, *i.e.*, if that customer were alone in the bookstore, (s)he would very much like to see all the time the display of the books corresponding to $\langle price_{c_i}, age_{c_i} \rangle$. A customer proxy surrounding a device, in this case, has the capability of rewriting the pair $\langle price, age \rangle$ being read by the device, according to a strategy that improves monotonically its individual satisfaction, without moving abruptly away from what was being shown prior to its arrival, which somehow represented the preferences of the community of agents surrounding the device prior to its arrival.

The communication among the customer proxies can occur through the pair $\langle price, age \rangle$. For example, agents can take turns to rewrite this pair, in a round-robin fashion. The strategy for agents to bring the pair closer to their preferences without disrupting a previously existing state of stability can be implemented as a tuple of numerical values within the real interval $[0, 1]$, corresponding to each attribute used to classify the contents to be shown by a device. In our concrete case, we have for each agent ag_{c_i} a corresponding pair $\langle \Delta_{c_i}^p, \Delta_{c_i}^a \rangle, \Delta_{c_i}^p, \Delta_{c_i}^a \in [0, 1]$. Every time the agent ag_{c_i} is granted the right to update the pair $\langle price, age \rangle$, it makes it the following way: (i) $price \leftarrow price + \Delta^p_{c_i} \times (price_{c_i} - price)$; (ii) $age \leftarrow age + \Delta^a_{c_i} \times (age_{c_i} - age)$.

The relative sensitivity of each agent with respect to each attribute used to determine the contents to be shown in the interactive devices can be calibrated empirically through the parameters $\Delta^j_{c_i}$. The result of a customer approaching a device, in this case, is that the contents shown in that device are gradually adjusted to the interests of that agent, without disregarding the tastes and interests of the other customers who were close to the device prior to the arrival of this last customer.

Intuitively, it is as if the attributes of contents generated an euclidean space, the actual contents being shown were located as a point in that space, each customer agent had the point of its most preferred contents also located in that same space, and the tuple $\langle \Delta^1_{c_i}, \Delta^2_{c_i}, ... \Delta^n_{c_i} \rangle$ of attribute-related parameters determined the power of agent ag_{c_i} to attract the contents shown to its preferences.

In Figure 4 we have a graphical representation of how it works. We have three customers, whose agents are named ag_{c_1}, ag_{c_2} and ag_{c_3}. Considering only price and age, let us assume that the most preferred contents for ag_{c_1} is given by $\langle 10, 10 \rangle$, the most preferred contents for ag_{c_2} is given by $\langle 20, 20 \rangle$ and the most preferred contents for ag_{c_3} is given by $\langle 10, 20 \rangle$. Let us also assume that the parameters related to agent ag_{c_1} are $\langle 0.5, 0.2 \rangle$, the parameters related to agent ag_{c_2} are $\langle 0.8, 0.5 \rangle$ and the parameters related to agent ag_{c_3} are $\langle 0.2, 0.7 \rangle$.

Let us finally assume that initially only the customer represented by ag_{c_1} was close to the display showing products, which lead it to show precisely the contents related to point $\langle 10, 10 \rangle$.

As soon as the customers represented by ag_{c_2} and ag_{c_3} approach the display, their influence start to update the contents being presented in the display. Agent ag_{c_2} "pushes" the contents towards $\langle 20, 20 \rangle$ with the strength provided by its relative parameters, and then agent ag_{c_3} "pushes" the contents towards $\langle 10, 20 \rangle$ with the relative strength provided by its own parameters, and then agent ag_{c_1} "pushes" the contents back towards $\langle 10, 10 \rangle$ with the strength provided by its relative parameters, and so on repeatedly. The contents shown are the ones captured asynchronously by the device, among the possibilities resulting from the "tra-

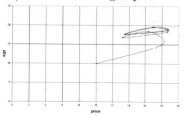

Fig. 4. Dynamics of Negotiation

jectory" of what to be shown generated by these values. In Figure 4, we see a line representing this trajectory, from the initial situation with only ag_{c_1} close to the display until the stable closed polygon that characterises the "orbit" of contents that attend the interests of all three agents.

5   Related Work

A general appraisal of the field of Ambient Intelligence, written by a researcher whose major contributions are connected to Artificial Intelligence and Multi-agent Systems, can be found in [14]. Another general appraisal of Ambient Intelligence can be found in [15], in which are proposed five "key technology features" of Ambient Intelligence:

- *Embedded:* multiple devices are integrated into the environment.
- *Context aware:* the environment, as an agent, recognises its human inhabitants, their activities and context.
- *Personalised:* the environment can adjust itself to the needs and interests of individual inhabitants.
- *Adaptive:* the environment can change in response to what is going on.
- *Anticipatory:* the environment can infer the desires, intentions and future actions of its inhabitants.

In [16,17] we have the notion of "ambient mediated" interaction between humans and software agents, which is akin to our approach. Human inhabitants of a responsive space are generally interested in the services that the space can provide to it, and would rather have access to those services automatically. It is expected, therefore, that humans consider irrelevant whether those services are the outcome of coordinated actions of a society of software agents. The interactions among software agents, between agents and the environment are, in that project, carefully constrained to tightly controlled protocols. Our work extends their results by giving room to more sophisticated patterns of interaction.

Other research work related to ours has been gradually reported in a series of papers [18,19,20,21]. Similar to our work, those researchers propose a framework in which software agents can negotiate based on their capabilities and goals and on context dependent information – e.g. information arising from sensors. Those authors, however, do not to consider the possibility of multiple human users sharing the same output – in which case this output should be of use to all concurrent users – or more convoluted negotiation protocols (their approach is basically first-come-first-served). The test bed proposed by those authors, nonetheless, is noteworthy: an active, context-aware arts museum (http://peach.itc.it/). Our proposal should be applicable to their scenario with great effectiveness, since active museums match perfectly the abstract setting we have taken into account.

In our work we have focused specifically in intelligent responsive environments which require sophisticated intelligent behaviour and interaction among the software agents that constitute them. A similar approach has been taken in [22]. Our work contrasts with the work presented in [22] by the way we account for spatial interaction. In [22] physical location rules the interactions among intelligent software agents, whereas in our work physical location is an attribute of "spaceless" information agents, who interact through a tuple space.

6   Conclusions, Discussion and Future Work

We presented Ambient Intelligence viewed from the perspective of Multi-agent Systems. We presented some concrete scenarios in which Ambient Intelligence is appropriate, and in which complex patterns of reasoning and interaction between digital devices and humans, as well as among digital devices (and their software counterparts), are useful to implement the desired functionalities of systems for Ambient Intelligence, thus suggesting that Multi-agent Systems can contribute to the design and implementation of complex responsive environments.

We have stressed along the article that these two areas – Ambient Intelligence and Multi-agent Systems – challenge and support each other with interesting problems and useful technical and conceptual tools to design and implement concrete systems. We have also introduced a generic architecture to build systems for Ambient Intelligence incorporating features of Multi-agent Systems. The *raison d'etre* of a generic architecture is reuse: one builds a generic architecture if it can be used in different instances of a class of problems. The class of problems we have in mind is somehow outlined in section 2, with a collection of representative cases.

The work presented here is in its preliminary stages. Our future work shall focus on the extension and refinements of the generic architecture presented here, based on empirical assessment of its application in the design and construction of concrete systems; the implementation of software modules that can actually speed-up and simplify the construction of different systems; and the extraction of formal properties of the architecture that allow us to verify properties related to model consistency and the avoidance of deadlocks and loops. As newcomers to the field of Multi-agent systems applied to Ambient Intelligence (and vice-versa), we must also insert our work more carefully into the context of existing related efforts, e.g. those found in [22,23].

References

1. Gaggioli, A.: User's Experience in Ambient Intelligence Systems. Ambient Intelligence: Conceptual and Practical Issues (mini-course, University of Haifa) (2005)
2. Ess, C.: Computer-mediated Communication and Human Computer Interaction. In: Luciano Floridi (ed.) The Blackwell Guide to Philosophy of Computing and Information, Oxford, UK, Blackwell (2004)
3. Engelbart, D.C.: Augmenting Human Intellect: A Conceptual Framework. Stanford Research Institute Technical Report AFOSR-3233 (1962)
4. McCarthy, J., Minsky, M.L., Rochester, N., Shannon, C.: A Proposal for the Dartmouth Summer Research Project on Artificial Intelligence. http://www-formal.stanford.edu/jmc/history/dartmouth/dartmouth.html (1955)
5. Berners-Lee, T.: Naming and Addressing: URIs, URLs.... http://www.w3.org/Addressing/ (2003)
6. Foundation for Physical Agents (FIPA): Device Ontology Specification. http://www.fipa.org/specs/fipa00091/XC00091C.pdf (2001)
7. World Wide Web Consortium (W3C): Composite Capabilities/Preferences Profile Public Home Page. http://www.w3.org/Mobile/ CCPP/ (2004)
8. Wooldridge, M.: An Introduction to MultiAgent Systems. John Wiley & Sons Ltd., England, U.K. (2002)
9. Carriero, N., Gelernter, D.: Linda in Context. CACM **32** (1989) 444–458
10. Swedish Institute of Computer Science: SICStus Prolog. (2005) http://www.sics.se/isl/sicstuswww/site/index.html, viewed on 10 Feb 2004 at 18.16 GMT.

11. Freeman, E., Hupfer, S., Arnold, K.: JavaSpaces: Principles, Patterns and Practice. Addison-Wesley, U.S.A. (1999)
12. Couderc, P., Banâatre, M.: Ambient Computing Applications: an Experience with the SPREAD Approach. In: Procs. of the 36th Hawaii Int'l Conf. on System Sciences (HICSS'03), IEEE Comp Soc (2003)
13. Picco, G., Murphy, A., Roman, G.C.: LIME: Linda Meets Mobility. In: Procs. of the 21st Int'l Conf. on Software Eng. (ICSE 1999), ACM Press (1999)
14. Shadbolt, N.: Editorial: Ambient Intelligence. IEEE Intell. Syst. **18** (2003) 2–3
15. Aarts, E.: Ambient Intelligence: A Multimedia Perspective. IEEE Intell. Systs. **19** (2004) 12–19
16. Misker, J.M., Veenman, C.J., Rothkrantz, L.J.: Groups of Collaborating Users and Agents in Ambient Intelligent Environments. In: Proc. 3rd Int'l Joint Conf. on Autonomous Agents & Multi-Agent Systems (AAMAS'04). Volume 3., New York, USA, ACM Press (2004)
17. Misker, J.M., Veenman, C.J., Rothkrantz, L.J.: Adaptive User Support in Agent Based Dynamic Environments. In: Advances in Pervasive Computing. (2004)
18. Busetta, P., Merzi, M., Rossi, S., Legras, F.: Real-time Role Coordination For Ambient Intelligence. In: Workshop on Representations and Approaches for Time-Critical Decentralized Resource/Role/Task Allocation. (2003)
19. Busetta, P., Zancanaro, M.: Open Social Agent Architecture for Distributed Multimedia. In: International Workshop on Agents at Work. (2003)
20. Busetta, P., Merzi, M., Rossi, S., Zancanaro, M.: Group Communication for Real-time Role Coordination and Ambient Intelligence. In: International Workshop on Artificial Intelligence in Mobile Systems – UbiComp'03. (2003)
21. Busetta, P., Kuflik, T., Merzi, M., Rossi, S.: Service Delivery in Smart Environments by Implicit Organizations. In: 1st Int'l Conf. on Mobile & Ubiquitous Systems (MobiQuitous). (2004)
22. Vizzari, G.: Dynamic Interaction Spaces and Situated Multi-Agent Systems: from a Multi-Layered Model to a Distributed Architecture. PhD Thesis – Universita degli Studi di Milano-Bicocca, Milan, Italy (2004)
23. Weyns, D., Holvoet, T.: A Formal Model for Situated Multi-Agent Systems. Fundamenta Informaticae **63** (2004) 1–34

An ACL for Specifying Fault-Tolerant Protocols

Nicola Dragoni, Mauro Gaspari, and Davide Guidi

Dipartimento di Scienze dell'Informazione, University of Bologna, Italy
{dragoni, gaspari, dguidi}@cs.unibo.it

Abstract. Agent Communication Languages (ACLs) have been developed to provide a way for agents to communicate with each other supporting cooperation in Multi-Agent Systems. In the past few years many ACLs have been proposed for Multi-Agent Systems and new standards are emerging such as FIPA ACL. Despite these efforts, an important issue in the research on ACLs is still open and concerns how these languages should deal with failures of agents in asynchronous Multi-Agent Systems. In this paper we present an asynchronous ACL which provide high-level mechanisms to deal with crash failures, one-to-many communication primitives and supports a fault-tolerant anonymous interaction protocol. To illustrate the expressive power of the language we show how it can be effectively used for the specification of fault tolerant protocols.

1   Introduction

Communication among software agents is an essential property of agency [1,2]. The power of agent systems strongly depends on inter-agent communication and as agents grow more powerful, their need for communication increases[3]. Agent Communication Languages (ACLs) have been developed to provide adequate inter-agent agent communication mechanisms. They allow agents to effectively communicate and exchange knowledge with other agents despite differences in hardware platforms, operating systems, architectures and programming languages. In the last decade many Agent Communication Languages have been proposed for Multi-Agent Systems (MAS), incorporating specific mechanisms of agent communication. Many of these communication mechanisms are based on *speech act theory*, which has originally been developed as a basic model of human communication [4]. The more promising ACLs that have adopted the speech act theory are KQML [5] and the FIPA ACL [6]. The goal of these languages is to support high-level, human like, communication between intelligent agents, exploiting *Knowledge-Level* features rather than symbol-level ones. They should support Knowledge-Level programming of MAS [7]: agents should concern with the use, request and supply of knowledge and not with symbol level issues such as the reliability, synchronization of competing requests, the allocation of resources or the physical allocation of agents on a network.

Despite these efforts, an important issue in the research on ACLs is still open and concerns how to deal with possible failures of agents. In this paper we address this issue proposing a Fault Tolerant Agent Communication Language

S. Bandini and S. Manzoni (Eds.): AI*IA 2005, LNAI 3673, pp. 237–248, 2005.

(FT-ACL) which deals with *crash* failures of agents. FT-ACL provides fault-tolerant versions of common conversation performatives and an anonymous interaction protocol based on fault-tolerant one-to-many requests for knowledge. Moreover FT-ACL has been designed for open architectures and deals with a dynamic set of competences and agents. In the design we provide special attention to the Knowledge-Level features of the ACL primitives as in [7], presenting a set of Knowledge-Level requirements that FT-ACL satisfies. To illustrate the expressive power of the language we show how it can be effectively used for the specification of fault tolerant protocols.

2   A Fault Tolerant Knowledge-Level ACL

The first steps towards the design of our fault tolerant ACL concern the identification of underlying failure model assumptions. These assumptions are then used in the specification of the communication primitives and of the related agents' infrastructure.

We assume a description of agents based on two levels: a *Knowledge-Level* which focuses on agents' competences and on the definition of the ACL primitives and abstracts from implementation details, and an *Architectural-Level* which specifies the agents' infrastructure showing how these competences and primitives are realized. This approach has several advantages. Firstly, this clear distinction allows to manage agents as abstract entities which operate at the Knowledge-Level executing *high level* communication primitives. All the implementation details, such as the interaction of the architectural components of an agent, synchronization and management of failures, are handled at the Architectural-Level. Secondly, it is possible to define a set of requirements that should be satisfied at the Knowledge-Level and that can be proved at the Architectural-Level.

Failure Model. The failure model we have adopted is based on a well known classification of process failures in distributed systems [8]. Following that model, we say that an agent is *faulty* in an execution if its behavior deviates from that prescribed by the algorithm it is running; otherwise, it is *correct*. The failure model we consider is *crash* failures of agents in a *fully asynchronous* Multi-Agent System: a faulty agent is *crashed* if it stops prematurely and does nothing from that point on. Before stopping, however, it behaves correctly. Note that considering only crash failures is a common fault assumption in distributed systems, since several mechanisms can be used to detect more severe failures and to force a crash in case of detection.

2.1   Knowledge-Level Description

Following the style of [7], an agent in the system has a symbolic (logical) name and a *virtual knowledge base* (VKB). The communication actions are asynchronous, allowing buffering of messages and supporting non blocking *ask* performatives. We also assume that each communication action contains information in a given knowledge representation formalism.

Let $\mathcal{A}_{ACL}$ be a countable set of agent names ranged over by $\hat{a}$, $\hat{b}$, $\hat{c}$,.... Let $VKB_{\hat{a}}$ be the virtual knowledge base of agent $\hat{a}$ which can be encoded in any knowledge representation formalism; w, w', w'' will range over VKB. We adopt the following abstract syntax for communication actions: $performative(\hat{a}, \hat{b}, p)$ where *performative* represents the communication action, $\hat{a}$ and $\hat{b}$ are the names of the recipient agent and of the sender agent respectively, and p is the contents of the message.

Agents react to messages received from other agents and from the user. Each agent has an associated *handler function* which maps the received message into the list of communication actions which must be executed when that message is received. $H_{\hat{a}}$ will be the handler function of agent $\hat{a}$. We assume that the handler function is enclosed in the VKB of an agent. The handler function is expressed by a set of Prolog-like rules $\{r_1, r_2 \ldots, r_n\}$ having the form:

$$handler(performative(\hat{a}, \hat{b}, p)) \leftarrow body \qquad (1)$$

where *body* is a sequence of literals $h_1 \wedge h_2 \ldots \wedge h_n$ in which each h_i can be a communication action, a dynamic primitive or a predicate on the VKB of the agent.

FT-ACL Primitives. FT-ACL includes a set of standard conversation performatives and supports an *anonymous interaction protocol* integrated with agent-to-agent communication. This allows an agent to perform a request of knowledge without knowing the name of the recipient agent and to continue the cooperation using agent-to-agent communication. More in detail, thanks to the anonymous interaction protocol an agent is able to:

- ask all agents in the system for some knowledge without knowing the names of the recipient agents and wait for all or some replies. This can be done by means of a performative *ask-everybody*.
- share its own knowledge with all the agents in the system without knowing their names. This can be done by means of the performatives *register* and *unregister*.

Moreover, FT-ACL supports a *dynamic* set of agents, allowing the creation of new agents and the termination of existing ones.

The failure model we have adopted requires to tackle new issues in the design of the ACL's communication primitives. Asynchronous and nonblocking communication primitives always succeed even if the target agent has crashed [7]. As soon as a communication primitive is executed the flow of control pass to the next instruction. This is a sound behaviour because when a communication action is executed it is not always possible to detect if the target agent has crashed. However, knowing that the target agent has crashed could be a relevant information for an agent to provide a fault tolerant behaviour.

To solve this problem we propose an high-level mechanism which associates specific failure continuations to communication primitives. When a communication primitive is called a failure continuation should be specified to deal with a possible failure, when the target agent fails the failure continuation is executed. This is different approach with respect to generic catch and throw mechanisms of programming languages (such as in Java or Lisp) because failure continuations are strongly related to the communication primitives and to the failure model we have adopted. In FT-ACL agents may react to relevant crash failures, while all the other exceptions are not considered at the knowledge level and are handled at the facilitator level. In FT-ACL, a failure continuation is associated to all the communication primitives that may need to deal with a possible failure of the target agents. This feature allows agents to react to unexpected crashes and thus to realize fault tolerant protocols.

The primitives of the language are shown in Table 1. The standard conversation performatives are a small subset of those defined in KQML and allow one-to-one agent interaction. Since ask primitives do not explicitly wait for answers a mechanism to specify the desiderated behaviour when a response is received is needed. This functionality is usually realized adding *:reply-to* and *:reply-with* parameters to the performatives (as in KQML) or defining the handler function to match answers with a template of the request (as in [7]). In FT-ACL we use a mechanism similar to the one defined above for dealing with crash failures: a success continuation allows an agent to specify the agent behaviour when it receives a response to a given request for knowledge or in general when the communication action succeeds. Thus the code that the agent must execute when it will receive a tell message containing the answer to a given request is specified together with the request, despite the performative is executed asynchronously.

Table 1. Primitives of FT-ACL

Standard conversation performatives:
ask-one($\hat{a}, \hat{b}, p$)[on_answer($body_1$) + on_fail($body_2$)]
insert($\hat{a}, \hat{b}, p$)[on_ack($body_1$) + on_fail($body_2$)]
tell($\hat{a}, \hat{b}, p$)
One-to-many performative:
ask-everybody($\hat{b}, p$)[on_answer($body_1$) + on_fail($body_2$)]
Support for anonymous interaction:
register($\hat{b}, p$)   unregister($\hat{b}, p$)
all-answers(p)
Support for creation and termination of agents:
create($\hat{b}, w$)   clone($\hat{b}$)
bye

Executing the performative *ask-one* an agent $\hat{b}$ asks an agent $\hat{a}$ for an instantiation of p which is true in the VKB of $\hat{a}$. This performative is associated with a success continuation *on_answer(body$_1$)* which is called when $\hat{b}$ receives the reply of the agent $\hat{a}$. As a consequence, the program $body_1$ is executed by $\hat{b}$. Instead, when $\hat{a}$ cannot reply because it is crashed, the failure continuation $on\_fail(body_2)$ is called and $\hat{b}$ executes the program $body_2$.

Executing the performative *insert*, an agent $\hat{b}$ tells an agent $\hat{a}$ to insert p in its VKB. A success continuation $on\_ack(body_1)$ can be associated to this primitive and is called when $\hat{a}$ has inserted p in its VKB and $\hat{b}$ has received an acknowledgement of this event. As a consequence, the program $body_1$ is executed by $\hat{b}$. Instead, if p cannot be inserted in $\hat{a}$'s VKB because $\hat{a}$ is crashed, then the failure continuation $on\_fail(body_2)$ is activated and $\hat{b}$ executes the program $body_2$. If the success continuation is missing agent $\hat{b}$ has no way to control that p is in the VKB of agent $\hat{a}$. On the other hand the stronger version of this performative allows us to approximate common knowledge.

The performative *tell* is similar to the *insert* primitive, but is less restrictive: an agent $\hat{b}$ simply sends some knowledge p to an agent $\hat{a}$ without requiring any information about the success of the performative. At the moment, no continuations can be associated to this performative, although the realization of a stronger version is possible.

The anonymous interaction protocol is implemented through the *ask-everybody* one-to-many performative: an agent which executes it does not need to know the names of all the agents which are interested in a query. In particular, the performative *ask-everybody* allows an agent $\hat{b}$ to ask all agents in the system which are able to deal with p for an instantiation of p which is true in their VKB. When $\hat{b}$ executes *ask-everybody*, an *ask-one* message is sent to all the agents interested in p (except $\hat{b}$). The performative is associated with the success continuation $on\_answer(body_1)$ which is called each time $\hat{b}$ receives a reply to the multicast query and it can remain active until all the replies are arrived. Instead, if no agents are able to reply because they are all crashed, then the failure continuation $on\_fail(body_2)$ is called. The success continuation remains active until it succeeds, allowing agents to realize different protocols. For example, if $\hat{b}$ wants to wait *all the answers* of the correct agents in the system which are able to deal with p, then it can do that executing the performative *ask-everybody* with

$$body_1 \stackrel{def}{=} body_3 \wedge all\text{-}answers(p) \wedge body_4 \tag{2}$$

where $all\text{-}answer(p)$ is a boolean predicate which returns *true* if all the *correct* agents have already replied about p or *false* if there is at least one *correct* agent which has not yet replied. Therefore each reply to the multicast query of $\hat{b}$ is handled by the program $body_3$, which is executed when the success continuation $on\_answer(body_1)$ is called. Instead the program $body_4$ is executed only when the predicate $all\text{-}answers(p)$ returns *true*, that is only when the last reply is arrived.

To show another example, consider an agent performative $ask\text{-}first(\hat{b}, p)$ which realizes the anonymous interaction protocol with the difference that $\hat{b}$ waits only for the first reply it receives and discards all the others. Let $body_3$ the program which has to be executed by $\hat{b}$ when the first reply arrives. Then the *ask-first* performative can be easily implemented simply associating the performative *ask-everybody* with the success continuation $on\_answer(body_3)$. So, when

$\hat{b}$ receives the first reply, the function *on_answer(body3)* is called, the program *body3* is executed and then the function becomes inactive. In this way, all the other replies are discarded. Of course, the program *body3* must not contain predicates which can block its complete execution (such as for example the predicate *all-answers*).

The multicast request performed by *ask-everybody* is forwarded to all the agents on the basis of agents' declarations. An agent $\hat{b}$ can declare its competences through the *register($\hat{b}$, p)* and *unregister($\hat{b}$, p)* primitives. The primitives *create*, *clone* and *bye* are provided to support an *open* and *dynamic* Multi-Agent System: new agents can be created from other agents in the system (for example to cooperate with the existing ones) and agents can leave the community when their tasks terminate. These primitives are well integrated with the anonymous interaction protocol. For example, if $\hat{d}$ is the clone of an agent $\hat{b}$ and $\hat{d}$ is able to deal with p, then the request *ask-everybody($\hat{b}$, p)* will also reach agent $\hat{d}$.

Table 2. Fault Tolerance in FT-ACL Communication Primitives

Performatives	Fault Tolerant Behaviour
ask-one($\hat{a}, \hat{b}$, p)	If $\hat{b}$ does not receive $\hat{a}$'s reply because $\hat{a}$ is crashed, then $\hat{b}$ does not wait the reply forever.
ask-everybody($\hat{b}$, p)	$\hat{b}$ does not wait the replies of dynamically crashed agents. If all the agents which have to reply are crashed, the performative does not succeed. However, $\hat{b}$ does not wait the replies forever and can continue its program.
insert($\hat{a}, \hat{b}$, p)	If $\hat{a}$ is crashed, then the primitive does not succeed. However, $\hat{b}$ can continue its computation knowing that p has not been inserted in $\hat{a}$'s VKB.

In Table 2 the fault tolerance of the FT-ACL communication performatives is summarized. Note that the performative *tell* is omitted because it is the only communication performative which does not require a fault tolerance behaviour: an agent which executes it simply sends a message to a recipient agent without care about the success of the sending.

Knowledge-Level Requirements. In [7] conditions are postulated which require a careful analysis of the underlying agent architecture in order to ensure Knowledge-Level behavior. We recall these *Knowledge-Level Programming Requirements* below extended to deal with crashes of agents (condition (4)).

(1) The programmer should not have to handle physical addresses of agents explicitly.
(2) The programmer should not have to handle communication faults explicitly.
(3) The programmer should not have to handle starvation issues explicitly. A situation of starvation arises when an agent's primitive never gets executed despite being enabled.

(4) The programmer should not have to handle *communication deadlocks* explicitly. A communication deadlock situation occurs when two agents try to communicate, but they do not succeed; for instance because they mutually wait for each other to answer a query [9] or because an agent waits a reply of a crashed agent forever.

Our ACL has been designed taking into account the above Knowledge-Level requirements. For example, condition (4) requires that no communication deadlocks can occur using FT-ACL. To satisfy this requirement we have designed fault tolerant ask performatives avoiding agents to wait for replies of crashed agents forever. In next Sections we will show how it is possible to definefault tolerant protocols in FT-ACL.

Dealing with Crash Failures of Agents: Failure Detectors. Since impossibility results for asynchronous systems stem from the inherent difficulty of determining whether a process has actually crashed or is only "very slow", Chandra and Toueg [10] propose to augment the asynchronous model of computation with a model of an *external failure detection mechanism* that can make mistakes. In particular, they model the concept of *unreliable failure detectors* for systems with *crash* failures.

The failure detectors are *distributed*: each process has access to a local *failure detector module*. Each local module monitors a subset of the processes in the system and maintains a list of those that it currently suspects to have crashed. Each failure detector module can make mistakes by erroneously adding or removing processes to its list of suspects. Failure detector mistakes should not prevent any correct process from behaving according to specification even if that process is (erroneously) suspected to have crashed by all the other processes.

2.2   Architectural-Level Description

We illustrate a generic agent architecture which is able to support FT-ACL. This architecture allows us to prove that the Knowledge-Level requirements holds at the Architectural Level. A generic agent is composed of three components (Figure 1): a *Knowledge-Base (KB)* component, a *Facilitator* component and a *Failure Detector* component.

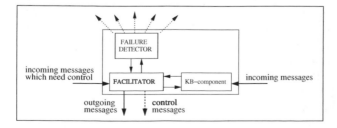

Fig. 1. Generic agent architecture which supports FT-ACL

The *KB-component* implements the VKB of an agent and its reactive behavior. It only deals with Knowledge-Level operations and it is able to answer requests from other agents. The other two components (*Facilitator* and *Failure Detector*) allow to support Knowledge-Level and fault tolerant communication respectively. Since a detailed discussion about the *KB-component* is out of the scope of the paper, we prefer to omit it and to focus on the remaining components.

To realize the anonymous interaction protocol we exploit a *distributed facilitator service* which is hidden at the Knowledge-Level and provides mechanisms for registering capabilities of agents and delivering messages to the recipient agents. Facilitators are distributed and encapsulated in the architecture of agents. Therefore each agent has its own local *facilitator component* which executes a distributed algorithm: it forwards control information to all the other local facilitators and delivers messages to their destinations. Finally, the *failure detector* component implements the distributed failure detector mechanism, enabling agents to support fault tolerant communication. All the run-time observations made by a local failure detector are communicated to the local facilitator, which will take them into account in all agent interactions. The failure detector component is fundamental to avoid infinite waits for replies of crashed agents (blocking the agent execution).

Observe that this is a generic agent architecture: the failure detector and the facilitator components are standard for all the agents in a Multi-Agent System, while the KB-component can be instantiated with different VKBs.

Example. To better illustrate the behaviours of the facilitator and failure detector components let focus on the execution of the agent primitive *ask-everybody*. Consider an agent $\hat{a}$ which executes *ask-everybody($\hat{a}$, q)[on_answers($body_1$) + on_fail($body_2$)]* to ask all agents in the system for some knowledge q. The program $body_1$ is defined as in the equation 2 of Section 2.1, so all the replies are handled by the success continuation *on_answers* which executes the program $body_3$ for each reply and the program $body_4$ when all the replies are arrived. The predicate *all-answers(p)* allows the agent $\hat{a}$ to perform this check. Note that, since *ask-everybody* realizes the anonymous interaction protocol, the list of agents which are able to provide an instantiation of q is not specified in the primitive. Instead, this list is stored in the facilitator component which is responsible to dynamically update it and to manage all the replies. Therefore, the predicate *all-answers(p)* is simply realized as a query to the local facilitator which consults its list and replies *true* is all the replies are arrived and *false* otherwise. Moreover, this list is dynamically updated with all the observations made by the local failure detector component, allowing the local facilitator to wait only for replies of *correct* agents. Therefore, we are sure that $\hat{a}$ will not wait for replies of crashed agents forever, but sooner or later the predicate *all-answers(p)* will return *true* (that is, all the correct agents have replied). Moreover, updating its list with the failure detector observations, the facilitator is able to handle the worst situation in which all the agents which have to reply are crashed. In this case the facilitator communicates this event to the KB-component and as a consequence the failure continuation *on_fail(body₂)* is called.

Ensuring Knowledge-Level Requirements. In [11,12] a formal specification of the agent architecture and of the FT-ACL primitives has been provided. The specification is realized by means of the *Algebra of Actors* [12,13], an object based algebra which represents a compromise between standard process algebras and the actor model [14]. Moreover, in [11] the formal model has been used to prove that the Knowledge-Level requirements are satisfied by our ACL.

3 Specification of Fault Tolerant Protocols

FT-ACL allows software designers to develop high level specifications of fault tolerant multi-agent system. This specification can then be translated in running program embedding FT-ACL in sequential programming languages. Since FT-ACL satisfies a set of well defined knowledge-level requirements the resulting multi-agent system will inherit these properties. Moreover, providing the appropriate failure continuations, FT-ACL can be effectively used to specify fault tolerant coordination protocols. We illustrate this concept providing a fault tolerant specification of the *Contract Net Protocol* and discussing the properties of the resulting agent's programs.

3.1 The Contract Net Protocol

The *Contract Net Protocol* [15] allows an agent to distribute tasks among a set of agents by means of negotiation. We only model a restricted version of the protocol with a single manager agent $\hat{a}$ and a set of workers $\hat{s}_1, ..., \hat{s}_n$ with $n \geq 1$. Moreover, we define a new agent primitive *ask-best* which allows to send a query to an agent of a presorted list L of agents. In particular, executing this performative a knowledge p is sent to the first agent in L. If that agent is not able to reply because crashed, then the message is sent to the second agent in L and so on. This performative can be programmed recursively with FT-ACL as follows:

---

ask-best([], $\hat{a}$, p)[on_answer($body_1$) + on_fail($body_2$)] = $body_2$
ask-best(L, $\hat{a}$, p)[on_answer($body_1$) + on_fail($body_2$)] =
        ask-one(first(L), $\hat{a}$, p)[on_answer($body_1$) + on_fail($body_3$)];
where
$body_3 \overset{def}{=}$ ask-best(rest(L), $\hat{a}$, p)[on_answer($body_1$) + on_fail($body_2$)]

A Contract Net can be defined by the set of agents $S = \{\hat{a}, \hat{s}_1, ..., \hat{s}_n\}$ running in parallel. The handler functions are defined as follows[1]:

---

[1] We use the special expressions **content** and **sender** to represent the content and the sender of a message respectively.

$H_{\hat{a}}$: handler(tell($\hat{a}$, Y , startCN)) ←
        ask-everybody($\hat{a}$, bid(task, Z))[on_answer($body_1$) + on_fail($body_2$)]
where
$body_1 \stackrel{def}{=}$ update(bid(**content**, **sender**)) ∧
        all-answers(bid(task, Z)) ∧
        best_bid(task, L) ∧
        ask-best(L, $\hat{a}$, dotask(task, R))[on_answer($body_3$) + on_fail($body_4$)]
$body_2 = body_4 \stackrel{def}{=}$ tell(Y, $\hat{a}$, ContractNetFailed)
$body_3 \stackrel{def}{=}$ update(done(**content**)) ∧
        tell(Y, $\hat{a}$, ContractNetOK)

$H_{\hat{s}_i}$: handler(ask-one($\hat{s}_i$, X, bid(T, Z))) ←
        bid(T, Z) ∧
        tell(X, $\hat{s}_i$, bid(T, Z))

    handler(ask-one($\hat{s}_i$, X, dotask(T, R))) ←
        dotask(T, R) ∧
        tell(X, $\hat{s}_i$, dotask(T, R))

When the manager $\hat{a}$ receives a *startCN* message, it exploits *ask-everybody* to perform a multicast request for bids on a given task. Then it starts waiting for answers. If all the agents $\hat{s}_i$ interested in the task are crashed, then $body_2$ is executed and a message of *ContractNetFailed* is sent to the starter of the protocol (another agent or the user) notifying the failure. When an agent $\hat{s}_i$ receives a query, it consults its VKB and replies with its bid. When $\hat{a}$ has received all the replies of the correct agents, then it exploits the fault tolerant performative *ask-best* to sends to the agent which has submitted the best bid a request for the execution of the task. In this interaction succeeds, the protocol ends successfully (message ContractNetOK in $body_3$). Otherwise, the request is sent to the second agent with the best bid (in the list L) and so on. Only when all the agents in L dynamically becomes crashed, the protocol fails and a *ContractNetFailed* message is sent to the starter of the protocol (program $body_4$). In all the other cases FT-ACL allows the program to tolerate agent crashes.

3.2   Properties of the Contract Net

We have shown that the defined protocol is able to tolerate agent crashes. However we can also infer more general properties of this Contract Net. In fact the Multi-Agent System we have defined inherits all the properties that follows from the Knowledge-Level requirements presented in Section 2.1. For example the following property holds:

Deadlock Free Property. The Fault Tolerant Contract Net Protocol is deadlock free (it follows from requirement (4)).

Moreover *liveness*[2] holds in the contract net if we assume that the manager agent does not crash. This follows from requirements (3) and (4). If we also assume that at least one worker does not crash, we can infer the following property:

Liveness Property. The Fault Tolerant Contract Net Protocol terminates executing the task.

4   Related Work and Conclusions

The goal of developing robust multi-agent systems has been addressed in the literature in the last years [16,17,18]. Some of the ideas presented by these authors are similar to the solutions we propose in our approach. For example the idea of introducing *sentinels* to intercept exceptions [18], is similar to our facilitator level which aims to hide most low level details at the agent level. The novelty of our approach is to embed some of the failure detection mechanisms in the ACL. On one hand we define a set of high-level communication primitives which are fault tolerant. On the other hand we provide a minimal interface which allows agents to deal with crash failures whenever this is necessary. Despite we define a set of fault tolerant primitives, we argue that in some situations agents should be able to explicitly deal with crash failures. This is in general true in distributed systems and we also believe in asynchronous multi-agent systems. FT-ACL is able to solve some crashes and exceptions autonomously and to hide them at the Knowledge-Level (this is similar to the domain-independent approach of [18]). But it also provides the ACL with a well defined interface which allows agent programmers to explicitly deal with a set of application dependent agent crashes that cannot be solved with general policies.

The main advantage of our approach with respect to current ACLs such as KQML [5] and the FIPA ACL [6] is that we provide a set of fault tolerant communication primitives which are well integrated at the Knowledge-Level. On the other hand most of the current ACLs do not provide a clear distinction between conversation and network primitives, these are often considered at the same level. Moreover, failures crashes and fault tolerance are often not present in the specifications. We have shown that FT-ACL can be successfully used to specify fault tolerant communication protocols such as the contract net one. In our approach we propose a set of communication primitives which implements a fault tolerant anonymous interaction protocol at the Knowledge-Level. This protocol is fully integrated with the dynamic nature of Open Services Architectures.

A promising application domain for FT-ACL is to support Web agents interaction. Agents are one of the main building blocks of the emerging Semantic Web infrastructure, and given the geographically distributed nature of the Internet, they should provide mechanisms to cope with possible failures of nodes or network partitions. In [19] we show how FT-ACL can be successfully used for these purposes.

---

[2] Liveness is informally defined as something good happens eventually *i.e.,* the contract net protocol is executed.

References

1. Chaib-draa, B., Dignum, F.: Trends in Agent Communication Language. Computational Intelligence **2** (2002)
2. Singh, M.P.: Agent communication languages: Rethinking the principles. IEEE Computer **31** (1998) 40–47
3. Luck, M., McBurney, P., Preist, C.: Manifesto for Agent Technology: Towards Next Generation Computing. Autonomous Agents and Multi-Agent Systems **9** (2004) 203–252
4. Searle, J.: Speech Acts. Cambridge University Press (1969)
5. Finin, T., Labrou, Y., Mayfield, J.: KQML as an Agent Communication Language. In: Software Agents. MIT Press (1997) 291–316
6. Foundation for Intelligent Physical Agents: Communicative Act Library Specification. (2001) http://www.fipa.org/specs/fipa00037.
7. Gaspari, M.: Concurrency and Knowledge-Level Communication in Agent Languages. Artificial Intelligence **105** (1998) 1–45
8. Mullender, S.: Distributed Systems. Addison Wesley (1993)
9. Singhal, M.: Deadlock Detection in Distributed Systems. IEEE Computer **22** (1989) 37–48
10. Chandra, T.D., Toueg, S.: Unreliable Failure Detectors for Reliable Distributed Systems. Journal of the ACM **43** (1996) 225–267
11. Dragoni, N., Gaspari, M.: Fault Tolerant Knowledge Level Communication in Open Asynchronous Multi-Agent Systems. Technical Report UBLCS-2005-10, Department of Computer Science, University of Bologna (ITALY) (2005)
12. Dragoni, N., Gaspari, M.: An Object Based Algebra for Specifying A Fault Tolerant Software Architecture. Journal of Logic and Algebraic Programming **63** (2005) 271–297
13. Gaspari, M., Zavattaro, G.: An Algebra of Actors. In: Proceedings of IFIP Conference on Formal Methods for Open Object-based Distributed Systems (FMOODS), Kluwer Academic Publisher (1999) 3–18
14. Agha, G.: Actors: a Model of Concurrent Computation in Distributed Systems. MIT Press (1986)
15. Smith, R.G.: The Contract Net Protocol: High Level Communication and Control in a Distributed Problem Solver . IEEE Transactions on Computers **29** (1980) 1104–1113
16. Shah, N., Chao, K., Anane, R., Godwin, N.: A Flexible Approach to Exception Handling in Open Multi-agent Systems. In: Proceedings of the 2nd International Joint Conference on Autonomous Agents and Multiagent Systems (AAMAS-03) Challenges'03 Workshop. (2003) 7–10
17. Parsons, S., Klein, M.: Towards Robust Multi-Agent Systems: Handling Communication Exceptions in Double Auctions. In: AAMAS, IEEE Computer Society (2004) 1482–1483
18. Klein, M., Rodríguez-Aguilar, J.A., Dellarocas, C.: Using Domain-Independent Exception Handling Services to Enable Robust Open Multi-Agent Systems: The Case of Agent Death. Autonomous Agents and Multi-Agent Systems **7** (2003) 179–189
19. Dragoni, N., Gaspari, M., Guidi, D.: Integrating Knowledge-Level Agents in the (Semantic) Web: an Agent-based Open Service Architecture. In: Proceedings of the 18th International FLAIRS Conference, AAAI Press (2005)

Experimental Evaluation of Hierarchical Hidden Markov Models

Attilio Giordana, Ugo Galassi, and Lorenza Saitta

Dipartimento di Informatica, Università del Piemonte Orientale,
Via Bellini 25g, Alessandria, Italy

Abstract. Building profiles for processes and for interactive users is a important task in intrusion detection. This paper presents the results obtained with a Hierarchical Hidden Markov Model. The algorithm discovers typical "motives" of a process behavior, and correlates them into a hierarchical model. Motives can be interleaved with possibly long gaps where no regular behavior is detectable. We assume that motives could be affected by noise,modeled as insertion, deletion and substitution errors. In this paper the learning algorithm is briefly recalled and then it is experimentally evaluated on three *profiling* case studies. The first case is built on a suite of artificial traces automatically generated by a set of given HHMMs. The challenge for the algorithm is to reconstruct the original model from the traces. It will be shown that the algorithm is able to learn HHMMs very similar to the original ones, in presence of noise and distractors. The second and third case studies refer to the problem of constructing a discriminant model for a user typing on a keyboard.

1 Introduction

Building profiles for processes and for interactive users is an important task in intrusion detection. This paper presents the results obtained with a recent induction algorithm [2], which is based on Hierarchical Hidden Markov Model [5]. The algorithm discovers typical "motives" [1] of a process behavior, and correlates them into a hierarchical model. Motives can be interleaved with possibly long gaps where no regular behavior is detectable. We assume that motives could be affected by noise due to non-deterministic causes. Noise is modeled as insertion, deletion and substitution errors according to a common practice followed in Pattern Recognition. A recent paper by Botta et al. [2] proposes a method for automatically inferring from sequences, and possibly domain knowledge, both the structure and the parameters of complex HHMMs.

In this paper, the learning algorithm proposed in [2] is briefly overviewed and then it is experimentally evaluated on three *profiling* case studies. The first case is built on a suite of artificial traces automatically generated by a set of given HHMMs. The challenge for the algorithm is to reconstruct the original model from the traces. It will be shown that the algorithm is able to learn HHMMs very similar to the original ones, in presence of noise and distractors.

---

[1] A motif is a subsequence of consecutive elementary events typical of a process.

S. Bandini and S. Manzoni (Eds.): AI*IA 2005, LNAI 3673, pp. 249–257, 2005.

The second and third case study refers to the problem of constructing a discriminant model for a user typing on a keyboard [1,3,7]. The results reported with a set of 20 different users are very encouraging.

2   The Hierarchical Hidden Markov Model

A Hierarchical Hidden Markov Model is a generalization of the Hidden Markov Model, which is a stochastic finite state automaton [9] defined by a tuple $\langle S, O, A, B, \pi \rangle$, where:

- S is a set of states, and O is a set of atomic events (observations),
- A is a probability distribution governing the transitions from one state to another. Specifically, any member $a_{i,j}$ of A defines the probability of the transition from state s_i to state s_j, given s_i.
- B is a probability distribution governing the emission of observable events depending on the state. Specifically, an item $b_{i,j}$ belonging to B defines the probability of producing event O_j when the automaton is in state s_i.
- π is a distribution on S defining, for every $s_i \in S$, the probability that s_i is the initial state of the automaton.

A difficulty, related to a HMM defined in this way, is that, when the set of states S grows large, the number of parameters to estimate (A and B) rapidly becomes intractable. A second difficulty is that the probability of a sequence being generated by a given HMM decreases exponentially with its length. Then, complex and sparse events become difficult to discover.

The HHMM proposed by Fine et al. [5] is an answer to both problems. On one hand, the number of parameters to estimate is strongly reduced by assigning a null probability to many transitions in distribution A, and to many observations in distribution B. On the other hand, the model allows a possibly long chain of elementary events to be abstracted into a single event, which can be handled as

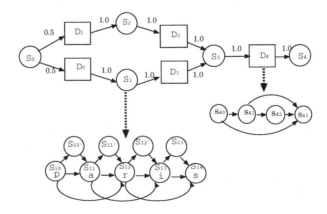

Fig. 1. Example of Hierarchical Hidden Markov Model. Circles denotes states with observable emission, whereas rectangles denote *gaps*.

a single item. This is obtained by exploiting the regular languages property of being closed under substitution, which allows a large finite state automaton to be transformed into a hierarchy of simpler ones.

An example of HHMM is given in Figure 1.

The advantage of the hierarchical structure, as defined in [5], may help very much inferring the entire structure of the automaton by means of an induction algorithm.

The research efforts about HHMMs mostly concentrate on the algorithms for estimating the probabilities governing the emission and the transition from state to state. Fine et al. [5] extend the classical Baum-Welch algorithm to the HHMM. In a more recent work, Murphy and Paskin [8] derive a linear (approximated) algorithm by mapping a HHMM into a Dynamic Bayesian Network.

3 Algorithm Overview

The basic algorithm [2] is bottom-up and constructs the HHMM hierarchy starting from the lowest level. The first step consists in searching for possible motives, i.e., short chains of consecutive symbols that appear frequently in the learning traces, and building an HMM for each one of them. This step is accomplished by means of classical methods used in DNA analysis [4,6]. As models of the motives are constructed independently from one another, it may happen that models for spurious motives are constructed. At the same time, it may happen that relevant motives are disregarded just because their frequency is not high enough. Both kinds of errors will be fixed at a second time. The HMMs learned so far are then used as feature constructors. Each HMM is labeled with a different *name* and the original sequences are rewritten into the new alphabet defined by the set of names given to the models. In other words, every sub-sequence in the input sequences, which can be attributed to a specific HMM, is replaced by the corresponding name.

The subsequences between two motives, not attributed to any model, are considered gaps and will be handled by means of special construct called *gap*. We will call *sequence abstraction* this rewriting process. After this basic cycle has been completed, an analogous learning procedure is repeated on the abstracted sequences. Models are now built for sequences of *episodes*, searching for long range regularities among co-occurrent motives. In this process, spurious motives not showing significant regularities can be discarded. The major difference, with respect to the first learning step, is that the models built from the abstract sequences are now observable Markov models. This makes the learning task easier and decreases its computational complexity. In this step, models (*gaps*) are built also for the long intervals falling between consecutive motives.

In principle, the abstraction step could be repeated again on the sequences obtained from the first abstraction step, building a third level of the hierarchy, and so on. However, up to now we considered only problems where two hierarchical levels are sufficient. After building the HHMM structure in this way, it can be refined using standard training algorithms [5,8]. However, two other refinement techniques are possible.

The first technique concerns the recovery of motives lost in the first learning phase because not having a sufficient statistical evidence. As said above, this missed information has actually been modeled by *gaps*. A nice property of the HHMM is that sub-models in the hierarchy have a loose interaction with one another, and so their structure can be reshaped without changing the global structure. Then, the model of a gap can be transformed into the model of a motif later on, when further data become available.

The second method consists in repeating the entire learning cycle using as learning set only the portion of the sequences where the instance of the previously learned HHMM have been found with sufficient evidence. Repeating the procedure allows more precise models to be learned for motives, because false motives will no longer participate to the learning procedure. The details about the implementation can be found in [2].

4   Evaluation on Artificial Traces

A specific testing procedure has been designed in order to monitor the capability of the algorithm of discovering "known patterns" hidden in trace artificially generated by handcrafted HHMMs. Random noise and spurious motives have been added to all sequences filling the gaps between consecutive motives, in order to make the task more difficult.

Three target HHMMs, each one constructed according to a two level hierarchy, have been used to generate a set of 72 learning tasks (24 for every model). Every learning task uses a set of 330 traces. 90% of the sequences contain an instance of a target HHMM that should be discovered by the learning program, whereas the 10% of the sequences contain spurious motives non generated by the target HHMM. The sequence length ranges from 80 to 120 elementary events.

The structure for the high level of the three models is shown in Figure 2. Every state at the high level emits a string (motif) generated by an HMM at the low level, indicated with a capital letter (A,B,C,D,E). A different HMM (F) has been used to generate spurious motives. The gaps between motives have been filled with subsequences containing random noise.

The evaluation of the obtained results has been done on the basis of the *Bayes classification error* between two (or more) HHMMs. Formally, given two HHMMs, λ_1 and λ_2, and the set L of all possible traces that can be generated by λ_1 or λ_2, the Bayes classification error $C(\lambda_1, \lambda_2)$ is defined as:

$$C(\lambda_1, \lambda_2) = \sum_{x \in L} [min(p(\lambda_1|x), p(\lambda_2|x)]p(x) \qquad (1)$$

being $p(\lambda_1|x)$ and $p(\lambda_2|x)$ the probability that, given a trace x, it has been generated by λ_1 or λ_2, respectively, and $p(x)$ the a priori probability of x. We notice that the upper-bound for $C(\lambda_1, \lambda_2)$ is 0.5, when λ_1 and λ_2 are identical. In general, for N models, the upper-bound is given by $(1 - 1/N)$.

In general, expression (1) cannot be computed because L is too large. Therefore, we adopted an approximate evaluation, made using a subset of L stochastically sampled.

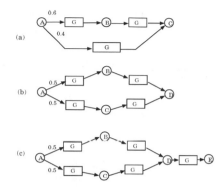

Fig. 2. HHMM used for evaluation on artificial data

Table 1. Bayes classification error between the target model and the learned model, versus the confusion among the basic motives (reported in the first line)

Motives	0.2	0.4	0.55
Model (a)	0.48	0.46	0.45
Model (b)	0.47	0.42	0.42
Model (c)	0.43	0.42	0.41

The role of Bayes classification error in the evaluation procedure is twofold. First, it is used to measure the quality of the learned models. A perfect learner should learn a model identical to the one used to generate the traces. Therefore, the closer to 0.5 the classification error (between it and the original model),the more accurate a learned model is considered.

Second, it is used to estimate the difficulty of the learning task. It is reasonable to assume that the difficulty of identifying a model hidden in a set of traces grows with the similarity among the motives belonging to the model and the spurious ones. Moreover, the difficulty grows also when the motives belonging to a same model become similar each other; in this case, in fact, it becomes more difficult to discover the correspondence between a motif and the hidden state it has been emitted from. Therefore, the experimentation has been run using different versions of models A, B, C, D, E, F with different Bayes classification errors among them.

The results obtained under three different conditions of difficulty are summarized in Table 1. The similarity between the six kinds of generated motives has been varied from 0.2 to 0.55. For every setting, the experiment has been repeated 8 times for each one of the three models. The reported results are the average over the 8 runs. In all cases the Bayes classification error has been estimated using a set of traces obtained by collecting 500 sequences generated from each one of the models involved in the specific comparison.

It appears that the performances suffer very little from the similarity among the motif models, and in all cases the similarity between the original model and the learned model is very high ($C(\lambda_1, \lambda_2)$, is close to 0.5).

5   User Profiling

User profiling is widely used to detect intrusions in computer networks or in telephony networks. The possibility of automatically building a profile for *users* or for *network services* reflecting their temporal behavior would offer a significant help to the deployment of adaptive Intrusion Detection Systems (IDSs).

The experiments described in the following investigate the possibility of automatically constructing a user profile from the logs of its activity. The task that has been selected consists in learning to identify a user from her typing style on a keyboard. The basic assumption is that every user has a different way of typing, which becomes particularly evident when she types words which are specifically important for her, such as her own name, or words referring to her job. This application has not been selected with the goal of challenging the results previously obtained [7,1,3], but because it is highly representative of the class of tasks we tackle, and the data are easy to acquire. In other words, if the methodology described so far succeeds in building up a HHMM for this kind of user profiling, it is likely that it will succeed in other cases as well. Two experiments, described in the following subsections, have been performed.

5.1   Key Phrase Typing Model

In the first experiment, the goal was to construct a model for a user typing a key phrase, discriminant enough to recognize the user among others. A selected sentence of 22 syllables has been typed many times on the same keyboard, while a transparent program recorded, for every typed key, the duration of each stroke and the delay between two consecutive strokes. Then, every repetition of the sentence generated a sequence, where every key stroke corresponded to an atomic event; the delay between two strokes was represented as a gap, whose length was set to the corresponding duration. Four volunteers provided 140 sequences each, and, for every one of them, a model has been built up using 100 traces (for each user) as learning set. The four learned models have been tested against the remaining 160 traces. For each model λ and for each trace s, the probability of λ generating s has been computed using the forward-backward algorithm [9]. Then, s has been assigned to the model with the highest probability. The results reported only one commission error and two rejection errors (no decision taken), when a trace was not recognized by any one of the models. The models were organized on two levels. The first one contained from 10 to 12 episodes separated by gaps. Even if the recognition rate is high, it does not seem realistic to use the acquired models to build up a deployable authentication system. In fact, a user profile based on a key phrase only is too restricted. The positive result is that a Markov model of a user typing on a keyboard seems to be appropriate.

5.2   Text Typing Model

The second experiment addressed the more general problem of modeling a user during a text editing activity. A corpus of several paragraphs, selected from newspapers and books, has been collected. The total number of words was 2280,

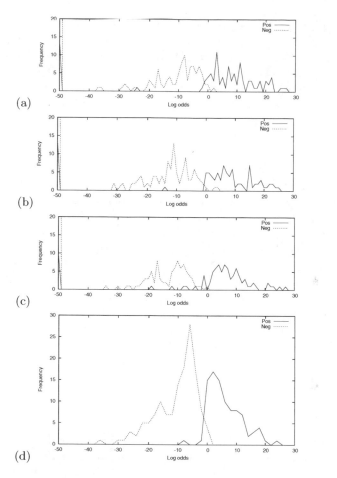

(a)

(b)

(c)

(d)

Fig. 3. User profiling statistics. Graphs (a), (b), (c) and (d) refer each one to a different user profile. The continuous line "Pos" reports the scoring, measured in log odds, for the sequences belonging to the profile (correct user). The dotted line "Neg" refers to the sequences not belonging to the profile (other users).

and the number of typed keys 14273. Again, four users typed the entire corpus in several different sessions, without any constraint, in order not to modify their natural typing style.

In this kind of application, a user model should be centered not on the specific words she types, but on the user typing style, which, in turns, depends on the position of the keys on the keyboard. Therefore, a standard keyboard subdivision into regions, used in dactylography, has been considered, and, on this basis, keys have been grouped into 10 classes. In this way, transition from one region of the keyboard to another should be emphasized. Afterwards, the sequences generated during a typing session have been rewritten by replacing every character with the name of the class it has been assigned to. Moreover, only the gap duration between strokes has been considered, disregarding the length of the key strokes themselves. Finally, long sequences deriving from an editing session have been segmented into shorter sequences, setting the breakpoint in correspondence of long gaps. The idea is that typical delays due to the user typing style cannot go beyond a given limit. Longer delays are imputable to different reasons, such as thinking or change of the focus of attention. In this way a set of about 1350 subsequences has been obtained. For every user, a subset of 220 subsequences has been extracted in order to learn the corresponding model. The remaining ones have been used for testing. As in the previous case, the probability of generating each one of the sequences in the test set has been computed for every model.

The results are summarized in Figure 3, where the distribution of the scoring rate on the test sequences is reported for every model. The scoring rated is measured in *log odds*[2]. The continuous line, labelled "Pos", represents the distribution of the scores assigned to the correct model (user), whereas the other one, labelled "Neg", represents the distribution of the scores assigned to all other models (users), considered together . The sequences on the extreme left have been rejected. It is evident from the figure that sequences belonging to the model are well separated from the other ones. Referring to the data in the test set, a monitoring system using the simple rule that, in a set of three consecutive sequences generated by a user at least two must have a score higher than '0', would give a perfect discrimination of the legal user without rising false alarms.

It is worth noting that the results have been obtained as a first shot, without requiring any tuning of the algorithm. This means that the method is robust and easy to apply to this kind of problems.

6   Conclusion

We have proposed a method for automatically synthesizing from traces complex profiles based on HHMMs. In preliminary tests on artificial datasets, the method succeeded in reconstructing non trivial two level HHMMs, whereas the results obtained on a task of user identification are very encouraging. It is worth noticing that, in this case, the goal was not to compete with the results obtained by task specific algorithms [1,3,7], but to test how a general-purpose algorithm performed on a non trivial task for which it was not directly customized. Even if this case study is just a preliminary investigation, the results are promising. In fact, the considered case is highly representative of many other similar problems found in intrusion detection systems. On the one hand, the results show that HHMM is a suitable tool for building profiles for users, or services, in this area. On the other hand, it appears that the methodology is effective, robust and easy to apply.

References

1. S. Bleha, C. Slivinsky, and B. Hussein. Computer-access security systems using keystroke dynamics. *IEEE Transactions on Pattern Analysis and Machine Intelligence*, PAMI-12(12):1217–1222, 1990.

---

[2]   The logarithm of the ratio between the probability that the observed sequence is generated by the model and the probability that it is generated by a random process.

2. M. Botta, U. Galassi, and A.Giordana. Learning complex and sparse events in long sequences. In *Proceedings of the European Conference on Artificial Intelligence, ECAI-04*, Valencia, Spain, August 2004.
3. M. Brown and S.J. Rogers. User identification via keystroke characteristics of typed names using neural networks. *International Journal of Man-Machine Studies*, 39:999–1014, 1993.
4. R. Durbin, S. Eddy, A. Krogh, and G. Mitchison. *Biological sequence analysis*. Cambridge University Press, 1998.
5. S. Fine, Y Singer, and N. Tishby. The hierarchical hidden markov model: Analysis and applications. *Machine Learning*, 32:41–62, 1998.
6. D. Gussfield. *Algorithms on Strings, Trees, and Sequences*. Cambridge University Press, 1997.
7. R. Joyce and G. Gupta. User authorization based on keystroke latencies. *Communications of the ACM*, 33(2):168–176, 1990.
8. K. Murphy and M. Paskin. Linear time inference in hierarchical hmms. In *Advances in Neural Information Processing Systems (NIPS-01)*, volume 14, 2001.
9. L.R. Rabiner. A tutorial on hidden markov models and selected applications in speech recognition. *Proceedings of IEEE*, 77(2):257–286, 1989.

Optimization of Association Rules Extraction Through Exploitation of Context Dependent Constraints

Arianna Gallo, Roberto Esposito, Rosa Meo, and Marco Botta

Dipartimento di Informatica, Università di Torino, Italy
{gallo, esposito, meo, botta}@di.unito.it

Abstract. In recent years, the KDD process has been advocated to be an iterative and interactive process. It is seldom the case that a user is able to answer immediately with a single query all his questions on data. On the contrary, the workflow of the typical user consists in several steps, in which he/she iteratively refines the extracted knowledge by inspecting previous results and posing new queries. Given this view of the KDD process, it becomes crucial to have KDD systems that are able to exploit past results thus minimizing computational effort. This is expecially true in environments in which the system knowledge base is the result of many discoveries on data made separately by the collaborative effort of different users. In this paper, we consider the problem of mining frequent association rules from database relations. We model a general, constraint-based, mining language for this task and study its properties w.r.t. the problem of re-using past results. In particular, we individuate two class of query constraints, namely "item dependent" and "context dependent" ones, and show that the latter are more difficult than the former ones. Then, we propose two newly developed algorithms which allow the exploitation of past results in the two cases. Finally, we show that the approach is both effective and viable by experimenting on some datasets.

1 Introduction

The problem of mining association rules and, more generally, that of extracting frequent sets from large databases has been widely investigated in the last decade [1,2,3,4,5,6,7]. These researches addressed two major issues: on one hand, performance and efficiency of the extraction algorithms; on the other hand, the exploitation of user preferences about the patterns to be extracted, expressed in terms of constraints.

Constraints are widely exploited also in data mining languages, such as in [8,9,10,4,7] where the user specifies in each data mining query, not only the constraints that the items must satisfy, but also different criteria to create groups of tuples from which itemsets will be extracted. Constraint-based mining languages are also the main key factor of inductive databases [11], proposed in order to leverage decision support systems. In inductive databases, the user explores

S. Bandini and S. Manzoni (Eds.): AI*IA 2005, LNAI 3673, pp. 258–269, 2005.

the domain of a mining problem submitting to the system many mining queries in sequence, in which subsequent queries are very often a refinement of previous ones. This constitutes for the system a huge computational workload and becomes a problem even more severe considering that these queries are typically instances of iceberg queries [12]. In such systems the intelligent exploitation of the queries previously submitted by the user becomes the key factor for a successful exploration of the problem search space [13]. Analogously, in inductive databases, it makes sense to try to exploit the effort already done by the DBMS in order to speed up the execution time of new queries. Furthermore, we suppose that the mining engine works in an environment similar to a data warehouse, in which database content updates occur rarely and in known periods of time. Thus, previous results are up to date and can be usefully exploited to speed up the execution of current queries.

In this paper, we propose and evaluate an "incremental" approach to mining that exploits the results of previous queries in order to reduce the response time to new queries. Of course, we suppose that the system relies on an optimizer who is entitled to recognize query equivalence and query containment relationships. [14] describes a prototype of such an optimizer and shows that its execution time is negligible (in the order of milliseconds).

We notice that several "incremental" algorithms have been developed in the data mining area [15,16], but they address a different issue: how to efficiently revise the result set of a mining query when the database source relations get updated with new data.

In all the previous works in constraint-based mining, a somewhat implicit assumption has always been made: properties on which users define constraints are functionally dependent on the item to be extracted, i.e., the property is either always true or always false for all the occurrences of a certain item in the database. In this case, it is possible to establish the satisfaction of the constraint considering only the properties of the item itself, that is, separately from the context of the database in which the item is found (e.g., typically the database transaction). In [14], we characterized the constraints on attributes that are functionally dependent on the items extracted and called them *item dependent* (ID). The exploitation of these constraints proves to be extremely useful for incremental algorithms.

In [14] another class of constraints, namely *context dependent* (CD), was introduced as well. CD constraints proved to be very difficult to be dealt with because, even when they hold within a transaction for a particular itemset, they do not necessarily hold for the same itemset but within another transaction.

Unfortunately, most of the state of the art algorithms [3,17,18], assume precisely that constraints do or do not hold for a given itemset database wide.

2   Preliminary Definitions and Notation

Let us consider a database instance D and let T be a database relation having the schema $TS=\{A_1, A_2, \ldots, A_n\}$. A given set of functional dependencies Σ over the attribute domains $dom(A_i)$, $i = 1..n$ is assumed to be known. We denote with Σ_{A_i} the set of attributes that are in the RHS of the functional dependencies with A_i as LHS.

For the sake of exemplification, we consider a fixed instance of the application domain. In particular, we will refer to a market basket analysis application in which T is a `Purchase` relation that contains data about customer purchases. In this context, TS is given by {`tr`, `date`, `customer`, `product`, `category`, `brand`, `price`, `qty`,`discount`}, where: `tr` is the purchase transaction identifier and the meaning of the other columns is the usual one for this kind of application. The Σ relation is {`product`→ `price`, `product` → `category`, `product` → `brand`, {`tr`, `product`} → `qty`, `tr` → `date`, `tr` → `customer`, {`tr`,`product`} → `discount`}. $\Sigma_{product}$, the set of attributes whose values depend on `product` is {`price`, `category`, `brand`}.

In writing a mining query, the user must specify, among the others, the following parameters:

- The *item attributes*, a set of attributes whose values constitute an item, i.e., an element of an itemset. In the language it is allowed to specify possibly different sets of attributes, one for the antecedent of association rules (body), and one for the consequent (head).
- The *grouping attributes* needed in order to decide how tuples are grouped for the formation of each itemset. This grouping, for the sake of generality and expressiveness of the language, can be decided differently in each query according to the purposes of the analysis.
- The *mining constraints* specify how to decide whether an association rule meets the user needs. Since we want to allow different constraints on the body and on the head of the association rules, we admit a distinct constraint expressions for each part of the rule.
- An expression over a number of *statistical measures* used to reduce the size of the result set and to increase the relevance of the results. This evaluation measures are evaluated only on the occurrences of the itemsets that satisfy the mining constraints.

By summarizing, a mining query may be described as

$$Q = (T, G, I_B, I_H, \Gamma_B, \Gamma_H, \Xi)$$

where: T is the database table; G is the set of grouping attributes; I_B and I_H are the set of item attributes respectively for the body and the head of association rules; Γ_B and Γ_H are boolean expressions of atomic predicates specifying constraints for the body and for the head of association rules; and Ξ is an expression on some statistical measures used for the evaluation of each rule.

We define an atomic predicate to be an expression in the form:

$$A_i \theta v_{Ai}$$

where θ is a relational operator such as $<, \leq, =, >, \geq, \neq$, and v_{Ai} is a value from the domain of attribute A_i. Ξ is defined to be a boolean expression in which each term has the form

$$\xi \theta v$$

where ξ is a statistical measure for the itemset evaluation, v is a real value, and θ is defined as above.

Examples of ξ are **support count** and **frequency**. The support count is the counting of the distinct groups containing the itemset. The itemset frequency is computed as the ratio between the itemset support count and the total number of database groups.

A mining engine, takes a query Q_i defined on an input relation T and generates a result set R_i.

Example 1. *The query*

$$Q=(Purchase, \{tr\}, \{product\}, \{product\},$$
category= 'clothes', category= 'clothes' and discount$\geq 10\%$,
support count≥ 20 AND confidence≥ 0.5)

over the **Purchase** *relation (first parameter) extracts rules formed by products in the body (third parameter) associated to products in the head (fourth parameter), where all the products in the rule have been sold in the same transaction (second parameter). Moreover, each product in the body must be of type "clothes" (fifth parameter) and be associated with discounted clothes (sixth parameter). Finally, the support count of the returned rules must be at least 20 and the confidence of the rules at least 0.5.*

An item dependent constraint is a predicate on an attribute A_i which lies in the dependency set of the schema of the rules (here denoted as $I_{BH} = I_B \cup I_H$, i.e. the union of the schema of the body and of the head), i.e., $\Sigma_{I_{BH}}$. As a consequence, being A_i in the dependency set of I_{BH}, its value can be determined directly (or indirectly, i.e., transitively) from the value of the association rules. In other words, the verification of this kind of constraint depends on the elements of the rule itself and not on other information stored in the transaction that make up the "context" of the rule. For instance, if we extract association rules on the values of the products frequently sold together in transactions, the category of the products does not depend on the transactions, but only on the products themselves. As explained in [14] (Lemma 1), an itemset satisfies an ID constraint either in all the instances of the database or in none of them.

On the contrary, the verification of a context dependent constraint depends on the contextual information that accompany the rules elements in the database. For instance, in our running example, the quantity of a product sold in a particular transaction depends on the product and on the transaction together. Therefore, a predicate on quantity is said to be a context dependent constraint and, in fact, its satisfaction changes depending on the particular transaction (the context). This implies that the support count might take any value ranging from 0 to the number of occurrences of that itemset in the database. In other words, when context dependent constraints are involved, we are obliged to evaluate the constraints on the fact table, where the contextual information can be retrieved.

3   An Incremental Algorithm for Item Dependent Constraints

In a previous work [14], we showed that in case a query contains only ID constraints, then we can obtain the result of a newly posed query Q_2 by means of set operations (unions and intersections) on the results of previously executed queries. We qualify this approach to itemset mining as *incremental* because instead of computing the itemsets from scratch it starts from a set of previous results. In this paper, we are interested, in particular, to study the situation of query containment, that is, when query Q_2 has a more restrictive set of constraints with respect to previous queries. In this case, it suffices to identify those rules in the previous results which satisfy the new constraints and report them all. We call this simple algorithm the ID incremental algorithm.

4   An Incremental Algorithm for Context Dependent Constraints

In this section we propose a new incremental algorithm, aiming at deriving the result of a new mining query Q_2 starting from a previous result R_1. This algorithm is able to deal with context dependent constraints, which, at the best of our knowledge, have not been tackled yet by any previous data mining algorithm [2,19,3,20,21,6].

Here we give a brief account of the algorithm behavior, describing it in greater details in the forthcoming sections. Initially, the algorithm reads rules from R_1 and builds a data structure to keep track of them. We call this structure the *BHF* (Body-Head Forest) (see Section 4.1). Then, the algorithm considers the items which satisfy the mining constraints in each group, and uses this information to update the BHF accordingly.

4.1   Description and Construction of the BHF

A BHF is a forest containing a distinguished tree (the body tree) and a number of other trees (head trees). The body tree is intended to contain the itemsets which are candidates for being in the body part of the rules. An important property of body trees is that an itemset B is represented as a single path in the tree and vice versa. The end of each path in the tree is associated to a head tree and to a (body) support counter.

The head tree rooted at the ending node of the path corresponding to itemset B is meant to keep track of those itemsets H that can possibly be used to form a rule $B \rightarrow H$. A head tree is similar to a body tree with the notably exception that there is no link pointing to further heads. A path in a head tree corresponds to an itemset H and is associated to a counter which stores the support of the rule.

Figure 1 gives a schematic representation of a BHF.

In the following we will make use of the following notation: given a node n belonging to a body tree or to a head tree, we denote with $n.child(i)$ the

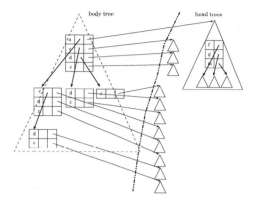

Fig. 1. Example of BHF

body (respectively the head) tree rooted in the node n in correspondence of the item i. For instance, in the root node of the BHF reported in Figure 1, there are four items, and three non-empty children; root.child(a) denotes the body node containing the items c, d, and z. In a similar way we denote the head tree corresponding to a particular item i in a node n using the notation n.head(i). We also assume that itemsets are sorted in an unspecified but fixed order. We denote with $I[k]$ the k-th element of the itemset I w.r.t. this ordering. Finally, in many places we adopt the standard notation used for sets in order to deal with BHF nodes. For instance, we write $i \in n$ in order to specify that item i is present in node n. Procedure insertRule describes how a rule is inserted in the

---

Procedure insertRule

Data   : root : the BHF root node
             $B \rightarrow H$: the rule to be inserted
headTree $\leftarrow$ insertBody(root, B, 1) ;
insertHead(headTree, H, 1);

BHF structure. The algorithm consists in two steps. In the first one the body of the rule is inserted in the body tree (see Function insertBody). In the second one the head is inserted and attached to the path found by the former function call (see Procedure insertHead). We notice that the hierarchical structure of the BHF describes a compressed version of a rule set. In fact, two rules $B_1 \rightarrow H_1$ and $B_2 \rightarrow H_2$ share a sub path in the body tree provided that B_1 and B_2 have a common prefix. Analogously they share a sub path in a head tree provided that $B_1 \equiv B_2$ and H_1 and H_2 have a common prefix.

4.2   Description of the Incremental Algorithm

Here, we assume that a BHF has been built out of the previous result set R_1. We explain how the counters in the structure are updated in order to reflect the support counters implied by Q_2.

Function insertBody

>   **Data**   : n : a BHF node; B : an itemset; k : an integer
>   **if** $B[k] \notin n$ **then**
> $n \leftarrow n \cup B[k]$
>   **end**
>   **if** $k < \text{size}(B)$ **then**
>   insertBody(n.child($B[k]$), $B, k + 1$)
>   **else**
>   return n.head($B[k]$)
>   **end**

Procedure insertHead

>   **Data**   : n : a BHF node; H : an itemset; k : an integer
>   **if** $H[k] \notin n$ **then**
> $n \leftarrow n \cup H[k]$
>   **end**
>   **if** $k < \text{size}(H)$ **then**
>   insertHead(n.child($H[k]$), $H, k + 1$)
>   **end**

In the following we will denote with:

-   $T_b'[g] \equiv \{i \mid (g, i) \in T_b'\}$ and with $T_h'[g] \equiv \{i \mid (g, i) \in T_h'\}$ the set of items in group g that satisfy the body constraints and the head constraints.
-   $\Pi_{\text{GID}}(T_b') \equiv \{g \mid (g, i) \in T_b'\}$ and with $\Pi_{\text{GID}}(T_h') \equiv \{g \mid (g, i) \in T_h'\}$ the set of GIDs in T_b' and in T_h'.
-   τ the support threshold chosen by the user
-   $B(r)$ the body of rule r and with $H(r)$ the head of rule r

For the sake of readability, we reported in Algorithm 4 a simplified version of the incremental algorithm which has the advantage of making its intended behavior clear. In fact, the implemented version greatly improves on the reported one by exploiting the hierarchical structure of BHF and the fact that there exists a single path in BHF for each B and at most $|B|$ paths for H. This allows the function to require $O(|B||H|)$ time in the worst case.

5   Results

The two incremental algorithms presented in this paper have been assessed on a database instance, describing retail data, generated semi-automatically. We generated a first approximation of the fact table (**purchases**) using the synthetic data generation program described in [22]. This data generation program has been run using parameters $|T| = 25$, $|I| = 10$, $N = 1000$, $|\mathcal{D}| = 10,000$, i.e., the average transaction size is 25, the average size of potentially large itemsets is 10, the number of distinct items is 1000 and the total number of transactions

Algorithm 4: Context Dependent (CD) incremental algorithm

Data   : BHF; pointers to T'_b, T'_h
Result : R_2
for *all GID* $g \in \Pi_{\text{GID}}(T'_b)$ **do**
| incrRuleSupp(BHF,$T'_b[g]$, $T'_h[g]$)
end
for *all rule* $r \in BHF$ **do**
| **if** $\Xi(r)$ **then**
| | $R_2 \leftarrow R_2 \cup r$
| **end**
end

Procedure incrRuleSupp

Data   : BHF; I_B: items in current transaction satisfying Γ_B; I_A: items in current transaction satisfying Γ_A
Result : It updates the support counters in the BHF
for *all* $r \in BHF$ **do**
| **if** $B(r) \subseteq T'_b[g]$ **then**
| | support(B(r))++;
| | **if** $H(r) \subseteq T'_h[g]$ **then**
| | | support(r)++;
| | **end**
| **end**
end

is 10.000. Then, we updated this initial table adding some more attributes, constituting the description (and the contextual information) on sales: some item dependent features (such as category of product and price) and some context dependent features (such as discount and quantity of sales). We generated these attributes values randomly, using a uniform distribution defined on the respective domains.

We note here how a single fact table suffices for the objectives of our experimentation. In fact, the important parameters from the viewpoint of the performance study of incremental algorithms are the selectivity of the mining constraints (which determine the volume of data to be processed from the given database instance) and the size of the previous result set. Figure 2(a) reports the performances of the item dependent incremental algorithm (ID) as the selectivity of the mining constraints changes. We experimented different constraints on the item dependent attributes, letting the constraints selectivity vary from 0% to 100% of the total number of items. In Figure 2(a) we sampled twenty points. Figure 2(b) tests the same algorithm, but it lets vary the number of rules in the previous result set. Again we sampled twenty points (in the range 0...3220). The two figures report the total amount of time needed by the algorithm to complete, subdividing it in the preprocessing time (spent in querying the database

266   A. Gallo et al.

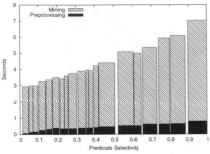
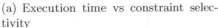
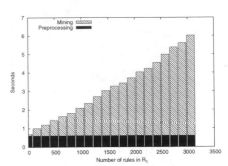

(a) Execution time vs constraint selectivity

(b) Execution time vs volume of previous result

Fig. 2. Empirical evaluation of the item dependent (ID) incremental algorithm

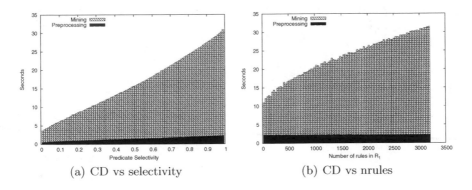

(a) CD vs selectivity

(b) CD vs nrules

Fig. 3. Empirical evaluation of the CD incremental algorithm

to retrieve and store in main memory the items that satisfy the constraints), and the core mining time (needed by the algorithm to read the previous result set and to filter out those rules that do not satisfy the constraints any more).

Figures 3(a) and 3(b) report the results on performances of the context dependent (CD) algorithm. The figures report again the total execution time, specifying how much time was spent for preprocessing and for the core mining task.

A couple of points are worth noting. The execution times of both algorithms increase almost linearly with the increase of the two parameters (constraints selectivity and previous results), but as it was expected the item dependent incremental algorithm runs much faster than its counterpart. In addition, evidence from another set of experiments (not reported here for space reasons) shows that the algorithms highly improve on our baseline miner algorithm that solves the problem of constraint-based mining in its most general version. Due to lack of space we do not describe this algorithm in details. In brief, the algorithm evaluates the mining constraints directly on the fact table, and supports the following features: fully support constraints (SQL-like predicates) on bodies and heads and correctly solves context dependent queries. This is an Apriori-like algorithm that keeps track of the groups in which each item satisfies the mining constraints. It adopts a work-flow similar to Partition [23] but uses BHF as data structure. Moreover, in order to support CD constraints the generalized algorithm builds a temporary source table which is usually much bigger than the original one. This algorithm takes about 700 seconds in the average case to build the complete result set which is more than an order magnitude higher than the time spent by the CD incremental algorithm on the same task.

We also ran a version of FPGrowth [24] on the same dataset, but using no constraints at all (since, at the best of our knowledge, CD constraints are not supported by any algorithm proposed so far in the literature). It takes, on average, about 21 seconds to complete. This is three times faster than the worst performance of the CD incremental algorithm and three times slower than the ID incremental one. We agree that this is only a very rough comparison and that things can change substantially accordingly to the size of the previous result set as well as with the support parameter given to FPGrowth. However, it is interesting to notice how suggests that it may be possible to combine an efficient algorithm like FPGrowth to build an initial result set, and an incremental one (supporting CD constraints) in order to solve constraint-based queries.

This further motivates the interest in incremental algorithms, since it is then possible to obtain an execution time that is still much smaller than the one required by the generalized constraint-based algorithm, and still allowing a general class of constraints to be supported.

6   Conclusions

In this paper we proposed a novel "incremental" approach to constraint-based mining which makes use of the information contained in previous results to answer new queries. The beneficial factors of the approach are that it uses both: the previous results and the mining constraints, in order to reduce the itemsets search space.

We presented two incremental algorithms. The first one deals with item dependent constraints, while the second one with context dependent ones. We note how the latter kind of constraints has been identified only recently and that there is very little support for them in current mining algorithms. However, the difficulty to solve mining queries with context dependent constraints can be partially overcome by combining the "traditional" algorithms proposed so far in the literature, and the context dependent incremental algorithm proposed in this paper.

In Section 5, we evaluated the incremental algorithms on a pretty large dataset. The results show that the approach reduces drastically the overall execution time. We believe the improvement to be absolutely necessary in many practical data mining applications, in data warehouses and inductive database systems.

An interesting direction for future research is the integration of condensed representations (which have been heavily studied in recent years) with the incremental techniques presented here. In fact, it would be desirable to take advantage of both: the improved readability of condensed patterns, and the speeds improvements of incremental algorithms. Moreover, to store condensed patterns means that incremental algorithms need to deal with smaller result sets. Then, it may be possible to obtain an even faster processing of incremental queries.

To this regard, the main problem to be faced is the interaction between novel (more restrictive) constraints and condensed patterns. In fact, even though the representative of a condensed set may not satisfy the new constraint, this not necessarily hold for all the elements of the condensed set. This means that, when such a situation occurs, it is not possible to simply remove the representative from the previous result set. On the contrary, the old dataset must undergo careful rewriting. While we expect that efficient solutions to the problem could be found, the extension of our algorithms to deal with these issues is not straightforward and deserve additional work.

References

1. Agrawal, R., Mannila, H., Srikant, R., Toivonen, H., Verkamo, A.I.: Fast discovery of association rules. In Fayyad, U.M., Piatetsky-Shapiro, G., Smyth, P., Uthurusamy, R., eds.: Knowledge Discovery in Databases. Volume 2. AAAI/MIT Press, Santiago, Chile (1995)
2. Srikant, R., Vu, Q., Agrawal, R.: Mining association rules with item constraints. In: Proceedings of 1997 ACM KDD. (1997) 67–73
3. Ng, R.T., Lakshmanan, L.V.S., Han, J., Pang, A.: Exploratory mining and pruning optimizations of constrained associations rules. In: Proc. of 1998 ACM SIGMOD Int. Conf. Management of Data. (1998) 13–24
4. Tsur, D., Ullman, J.D., Abiteboul, S., Clifton, C., Motwani, R., Nestorov, S., Rosenthal, A.: Query flocks: A generalization of association-rule mining. In: Proceedings of 1998 ACM SIGMOD Int. Conf. Management of Data. (1998)
5. Chaudhuri, S., Narasayya, V., Sarawagi, S.: Efficient evaluation of queries with mining predicates. In: Proc. of the 18th Int'l Conference on Data Engineering (ICDE), San Jose, USA (2002)
6. Perng, C.S., Wang, H., Ma, S., Hellerstein, J.L.: Discovery in multi-attribute data with user-defined constraints. ACM SIGKDD Explorations 4 (2002) 56–64
7. Wang, H., Zaniolo, C.: User defined aggregates for logical data languages. In: Proc. of DDLP. (1998) 85–97
8. Imielinski, T., Virmani, A., Abdoulghani, A.: Datamine: Application programming interface and query language for database mining. KDD-96 (1996) 256–260
9. Meo, R., Psaila, G., Ceri, S.: A new SQL-like operator for mining association rules. In: Proceedings of the 22st VLDB Conference, Bombay, India (1996)
10. Han, J., Fu, Y., Wang, W., Koperski, K., Zaiane, O.: DMQL: A data mining query language for relational databases. In Proc. of SIGMOD-96 Workshop on Research Issues on Data Mining and Knowledge Discovery (1996)
11. Imielinski, T., Mannila, H.: A database perspective on knowledge discovery. Communications of the ACM 39 (1996) 58–64
12. Fang, M., Shivakumar, N., Garcia-Molina, H., Motwani, R., Ullman, J.: Computing iceberg queries efficiently. In: Proceeding of VLDB '98. (1998)
13. Sarawagi, S.: User-adaptive exploration of multidimensional data. In: Proc. of the 26th Int'l Conf. on Very Large Databases (VLDB), Cairo,Egypt (2000) 307–316

14. Meo, R., Botta, M., Esposito, R.: Query rewriting in itemset mining. In: Proceedings of the 6th International Conference On Flexible Query Answeringd Systems. LNAI (to appear), Springer (2004)
15. Cheung, D.W., Han, J., Ng, V.T., Wong, C.Y.: Maintenance of discovered association rules in large databases: an incremental updating technique. In: ICDE96 12th Int'l Conf. on Data Engineering, New Orleans, Louisiana, USA (1996)
16. Labio, W., Yang, J., Cui, Y., Garcia-Molina, H., Widom, J.: Performance issues in incremental warehouse maintenance. In: Proceedings of Twenty-Sixth International Conference on Very Large Data Bases. (2000) 461–472
17. Leung, C.K.S., Lakshmanan, L.V.S., Ng, R.T.: Exploiting succinct constraints using fp-trees. ACM SIGKDD Explorations **4** (2002) 40–49
18. Bucila, C., Gehrke, J., Kifer, D., White, W.M.: Dualminer: a dual-pruning algorithm for itemsets with constraints. In: Proc. of 2002 ACM KDD. (2002) 42–51
19. Bayardo, R., Agrawal, R., Gunopulos, D.: Constraint-based rule mining in large, dense databases. In: Proc. of the 15th Int'l Conf. on Data Engineering. (1999)
20. Lakshmanan, L.V.S., Ng, R., Han, J., Pang, A.: Optimization of constrained frequent set queries with 2-variable constraints. In: Proceedings of 1999 ACM SIGMOD Int. Conf. Management of Data. (1999) 157–168
21. Raedt, L.D.: A perspective on inductive databases. ACM SIGKDD Explorations **4** (2002) 69–77
22. Agrawal, R., Srikant, R.: Fast algorithms for mining association rules in large databases. In: Proceedings of the 20th VLDB Conference, Santiago, Chile (1994)
23. Savasere, A., Omiecinski, E., Navathe, S.: An efficient algorithm for mining association rules in large databases. In: Proc. of the 21st VLDB Conf. (1995)
24. Han, J., Pei, J., Yin, Y.: Mining frequent patterns without candidate generation. In: Proc. of ACM SIGMOD 2000, Dallas, TX, USA (2000)

Automata Slicing for Diagnosing Discrete-Event Systems with Partially Ordered Observations

Alban Grastien[1], Marie-Odile Cordier[1], and Christine Largouët[2]

[1] Irisa, University of Rennes 1, Campus de Beaulieu, 35 042, Rennes Cedex, France
{agrastie, cordier}@irisa.fr
[2] University of New Caledonia, BP. 4477, 98847, Nouméa Cedex, New Caledonia
largouet@univ-nc.nc

Abstract. When dealing with real systems, it is unrealistic to suppose that observations can be totally ordered according to their emission dates. The partially ordered observations and the system are thus both represented as finite-state machines (or automata) and the diagnosis formally defined as the synchronized composition of the model with the observations. The problem we deal with in this paper is that, taking into account partially ordered observations rather than sequential ones, it becomes difficult to consider the observations one after the other and to incrementally compute the global diagnosis.

In this paper, we rely on a slicing of the observation automata and propose to compute diagnosis slices (for each observation slice) before combining them to get the global diagnosis. In order to reach this objective, we introduce the concept of *automata chain* and define the computation of the diagnosis using this chain, first in a modular way and then, more efficiently, in an incremental way. These results are then extended to the case where observations are sliced according to temporal windows. This study is done in an off-line context. It is a first and necessary step before considering the on-line context which is discussed in the conclusion.

1 Introduction

It is established that diagnosing dynamical systems, represented as discrete-event systems [1] amounts to finding what happened to the system from existing observations [2,3,4,5,6]. In this context, the diagnostic task consists in determining the trajectories (a sequence of states and events) compatible with the observations. When dealing with real systems, it is unrealistic to suppose that observations can be totally ordered according to their emission dates. The partially ordered observations and the system are thus both represented as finite-state machines (or automata) and the diagnosis formally defined as the synchronized composition of the model with the observations.

A problem that can be encountered is the size of the observation automaton, due to the temporal uncertainties on the observations or/and the duration of the observation recording. For instance, we may want to compute an a posteriori diagnosis from log files of observations during a few days period, as in the domain

S. Bandini and S. Manzoni (Eds.): AI*IA 2005, LNAI 3673, pp. 270–281, 2005.

of telecommunication networks. It becomes difficult to consider the observations one after the other and to incrementally compute the global diagnosis. In this article, we propose a way to avoid this global computation by considering an automata slicing for the observations and building the diagnosis incrementally on successive slices of observations. The problem of building the sliced observation automata is not considered in this paper where we consider it as given.

After a brief reminder of the definitions about automata (section 2), we introduce, in section 3, the concept of *automata chain*, to represent an automaton by a sequence of automata slices. We provide the properties such an automata chain has to satisfy to be a *correct slicing* and define a *reconstruction* operation to get the global automaton back. Then, we demonstrate, provided the observations are correctly sliced, that the diagnosis can be correctly (section 4) and incrementally (section 5) computed from the observation slices. In section 6, these results are extended to the case where observations are sliced according to time, i.e according to *temporal windows*. We here focus on the off-line diagnosis context; the extension to the on-line diagnosis context is discussed in the conclusion.

2   Preliminaries: Automata and Trajectories

In this paper, we are more particularly interested in diagnosing reactive systems. Reactive systems are event-driven since their behaviour evolves with the occurrence of events and can cause by propagation a succession of state changes [2]. In this approach, the behavioural model of the system is represented by finite state machines. This section thus recalls some basic notions about automata and trajectories.

Definition 1 (Automaton). *An* automaton A *is a tuple* (Q, E, T, I, F) *where:*

- Q *is the finite set of states;*
- E *is the finite set of events;*
- $T \subseteq (Q \times 2^E \times Q)$ *is the finite set of transitions; a transition t is a tuple (q, l, q') such that t connects q to q' on the label l, with $l \in 2^E \setminus \{\emptyset\}$ a non-empty subset of events;*
- I *is the finite set of initial states $(I \subseteq Q)$; and*
- F *is the finite set of final states $(F \subseteq Q)$.*

Labels over transitions should not be empty. We consider that $\forall q \in Q$, the transition $(q, \emptyset, q)$ is a transition of T.

A *path between the states* q_0 *and* q_m of an automaton $A = (Q, E, T, I, F)$ is the couple $((q_0, \dots, q_m), (l_1, \dots, l_m))$, where $(q_0, \dots, q_m)$ is the finite sequence of states and $(l_1, \dots, l_m)$ the sequence of labels, such that:

- $\forall i \in \{0, \dots, m\}$, $q_i \in Q$, and
- $\forall i \in \{1, \dots, m\}$, $t_i = (q_{i-1}, l_i, q_i) \in T$.

A *trajectory* denoted $traj$ of an automaton A is a path $((q_0, \dots, q_m), (l_1, \dots, l_m))$, where $q_0 \in I$ and $q_m \in F$.

Two automata A and A' are equal ($A = A'$) if their trajectory sets are equal. We call *simplified automaton of A* the automaton $A' = A$ where all the states and transitions that do not appear in at least one trajectory have been removed. In the following, when computing new automata, only simplified ones are considered.

Definition 2 (Synchronization of labels). *Given l_1 a label from E_1 and l_2 a label from E_2, l_1 and l_2 are said to be synchronized iff $l_1 \cap (E_1 \cap E_2) = l_2 \cap (E_1 \cap E_2)$. The synchronization l, denoted $\Theta(l_1, l_2)$, is the label $l_1 \cup l_2$ on the set of events $E_1 \cup E_2$.*

Two labels can be synchronized if the synchronization events ($E_1 \cap E_2$) are common to both labels. Note that $l_1 = l \cap E_1$ and $l_2 = l \cap E_2$.

Definition 3 (Synchronization of automata). *Let $A_1 = (Q_1, E_1, T_1, I_1, F_1)$ and $A_2 = (Q_2, E_2, T_2, I_2, F_2)$ be two automata. The synchronization of A_1 and A_2, denoted $A_1 \otimes A_2$, is the automaton $A = (Q, E, T, I, F)$ such that:*

- $Q = Q_1 \times Q_2$,
- $E = E_1 \cup E_2$,
- $T = \{((q_1, q_2), l, (q_1', q_2')) \mid (q_1, l \cap E_1, q_1') \in T_1 \wedge (q_2, l \cap E_2, q_2') \in T_2\}$,
- $I = I_1 \times I_2$, and
- $F = F_1 \times F_2$.

The synchronization consists in trigerring simultaneously the two transitions having the same synchronization labels in both automata.

3   Automata Chain

In this section we introduce the concept of *automata chain* whose goal is to represent an automaton into pieces. The correct slicing of an automaton is defined as well as the automaton reconstruction which is the automaton obtained after the reconstruction of an automata chain. A new synchronization operation, performed on automata chains, is then presented.

Definition 4 (Automata chain). *A sequence of automata $(A^1, \ldots, A^n)$ with $A^i = (Q^i, E^i, T^i, I^i, F^i)$ is called automata chain, and denoted $\mathcal{E}_A$, if:*

- $\forall i, j, \ E^i = E^j$,
- $\forall i, j, \ j > i, \forall q, \ q \in Q^i \cap Q^j \Rightarrow q \in F^i \wedge q \in I^{i+1}$, and
- $\forall i, j, \forall q, q', \ if \ \{q, q'\} \subseteq Q^i \cap Q^j \ then \ \forall p, \ path \ of \ A^i \ between \ q \ and \ q', \ p \ is \ also \ a \ path \ of \ A^j.$

In the following, the superscript i refers to the ith automaton of the chain. An automata chain is given Figure 1. To simplify, the labels over the transitions are not represented. By definition, a state must not appear in two different automata of the chain except if it belongs to the boundaries of two successive automata, i.e the state is a final state of the former and an initial state of the later. The last item of the previous definition requires similar path between the states on

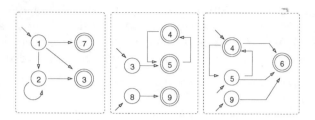

Fig. 1. Chain of three automata

the boundary of two consecutive automata (see for example the states 4 and 5 for the second and third automata of the chain). The third condition of the definition is necessary to obtain the Property 1 (defined later, see the proof in annex).

Definition 5 (Trajectory reconstruction). *Let* $traj^i = ((q_0^i, \ldots, q_{mi}^i), (l_1^i, \ldots, l_{mi}^i))$ *be* n *trajectories such that* $\forall i$, $q_{mi}^i = q_0^{i+1}$. *Then the trajectory* $traj$ *resulting from the reconstruction of the* n *trajectories* $traj^i$, *is defined by:* $traj = ((q_0^1, \ldots, q_{m1}^1, q_1^2, \ldots, q_{m2}^2, \ldots, q_1^n, \ldots, q_{mn}^n), (l_1^1, \ldots, l_{m1}^1, l_1^2, \ldots, l_{m2}^2, \ldots, l_1^n, \ldots, l_{mn}^n)).$

Definition 6 (Automata chain trajectory). *Let* $\mathcal{E}_A$ *be an automata chain* $(A^1, \ldots, A^n)$. *A* trajectory *of* $\mathcal{E}_A$ *is any trajectory obtained by the reconstruction of any* n *trajectories* $traj^i$ *from each of the* n *automata* A^i.

An example of trajectory on the automata chain presented Figure 1 is $((1, 2, 2, 2, 3, 5, 4, 5, 6), l)$ where l is the sequence of labels of the transitions.

Definition 7 (Correct slicing). *Let* A *be an automaton and* $\mathcal{E}_A = (A^1, \ldots, A^n)$ *be an automata chain.* $\mathcal{E}_A$ *is a* correct slicing *of* A *iff the set of trajectories of* $\mathcal{E}_A$ *is equal to the set of trajectories of* A. *We denote* $Sli(A)$ *a correct slicing of* A *into an automata chain* $\mathcal{E}_A$ *such that* $\mathcal{E}_A = Sli(A)$.

The chain in Figure 1 is a correct slicing of the automaton of Figure 2.

The reconstruction operation builds an automaton (see Figure 2) from the sequence of automata of an automata chain (see Figure 1). In a first step, all the states and transitions are kept, the initial states being the initial states of the

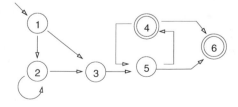

Fig. 2. The automata chain $\mathcal{E}_A$ presented in Figure 1 is one of the correct slicings of this automaton. It can be obtained (see Property 1) by reconstruction of $\mathcal{E}_A$.

first automaton (state 1) and the final states being the final states of the last one (states 4 and 6). In a second step, the states which are not reachable from these new initial states (as states 8, 9) or not leading to a final state (as state 7) are deleted as well as the transitions from or to these deleted states.

Definition 8 (Automaton reconstruction). *Let $\mathcal{E}_A = (A^1, \ldots, A^n)$ be an automata chain with $A^i = (Q^i, E^i, T^i, I^i, F^i)$. We call* reconstruction *of the chain $\mathcal{E}_A$, the simplified automaton obtained from $A_R = (Q_R, F_R, T_R, I_R, F_R)$ defined as follows:*

- $Q_R = Q^1 \cup \ldots \cup Q^n$,
- $E_R = E^1 = \ldots = E^n$,
- $T_R = T^1 \cup \ldots \cup T^n$,
- $I_R = I^1$, *and*
- $F_R = F^n$.

Property 1. *Let A be an automaton and $\mathcal{E}_A$ an automata chain. If $\mathcal{E}_A$ is a correct slicing of A, then A is obtained by the reconstruction of $\mathcal{E}_A$.*

Proof: The proof is given in Annex.

The reconstruction of $\mathcal{E}_A$ is denoted $Sli^{-1}(\mathcal{E}_A)$. If $\mathcal{E}_A$ is a slicing of A, then $A = Sli^{-1}(\mathcal{E}_A)$ (Property 1). We now see how the size of the automata chain can be reduced by refinement without loss of information.

Definition 9 (I-refined (F-refined) automata chain). *An automata chain $\mathcal{E}_A = (A^1, \ldots, A^n)$ with $A^i = (Q^i, E^i, T^i, I^i, F^i)$ is called* I-refined *(resp. F-refined) iff $\forall i, I^{i+1} \subseteq F^i$ (resp. $F^i \subseteq I^{i+1}$).*

Definition 10 (I-Refinement). *Let $\mathcal{E}_A = (A^1, \ldots, A^n)$ be an automata chain with $A^i = (Q^i, E^i, T^i, I^i, F^i)$. We call* I-refinement *of $\mathcal{E}_A$ a sequence $\mathcal{E}_{A'} = (A'^1, \ldots, A'^n)$ such that $\exists q, \exists i > 1, \ q \in I^i \land q \notin F^{i-1}$ with:*

- $\forall j \neq i, \ A'^j = A^j$,
- A'^i *is the simplified automaton from $(Q^i, E^i, T^i, I^i \setminus \{q\}, F^i)$.*

F-refinement can be defined in an analog way as I-refinement. We use the generic term of refinement to either I-refinement or F-refinement.

Property 2. *Let $\mathcal{E}_A$ be an automata chain. The sequence of automata $\mathcal{E}_{A'}$ obtained by refinement of $\mathcal{E}_A$ is a chain. Moreover, the refinement operation on automata chain preserves the equality of the reconstructed automata.*

Proof. It is obvious that the trajectories of $\mathcal{E}_{A'}$ are trajectories of $\mathcal{E}_A$. Let $traj$ be a trajectory of $\mathcal{E}_A$. Then, there exists $traj^1, \ldots, traj^n$, trajectories such that $traj^i = ((q_0^i, \ldots, q_{mi}^i), (l_1^i, \ldots, l_{mi}^i))$ and $q_{mi}^i = q_0^{i+1}$. $\forall i, q_0^i$ is a state of F^{i-1} and so, this state cannot be removed by I-refinement. $\forall i, q_{mi}^i$ is a state of I^{i+1} and so, this state cannot be removed by F-refinement. Then, $traj$ is a trajectory of $\mathcal{E}_{A'}$.

A refinement enables us to get a smaller equivalent automata chain. The I-refined automata chain obtained by successive I-refinements of the automata chain Figure 1 is presented Figure 3. The refinement operation is specially useful in the incremental synchronization (presented later, Section 5).

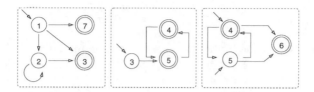

Fig. 3. I-refined automata chain ($I^{i+1} \subseteq F^i$)

Our interest is now the synchronization of an automata chain with an automaton.

Definition 11 (Prefix(suffix)-closed automaton). *Let $A = (Q, E, T, I, F)$ be an automaton. We call* prefix-closed *(resp.* suffix-closed*) automaton of A, denoted A^+ (resp. A^-), the automaton A whose all states are final: $F^+ = Q$ (resp. initial: $I^- = Q$).*

We denote $A^\#$, the automaton which is both prefix-closed and suffix-closed ($A^\# = A^{+^-} = A^{-^+}$).

Definition 12 (Automata chain synchronization). *We call* synchronization *of an automata chain $\mathcal{E}_A = (A^1, \dots, A^n)$ with an automaton M the sequence denoted $\mathcal{E}_A \otimes M$ defined by: $\mathcal{E}_A \otimes M = (A^1 \otimes M^+, A^2 \otimes M^\#, \dots, A^{n-1} \otimes M^\#, A^n \otimes M^-)$.*

When the state q of I^i ($i \neq 1$) is reached, the current state of M is not necessarily an initial state of M. Thus, the synchronization uses the suffix-closure of the automaton M. For the same reason, the prefix-closure of M is used.

Property 3. *Let $\mathcal{E}_A$ be an automata chain and M an automaton, then $\mathcal{E}_A \otimes M$ is an automata chain.*

Proof. We denote $\mathcal{E}_A = (A^1, \dots, A^n)$ with $A^i = (Q^i, E^i, T^i, I^i, F^i)$. Let $M = (Q_M, E_M, T_M, I_M, F_M)$. We note $\mathcal{E}_A \otimes M = (A^1_\otimes, \dots, A^n_\otimes)$ with $A^i_\otimes = (Q^i_\otimes, E^i_\otimes, T^i_\otimes, I^i_\otimes, F^i_\otimes)$.

- $\forall i, j, \ E^i_\otimes = E^j_\otimes = E \cup E_M$,
- $\forall i, j, \ j > i, \forall (q, q_M), \ (q, q_M) \in Q^i_\otimes \cap Q^j_\otimes$
  - $q \in F^i \Rightarrow (q, q_M) \in F^i_\otimes$,
  - Either $j = i+1$, and then $(q, q_M) \in Q^{i+1}_\otimes$ ((q, q_M) has not been removed by the simplification). $q \in I^{i+1} \Rightarrow (q, q_M) \in I^{i+1}_M$. Or $j > i+1$ and then $q \in I^{i+1} \cap F^{i+1}$ and $(q, q_M) \in I^{i+1}_M \cap F^{i+1}_M$, and so, (q, q_M) is not removed by the simplification of the automaton.
- $\forall i, j, \ \ \forall \{(q_0, q_{M0}), (q_m, q_{Mm})\} \ \subseteq \ Q^i_\otimes \cap Q^j_\otimes$. Let p be a path on $A^i_\otimes$ so that $p = (((q_0, q_{M0}), \dots, (q_m, q_{Mm}))(l_1, \dots, l_m))$. Then, $((q_{M0}, \dots, q_{Mm}), (l_1 \cap E_M, \dots, l_m \cap E_M))$ is a path on M, and $((q_0, \dots, q_m), (l_1 \cap E, \dots, l_m \cap E))$ is a path on A^i and so on A^j (since $\{q_0, q_m\} \subseteq Q^i \cap Q^j$). Thus, p is a path on $A^j_\otimes$.

Property 4. *Let $\mathcal{E}_A$ be an automata chain and $M = (Q_M, E_M, T_M, I_M, F_M)$ then $\mathcal{E}_A \otimes M$ is a correct slicing of $Sli^{-1}(\mathcal{E}_A) \otimes M$.*

Proof. We use the same notation as in the previous proof. Let $traj_\otimes = ((q_0, \ldots, q_m), (l_1, \ldots, l_m))$, a trajectory of $Sli^{-1}(\mathcal{E}_A) \otimes M$ so that $q_i = (q_i^A, q_i^M)$ and $l_i = \Theta(l_i^A, l_i^M,)$. Then $traj = ((q_0^A, \ldots, q_m^A), (l_1^A, \ldots, l_m^A))$ (resp. $traj^M = ((q_0^M, \ldots, q_m^M), (l_1^M, \ldots, l_m^M)))$ is a trajectory of $Sli^{-1}(\mathcal{E}_A)$ (resp. M). Then, $\exists f$ so that $traj^j = ((q_{f(j)}^A, \ldots, q_{f(j+1)}^A), (l_{f(j)+1}^A, \ldots, l_{f(j+1)}^A))$ is a trajectory of A^j with $traj$ is the reconstruction of the n trajectories $traj^j$. Then, $traj_\otimes^j = ((q_{f(j)}, \ldots, q_{f(j+1)}), (l_{f(j)+1}, \ldots, l_{f(j+1)}))$ is a trajectory of $A^j \otimes M^\#$ ($A^1 \otimes M^+$ for $j = 1$, $A^n \otimes M^-$ for $j = n$), and $traj_\otimes$ is a trajectory of $\mathcal{E}_A \otimes M$.

In the same way, we can prove that any trajectory of $Sli^{-1}(\mathcal{E}_A \otimes M)$ is a trajectory of $Sli^{-1}(\mathcal{E}_A) \otimes M$. Then, $\mathcal{E}_A \otimes M$ is a correct slicing of $Sli^{-1}(\mathcal{E}_A) \otimes M$.

4   Diagnosis by Slices

This section proposes to use the formalism of automata chains to represent the observations and to compute, given Property 4, the system diagnosis. The section 5 then presents how to compute the diagnosis incrementally.

Let us first recall the definitions used in the domain of discrete-event systems diagnosis where the system is traditionally modelled by an automaton.

Definition 13 (Model). *The model of the system, denoted Mod, is an automaton $(Q^{Mod}, E^{Mod}, T^{Mod}, I^{Mod}, F^{Mod})$. I^{Mod} is the set of possible states at t_0. All the states of the system may be final, thus $F^{Mod} = Q^{Mod}$. The set of observable events of the system is denoted $E_{Obs}^{Mod} \subseteq E^{Mod}$.*

The model of the system describes its behaviour and the trajectories of *Mod* represent the evolutions of the system. Let us remark that we do not have any information on the final states of *Mod*, and so $Mod^+ = Mod$ and $Mod^\# = Mod^-$.

Let us turn to observations and diagnosis definitions. We consider that the observable events are observed by sensors and sent via communication channels to an unique supervisor. Therefore, the observations are subject to uncertainties: the clocks of the sensors are not synchronized (see for instance [7]), the transfer policy and duration are variable or partially unknown, some observations may even be lost, etc. Generally, we don't know the total order on the observations emitted by the system. Consequently, the observations are represented by an automaton, each trajectory of which represents a possible order of emission of the observations.

Definition 14 (Observation automaton). *The observation automaton, denoted Obs_n, is an automaton describing the observations emitted by the system during the period $[t_0, t_n]$.*

Definition 15 (Diagnosis). *The diagnosis, denoted Δ_n, is an automaton describing the possible trajectories on the model of the system compatible with the observations sent by the system during the period $[t_0, t_n]$.*

The diagnosis can be formally defined as resulting from the synchonization of the automaton representing the model (Mod), and the automaton representing the observations Obs_n on the period $[t_0, t_n]$. We have:

$$\Delta_n = Obs_n \otimes Mod \tag{1}$$

Using Property 4, the diagnosis by slices can be computed. The idea is to compute diagnosis slices, corresponding to observations slices. The global diagnosis can be reconstructed from the diagnosis automata chain that is obtained.

Definition 16 (Diagnosis by slices - Diagnosis slice). *Let Mod be the system model and Obs_n the observation automaton. Let $\mathcal{E}_{Obs_n} = (Obs^1, \ldots, Obs^n)$, be a correct slicing of Obs^n. The synchronization (see definition 12) of $\mathcal{E}_{Obs_n}$ with Mod, i.e $\mathcal{E}_{Obs_n} \otimes Mod = (Obs^1 \otimes Mod, Obs^2 \otimes Mod^{\#}, \ldots, Obs^n \otimes Mod^{\#})$ is the diagnosis by slices of the system.*

It can be denoted by the diagnosis automata chain $(\Delta^1, \ldots, \Delta^n)$, where Δ^i is called the ith diagnosis slice of the system.

Using Property 4, it can be proved that the diagnosis by slices of a system, here $\mathcal{E}_{Obs_n} \otimes Mod$, correctly represents the diagnosis computed on the global observations since the reconstruction of $\mathcal{E}_{Obs_n} \otimes Mod$ equals the global diagnosis:

Result 1. $\Delta_n = Sli^{-1}(\mathcal{E}_{Obs_n} \otimes Mod)$

5   Incremental Diagnosis

In the diagnosis by slices as presented above, the ith diagnosis slice, Δ^i, is computed independently from the others, by synchronizing the ith observation slice from the chain $\mathcal{E}_{Obs_n}$, Obs^i, with the system model $Mod^{\#}$. One of the interests of the observation slicing is to make the parallelized computation of each diagnosis slice possible. In this section, we focus on another approach, which elaborates an incremental diagnosis, using Δ^{i-1} to restrict the set of initial states of Mod when computing Δ^i [1]. In this section we first present a new definition of the synchronization for the incremental case and tackle the specific problem of incremental diagnosis.

Definition 17 (Restriction). *Let $A = (Q, E, T, I, F)$ be an automaton. The automata restriction of A by the states of I', denoted $A[I']$, is the automaton $A' = (Q, E, T, I \cap I', F)$.*

In the incremental synchronization the set of initial states of an automaton of the chain is restricted by the set of final states of its predecessor.

Definition 18 (Incremental synchronization). *The incremental synchronization of the automata chain $\mathcal{E}_A = (A^1, \ldots, A^n)$ with the automaton M, denoted $\mathcal{E}_A \odot M$ is defined as $(A'^1, \ldots, A'^m)$ with $A'^i = (Q'^i, E', T'^i, I'^i, F'^i)$ and:*

---

[1] We could conversely use Δ^i to restrict the set of final states of Mod when computing the diagnosis Δ^{i-1}.

- $A'^1 = A^1 \otimes M^+$,
- $\forall i \in \{2, \ldots, n-1\}$, $A'^i = (A^i \otimes M^{\#})[F'^{i-1}]$ and
- $A'^n = (A^n \otimes M^-)[F'^{n-1}]$.

Property 5. *Let $\mathcal{E}_A$ be an automata chain and M an automaton. Then $\mathcal{E}_A \odot M$ is the automata chain obtained by successive I-refinements of $\mathcal{E}_A \otimes M$.*

Proof. It is clear that the chain of automata $\mathcal{E}_A \odot M$ can be obtained by successive I-refinements of $\mathcal{E}_A \otimes M$ since the definition is identical except the removal of initial states q_i of the ith automaton not in the set of final states of the $(i-1)$th automaton. It is also clear that $\mathcal{E}_A \odot M$ is I-refined since we have $\forall i$, $I^i \subseteq F^{i-1}$.

Property 6. *Let $\mathcal{E}_A$ be an automata chain and $M = (Q_M, E_M, T_M, I_M, F_M)$ an automaton. We have $Sli^{-1}(\mathcal{E}_A \odot M) = Sli^{-1}(\mathcal{E}_A \otimes M)$.*

This can be proved using Property 2 and Property 5.

Given this new definition of synchronization, a formalization of incremental diagnosis can be proposed. Provided that $\mathcal{E}_{Obs_n} = (Obs^1, \ldots, Obs^n)$ is a correct slicing of Obs_n we have: $\Delta_n = Obs_n \otimes Mod = Sli^{-1}(\mathcal{E}_{Obs_n} \odot Mod)$.

We note $\forall i$, $\mathcal{E}_{Obs_i} = (Obs^1, \ldots, Obs^i)$, the automata chain of the first i observations automata. Let $i < n$, and $\mathcal{E}_{\Delta_i} = (\Delta^1, \ldots, \Delta^i)$ the automata chain resulting from the incremental synchronization of $\mathcal{E}_{Obs_i}$ with the system model Mod. We can incrementally compute $\mathcal{E}_{\Delta_{i+1}} = \mathcal{E}_{Obs_{i+1}} \odot Mod$ as follows:

Result 2. $\mathcal{E}_{\Delta_{i+1}} = (\Delta^1, \ldots, \Delta^i, \Delta^{i+1})$ *with $\Delta^{i+1} = (Obs^{i+1} \otimes Mod^{\#})[F_\Delta^i]$ where F_Δ^i is the set of final states of Δ^i.*

This result comes from the fact that $Mod^- = Mod^{\#}$ (all the states in Mod are final states). Thus it is possible to compute the automata chain that represents the diagnosis in an incremental way by synchronizing the one after the other each of the automata of the observation chain.

We note Obs_i the reconstruction of $\mathcal{E}_{Obs_i}$. Then:

Result 3. *Let $\Delta_i = Sli^{-1}(\mathcal{E}_{\Delta_i})$. Then, $\Delta_i = Obs_i \otimes Mod$.*

6   Temporal Windows Diagnosis

It has been proved above that, at the condition to have a correct slicing of the observation automaton, it is possible to incrementally compute the global system diagnosis by considering in sequence the slices of observations and computing for each of them its diagnosis slice. In this section, we show that this result can be instantiated to the case where the observation automaton is sliced according to time, according to temporal windows. Firstly, we extend the definition of *correct slicing* to *temporally correct slicing* by requiring temporal properties. Then, the incremental computation is demonstrated as valid on temporal windows which correctly slice the observation automaton.

Definition 19 (Correct sequence of temporal windows). *Let t_i be time instants and $[t_0, t_n]$ be the global diagnosis temporal window. A sequence of temporal windows is correct w.r.t $[t_0, t_n]$ iff it is a sequence $\mathcal{W} = (\mathcal{W}_1, \ldots, \mathcal{W}_i, \ldots, \mathcal{W}_n)$ such that $\forall i \in \{1, \ldots, n\}$, $\mathcal{W}_i = [t_{i-1}, t_i]$.*

Definition 20 (Temporally correct slicing). *Let Obs_n be the observation automaton on $[t_0, t_n]$. The automata chain $\mathcal{E}_{Obs_n} = (Obs^{\mathcal{W}_1}, \ldots, Obs^{\mathcal{W}_n})$ is a temporally correct slicing of Obs_n according to $\mathcal{W} = (\mathcal{W}_1, \ldots, \mathcal{W}_i, \ldots, \mathcal{W}_n)$ iff:*

- *the slicing is correct;*
- *$\mathcal{W}$ is a correct sequence of temporal windows w.r.t $[t_0, t_n]$; and*
- *for each trajectory in $Obs^{\mathcal{W}_i}$, the transitions have occured during $[t_{i-1}, t_i]$ (i.e the observations labelling the transitions have been emitted by the system in $\mathcal{W}_i$).*

Let us remark that, for any $i \in \{1, \ldots, n\}$, the initial states of $Obs^{\mathcal{W}_i}$ are possible states at $t_{i\ 1}$ and that the final states of $Obs^{\mathcal{W}_i}$ are possible states at t_i. Note also that, if a final state of a temporal window can be reached by two trajectories, it is required that both trajectories have occured during the temporal window, i.e the final state is a possible state in t_i whatever the trajectory used to get it.

The results of section 4 can be used in the case of temporally correct slicing. Let us denote $\forall i$, $\mathcal{E}_{Obs_{\mathcal{W}_i}} = (Obs^{\mathcal{W}_1}, \ldots, Obs^{\mathcal{W}_i})$. Let $i < n$, and $\mathcal{E}_{\Delta_{\mathcal{W}_i}} = \mathcal{E}_{Obs_{\mathcal{W}_i}} \odot Mod = (\Delta^{\mathcal{W}_1}, \ldots, \Delta^{\mathcal{W}_i})$. Then, $\mathcal{E}_{\Delta_{\mathcal{W}_{i+1}}} = \mathcal{E}_{Obs_{\mathcal{W}_{i+1}}} \odot Mod$ can be computed as follows:

Result 4. $\mathcal{E}_{\Delta_{\mathcal{W}_{i+1}}} = (\Delta^{\mathcal{W}_1}, \ldots, \Delta^{\mathcal{W}_i}, \Delta^{\mathcal{W}_{i+1}})$ *with* $\Delta^{\mathcal{W}_{i+1}} = (Obs^{\mathcal{W}_{i+1}} \otimes Mod^{\#})[F_{\Delta}^{\mathcal{W}_i}]$ *where $F_{\Delta}^{\mathcal{W}_i}$ is the set of final states of $\Delta^{\mathcal{W}_i}$.*

Let $Obs_{\mathcal{W}_i}$, the automaton provided by the reconstruction operation on $\mathcal{E}_{Obs_{\mathcal{W}_i}}$. $Obs_{\mathcal{W}_i}$ represents the observations emitted on the period $[t_0, t_i]$.

Result 5. *Let $\Delta_{\mathcal{W}_i} = Sli^{-1}(\mathcal{E}_{\Delta_{\mathcal{W}_i}})$. Then, $\Delta_{\mathcal{W}_i} = Obs_{\mathcal{W}_i} \otimes Mod$ is the diagnosis of the period $[t_0, t_i]$.*

The incremental computation of diagnosis from temporal windows seems promising firstly because the diagnosis gives then the possible states of the system at time t_i w.r.t the (possibly uncertain) observations gathered at time t_i. Another good reason appears when turning into an on-line diagnosis context. The observation automata chain has now to be built on-line, i.e without knowing by advance the whole set of observations gathered on the global diagnosis window. This point will not be examined in this paper but it can be shown that taking advantage of temporal information, it is easier, on-line, to build temporally correct slicing than only correct slicing. Observations, which should be considered as possible in the general case, can be discarded as not satisfying the temporal constraints collected on the system behaviour (as delays between observations emission and reception; communication channels politics...).

7   Conclusion

In this paper, we formalized the incremental computation of diagnosis for discrete-event systems. We introduced and defined the concept of automata chain that enables us to handle slices of observations and slices of diagnosis rather than global observations and global diagnosis. We proved that the diagnosis can be computed, by using automata chain, in a modular way and, more efficiently, in an incremental way. We then presented how the results can be extended to the case where observations are sliced according to temporal windows.

In the diagnostic literature the notion of incremental diagnosis is relatively new. It can be explained by the fact that, in most cases, observations are supposed to be totally ordered, received without delays, and without any loss. In these cases, the problem of slicing the observations does not exist. In [2] however, the authors examine the case where observations are uncertain and represented by partially ordered graphs. In the case of decentralized systems, Pencolé *et al.* [7] consider the incremental diagnosis computation applied to the on-line diagnosis for telecommunication networks. The property of *safe window* is defined and algorithms are given in the case where the temporal windows satisfy this property. Extensions to more complicated cases are proposed. Compared to this, our proposal is more general and give a formal view of the problem which allows to better situate the algorithmic approach proposed in [7]. In [8] an incremental approach of diagnosis is considered from a model-checking point of view.

Our study exhibits the (non trivial) correctness properties that the observation slicing, in an automata chain, has to satisfy in order to guarantee the completeness of the diagnosis computation. This first step is then essential before considering the incrementality of on-line diagnosis computation.

The next step will consider the building of the observations automata chain in the context of off-line and then on-line diagnosis. The case of on-line diagnosis is particularly interesting since the goal is to dynamically build an automata chain without having all the observations. As seen at the end of section 6, this task can take profit of temporal information known on the system, even if, for complexity reasons, these temporal constraints are not encoded in the system model. Another interesting point is to use the concept of automata chains for the diagnosis of reconfigurable systems.

Annex

Proof (Property 1). Let $A = (Q, E, T, I, F)$ be an automaton and $\mathcal{E}_A = (A^1, \ldots, A^n)$ an automata chain with $A^i = (Q^i, E^i, T^i, I^i, F^i)$ so that $\mathcal{E}_A$ is a correct slicing of A. Let $A_R = (Q_R, E_R, T_R, I_R, F_R)$ be the reconstruction of $\mathcal{E}_A$. We have to prove that the set of trajectories of A (which is the same as the set of trajectories of $\mathcal{E}_A$) equals the set of trajectories of A_R.

Let $\mathcal{E}_{A_{1,2}} = (A^1, A^2)$. $\mathcal{E}_{A_{1,2}}$ is an automata chain. Let $A_{1,2}$ be the reconstruction of $\mathcal{E}_{A_{1,2}}$. Let us consider a transition (q, l, q') of $A_{1,2}$.

Remark 1:$\{q, q'\} \subseteq Q^1$ or $\{q, q'\} \subseteq Q^2$ (because $(q, l, q') \in T_{1,2} = T^1 \cup T^2$). Consequently, if a state does not belong to Q^2 (resp. Q^1), it belongs to Q^1 (resp.

Q^2) and its predecessor too. Moreover, if a path on $A_{1,2}$ goes from a state from Q^1 to a state from Q^2, there exists at least one state on the path belonging to $Q^1 \cap Q^2$.

Remark 2: $\forall j \in \{1, 2\}$, $\{q, q'\} \subseteq Q^j \Rightarrow (q, l, q') \in T^j$.

i) $\forall traj = ((q_0, \ldots, q_m), (l_1, \ldots, l_m))$, trajectory of $\mathcal{E}_{A_{1,2}}$, then $traj$ is also a trajectory of $A_{1,2}$ since (by definition) any transition of A^1 or A^2 is a transition of $A_{1,2}$, $q_0 \in I^1$ and $q_m \in F^2$.

ii) $\forall traj = ((q_0, \ldots, q_m), (l_1, \ldots, l_m))$, trajectory of $A_{1,2}$. Let k be the smallest value in $\{0, \ldots, m\}$ so that $q_k \in Q^1 \cap Q^2$ (k exists due to Remark 1).
$\forall i \leq k$, $q_i \in Q^1$, so $traj^1 = ((q_0, \ldots, q_k), (l_1, \ldots, l_k))$ is a trajectory of A^1 (cf. Remark 2).

Let us now prove that $\forall i > k$, $q_i \in Q^2$. Let us suppose it exists j, the smallest value so that $j > k$ and $q_j \notin Q^2$. $q_j \in Q^1$ and, due to Remark 1, $q_{j-1} \in Q^1 \cap Q^2$. For the same reason as for k, $\exists l$ the smallest value so that $l > j$ and $q_l \in Q^1 \cap Q^2$. The path $p = ((q_{j-1}, \ldots, q_l), (l_j, \ldots, l_l))$ is a path of A^1. But, since q_{j-1} and q_l are both belonging to $Q^1 \cap Q^2$, p is also a path of A^2. It implies that q_j is a state of Q^2, which is in contradiction with the existence of j. So, $\forall i > k$, $q_i \in Q^2$. And $traj^2 = ((q_k, \ldots, q_m), (l_{k+1}, \ldots, l_m))$ is a trajectory of A^2. $traj$ is built by reconstruction of $traj^1$ and $traj^2$. It is then a trajectory of $\mathcal{E}_{A_{1,2}}$.

Since the trajectories of $A_{1,2}$ and (A^1, A^2) are equal, $\mathcal{E}_A$ and $(A_{1,2}, A^3, \ldots, A^n)$ have the same trajectories. We define recursively $\forall i > 2$, $A_{1,i}$ the reconstruction of $(A_{1,i-1}, A^i)$. Then, we prove recursively that $\mathcal{E}_A$ has the same trajectories as $(A_{1,i}, A^{i+1}, \ldots, A^n)$ in particular $(A_{1,n}) = (A_R)$. So, $\mathcal{E}_A$ and A_R have the same trajectories. As $\mathcal{E}_A$ is a correct slicing of A, $A = A_R$.

References

1. Cassandras, C.G., Lafortune, S.: Introduction to Discrete Event Systems. Kluwer Academic Publishers (1999)
2. Baroni, P., Lamperti, G., Pogliano, P., Zanella, M.: Diagnosis of large active systems. Artificial Intelligence **110** (1999) 135–183
3. Cordier, M.O., Thiébaux, S.: Event-based diagnosis for evolutive systems. In: 5th International Workshop on Principles of Diagnosis (DX-94). (1994) 64–69
4. Barral, C., McIlraith, S., Son, T.: Formulating diagnostic problem solving using an action language with narratives and sensing. In: International Conference on Knowledge Representation and Reasoning (KR'2000). (2000) 311–322
5. Console, L., Picardi, C., Ribaudo, M.: Diagnosis and diagnosability analysis using PEPA. In: 14th European Conference on Artificial Intelligence (ECAI-2000), Berlin, Allemagne (2000) 131–135
6. Lunze, J.: Discrete-event modelling and diagnosis of quantized dynamical systems. In: 10th International Workshop on Principles of Diagnosis (DX-99), Loch Awe, Écosse, Royaume Uni (1999) 147–154
7. Pencolé, Y., Cordier, M.O., Rozé, L.: Incremental decentralized diagnosis approach for the supervision of a telecommunication network. In: 12th International Workshop on Principles of Diagnosis (DX'01). (2001) 151–158
8. Cordier, M.O., Largouët, C.: Using model-checking techniques for diagnosing discrete-event systems. In: 12th International Workshop on Principles of Diagnosis (DX'01). (2001) 39–46

Configurations for Inference from Causal Statements: Preliminary Report

Philippe Besnard[1], Marie-Odile Cordier[1], and Yves Moinard[1]

IRISA, Campus de Beaulieu, 35042 Rennes cedex, France
{besnard, cordier, moinard}@irisa.fr

Abstract. Our aim is to provide a rigorous logical framework for describing causal relations (involved in reasoning tasks such as diagnosis). We propose a framework which is minimal in that only a few properties, hopefully uncontroversial, are imposed upon it. Our semantics of a causal relation is based on collections of possible cases, called "configurations".

We mention several features which causation makes undesirable despite commonly held beliefs. We show how our logic avoid such pitfalls and generally conforms with a strict view of causation.

1 Motivation

Causation as entertained here concerns the usual relationship that may hold between states of affairs (thus departing from the concept favored by many who focus on events —up to the point of insisting that causation is based on events[1]). For the relationship to hold, the cause must be what brings about the effect. Here, the cause always brings about the effect (ruling out that "smoking causes cancer" may count as true). Such a strict reading makes a probabilistic interpretation of causation [6] (whether the probabilities are subjective or not) less appealing but is more sympathetic to the celebrated counterfactual analysis of causation [3]. As is well-known, the idea of causal dependence is thus originally stated in terms of events (where c and e are two distinct possible events, e causally depends on c if and only if c occurs counterfactually implies e occurs and c does not occur counterfactually implies e does not occur) but facts have now been reinstated [5] (cf causation involving negative existential facts: "she didn't get a speeding ticket because she was able to slow down early enough", that cannot be expressed in terms of events because nothing happened). Although the counterfactual analysis of causation is meant to address the issue of truth for causation, the aim here is not a logic of causation: The purpose is not to give truth conditions for causal statements in terms that do not themselves appeal to causal concepts. The aim is instead to provide truth-preserving conditions between causal statements. E.g., the logic will distinguish between a pair of statements essentially related as cause and effect and a pair of statements which are merely effects of a common

---

[1] The event-based view is far from uncontroversial: The gravitational attraction of the moon is said to cause tides although no event but a principle, is given as the cause.

S. Bandini and S. Manzoni (Eds.): AI*IA 2005, LNAI 3673, pp. 282–285, 2005.

cause (correlations being not confused with instances of causation —something conceptually troublesome for probabilistic approaches).

When dealing with a cause (e.g., looking for something which could explain certain facts), cases involving some effect due to that cause are precious as such cases contribute to what the cause is. Accordingly, they must be reasoned upon if inference about causes is to take place. It thus seems like a good logic for causes would arise from a semantics based on collections of cases, to be called configurations that gather instances of a given cause yielding some effect(s).

The setting of configurations is what permits to discriminate correlations from instances of causes: Should α and β be equivalent for example, no possibility exists that one be true but the other false; when it comes to describing causation with respect to δ, nothing requires to mention β for the reason that configurations are only supposed to take causation but not truth into account (if δ causes the single effect α, to be written δ $causes$ $\langle\alpha\rangle$ in our formalism, each configuration for δ must mention α as δ causes α but it need not be so for β —because δ does not cause β, regardless of the fact that β is true exactly when α is).

Now, α $causes$ $\langle\beta_1,\ldots,\beta_n\rangle$ means that the effects caused by α consist exactly of $\beta_1,\ldots,\beta_n$ where each β_i is the effect caused by a certain occurrence of α. Importantly, it is thus possible to express that a cause has alternative effects like in the next example: "Turning the wheel causes the car to go left or right". Among the configurations for "turning the wheel", some must include "the car goes left" and the others must include "the car goes right". [2]

A formula α $causes$ $\langle\beta_1,\ldots,\beta_n\rangle$ states that our causal knowledge includes the fact that α has $\{\beta_1,\ldots,\beta_n\}$ as an exhaustive set of alternative effects. Here, "exhaustive" means that $\{\beta_1,\ldots,\beta_n\}$ accurately describes a set of alternative effects of a given kind (while not precluding the existence of other kinds of effects, to be specified by means of other causal formulas). Discretizing temperatures to simplify matters, flu $causes$ $\langle t_{38}, t_{39}, t_{40}\rangle$ illustrates the point here: Adding t_{37} or removing t_{40} would modify the intended meaning for the disease called flu. However, adding formulas such as flu $causes$ $\langle fatigue\rangle$ is possible. In short, from such causal formulas together with classical formulas, some consequences are to be formally derived according to the contents of the causal configurations.

The replacement of equivalents (δ $causes$ $\langle\alpha\rangle$ and $\alpha \leftrightarrow \beta$ entail δ $causes$ $\langle\beta\rangle$) must fail, here is an example adapted from Mellor. "Laura Welch being George Bush's wife" is equivalent with "Laura Welch being the First Lady". However, "George Bush has won the election is the cause for Laura Welch being George Bush's wife" is absurd and fails to be equivalent with "George Bush has won the election is the cause for Laura Welch being the First Lady" which is true. A few other commonly held beliefs[3] fail, but lack of space prevents us to discuss them.

---

[2] A cause with alternative effects is not formalized here as a cause with a single disjunctive effect because the latter notion seems shaky. About the example that Suzy may throw a rock at a glass bottle and Billy may throw a rock at another glass bottle, some authors deny that the disjunctive item "Suzy's bottle shatters or Billy's bottle shatters" is apt to be caused: There is no such thing as a disjunctive effect.

[3] Transitivity is highly controversial, with some prominent authors defending it [2] [4].

2   Formal Development

The language of classical propositional logic is extended with formulas built from causal operators *causes* having multiple arguments: α *causes* $\langle \beta_1, \ldots, \beta_n \rangle$ where α and $\beta_1, \ldots, \beta_n$ are atomic formulas of classical propositional logic. Henceforth, there are no disjunctive effects (see footnote 2). Instead, α *causes* $\langle \beta, \gamma \rangle$ can intuitively be taken to mean that α causes β or γ.

Arbitrary formulas are allowed: e.g., $(a\ causes\ \langle c \rangle) \rightarrow \neg(b\ causes\ \langle c, d \rangle) \ldots$

$\mathcal{I}$ denoting the set of interpretations in classical propositional logic, a subset of $2^{\mathcal{I}}$ is called a *configuration* (cases of reference between a cause and its effects).

A *causal interpretation* is a pair $\langle \mathcal{S}, I \rangle$ where I is an interpretation in classical propositional logic, $\mathcal{S}$ is a family (indexed by the propositional atomic formulas) of configurations. I.e., $I \in \mathcal{I}$ and $\mathcal{S} = \{S_\alpha, S_\beta, \ldots\}$ where $S_\alpha \subseteq 2^{\mathcal{I}}, S_\beta \subseteq 2^{\mathcal{I}}, \ldots$ as $\alpha, \beta, \ldots$ is a list of all propositional atomic formulas.

A causal interpretation $C = \langle \mathcal{S}, I \rangle$ *satisfies* a formula γ (written $C \Vdash \gamma$ which can also be read as γ is true in C) according to the following recursive rules:

$C \Vdash \neg\delta$	iff $C \not\Vdash \delta$
$C \Vdash \delta \vee \epsilon$	iff $C \Vdash \delta$ or $C \Vdash \epsilon$
$C \Vdash \delta \rightarrow \epsilon$	iff $C \not\Vdash \delta$ or $C \Vdash \epsilon$
$C \Vdash \delta \wedge \epsilon$	iff $C \Vdash \delta$ and $C \Vdash \epsilon$
$C \Vdash \alpha$	iff $I \models \alpha$ for α propositional atomic formula

$$C \Vdash \delta\ causes\ \langle \gamma_1, \ldots, \gamma_n \rangle \text{ iff } \begin{cases} I \not\models \delta \wedge \neg\gamma_1 \wedge \ldots \wedge \neg\gamma_n \text{ and } \mathcal{S} \text{ is such that:} \\ \forall X \in S_\delta \quad \exists\gamma_i \quad X \models \gamma_i \ \& \ \exists Y \in S_{\gamma_i} \quad X \models Y \\ \forall\gamma_i \quad \exists X \in S_\delta \quad X \models \gamma_i \ \& \ \exists Y \in S_{\gamma_i} \quad X \models Y \end{cases}$$

where the symbol $\models$ denotes satisfaction in classical propositional logic.

As the configuration S_δ is supposed to list the cases involving the particular cause δ, the requirement $\forall X \in S_\delta \quad \exists\gamma_i \quad X \models \gamma_i$ expresses that there is no case in which δ causes none of $\gamma_1, \ldots, \gamma_n$ and the requirement $\forall\gamma_i \quad \exists X \in S_\delta \quad X \models \gamma_i$ expresses that each of $\gamma_1, \ldots, \gamma_n$ does exist as an effect of δ. The cases gathered in the causal configuration for δ provide all and only the effects caused by δ.

The subcondition $\exists Y \in S_{\gamma_i} X \models Y$ ensures that the causal configuration for γ_i includes a case that gathers the specific effects of γ_i when γ_i is caused by δ.

Back to the example (flu causes some high temperature), let $40°$ cause shiver. Take $C = \langle \mathcal{S}, I \rangle$ where $I = \emptyset$ (i.e., $I \models \neg flu$ and so on) and $\mathcal{S}$ be such that

$$S_{flu} = \{\{t_{38}\}, \{t_{39}\}, \{t_{40} \wedge shiver\}\} \qquad S_{t_{40}} = \{\{shiver\}\}$$
$$S_{t_{38}} = S_{t_{39}} = S_{shiver} = \{\{\top\}\} \qquad S_\top = \emptyset$$

- Let us verify $C \Vdash t_{40}\ causes\ \langle shiver \rangle$. So, we check $C \Vdash \delta\ causes\ \langle \gamma_1, \ldots, \gamma_n \rangle$ when δ is t_{40} and $\gamma_1 = shiver$ (with $n = 1$).
  - As to the first condition, $I \not\models \delta \wedge \neg\gamma_1 \wedge \ldots \wedge \neg\gamma_n$ because $I \models \neg t_{40}$.
  - The second condition $\forall X \in S_\delta \exists\gamma_i X \models \gamma_i \ \& \ \exists Y \in S_{\gamma_i} X \models Y$ is then instantiated by: $X = \{shiver\}$ and $\gamma_i = shiver$. Hence, $X \models \gamma_i$ holds. It remains to find $Y \in S_{\gamma_i}$ satisfying $X \models Y$. Clearly, $Y = \{\top\}$ will do.
  - The third condition $\forall\gamma_i \exists X \in S_\delta X \models \gamma_i \ \& \ \exists Y \in S_{\gamma_i} X \models Y$ is similar to the second condition because γ_i can only be *shiver* due to $n = 1$.

- Let us now check $C \not\Vdash t_{40}$ *causes* $\langle \top \rangle$. As above, $X = \{shiver\}$ and it is enough to consider the second condition: Its rightmost part $\exists Y \in S_{\gamma_i}\ X \models Y$ fails because γ_i is $\top$ but $S_\top$ is empty (hence there is no Y in S_{γ_i}).
- Let us verify $C \Vdash flu$ *causes* $\langle t_{38}, t_{39}, t_{40} \rangle$. Stated otherwise, we check $C \Vdash \delta$ *causes* $\langle \gamma_1, \ldots, \gamma_n \rangle$ when δ is flu while $\langle \gamma_1, \ldots, \gamma_n \rangle$ is $\langle t_{38}, t_{39}t_{40} \rangle$.
  - Of course, $I \not\models \delta \wedge \neg\gamma_1 \wedge \ldots \wedge \neg\gamma_n$ because $I \models \neg flu$.
  - The second condition requires to check three values for X as follows:

    $\begin{array}{llll} X = \{t_{38}\} & \text{take } \gamma_i = t_{38} \text{ then } S_{\gamma_i} = \{\top\} & \text{hence } Y = \top \\ X = \{t_{39}\} & \text{take } \gamma_i = t_{39} \text{ then } S_{\gamma_i} - \{\top\} & \text{hence } Y = \top \\ X = \{t_{40} \wedge shiver\} & \text{take } \gamma_i = t_{40} \text{ then } S_{\gamma_i} = \{shiver\} & \text{hence } Y = shiver \end{array}$

  - Lastly, the third condition requires to check three values for γ_i as follows:

    $\begin{array}{llll} \gamma_i = t_{38} \text{ take } X = \{t_{38}\} & \text{then } S_{\gamma_i} = \{\top\} & \text{hence } Y = \top \\ \gamma_i = t_{39} \text{ take } X = \{t_{39}\} & \text{then } S_{\gamma_i} = \{\top\} & \text{hence } Y = \top \\ \gamma_i = t_{40} \text{ take } X = \{t_{40} \wedge shiver\} & \text{then } S_{\gamma_i} = \{shiver\} & \text{hence } Y = shiver \end{array}$

$C \not\Vdash flu$ *causes* $\langle t_{38}, t_{39} \rangle$ because the second condition fails: There is $X \in S_{flu}$ (i.e. $X = \{t_{40} \wedge shiver\}$) for which no γ_i (i.e. neither t_{38} nor t_{39}) obeys $X \models \gamma_i$.

Note that $C \not\Vdash flu$ *causes* $\langle t_{37}, t_{38}, t_{39}, t_{40} \rangle$ because the third condition fails: There exists γ_i (namely, $\gamma_i = t_{37}$) such that no $X \in S_{flu}$ satisfies $X \models \gamma_i$.

3   Inferring Causal Predictions and Explanations

There are two ways to reason from causes and effects. One is merely deduction: From what is known to be true and what is known to cause what, infer what else is true. The other is abduction: From what is observed and what is known to cause what, infer what could explain the current facts. Either task ignores discovering causal relationships: These are postulated (abductive/deductive premises).

The above account of causes being rather strict, our logic can serve as a basis for both tasks. As for deduction, the premises consist of facts and causal statements whereas the conclusions are statements expected to be true by virtue of the premises. E.g. $(\alpha \vee \beta) \wedge \delta$ together with δ *causes* $\langle \gamma \rangle$ yield $(\alpha \vee \beta) \wedge \gamma \wedge \delta$.

As for inferring what could be a cause of a given fact, consider the information stating that δ causes either α or β or γ. Consider further that β happens to be the case (it is a fact). In the light of the information available, it seems right to infer *at least tentatively* that δ is a possible cause of β being true. In fact, δ *causes* $\langle \alpha, \beta, \gamma \rangle$ makes it possible to regard δ as a causal explanation for α.

References

1. Besnard Ph. & Cordier M.-O. Inferring Causal Explanations. In Hunter & Parsons, editors, *ECSQARU-99*, pp. 55–67, LNAI Vol. 1638, Springer, 1999.
2. Hall N. Causation and the Price of Transitivity. *J. of Philosophy* 97:198–222, 2000.
3. Lewis D. Causation. *Journal of Philosophy* 70:556–567, 1973.
4. Lewis D. Causation as Influence. *Journal of Philosophy* 97:182–197, 2000.
5. Mellor D. H. *The Facts of Causation*. Routledge, 1995.
6. Pearl J. *Causality*. Cambridge University Press, 2000.
7. Shafer G. *The Art of Causal Conjecture*. MIT Press, 1996.

Laying the Foundations for a Formal Theory of Drama

Rossana Damiano[1], Vincenzo Lombardo[1], and Antonio Pizzo[2]

[1] Dipartimento di Informatica and CIRMA,
Cso Svizzera, 185 Torino, Italy
[2] DAMS and CIRMA, Via S. Ottavio 20, Torino Italy

Abstract. The goal of this research is to lay the foundations for a formal theory of drama, that abstracts from the procedural and interactive aspects involved in the generation of dramatic content. The theory characterizes dramatic qualities by reconciling the structural accounts provided by traditional drama analysis with an agent-based perspective on characters.

1 Motivations and Formalization

In the design of AI systems for communication and entertainment, much attention has been devoted to the dramatic qualities exhibited by interactive applications. Typical applications span from artificial characters for entertainment and instruction, to interactive systems for storytelling and drama [1,2,3]. The aim of this paper is to lay the foundations of a formal theory that systematizes the basic aspects of drama in a direct and explicit model, with an immediate integration with agent-based theories. The theory, called *Drammar*, abstracts from the interactive and procedural aspects of drama generation, and is intended as the starting point for specifying, implementing and evaluating practical storytelling systems in a principled way.

The notions of direction, character and plot, pervasive throughout the literature on drama analysis since Aristotle, are the three main components of the drama ontology incorporated in Drammar. The goal of a drama is to make audience perceive what is intuitively called a "story" by displaying the actions of some *characters* in conflict; actions are organized in a *plot*; the plot moves toward a *direction*. Concerning the structure of drama, it has been a well known convention to segment the list of actions that form a drama into a number of units or sections [6]. Such units, despite terminological disparities, are of the same nature, so that some authors define drama as a recursive or "fractal" structure [7].

Drammar is structured in two levels: the *actional* level models the intentional behaviour of the characters in a plot as intelligent, goal-directed agents. The *directional* level accounts for dramatic meaning, abstracting from the intentionality of the characters through the use of attributes that model the effect of plot incidents onto the characters' rational and emotional state. The *drama direction* is a change function that transforms the rational and emotional state of a character into a different state [4]. Such states are defined through values assigned to a number of *attributes* of the characters (or *dramatis personae*), defined as a set of attributes. The set of attributes defining a character combines a rational, BDI perspective with an emotional component.

S. Bandini and S. Manzoni (Eds.): AI*IA 2005, LNAI 3673, pp. 286–289, 2005.

A *Dramatis_persona* $CHAR$ is a pair $\langle ATT, POLARITY \rangle$, where ATT is a subset of a $POOL$ of attributes; $POLARITY$ is a set of pairs $\langle x, v_x \rangle$, where $x \in ATT$ e $v_x \in \{+,-\}$. All the attributes in ATT are assigned a value in $POLARITY$ and for each attribute only one assignment is permitted.

The Direction is a function D that specifies the value changes of the characters' attributes after the execution of the plot. So, the domain of the direction function is a State (where a State is a set of Polarities of attributes), and the co-domain is another State. So, let a State be $\bigcup_i CHAR_i.POLARITY$:

$$D : State_i \rightarrow State_f$$

The relationship between the value changes of the rational/emotional states of the characters and the actual actions and events listed in a drama is stated at the actional level through the notion of *drama goal*. The drama goal is the world state that realizes the Direction, and it is operatively specified as the achievement or the negation of the goal of a certain character, namely the drama protagonist.

The Plot is the component that carries out the polarity inversions described by the Direction function. The Plot is a sequence of elementary units called called *Beats*, pure actional units formed by a action-reaction pair [6]. Notice that some Beat may not change any attribute value, but every change does occur in some Beat.

The three components described above form a Drama-unit, that represents by itself all the basic aspects of drama. Formally, a Drama-unit is a triple:

- *Dramatis_personae* is a finite set of Dramatis_persona;
- *Direction* is a function D defined as above;
- *Plot* is a list of Beats $\langle B_1, B_2, \ldots, B_m \rangle$,

and the condition holds that at least one attribute inverts its polarity.

In Drammar, drama-units are subdivided into smaller drama-units, resulting in a tree of drama-units. The leaves of this tree are directly connected to beats, and its root is the properly called drama, the highest-level unit that subsumes the entire sequence of beats, and is not subsumed by other drama-units. The units of the drama and their directions are combined in a drama-specific progression related with the emotional engagement of the audience via the protagonist's fate. Dramatic actions in the plot trace a curve related to the fulfilment of the direction. Each drama-unit, with its goal, has both a temporal position and a *dramatic value* within the plot. This value is given by the number of value changes that occur within the unit, either in a beat directly included by the unit or in a beat included in one of its sub-units.

2   An Example

We apply the formal system Drammar to the definition of a linear drama, the well-known Hitchcock's North by Northwest [8] (see the table in Figure 1). North by Northwest is about a middle-aged advertising executive Roger Thornhill who is mistaken for the (non-existent) government agent George Kaplan by a gang of spies lead by Mr Vandamm. He gets involved in a series of misadventures and is pursued across the States

ID	Description	Drama Goal	Attribute	Value	Attribute-type	Dramatic Value
1	R. mistaken for Kaplan and kidnapped by Vandamm's gang	Kidnapped (Roger) True	Distress	+	EMOTION.well-being	1
2	R. gets aware of mismatch and tries get out of trouble	Involved (Roger) True	Individualism	-	BELIEF.norms	20
2.1	R. meets Vandamm	Agreement (Roger,Vandamm) False	Disappointment	+	EMOTION.prospect-based	4
2.1.1	Vandamm addresses R. as Kaplan	Mentioned (Vandamm,Kaplan) True	Distress	+	EMOTION.well-being	1
2.1.2	Vandamm threatens R. of death	Threatened (Vandamm,Roger) True	Anger	+	EMOTION.well-being/attribution	1
2.1.3	Vandamm's gang tries to kill R.; R. escapes	Killed (gang, Roger) False	Relief	+	EMOTION.prospect-based	1
2.2	Nobody believes R.; R. accused of shooting Townsend	Outcast (Roger) True	Isolation	+	BELIEF.world-state	4
2.2.1	R.'s report not believed by anybody	Discredited (Roger) True	Anger	+	EMOTION.well-being/attribution	1
2.2.2	R. leaves his mother	Left (Roger.Mother) True	Submission	-	BELIEF.social	1
2.2.3	R. is believed to have killed Townsend	Falsely_accused (Roger.assassination) True	Disappointment	+	EMOTION.prospect-based	1
2.3	R. escapes police, meets Eve, seduction, fake appointment	Seduced (Eve.Roger) True	Love	+	EMOTION.attraction	6
2.3.1	R. runs away by train	Caught (Roger.Train) True	Relief	+	EMOTION.prospect-based	1
2.3.2	E. hides R. from police in the cabin	Hidden (Roger) True	Gratitude	+	EMOTION.well-being-attribution	1
2.3.3	R. and E. sleep together	Had_sex (Roger.Eve) True	Satisfaction	+	EMOTION.prospect-based	1
2.3.4	E. fixes the fake appointment with Kaplan	Deceived (Eve,Roger)True	Hope	+	EMOTION.prospect-based	1
2.3.5	Airplane tries to kill R.	Meeting (Roger,Kaplan) False	Disappointment	+	EMOTION.prospect-based	1
2.4	R. calls E.'s bluff and Professor explains	Explain (Professor,Roger) True	Anger	+	EMOTION.well-being-attribution	5
2.4.1	R. discloses E.	Deceive (Eve,Roger) False	Reproach	+	EMOTION.attribution	1
2.4.2	R. finds about Vandamm and E.	Unmasked (Roger.Vandamm) True	Anger	+	EMOTION.well-being-attribution	1
2.4.3	R. arrested and meets Prof.	Meeting (Professor,Roger) True	Truth	+	BELIEF.world-state	1
2.4.4	E.'s identity revealed	Revealed (Eve's identity,Roger) True	Pity	+	EMOTION.fortune-of-others	1
3	R. takes revenge	Married (Roger,Eve) True	Family	+	BELIEF.norms	8
3.1	E. pretends shooting R. at M. Rushmore	Collaboration (Roger,Eve) True	Relationship	+	BELIEF.social	3
3.1.1	E. fake-shoots R.	Deceived (Roger,Vandamm) True	Satisfaction	+	EMOTION.prospect-based	1
3.1.2	E. to leave with Vandamm	Coupled (Roger,Eve) True	Love	+	EMOTION.attraction	1
3.2	Chase and fight at M. Rushmore	Saved (Roger.Eve) True	Gratification	+	EMOTION.well-being/attribution	4
3.2.1	R. escapes from hospital	Rebellion (Roger,Professor) True	Independence	+	BELIEF.normative	1
3.2.2	Leonard discloses Eve's secret	Informs (Leonard,Vandamm, Eve's trick) True	Fear	+	EMOTION.prospect-based	1
3.2.3	R. kills Leonard on M. Rushmore	Killed (Roger,Leonard) True	Relief	+	EMOTION.prospect-based	1

Fig. 1. Analysis of North by Northwest

by both the spies and the government whilst being helped by a beautiful blonde Eve Kendall. Eventually, he will discover that Eve is an undercover CIA agent and together they will defeat the evil gang, on a thrilling sequence on the Mount Rushmore.

The first column, ID, reports the hierarchical structure of Drama-units in North by Northwest (the table rows); the levels of the hierarchy correspond to acts, sequences and scenes in the standard filmic terminology. The second column, Description, contains an informal description of each Drama-unit. The third column, Drama goal, reports the drama goal through which the direction of a unit is accomplished. For example, Act 2 leads to a state in which the moral standards of the protagonist, Roger Thornill, have been affected, so as to make him more inclined to help the others (the predicate "Involved (Roger)" becomes true). This goal is in turn accomplished trough the drama-goals of the sub-units of that unit: Roger's individualism is affected by the need to take himself out the troubles he got into (Sequences 2.1 and 2.2), by Eve's seduction (2.3) and by the awareness of a conflict between the CIA and Vandamm (2.4).

The last three columns, Attribute, Value and Attribute-type, describe the direction of each Drama-unit. For example, in Act I, Roger falls into an emotional state of distress as a consequence of being kidnapped by Vandamm's gang, setting the "distress" attribute to +; in the second act, Roger's "individualism" is set +. The subtype of each attribute is expressed by the dot notation: for example, "BELIEF.norms" referred to "individualism" means that this attribute belongs to the normative component of the character's beliefs, which are part of the rational component of the character. For emotions, the notation refers to the emotional classes described in OCC model [5].

3   Conclusions and Future Work

The definition of drama proposed in this paper is a first step toward a comprehensive formal system for analyzing and generating drama. The current theory leaves to future research the task of identifying the instruments by which the formal model may be incorporated into practical systems.

The theory describes drama as an off-line object, and does not specifically address the interactive generation of drama. The extension of the provisional model to the non-linear case, where the list of units in the plot is not pre-determined, represents another line of research in the development of a comprehensive theory.

References

1. Bryan Loyall, A., Bates, J.: Personality-rich belivable agents that use language. In Lewis Johnson, W., ed.: Proc. of the First Int. Conference on Autonomous Agents. (1997)
2. Staller, A., Petta, P.: Towards a tractable appraisal-based architecture. In Canamero, D., Numaoka, C., Petta, P., eds.: Workshop: Grounding Emotions in Adaptive Systems. (1998)
3. Cavazza, M., Charles, F., Mead, S.: Interacting with virtual characters in interactive storytelling. In: Proc. of AAMAS02 (2002)
4. Egri, L.: The Art of Dramatic Writing. Simon and Schuster, New York (1960 (1946))
5. A. Ortony, G.C., Collins, A.: Cognitive Stucture of Emotions. Cambrige Univ. Press (1988)
6. McKee, R.: Story. Harper Collins, New York (1997)
7. Lavandier, Y.: La dramaturgie. Le clown et l'enfant, Cergy (1994)
8. E.Lehman: North by Northwest. Directed by A. Hitchcock. Photographed by R. Burks. With C. Grant, E. M. Saint, J. Mason. Metro Goldwyn Mayer (1959)

A Semantic Kernel to Exploit Linguistic Knowledge

Roberto Basili, Marco Cammisa, and Alessandro Moschitti

University of Rome "Tor Vergata", Computer Science Department,
00133 Roma, Italy
{basili, cammisa, moschitti}@info.uniroma2.it

Abstract. Improving accuracy in Information Retrieval tasks via semantic information is a complex problem characterized by three main aspects: the *document representation* model, the *similarity estimation* metric and the *inductive algorithm*. In this paper an original kernel function sensitive to external semantic knowledge is defined as a document similarity model. This *semantic* kernel was tested over a text categorization task, under critical learning conditions (i.e. poor training data). The results of cross-validation experiments suggest that the proposed kernel function can be used as a general model of document similarity for IR tasks.

1   Introduction

Machine learning approaches to specific Information Retrieval (IR) tasks (e.g. ad-hoc document retrieval, text classification, text clustering or question answering) are characterized by three main design choices: a *document representation* model, a *similarity estimation* metric and an *inductive algorithm* that derives the decision function (e.g. category membership).

First, the *feature-based representations* are modeled as *bag of words* made by the terms (or *lexical tokens*) as they appear in the source documents. Data sparseness usually affects this representation as no matching is possible when semantically related but not identical tokens are used. This is particularly true when only small training data sets are available. Attempts to overcome this limitation have inspired several research lines that try to extend the *bag of word* representation with more expressive information: term clusters [1], query expansion via statistical corpus-driven (e.g. [2]) or thesauri-driven term expansion (e.g. [3]).

Second, vector space models make use of *document similarity metrics* [4] between information units (e.g. documents and queries) by mapping the latter in feature vectors whose components are the weights associated with features. The cosine similarity between normalized vectors is the most widely adopted model.

Third, *machine learning* (ML) *algorithms*, e.g. K-Nearest Neighbor [5] and Support Vector Machines [6], are widely used in supervised settings for text categorization, filtering or in user-relevance feedback.

S. Bandini and S. Manzoni (Eds.): AI*IA 2005, LNAI 3673, pp. 290–302, 2005.

Any ML model for IR should thus benefit from *all* the three design choices. Promising methods for one of the above choices are not sufficient alone to improve the overall accuracy, when not adequately modeled along the other two problem dimensions. For example, semantic information about lexical tokens is expected to improve the similarity estimation as wider (e.g. by using term clusters) or more precise (e.g. by using sense disambiguated words) feature matching is supported. However, every large scale evaluation in IR (ad-hoc retrieval, e.g. [7], or text categorization, e.g. [8]) has shown that this extended information provides poor or no benefit at all (see [9] for a more recent and extensive investigation).

The main problem of term cluster based representations seems the unclear nature of the relationship between the word level and the cluster level matching. Even if (semantic) clusters tend to improve the Recall, lexical tokens are, on a large scale, more accurate (e.g. [10]). When term clusters and simple words are combined, the mixed statistical distributions of individual tokens and sets may be inconsistent with the original ones.

In [3,11] term clusters are obtained through the synonymy information derivable from WordNet [12]. The empirical evidence is that the misleading information due to the choice of wrong (local) senses causes the overall accuracy to decrease. Word sense disambiguation (WSD) was thus applied beforehand by indexing document by means of disambiguated senses, i.e. synset codes [11,13,3,14,10]. However, even the state-of-art methods for WSD do not improve accuracy because of the inherent noise introduced by disambiguation mistakes.

Sense disambiguated corpora have been also used to study the relationship between sense and topical information (e.g. IRSemcor, [15]). These benchmarks suggest that there is no systematic correlation between semantic phenomena (e.g. regular polisemy) and topical relatedness, as different domains (or queries) are sensitive to different forms of semantic similarity. Word semantic similarity cannot be directly adopted as a general criteria for computing document (i.e. topical) similarity. Again, extended document representations are more dangerous than beneficial if it is not adequately modeled in the resulting metric space. The semantic expansion of features seems to require a corresponding careful adaptation of both the document similarity model and the adopted learning paradigm.

In this paper, a model for document similarity based on the similarity among words in WN is defined and its application to a supervised text classification task is used for empirical assessment. The WN based word similarity provides semantic expansions of lexical tokens traditionally used as features for a document (Section 2). A corresponding novel vector space model is then proposed where features are pairs of similar words (Section 3). Intuitively, every document d is represented through the set of all pairs $< t, t' >$ originating by terms $t \in d$ and some words t' *enough similar* to t. In this space the same pairs found in different documents contribute to their similarity, even if originating tokens are different. No sense is *a priori* pruned from a document representation but sense matching is triggered only when document matching is carried out.

Such space may be composed by $O(|V|^2)$ dimensions, where V is the corpus vocabulary. If we consider only the WN nouns, the space may contain about 10^{10} features. This critical complexity impacts on the learning algorithm. However, kernel methods can be applied as they can represent feature spaces implicitly. Among kernel-based learners, Support Vector Machines (SVMs) [16] have shown to achieve high accuracy by dealing effectively with many irrelevant features. Here, the selection of the suitable pairs is left to the SVM learning. Therefore, no sense disambiguation is imposed *a priori*, but sense selection is carried out *on the fly*. The overall model is thus distinct from most of the previous work in language-oriented IR.

The improvements in the overall accuracy observed over a TC task (Section 4) make this model a promising document similarity model for general IR tasks: unlike previous attempts, it makes sense of the adoption of semantic external resources (i.e. WN) in IR.

2   A Semantic Similarity Measure

Semantic generalizations overcome data sparseness problems in IR as contributions from different but semantically similar words are still available.

Methods for corpus-driven induction of semantically inspired word classes have been widely used on language modeling and lexical acquisition tasks (e.g. [17]). The main resource employed in most works is WordNet [12]. The WordNet noun hierarchy represents lexicalized concepts (or senses) organized according to an *"is-a-kind-of"* relation. A concept s, labeled with words w used to denote it, is thus called a *synset*, $syn(s)$. Words w are synonyms under the specific dimension captured by s and every synset s is a (lexical) sense for all the members $w \in syn(s)$.

The noun hierarchy is a direct acyclic graph[1]. The *direct_isa* relation defined by edges in the graph can be extended via a transitive closure to determine the overall *isa* relation between pairs of synsets. In line with [17] we denote by $\bar{s}$ the set of nodes in the hierarchy dominated by s, i.e. $\{c | c \; isa \; s\}$. By definition $\forall s \in \bar{s}$.

The automatic usage of WordNet for NLP and IR tasks has proved to be very complex. First, how the topological distance between senses is related to their corresponding conceptual distance is unclear. The pervasive lexical ambiguity is also problematic as it impacts on the measure of conceptual distances between word pairs. Moreover, the approximation of concepts by means of their shared generalizations in the hierarchy implies a conceptual loss that impacts on the target IR (or NLP) tasks. Similar words play different roles in IR tasks, so that equivalence cannot be imposed in general. This depends on the lack of semantic properties needed to select the word topical roles. It is thus difficult to decide the degree of generalization at which the conflation of senses into single features

---

[1] As only the 1% of its nodes own more than one parent in the graph, most of the techniques assume the hierarchy to be a tree, and treat the few exceptions heuristically.

can be effective for IR. Attempts to automatically determine suitable levels (as 'cuts' in the hierarchy) has been proposed in [18] with justifications derived from corpus statistics. For several tasks (e.g. in TC) this is unsatisfactory: different contexts (e.g. documents) may require different generalizations of the same word as they independently impact on the suitable document similarity. This is one of the limitations of corpus-driven metrics, like the one proposed by [19].

A flexible notion of semantic similarity is the *Conceptual Density* (*CD*) measure, early introduced in [20]. It depends on the generalizations of word senses not referring to any fixed level of the hierarchy. The measure used in this paper corresponds to the *CD* variant defined in [21], applied to semantic tagging and lexical alignment for ontology engineering. *CD* defines a distance between lexicalized concepts according to the topological structure of WordNet and can be seemingly applied to two or more words.

Conceptual Density (*CD*) makes a guess about the proximity of senses, s_1 and s_2, of two words u_1 and u_2, according to the information expressed by the (minimal, i.e. maximally dense) subhierarchy, $\bar{s}$, that includes them. Let S_i be the set of generalizations for at least one sense s_i for the word u_i, i.e. $\{s | s_i \in \bar{s}\}$. Given two words u_1 and u_2, their *CD* is formally defined as:

$$CD(u_1, u_2) = \begin{cases} 0 & \text{iff } S_1 \cap S_2 = \emptyset \\ max_{s \in S_1 \cap S_2} \frac{\sum_{i=0}^{h} \mu(\bar{s})^i}{|\bar{s}|} & \textbf{otherwise} \end{cases} \quad (1)$$

where:

- $S_1 \cap S_2$ is the set of WN shared generalizations (i.e. the common hypernyms) for u_1 and u_2
- $\mu(\bar{s})$ is the average number of children per node (i.e. the branching factor) in the actual sub-hierarchy $\bar{s}$. $\mu(\bar{s})$ depends on WordNet and in some cases its value can approach 1.
- $|\bar{s}|$ is the number of nodes in the sub-hierarchy $\bar{s}$. This value is statically estimated from WN and it is a negative bias for higher level generalizations (i.e. larger $\bar{s}$).
- h is the depth of the *ideal* WN subtree able to represent the lexical senses s_1 and s_2 of the two words. This value is actually estimated by:

$$h = \begin{cases} \lfloor log_{\mu(\bar{s})} 2 \rfloor & \text{iff } \mu(\bar{s}) \neq 1 \\ 2 & \textbf{otherwise} \end{cases} \quad (2)$$

where h expresses, given the average branching factor $\mu(\bar{s})$ at $\bar{s}$, the minimal number of levels needed to have s_1, s_2 represented in the leaves. Eq. 2 prevents the logarithm to assume an infinite value in cases $\mu(s)$ is exactly 1.

Conceptual density models the semantic distance as the density of the most dense generalization $\bar{s}$ such that $s \in S_1 \cap S_2$. The *density* of $\bar{s}$, is the ratio between the number of its useful nodes and $|\bar{s}|$. Useful nodes are those referring to senses of the involved words, i.e. s_1 and s_2. The density accounts for the branching factor local to $\bar{s}$: the higher is $\mu(\bar{s})$, the lower is the hierarchy height (h) sufficient to represent lexical senses (s_1 and s_2) with the highest density. If u_1 and u_2 are synonyms, the similarity measure gives 1, i.e. the highest similarity. Notice that for each pair, $CD(u_1, u_2)$ determines the similarity according to *the closest lexical senses*, s_1, $s_2 \in \bar{s}$: the remaining senses of u_1 and u_2 are irrelevant, with a resulting semantic disambiguation side effect. It must be noticed that Eq. 1 is the binary version of the general model defined in [21].

3   A WordNet Kernel for Document Similarity

Term similarity is used in the design of the document similarity which is the core function of most learning algorithms for TC. Document similarity models based on string matching do not support functions much different from the (inner) products between weights (of matching terms). The term similarity proposed in Eq. 1 is defined for all term pairs of a target vocabulary and has two main advantages: (1) the relatedness of each term occurring in the first document can be computed against *all* terms in the second document, i.e. all different pairs of similar (not just identical) tokens can contribute and (2) if we use all term pair contributions in the document similarity we obtain a measure consistent with the term probability distributions, i.e. the sum of all term contributions does not penalize or emphasize arbitrarily any subset of terms.

In order to model all pair contributions, we will still define a document similarity function as an inner product but in a new vector space where, intuitively, the dimensions are all possible pairs in the initial vocabulary and the weights of such components depend on the term similarity function. The next section presents more formally the above idea.

3.1   A *semantic* Vector Space

Given two documents d_1 and $d_2 \in D$ (the document-set) we define their similarity as:

$$K(d_1, d_2) = \sum_{w_1 \in d_1, w_2 \in d_2} (\lambda_1 \lambda_2) \times \sigma(w_1, w_2) \tag{3}$$

where λ_1 and λ_2 are the weights of the words (features) w_1 and w_2 in the documents d_1 and d_2, respectively and σ is a term similarity function, e.g. the conceptual density defined in Section 2.

To prove that Eq. 3 is a valid kernel[2] is enough to show that it is a specialization of the general definition of convolution kernels formalized in [23]. Hereafter, we report such definition: let $X, X_1, .., X_m$ be separable metric spaces, $x \in X$ a structure and $\boldsymbol{x} = x_1, ..., x_m$ its parts, where $x_i \in X_i \forall i = 1, .., m$. Let R be a relation on the set $X \times X_1 \times .. \times X_m$ such that $R(\boldsymbol{x}, x)$ is "true" if $\boldsymbol{x}$ are the

---

[2] An alternative way to prove the validity of the Mercer's conditions was shown in [22]. It is enough to observe that the kernel $K(d_1, d_2)$ can be written as $\boldsymbol{\lambda_1} W \cdot W' \boldsymbol{\lambda_2}$, where $\boldsymbol{\lambda_1}$ and $\boldsymbol{\lambda_2}$ are the vectors of weights associated with d_1 and d_2, and W and W' are the matrix and its transposed of the WordNet term similarities. Clearly, $P = W \cdot W'$ is positive semi-definite, thus $K(d_1, d_2) = \boldsymbol{\lambda_1} P \boldsymbol{\lambda_2}$ satisfies the Mercer's conditions. Note that this proof does not show that our kernel is a convolution kernel.

parts of x. We indicate with $R^{-1}(x)$ the set $\{x : R(x, x)\}$. Given two objects x and $y \in X$ their similarity $K(x, y)$ is defined as:

$$K(x, y) = \sum_{x \in R^{-1}(x)} \sum_{y \in R^{-1}(y)} \prod_{i=1}^{m} K_i(x_i, y_i) \qquad (4)$$

If we consider X as the document set (i.e. $D = X$), $m = 1$ and $X_1 = V$ (i.e. the vocabulary of our target document corpus) we derive that: $x = d$ (i.e. a document), $x = x_1 = w \in V$ (i.e. a word which is a part of the document d) and $R^{-1}(d)$ is the set of words in the document d. As $\prod_{i=1}^{m} K_i(x_i, y_i) = K_1(x_1, y_1)$, we can define $K_1(x_1, y_1) = K(w_1, w_2) = (\lambda_1 \lambda_2) \times \sigma(w_1, w_2)$ to obtain exactly the Eq. 3.

The above equation can be used in the learning algorithm of support vector machines as illustrated by the next section.

3.2   Support Vector Machines and Kernel Methods

Given the vector space in $\mathbb{R}^\eta$ and a set of positive and negative points, SVMs classify vectors according to a separating hyperplane, $H(x) = \omega \cdot x + b = 0$, where x and $\omega \in \mathbb{R}^\eta$ and $b \in \mathbb{R}$ are learned by applying the *Structural Risk Minimization principle* [16]. From the kernel theory we have that:

$$H(x) = \left(\sum_{h=1..l} \alpha_h x_h \right) \cdot x + b = \sum_{h=1..l} \alpha_h x_h \cdot x + b =$$

$$= \sum_{h=1..l} \alpha_h \phi(d_h) \cdot \phi(d) + b. \qquad (5)$$

where, d is a classifying document and d_h are all the l training instances, projected in x and x_h respectively. The product $K(d, d_h) = <\phi(d) \cdot \phi(d_h)>$ is the *Semantic WN-based Kernel (SK)* function associated with the mapping ϕ.

Eq. 5 shows that to evaluate the separating hyperplane in $\mathbb{R}^\eta$ we do not need to evaluate the entire vector x_h or x. Actually, we do not know even the mapping ϕ and the number of dimensions, η. As it is sufficient to compute $K(d, d_h)$, we can carry out the learning with Eq. 3 in the $\mathbb{R}^n$, avoiding to use the explicit representation in the $\mathbb{R}^\eta$ space. The real advantage of the Eq. 3 is that we can consider only the word pairs associated with non-zero weight, i.e. we can use a sparse vector computation. Additionally, to have a uniform score across different document size, the kernel function can be normalized as follows:

$$SK'(d_1, d_2) = \frac{SK(d_1, d_2)}{\sqrt{SK(d_1, d_1) \cdot SK(d_2, d_2)}} \qquad (6)$$

It should be noted that, the sparse evaluation also has a quadratic time complexity which is much less efficient than the linear complexity of the traditional document similarity. This, prevents the use of large document sets in the experiments. Moreover, as we claim that the general prior knowledge provided by WordNet can be effective only in poor training data conditions, we carried out cross-validation experiments on small subsets of the well known TC corpus 20 NewsGroups (20NG). It is available at `www.ai.mit.edu/ people/jrennie/ 20Newsgroups/` and contains a general terminology which is mostly covered by in WN.

4   Experiments

The use of WordNet (WN) in the term similarity function introduces a prior knowledge whose impact on the Semantic Kernel (SK) should be assessed experimentally. The main goal is to compare the traditional Vector Space Model kernel against SK, both within the Support Vector learning algorithm.

The high complexity of the SK is due to the large dimension of the similarity matrix, i.e. in principle any pair of WN words have a non null similarity score. However, it has to be evaluated only once. Moreover, we are not interested to large collections of training documents as simple *bag-of-words* models are in general very effective [9], i.e. they seems to model well the document similarity needed by the learning algorithm. For any test document, in fact, a set of support vectors can be found able to suggest similarity according to a simple string matching model. In other words, training documents are available including a large number of terms found in the target test document. We selected small subsets from the 20NewGroups collection, instead, and, in order to simulate critical learning conditions, experiments were run on training sets of increasing size.

4.1   Experimental Set-Up

In order to get statistically significant results, 10 different samples of 40 documents were randomly extracted, from 8 out of the 20 categories of the Usenet newsgroups collection. The training was carried out over the 10 distinct samples. For each learning phase, one sample was used as a validation set and the remaining 8 as test-set. This means that we run 80 different experiments for each model.

The classifier runs were carried out by using the SVM-light software [6] (available at `svmlight.joachims.org`) with the default linear kernel on the token space adopted as the baseline evaluations. The semantic kernel SK was implemented inside SVM-light.

The SK kernel (in Eq. 3) was applied with $\sigma(\cdot, \cdot) = CD(\cdot, \cdot)$ (Eq. 1), i.e. it is sensitive only to noun information. Accordingly, part of speech tagging was applied. However, verbs, adjectives and numerical features were used in all the experiments: in the space of lexical pairs, they have a null similarity with respect to any other word.

The classification performances were evaluated using the f_1 measure[3] for single arguments and the MicroAverage for the final classifier pool [24]. The performance are expressed as the mean and the standard deviation over 80 evaluations.

---

[3] f_1 assigns equal importance to Precision P and Recall R, i.e. $f_1 = \frac{2P \cdot R}{P+R}$.

Given the small number of documents careful SVM parameterization was applied. Preliminary investigation suggested that the trade-off (between the training-set error and margin) parameter, (i.e. c option in SVM-light) optimizes the f_1 measure for values in the range $[0.02, 0.32]^4$. We noted also that the cost-factor parameter (i.e. j option) is not critical, i.e. a value of 10 always optimizes the accuracy. Finally, feature selection techniques and weighting schemes were not applied in our experiments, as they cannot be accurately estimated from the small training data available.

4.2 Cross Validation Results

The SK (Eq. 3) was compared with the linear kernel which obtained the best f_1 measure in [6]. Table 1 reports the first comparative results for three categories (about 15 training documents each). Global results were obtained by averaging over 80 runs of the same size. The *Mean* and the *Std. Dev.* of f_1 are reported in Column 2 (for linear kernel SVMs), Column 3 (SK as in Eq. 3 without applying POS information, i.e. no noun selection applied) and Column 4 (SK with the use of POS information). The last row shows the Microaverage performance for the above three models.

Table 1. SVM performance using the linear and the Semantic Kernel over 3 categories of 20NewsGroups with 40 documents of training data

Category	Bow	SK	SK-POS
Atheism	59.6±11.2	63.7±10.7	63.0±9.6
Talk.Relig.	63.5±10.6	66.0±7.8	64.9±8.5
Comp.Graph.	85.3±8.3	86.7±7.4	85.7±9.8
MicroAvg. f_1	68.6±5.0	72.2±5.4	71.4±5.5

In order to asses these findings we repeated the evaluation over 8 20New-Groups categories (about 5 documents each). The results are reported in Table 2.

All the results confirm that SK outperforms the best bow linear kernel of about 4% as in critical learning conditions the semantic contribution of the SK recovers with useful information. In particular, during the similarity estimation, a word in a document activates 60.05 pairs (i.e. the other words in the matching document), on average. This is particularly useful to increase the amount of information available to the SVM. Noise due to semantic ambiguity seems not harmful to the SVM learner.

First, only the useful information seems to be made available by the training examples: similar words according to the correct senses appear in the positive examples so that only the useful pairs are amplified. Moreover, noisy information seems to be tolerated by the robustness of the learning SVM algorithm. Irrelevant pairs (senses emerging by mistakes) have a smoother distribution and are neglected by the SVM algorithm.

---

[4] We used all the values from 0.02 to 0.32 with step 0.02.

Table 2. Performance of the linear and Semantic Kernel with 40 training documents over 8 categories of 20NewsGroups collection

Category	bow	SK	SK-POS
Atheism	29.5±19.8	32.0±16.3	25.2±17.2
Comp.Graph	39.2±20.7	39.3±20.8	29.3±21.8
Misc.Forsale	61.3±17.7	51.3±18.7	49.5±20.4
Autos	26.2±22.7	26.0±20.6	33.5±26.8
Sport.Baseb.	32.7±20.1	36.9±22.5	41.8±19.2
Sci.Med	26.1±17.2	18.5±17.4	16.6±17.2
Talk.Relig.	23.5±11.6	28.4±19.0	27.6±17.0
Talk.Polit.	28.3±17.5	30.7±15.5	30.3±14.3
MicroAvg. f_1	31.5±4.8	34.3±5.8	33.5±6.4

Second, the Standard Deviations tend to assume high values. However, given the high number of samples the results are statistically reliable. To verify such hypothesis, we carried out the Normal Distribution confidence test on the 80 samples. The stochastic variable observed in each sample was the differences between the Microaverage of SK and bow models. The result shows that SK reaches higher Microaverage than the baseline at 99% of confidence level.

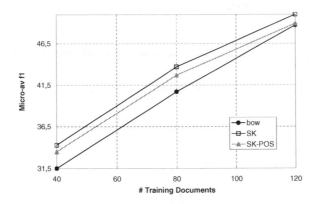

Fig. 1. MicroAverage f_1 of SVMs using bow, SK and SK-POS kernels over the 8 categories of 20NewsGroups

Third, a study on the impact of training data set size on the learning accuracy has been carried out for the three above models: bag-of-$words$ (bow), SK and SK-POS. Figure 1 shows the derived leaning curves over training data set of increasing size (5,10 and 15 documents for each category).

As expected the advantage of SK tends to reduce when more training data is available. However, the improvements keep not negligible. The SK model (without POS information) still preserves about 3% improvement. The similarity matching possibly allowed between noun-verb pairs still captures semantic information useful for topical similarity.

Finally, an experiment with 3 categories (compare with Table 1) was made by discarding all string matchings from SK. Only words having different surface forms were allowed to give contributions to Eq. 3. An important outcome is that the SK converges to an f_1 value of 50.2%. This shows that the word similarity provided by WN is consistent and effective to TC.

5   Related Work

The IR work related to this study focus on similarity (clustering) models for embedding statistical and external knowledge in document similarity.

In [25] a *Latent Semantic Indexing* analysis was used for term clustering. The algorithm, as described in [26], assumes that values x_{ij} in the transformed term-term matrix represents the similarity (> 0) and anti-similarity between terms i and j. Evaluation of query expansion techniques showed that positive clusters can improve Recall of about 18% for the *CISI* collection, 2.9% for *MED* and 3.4% for *CRAN*. Furthermore, the negative clusters, when used to prune the result set, improve the precision.

In [1], a feature selection technique that clusters similar features/words, called the Information Bottleneck (IB), is applied to TC. Support Vector Machines trained over clusters were experimented on three different corpora: *Reuters-21578*, WebKB and 20NewsGroups. Controversial results are obtained as the cluster based representation outperformed the simple *bag-of-words* only on the latter collection ($>3\%$).

The use of external semantic knowledge seems to be more problematic in IR as the negative impact of semantic ambiguity [11]. A WN-based semantic similarity function between noun pairs is used to improve indexing and document-query matching. However, the WSD algorithm had a performance ranging between 60-70%, and this made the overall semantic similarity not effective.

Other studies using semantic information for improving IR were carried out in [13] and [3,14]. Word semantic information was here used for text indexing and query expansion, respectively. In [14] it is shown that semantic information derived directly from WN without a priori WSD produces poor results.

The above methods are even more problematic in TC [9]. Word senses tend to systematically correlate with the positive examples of a category. Different categories are better characterized by different words rather than different senses. Patterns of lexical co-occurrences in the training data seems to suffice for automatic disambiguation. [27] uses WN senses to replace simple words without word sense disambiguation and small improvements are derived only for a small corpus. The scale and assessment provided in [10] (3 corpora using cross-validation techniques) showed that even accurate disambiguation of WN senses (about 80% accuracy on nouns) does not improve TC.

An approach similar to the one proposed in this article, is the use of term proximity to define a semantic kernel [28]. Such semantic kernel was designed as a combination of the Radial Basis Function kernel with the term proximity matrix. Entries in this matrix are inversely proportional to the length of the

WN hierarchy path linking the two terms. The performance, measured over the 20NewsGroups corpus, showed an improvement of 2% over the *bag-of-words*. The main difference with our approach are the following: first, the term proximity is not fully sensitive to the information of the WN hierarchy. For example, if we consider pairs of equidistant terms, the nearer to the WN top level a pair is the lower similarity it should receive, e.g. *Sky* and *Location* (hyponyms of *Entity*) should not accumulate similarity like *knife* and *gun* (hyponyms of *weapon*). Measures, like CD, that deal with this problem have been widely proposed in literature (e.g. [19]) and should be always applied. Second, the description of the resulting space is not given and the choice of the kernel is not justified in terms of document similarity. The proximity matrix is a way to smooth the similarity between two terms but its impact on learning is unclear. Finally, experiments were carried out by using only 200 features (selected via Mutual Information statistics). In this way the contribution of rare or non statistically significant terms is neglected. In our view, the latter features may give, instead, a relevant contribution once we move in the SK space generated by the WN similarities.

Other work using corpus statistc knowledge, e.g. latent semantic indexing, for retrieval was carried out in [29,30].

6   Conclusions

The introduction of semantic prior knowledge in IR has always been an interesting subject as the examined literature suggests. In this paper, we used the conceptual density function on the WordNet hierarchy to define a document similarity metric. Accordingly, we defined a semantic kernel to train a Support Vector Machine classifiers. Cross-validation experiments over 8 categories of 20NewsGroups over multiple samples have shown that in critical training data conditions, such prior knowledge can be effectively used to improve (about 3 absolute percent points, i.e. 10%) the TC accuracy.

These promising results enable a number of future researches: (1) larger scale experiments with different measures and semantic similarity models (e.g. [19]); (2) domain-driven specialization of the term similarity, by selectively tuning WordNet to the target categories, (3) optimization driven by prior feature selection, and (4) extension of the semantic similarity by a general (i.e. non binary) application of the conceptual density model, e.g. use the most important category terms as prior bias for the similarity score.

References

1. Bekkerman, R., El-Yaniv, R., Tishby, N., Winter, Y.: On feature distributional clustering for text categorization. In proceedings of SIGIR'01, New Orleans, Louisiana, United States, ACM Press (2001)
2. Strzalkowski, T., Carballo, J.P.: Natural language information retrieval: TREC-6 report. In: Text REtrieval Conference. (1997)
3. Voorhees, E.M.: Using wordnet to disambiguate word senses for text retrieval. In proceedings of SIGIR'93. Pittsburgh, PA, USA, 1993

4. Salton, G.: Automatic text processing: the transformation, analysis and retrieval of information by computer. Addison-Wesley (1989)
5. Yang, Y.: Expert network: effective and efficient learning from human decisions in text categorisation and retrieval. In proceedings of SIGIR'94, Dublin, IE (1994)
6. Joachims, T.: Making large-scale SVM learning practical. In Schölkopf, B., Burges, C., Smola, A., eds.: Advances in Kernel Methods - Support Vector Learning. (1999)
7. Strzalkowski, T., Carballo, J.P., Karlgren, J., Tapanainen, A.H.P., Jarvinen, T.: Natural language information retrieval: TREC-8 report. In: Text REtrieval Conference. (1999)
8. Lewis, D.D.: An evaluation of phrasal and clustered representations on a text categorization task. In proceedings of SIGIR'92, Kobenhavn, DK (1992) 37–50
9. Moschitti, A.: Natural Language Processing and Automated Text Categorization: a study on the reciprocal beneficial interactions. PhD thesis, Computer Science Department, Univ. of Rome "Tor Vergata" (2003)
10. Moschitti, A., Basili, R.: Complex linguistic features for text classification: a comprehensive study. In proceedings of ECIR'04, Sunderland, UK, Springer Verlag (2004)
11. Smeaton, A.F.: Using NLP or NLP resources for information retrieval tasks. In Strzalkowski, T., ed.: Natural language information retrieval. Kluwer Academic Publishers, Dordrecht, NL (1999)
12. Fellbaum, C.: WordNet: An Electronic Lexical Database. MIT Press. (1998)
13. Sussna, M.: Word sense disambiguation for free-text indexing using a massive semantic network. In proceedings of CKIM'93. (1993)
14. Voorhees, E.M.: Query expansion using lexical-semantic relations. In proceedings of SIGIR'94, Dublin, Ireland, (1994)
15. Fernandez-Amoros, D., Gonzalo, J., Verdejo, F.: The role of conceptual relations in word sense disambiguation. In proceedings of the 6th international workshop on applications of Natural Language for Information Systems (NLDB 2001). (2001)
16. Vapnik, V.: The Nature of Statistical Learning Theory. Springer (1995)
17. Clark, S., Weir, D.: Class-based probability estimation using a semantic hierarchy. Computional Linguistics (2002)
18. Li, H., Abe, N.: Generalizing case frames using a thesaurus and the mdl principle. Computational Linguistics (1998)
19. Resnik, P.: Selectional preference and sense disambiguation. In proceedings of ACL Siglex Workshop on Tagging Text with Lexical Semantics, Why, What and How?, Washington, April 4-5, 1997. (1997)
20. Agirre, E., Rigau, G.: Word sense disambiguation using conceptual density. In proceedings of COLING'96, pages 16–22, Copenhagen, Danmark. (1996)
21. Basili, R., Cammisa, M., Zanzotto, F.M.: A similarity measure for unsupervised semantic disambiguation. In proceedings of Language Resources and Evaluation Conference. (2004)
22. Cristianini, N., Shawe-Taylor, J.: An introduction to Support Vector Machines. Cambridge University Press (2000)
23. Haussler, D.: Convolution kernels on discrete structures. Technical report ucs-crl-99-10, University of California Santa Cruz (1999)
24. Yang, Y.: An evaluation of statistical approaches to text categorization. Information Retrieval Journal (1999)
25. Kontostathis, A., Pottenger, W.: Improving retrieval performance with positive and negative equivalence classes of terms (2002)

26. Deerwester, S.C., Dumais, S.T., Landauer, T.K., Furnas, G.W., Harshman, R.A.: Indexing by latent semantic analysis. Journal of the American Society of Information Science (1990)
27. Scott, S., Matwin, S.: Feature engineering for text classification. In Bratko, I., Dzeroski, S., eds.: Proceedings of ICML'99, San Francisco, US (1999)
28. Siolas, G., d'Alch Buc, F.: Support vector machines based on a semantic kernel for text categorization. In proceedings of IJCNN'00, IEEE Computer Society (2000)
29. Cristianini, N., Shawe-Taylor, J., Lodhi, H.: Latent semantic kernels. J. Intell. Inf. Syst. (2002)
30. Kandola, J., Shawe-Taylor, J., Cristianini, N.: Learning semantic similarity. In NIPS'02 - MIT Press. (2002)

Building a Wide Coverage Dynamic Grammar

Alessandro Mazzei and Vincenzo Lombardo

Dipartimento di Informatica, Università di Torino,
c.so Svizzera, 185 10149, Torino, Italy
{mazzei, vincenzo}@di.unito.it

Abstract. Incremental processing is relevant for language modeling, speech recognition and language generation. In this paper we devise a dynamic version of Tree Adjoining Grammar (DVTAG) that encodes a strong notion of incrementality directly into the operations of the formal system. After discussing the basic features of DVTAG, we address the issue of building of a wide coverage grammar and present novel data on English and Italian.

1 Introduction

Incrementality is a largely held assumption that constrains the language processor to parse the input words from left to right, and to carry out a semantic interpretation of the partial structures [1]. Most of the approaches to incremental parsing assume some standard syntactic formalism (e.g. context-free grammar) and address the issue of incrementality in the parsing algorithm [2]. An alternative approach (*incrementality in the competence*) is to encode incrementality in the operations of a formal system. Competence and some performance issues are addressed by the same model, derivation and parsing share the same mechanism, and we can use the two terms interchangeably (we can generically talk of a *syntactic process*, cf. [3]).

The detailed specification of the incremental syntactic process is often addressed by assuming a parsimonious version of incrementality that we can call *strong connectivity* [4]. Strong connectivity constrains the syntactic processor to maintain a fully connected structure throughout the whole process and is supported by a large amount of psycholinguistic evidence [5,6] as well as linguistic facts [7]. The syntactic process consists in attaching each word from left to right to the existing unique structure, called the *left-context*, that spans the previous words in the string.

Tree Adjoining Grammars (TAG) is a well known family of formalisms. Recently the results of some psycholinguistic experiments have suggested that the adjoining mechanism of TAG can be used to fulfill the to the strong connectivity hypothesis (*adjoining mechanism hypothesis*) [6].

A natural way of viewing the syntactic process is a dynamic system, that is a system that evolves in time through a number of steps. A *dynamic grammar* views the syntactic process as a sequence of transitions between adjacent states S_{i-1} and S_i while moving from left to right on the string of terminals [8].

S. Bandini and S. Manzoni (Eds.): AI*IA 2005, LNAI 3673, pp. 303–314, 2005.

Thus, it naturally fulfills the incrementality in the competence and the strong connectivity hypotheses. In [9] it has been proposed a constituency based dynamic grammar, called *Dynamic Version of TAG* (DVTAG), that fulfills the hypotheses of *incrementality in the competence, strong connectivity, adjoining mechanism*. DVTAG is TAG-related, since it shares some basic properties with LTAG formalism, i.e. the extended domain of locality, the lexicalization and the adjoining mechanism [9].

The focus of this paper is on the applicability of DVTAG into a realistic context. In particular, we build two wide coverage DVTAGs for English and Italian respectively, through extraction from treebank.

2   LTAG, Dynamic Grammars and DVTAG

In Fig. 1 we can see the DVTAG derivation of the sentence *John loves Mary madly*. Like LTAG [10], a Dynamic Version of Tree Adjoining Grammar (DVTAG) consists of a set of elementary trees, divided into initial trees and auxiliary trees, and attachment operations for combining them. Lexicalization is expressed through the association of a lexical *anchor* with each elementary tree. With the aim to consider the lexical dependencies between the lexical items, each node in the elementary trees is augmented with a feature indicating the lexical head that projects the node. The head variable is a variable in logic terms: $\_v_3$ will be unified with the constant *loves* in the derivation of Fig. 1. The derivation process in DVTAG builds a constituency tree by combining the elementary trees via some operations that are illustrated below. DVTAG implements the incremental

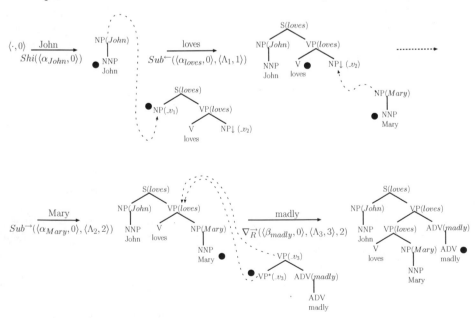

Fig. 1. The DVTAG derivation of the sentence *John loves Mary madly*

process by constraining the *derivation process* to be a series of steps in which an elementary tree is combined with the partial tree spanning the left fragment of the sentence. The result of a step is an updated partial structure. Specifically, at the processing step i, the elementary tree anchored by the i-th word in the sentence is combined with the partial structure spanning the words from 1 to $i-1$ positions; the result is a partial structure spanning the words from 1 to i. In DVTAG the derivation process starts from an elementary tree anchored by the first word in the sentence and that does not require any attachment that would introduce lexical material on the left of the anchor (such as in the case that a Substitution node is on the left of the anchor). This elementary tree becomes the first left-context that has to be combined with some elementary tree on the right. At the end of the derivation process the left-context spans the whole sentence, and is called the *derived tree*: the last tree of Fig.1 is the derived tree for the sentence *John loves Mary madly*.

In DVTAG we always combine a left context with an elementary tree, then there are seven attachment operations. Standard LTAG adjoining is split into two operations: *adjoining from the left* and *adjoining from the right*. The type of adjoining depends on the position of the lexical material introduced by the auxiliary tree with respect to the material currently dominated by the adjoined node (which is in the left-context). In Fig. 1 we have an adjoining from the right in the case of the left auxiliary tree anchored by *madly*, and in Fig. 2 we

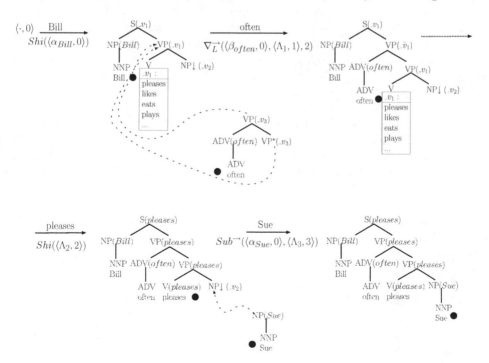

Fig. 2. The DVTAG derivation of the sentence *Bill often pleases Sue*

have an adjoining from the left in the case of the left auxiliary tree anchored by *often*. Inverse operations account for the insertion of the left-context into the elementary tree. In the case of *inverse substitution* the left-context replaces a substitution node in the elementary tree; in the case of *inverse adjoining from the left* and *inverse adjoining from the right*, the left-context acts like an auxiliary tree, and the elementary tree is split because of the adjoining of the left context at some node[1]. In Fig. 1 we have an inverse substitution in the case of the initial tree anchored by *John*. Finally, the *shift* operation either scans a lexical item which has been already introduced in the structure or derives a lexical item from some predicted preterminal node. The grounding of the variable $\_v_1$ in Fig. 2 is an example of shift.

It is important to notice that, during the derivation process, not all the nodes in the left-context and the elementary tree are accessible for performing operations: given the $i-1$-th word in the sentence we can compute a set of accessible nodes in the left-context (the *left-context fringe*); also, given the lexical anchor of the elementary tree, that in the derivation process matches the i-th word in the sentence, we can compute a set of accessible nodes in the elementary tree (the *elementary tree fringe*). To take into account of this feature, the elementary tree in DVTAG are dotted tree, i.e. a couple $\langle \gamma, i \rangle$ formed by a tree γ and an integer i denoting the accessible fringe[2] of the tree [11].

The DVTAG derivation process requires the full connectivity of the left-context at all times. The extended domain of locality provided by LTAG elementary trees appears to be a desirable feature for implementing full connectivity. However, each new word in a string has to be connected with the preceding left-context, and there is no *a priori* limit on the amount of structure that may intervene between that word and the preceding context. For example, in a DV-TAG derivation of *John said that tasty apples were on sale*, the adjective *tasty* cannot be directly connected with the S node introduced by *that*; there is an intervening NP symbol that has not yet been predicted in the structure. Another example is the case of an intervening modifier between an argument and its predicative head, like in the example *Bill often pleases Sue* (see Fig.2). The elementary tree *Bill* is linguistically motivated up to the NP projection; the rest of the structure depends on connectivity. These extra nodes are called *predicted nodes*. A predicted preterminal node is referred by a set of lexical items, that represent a *predicted head*. So, the extended domain of locality available in LTAG has to be further extended. In particular, some structures have to be predicted as soon as there is some evidence from arguments or modifiers on the left.

The notion of predicted nodes is crucial for the linguistic appealing of the formalism. Indeed DVTAG does not assume any linguistic theory *a priori*. Similar

---

[1] In [9] there is shown the importance of the inverse operation to obtain the correct cross-serial dependencies in DVTAG.

[2] In the picture we represent the integer using a dot. Note that *fringe* and *dotted tree* are two concepts borrowed from parsing as a consequence of the dynamic nature of DVTAG.

to LTAG, DVTAG allows for the specification of a number of linguistic principles licensing the elementary trees. The mathematical properties of TAG are a consequence of the finiteness of the size of the lexicon, then the linguistic principles have to guarantee (more or less implicitly) this property [12]. In DVTAG there is no *a priori* limit on the number of predicted nodes, an then there is not a limit on the size of the grammar. The notion of predicted nodes is also crucial for the applicability of DVTAG a real context. Several works have showed that the most important factor in TAG parsing complexity is the size of the grammar [13] [14], and for a wide coverage DVTAG predicted nodes could produce a very huge grammar [15]. Our hypothesis is that DVTAG respects the constraint on the finiteness of the lexicon because there is an empirical limit on the number of predicted heads. This limit can be obtained by the observation of the experimental data: several work confirmed that the number of predicted heads necessary to guarantee the strong connectivity is relatively low [16,17].

In the next sections we address the problem of building a linguistic motivated wide coverage DVTAG for English and Italian. As a side result of these experiments we present a number of preliminary results that empirically verify the hypothesis about the limited number of predicted heads.

3   Building a Wide Coverage DVTAG

A way to build a wide coverage grammar is to manually write the grammar. For instance, XTAG [18] is an ongoing project to produce a hand written wide coverage LTAG for English. In [15] and [11] we have discussed the possibility of transforming the XTAG grammar into a DVTAG using a non-constrained transformation. These experiments have showed the DVTAG produced in this way is not adequate for an applicative context. The key point is the size of the grammar. Indeed the non-constrained transformation did not take into account any empirical principle to construct the DVTAG elementary trees. In this paper we pursue a different approach.

As large size treebanks are becoming widely available (among others Penn treebank [19]) a new way is the automatic extraction of wide coverage grammar from a treebank [20,21]. Here we investigate on the possibility of extracting a large DVTAG from a treebank. In particular, exploiting the formal relation between LTAG and DVTAG (cf. [11]) we propose a two steps algorithm. In the first step we use a LTAG extractor; in the second step we transform the LTAG produced in the first step into a DVTAG. To pursue this strategy we use the LTAG extractors described in [20] and [14] for English and Italian respectively. Both these extractors have been used to test the relation between the time complexity of the parsing and the size of LTAG lexicon [13,14]. The Italian LTAG extractor has been also used to test the relation between the coverage of extracted LTAG and the genre of the extraction corpus [22].

In section 3.1 we briefly describe the basic issues of an algorithm to automatically extract a LTAG from a treebank. In section 3.2 we define the *left-association*, an operation that allows us to increase a DVTAG lexicon with new wider elementary trees. In section 3.3 we describe an algorithm to transform a LTAG automatically extracted into a DVTAG based on the left-association. In section 3.4 and in section 3.5 we report some data for DVTAG automatically extracted from an English treebank and from an Italian treebank respectively: we provide an explorative analysis of this data with the aim to test the reliability of the grammars produced.

3.1   Extracting a LTAG from a Treebank

All the algorithms for automatic extraction of a LTAG from a treebank share a basic feature. They produce a LTAG grammar that covers the treebank, and at the same time they assign a derivation tree D_T to each tree T of the treebank ([20] [21]). Each derivation tree D_T contains all the elementary trees that the algorithm extracts from each derived tree T. The derivation trees D_T play a key role in the definition of a probabilistic model for the treebank grammar [23]. Now we describe the basic feature of the algorithm (henceforth LexTract) proposed in [20] for the extraction of a wide coverage LTAG from Penn treebank. A quite similar algorithm has been used for the extraction of a wide coverage LTAG from an Italian dependency treebank [14]. LexTract can be essentially described as a two steps procedure. In the first step, each constituency tree T of the treebank is converted into a set of elementary trees $\gamma_1^T ... \gamma_n^T$. By using a head-table and a modifier-table, the algorithm identifies the head and modification relations between the nodes of constituency tree. The algorithm uses the head-modifier annotation together with a set of prototypical tree templates (a sort of extended projection skeletons) to extract a set of elementary trees that derives the constituency tree. In the second step, using the elementary trees $\gamma_1^T ... \gamma_n^T$ produced in the first step, each constituency tree T of the treebank is converted into a derivation tree.

3.2   Left-Association

The left-association takes as input two DVTAG elementary trees, called the **base tree** and the **raising tree** respectively, and returns a new DVTAG elementary tree, the **raised tree**[3]. The operation produces the raised tree by grafting the base tree into the raising tree, and replacing the left-anchor of the raising tree with a new head-variable. Left-association can be performed during the parsing/derivation process (i.e. on-line, cf. [17]) or with the goal to extend the lexicon (i.e. off-line). In this paper we are exploring the consequences of increasing the role of the competence grammar, then we use this operation off-line. The raised tree produced by the left-association displays a larger number of predicted nodes in comparison with the base tree. The raised tree has zero or more predicted heads: the raised tree has one more predicted head that projects a number of the predicted nodes in the raised tree (cf. Fig. 4).

---

[3] There are some similarities between left-association and the CCG type raising operation [3], because in both cases some root category X is raised to some higher category Y.

3.3   Converting an Automatically Extracted LTAG into a DVTAG

The left-association can be used to transform an automatically extracted LTAG into a DVTAG. For each tree T in the treebank, we define a relation, called *left-corner* relation, on the nodes belonging to D_T. We say that γ_k γ_l are in the left-corner relation if in D_T γ_k is the left-most child of γ_l, and if the root node label of γ_k is different from the root node label of γ_l. If two nodes γ_k γ_l of D_T are in the left-corner relation, we use the left-association on the respective trees to build a new DVTAG elementary tree.

Conversion Algorithm

[**step 1:**] We extract the LTAG $\gamma_1^T...\gamma_n^T$ and the derivation D_T from T (i.e. $derived(D_T) = T$). We build the dotted trees $\langle\gamma_1^T, 0\rangle...\langle\gamma_n^T, 0\rangle$ augmenting each non terminal node in γ_i $i \in 1...n$ with a head feature that contains the lexical item projecting the node (Fig. 3).

[**step 2:**] To produce $\langle\delta_1, 0\rangle...\langle\delta_m, 0\rangle$ we apply the transitive closure of the left-association on $\langle\gamma_1, 0\rangle...\langle\gamma_n, 0\rangle$.

The application of the transitive closure of left-association is subject to a **closure condition**. The sequence of raising tree in the transitive closure of the left-association, applied to some base tree $\langle\delta, 0\rangle$, has to respect the left-corner relation.

The adequacy of the closure condition is motivated by the presence of the adjoining operation, which factorizes recursion. So, adjoining should account for repetitions of the root category outside of the left-association. But, since DVTAG respects the strong connectivity hypothesis, not all the cases of recursion in LTAG derivation tree are generable in DVTAG also using the predicted nodes (cf. [11]). Then, in some cases the generative power of the DVTAG produced with the conversion algorithm is not equal to the generative power of the original

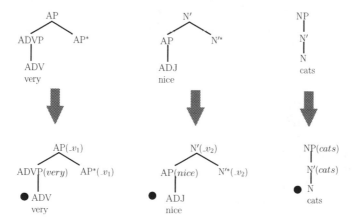

Fig. 3. First step of the conversion from a LTAG to a DVTAG: each nodes is augmented with a head variable

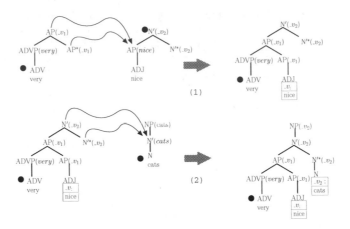

Fig. 4. Second step of the conversion from a LTAG to a DVTAG: iteration of the left-association

LTAG extracted. However, our final goal in this work is to provide an exploratory analysis of a realistic DVTAG. In comparison with this task, we assume as a working hypothesis that the difference on the generative power between LTAG and DVTAG is not substantially relevant.

In the next sections we apply the conversion procedure described above to two LTAG automatically extracted from an English and Italian treebanks respectively. We compare the properties of the DVTAG extracted with the data reported in [16], based on *Connection Path Grammars* (CPG). Similar to DV-TAG, CPG is a dynamic constituency grammatical formalism, but there are some crucial differences between them. DVTAG uses linguistically motivated elementary trees and uses adjoining to factorize recursion. In contrast, CPG uses elementary structures motivated uniquely by the constraint of strong incrementality. However, similarly to DVTAG CPG includes the notion of predicted heads, and then can be used as a baseline.

3.4   Extraction of an English DVTAG from Penn Treebank

By applying the LexTract[4] on the sections 02-21 of the Wall Street Journal part of the Penn treebank II (39,832 sentences, 950,026 words), we have obtained $841,316$ LTAG (non distinct) elementary trees[5], corresponding to $5,268$ (distinct) templates. The DVTAG conversion algorithm on these LTAG elementary trees, produces a DVTAG (henceforth DVPenn) with $840,450$ (non distinct) elementary dotted trees corresponding to $12,026$ (distinct) dotted templates. In Table 1 we have reported the number of dotted trees with respect to the number of left-association in DVPenn. Moreover we have reported the also the

---

[4] We wish to thank Fei Xia, that kindly let us to use her program.

[5] The number of elementary tree is different in comparison with the number of token words because LexTract does not extract trees anchored by punctuations.

Table 1. Number of (non distinct) DVTAG elementary dotted trees with respect to the number of left-associations for the DVPenn grammar

# of iterations of left-association	# DVPenn dotted trees	% DVPenn dotted trees	% Connection paths
0	764,359	90.95	82,33
1	75,125	8.94	15,26
2	959	0.11	2,28
3	7	0.00	0.13
Total:	840,450		

Table 2. Number of DVTAG templates with respect to the number of left-associations for the DVPenn grammar

# of iteration of left-association	# DVPenn dotted templates	% DVPenn dotted templates	# Connection paths
0	4,947	41.13	
1	6,329	52.63	
2	743	6.18	
3	7	0.06	
Total:	12,026		1,896

percentage of CPGs with respect to the number of *headless* as reported in [16]. Note that we have used the percentage because in in [16] it has been used a fraction of the WSJ of ∼100,000 words: then their corpus is ten times smaller with respect to corpus used in this experiment. Comparing the percentage of dotted trees in DVPenn to the percentage of connection path in the CPG extracted from Penn, we note that both the grammars have really few elementary structures with more than two predicted heads (∼0.001% and 0.13% for DVPenn and CPG respectively). Moreover, most of the structures do not use predicted heads (90,95% and 82,33% for DVPenn and CPG respectively). In Table 2 we have reported the number of dotted templates with respect to the number of left-association in DVPenn[6]. In this case, the maximum percentage of dotted templated (52,63 %) are left-associated only once. Also if the corpus used in [16] is smaller with respect to our corpus, the total number of templates extracted is not really different for CPG, LTAG and DVTAG, 1,896 5,268 12,026 respectively. This fact could suggest that the number of structures necessary to fulfill strong connectivity is not really huge, but more experiments on the properties of the extracted grammars are necessary. For example to assess the quality of the grammars it is necessary to test their *coverage*.

---

[6] In this measure we do not have the complete data for CPG.

Table 3. Number of DVTAG trees with respect to the number of left-association, for the DVTUT grammar

# of iterations of left-association	# DVTUT dotted trees	% DVTUT dotted trees	% Connection paths
0	37,382	92.39	82,33
1	3,059	7.56	15,26
2	22	0.05	2,28
3	0	0.00	0.13
Total:	40,463		

However the results of the experiment show that for the Penn treebank only few dotted trees have more than two predicted heads. Moreover, this result is in accord with a precedent test performed with connection path grammars [16]. In the next section we replicate this experiment using an Italian treebank.

3.5   Extraction of an Italian DVTAG from TUT

The Turin University Treebank (TUT) is an ongoing project of the University of Turin on the construction of a dependency style treebank for Italian [24]: each sentence is semi-automatically annotated with dependency relations that form a tree, and relations are of morphological, syntactic and semantic types. The corpus is very varied, and contains texts from newspapers, magazines, novels and press news. Its current size is 1,800 annotated sentences (40,470 words). In order to extract the LTAG grammar, we have converted the TUT treebank dependency format to a constituency format[7], and then we have adapted the LexTract algorithm described above (for the details of the algorithms see [14]).

We have used the DVTAG extraction algorithm by applying the TUT LTAG extractor on the whole TUT corpus. From the 167 out 1800 sentences are discarded because they represent linguistic constructions that the extractor is not yet able to take into account. From the remanent 1683 sentences, the LTAG extractor produces (non distinct) $43,621$ elementary trees corresponding to $1,212$ (distinct) templates, while the DVTAG extractor produces 40,463 dotted trees corresponding to $1,614$ dotted templates (henceforth DVTUT grammar).

In Table 4, we have reported the number of templates with respect to the number of left-association. The total number of dotted templates is 1,614: 844 are no left-associated, 752 are left-associated only once, 18 are left-associated two times. The percentage values for zero or one left-associations is quite close (52% vs. 46.59%), while the number of two times left-associated templates is very small (1,12%). In the last raw of the table, we have compared the total number of templates with the total number of *connection path type* (i.e. template) reported in [16]. Note that also if the size of the TUT is less than the

---

[7] The constituency format is not yet compliant with the Penn treebank format.

Table 4. Number of DVTAG templates with respect to the number of left-association, for the DVTUT grammar

# of iterations of left-association	# DVTUT dotted templates	% DVTUT dotted templates	# Connection Path templates
0	844	52.29	
1	752	46.59	
2	18	1.12	
Total:	1,614		1,896

half of the corpus used in [16] (40,470 versus ~100,000 words respectively), the number of templates is quite similar. However as well as for the experiment on the Penn treebank, the results of this experiment are in accord with the results of [16].

4   Conclusions

In this paper we have provided the basic features of the DVTAG formalism. We have analyzed the theoretical and applicative problems related to the notion of predicted heads. Moreover, we have defined an algorithm to extract a DVTAG from a treebank based on a generic LTAG extractor. We have used this algorithm to produce two wide coverage DVTAGs for English and Italian. Analyzing these grammars, as a side result we have found that the DVTAG elementary trees extracted from the treebanks have very few predicted heads. In a future work we want to extend the analysis of the extracted grammars taking into account of their coverage [22].

References

1. Marslen-Wilson, W.: Linguistic structure and speech shadowing at very short latencies. Nature 244 (1973) 522–523
2. Abney, S.P., Johnson, M.: Memory requirements and local ambiguities of parsing strategies. Journal of Psycholinguistic Research 20 (1991) 233–250
3. Steedman, M.J.: The syntactic process. A Bradford Book, The MIT Press (2000)
4. Stabler, E.P.: The finite connectivity of linguistic structure. In Clifton, C., Frazier, L., Reyner, K., eds.: Perspectives on Sentence Processing. Lawrence Erlbaum Associates (1994) 303–336
5. Kamide, Y., Altmann, G.T.M., Haywood, S.L.: The time-course of prediction in incremental sentence processing: Evidence from anticipatory eye movements. Journal of Memory and Language Language 49 (2003) 133–156
6. Sturt, P., Lombardo, V.: Processing coordinated structures: Incrementality and connectedness. Cognitive Science 29 (2005) 291–305
7. Phillips, C.: Linear order and constituency. Linguistic Inquiry 34 (2003) 37–90

8. Milward, D.: Dynamic dependency grammar. Linguistics and Philosophy 17 (1994) 561–604
9. Lombardo, V., Sturt, P.: Towards a dynamic version of TAG. In: TAG+6. (2002) 30–39
10. Joshi, A., Schabes, Y.: Tree-adjoining grammars. In Rozenberg, G., Salomaa, A., eds.: Handbook of Formal Languages. Springer (1997) 69–123
11. Mazzei, A.: Formal and empirical issues of applying dynamics to Tree Adjoining Grammars. PhD thesis, Dipartimento di Informatica, Università degli studi di Torino (2005)
12. Frank, R.: Phrase Structure Composition and Syntactic dependencies. The MIT Press (2002)
13. Sarkar, A., Xia, F., Joshi, A.: Some experiments on indicators of parsing complexity for lexicalized grammars. In: COLING00. (2000)
14. Mazzei, A., Lombardo, V.: Building a large grammar for italian. In: LREC04, Lisbon (2004) 51–54
15. Lombardo, V., Mazzei, A., Sturt, P.: Competence and performance grammar in incremental parsing. In: Incremental Parsing: Bringing Engineering and Cognition Together, Workshop at ACL-2004, Barcelona (2004) 1–8
16. Lombardo, V., Sturt, P.: Incrementality and lexicalism: A treebank study. In Stevenson, S., Merlo, P., eds.: Lexical Representations in Sentence Processing. John Benjamins (2002)
17. Schneider, D.: Parsing and incrementality. PhD thesis, University of Delaware, Newark (1998)
18. Doran, C., Hockey, B., Sarkar, A., Srinivas, B., Xia, F.: Evolution of the xtag system. In Abeillé, A., Rambow, O., eds.: Tree Adjoining Grammars. Chicago Press (2000) 371–405
19. Marcus, M., Santorini, B., Marcinkiewicz, M.A.: Building a large annotated corpus of english: The penn treebank. Computational Linguistics 19 (1993) 313–330
20. Xia, F.: Automatic Grammar Generation from two Different Perspectives. PhD thesis, Computer and Information Science Department, Pensylvania University (2001)
21. Chen, J.: Towards Efficient Statistical Parsing using Lexicalized Grammatical Information. PhD thesis, Computer and Information Science Department, University of Delaware (2001)
22. Mazzei, A., Lombardo, V.: A comparative analysis of extracted grammars. In: 16th European Conference on Artificial Intelligence, ECAI04, Valencia (2004) 601–605
23. Joshi, A., Sarkar, A.: Tree adjoining grammars and their apllication to statistical parsing. In Bod, R., Scha, R., Sima'an, K., eds.: Data-Oriented Parsing. CSLI Publications (2003) 255–283
24. Bosco, C., Lombardo, V., Vassallo, D., Lesmo, L.: Building a treebank for italian: a data-driven annotation schema. In: LREC00, Athens (2000) 99–105

A Linguistic Inspection of Textual Entailment

Maria Teresa Pazienza[1], Marco Pennacchiotti[1], and Fabio Massimo Zanzotto[2]

[1] University of Roma Tor Vergata, Via del Politecnico 1, Roma, Italy
{pazienza, pennacchiotti}@info.uniroma2.it
[2] DISCo, University of Milano Bicocca, Via B. Arcimboldi 8, Milano, Italy
zanzotto@disco.unimib.it

Abstract. Recognition of textual entailment is not an easy task. In fact, early experimental evidences in [1] seems to demonstrate that even human judges often fail in reaching an agreement on the existence of entailment relation between two expressions. We aim to contribute to the theoretical and practical setting of textual entailment, through both a linguistic inspection of the textual entailment phenomenon and the description of a new promising approach to recognition, as implemented in the system we proposed at the RTE competition [2].

1 Introduction

Several applications like Question Answering (QA) and Information Extraction (IE) strongly rely on the identification in texts of fragments answering specific user information needs. For example, given the question : *Who bought Overture?* a QA system should be able to extract and return to the user forms like *Yahoo bought Overture, Yahoo owns Overture, Overture acquisition by Yahoo*, all of them conveying equivalent or inferable meaning. A huge amount of linguistic and semantic knowledge is needed in order to find equivalences and similarities both at lexical and syntactic levels. Both the study of syntactic alternation and normalization phenomena [3], and the use of semantic and lexical resources, such as WordNet [4], could be useful to disentangle the problem from a linguistic perspective. On the contrary, most applications adopt statistical approaches, looking at collocation and co-occurrence evidences, avoiding deeper and complex linguistic analysis.

Whatever the approach is, what still lacks in the NLP community (as underlined in [3]) is the identification of a common framework in which to analyse, compare and evaluate these different techniques. Indeed, even if shared test beds and common roots for specific applications already exist (e.g., TREC competition for QA [5] and MUC [?] for IE), there is an emerging need for gathering together researches and methodologies that share the underlying common goal of equivalence/similarity recognition among surface forms.

In this direction, the *textual entailment* task has been recently proposed in [3] as a new framework, whose aim is to capture the common *core* shared by most NLP applications.

Roughly, textual entailment can be defined as an oriented relation, between the text T and the hypothesis H. T is said to entail H if the meaning of H can

S. Bandini and S. Manzoni (Eds.): AI*IA 2005, LNAI 3673, pp. 315–326, 2005.

be inferred from the meaning of T. For example the sentence *Yahoo bought Overture* entails *Overture acquisition by Yahoo*. A system able to recognize textual entailment relations could be thus intended as the core of any NLP architecture whose aim is to extract an information need from textual material, looking at equivalence and more sophisticated subsumption phenomena.

Recognition of textual entailment is not an easy task. In fact, early experimental evidences in [1] seems to demonstrate that even human judges often fail in reaching an agreement on the existence of entailment relation between two expressions. In [1] it is shown that three judges could not reach an agreement in 233 over 759 cases of entailment template forms like T:[X punish Y] *entails* H:[X conquers Y]. Despite the intrinsic difficulties of the task, the recent first *Recognition of Textual Entailment* (RTE) competition [2] has seen the participation of a variety of systems, whose performance have been evaluated over a common test bed of T-H entailment pairs. The average accuracy performance of the proposed systems is still less than 60%.

We aim to contribute to the theoretical and practical setting of textual entailment, through both a linguistic inspection of the textual entailment phenomenon and the description of a new promising approach to recognition, as implemented in the system we proposed at the RTE competition [7].

2 Textual Entailment

2.1 Definitions

Textual Entailment is formally defined [3] as a relationship between a coherent text T and a language expression, the hypothesis H. T is said to entail H ($T \Rightarrow H$) if the meaning of H can be inferred from the meaning of T. An *entailment function* $\mathcal{E}(T, H)$ thus maps an *entailment pair* $T - H$ to a true value (i.e., *true* if the relationship holds, *false* otherwise). Alternatively, $\mathcal{E}(T, H)$ can be also intended as a probabilistic function mapping the pair $T - H$ to a real value between 0 and 1, expressing the confidence with which a human judge or an automatic system estimate the relationship to hold.

In this perspective, two types of entailment can be identified:

- *Paraphrasing*: T and H carry the same fact, expressed with different words. For example *Yahoo acquired Overture* and *Yahoo bought Overture*.
- *Strict entailment*: T and H carry different facts, where the latter can be inferred from the former, as it is the case for *Yahoo bought Overture* and *Yahoo owns Overture*.

In textual entailment, the only restriction on T and H is to be meaningful and coherent linguistic expressions: simple text fragments, such a noun phrase or single words, or complete sentences. In the first case, entailment can be verified simply looking at synonymy or subsumption relation among words. For example the entailment *cat* $\Rightarrow$ *animal* holds, since the meaning of the hypothesis (*a cat exists*) can be inferred from the meaning of the text (*an animal exists*). In the latter case, deeper linguistic analysis are required, as sentential expression express complex facts about the world. In this paper we will focus on sentential entailment, as it reveals the most challenging and practical issues.

In view of using entailment recognition methods in real NLP applications, two main tasks can be identified: entailment pattern *acquisition* and entailment *recognition*. Entailment patterns, as defined in [3], are formed by a T template and an H template, that is, two language expressions accompanied with syntactic properties and possible free slots. For example, the pattern $X_{subj} : buys : Y_{obj} \rightarrow X_{subj} : owns : Y_{obj}$ states that for any syntactically coherent instantiation of X and Y, entailment holds.

Entailment pattern acquisition aims at collecting these generalized forms, carefully inspecting textual corpora, using different techniques ranging from statistical counts to linguistic analysis [1,8,9]. Then they will be used to retrieve entailment relations in new texts, as needed for specific applications.

Entailment recognition aims at verifying if an entailment relation holds (possibly with a degree of confidence) between two linguistic expressions. Unlike patterns acquisition, in the recognition task the textual material of T and H is given. The use of linguistic resources and analysis can be thus preferred [10].

2.2   Type of Entailment

From an operational point of view, three types of entailment can be defined:

- *semantic subsumption.* T and H express the same fact, but the situation described in T is more specific than the situation in H. The specificity of T is expressed through one or more semantic operations. For example in the sentential pair H:[the cat eats the mouse], T:[the cat devours the mouse], T is more specific than H, as *eat* is a semantic generalization of *devour.*
- *syntactic subsumption.* T and H express the same fact, but the situation described in T is more specific than the situation in H. The specificity of T is expressed through one or more syntactic operations. For example in the pair H:[the cat eats the mouse], T:[the cat eats the mouse in the garden], T contains a specializing prepositional phrase.
- *direct implication.* H expresses a fact that is implied by a fact in T. For example H:[The cat killed the mouse] is implied by T:[the cat devours the mouse], as it is supposed that *killed* is a precondition for *devour*.[1]

Despite the two types of subsumption entailment, *direct implication* underlies deeper semantic and discourse analysis. In most cases, as implication concerns two distinct facts in T and H, and as facts are usually expressed through verbs, it follows that the implication phenomenon is strictly tied to the relationship among the T and H verbs. In particular, it is interesting to notice the temporal relation between T and H verbs, as described in [4]. The two verbs are said to be in *temporal inclusion* when the action of one verb is temporally included in the action of the other (e.g. *snore→sleep*). *Backward-presuppoasition* stands when the H verb happens before the T verb (*win* entails *play*). Finally, in *causation*

---

[1] In [3] syntactic subsumption roughly corresponds to the *restrictive extension* rule, while direct implication and semantic subsumption to the *axiom rule*.

a stative verb in H necessarely follows a verb of change in T (e.g. *give→have*). In this case, the temporal relation is thus inverted with respect to backward-presupposition. Such considerations leave space to the application of temporal and verb analysis techniques both in the acquisition and recognition tasks.

3   Modelling Textual Entailment as Syntactic Graph Similarity

In this section we introduce the model of the running system for entailment *recognition* we presented at the RTE competition [7], based on the idea that entailment recognition can be modelled as a graph matching problem. Given a set of pairs $T - H$, the task consists in predicting if entailment holds or not, possibly accompanying the prediction with a confidence score.

As textual entailment is mainly concerned with syntactic aspects (as outlined in [3]), a model aiming at entailment recognition should basically rely on lexical and syntactic techniques, accompanied only with shallow semantic analysis.

We decided to model the entailment pair $T - H$ as two *syntactic graphs* augmented with lexical and shallow semantic information. Each graph *node* represents a phrase of the sentence, accompanied by its syntactic, morphological and semantic information. Each graph *edge* expresses a syntactic relation among phrases. Recognition can be thus intended as a process of comparison between two graphs: the more similar the graphs are, higher it is the probability of entailment. A *similarity measure* among graphs can be intended as a measure of entailment, and *graph matching theory* can be used as a tool to verify if entailment relation holds.

3.1   Graph Matching and XDG Basic Concepts

Graph matching theory aims at evaluating the similarity between two graphs. The power of graph matching is in the generality of graphs, as they can be used to represent roughly any kind of objects. Graph nodes usually represent object parts, while edges represent relations among parts. Matching algorithms are then used to recognize how similar two object are, looking at the structural similarity of their graph representation. Basic definitions of graph matching theory are those reported in [11]:

Definition 1. *A graph is defined as tuple* $G = (N, E, \mu, \nu)$, *where N is the finite set of labelled nodes, E the finite set of labelled edges connecting the nodes in N, $\mu : N \to L_N$ the function that assigns labels to nodes, and $\nu : E \to L_E$ the function that assigns labels to edges.*

Definition 2. *A graph isomorphism is a bijective function $f : N \to N'$, from a graph $G = (N, E, \mu, \nu)$ to a graph $G' = (N', E', \mu', \nu')$, such that:*

- $\mu(n) = \mu'(f(n))$ *for all $n \in N$*
- *for any edge $e \in E$ connecting two nodes n_1, n_2, it exists a edge e' connecting $f(n_1), f(n_2)$, and vice versa.*

Definition 3. *A subgraph isomorphism is an injective function* $f : N \rightarrow N'$, *from* $G = (N, E, \mu, \nu)$ *to* $G' = (N', E', \mu', \nu')$, *if it exists a subgraph* $S \subseteq G'$ *such that* f *is a graph isomorphism from* G *to* S.

Definition 4. *A graph* G *is called* common subgraph *between two graphs* G_1 *and* G_2 *if it exist a subgraph isomorphism from* G_1 *to* G *and from* G_2 *to* G.

Definition 5. *The common subgraph* G *of* G_1 *and* G_2 *with the highest number of nodes is called the* maximal common subgraph *(mcs(G_1, G_2))*.

The concept of *maximal common subgraph (mcs)* is often central in the definition of a *similarity measure*. In fact, in real applications errors and distortions in the input graphs can easily appear. Consequently, as perfect matching between two object is often impossible, graph matching algorithms must be error tolerant, returning as result a degree of similarity between graphs, rather than a deterministic matching answer.

In the context of textual entailment, graph matching theory must be applied to two graphs representing the syntactic structure of T and H, together with relevant lexical information. As useful syntactic representation we decided to use the extended dependency graph (XDG) [12]. An XDG is basically a dependency graph whose nodes C are *constituents* and whose edges D are the *grammatical relations* among the constituents, i.e. $\mathcal{XDG} = (C, D)$. Constituents, i.e. $c \in C$, are classical syntactic trees with explicit *syntactic heads*, i.e. $h(c)$, and *potential semantic governors*, i.e. $gov(c)$. A constituent can be either *complex* or *simple*. A *complex constituent* is a tree containing other constituents as sons. A *simple constituent* represent a leaf node, i.e., a token span in the input sentence, that carries information about lexical items (surface form, lemma, morphology, etc.). Dependencies in $(h, m, T) \in D$ represent typed (where T is the type) and ambiguous relations among a constituent, the *head* h, and one of its *modifiers* m. Ambiguity is represented using *plausibility* (between 0 and 1).

The syntactic analysis of entailment pairs has been carried out by Chaos [12], a robust modular parser based on the XDG formalism.

3.2   Adapting XDG and Graph Matching to Textual Entailment

Entailment recognition can thus be intended as a matching process among the two XDG graphs representing the hypothesis and the text, where nodes are the set of constituents C and edges are the set of dependencies D.

Concerning the XDG formalism, it is necessary to define the specific kind of information that a graph devoted to entailment recognition must hold. Then, it must be verified if XDG graphs are able to capture all these information. The three type of entailment outlined in Sec. 2.2 require, in order to be detected:

- *syntactic information*. In general, graphs that have similar syntactic and surface structure are likely to express the same fact. Moreover, syntactic addition to the T graph with respect to H can reveal a strict entailment relation, as capturing *syntactic subsumption entailment*. Finally, syntactic variations such as nominalization and active/passive transformations must be treated as invariant operations on graphs.

- *shallow lexical-semantic information.* Syntactic similarity can be supported by lexical-semantic information needed to grasp *semantic subsumption entailment*, such as verb and noun generalization, antinomy and synonymy. Moreover, *direct implication* requires the recognition of verb entailments.

The XDG formalism captures all needed information, as syntactic dependencies are explicitly represented, and lexical information about nodes are carefully treated.

A classical graph matching problem and textual entailment present similarities:

- In both cases there are complex objects to be matched.
- In order to tackle errors and distortion, in both tasks it is preferred to adopt a similarity measure able to express the degree of similarity between two object (e.g. using *mcs*), rather than a deterministic value.

However, some peculiar properties of textual entailment make necessary major adaptations of the standard graph matching methodology:

- *Node complexity.* In the graph theory nodes are matched simply looking at their *label level*. In textual entailment node similarity can not be reduced to a surface analysis, as both morphological and semantic variations must be taken into account. Textual entailment nodes are not atomic, since they represent complex constituents that can be further divided in sub-constituents for deeper lexical-semantic analysis. For these two reasons, matching between two nodes is a complex process. It is necessary to evaluate a graded level of linguistically motivated *node semantic similarity* $sm(c_h, c_t)$.
- *Edge complexity.* Edges are complex structures too: their matching must be evaluated looking also at the type of dependency they express. A graded *syntactic similarity* $ss(c_h, c_t)$ has then to be defined to capture this aspects.
- *Transformation invariance.* Textual entailment must account for graph invariant transformations: specific type of syntactic phenomena (nominalization, active/passive transformation, etc.) should be properly treated. Two graphs representing syntactic variations of the same fact, while structurally dissimilar, should be considered as equivalent.
- *Asymmetry.* Textual entailment, unlike the classical graph problems, is not symmetric, since it represents a direct relation of subsumptiom from T to H. By consequence, the *graph isomorphism* definition must be further refined in a more specific notion of *XDG subsumption isomorphism*.

In view of these observations, definition in Sec.3.1 are extended as follows.

Definition 6. *An* XDG subsumption isomorphism *is an oriented relation from a text* $\mathcal{XDG}_T = (C_T, D_T)$ *to an hypothesis* $\mathcal{XDG}_H = (C_H, D_H)$ *(*$\mathcal{XDG}_H \preceq \mathcal{XDG}_T$*), expressed by two bijective functions:*

- $f_C : C_T \to C_H$
- $f_D : D_T \to D_H$

where f_C and f_D describe the oriented relation of subsumption between con-stituents (nodes) and dependencies (edges) of H and T.

f_C and f_D play the role of function f in the definition of *graph isomorphism* in Sec.3.1. Unluckily, due to the *node and edge complexity* factors, a definition of f_C and f_D can not be easily stated as for f. Sec.3.3 will thus give an extensive description on how these two functions are modelled.

Definition 7. *A* subgraph subsumption isomorphism *between* $\mathcal{XDG}_H$ *and* $\mathcal{XDG}_T$, *written as* $\mathcal{XDG}_H \sqsubseteq \mathcal{XDG}_T$, *holds if it exists* $\mathcal{XDG}'_T \subseteq \mathcal{XDG}_T$ *so that* $\mathcal{XDG}_H \preceq \mathcal{XDG}'_T$.

Isomorphic subsumption aims to capture cases 1 and 3 described in Sec.2.2, while *subgraph subsumption isomorphism* corresponds to case 2 in Sec.2.2.

As in graph matching theory, an *mcs* must be defined in order to cope with distortions and errors in the input graphs mainly introduced by syntactic parser erroneous interpretations.

Definition 8. *The* maximal common subsumer subgraph *(mcss) between* $\mathcal{XDG}_H$ *and* $\mathcal{XDG}_T$ *is the graph with the highest number of nodes, among all the subgraph of* $\mathcal{XDG}_H$ *which are in isomorphic subgraph subsumption with* $\mathcal{XDG}_T$.

3.3   Graph Syntactic Similarity Measure for Textual Entailment

The similarity measure $\mathcal{E}(\mathcal{XDG}_T, \mathcal{XDG}_H)$, used to estimate the degree of confidence with which $\mathcal{XDG}_H$ and $\mathcal{XDG}_T$ are in entailment relation, must be modelled on the subsumption between nodes and edges in T and H, grasping the notion of *mcss*. Four main steps are required:

1. *Model the bijective function* $f_C : C'_T \to C'_H$, that maps constituents in $C'_H \subseteq C_H$ to subsuming constituents in $C'_T \subseteq C_T$. A semantic similarity $sm(c_h, c_t)$ must be accompanied to each mapping. For example in the pair H:[the cat eats the mouse], T:[the cat devours the mouse], *eats* could be mapped in *devours*.
2. *Model the bijective function* $f_D : D'_T \to D'_H$, that maps dependencies in $D'_H \subseteq D_H$ to dependencies in $D'_T \subseteq D_T$. A syntactic similarity $ss(c_h, c_t)$ is then derived to better capture the implications of such mappings.
3. *Find the mcss*, that is, the common subgraph identified by f_C and f_D. The *mcss* must be accompanied with an overall similarity, deriving from the *sm* and *ss* of its nodes and edges.
4. *Model* $\mathcal{E}(XDG_T, XDG_H)$ using *mcss* and the two input graphs $\mathcal{XDG}_H$ and $\mathcal{XDG}_T$. Textual entailment between a pair $T - H$ will be thus predicted verifying $\mathcal{E}(XDG_T, XDG_H)$ against a manually tuned threshold.

Node Subsumption. The node subsumption function f_C must identify constituents in C_H that can be mapped to constituents C_T. We will define the function with a set A containing the *anchors*, i.e. the correspondences between the constituents of C_H and C_T. The set A will thus represent the nodes of the *mcss*.

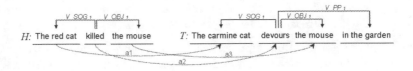

Fig. 1. A complete example of entailment pair, represented in the XDG formalism. Solid lines indicate grammatical relations D (with *type* and *pluusibility*); dotted lines indicate anchors a_i between H and T constituents.

In A, each constituent $c_h \in C_H$ is associated, if possible, to its most similar constituent $c_t \in C_T$ (that is, the c_t that most likely subsumes c_h). The definition follows:

Definition 9. *Given the anchors $a = (c_h, c_t)$ as linking structures, connecting constituents $c_h \in C_H$ to constituents $c_t \in C_T$ and a function of semantic similarity $sm(c_h, c_t) \in (0, 1]$ expressing how much similar c_h and c_t are looking at their lexical and semantic properties, the set of anchors A is:*

$$A = \{(c_h, c_t) | c_h \in C_H, c_t \in C_T, sm(c_h, c_t) = \max_{c \in C_T} sm(c_h, c) \neq 0\}$$

If a subsuming c_t can not be found for a c_h (i.e. $\max_{c \in C_T} sm(c_h, c) = 0$), then c_h has no anchors. For example in the entailment pair of Fig. 1, f_C produces the mapping pairs *[The red cat - The carmine cat]*, *[killed - devours]*, *[the mouse - the mouse]*.

The semantic similarity $sm(c_h, c_t)$ is derived on the basis of the syntactic type of c_h, that is, if it is a noun-prepositional phrase $sm(c_h, c_t) = sm_{np}(c_h, c_t)$ or a verb phrase $sm(c_h, c_t) = sm_{vp}(c_h, c_t)$. If c_h is a noun-prepositional phrase, similarity $sm_{np}(c_h, c_t)$ is evaluated as:

$$sm_{np}(c_h, c_t) = \alpha * s(gov(c_h), gov(c_t)) + (1 - \alpha) * \frac{\sum_{s_h \in S(c_h)} \max_{s_t \in S(c_t)} s(s_h, s_t)}{|S(c_h)|}$$

where $gov(c)$ is the governor of the constituent c, $S(c_h)$ and $S(c_t)$ are the set simple constituents excluding the governors respectively of c_h and c_t, and $\alpha \in [0, 1]$ is an empirically evaluated parameter used to weight the importance of the governor. In turns, $s(s_h, s_t) \in [0, 1]$ expresses the similarity among two simple constituents: it is maximal if they have same surface or stem (e.g. *cat* and *cats*), otherwise a semantic similarity weight $\beta \in (0, 1)$ is assigned looking at possible WordNet relations (synonymy, entailment and generalization).

If c_h is a verb phrase, different *levels* of similarity are taken into consideration, according to the semantic value of its modal. For example *must go-could go* should get a lower similarity than *must go-should go*. A verb phrase is thus composed by its governor *gov* and its modal constituents *mod*. The overall similarity is thus:

$$sm_{vp}(c_h, c_t) = \gamma * s(gov(c_h), gov(c_t)) + (1 - \gamma) * d(mod(c_h), mod(c_t))$$

where $d(mod(c_h), mod(c_t)) \in [0, 1]$ is empirically derived as the semantic distance between two modals (e.g., *must* is nearer to *should* than to *could*) (classified as generic auxiliaries, auxiliaries of possibility and auxiliaries of obligation).

Edge Subsumption. Once f_C is defined the existence of the bijective fuction f_D can be easly verified by construction. The edge subsumption function f_D maps $(c_h, c_h', T_h) \in D_H$ to $f_D(c_h, c_h', T_h) = (c_t, c_t', T_t) \in D_T$ if $T_h = T_t$ and $(c_h, c_t), (c_h', c_t') \in A$. The set of mapped D_H will thus represent the edges linking the nodes of the *mcss*.

The definition of f_D gives the possibility of investigating the external *syntactic similarity* $ss(c_h, c_t)$ of a given anchor $(c_h, c_t) \in A$. This should capture how similar are the relations established by elements in the anchor. Our syntactic similarity $ss(c_h, c_t)$ depends on the semantic similarity of the constituents connected with the same depencency to c_h and c_t in their respective $\mathcal{X}D\mathcal{G}$s, that is, the set $A(c_h, c_t)$ defined as:

$$A(c_h, c_t) - \{(c_h', c_t') \in A | f_D(c_h, c_h', T) = (c_t, c_t', T)\}$$

For example in Fig. 1, $A(killed, devours) = \{([the\_red\_cat], [the\_carmine\_cat]), ([the\_mouse], [the\_mouse])\}$. The syntactic similarity $ss(c_h, c_t)$ is then defined as:

$$ss(c_h, c_t) = \frac{\displaystyle\sum_{(c_h', c_t') \in A(c_h, c_t)} sm(c_h', c_t')}{|D_H(c_h)|}$$

where $D_H(c_h)$ are the dependencies in D_H originating in c_h.

Similarity Measure. Once nodes and edges of the *mcss* have been identified through f_C and f_D, an overall similarity $S(mcss)$ is evaluated for *mcss*. $S(mcss)$ must express how much similar the two subgraphs $\mathcal{X}D\mathcal{G}'_T$ and $\mathcal{X}D\mathcal{G}'_H$ in isomorphic subsumption are, both from a syntactic and a semantic point of view.

For each pair $(c_h, c_t) \in A$ a global similarity S is thus derived as:

$$S(c_h, c_t) = \delta * sm(c_h, c_t) + (1 - \delta) * ss(c_h, c_t)$$

where δ is a manually tuned parameter. The, similarity measure $\mathcal{E}(\mathcal{X}DG_T, \mathcal{X}DG_H)$ can be evaluated in analogy to the measure described in 3.1. In this specific case, numerator and denominator will not be expressed as number of nodes, but as probabilities, since, as stated before, textual entailment must account for node and edges complexity. Numerator will thus be the overall *mcss* similarity . The denominator will express the best case, in which *mcss* corresponds to $\mathcal{X}DG_H$, and all nodes and edges match with probability 1 to elements of a hypothetic T.

$$\mathcal{E}(\mathcal{X}DG_T, \mathcal{X}DG_H) = \frac{S(mcss)}{|C_H|} = \frac{\displaystyle\sum_{(c_h, c_t) \in A} S(c_h, c_t)}{|C_H|}$$

3.4   Graph Invariant Transformations

Entailment pairs are often expressed through syntactic variations, as:

H:[The cat killed the mouse], T:[The killing of the mouse by the cat]

We had thus to model the most important variation phenomena in our system, in order to cope with pairs with different syntactic structures used that express the same fact. Before the graph matching procedure, a set of graph transformation rules have been applied to $\mathcal{XDG}_H$ and $\mathcal{XDG}_T$, in order to bring to a normalized form sentences that have a syntactic variation. For example in the abovementioned example, the text is brought back to the normal form T:[the cat killed the mouse]. We modelled the following type of invariant transformation:

- *nominalization in T*. Different cases such as T:[The killing of the mouse by the cat] and T:[The cat is the killer of the mouse] are treated. Only nominalization of T is taken into consideration, as usually in entailment relations nominalization happens only in T;
- *passivization in H or T*. Passive sentences are brought to active forms.
- *negation in H or T*. If one sentence is the negative form of the other, the two sentences are recognized to be not in entailment (*negative subsumption*).

4   Experimental Setting and Result Analysis

The RTE challenge has been the first test to verify the performances of our system. The data set used for the competition was formed by three sets of entailment pairs. A First development set, composed by 287 annotated pairs; a *Second development set*, composed by 280 annotated pairs; a *Test set*, composed by 800 non annotated pairs. In the first two sets the true value of entailment was given, in order to model and tune the systems participating at the competition. The test set was used for evaluation. We used the first development set to tune parameters of the model (α, β, γ, δ) and the second development set to verify the validity of the model, while the test set was used for the competition. Participating systems were evaluated over the test set: a prediction value ($True/False$) and an associated degree of confidence on the prediction $c \in [0, 1]$ have been provided for each pair. Two measures were used for evaluation: *accuracy* (fraction of correct responses) and the *confidence-weighted score (cws)* as defined in [2].

Performance of our system where on the average of those reported by other participants (cws 55,70%). Results are shown on Table 1 . In fact, pairs of development and test sets have been collected by human annotators, looking at typical NLP *tasks*: Information Retrieval (IR), Information Extraction (IE), Comparable Documents (CD), Reading Comprehension (RC), Question Answering (QA), Machine Translation (MT), Paraphrase Acquisition (PP). As different application envision different types of linguistic expression and consequently different types of entailment, it is predictable to obtain different performances for pairs collected in different ways.

Table 1. RTE competition results on data set (800 entailment pairs). On the left, overall results. On the right, results ordered by task.

Measure	Result
cws	0.5574
accuracy	0.5245
precision	0.5265
recall	0.4975
f	0.5116

$TASK$	cws	accuracy
CD	0.8381	0.7651
IE	0.4559	0.4667
MT	0.5914	0.5210
QA	0.4408	0.3953
RC	0.5167	0.4857
PP	0.5583	0.5400
IR	0.4405	0.4444

At a first glance, results in Table 1 seems to show low accuracy and cws. In truth, performances are in line with those obtained by other systems, driving at least to two conclusions. Firstly, the task of entailment recognition seems inherently hard, as outlined in Sec.1. Secondly, low results indicate that research on entailment is only at an early stage and that system proposed must be considered as prototypical architectures implementing on-going studies.

More in particular, it is interesting to analyze results looking at the performance obtained on the different tasks. As Table 1 shows, our system performed quite well on the CD task, while worst performance were achieved in QA and IR. Such large difference is not surprising, as a comparison of the pairs of each tasks reveals. CD pairs are characterized by having T and H syntactically and lexically very similar, e.g.:

T: [The first settlements on the site of Jakarta were established at the mouth of the Ciliwung, perhaps as early as the 5th century AD.]
H: [The first settlements on the site of Jakarta were established as early as the 5th century AD.]

IR and QA pairs are much more complex to recognize, as they are usually formed by a brief H statement and a long an complex T sentence, e.g.:

T: [A former police officer was charged with murder Thursday in the slaying of a college student who allegedly had threatened to expose their sexual relationship, authorities said.]
H: [Ex-cop Rios killed student.]

As the graph method we adopted is strongly based on the comparison of the syntactic graphs of T and H, it follows that it is most suited to the CD task, as the system can easily find anchors and carry out the reasoning. On the contrary, for IR and QA task statistical approaches to entailment recognition would maybe be the only strategy to approach the task.

In general, as expected, the system has been able to successfully recognize entailment when the relation between T and H was expressed through syntactically *recognizable* operations (e.g., invariant transformations and constituent generalizations/synonymy):

T: [Korean Seoul, formally Soul-t'ukpyolsi ("Special City of Seoul"), largest city and
capital of the Republic of Korea (South Korea), ...]
H: [The capital and largest city of South Korea is Seoul.]

5   Conclusions and Future Works

While a very important results must be considered the overall methodological
definition of the task and the theoretical defintions given in Sec.2, early experimental results show that further improvement are needed, in particular to cover
entailment cases that can be grasped only by statistical techniques. Future works
thus envision a deeper analysis of entailment pairs in the perspective of the classifications proposed, in order to identify specific entailment patterns that could
be associated to each specific entailment type. Moreover, the fertile combination
of statistical and linguistic methods for both recognition and acquisition could
be a promising area of investigation.

References

1. Szpektor, I., Tanev, H., Dagan, I., Coppola, B.: Scaling web-based acquisition
   of entailment relations. In Lin, D., Wu, D., eds.: Proceedings of EMNLP 2004,
   Barcelona, Spain, Association for Computational Linguistics (2004) 4148
2. Dagan, I., Glickman, O., Magnini, B.: The pascal recognising textual entailment
   challenge. In: PASCAL Challenges Workshop, Southampton, U.K (2005)
3. Dagan, I., Glickman, O.: Probabilistic textual entailment: Generic applied modeling of language variability. In: Learning Methods for Text Understanding and
   Mining, Grenoble, France (2004)
4. Miller, G., Beckwith, R., Fellbaum, C., Gross, D., Miller, K.: Five papers on wordnet. Technical Report CSL Report 43, Princeton University (1990)
5. Voorhees, E.M.: Overview of the trec 2003 question answering track. In: TREC.
   (2003) 5468
6. Proceedings of the Seventh Message Understanding Conference (MUC-7), Virginia
   USA, Morgan Kaufmann (1998)
7. Pazienza, M.T., Pennacchiotti, M., Zanzotto, F.M.: Textual entailment as syntactic
   graph distance: a rule based and a svm based approach. In: PASCAL Challenges
   Workshop, Southampton, U.K (2005)
8. Barzilay, R., McKeown, K.: Extracting paraphrases from a parallel corpus. In:
   Proceedings of the 39th ACL Meeting, Toulouse, France (2001)
9. Lin, D., Pantel, P.: DIRT,discovery of inference rules from text. In: Knowledge
   Discovery and Data Mining. (2001) 323328
10. Hagege, C., Roux, C.: Entre syntaxe et smantique : normalisation de la sortie de
    lanalyse syntaxique en vue de lamlioration de lextraction dinformation a partir de
    textes. In: TANL 2003, Batz-sur-Mer,France (2003)
11. Bunke, H.: Graph matching: Theoretical foundations, algorithms, and applications.
    In: Vision Interface 2000, Montreal, Springer-Verlag (2000) 8288
12. Basili, R., Zanzotto, F.M.: Parsing engineering and empirical robustness. Natural
    Language Engineering 8/2-3 (2002)

Multigranular Scale Speech Recognizers: Technological and Cognitive View

Francesco Cutugno, Gianpaolo Coro, and Massimo Petrillo

Department of Physics, University Federico II, Naples, Italy
{cutugno, coro, massimo.petrillo}@na.infn.it

Abstract. We propose a Multigranular Automatic Speech Recognizer. The hypothesis is that speech signal contains information distributed on more different time scales. Many works from various scientific fields ranging from neurobiology to speech technologies, seem to concord on this assumption. In a broad sense, it seems that speech recognition in human is optimal because of a partial parallelization process according to which the left-to-right stream of speech is captured in a multilevel grid in which several linguistic analyses take place contemporarily. Our investigation aims, in this view, to apply these new ideas to the project of more robust and efficient recognizers.

1 Introduction

Many works available from various scientific fields ranging from neurobiology to experimental phonetics seem to concord on the idea that speech signal contains information distributed on more different time scales and that, in order to process it properly, it is necessary that more parallel cognitive functions operate a chunking on the unfolding of the information over time. It seems that speech recognition in human can success because of a partial parallelization process according to which the left-to-right stream of speech is captured in a multilevel grid in which several linguistic analyses take place contemporarily. Evidence of parallelized speech processing can be seen in many authors like Poeppel [1]. In recent speech perception theories (Hawkins, Smith [2]) the existence of a multimodal sensory experience is stated being processed and transformed into different type of linguistic and non linguistic knowledge. These ideas have rapidly influenced many researchers involved in ASR (Automatic Speech Recognition) projects (Wu [3], Chang [4], Greenberg [5]). Newer ideas like "syllabic pre-segmentation", "word n-gram statistical combination", "parallel and multiscale speech coding" have been introduced in speech processing (similar concepts were also present, in Erman et al. [6]).

2 Multigranular Automatic Recognition

Modern approaches to Automatic Speech Recognition are typically classified on the base of different identification of the so called "Base Unit" of Speech (the minimal form of acoustic and linguistic information around which human speech recognition is organized). Supported by perceptive experimental results and application efficiency,

S. Bandini and S. Manzoni (Eds.): AI*IA 2005, LNAI 3673, pp. 327–330, 2005.

the most common approach is the "phonetic" one: it is hypothesized that a sequence of phones is sufficient to recognize a word. Hereby we mean by phone one or more acoustic instances of the abstract classes of speech sound known as "phonemes".

A possible alternative is to identify the Base Unit with the syllable. Even in this case a number of perceptive experiments give support [7]. We refer here a syllable as a group of phones strongly connected each other by dynamic constraints and by temporal evolution of the articulatory apparatus.

In the rest of this article we propose a third approach, following the idea of a "multigranular" recognizer and refusing to use a single type of Base Unit. We will attempt a first design of a framework in which two o more linguistic units, directly connected to different time scaled processes, could generate a multilevel lattice taking into account all the information available in speech signal during the speech recognition process: phones and syllable could constitute the first two levels of analysis directly followed by words and other events. Collateral to the theoretical discussion on the Base Unit, is the problem of the choice of the "technical" instruments for the recognition. The statistical approach is the most used, but some alternatives must be evaluated: the redundancy, present in the acoustic signals, has to be "swindled" in order to reduce complexity, and, furthermore, we also want control the speech recognition process at every step.

Experimental evidence brings us to think that systems like Hidden Markov Models (HMMs) can extract recognition-useful information with less variables than other systems, while many authors prefer a "hybrid approach", that makes use of a Neural Network for the recognition of single linguistic units, followed by a lexicon for word decoding.

Assume now we have a stochastic recognizer (HMM, Neural Network etc.) for every linguistic unit (phone, syllable, word etc.) and let's see how we can melt together the single "grain" recognitions, in order to get the most probable spoken word.

We could build a "lattice" linking linguistic units of the same type, that would represent any possible pronunciation of the words in a reference dictionary.

For example we could think about a "phone lattice": every node will represent a single phone and every arc the probability of moving from a phone to the successive (this is the "classic approach" lexicon). By means of the sequence of recognitions, performed by the previous statistical system, we will get an "optimal" walk through the lattice and so the most probable phrase or word. At the same way, we can imagine a syllable based lattice or a word based lattice.

Arc weights are chosen on the basis of a statistical analysis on a reference corpus and correspond to the succession frequency between two linguistic units.

The number of arcs and their topology in the lattice are clearly different in this three models: while in the phones lattice each node has at least, in principle, a connection with any other unit in the set, not every syllable (or word) can be put before any other.

Statistics on English showed that only few syllable from all possible ones are most used during a natural speech conversation [8], so this should be also the case in Italian, were we know bi-syllable as most used words. This kind of analysis could result in a pruning of the possible combination of syllables or words and a loss of complexity.

From a theoretical point of view a multigranular recognizer should take into account all the three lattices, acting on the basis of their behaviour. The lattices should also be able to communicate each other. A first, rough, idea could be that all the three lattices acted in parallel with the decision basing on the "best scoring" lattice.

This approach is very expensive, in terms of computational complexity, so it's better finding alternative methods.

A possible choice, that we propose in this paper, sees that the system operating always in a single level (starting for example from the less complex) and, only depending upon heuristic evaluations, foresees the passage to another level until another change or the end of the recognition (Fig. 1) is reached.

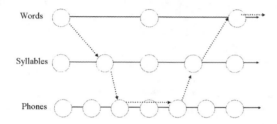

Fig. 1. Recognition process of an ideal Multigranular Recognizer

The heuristic evaluation could be based upon parameters as noise level, or complexity of the level lattice, letting the system to rise or fall also in a "multigranular" scale, according to the belief, explained above, that different granular-levels can vary lattice complexity, and that there are more convenient levels, given a particular situation, that let us recognize a word without the classification of each single phone or syllable. Think about a situation in which, based on the knowledge retrieved from a corpus, a grammar tells us that there is a particular word, into the vocabulary, that starts with the yet recognized phones or syllable and that frequently follows the previously recognized words. On the basis of a heuristic evaluation, the system could infer the correct word without exploring the not-yet recognized phones or syllables, as usually the Viterbi algorithm does in this type of lattices.

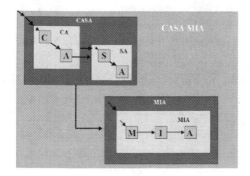

Fig. 2. Statechart Multigranular ASR

The idea we propose here involves the use of a special language: the Statechart [9]. Statechart extends the classical notion of Finite Automata by means of the following concepts: **Hierarchy, Concurrency** and **Transmitted Communication** Every state of an Automata is allowed to include other finite automata (**OR** States) and more automata can act in parallel (**AND** states) communicating with the exchange of messages . We want to stress indeed that this is not the only possible implementation of the model, alternatives are still in study. Starting from the statechart concept we show an implementation scheme of a multigranular ASR. Hierachy is central in the model and this is achieved by nested OR states (Fig. 2). This model exploits the varying complexity and performances potentials of several recognizers, in order to take advantage from the best combination. A big weight is given to the heuristic function that has to choose the way, and hierarchy allows a better management of lattices than the parallel model.

3   Discussion

The necessity of a multigranular model derives from a gap between human and machine spontaneous speech recognition. Modern ASR are not able to emulate human auditory system, moreover they are usually based on a single linguistic unit and completely separate from the perceptual behaviour. Models yet developed in this way let us think that the whole system could result in a more robust to interferences one (Wu [3]). We have proposed a new theoretical model, though also an idea of implementation have been discussed, towards a speech multigranular processing.

References

1. Poeppel, D.: The Analysis of Speech in Different Temporal Integration Windows: Cerebral Lateralization as 'Asymmetric Sampling in Time'. Speech Communication 41 (2003) 245-255
2. Hawkins, S., Smith, R.: Polysp: a Polysystemic, Phonetically-Rich Approach to Speech Understanding. Rivista di Linguistica, (2001) 99-189
3. Wu., S. L.: Incorporating Information from Syllable-Length Time Scales into Automatic Speech Recognition. ICSI PhD. Thesis (1998)
4. Chang, S.: A Syllable, Articulatory-Feature and Stress-Accent model of Speech Recognition. PhD. Dissertation, Department of Electrical Engineering and Computer Sciences, University of California, Berkeley (2002)
5. Greenberg, S.: Understanding Speech Understanding: Towards a Unified Theory of Speech Perception. ESCA Workshop on Auditory Basis of Speech Perception, (1996) 1-8
6. Erman L.D., Hayes-Roth F., Lesser V.R., Reddy R. The Hearsay-II Speech-Understanding System: Integrating Knowledge to Resolve Uncertainty. ACM Computing Surveys 12(2) (1980)
7. Dominic W. Massaro. Preperceptual images, processing time and perceptual units in auditory perception. Psychological Review, 79(2) (1972) 124-145
8. Greenberg, S.: On the Origins of Speech Intelligibility. ESCA Workshop for Robust Speech Recognition for Unknown Communication Channels, (1997) 23-32
9. Maggiolo-Schettini, A., Peron, A., Tini, S.: A Comparison of Step-Semantics of Statecharts. Theoretical Computer Science (2003) 465-498

Towards a General Framework for Substitutional Adaptation in Case-Based Reasoning

Sara Manzoni, Fabio Sartori, and Giuseppe Vizzari

Department of Informatics, Systems and Communication,
University of Milano-Bicocca,
Via Bicocca degli Arcimboldi 8 20126 Milan, Italy
Tel: +39 02 64487835; Fax: + 39 02 64487839
{manzoni, sartori, vizzari}@disco.unimib.it

Abstract. Adaptation is one of the most problematic steps in the design and development of Case Based Reasoning (CBR) systems, as it may require considerable domain knowledge and involve complex knowledge engineering tasks. This paper describes a general framework for substitutional adaptation, which only requires analogical domain knowledge, very similar to the one required to define a similarity function. The approach is formally defined, and its applicability is discussed with reference to case structure and its variability. A case study focused on the adaptation of cases related to truck tyre production processes is also presented.

1 Introduction

The acquisition of knowledge required to implement the capability of adapting the solution to a past case in a different, although similar, situation is a general issue in the development of Case Based Reasoning (CBR) systems (see, e.g., [1]). CBR approach allows to tackle problems still not well understood, in which it is not possible to build a theory or a model supporting the problem solving activity. In general, in these situations it is also difficult to develop a method to adapt the solution of the retrieved case to the case the target case that has to be solved. In particular, even if the required knowledge is actually available, it is a complex knowledge engineering task to acquire, represent and implement it into a specific adaptation module.

A taxonomy of various approaches to case adaptation can be found in [2], and two main categories of adaptation approaches are identified. *Transformational* approaches provide the modification of the solution of a retrieved case to better fit the new situation (through the *substitution* of certain solution features or even the modification of its *structure*). *Generative* adaptation schemes instead build from scratch part of the solution, according to current case description features and the description of the reasoning process that led to the solution of the retrieved best–matching case. In general, whatever adaptation approach is selected, the involved knowledge is strictly domain specific and it cannot be simply generalized.

S. Bandini and S. Manzoni (Eds.): AI*IA 2005, LNAI 3673, pp. 331–342, 2005.

The aim of this paper is to present a general framework for substitutional approach to adaptation which only requires and exploits *analogical* knowledge, that is, domain knowledge that is already employed by the CBR system in order to evaluate differences and similarity between cases. The underlying idea of the here presented approach considers that past cases may give an indication on how to adapt the solution of the retrieved case given the difference among its description and the one related to the current problem. The difference among current and retrieved case descriptions is used as a criteria to select from the Case Base pairs of representatives of these cases, whose solutions (and more precisely, the difference among their solutions) are aggregated to define the way to adapt the solution of the retrieved case to solve the current one.

The following Section introduces the context of this work and describes other adaptation approaches that can be found in the literature, while Section 3 formally describes the proposed approach and discusses its applicability. A case study in which this framework was applied for the development of an adaptation module for a CBR system supporting the design of a production process will then be introduced. Conclusions and future developments will end the paper.

2   Context and Related Work

Case adaptation is a very complex task: in fact, CBR is often selected as a problem solving method for situations in which a theory or model allowing to construct the solution of a given problem cannot be defined due to lack of knowledge. In these situations it is also very difficult to have a theory of adaptation, a set of mechanisms defining how to modify the solution of a case similar to the current one according to differences in their descriptions. The *null adaptation* approach (i.e. leaving the adaptation up to the user, or do not perform adaptation at all) is often selected, while relevant experiences in the modelling and design of adaptation models describe complex knowledge models requiring considerable knowledge engineering effort to be effectively implemented (see, e.g., [3,4]).

Several works can be found in the literature that aim at describing possible approaches for the modelling and design of adaptation modules, and some of them are aimed at the development of general approaches and methodologies for case adaptation. In [5] it is described an attempt to combine retrieve and adaptation steps into a unique planning process, leading to the problem solution starting from the current problem description. In this way the general issue of adaptation is reformulated in terms of plan adaptation. Several other approaches provide the learning of adaptation rules from the case base itself [6]. In particular, while some of these approaches reify episodes of adaptation into cases and adopt a second CBR system devoted to this single step of the overall cycle (see, e.g. [7]), other ones adopt a hybrid strategy, including both such a CBR-based adaptation and rule-based modifications of the retrieved solution (see, e.g., [8]). Another relevant example of adaptation strategy provides the exploitation of domain specific relationships among cases (i.e. case dominance) to provide an adaptation heuristics supporting case-based estimation [9]. In particular, this approach exploits pairs of past solved cases presenting some specific difference with respect to the current one, in order to derive an adaptation to the retrieved case solution.

3   Framework for Substitutional Adaptation

The basic assumption of the CBR approach is that "similar cases of a certain problem have similar solutions": given the description of a new instance of a problem, one may search the set of previous experiences for a solved case characterized by a similar description and adapt its solution to the current situation. The first part of this process (i.e. to search for a similar case) relies essentially on the concept of similarity and knowledge related to the capability to compare cases. The second part is instead related to the capability to derive a modification to be applied to the solution of the retrieved case, from the descriptions of the current and retrieved ones in order to adapt the solution of the latter to be suitable for the current target case.

The rationale on which the proposed approach is based is that "similar differences among case descriptions imply similar differences among their solutions". In other words the same base of previously solved problem instances can also be queried for pairs of cases representing respectively the current and the retrieved case. These pairs are characterized by the fact that their descriptions present similar differences to the one that holds between the current and the retrieved cases. The differences among their solutions can thus be considered as indicators of the modification to be applied to the solution of the retrieved case to obtain the new one. A diagram describing this adaptation scheme is shown in Figure 1. The current and retrieved cases are respectively denoted by c_c and r_c, while r_{c_c} and r_{r_c} indicate their representatives; mod_c represents the modification to be applied to the solution of r_c in order to adapt it to the current case, and it is obtained as an aggregation of the differences among solutions of the representatives (i.e., $mod_1, \ldots, mod_n$).

In the following we will describe this approach in details and we will discuss its applicability.

3.1   Formal Description

In a CBR method, a case is a three–tuple $\langle d, s, o \rangle$, where d is the set of features that describe the specific instance of the problem, s is the set of attributes that characterize its solution, and o is the set of attributes describing the outcome obtained by the application of the solution s to the problem d. Given a Case Base CB, with $d(c)$, $s(c)$ and $o(c)$ we respectively denote the description, solution and outcome of a case $c \in CB$.

A case representation may provide a flat, fixed set of case descriptors or a more structured and possibly heterogeneous organization (see, e.g., [10,11]); however a case description can always be reduced to a finite set of features (e.g. a tree structured case can be reduced to a vector including only the leaves). In the following we are thus going to consider a case as a finite set of features

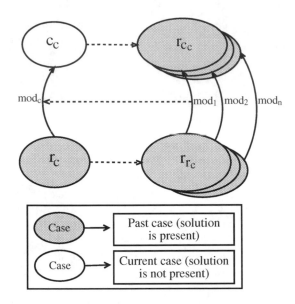

Fig. 1. Pairs of past cases representing the current and the retrieved one can be used to adapt the retrieved solution

$\{c_1, \ldots, c_k\}$; moreover it will be assumed that cases have an homogeneous description d. Under these conditions a case having k attributes can be considered as a vector of a k-dimensional space; in this way it is possible to obtain from pairs of cases a vector indicating the (vectorial) difference among their description parts. Given $a, b \in CB$ having an homogeneous description d (with $l < k$ the number of attributes composing d), the distance vector among them can be defined as

$$dist(a,b) = \Big(\big(dist_1(a_1, b_1)\big), \ldots, \big(dist_l(a_l, b_l)\big)\Big) \qquad (1)$$

where $dist_i$ represents the function that measures the distance among attributes at the i-th position in the case description d (e.g. normal difference for numeric attributes, specifically defined function for symbolic attributes). It must be noted that in general $dist(a, b) \neq dist(b, a)$.

Let us consider two cases $c_c \in CB$ and $r_c \in CB$, having an homogeneous description (i.e. a description providing the same number and type of features), and representing respectively the current case and the best–matching case in the Case Base according to the similarity function computation. It is possible to obtain pairs of case representatives $\langle r_{c_c}, r_{r_c} \rangle$ so that

$$r_{c_c}, r_{r_c} \in CB, \|dist(c_c, r_c) - dist(r_{c_c}, r_{r_c})\| < \epsilon \qquad (2)$$

In other words these representatives (that are case belonging to the case base CB) are not selected because they are similar to the current and retrieved case, but because the difference among their description is similar to the one that holds between the descriptions of c_c and r_c. The vector norm of difference among vector $a = dist(c_c, r_c)$ and $b = dist(r_{c_c}, r_{r_c})$ can be computed in this way

$$\sum_{i=1}^{l} \left(w_i \cdot diff_i(a_i, b_i) \right) \tag{3}$$

where $diff_i$ represents the function adopted to evaluate differences among the i-th distances in case descriptions, whose relevance is modulated by means of weighs w_i; they are strictly related to $dist_i$ functions, but these are bound to have $\mathbb{R}^+$ as codomain. However this is just one possible way to evaluate the similarity of two differences among cases, and according to specific domain knowledge this kind of evaluation might assume a different form. An intuitive graphical representation of this method to select representatives is shown in Figure 2.

It must be noted that representatives are identified according to $dist_c = dist(c_c, r_c)$, which is a vector distance. More precisely, two cases a and b are chosen respectively as representatives of the current case c_c and the retrieved case r_c because of the similarity among their vector distance $dist(a, b)$ and $dist_c$ according to a given norm, such as the one defined in equation 3, and a threshold value ϵ. However, in general, nothing can be said on the possibility of inverting a and b and still having a pair of representatives. This is due to the fact that $dist(a, b) \neq dist(b, a)$, and thus the there is no indication on $\|dist(c_c, r_c) - dist(b, a)\|$.

Given this method for defining pairs of cases which, according to the differences among their descriptions, can be considered representatives of the current and retrieved cases, it is possible to denote the set of these representatives by $Rep_{(c_c, r_c, \epsilon)}$. According to the previously introduced principle "similar differences among case descriptions imply similar differences among their solutions" every pair of representatives of this set may give an indication on the modification to be applied to the retrieved case solution. To derive in an automatic way a modification to be applied to the retrieved case in order to obtain the solution to the current one, is not trivial and some specific conditions must be specified. First of all, we focus on those representatives whose solutions are homogeneous to $s(r_c)$ (i.e. whose solution has the same structure of the one specified by the retrieved case), which will be denoted by $HRep_{(c_c, r_c, \epsilon)}$. Thanks to this homogeneity, given a case c in $HRep_{(c_c, r_c, \epsilon)}$, its solution part is a vector of attributes $s(c) = \{s_1, \ldots, s_j\}$. Given s and s' vectors representing solutions to two different cases, the difference vector among s and s' can be defined as

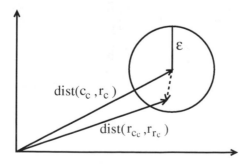

Fig. 2. A diagram illustrating the representative selection mechanism

$$mod(s, s') = \big(dist_1(s_1, s'_1), \ldots, dist_j(s_j, s'_j)\big) \tag{4}$$

where these $dist_i$ functions are analogous to those introduced for the computation of distance among cases in equation 1, with analogous considerations with reference to numeric and symbolic attributes. In other words, while distances and related modifications to numerical attributes can be easily computed, symbolic attributes require the definition of specific functions to compute this distance. Moreover, in this case we want to exploit this value to obtain indications on how to modify such an attribute in an adaptation scheme. The management and adaptation of symbolic attributes in case solution will be the object of future works, and we will now focus on numeric ones.

Considering that $s_1, \ldots, s_j$ are numerical attributes, it is possible to define the vector $mod(c_c, r_c)$ representing the modification to be applied to the retrieved case solution as a vectorial aggregation of the differences between solutions of case representatives. More precisely, given $H = HRep_{(c_c, r_c, \epsilon)}$,

$$mod(c_c, r_c) = \Big(\sum_{\langle c,r \rangle \in H} \big(f_{cr} \cdot dist_1(c, r)\big), \ldots, \sum_{\langle c,r \rangle \in H} \big(f_{cr} \cdot dist_j(c, r)\big) \Big) \tag{5}$$

where c and r respectively represent the current and retrieved case (in fact $\langle c, r \rangle \in HRep_{(c_c, r_c, \epsilon)}$). The multiplicative factor f_{cr} represents instead the relevance of the pair of representatives $\langle c, r \rangle$ in determining the overall adaptation vector mod_c. This factor can be a constant (e.g. $\frac{1}{|HRep_{(c_c, r_c, \epsilon)}|}$), or a function encapsulating domain knowledge which allows to distinguish pairs of representatives. The vector mod_c represents the modification to be applied to the solution of the retrieved case in order to obtain the new solution for the current case.

A schematic illustration of the whole process of representatives selection and aggregation of modifications to compose the adaptation vector is shown in Figure 3. In particular, $dist$ and mod blocks are respectively related to equation 3 and 4, while the $Aggreg.$ block is related to equation 5.

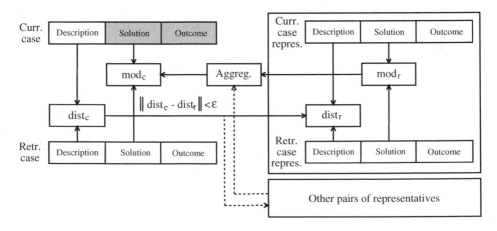

Fig. 3. A diagram illustrating in details the proposed adaptation framework

3.2   Applicability of the Proposed Approach

In the previous Section the proposed framework for substitutional adaptation has been formally described; some constraints on the structure of cases on which this framework can be applied were briefly introduced, but this section will discuss the applicability of this approach, with specific reference to two main aspects, that are case structure and the type of attributes that compose its solution part.

With reference to case structure, hierarchical and even graph–based approaches are being growingly considered and adopted for case representation, due to their expressive power and suitability to represent complex case descriptions, but flat structures are still commonly adopted for CBR systems development. This kind of representation provides the description of a case in terms of a fixed number of attribute–value pairs. This kind of structure does not present particular problems with respect to this approach. In this framework, cases having a non-flat structure (e.g. hierarchies) do not present different problems, provided that their structure is fixed and not variant from case to case. In fact this kind of structures can be reduced to a flat set of attribute-value pairs composing the case base (e.g. leaves of a tree–structured case).

The actual crucial factor for the approach applicability is the variability of the case structure. If the case base is made up of non-homogeneous cases, presenting different descriptions or solutions, the previously introduced mechanisms for the computation of distances introduced in equation 1 must be modified. While there are existing approaches focused on the computation of similarity among the heterogenous descriptions of cases (see, e.g., [10,12,11]), which could be adopted in this case to measure distances, the problem of computing differences among solutions (equation 4) and especially to exploit them in order to obtain an adaptation of the retrieved case solution (equation 5) is the object of current and future works. Moreover this goes beyond the simple substitutional adaptation approach, and possibly provides a structural modification of the proposed solution.

The simplest strategy for the application of this approach in a flexible case situation is to limit the search for representatives to those cases whose structure provides description and solution parts that are homogeneous to the one provided by the current and retrieved case. In this way, the flexibility of case representation is not exploited (cases with a different structure are simply ignored by the adaptation mechanism), and the situation is reduced to a homogeneous scenario.

Another relevant aspect is determining the applicability of the approach is the type of attributes that compose the solution part of the case. The introduced approach can manage numeric attributes in a very simple way, while symbolic attributes require some additional work in order to be managed automatically. The main issue is the aggregation of differences among values related to a symbolic attribute in solutions of case representatives in order to derive that component of the adaptation vector. To manage this operation in an automatic way a sort of algebra for that kind of symbolic attribute should be defined. Another possible approach is to perform adaptation only for numeric attributes and report the user on the set of possible modifications on symbolic attributes related to the identified representatives, leaving him/her the choice on that component of the adaptation vector.

It must be noted that the only domain knowledge exploited in this process, and thus required by the approach, is essentially related to the capability to measure differences among cases and their attributes (i.e. *dist* and *diff* functions in equations 1, 3 and 4) and to attribute relevance (i.e. weights in equation 3 and multiplicative factors in equation 5) to these differences, in other words *analogical* knowledge. Essentially this kind of approach does not require the typical additional knowledge (e.g. procedural domain knowledge) required to implement an adaptation module. However it also allows to include some specific domain knowledge, for instance to select which pairs of representatives have more influence on the overall modification to be applied to the retrieved case solution. A more through analysis of possible ways to integrate this approach with non-analogical domain knowledge (e.g. partial heuristics or procedural knowledge), is also object of current and future developments.

4   A Case Study: P-Truck Curing

The case study which will be presented in this Section is related to the design and development of P–Truck Curing, a Case Based Reasoning system supporting the design of the curing phase for truck tyre production. A truck tyre is composed of both rubber compounds and metallic reinforcements: the former are responsible for all the thermal and mechanical properties of the tyre; on the other hand, metallic reinforcements give it the necessary rigidity. Once all the semi–manufactured parts are assembled into a semi–finished product (in jargon called *green–tyre*), the latter undergoes a thermal treatment (vulcanization) that activates reactions between polymers, in order to give it the desired properties, such as elasticity, strength, and stability. The curing process provides different phases of external or internal heating, and internal inflation of the green–tyre carcass. To design a curing process the expert evaluates the characteristics of the green–tyre and then, for every step of the process, he/she decides starting instant and duration, temperature and pressure of the involved fluids. Variants to standard procedures can also be suggested (for instance to slightly modify the typical value of factory dependent parameters). Problem analysis began with meetings and interviews with expert curing process designers, also referred to as curing technologists. Early stages of knowledge acquisition made clear that any of these experts uses to store information related to curing processes, designed both by himself/herself and by other technologists. These notes concern incidental problems, adopted solutions, variants of process and results, both positive and negative, about tyre curing. When a technologist has to design a new curing process he/she uses these information and his/her experience to define its details, without starting from scratch or using formally well–defined rules. A CBR system is thus a suitable approach to model this problem solving method.

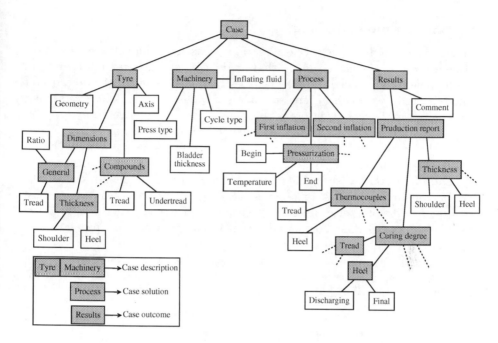

Fig. 4. Case structure: the diagram shows a partial view of the tree–structure related to a case

Figure 4 shows a partial view of the case structure, which is hierarchical and fixed. In particular the high-level components of this structure are related to tyre (e.g. dimensions, composition) and curing machinery (e.g. temperature and fluids), which compose the case description, curing process specification, that represents case solution, and process evaluation, which is related to case outcome. A detailed description of P–Truck Curing is out of the scope of this paper and can be found in [13]; this Section will instead focus on a description of how the previously introduced framework for substitutional adaptation was applied to this specific situation.

A CBR approach was adopted because of its suitability to represent expert's decision making process but also because knowledge on the domain (in particular procedural knowledge) is very limited. As previously specified, a green–tyre is a composite object, and even if some basic principles are known (e.g. thicker parts of a tyre require more energy to reach an optimal curing degree), to compose them in order to obtain a globally optimal process result is a very complex task. For instance, different tyre parts could require a completely different process modification (i.e. sidewalls are thinner and thus require less energy, while shoulders are thicker and require more), and some components do not have a clear influence on the global result (e.g. metallic parts). Nonetheless the adopted approach aims to supply to the designer an indication of how to adapt the retrieved solution to the current case according to past experiences.

4.1   Curing Process Adaptation

The adaptation to the retrieved case solution is based on pairs of past cases presenting differences similar to the one that holds between the current case and the retrieved one. In particular, for every field which is different in the description of the retrieved case a pair of representatives having the same difference among their description is chosen, in order to define a part of the overall adaptation which is due to that specific difference. The choice is based on a numerical evaluation of the cases composing the pair (i.e. successful cases are more likely chosen as representatives). The idea is to consider differences that cause the adaptation step, and discover what such differences meant in the past in terms of differences in case solutions. These differences are indicators of how the retrieved case should be modified to better fit the new situation. These consideration must be considered as specific domain knowledge that has an influence on representatives selection and modification aggregation.

Consider the adaptation scenario described in Table 1; a simplified version of curing case is presented, for sake of simplifying the example and also for confidentiality reasons. The described attributes are related to

- elements of case description: tyre thickness and axis, curing press inflating fluids and bladder thickness;
- case solution: curing process duration;
- outcome: numeric evaluation of process results.

Elements c_c and r_c represent respectively the current and retrieved case, while $a, b, c, d, e \in CB$ are cases belonging to the case base. The pairs $\langle a, b \rangle$ and $\langle e, d \rangle$ are selected as representatives of c_c and r_c, in fact the first pair presents the same difference in tyre thickness, while the second presents the same difference in the inflating fluids exploited by the curing machinery. While the solutions related to the first pair indicate that the duration of the retrieved case should be reduced $(s(a) - s(b) = -1.1)$, the other pair suggests to increase it $(s(e) - s(d) = 0.1)$. According to multiplicative factors specified for equation 5, and thus to specific domain knowledge, a combination of the two modifications will determine the overall adaptation to be applied to $s(r_c)$. In particular, in this case, tyre thickness is considered a more important factor than the adopted inflating fluid, so the overall modification will decrease the process duration but less than the only pair $\langle a, b \rangle$ would suggest.

Table 1. A sample adaptation scenario for P-Truck Curing

	Thickness	Axis	Fluid	Chamber	Duration	Result
c_c	40	T	H_2O	8		
r_c	41	T	N	8	48.3	7
a	42	T	N	6	53.8	6
b	43	T	N	6	54.9	6
c	45	T	H_2O	8	57	5
d	43	T	N	8	55	7
e	43	T	H_2O	8	55.1	6

5   Conclusions and Future Developments

In this paper a general framework for substitutional adaptation based on analogical knowledge was introduced and formally described. Its applicability was discussed with specific reference to the structure of cases and their variability, and also with reference to the types of attributes of case solution part. The main feature of this approach is that the only kind of knowledge required to implement it is related to the capability to measure differences and distances among cases and to define the relevance of these measures. Thanks to this kind of knowledge it is possible to select representatives of current and retrieved cases, and exploit the differences among their solutions to adapt the retrieved case solution.

The approach is actually the generalization of a concrete experience described as a case study, which provides the adaptation of cases related to truck tyre production processes. The module was designed and developed in close collaboration with expert curing process designers, which validated the approach. The module is currently being tested and effectively applied in order to fine-tune the related parameters. This adaptation scheme is also being considered for application in other projects providing the adoption of CBR as problem solving method.

Current and future works related to this framework are aimed at a more through analysis of possible ways to integrate additional domain knowledge (e.g. partial heuristics, incomplete procedural knowledge) in the adaptation scheme, and also on possible ways to support the generalization of adaptation experiences and their reification into more comprehensive forms of adaptation knowledge, towards the construction of domain specific adaptation theories and models.

The approach is focused on substitutional adaptation, and it is not well suited to manage and exploit variability in case structure. The exploitation of the basic principle of this approach in the context of structural or generative adaptation scenarios is also object of future investigations.

References

1. Kolodner, J.: Case-Based Reasoning. Morgan Kaufmann, San Mateo (CA) (1993)
2. Wilke, W., Bergmann, R.: Techniques and Knowledge Used for Adaptation During Case-Based Problem Solving. In: IEA/AIE (Vol. 2). Volume 1416 of Lecture Notes in Computer Science., Springer (1998) 497–506
3. Bandini, S., Manzoni, S.: CBR Adaptation for Chemical Formulation. In: ICCBR. Volume 2080 of Lecture Notes in Computer Science., Springer (2001) 634–647
4. Smyth, B., Keane, M.T.: Adaptation-Guided Retrieval: Questioning the Similarity Assumption in Reasoning. Artif. Intell. **102** (1998) 249–293
5. Fuchs, B., Lieber, J., Mille, A., Napoli, A.: Towards a Unified Theory of Adaption in Case-Based Reasoning. In: ICCBR. Volume 1650 of Lecture Notes in Computer Science., Springer (1999) 104–117
6. Hanney, K., Keane, M.T.: The Adaption Knowledge Bottleneck: How to Ease it by Learning from Cases. In: ICCBR. Volume 1266 of Lecture Notes in Computer Science., Springer (1997) 359–370
7. Jarmulak, J., Craw, S., Rowe, R.: Using Case-Base Data to Learn Adaptation Knowledge for Design. In: IJCAI, Morgan Kaufmann (2001) 1011–1020

8. Leake, D.B., Kinley, A., Wilson, D.C.: Acquiring Case Adaptation Knowledge: a Hybrid Approach. In: AAAI/IAAI, Vol. 1. (1996) 684–689
9. McSherry, D.: An Adaptation Heuristic for Case-Based Estimation. In: EWCBR. Volume 1488 of Lecture Notes in Computer Science., Springer (1998) 184–195
10. Bergmann, R., Stahl, A.: Similarity Measures for Object-Oriented Case Representations. In: EWCBR. Volume 1488 of Lecture Notes in Computer Science., Springer (1998) 25–36
11. Ricci, F., Senter, L.: Structured Cases, Trees and Efficient Retrieval. In: EWCBR. Volume 1488 of Lecture Notes in Computer Science., Springer (1998) 88–99
12. Manzoni, S., Mereghetti, P.: A Tree Structured Case Base for the System P–Truck Tuning. In: UK CBR workshop at ES 2002, Cambridge, 10 december, 2002, University of Paisley (2002) 17–26
13. Bandini, S., Colombo, E., Sartori, F., Vizzari, G.: Case Based Reasoning and Production Process Design: the Case of P-Truck Curing. In: ECCBR. Volume 3155 of Lecture Notes in Computer Science., Springer (2004) 504–517

A Consumer Interest Prediction System from Transaction Behaviors in Electronic Commerce[*]

Chien-Chang Hsu and Wen-Yu Chien

Department of Computer Science and Information Engineering,
Fu-Jen Catholic University, 510 Chung Cheng Rd.,
Hsinchuang, Taipei, Taiwan 242

Abstract. Consumer interest prediction usually uses transaction behaviors for predicting consumer's goal and interested items. The correct prediction heavily depends on the complete information of user profiles. The prediction system may conduct wrong prediction if it only uses the static, passive, incomplete, and out-of-date consumer transaction information to do the prediction. This paper proposes a consumer interest prediction system from transaction behaviors in electronic commerce. The system contains three modules, namely, transaction analyzer, transaction case library, and plan predictor. The transaction analyzer monitors the interactions of the consumer in the application systems. The transaction case library stores instances of consumer transaction behaviors in electronic commerce. The plan predictor integrates induction and decision theories for predicting consumer interest.

1 Introduction

Consumer interest prediction usually uses transaction behaviors for predicting consumer's goal and possible transaction behaviors in electronic commerce [1]. The correct prediction may provide a shortcut to compute business tasks and make it easy for the consumer to complete transaction operations in electronic commerce. It can reduce the time and money of consumers for surfing in the Internet and finding right web pages and preferred products. Moreover, the correct prediction also eliminates unnecessary service requests of the website to reduce the system overhead. However, the correct prediction heavily depends on the complete information of user profiles. Many systems usually use consumer-provided preference and/or past transaction information for predicting consumer interest.

This paper proposes a consumer interest prediction system from transaction behaviors in electronic commerce. The system combines online transaction behaviors and past business transaction history of consumers for interest prediction. The system contains three modules, namely, transaction analyzer, transaction case library, and plan predictor. The *transaction analyzer* monitors the interactions of the consumer in the application systems. Specifically, the transaction analyzer collects the interactions performed by the consumer using the application interface and peripheral devices. It

---

[*] This project is partly supported by National Science Council of ROC under grants NSC 94-2745-E-030-004-URD.

S. Bandini and S. Manzoni (Eds.): AI*IA 2005, LNAI 3673, pp. 343–346, 2005.

captures the user interactions from the interaction message. It then filters the user operations from the user interactions and recognizes the behavior patterns. The *transaction case library* stores instances of consumer transaction behaviors in electronic commerce. Each case contains four types of transaction information, that is, browsing, searching, buying, and payment. The *plan predictor* integrates induction and decision theories for predicting consumer interest. The plan predictor selects the most relevant cases as the candidate cases by evaluating the information relevance from the case library. Subsequently, the induction theory induces the most relevant cases with the same transaction type into a decision tree. The decision theory uses the expected utility to evaluate the feature relevance of the induction three. Finally, the plan predictor prunes the node with lower expected utility of the induction tree to conclude the prediction.

2   System Architecture

The interest prediction system contains three modules, namely, transaction analyzer, transaction case library, and plan predictor. The transaction analyzer is responsible for monitoring the interactions of the consumer and recognizing the behavior patterns. First, it monitors customer operations by extracting customer operations from the interaction message between the customer and the system. It then uses Bayesian belief networks to eliminate unnecessary customer operations. Finally, it uses the RBF (Radial Basis Function) neural model as the behavior pattern classifier for recognizing the customer behavior from the interaction message.

The transaction case library stores instances of consumer transaction behaviors in electronic commerce. Each case contains four types of transaction information, that is, browsing, searching, buying, and payment [4].

The plan predictor conducts the following tasks. First, it retrieves the nearest and most relevant cases from the case library between the consumer transaction data and case library. The plan predictor then induces these cases with the same transaction type into induction trees. It then uses the expected utility to evaluate the nodes of the induction tree. Finally, the plan predictor prunes the node with lower expected value of the induction tree to conclude the prediction.

3   Transaction Analyzer

The transaction analyzer performs two tasks, namely, customer operation monitoring and behavior patterns recognition. The *customer operation monitoring* observed customer operations by extracting customer operations from the interaction message between the customer and the system. The transaction analyzer uses the web page scripts and cookies to capture the interaction events in each session. *The behavior pattern recognition* uses the Bayesian belief networks to exclude redundant and irrelevant operations. Redundant operations are those which the customer use the same operation for the same subtask. Moreover, the irrelevant operations are those that are not effective in performing the subtask. Redundant and unnecessary operations can be removed by computing the joint probability of the operations according to the causal relations of the Bayesian belief network. Finally, it uses the RBF neural model as the behavior pattern classifier for discriminating the customer behavior from the interaction message. The RBF neural model contains three layers, namely, the input, hidden, and output layers. The input of the interaction information includes the interaction events, focus object, request method, and query items. The node of output layer represents the transaction behaviors. The number of node in the output layer varies according to the behavior patterns in the business tasks [2].

4 Plan Predictor

The plan predictor conducts two tasks, namely, nearest cases retrieval and consumer interest prediction. The *nearest cases retrieval* uses the backpropagation neural networks to project the case library into the two-dimensional geometrical feature space. It uses the value of first hidden layer to project the input vector into the geometrical feature space. It then transforms the consumer transaction data into the same feature space to evaluate the surrounded cases. Moreover, it selects the cases that enclosed the consumer transaction data in the nearest closed region as the nearest cases. The *consumer interest prediction* selects the candidate cases by measuring the information relevance (IR) of the nearest cases.

$$IR = 1 - \frac{\sum (v * w_v + i * w_i + d * w_d + p * w_p)}{n}, \tag{1}$$

where v, f, s, and p are the value difference, importance difference, distance difference, and popularity difference of the nearest cases. w_v, w_i, w_d, and w_p are the weights of above factors. n is the number of feature in the case. It selects the cases with higher IR value as the candidate cases for predicting the consumer interest [4]. The plan predictor then induces the cases in the same transaction type for constructing the induction tree. Each nonterminal node in an induction tree represents the goal of the candidate cases. Each outgoing link from a node represents a value for the node. Each leaf of an induction tree stores the surface feature similarity of each candidate case. The plan predictor then computes the expected utility of each feature value recursively by the following equation.

$$EU(A_j) = \sum_{k=1}^{n} EU(A_{jk}) * IR(A_j \to A_{jk}) * P(A_j \to A_{jk}) \tag{2}$$

where A_{jk}, n, $IR(A_j \to A_{jk})$, and $P(A_j \to A_{jk})$ are the kth child node of feature node A_j, numbers of children of feature node A_j, information relevance of the feature value represented by link $A_j \to A_{jk}$, and probability of the feature value represented by link $A_j \to A_{jk}$. Moreover, the calculation of expected utility starts by setting the expected utility of the leaf node C_i to C_i's similarity, i.e., $EU(C_i)=S_i$, where S_i represents the similarity of case C_i to the given problem p. The $EU(C_i)$ is then backed up to its father node by Equation (2) to compute its father's expected utility. This process repeats until it reaches the root node. Finally, the predictor prunes the nodes whose EU are below a threshold. The leaf nodes of the pruned induction tree, that is, the goal of the cases, are extracted as the prediction of consumer interest [3].

5 Conclusions

This paper proposes a consumer interest prediction system from transaction behaviors in electronic commerce. The system combines online transaction behaviors and past business transaction history of consumers for interest prediction. The system contains three modules, namely, transaction analyzer, transaction case library, and plan predictor. The transaction analyzer monitors the interactions of the consumer in the application systems. The transaction case library stores instances of consumer transaction behaviors in electronic commerce. The plan predictor projects the case library into the two-dimensional geometric feature space. It then selects the most relevant cases as the candidate cases by evaluating the information relevance from the nearest cases. Subsequently, the induction theory induces the most relevant cases with the same transaction type into a decision tree. The decision theory uses the expected utility to evaluate the feature relevance of the induction three. Finally, the plan predictor prunes the node with lower expected utility of the induction tree to conclude the prediction. In summary, the proposed interest prediction system exhibits the following features. First, the proposed system projects case library into the two-dimensional geometrical plane. It is appropriate for the designer to examine the data and to make decisions from the spread plane of the data. Second, the selection nearest cases in the geometrical plane can relieve the overhead of the system to examine the whole case library. It only investigates the cases that encompass the consumer transaction data. Third, the computation of information relevance provides the shortcut to filter irrelevant and noisy cases. It also reduces the computation overhead to construct the induction trees. Finally, the interest prediction is effective with the help of feature expected utility. The system can tackle multiple cases by pruning the useless branch of the induction tree for achieving the interest prediction.

References

1. Claypool, M., Brown, D., Le, P., Waseda, M.: Inferring User Interest. IEEE Internet Computing, 5(6) (2001) 32-39
2. Hsu, C. C., Deng, C. W.: An Intelligent Interface for Customer Behaviour Analysis from Interaction Activities in Electronic Commerce. In: Orchard, R., Yang, C. S., Ali, M. (eds.): Innovations in Applied Artificial Intelligence, Lecture Notes in Computer Science, Vol. 3029. Springer, Berline Heidelberg New York (2004) 315-324
3. Hsu, C. C., Ho, C. S.: A New Hybrid Case-based Architecture for Medical Diagnosis. Information Science 166(1-4) (2004) 231-247
4. Tian, Y. J.: The Design and Implementation of an Automatic Case Library Construction System. Master Thesis of Fu-Jen Catholic University (2005)

Dealing with Different Languages and Old Profiles in Keystroke Analysis of Free Text

Daniele Gunetti, Claudia Picardi, and Giancarlo Ruffo

Department of Informatics, University of Torino,
corso Svizzera 185, 10149 Torino, Italy
{gunetti, picardi, ruffo}@di.unito.it

Abstract. In this paper we show experimentally that typing dynamics of free text provide useful information for user identification and authentication even when a long time has passed since typing profiles of users were formed, and even when users are writing in a language different from the one used to form their profiles. Hence, we argue that keystroke analysis can be an effective aid in different areas where ascertaining user identity is important or crucial, including Computer Security and User Modeling.

1   Introduction

Biometric features (such as retinal or iris patterns, fingerprints, palm topology, hand geometry, wrist veins and thermal images, voiceprints and handwritten signatures) can be conveniently used to ascertain personal identity [1]. When people are using a computer, a biometric such as keystroke dynamics is particularly appealing, since it can be sampled without the aid of special tools, just the keyboard of the computer where the biometric analysis has to be performed. User identification through typing rhythms is however a difficult task, for several reasons:

1. Keystrokes, unlike other biometric features, convey an unstructured and very small amount of information. From two consecutive keystrokes we may just extract the elapsed time between the release of the first key and the depression of the second (the so-called *digraph latency*) and the amount of time each key is held down (the *keystroke duration*): a pretty shallow kind of information.
2. This information may vary not only because of the intrinsic instability of behavioral characteristics, but even because different keyboards can be used, because of different environmental conditions and, above all, because typing rhythms depend also on the entered text.
3. Even if users' profiles are accurate, and provide a high level of identification accuracy, such profiles may become obsolete, as typing habits and skills may change over time (unlike, of course, physiological biometrics such as fingerprints or retinal and iris patters).
4. Within their normal activity, users may want to enter text in a language different from the one used to form users' profiles (this is certainly the case for all computer science researchers that are not of English mother tongue). So that one may wonder what happens of the possibility to identify users through keystroke dynamics in such cases.

S. Bandini and S. Manzoni (Eds.): AI*IA 2005, LNAI 3673, pp. 347–358, 2005.
© Springer-Verlag Berlin Heidelberg 2005

In [3] we showed that keystroke analysis can be used to ascertain personal identity with a very high level of accuracy in the case of fixed text, and in [4] we showed that the same can be done even when users are entering free text.

In this paper we perform a further step, and address experimentally points 3) and 4) above: is it possible to identify a user through the way he types on a keyboard, even if a long time (e.g., more than one year) has passed since when her typing profile was formed? Is it possible to do so even when the user is entering text in a language different from the one used to form his profile?

We provide positive answers to both questions through a set of experiments that involved 30 volunteers. After more than one year and a half, our keystroke analysis system is still able to identify them with a good level of accuracy, even when they are entering free text in a language different from the one used to form users' profiles. As far as we know, this is the first study showing that the analysis of typing rhythms can be used to ascertain personal identity even when users' profiles have not been updated for a long time, and different languages are involved.

2   Keystroke Analysis

Keystroke analysis can be seen as a form of Pattern Recognition (as in fact most of the other biometric techniques). As such, it involves *representation* of input data measures, *extraction* of characteristic features and *classification* or *identification* of patterns data so as to decide to which pattern class these data belong [8]).

In the case of typing rhythms, input data is usually represented by a sequence of typed keys, together with appropriate timing information expressing the exact time at which keys have been depressed and released, in order to compute the duration of keystrokes and the latency of digraphs. The extraction of these two features turns a sequence of keystrokes into a *typing sample*. Since features are measured in the form of real or integer numbers, a typing sample can be seen as a pattern vector representing a point in an n-dimensional Euclidean space. Appropriate algorithms are then used to classify a typing sample among a set of pattern classes, each one containing information about the typing habits of an individual. Pattern classes are often called *profiles* or *models*, and they are built using earlier typing information gathered from the involved individuals.

In order to deal with the instability of typing rhythms,[1] most research in the field of keystroke analysis limited the experiments to samples produced from a unique pre-defined text (e.g.[14,13,5,17,3,12]) or from a small number of different, but still pre-defined texts (e.g.[15,10,4]). However, a large part of the interest in keystroke analysis lies in the possibility to use what stems from the normal use of a computer: the typing rhythms of free text. Of course, in this case the aforementioned variability of keystroke dynamics is akin to get worse, since the timings of a sequence of keystrokes may be influenced in different ways by the keystrokes occurring before and after the one currently issued.

The literature about keystroke analysis of true free text is quite limited. Analysis of "true" free text is attempted in [16], where the authors test different methods to measure

---

[1] After all, when typing we have a very little control on the speed we hit a sequence of keys, and we have even less control on the number of milliseconds we hold down a key.

similarities and differences among typing samples of 31 users. The aim of this research was to experiment in keystroke analysis with both fixed and free text, but when different texts are used for the users' profiles and the samples to be classified, outcomes fall to an absolutely unsatisfactory 23% of correct classification.

In [6] four users are monitored for some weeks during their normal activity on computers, so that thousands of digraphs latencies can be collected. Authors use both statistical analysis and different data mining algorithms on the users' data sets, and are able to reach an almost 60% of correct classification. Authors' approach is improved in [7], both in the outcomes and in the number of users (35) involved, collecting over three months of continuous monitoring more than 5 millions keystrokes from the users.

3 Computing the Distance Between Two Typing Samples

Suppose we are given two typing samples, and we want to decide if they come from the same user. We may use a distance measure that returns a real number indicating the similarities and differences between the typing rhythms "recorded" in the two samples. Intuitively, the lower the number the higher the similarities, and in particular we expect two typing samples coming from the same individual having, on the average, a distance smaller than two samples entered by different individuals. The distance measure we will use was introduced in [3] and showed the best outcomes among all systems performing user authentication through the keystroke analysis of fixed text. We refer to [3] for a thorough description of the measure and its properties.

The only timing information we measure in our experiments is the time elapsed between the depression of the first key and the depression of the second key of each digraph. We call such interval the *duration* of the digraph. If the typed text is sufficiently long, the same digraph may occur more than once. In such case, we report the digraph only once, and we use the mean of the duration of its occurrences.

Since we want to be able to deal with typing samples of free text, in order to compare two samples we must extract the information they have in common: in our case, this information will be represented by the digraphs shared by the two samples, together with their durations. As an example, suppose the following two texts **E1** = *mathematics* and **E2** = *sympathetic* have been entered. A possible outcome of the sampling may be the following, where the number between each pair of letters represents the duration in milliseconds of the corresponding digraph:

E1: m 285 **a** 164 **t** 207 **h** 195 **e** 221 **m** 149 **a** 230 **t** 156 **i** 184 **c** 100 **s**

E2: s 220 **y** 110 **m** 215 **p** 242 **a** 128 **t** 250 **h** 201 **e** 325 **t** 270 **i** 136 **c**

After having merged together multiple occurrences of the same digraph, and sorted the digraphs w.r.t. their typing speed, typing samples can be more conveniently represented as in Table 1. The digraphs shared by **E1** and **E2** are: **ti, ic, he, at** and **th**.

Given any two typing samples **S1** and **S2**, each one sorted with respect to the typing speed of its digraphs, we define the *distance* of **S2** w.r.t. **S1** (in short: d(**S1**,**S2**)), as the sum of the absolute values of the distances of each digraph of **S2** w.r.t. the position of the same digraph in **S1**. When computing d(**S1**,**S2**), digraphs that are not shared

Table 1. Digraphs and durations for samples **E1** and **E2**

Sample **E1**

digraph	duration
cs	100
ti	156
ic	184
he	195
at	197
th	207
ma	217
em	221

Sample **E2**

digraph	duration
ym	110
at	128
ic	136
he	201
mp	215
sy	220
pa	242
th	250
ti	270
et	325

E1				**E2**	
ti	156	d = 3		at	128
ic	184	d = 0		ic	136
he	195	d = 0		he	201
at	197	d = 1		th	250
th	207	d = 4		ti	270

Fig. 1. Computation of the distance of two typing samples

between the two samples are simply removed. It is clear that d(**S1,S2**) = d(**S2,S1**), and that from the above definition, we may compute the distance between any two typing samples, provided they have some digraphs in common (which is normally the case for texts sufficiently long). Figure 1 illustrates pictorially the computation of the distance between our examples **E1** and **E2**. We have:

d(**E1,E2**) = 3+0+0+1+4 = 8.

Given any two typing samples, the maximum distance they may have is when the shared digraphs, sorted by their typing speed, appear in reverse order in one sample w.r.t. the other sample. Hence, if two samples share N digraphs, it is easy to see that the maximum distance they can have is given by:

$N^2/2$ (if N is even); $(N^2-1)/2$ (if N is odd).

The above value can be used as a normalization factor of the distance between two typing samples sharing N digraphs, dividing their distance by the value of the maximum distance they may have. In this way it is possible to compare the distances of pairs of samples sharing a different number of digraphs: the normalized distance d(**S1,S2**) between any two samples **S1** and **S2** is a real number between 0 and 1. Measure d returns 0 when the digraphs shared by the two samples are exactly in the same order w.r.t. their duration, and returns 1 when the digraphs appear in reverse order (d(**S1,S2**) is also set to 1 if S1 and S2 do not share any digraph).

In the case of our example, the maximum distance between typing samples sharing N=5 digraphs is: $(5^2-1)/2 = 12$, and hence the normalized distance between **E1** and **E2** is $8/12 = 0.66666$. In the rest of this paper, when speaking of the distance of two typing samples, we will always refer to their normalized distance.

Readers may have noticed that the distance measure just described completely overlooks any absolute value of the timings associated to the samples. Only the relative positions (which is of course a consequence of the typing speed) of the digraphs in the two samples are taken into consideration.[2] The rationale behind this measure is that, for a given individual, typing speed may greatly vary as a consequence of changes in the psychological and physiological conditions of the subject, but we may expect the changes to affect homogeneously all the typing characteristics in a similar way: if the individual types the word *on* more slowly that the word *of*, this is likely to remain unchanged even in different conditions.

4 Gathering of the Typing Samples

More than one year and a half ago, we asked 30 volunteers to provide 15 typing samples each one. All the people participating to the experiments were native speakers of Italian, and were asked to provide samples written in Italian. Though with varying typing skills, all volunteers were well used to type on normal computer keyboards.

All users were instructed to provide no more than one sample per day, and in general typing samples were produced on a very irregular basis: some of the samples were provided pretty frequently, whereas for other samples two or three weeks, or even more than one or two months passed between the production of a sample and the next one.

Volunteers could provide the samples from their computer, through an HTML form with a text area of 780 characters to be filled by the users and submitted to the collecting server. A client side Javascript was used to record the time (in milliseconds) when a key was depressed, together with the ascii value of the key. People used their office computers or their notebooks to produce the samples, which were provided both in Windows and Unix environments, using both Explorer and Netscape browsers.

Volunteers were asked to enter the samples in the most natural way, more or less as if they were writing an e-mail to someone. They were completely free to choose what to write, and the only limitations were of not typing the same word or phrase repeatedly in order to fill the form, and not to enter the same text in two different samples. On

---

[2] On the contrary, both the approaches described in [16] and [6] are based on the computation of the mean and standard deviation of digraphs latency (though the adopted classification algorithm is different in the two works). It may be the case that the differences among the typing habits of individuals entering unconstrained text are not well grasped by numerical information such as mean and standard deviation. This would account for the poor outcomes on free text reported in the aforementioned papers. It must be noted that the accuracy of a method is of course also related to the length of the samples under analysis. However, works described in [16] and [6] do not provide precise information on the length of the samples used in the experiments.

the contrary, we suggested people to write about different subjects in each sample, their job, movies, holidays, recipes, family, and so on: everything they liked. People were free to make typos, and to correct them or not. Corrections could be made by using the backspace key or the mouse, as preferred. People were free to pause in every moment when producing a sample, for whatever reason and as long as they wanted. No sample provided by the volunteers was rejected, for any reason.

One year and a half after the last sample of each volunteer was provided, at the same conditions described above, we asked the 30 volunteers to provide other two samples, one in Italian, and another one in English. Note that all people participating to the experiments are more or less used to write in English, since they are colleagues and PhD students. Every Italian sample was still long about 780 characters, while English samples had to be long about twice (i.e. about 1560 chars each one), so that when they are matched to samples in users' profiles (which are in Italian), a sufficient number of shared digraphs is available.

5   The Experiments

By using the distance measure described in Section 3, we want to see if, after more than one year and a half, users can still be recognized through their typing rhythms, and if this is possible even when new samples are typed in a language different from the one used to form the profiles. Therefore, we try to exploit the distance for user identification and user authentication.

5.1   User Identification

In our approach, a user's profile is simply made of a set of typing samples provided by that user. Hence, suppose we are given a set of users' profiles and a new typing sample from one of the users, so that we want to identify who actually provided the sample. If the measure defined in Section 3 works well, we may expect the computed distance between two samples of the same user to be smaller than the distance between two samples coming from different users. As a consequence, we may expect the mean distance of a new sample X from (the samples in) the profile of user U to be smaller if X has been provided by U than if X has been entered by someone else.

Hence, suppose we have three users A, B and C, with, say, 3 typing samples each one in their profiles (so that, for example, A's profile contains typing samples A_1 and A_2 and A_3). Moreover, suppose a new typing sample X has been provided by one of the users, and we have to decide who entered the sample. We may compute the mean distance (let us call it md for short) of X from each user's profile as the mean of the distances of X from each sample in the profile (e.g., md(A,X) = (d(A_1,X) + d(A_2,X) + d(A_3,X))/3) and decide that X belongs to the user with the smallest mean distance among the three. This rule has been tested using the old samples provided by the 30 users as users' profiles, while the two new samples in Italian and English are the ones to be classified. The outcomes of this experiment are reported in Table 2, where a 90% of correct classification is reached in the case of the English samples, and a slightly better outcome is reached for the Italian samples. That is, users are in most cases correctly identified by their typing habits even after a year and a half, and even when using a

Table 2. Experimental results in user identification

language of the sample	Italian	English
Tot. n. of classification attempted	30	30
Tot. n. of errors	2	3
% of correct classification	93.33%	90%

different language. Two out of the 5 classification errors made by the system concern the same user: both his samples are not correctly identified as belonging to him. It may be the case that the typing skills of that user changed sufficiently to make his old typing profile useless.

5.2 User Authentication

The identification rule described above can be used to authenticate users simply by marking the samples with an identity: a new sample X claimed to come from user A is authenticated as belonging to A if md(A,X) is the smallest among all known users. Now, the system can be evaluated w.r.t. two kinds of mistakes it can make: 1) the *Impostor Pass Rate (IPR)*, which is the percentage of cases in which a sample X from an unknown individual is erroneously attributed to one of the users of the system; 2) the *False Alarm Rate (FAR)*, which is the percentage of cases in which a sample belonging to some user is not identified correctly.

From Table 2 it is easy to see that our system shows a FAR of 8.33%: 5 samples out of 60 are not correctly attributed to the user who provided them. But what about the IPR? If there are 30 users in the system, it is simply (100/30)% = 3.33%. In fact, an impostor pretending to be a legal user A, has a chance out of 30 that the sample she provides is closer to A's profile than to any other profile known to the system. We may improve such *basic performance* by observing the following. Suppose again that we have 3 users A, B and C, and a new sample X to be classified, so that we compute:

md(A,X) = 0.419025,   md(B,X) = 0.420123,   md(C,X) = 0.423223.

and hence X is classified as belonging to user A. However, suppose that the mean of the distances of the samples forming the model of A (denoted by m(A)) is:

$d(A_1,A_2) = 0.312378$; $d(A_1,A_3) = 0.304381$; $d(A_2,A_3) = 0.326024$;
m(A) = (0.312378 + 0.304381 + 0.326024)/3 = 0.314261

Then, we may expect another sample of A to have a mean distance from the model of A similar to m(A), which is not the case for X in the example above. Even if X is closer to A than to any other user's profile in the system, it should be rejected.

To deal with such situations, we restate the classification rule as follow: a new sample X claimed to belong to user A is classified as belonging to A if and only if:

1. md(A,X) is the smallest w.r.t. any other user B and
2. md(A,X) is *sufficiently* closer to m(A) than to any other md(B,X) computed by the system. Formally:
   md(A,X) < m(A) + $|k(md(B,X) - m(A))|$ for any user B, and for some k such that $0 < k \leq 1$.

Table 3. Experimental results in user authentication: 1740 impostors attacks; 60 legal connections

language	k = 0.95		k = 0.90	
of samples	IPR	FAR	IPR	FAR
Italian	2.53%	6.67%	1.84%	6.67%
	(22/870)	(2/30)	(16/870)	(2/30)
English	2.53%	13.33%	1.49%	16.67%
	(22/870)	(4/30)	(13/870)	(5/30)
totals	2.53%	10%	1.67%	11.67%
	(44/1740)	(6/60)	(29/1740)	(7/60)

If a user A meeting the above rules does not exist, X is rejected. Clearly, different values for k provide different trade-offs between IPR and FAR. Smaller values of k will allow to reject more samples from impostors, but could cause more false alarms. For $k = 1$, we fall back to the plain classification rule of Section 5.1. Table 3 reports the outcomes of the experiments in user authentication for two different values for k. The system can be tested 1740 times for attacks from impostors: the profile of each user, in turn, is removed from the system, and the Italian and English samples of that (now unknown) individual are used to attack all users in the systems (so we have $2 \cdot 29 \cdot 30 = 1740$ impostors' attacks). Hopefully, the system should reject the attacking samples. Moreover, the system is tested 60 times with legal samples claimed to belong to the users who actually provided them.[3]

From the table we see that, for example in the case of $k = 0.90$, the system shows an IPR that is about a half of the IPR for the basic classification rule with 30 legal users. The cost is in the worsening of the ability to identify legal users, since two more legal samples are rejected w.r.t. the basic classification method. From the outcomes we also see that Italian samples appear easier to authenticate correctly, since they provide a smaller FAR than English samples. On the other hand, English samples provide a better IPR. This is probably not by chance. Users' profiles were provided in Italian, so that legal users are more easily recognized if they write in Italian, as well as impostors are spotted if they write in a language different from that of the profiles.

6   Discussion and Applications

In [4] we showed experimentally that, on the average, typing samples of different texts provided by the same individual are more similar than typing samples of the same text provided by different individuals. In other words, it was shown that keystroke analysis of free text, though more difficult than static keystroke analysis, can still be achieved. In this paper we perform a further step by showing that the analysis of typing rhythms can be an effective aid to ascertain user identity even in "hard" conditions, as it is when the system has to rely on old users profiles, and/or users may type in different languages.

---

[3] In brackets are the corresponding numerical values: for example, for $k = 0.90$, we have 16 successful attacks out of 870, using an Italian sample.

In fact, an additional evidence of the ability of the distance measure used in this paper to discriminate among users can be obtained by computing the following mean distances for the 30 Italian and 30 English samples gathered in our experiments:

1. the mean distance between any two Italian samples provided by the volunteers in our experiments (of course, only samples from different individuals can be compared, as every volunteer provided only one Italian and one English sample);
2. the mean distance between any two English samples provided by the volunteers in our experiments (again, only samples from different individuals are compared);
3. the mean distance between any two samples of different languages, provided by different individuals;
4. the mean distance between samples of different languages provided by the same individual.

The above means are reported in Table 4,[4] and from such values we see that typing samples of different text and different languages provided by the same individual (column 4) are, on the average, more similar than typing samples of different text but same language provided by different individuals (columns 1 and 2). Of course, even samples of different text and languages, coming from different individuals, have in general a larger distance between each other (column 3).

Table 4. Mean distances between different groups of samples

mean 1 (435)	mean 2 (435)	mean 3 (870)	mean 4 (30)
0.5302	0.5341	0.5228	0.4061

We note that, in our approach, the ability to perform keystroke analysis when different languages are involved is clearly related to the fact that such languages share some legal digraphs.[5] For example, in our experiments, an English sample shares on the average 142 different digraphs with a sample in users profiles, whereas such number is 139 when only Italian samples are involved. However, an average English sample is long about twice an Italian sample and, of course, the longer the involved samples, the larger the number of shared digraphs. Hence, samples written in different languages can be compared with our technique as long as the two languages share some legal digraphs, and the samples are sufficiently long. For a given length of the samples, the more similar the two languages, the larger the number of digraphs shared by the corresponding samples, and the more accurate the distance between them computed by the measure. Thus, the distance between two samples of a given length written in, say, Italian and Spanish (that are very similar languages), is likely to be more meaningful than the distance between samples of the same length written in Italian and English. Clearly, our method

---

[4] In brackets we report the number of distances between samples used to compute the corresponding mean distance. For example, 30 Italian samples from different individuals can be matched in $29 \cdot 30 / 2 = 435$ different pairs.

[5] That is, digraphs that occur in words belonging to the language.

stops being useful when the languages involved (or just the texts used to produce two samples that must be compared) share a very small number of legal digraphs.

The outcomes of our experiments both in user identification and authentication outperform other results reported in the literature on keystroke analysis of free text, and are in many cases comparable to works that limited the experiments to fixed text.[6] However, we are well aware that a thorough and meaningful evaluation of any biometric system can only be obtained by testing it in real conditions, with as many individuals as possible. Of course, such an evaluation is much more time/budget/resources consuming than an *ad oc* experiment involving a few volunteers.

Unlike other biometric techniques, that require special devices and may be intrusive (like a light that must be directed through the cornea of the eye), keystroke analysis of free text is harmless and can be performed transparently to the users during their normal activity on a computer. The ability to check personal identity through a continuous or periodic monitoring of typing rhythms of individuals may be useful in different applications, and we illustrate two of them below.

Intrusion detection. The generation of false alarms is an endemic problem within intrusion detection [2]. In principle, keystroke analysis can be used to notice possible anomalies in the typing dynamics of individuals connected to the system, that may be intruders. However, the inaccuracy of the analysis may itself be the source of false alarms or undetected intrusions. On the contrary, if keystroke analysis is used in conjunction with other techniques, it may be useful to mitigate the problem of false alarms, by providing an additional evidence of identity, as we showed in [11].

Intrusions are often successful because no monitoring procedure is active, and because different form of intrusions are used. Hence, it is important to "attack the attackers" with different and complementary techniques, in order to improve the chances to detect them reliably and quickly. Experiments in this paper show that keystroke analysis can be a valid aid to intrusion detection even when individuals have not used their account for a long time, or are using language different from the one they used to form their typing profile (this last ability is particularly important since, for example, more and more people writing text with a computer may use their own language when communicating with others understanding the same language, but use English as the "Lingua Franca" to communicate with the rest of the world.)

User identification over the Internet. The ability to identify users through their typing habits can be used to achieve some form of User and Usage Modeling [9], in order to be able to offer personalized graphical interfaces, services and advertising to users on their return on a Web site visited previously [18]. Keystroke analysis would in particular be of great help to identify returning users of web sites that provide mailing lists, forums, chat lines and newsgroups access. The use of such services produces a large amount of typed text, whose typing rhythms can be stored and used to identify people on their return to the site, especially when no form of registration is required to visit the site and use its services.

---

[6] See, e.g., [3] and [4] for a comprehensive description of methods and performances of different approaches to keystroke analysis.

User tracking over the Internet through the analysis of typing rhythms would find an interesting application also within the investigation of illegal activities that use the web (e.g., newsgroups and anonymous mailing services) to exchange information. At the very least, the analysis of the typing rhythms coming from different anonymous accounts and web connections would be useful to restrict and direct investigations on a subset of the individuals under observation.

7 Conclusion

In this paper we have shown that keystroke analysis of free text can be a useful tool for user identification and authentication even when we have to rely on dated information, and the typing samples to be analyzed are written in a language different from the one used to form users' profiles. Our method avoids any form of overfitting, and does not rely on the classical training-testing approach that may require the system to be tuned anew when a different set of users' profiles is involved. We used in our experiments a pretty large amount of typing data; actually, we believe that keystroke analysis of free text cannot be performed with very short samples, as they do not provide a sufficient amount of timing information to allow accurate discrimination among legal users and impostors. On the contrary, if relatively long sample texts are considered, keystroke analysis can become a valid tool to ascertain personal identity.

Keystroke dynamics is a natural kind of biometric available on computers, and it is still available after the initial authentication step. Thus, the ability to exploit the typing rhythms of individuals even in difficult situations like those described in this paper is important, as it may improve the possibility of making computers safer and easier to use.

Acknowledgements. We want to thank all the volunteers in our Department who contributed to our research. This work has been partially funded by the Italian FIRB 2001 project "Web MiNDS" (project number RBNE01WEJT).

References

1. J. Ashbourn. *Biometrics: Advanced Identity Verification. The Complete Guide.* Springer, London, GB, 2000.
2. S. Axelsson. The Base-rate Fallacy and the Difficulty of Intrusion Detection. *ACM Transactions on Information and System Security*, 3(3):186–205, 2000.
3. F. Bergadano, D. Gunetti and C. Picardi. User authentication through keystroke dynamics. *ACM Trans. on Information and System Security*, 5(4), 2002.
4. F. Bergadano, D. Gunetti and C. Picardi. Identity Verification through Dynamic Keystroke Analysis. *Journal of Intelligent Data Analysis*, 7(5), 2003.
5. M. E. Brown and S. J. Rogers. User identification via keystroke characteristics of typed names using neural networks. *Int. J. of Man-Machine Studies*, 39:999–1014, 1993.
6. P. Dowland, S. Furnell and M. Papadaki. Keystroke Analysis as a Method of Advanced User Authentication and Response. In *Proc. of of IFIP/SEC 2002 - 17th Int. Conf. on Information Security*, Cairo, Egypt, 2002.
7. P. Dowland, and S. Furnell. A Long-term Trial of Keystroke Profiling using Digraph, Trigraph and Keyword Latencies. In *Proc. of of IFIP/SEC 2004 - 19th Int. Conf. on Information Security*, Toulouse, France. Kluwer, 2004.

8. R. O. Duda, P. E. Hart and D. G. Stork. *Pattern Classification (2nd ed.)*. John Wiley, 2000.
9. J. Fink and A. Kobsa. A Review and Analysis of Commercial User Modeling Servers for Personalization on the World Wide Web. *User Modeling and User-Adapted Interaction*, 10(3-4):209-249, 2002.
10. S. Furnell, J. Morrissey, P. Sanders, and C. Stockel. Applications of keystroke analysis for improved login security and continuous user authentication. In *Proc. of the Information and System Security Conf.*, 1996.
11. D. Gunetti and G. Ruffo. Intrusion Detection through Behavioural Data. In *Proc. of the Third Symp. on Intelligent Data Analysis*, LNCS, Springer-Verlag, 1999.
12. N. Clarke, S. Furnell, B. Lines and P. Reynolds. Using Keystroke Analysis as a mechanism for Subscriber Authentication on Mobile Handsets. In *Proc. of the 18th IFIP/SEC 2003 Conf.*, Athens, Greece, 2003. Kluwer.
13. R. Joyce and G. Gupta. User authorization based on keystroke latencies. *Comm. of the ACM*, 33(2):168–176, 1990.
14. J. Leggett and G. Williams. Verifying identity via keystroke characteristics. *Int. J. of Man-Machine Studies*, 28(1):67–76, 1988.
15. J. Leggett, Gl. Williams and M. Usnick. Dynamic identity verification via keystroke characteristics. *Int. J. of Man-Machine Studies*, 35:859–870, 1991.
16. F. Monrose and A. Rubin. Authentication via keystroke dynamics. In *Proc. of the 4th ACM Computer and Communications Security Conf.*, 1997. ACM Press.
17. M. S. Obaidat and B. Sadoun. A simulation evaluation study of neural network techniques to computer user identification. *Information Sciences*, 102:239–258, 1997.
18. M. Perkowitz and O. Etzioni. Adaptive Web Sites: Conceptual Framework and Case Study. *Artificial Intelligence*, 118(1,2):245–275, 2000.

Learning Path Generation by Domain Ontology Transformation

Roberto Pirrone[1], Giovanni Pilato[2], Riccardo Rizzo[2], and Giuseppe Russo[1]

[1] DINFO - University of Palermo, Viale delle Scienze 90128 Palermo, Italy
[2] ICAR - Italian National Research Council, Viale delle Scienze 90128 Palermo, Italy
pirrone@unipa.it, {pilato, ricrizzo}@pa.icar.cnr.it

Abstract. An approach to automated learning path generation inside a domain ontology supporting a web tutoring system is presented. Even if a terminological ontology definition is needed in real systems to enable reasoning and/or planning techniques, and to take into account the modern learning theories, the task to apply a planner to such an ontology is very hard because the definition of actions along with their preconditions and effects has to take into account the semantics of the relations among concepts, and it results in building an *ontology of learning*. The proposed methodology is inspired to the Knowledge Space Theory, and proposes some heuristics to transform the original ontology in a weighted graph where the A* algorithm is used to find the path. The proposed approach is applied to the implementation of a web based tutoring system about the Java programming language.

1 Introduction

The task of knowledge management for an e-learning application aimed to satisfy users requests by the generation of personalized learning paths, relies on the definition of a domain ontology structuring the concepts related to the course domain. An ontology can be defined as a way to specify concepts and relations among them [1], and a learning path between concepts is thus constrained by such relations.

The correct definition of the ontological structures that are involved in an e-learning process has been a greatly debated topic in recent years. Stojanovic and his collegues [2] devise three ontology types to provide a correct definition of a learning material: content, context, and structure. In the work of Panteleyev [3] up to five ontological levels or *layers* are defined: standard layer (basic concepts definition) relations layer (relations among concepts) logical layer (axioms to define concepts and relations) action layer (action definition) and methods layer (definition of sequences of action executions). These approaches, like many others, make use of the semantic web paradigm to build domain ontologies: the use of XML and RDF can provide interoperability between learning objects following different annotation standards such as IEEE LOM and IMS. In this direction is oriented the work by Nejdl [4] where the framework EDUTELLA is proposed

S. Bandini and S. Manzoni (Eds.): AI*IA 2005, LNAI 3673, pp. 359–369, 2005.

as a peer-to-peer infrastructure to share information between distributed repositories of RDF metadata by means of a common data model (ECDM: Edutella Common Data Model). In all the previous works, knowledge is managed in the framework of a suitable RDF schema where concepts and relations are defined: the core of these works is the organization of learning materials, and not so much attention is devoted to the use of a particular learning theory. All the implementations inspired to these ideas result in simple curriculum systems. An interesting approach in the opposite direction can be represented by the GetSmart system [5] where a constructivist environment is proposed, which is based on the integration of a searching tool, a curriculum tool, and a concept map to obtain a visual arrangement of information. Marshall observes that concept maps are crucial to obtain mental schemata construction that is the core concept in the constructivist theory, but this is not completely true. At least two knowledge organization levels are needed to obtain a learning system centered on the student needs: an ontological structure of knowledge, and a concept map. Concept maps are intuitive interaction systems allowing the student to browse information according to his preferences, but also capable to implement a not so strong guidance procedure. Ontologies allow knowledge structuring, and management finalized to several goals such as abstract definition of a learning theory used to inspire the real system, user modeling, and planning personalized learning paths. XML based ontologies are not so flexible to address all these tasks in a simple way. A linguistic approach that makes use of a terminological knowledge base is preferable because of the possibility to easily implement predicates between concepts allowing to extract other knowledge by means of reasoning or planning techniques.

This work deals with a domain ontology for a web based tutoring system, and it is particularly focused on a possible strategy to transform its structure to obtain simple generation of learning paths. In a generic domain ontology it is possible to devise two kinds of relations between concepts: *structural*, and *navigation* relations. Structural relations are the classical specialization and subsumption predicates plus some predicates related to the specific structure of the arguments in the knowledge domain. As an example, in a history domain, events have to be correlated to dates, while in a OOP domain, classes have to hold information about their methods. Navigation relations are related to the logical links between different pieces of knowledge: an argument is a prerequisite for another one, two arguments are related in a some way and so on. Moreover, given a concept, not all the other ones related to it concur in the same way to its explanation, so the links have to be tagged with respect to concepts relevance. A planning approach is needed to obtain an articulated learning path from such an ontology, but direct application of classical action-state planners is very hard because one has to define wich are the most suitable actions to implement, with their preconditions and effects. It is not possible to simply follow the relations because they have different semantics, so it should be needed to define a set of actions as functions of the links traversal. Such actions are *learning actions* so an ontology about a particular learning process should be defined.

In this paper, authors were inspired by the Knowledge Space Theory (KST) [6] to obtain a transformation from the original ontology defined in the OpenCyc [7] knowledge base to a weighted graph where the A* algorithm was applied to determine learning paths. KST is a classical theory about knowledge structuring to support learning, and in particular to devise what the student already knows about a certain topic, and what she/he wants to know. A natural language dialog session with the student elicits these sets of concepts and allows for an initial pruning of not useful relations. A suitable heuristics has been employed to obtain arcs' weights from the semantics of each relation in the ontology, the absolute relevance of each concept in the domain, and a dynamic term describing the subjective relevance of each concept with respect to the student's goal. Finally, a map that represents and organizes a set of concepts in a spatial way is used to visualize the path inside the whole arrangement of learning materials. In the following discussion this map will be referred as a concept map. A path may not be a unique trajectory, but it can be visualized with ramifications due to the level of detail needed to explain the goal topic: this is not in contrast with any modern learning theory, and in particular it accounts for a constructivist approach to the problem. The presented methodology is quite general, and the implementation for an ontology describing the Java programming language is detailed throughout the paper.

The rest of the paper is arranged as follows. Section 2 provides some brief remarks about the Knowledge Space Theory, and the OpenCyc knowledge base. In section 3 the ontology-to-graph transformation is detailed, while in section 4 the implementation of the whole interaction cycle is explained, starting from the dialog with the student, until the visual presentation of the path. Finally in section 5 some conclusions are drawn, and future work is discussed.

2   Theoretical Background

The proposed methodology is based on the use of the KST as a framework to devise the starting point of the path to reach the goal, using natural language dialog system to capture the intentions of the user. Another fundamental component of the implemented system is the OpenCyc knowledge base that has been used because of the presence of truly general concepts and relations which can be considered as a sort of root for quickly develop a new ontology. In the presented work this statement is true both for the domain ontology, and the *ontology about graphs* which has been defined in order to perform the transformation, and to apply the A* algorithm. In this section a brief review of these two topics is reported.

2.1   Knowledge Space Theory

The KST was proposed by Doignon and Falmagne [6][8][9], and is a theoretical framework in the field of student modelling. KST is a psychological model for structuring domains of knowledge and offers a mean to formally describe the structure of a given knowledge domain based on prerequisite relationships [10]. According to the KST, a field of knowledge can be decomposed into items:

an item is a notion or skill to be learned. An item may also be presented as a task, which the student has to perform if the goal is to assess procedural and/or strategic knowledge. A field of knowledge is characterized by a set of items called a domain. A domain is the set of all items making up a particular subject matter. A student is considered to have learned the domain when she is capable to solve problems corresponding to all the items of the domain. Each student can be described by her knowledge state, i.e the collection of items the student is capable to solve. Knowledge states are related to a specific student and a particular domain. Besides, a students knowledge state changes during time, and the goal of learning is that, in the end, it should correspond to the complete domain. It is worthwhile to point out that, since there exist prerequisite relationships between the items, not all possible subsets of items are knowledge states. The collection of feasible knowledge states for a particular domain is called knowledge space. Such a knowledge space contains the empty set $\emptyset$ and the complete item set Q as elements, and, for any two knowledge states K, K' belonging to the knowledge space K_s, their union $K \bigcup K'$ is also a member of K_s [8]. The application of the knowledge space framework for tutoring tasks, leads to the possibility of obtaining learning paths which describe the students possible paths form the total novice learner (identified by the empty set $\emptyset$) through the knowledge space to the complete expert of the domain (identified by the knowledge state Q) [11].

2.2 OpenCyc

In the last years, the Cycorp, Inc company has developed the Cyc knowledge base (KB) which has a very large ontology constituted by over one hundred thousands atomic terms axiomatized by a set of over one million assertions fixed in nth-order predicate calculus. The Cyc KB, at present, is the largest and most complete general knowledge base, equipped with a good performing inference engine [12]. OpenCyc is suitable for automated logical inference to support knowledge-based reasoning applications, it also supports interoperability among software applications, it is extensible, provides a common vocabulary, and is suitable for mapping to/from other ontologies. Cyc collections are natural kinds or classes. The collections are opposed to mathematical sets; their instances have some common attribute(s). Each Cyc collection is similar to a set since it may have elements, subsets, and supersets, and may not have parts or spatial or temporal properties. The differences between a mathematical set and a Cyc collection are the following: the former can be constituted by an arbitrary set of uncorrelated things; besides two sets with the same elements are considered equal. The latter is characterized by the fact that the instances of a collection will have some common features; besides two Cyc collections can have all the same instances without being identical.

3   The Proposed Methodology

In this work a three-level schema to model course topics is adopted. At the lowest level, information is aggregated as a set of HTML documents which can represent single learning objects (e.g. a Java documentation page) or a composition of them as in the case of lessons. The intermediate representation is achieved by a concept map that is implemented as a SOM used to cluster documents in a Vector Space Representation using a measure of the similarity between the documents. A concept map is trained in an unsupervised way, and it is labelled with some *landmark concepts* that are used to bridge the gap with the symbolic level. The concept map owns an implicit representation of logical relations between concepts, and allows easy integration of new clusters standing for new concepts that can be instantiated at the symbolic level together with their relations with the nearest regions. Finally, the linguistic representation of the domain ontology is provided, where the landmark concepts play the role of atomic assertions inside the knowledge base.

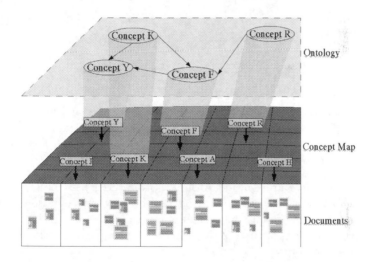

Fig. 1. Three-levels information organization

All the information and the structures of the concepts in the implemented Java ontology (relations, terms, constraints, applications an so on), are organized and verified starting from the official Sun Microsystems document presenting the main language characteristics and the Java structure. Java is a strongly typed language; every variable and every expression has a type that is known at compile time. The Java Ontology reflects this feature: the ontology is strongly connected, every concept is related to one or many others via a few relations. Figure 2 illustrates a portion of the ontology as a UML class diagram. The domain-specific theory has been partitioned essentially in two levels: the *structure* level and the *navigation* level. The first level realizes a structural definition of the ontology concepts, in terms of composition, definition of properties and all the other structural relations needed to represent the world. The navigation level gives the opportunity to tie down different concepts allowing the student to improve her/his knowledge. Structural level predicates are:

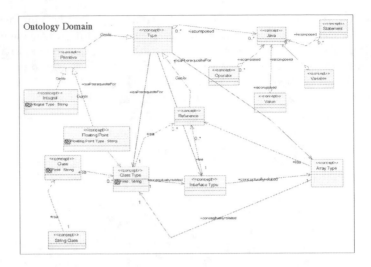

Fig. 2. A portion of the Java ontology

- *(#$isComposed #$Thing1 #$Thing2)*: *Thing2* is part of *Thing1*;
- *(#$genls #$Collection1 #$Collection2)*: OpenCyc inheritance predicate;
- *(#$isaMethodOf #$Method #$Thing)*: an element of the Cyc collection *Method* a method defined in class *Thing*;

The previous predicate are Ground Atomic Forms (GAF) in the OpenCyc vocabulary; they are just used to describe a fact in the representation. This is a very important starting point, but a formulation like this is still incomplete in term of accuracy and importance of the concepts. A couple of relations is defined to navigate the ontology:

- *(#$isaPrerequisiteFor #$Thing1 #$Thing2)*: *Thing1* is a prerequisite to learn about *Thing2*;
- *(#$conceptuallyRelated #$Thing1 #$Thing2)*: *Thing1* and *Thing2* are related in some way;

The predicate *isaPrerequisiteFor* has been implemented to provide a backbone structure inside the ontology ensuring the possibility of extracting meaningful learning paths on the basis of a sequence of precedence relations. The *conceptuallyRelated* predicate is just an alternative way to explore the ontology: this is a less strong relation than *isaPrerequisiteFor*, but it enables free exploration of the ontology in response to a query like "what about ... ?". To avoid the combinatorial explosion of search paths resulting from the direct exploration of the ontology a tag system has been introduced where every concept has an index representing his importance with respect to all the others. This tag is implemented with the relation *(#$WeightRelation #$Thing (#$Unity SubLRealNumber))*. This system presents two advantages: the selection of a navigation trajectory can be implemented simply choosing, in a first approximation, the concept with a higher tag, and in the same way it is possible to introduce a heuristic criterion in the planning module. The tag system is related to the number of occurrences of a concept in the master document from which the ontology has been built. This *citation weight* can be assumed as an absolute relevance measure of the concept.

The ontology-to-graph transformation is performed according to the Knowledge Space Theory formulation of learning path: the student is characterized by a *knowledge state* defined as the set of concepts she/he knows at a certain time, and she/he can move to another state by evaluating what she/he is ready to learn. In the original KST this is performed by questioning the user about topics directly related with the ones defining her current state. The ontology structure allows to define knowledge states in the same manner as in KST, and transitions between states take place moving across the navigation relations. The natural language dialog interaction is used to determine the initial state, and the goal. The transformation proceeds in this way:

- mapping of the original ontology in an ontology describing a graph;
- extraction of the path from the graph.

The mapping step starts with the of the process of pruning of the prerequisite concepts of the initial state: these are the things that the student already knows. Successively a heuristic weighting is performed according to the following procedure. Two concepts c_i and c_j have a citation weight respectively w_i and w_j. The global weight w_{ij} of the arc connecting them in the graph is computed as:

$$w_{ij} = \frac{w_i w_j}{M_W}(f(d_s)w_0^S + f(d_g)w_0^N) \tag{1}$$

Here M_W is maximum value of the citation weight, $f(d_s)$ and $f(d_g)$ are two weighting functions depending respectively on the distance from the starting point, and from the goal, while w_0^N and w_0^S are the initial values of the navigation, and structure relations that can eventually connect c_i and c_j. This means that in the initial part of the path, navigation links will be preferred due to the need to go far away the initial knowledge state: in fact in this phase the student is in region of the knowledge space she is more confident. On the contrary, in the neighbourhood of the goal state, structure links are preferred because they represent well defined relationships between concepts. These relations are precisely defined in the ontology, and are taken from the domain structure. The resulting graph is represented by means of two predicates:

- *(#$onPath #$Thing Path-Generic)*: *Thing* is part of path defined in the graph whose Cyc type is *Path-Generic*;
- *(#$pathConnection #$Thing1 #$Thing2 Path-Generic)*: *Thing1* and *Thing2* are connected inside the graph.

The A* algorithm is then applied to the resulting graph (see figure 3). In the implementation, the A* heuristic h is proportional to d_g, and it verifies all the monotonicity conditions required by the algorithm.

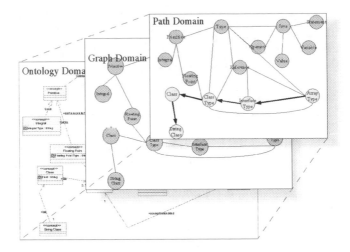

Fig. 3. Ontology-to-graph transformation

4   System Implementation and Results

An example of dialogue is reported in order to show the approach used to obtain information for the realization of the learning path. A session starts chatting with a conversational agent: the A.L.I.C.E. chat-bot (http://www.alicebot.org) which an XML DTD called AIML to perform pattern matching on a repository of request/answer pairs. Conversations have to be redirected to the knowledge base in order to obtain information about the learning requests issued to the system. A properly modified version of the CyN chat-bot [13] has been used to make a bridge with Cyc. The original version of CyN is based on the A.L.I.C.E. and allows to add the "common sense" to a chat-bot. With this solution it is possible to access the OpenCyC Common Sense Knowledge Base simply using an enhanced version of AIML. The chat-bot tries to guide the user to explain her needs, and the actual level of comprehension of the topic. Logs from the dialog are used to extract concepts for the ontology, and the inferential engine uses them to extract the learning path. In figure 4 is reported an example of dialog.

As it can be seen, the dialogue is inspired to the Knowledge Space Theory because the user answers lead to the questions formulation. In fact, to build of the knowledge structures of KST, the way the user answers to the query of the system is taken into account. Besides, it is supposed that, if a student correctly answers to the system questions, probably she masters that particular argument. In this case, the dialogue proceeds through those concepts that are more known or that are more interesting for the user as it is the case for the KST. From the analysis of the previous dialog, the following sets have been extracted:

- set A: the Goal: *Interface* ;
- set B: Subjects which are known on not interesting for the user: *Type, Keyword, ClassLiteral, InterfaceType, ClassType*;

```
User: HI TUTORJ

Chat-bot: HI STUDENT DO YOU WANT KNOW ANYTHING ABOUT JAVA? U: YES. I AM INTERESTED IN INTERFACE

C: TO OBTAIN THE LESSON ABOUT THE CONCEPT OF INTERFACE YOU MUST KNOW SOMETHING ABOUT InterfaceType, Class

ARE YOU INTERESTED IN ONE OF THESE?

U: YES I DO. I WANT TO KNOW SOMETHING ABOUT InterfaceType

C: OK. InterfaceType IS RELATED TO ClassType AND ArrayType

U:OK. I AM INTERESTED IN THE CONCEPT OF ClassType

C: TO OBTAIN THE LESSON ABOUT THE CONCEPT OF ClassType YOU MUST KNOW SOMETHING ABOUT Type

U: NO, THANKS I WANT TO KNOW WHAT IS AN Interface?

C: OK. Interface IS Keyword, ClassLiteral, InterfaceType, ClassType. DO YOU WANT TO KNOW SOMETHING ABOUT ONE OF

THESE?

U: NO, TELL ME ALL ABOUT Interface?

C: Interface :

IS A PREREQUISITE FOR : InterfaceDeclaration,

IS COMPOSED BY : ExtendInterface, InterfaceBody, InterfaceIdentifier, InterfaceModifier,

IS A : Keyword, ClassLiteral, InterfaceType, ClassType,

IS RELATED TO :

ARE YOU INTERESTED IN ONE OF THESE?

U: TELL ME SOMETHING ABOUT InterfaceDeclaration

C: InterfaceDeclaration IS COMPOSED BY InterfaceBody, InterfaceIdentifier, InterfaceModifier, Interface

U: OK, PLEASE GIVE ME A LEARNING PATH.
```

Fig. 4. A dialog example

- set C: Arguments which are interesting for the user: *InterfaceType, ClassType, InterfaceDeclaration, Interface*;
- set D: Prerequisites of the set A$\cup$C (given by the CyC ontology): *null*;
- set E: the set D-B: *null* ;

The lerning path will therefore start form the initial state defined by E, and it will stop in the concept belonging to A. The obtained path in Cyc is reported in figure 5.

The visual interface reproducing the path is reported in figure 6. It is inspired to the StarryNight visualization tool (http://rhizome.org/starrynight) which gives an immediate feedback to the user about the topics holding the greatest amount of information by means of the star cluster metaphor. The

```
(isaPrerequisiteFor Class InterfaceDeclaration)
(iscomposed InterfaceDeclaration InterfaceModifier)
(iscomposed InterfaceDeclaration InterfaceIdentifier)
(iscomposed InterfaceDeclaration InterfaceBody)
(iscomposed InterfaceDeclaration Interface)
(isaPrerequisiteFor Interface InterfaceDeclaration)
(iscomposed Interface InterfaceDeclaration)
```

Fig. 5. Cyc generation of the path

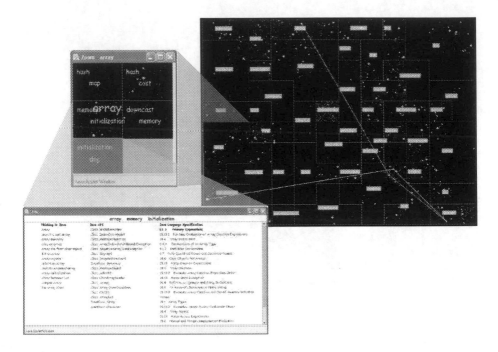

Fig. 6. Learning path visualization

implemented interface is split into areas addressing the different landmark concepts. Clicking on a single area, the user can highlight more terms that have been clustered close to the landmark. Finally, from each term it is possible to obtain a pop-up window linking javadoc, lessons, and other learning material. The user is not constrained to follow the highlighted path, but he can also freely browse all the documents in the map.

5   Conclusions

A methodology has been presented to automatically extract learning paths from a domain ontology, via a transformation of the ontology itself in a suitable weighted graph. The graph can be managed using an A* path finding algorithm. Direct use of a classical planner on the ontology implies the definition of actions along with their preconditions and effects in terms of the relations semantics: this leads to the definition of an ontology of learning. The presented methodology avoids this problem, and makes the system responsive because no re-planning is necessary. Moreover the explained technique is grounded on a well known theory of knowledge management to support learning.

Future work will regard the development of an integrated system to support the application of the methodology to different domains. Other work will regard the extension of the system to a IMS SCORM compliant framework for documents annotation.

References

1. Staab, S., Studer, R., Schnurr, H., Sure, Y.: Knowledge Processes and Ontologies. IEEE Intelligent Systems **16** (2001) 26–34
2. Stojanovic, L., Staab, S., Studer, R.: Elearning based on the semantic web. In: Proc. of World Conference on the WWW and Internet WebNet2001, Orlando, Florida, USA (2001)
3. Panteleyev, M., Puzankov, D., P.V.Sazykin, Sergeyev, D.: Intelligent educational environments based on the semantic Web technologies. In: Proc. of 2002 IEEE International Conference on Artificial Intelligence Systems (ICAIS 2002), Divnomorskoe, RUSSIA, IEEE Computer Society Press (2002) 457–462
4. Nejdl, W., Wolf, B., Qu, C., Decker, S., Sintek, M., Naeve, A., Nilsson, M., Palmér, M., Risch, T.: EDUTELLA: A P2P Networking Infrastructure Based on RDF. In: Proc. of the 11th World Wide Web Conference, ACM Press (2002) 604–615
5. Marshall, B., Zhang, Y., Chen, H., Lally, A., Shen, R., Fox, E., Cassel, L.: Convergence of knowledge management and e-learning: the GetSmart experience. In: Proc. of Joint Conference on Digital Libraries 2003, Houston, TX, IEEE Computer Society Press (2003) 135–146
6. Falmagne, J., Doignon, J., Koppen, M., Vilano, M., Johannesen, L.: Introduction to knowledge spaces: How to build, test, and search them. Psycological Review **97** (1990) 201–224
7. Lenat, D., Guha, R.: Building Large Knowledge Bases. Addison-Wesley, Reading MA, USA (1990)
8. Albert, D., Hockemeyer, C.: Adaptive and Dynamic Hypertext Tutoring Systems Based on Knowledge Space Theory. Artificial Intelligence in Education: Knowledge and Media in Learning Systems, Frontiers in Artificial Intelligence and Applications **39** (1997) 553–555
9. Harp, S., Samad, T., Vilano, M.: Modeling student knowledge with self-organizing feature maps. IEEE Trans. on Systems, Man and Cybernetics **25** (1995) 727–737
10. Albert, D., Hockemeyer, C.: Applying demand analysis of a set of test problems for developing adaptive courses. In: Proc. of International Conference on Computers in Education. Volume 1. (2002) 69–70
11. Hockemeyer, C., Held, T., Albert, D.: Rath: A relational adaptive tutoring hypertext www-environment based on knowledge space theory. In: Proc. of Computer Aided Learning and Instruction in Science and Engineering (CALISCE'98), Göteborg, Sweden (1998) 417–423
12. Reed, S.L., Lenat, D.B.: Mapping Ontologies into Cyc (2002)
13. Coursey, K.: Living in CyN: Mating AIML and Cyc together with Program N (2004)

A Multidimensional Framework for the Representation of Ontologies in Adaptive Hypermedia Systems

Francesca Carmagnola, Federica Cena, Cristina Gena, and Ilaria Torre

Dipartimento di Informatica, Università di Torino,
Corso Svizzera 185, Torino, Italy
{carmagnola, cena, cgena, torre}@di.unito.it

Abstract. [1]This paper introduces a semantic framework for adaptive systems. The core is a multidimensional matrix whose different planes contain the ontological representation of different types of knowledge. On these planes we represent user features, her actions, context, device, domain, adaptation goals and methods. The intersection between planes allows us to represent and managing semantic rules for inferring new user features or defining adaptation strategies. We exploit OWL to represent taxonomic knowledge and SWRL for rules.

1 Introduction

The Semantic Web aims at representing information in the WWW in a way such that machines can use it for automation, integration and reuse of knowledge across applications. The advantage of such an approach can be particularly useful in the field of adaptive hypermedia systems. These systems typically reflect some features of the user in the user model and apply this model to adapt various aspects of the system (content, interface, navigation, etc) to the user [6].

Current adaptive systems may also take into account other features, besides the user model, such as the context of interaction, the device, etc...

Usually the corpus of the documents and services the system can adapt is already known at the design time and can be defined as a *closed corpus of adaptation* [8]. The application of Semantic Web technologies to adaptive systems and the use of shared ontologies and metadata to describe resources can contribute to extend the closed corpus to an *open corpus of adaptation*. Thus, external documents and resources, which are semantically annotated, can be considered during the adaptation to the users. Furthermore, representing the user model with a semantic formalism and shared ontologies can be the base for building a user model server: a server that enables the reuse of user models, user modeling knowledge, and adaptation strategies across applications [12].

Different adaptive systems can query the same user model server, be provided with the user model and share the common knowledge.

This paper describes an ontology-based framework for adaptive hypermedia systems which aims at providing a methodological approach for the semantic definition of two types of knowledge:

---

[1] We are very grateful to Luca Console for having helped us during the development of the project and for his fruitful suggestions.

S. Bandini and S. Manzoni (Eds.): AI*IA 2005, LNAI 3673, pp. 370–380, 2005.
© Springer-Verlag Berlin Heidelberg 2005

(i) knowledge regarding what has to be adapted, which features (of the user, context, etc.) the system has to take into account to perform adaptation and how (adaptation methods and techniques);

(ii) knowledge regarding adaptation strategies and rules for inferring new knowledge.

Following the 'equation' *ontology= (i) taxonomy + (ii), axioms,* (see for example the RuleML Initiative [4]), we represent (i) the declarative descriptions of user models, domain knowledge, etc., with taxonomies expressed in a standard semantic markup language for the Semantic Web, OWL[2], and (ii) the inference rules with SWRL[3], a W3C proposal for a semantic rule language.

2 Goals of the Project and Choices for Semantic Knowledge Representation

While many works in the user modeling and adaptation community exploit ontologies, in the form of taxonomies, to describe application domains and some recent ones adopt them to represent user models, devices features, context of interaction, etc. [8], [11], the semantic representation of reasoning strategies is still little addressed. In our project we use both taxonomies and reasoning strategies.

As far as taxonomies are concerned, we use them since they allow to represent and share conceptualizations of a certain knowledge domain [10] and contain a large set of pertinent concepts (entities, attributes) and the relations among them (IS_A, PART_OF, PORPUSE_OF, etc...).

The formalisms through which taxonomies may be expressed can be not XML-based, such as Kl_ONE [5] Lloom[4], Flogic[5]; or XML-based, such as XOL[6] (Ontology eXchange Language), SHOE[7] (Simple HTML Ontology Extension), OML[8] (Ontology Markup Language), OIL (Ontology Interchange Language)[9], DAML (DARPA Agent Markup Language)[10], DALM + OIL[11], OWL (Web Ontology Language). Among them OIL, DAML, OWL are compatible with web standard languages (RDF, RDF Schema) and give a support to reasoning strategies.

Regarding the representation language, we opted for OWL for two main reasons:

- it is the new standard ontology language of the Semantic Web, defined by W3C, and developed as revision of the previous DAML+OIL[12];
- having a set of powerful primitives, mostly derived from description logic, it provides more expressive power than RDF and RDF schema.

---

[2] http://www.w3.org/TR/owl-features/
[3] http://www.w3.org/Submission/SWRL/
[4] http://www.isi.edu/isd/LOOM/LOOM-HOME.html
[5] http://www.informatik.uni-freiburg.de/~dbis/Publications/95/flogic-jacm.html
[6] http://www.ai.sri.com/pkarp/xol/
[7] http://www.cs.umd.edu/projects/plus/SHOE/
[8] http://www.ontologos.org/OML/OML%200.3.htm
[9] http://www.ontoknowledge.org/oil/
[10] http://www.daml.org/
[11] http://www.w3.org/TR/daml+oil-reference
[12] http://www.w3.org/TR/daml+oil-reference

What lacks in taxonomies is a set of reasoning mechanisms (which might be expressed by means of rules) to make inferences, and to extract useful information.

Thus, rule systems require taxonomies in order to have a shared definition of the concepts and relations mentioned in the rules, and taxonomies require a rule system to derive/use further information that cannot be captured by them. Rules allow also to add expressiveness to the representation formalism, to reason on the instances, and they can be orthogonal to the description logic taxonomies are typically based on.

Moreover, an ontology based on taxonomies and rules can provide humans (and machines) with rational explanations of system behaviour, thus improving their trust on the system. In the specific case of the Semantic Web, this is a relevant aspect for the so-called *proof layer*, which involves the "deductive process as well as the representation of proofs in Web Languages and proof validation"[2]. In this way, the proof presentation can be considered as a way for humans/machine to retrace the derivation of answers.

To achieve these goals, rules have to be expressed using semantic formalisms as well as taxonomies.

In our project, we exploit SWRL, a Semantic Web Rule Language combining OWL and RuleML[13]. In particular, SWRL is a combination of OWL Description Logic, OWL Lite and the Unary/Binary Datalog RuleML, and extends the set of OWL axioms to include Horn-like rules.

As described in the W3C proposal cited above, model theoretic semantics of SWRL is an extension of the semantics for OWL: it defines "bindings", which are extensions of OWL interpretations that map variables to elements of the domain: a rule is satisfied by an interpretation if every binding that satisfies the antecedent also satisfies the consequent. Therefore, OWL classes can be used as predicates in rules, and rules and ontology axioms can be freely mixed.

Like RuleML, SWRL allows interoperability with major rules systems (commercial and not): CLIPS, JESS, etc…

Summarizing, a semantic representation of rules has different purposes, in particular:

- it enables knowledge sharing between software agents and human designers;
- it enables to compare and evaluate rules, detect incompatibilities, validate or eventually refuse them both in the design phase and in the exploitation phase;
- in the field of adaptive systems, it allows to give explanations about the generation of inferences of new user features; the system adaptive behaviour and the strategies of adaptation

3   Description of the Framework

The framework we propose aims at supporting the visual design, the semantic representation of knowledge bases and rules, and their implementation in adaptive hypermedia systems based on symbolic reasoning.

In addition to the above reasons, the choice of using a semantic formalism in order to define the framework arises from the evidence that user features are common to different applications and, if semantically described, they can be shared among them

---

[13] http://www.ruleml.org/

(consider for example the feature "user expertise": it is used by almost all adaptive systems). Defining these dimensions once for all represents an interesting opportunity in terms of reduced design costs and optimization of results. Moreover, the ontological representation of user, device, context and domain models also arises from the diffusion of this kind of taxonomies on the web (the last one in particular), and the possibility to link such taxonomies and integrating them with semantic web technologies and Web Services[14].

For the definition of this semantic framework we developed a multidimensional matrix, as in [14], composed of different planes. Each plane contains the ontological representation of a specific type of knowledge. In particular we have:

- user model taxonomy
- user actions taxonomy
- domain taxonomy
- device taxonomy
- context taxonomy
- adaptation goals taxonomy
- adaptation methods taxonomy

Regarding rules, the framework semantically represents and manages the typical and relevant rules in adaptive hypermedia systems:

- *user modeling rules* (which can be considered as *derivation rules*) that add knowledge about a user, inferring new user features from other features,
- *adaptation rules* (which can be considered as *reaction rules*) that define the strategies of adaptation, taking into account domain features, system adaptation goals, user features, context and the device in use.

Being a framework, the taxonomies on the planes have to be application independent and modular, so they can be reused among different domains and applications.

In some planes we exploit and extend shared ontologies (in particular CC/PP[15] for the device, Ubisword[16] for the user and the context features, the Open Directoy Project for the domain[17]), since they are easier to map, public available and better known.

Each taxonomy is defined at *different levels*: at the first level there is the definition of general concepts. For example, for the *domain taxonomy*, the first level includes macro domains such as: tourist domain, financial domain, e-learning domain, etc...; for the *adaptation-goals taxonomy*, the first level specifies general goals such as: inducing/pushing; informing, explaining, suggesting/recommending, guiding, assisting/helping [14], and so on for all the ontologies. At the following levels there are specialized concepts. For example, in the *tourist domain*, the next levels can include tourist categories (lodging, places, etc...), while in the *adaptation-goals taxonomy* they can include more specific goals such as explaining to support learning or to clarify, to teach new concepts or to correct mistakes, etc...

---

[14] http://www.w3.org/TR/ws-arch/

[15] http://www.w3.org/Mobile/CCPP/

[16] http://www.u2m.org/

[17] http://dmoz.org

Thanks to this modular structure, the framework can be used by different applications, which can select a sub-part of the most generic taxonomy, in the considered planes, and instantiate only the concepts they are interested in.

The basic idea of the matrix is that user modeling and adaptation rules can be defined on the points of intersection between planes.

Given for example the leaf of the taxonomic tree *"explaining → explaining to support learning → teaching new concepts"*, the idea is that the *adaptation rule* for reaching this goal can be defined taking into account the knowledge domain, the user's current knowledge, her preferences and, possibly, her learning style (e.g. top-down vs. bottom-up), her current cognitive load, the current device (e.g. PDA, desktop pc) and context conditions (e.g. the noise level in the room). Finally, the definition of adaptation rules requires considering the set of available adaptation methods and techniques (such as hiding text, stretch text, audio annotations, direct guidance, etc.). Since all of these features are classes represented inside taxonomies in different planes, it can be perceived that the definition of the rule derives from the intersection of such planes in correspondence of the involved classes.

This methodology can be exploited to define all the rules addressed by the framework,clearly taking into account the appropriate planes. As previously seen, the added value of using a semantic formalism to express rules consists mainly in enabling knowledge sharing both between software agents and human designers and in allowing to give explanations about the generation of inferences system adaptive behaviour.

User Modeling Rules. For this kind of derivation rules, which allow an adaptive system to infer new knowledge about the user, we consider:

- on the X_1-plane, the taxonomy of the *user's actions* on the system (selection, bookmark, print, etc...);
- on the X_2-plane, the taxonomy of the possible *domain features* (business, tourist, e-learning, shopping);
- on the X_3-plane, the taxonomy of the *user model* (demographic features, psychographic features, cognitive features, preferences, interests, etc...);

From the intersection of dimensions on these planes we can define user-modeling rules in the form of:

> *If ((X₁Plane user actions=a₁, a₂,... aₙ)*
>   *AND (X₂Plane domain_feature= b₁, b₂,...bₙ)*
>   *AND(X₃Plane explicit_user_features= c₁,c₂,...,cₙ)*
>   *Then (inferred_user_features= i₁,i₂,...,iₙ)*

in which the *Left Hand Side* specifies classes or properties of classes that contribute to define the value of the inferred user's feature, which constitute the *Right Hand Side*. For example:

> *If ((X₁Plane user actions= bookmark)*
>   *AND (X₂Plane domain feature=pub)*
> *AND(X₃Plane explicit_user_features=role:clerk, age: 35<x<45, gender:F)*
>   *Then (inferred_user_feature=user's propensity to spend: medium-low)*

The matrix representation for this rule is showed in **Fig. 1**. This rule lets to infer the user's feature *propensity to spend* as a match between dimensions of each plane. In

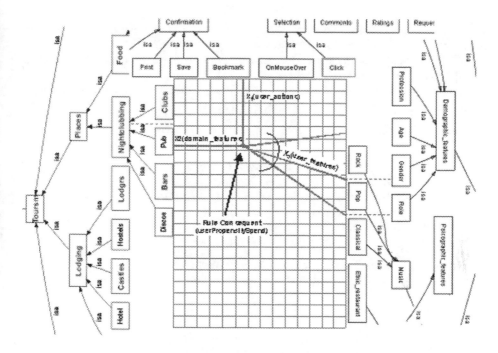

Fig. 1. A matrix for inferring user propensity to spend

particular we assume that *propensity to spend* derives from the observation of variables such as user actions, domain features (as objects of users actions) and from specific user features (age, gender and role).

Giving that, the rule means that: if a user makes actions like bookmarking pages and the pages she has bookmarked regard pubs (in the turist/town domain) and the user is a female, with an age between 35 and 45 years and she is a clerk, then we can infer that her propensity to spend may be medium-low.

Notice that, at this moment, we do not manage uncertainty or probability distributions of values, but we are working on defining a taxonomy of uncertainty factors and referencing it in SWRL.

Adaptation Rules. As already explained, the above methodology can be used to define the adaptation rules as well, clearly changing the planes to take into account. Given that the aim of this matrix is to define the right adaptation techniques to reach a specific adaptation goal, given some available methods, a user, a device, a domain and a context, the taxonomies taken into account are the following:

- on the Z_1-plane, we place the taxonomy of the *adaptation goals* (adaptation of content, interface, amount of information, detail level, etc.);
- on the Z_2-plane we place the taxonomy of the *adaptation methods* (link removal, additional explanation, etc), defined following both Kobsa et. al. [13] and Brusilovsky [6] classifications.
- on the Z_3-plane, we have the taxonomy of *context conditions* (e.g. time of the day, movement conditions,.)

- on the Z_4-plane, the taxonomy of the *user model* integrated/updated with the user's dimensions inferred by the previous user modeling rules.
- on the Z_5-plane we place the taxonomy of *devices* that can be used by the user (PDA, PC, mobile phone, on-board system, DTT, etc.);
- on the Z_6-plane we place the taxonomy which describes the possible *domain feature* (business, tourist, e-learning, shopping).

The definition of the adaptation rule drives from the intersection of such planes:

> *If* $((Z_1 Plane\ adaptation\ goals = a_1,\ a_{2,...} a_n)$
>   *AND* $(Z_2 Plane\ adaptation\ methods = b_1,\ b_{2,...}\ b_n)$
>   *AND* $(Z_3 Plane\ context\ condition = c_1,\ c_{2,...}\ cn_3)$
>   *AND* $(Z_4 Plane\ user\_features = d_1,\ d_{2,...},\ d_n)$
>   *AND* $(Z_5 Plane\ device = e_1,\ e_{,...},e_n)$
>   *AND* $(Z_6 Plane\ domain = f_1,\ f_{2,...},f_n))$
> *Then* $(adaptation\ techniques = g_1,\ g_{2,...},\ g_n)$

in which the *Left Hand Side* specifies the conditions to be satisfied and the *Right Hand Side* identifies the adaptation techniques for a correct method application.

For example:

> *If* $((Z_1 Plane\ adaptation\ goal = emphasize\ an\ item)$
>   *AND* $(Z_2 Plane\ adaptation\ methods = font\ enhancement,\ highlighting)$
>   *AND* $(Z_3 Plane\ context\ condition = night,\ movement)$
>   *AND* $(Z_4 Plane\ user\_features = age:>65)$
>   *AND* $(Z_5 Plane\ device = PDA)$
>   *AND* $(Z_5 Plane\ domain = \backslash any)$
> *Then* $(adaptation\ techniques = font\ enhancement: +3)$

According to this rule, having an elderly user in a nightly and mobile context, the system has to enlarge the font size in order to emphasise an item and to make it more readable.

As explained in section 2, taxonomies on the planes are written in OWL, while rules, at the intersection of planes, are written in SWRL.

A final consideration regards the explanation of how taxonomies and rules are employed to finally produce the User Model, Domain Model, Device Model, etc. of a specific application.

First of all we must underline that each component of the framework is ontologically represented as a class. Thus we have for example the User Model Class, the Domain Model Class, the Device Model Class, etc... each one characterized by a set of properties, that are the user features, the domain features, etc... so a specific user model represents an instance of the User Model Class.

Each property is mapped on the classes represented on the corresponding taxonomy.

For example, the *User Model* property "Age" is mapped on the Class Age of the *User Model Taxonomy*. And the values of properties are the instances of the Classes in the corresponding taxonomy.

Inference and adaptation rules are written exactly taking into account the properties of the models, which are mapped on the taxonomies. The next section will provide an example.

4 An Example of Application of the Framework

We are currently testing the proposed methodology with an application, UbiquiTo [1], we previously developed. This application is a *multi-device* adaptive guide that offers personalized tourist information. Therefore, the instantiation of the taxonomies on planes is restricted to the classes related to such features of the application.

For example, regarding the matrix for inferring user features, on the *domain Plane*, we consider the classes of the tourist domain (e.g., Lodging, Places, Arts, etc.). However, in Class Lodging, for instance, we do not instantiate the subclass "Castles", since UbiquiTo does not address it.

The same approach has been adopted for all the planes considered in the matrix. As said in section 3, some taxonomies are based on and extend public and shared ontologies (CC/PP for the device, Ubisword for the user and the context features, Open Directoy Project for the domain).

To support the development of the taxonomies and the translation in Owl, we use the free tool Protégé 3.0[18]. As it is a standard language we do not provide an example here. Instead, in the following we show an example of SWRL code for representing the above defined rule (see Fig.1), which derives user's "propensity_to_spend" starting from other user's features and user's actions on a specific domain.

// Definition of the taxonomies involved in the rule
```
    <swrl:Variable rdf:ID="user"/>
    <swrl:Variable rdf:ID="actions"/>
    <swrl:Variable rdf:ID="domain"/
    <ruleml:Imp>
```

//Begin of the antecedent

// Definition of the URL of taxonomies
```
    <ruleml:body rdf:parseType="Collection">
    <swrl:classAtom>
     <swrl:classPredicate rdf:resource="URLOntology User"/>
     <swrl:argument1 rdf:resource="#user"/>
    </swrl:classAtom>
    <swrl:classAtom>
     <swrl:classPredicate rdf:resource="& URLOntology Action "/>
     <swrl:argument1 rdf:resource="#actions"/>
    </swrl:classAtom>
    <swrl:classAtom>
     <swrl:classPredicate rdf:resource="& URLOntology Domain"/>
     <swrl:argument1 rdf:resource="#domain"/>
    </swrl:classAtom>
```

// Definition of the property "age" mapped on the user model taxomomy"
```
    <swrlx: datavaluePropertyAtom swrlx:property="age">
    <ruleml:var>user</ruleml:var>
```

---

[18] http://protege.stanford.edu/

// Instatiation of the property "age" (value 35<x<45)
```
    <owlx:DataValue owlx:datatype="&xsd;integer">35<x<45</owlx:DataValue>
    </swrlx:datavaluedPropertyAtom>
```

// Definition of the property "role"
```
    <swrlx:individualPropertyAtom swrlx:property="role">
    <ruleml:var>user</ruleml:var>
```

// Instatiation of the property "role" (value clerk)
```
    <owlx:Individual owlx:name="clerk"/>
    </swrlx:individualPropertyAtom>
```

// Definition of the property "gender" of the user model
```
    <swrlx:individualPropertyAtom swrlx:property="gender">
    <ruleml:var>user</ruleml:var>
```

// Instatiation of the property "gender" of the user model (value female)
```
    <owlx:Individual owlx:name="female"/>
    </swrlx:individualPropertyAtom>
```

// Definition of the property "bookmark" of the user actions
```
    <swrlx:individualPropertyAtom swrlx:property="bookmark">
    <ruleml:var>actions</ruleml:var>
```

// Instatiation of the property "bookmark" of the user actions*(value yes)*
```
    <owlx:Individual owlx:name="yes"/>
    </swrlx:individualPropertyAtom>
```

// Definition of the property "pub" of the domain
```
    <swrlx:individualPropertyAtom swrlx:property="pub">
    <ruleml:var>domain</ruleml:var>
```

// Instatiation of the property "pub" of the domain (value yes)
```
    <owlx:Individual owlx:name="yes"/>
    </swrlx:individualPropertyAtom>
```

//relation between an action (mapped on the user actions *taxonomy) and a domain object (mapped on the domain taxonomy)*
```
    <swrl:individualPropertyAtom>
    <swrl:propertyPredicate rdf:resource="Uri#actions;objectOfAction"/>
    <swrl:argument1 rdf:resource="uri#actions"/>
    <swrl:argument2 rdf:resource="uri#domain"/>
    </swrl:individualPropertyAtom>
```

//End of antecedent
```
    </ruleml:body>
```
//Begin of the consequent
```
    <ruleml:head rdf:parseType="Collection">
    <swrl:individualPropertyAtom>
```

//Definition of new user's feature (propensity to spend) that emerges at the point of intersection between planes
    <swrl:propertyPredicate rdf:resource="&URI;propensityToSpent"/>
    <ruleml:var>user</ruleml:var>

//Instatiation of the inferred feature "propensityToSpend" of the user model (value medium-low)
    <owlx:Individual owlx:name="medium low"/>
</swrlx:individualPropertyAtom>
    <swrl:argument1 rdf:rcsource="#user"/>
    <swrl:argument2 rdf:resource="#actions"/>
    <swrl:argument3 rdf:resource="#domain"/>
    </swrl:individualPropertyAtom>

5 Conclusion and Related Work

In the recent years the User Modeling and Adaptive Hypermedia community has been approaching to Semantic Web technologies. Frasincar and Houben, for example, developed a methodology for the design of intelligent web information systems in the Web [9]. In this work, device capabilities are specified by means of CC/PP, while adaptation aspects, application domain, adaptivity conditions and update rules are expressed in RDFS. One of the most interesting aspects of their methodology is the design of the Application Model, which is concerned with the navigational aspects of the hypermedia presentation. They extended their Conceptual Model, expressed in RDFS, with navigational views, considered as slices of one ore more concepts from the Conceptual Model. Heckmann and Krueger [11] developed an XML-based markup language, UserML, and its corresponding ontology, UbisWorld, to communicate user models in a ubiquitous computing environment. Every UserML document can be divided into MetaData, UserModel, InferenceExplanations, ContextModel and Environment Model. The main aim of this representation is that different user modeling applications could use the same framework and keep their individual user model elements. Dolog et al. [8] developed an adaptive learning application using Semantic Web technologies. Learning resources are described by means of shared ontologies (Dublin Core and Learning Objects Metadata) with their RDF bindings and reasoning and adaptation are realized by using TRIPLE, a rule-based query language for the semantic web. Then, they also extended the adaptation capability of the systems to a global *external* context of semantically annotated resources, and they used TRIPLE to make ontology mapping, query relaxation, result filtering and finally to generate recommendations.

Respect to these works, the main contribution of our project is the definition of an *ontological framework* for managing *rules* and *taxonomies* in an *integrated, semantic* and *visual* way. In this framework we exploit the semantic formalism SWRL for the definition of reasoning capabilities and adaptation strategies integrating it with OWL, the standard language for the Semantic Web, which we exploit for the declaration of the knowledge base. Thus, through our framework, the development of an adaptive system may benefit from the availability of: i) shared ontologies regarding the user model, domain model, adaptation methods, etc. which the specific application can instantiate and extend, if necessary, ii) the *matrix tool* for representing, in a unified way, all the knowledge the system is based on, iii) standard and integrated languages for representing knowledge, iiii) implementation support, given by the possibility to convert OWL and SWRL to the syntax of rule engines such as CLIPS and Jess.

As regards future work, we are going to apply this methodology to other adaptive applications (e.g., [3], [7]) in order to evaluate if our approach is useful in different application domains and successful with different adaptation techniques. Regarding the extension of the framework, we are developing rules to integrate XSLT transformation in our resource and generate different kind of interfaces directly from our model. Moreover we are working to manage uncertainty defining a taxonomy of uncertainty factors and referencing it in SWRL. Finally, we are working on the extension of taxonomies on each plane.

References

1. Amendola I., Cena F., Console L., Crevola A., Gena C., Goy A., Modeo S., Perrero M., Torre I., Toso A.: UbiquiTO: A Multi-device Adaptive Guide. Proc. of Mobile HCI 2004, Lecture Notes in Computer Science, 3160 (2004) 409-414
2. Antoniou, G., Van Harmelen F.: A Semantic Web Primer. The MIT Press, Cambridge, MA, (2004)
3. Ardissono L, Gena C., Torasso P., Bellifemine F., Chiaretto A., Difino A., Negro A. : Generation of personalized Electronic Program Guides. LNCS n. 2829. AI*IA 2003, Springer Verlag, (2003) 474-486
4. Boley, H., S. Tabet, and G. Wagner.: Design Rationale of RuleML: A Markup Language for Semantic Web Rules. Proc.of the First Semantic Web Working Symposium, SWWS'01, Stanford, CA, (2001) 381-402
5. Brachman R.J. , Schmolze J.: An Overview of the KL-ONE Knowledge Representation System. Cognitive Sci 9(2) (1985)
6. Brusilovsky P.L.: Methods and Techniques of Adaptive Hypermedia. In User Modeling and User-Adapted Interaction 6 (1996) 87–129
7. Cena, F., Torre, I.: Increasing Performances and Personalization in the Interaction with a Call Center System. Proc. of the 8th ACM International Conference on Intelligent User Interfaces, Funchal, Madeira, Portugal, (2004), 226-228
8. Dolog, P., Henze, N., Nejdl, W., Sintek, M.: The Personal Reader: Personalizing and Enriching Learning Resources using Semantic Web Technologies. Proc. of the AH 2004, Eindhoven, The Netherlands, LNCS, Springer Verlag (2004) 85-94
9. Frasincar F., Houben G.: Hypermedia Presentation Adaptation on the Semantic Web. Proc. of the AH 2002, LNCS, Springer Verlag (2002) 85-94
10. Gruber R.: Toward Principles for the Design of Ontologies Used for Knowledge Sharing. Stanford Knowledge Systems Laboratory Technical Report KSL (1993) 93-04
11. Heckmann D. and Krueger A.: A User Modeling Markup Language (UserML) for Ubiquitous Computing, in LNCS 2702, Springer Verlag (2003), 393 - 397
12. Kay, J., Kummerfeld, R., Lauder P.: Personis: A Server for User Models. Proc. of the AH, LNCS, Springer Verlag (2002) 203-212
13. Kobsa, A., Koenemann, J., Pohl, W.: Personalized Hypermedia Presentation Techniques for Improving Online Customer Relationships. The Knowledge Engineering Review 16(2) (2001) 111-155
14. Torre I.: Goals, tasks and Application domains as the guidelines for defining a framework for User modeling. In User Modeling 2001, LNCS, Springer Verlag (2001) 260-262

A Conversational Agent Based on a Conceptual Interpretation of a Data Driven Semantic Space

Francesco Agostaro[1], Agnese Augello[1], Giovanni Pilato[2], Giorgio Vassallo[1], and Salvatore Gaglio[1]

[1] DINFO-Dipartimento di Ingegneria Informatica,Università degli studi di Palermo,
Viale delle Scienze - Edificio 6, 90128 Palermo, Italy
{agostaro, gvassallo, gaglio}@unipa.it, augello@csai.unipa.it
[2] ICAR - Istituto di Calcolo e Reti ad Alte Prestazioni,
CNR - Consiglio Nazionale delle Ricerche, Viale delle Scienze - Edificio 11,
90128 Palermo, Italy
g.pilato@icar.cnr.it

Abstract. In this work we propose an interpretation of the LSA framework which leads to a data-driven "conceptual" space creation suitable for an "intuitive" conversational agent.

The proposed approach allows overcoming the limitations of traditional, rule-based, chat-bots, leading to a more natural dialogue.

1 Introduction

Natural language dialogue interfaces, like chat-bot systems, are simple to build and they can be used as interfaces for a large set of applications (entertainment, educational and e-learning platforms, research engines, e-commerce web-site navigation systems and so on). However the pattern matching rules they are based on are often too restrictive. Many approaches try to integrate the simple technology of chat-bot systems, with more sophisticated techniques[15,16,17,18]. In [19] a dialogue system has been implemented, which inherits from the chat-bots systems the robustness and the locality of pattern-matching based dialogue management, but uses an ontological model in order to abstract dialogue-acts from the specific inputs. Another attempt to improve the human features of chat-bots has been realized with the CyN project [13], whose aim is to link the pattern matching interpreter of a well-known conversational system, Alice[3], to OpenCyc[14], the largest commonsense knowledge base available today.

In recent years a paradigm, named Latent Semantic Analysis (LSA), useful to extract and represent the meaning of words by statistical computations applied to a large corpus of texts, has been proposed [11]. LSA is based on the *vector space method*: given a text corpus of N documents and M words, the LSA paradigm defines a mapping between the M words and the N documents into a continuous vector space S, where each word w_i is associated to a vector U_i in S, and each document d_j is associated a vector V_j in $S[6]$. The S vector space is a "semantic space", since semantics conveyed by the presence of the i-th word

S. Bandini and S. Manzoni (Eds.): AI*IA 2005, LNAI 3673, pp. 381–392, 2005.

in the j-th document can be measured by taking the dot product between U_i and V_j. In fact, if we apply LSA to a large information conveying text corpus, segmented in N documents, we obtain a word-document co-occurrence $M \times N$ matrix A (i.e. the (i, j) entry is the count of occurrences of the i-th word within the j-th document).

The Latent Semantic methodology has been also applied to a community of traditional Alice chat-bots[1,2]. In particular, each chat-bot had a specific knowledge on one single topic[1], then a semantic space was created, in which the knowledge bases of the chat-bots have been vector-coded, allowing them to estimate their own competence about questions asked by the user.

In this paper we show that a particular interpretation of the Latent Semantic Analysis paradigm helps to better design an human-like conversational agent (here called *LSA-bot*).

It is well known that the Latent Semantic Analysis technique is capable of simulating several human cognitive phenomena (word-categorization, sentence-word semantic priming, discourse comprehension, judgments of essay quality, etc.)[11]. Besides, under specific hypotheses, the co-occurrence matrix A can be considered as a sample set, by which a word-document co-occurrence probability distribution can be inferred by means of an estimator. This can be achieved by taking a Truncated Singular Value Decomposition (TSVD) approximation of the original matrix.

In order to ensure estimator's sufficiency, a pre-processing on the original matrix A has to be performed before evaluating its approximation. We show that singular vectors of the approximated matrix can be interpreted as orthonormal basis vectors of a "conceptual" space. This "conceptual" space is entirely data driven, since it has been constructed by processing a matrix automatically arranged from the raw text corpus. Moreover we do not need to introduce any hierarchical structure, since orthonormality of basis vectors ensures independency among the vectors which generate the conceptual space, so that domains may not be included in its algebraic structure (as required, for example, in Gardenfors conceptual spaces[8]).

This approach allows to overcome the limitations of classic pattern matching based chat-bot thanks to the intuitive/associative capabilities provided by a data driven, automatically constructed, "conceptual" space. In fact this space has the same psychological basis claimed by the LSA [11] and therefore this choice allows to code somehow the intuitive/associative component of human brain. The knowledge base of the LSA-bot is sub-symbolically coded in the "conceptual" space, then the association capability is implemented by mapping the user's question in the same conceptual space and comparing the coded query with the sub-symbolically coded elements of the knowledge base. Experimental trials and comparisons have been carried out by using the cosine measure between the user query vector and each of the vectors representing the answers contained in the LSA-bot knowledge base. Answers that turn out to be closest to the query vector are then shown to the user.

The remainder of the paper is organized as follows: in section 2 it is described the proposed "conceptual" interpretation of data-driven semantic space; in section 3 it is illustrated the realization of a chat-bot with "intuitive" capabilities obtained mapping its knowledge in the created "conceptual" space, the dialogue implementation, the experimental results concerning also a comparison with the traditional Alice architecture[3]. Then, in section 4, conclusions and future work are outlined.

2   Data-Driven Conceptual Space Creation

2.1   Theoretical Background: The LSA Paradigm

In recent years a paradigm, named Latent Semantic Analysis (LSA), useful to extract and represent the meaning of words by statistical computations applied to a large corpus of texts, has been proposed [11]. LSA is based on the *vector space method*: given a text corpus of N documents and M words, the LSA paradigm defines a mapping between the M words and the N documents into a continuous vector space S, where each word is associated to a vector in S, as well as each document is associated a vector in S[6]. The S vector space is a "semantic space", since semantics conveyed by the presence of the i-th word in the j-th document can be measured by taking the dot product between the vector representing the word and the vector representing the document.

Let us consider a corpus made of N text documents, and let M be the number of words in the whole corpus (counting each word only once even if it occurs more than once). Then let A be the $M \times N$ matrix whose (i, j) entry is the count of the occurrences of the i-th word in the j-th document. Hence A_{ij} is the (not normalized) occurrence frequency of the i-th word within the j-th document. As a consequence the i-th row of the matrix A can be interpreted as representative of the i-th word's behaviour within the entire corpus, while the j-th column of the matrix A can be interpreted as representative of the j-th document within the entire corpus [11,6].

However this approach presents some drawbacks. In fact the vectors representing words and the vectors representing documents belong to different vector spaces, respectively to $\mathbb{R}^N$ and to $\mathbb{R}^M$. It's experimentally verified [10] that these vectors are very sparse, and that M and N can reach very large values. The *Truncated Singular Value Decomposition* (TSVD) technique is considered a standard technique in order to overcome these drawbacks [11,5]. First, the *Singular Value Decomposition* of the matrix A is performed, i.e. the matrix A is decomposed in the product $A = U\Sigma V^T$, where U is a column-orthonormal[1] $M \times N$ matrix, V is a column-orthonormal $N \times N$ matrices and Σ is a $N \times N$ diagonal matrix, whose elements are called *singular values* of A. The columns of U are called *left singular vectors* of A and the columns of V are called *right singular vectors* of A. We can suppose, without loss of generality, that A's singular values are

---

[1] i.e. the dot product of two different columns of U is 0, while each column squares to 1

ranked in decreasing order, since Singular Value Decomposition also holds if we perform permutations of singular values along with the correspondent rows in U and V [5].

Let R be a positive integer with $R < N$, and let $\tilde{U}$ be the $M \times R$ matrix obtained from U by suppressing the last $N - R$ columns, $\tilde{\Sigma}$ the matrix obtained from Σ by suppressing the last $N - R$ rows and the last $N - R$ columns and $\tilde{V}$ be the $N \times R$ matrix obtained from V by suppressing the last $N - R$ columns. Then $\tilde{A} = \tilde{U} \tilde{\Sigma} \tilde{V}^T$ is a $M \times N$ matrix of rank R. It can be shown [5] that $\tilde{A}$ is the best rank R approximation of the matrix A (among the $M \times N$ matrices) with respect to the metric obtained by assuming as distance among two arbitrary matrices X and Y the non-negative real number $d_F(X, Y) = \sqrt{\sum_{i=1}^{M} \sum_{j=1}^{N} (X_{ij} - Y_{ij})^2}$. This is the *Frobenius distance* between the two matrices X and Y. The matrix $\tilde{A}$ is said to be obtained from the matrix A by *Truncated Singular Value Decomposition* (TSVD), where the term "truncated" recalls that we obtained $\tilde{A}$ by suppressing the smallest $N - R$ singular values of A along with the corresponding columns of U and V. The $i - th$ row of the matrix $\tilde{U}$ may be considered as representative of the $i - th$ word, while the j-th word of the matrix $\tilde{U}$ may be considered as representative of the j-th document. Appropriateness of the presence of the i-th word within the j-th document can be measured by the cosine between the two vectors representing the word and the document.

2.2   A Proposal of a "Conceptual" Interpretation of the Semantic Space

In this subsection we propose a "conceptual" interpretation of the orthonormal bases of the semantic space constructed with the technique outlined above. In this way, the semantic space can be regarded as a "conceptual" space. The term "conceptual space" may be misleading, since it recalls the well known Gardenfors conceptual spaces [8]. Our conceptual spaces are substantially different, since they are automatically constructed by subsymbolic processing of the raw sample data. On the contrary, Gardenfors spaces have to be "manually" constructed by extracting from the knowledge base the quality dimensions, so they are not suitable in order to represent the knowledge base of a conversational interface.

If we normalize the matrix A described in the previous subsection, dividing it by the sum of all its elements, A can be considered as a sample set, by which a word-document co-occurrence probability distribution can be inferred by means of an estimator. Each sample can be considered as an instance of a stochastic variable. Since the number of these variables is very large, in order to infer a probability distribution from the sample set, we should use an *estimator*, i.e. a function of the aforementioned stochastic variables. We would like this estimator to be *sufficient*, i.e. it should "catch" from the sample data only the information which is relevant with respect to latent semantics, neglecting other features that are related to the particular instances of the stochastic variables. In other words, we suppose that the matrix A of the sample data can be decomposed in the sum of two matrices, $A = \Psi + N$, where the matrix Ψ contains only the sample data which are relevant to latent semantics, while N contains all the other data. We would like the estimator to give Ψ as a result if its arguments are instantiated with the actual sample data in A. A possible estimator is obtained by the TSVD technique described above.

Unfortunately, the application of TSVD does not yield a sufficient estimator. It can be shown [12] that a sufficient estimator can be obtained by evaluating the best rank R approximation to A with respect to the *Hellinger distance*, defined by

$$d_H(X,Y) = \sqrt{\sum_{i=1}^{M}\sum_{j=1}^{N}(\sqrt{X_{ij}} - \sqrt{Y_{ij}})^2}$$

Therefore, in order to ensure estimator's sufficiency, a pre-processing on the original matrix has to be performed before evaluating its approximation, namely each entry of the A matrix has to be replaced with its square root.

Calling B the pre-processed matrix, within the R-dimensional semantic space obtained by TSVD on the matrix B, the rows of the matrix $\tilde{U}$ and the rows of matrix $\tilde{V}$ represent the vector coding of the words and of the documents respectively.

The sufficiency of this estimator allows us (by inference) to interpret the singular vectors of B as probability distributions (and TSVD is compatible with this semantic, since B's singular vectors all square to 1). We wish to point out the relationship between the orthonormality of $\tilde{U}$'s and $\tilde{V}$'s columns, and the independence between them.

The original matrix represents relationships between words and documents. The two matrices U and V obtained after decomposition reflect a breakdown of the original relationships into linearly-independent vectors[4]. This independent R dimensions of the $\mathbb{R}^R$ space can be tagged in order to interpret this space as a "conceptual" space. Since these vectors are orthogonal, they can be regarded as principal axes, and so they can be regarded as axes which represent the "fundamental" concepts residing in the data driven space generated by the LSA, and can be tagged according to this interpretation.

2.3 An Example of "Conceptual" Axis Tagging

To clarify the procedure of the conceptual axes tagging, the technique proposed in the previous subsection has been applied to the well-known example reported in [11].

In this example the documents for the matrix construction are the titles of nine technical memoranda, five concerning human computer interaction (HCI), and four concerning mathematical graph theory. These topics are conceptually rather disjoint[11].

In the table 1 the list of the titles is presented. The extracted terms are highlighted in italics.

Table 1. The document used for the matrix construction

Titles of nine technical memoranda

c1: *Human* machine *interface* for ABC *computer* applications
c2: A *survey* of *user* opinion of *computer system responce time*
c3: The *EPS user interface* management *system*
c4: *Systen* and *human system* engineering testing of *EPS*
c5: Relation of *user* perceived *responce time* to error measurement

m1: The generation of random, binary, ordered *trees*
m2: The intersection *graph* of paths in *trees*
m3: *Graph minors* IV: Widths of *trees* and well-quasi-ordering
m4: *Graph minors*: A *survey*

Table 2. Results of the proposed approach for the $k = 1$ axis

WORDS	SQUARE-VALUES
system	$2,753E - 01$
user	$2,203E - 01$
time	$1,054E - 01$
response	$1,054E - 01$
computer	$7,898E - 02$
EPS	$6,858E - 02$
survey	$6,189E - 02$
interface	$4,470E - 02$
human	$3,380E - 02$
graph	$2,907E - 03$
minors	$2,159E - 03$
trees	$4,671E - 04$

Table 3. Results of the proposed approach for the $k = 2$ axis

WORDS	SQUARE-VALUES
graph	$4,226E - 01$
trees	$2,719E - 01$
minors	$2,178E - 01$
survey	$5,123E - 02$
system	$1,190E - 02$
EPS	$1,069E - 02$
human	$6,144E - 03$
interface	$5,863E - 03$
user	$1,256E - 03$
time	$2,359E - 04$
response	$2,359E - 04$
computer	$9,355E - 05$

In order to consider the obtained matrix as a probability distribution each entry has been divided by the sum of all the matrix entries. Then the matrix obtained by performing the square root of each element is computed.

The truncated singular value decomposition with $R = 2$ is then performed.

The obtained tagging is reported in Tables 2, 3: as it can be seen the first three tags for the $k = 1$ axis are *system, user, interface* which reflect the HCI topic, while the first three words for the $k = 2$ axis are *graph, trees, minors* which are related to the mathematical graph theory topic. So the two concepts related to the topics turn out to be correctly separated, thus identifying the principal axes of the "conceptual" space.

3   Mapping of a Chat-Bot Knowledge in the Created "Conceptual" Space

The automatic, data driven, creation of the "conceptual" space allows to design a natural, human-like, conversational agent.

The agent, called *LSAbot*, has an "intuitive" capability, modelled as an association mechanism. This is obtained by mapping its knowledge base into the automatically built conceptual space.

In the following, the whole procedure (from the automatic creation of the conceptual space up to the realization of LSAbot) is presented. Then LSAbot's performances are compared with a traditional Alice[3] chat-bot's ones. Alice (Artificial Linguistic Internet Computer Entity) is a well-known artificial intelligence natural language chat robot based on an experiment specified by Alan M. Turing in 1950. The Alice software utilizes AIML(Artificial Intelligence Mark-up Language), an XML-like language designed for creating stimulus-response chat robots.

The Alice chat-bot knowledge base is composed of question-answer modules, called categories and structured with AIML. The question, or stimulus, is called the "pattern". The answer, or response, is called the "template". The dialogue is based on algorithms for automatic detection of patterns in the dialogue data.

3.1   Data-Driven Conceptual Space Creation

It is well known from theory that, in order to effectively apply the LSA technique, a very large corpus of documents is required[11].

Therefore a text corpus composed of 1574 English euro-parliament documents and 910 templates of the Alice[3] standard knowledge set have been used. The sentences include greetings, definition of terms knowledge, notions about artificial intelligence and computers.

After a pre-processing of the documents, which consists in removing all the stop-words (i.e. words that do not carry semantic information like articles, prepositions and so on), a set of 101424 word forms has been obtained (no stemming has been performed).

Hence a 101424 × 2484 terms-documents matrix has been created, whose generic entry a_{ij} is the count of occurrences of the *i-th*word in the *j-th* document.

The matrix has been then normalized and each entry has been replaced with it square root value, obtaining a new matrix B. Then the TSVD with $R = 100$ has been performed in order to find the best approximation of A according to the Hellinger distance.

Each row of the matrix $\tilde{U}$ represents the sub-symbolic coding of each of the 101424 terms, and each row of the matrix $\tilde{V}$ represents the sub-symbolic coding of the 2484 documents: the first 1574 rows represent the euro-parliament documents and the last 910 rows represent the Alice standard templates.

The 2484 vectors associated to the documents used for the conceptual space construction make up the sub-symbolic coding of the LSAbot knowledge base.

3.2 Dialogue Implementation

After mapping the chat-bot knowledge base onto the conceptual space, the conversation between the user and the chat-bots can take place. The query of the user is coded, in the same conceptual space, as a sum of the vectors representing the terms which compose the query[7], normalized with respect to the Euclidean norm.

The similarity between this vector and the vectors representing the sentences in the conversational agent's knowledge base is then evaluated using the cosine similarity measure between each sentece's vector and the user query vector.

Let q be the user query and $\boldsymbol{q}$ its associated vector, let s be one of the knowledge base sentences and $\boldsymbol{s}$ its corresponding vector; the similarity between the query and the sentence can be evaluated as:

$$sim(q,s) = cos(\vartheta) = \frac{\boldsymbol{q} \cdot \boldsymbol{s}}{\|\boldsymbol{q}\| \, \|\boldsymbol{s}\|} \tag{1}$$

where $|\boldsymbol{q}|$ and $|\boldsymbol{s}|$ are the modules of the query vector and of the sentence vector respectively.

Then, whenever the user asks a question, LSAbot answers with the sentence of its knowledge base which minimizes the cosine with the question vector.

3.3 Experimental Results and Comparison with Alice

To test the effectiveness of the approach, the LSAbot performances have been compared with the performances of the traditional Alice[3] architecture by using a sample of questions submitted to the system.

The results have been evaluated analyzing the answers given by both the LSAbot and the Alice traditional chat-bot to the user questions.

Here we call, for the sake of clarity:

- *correct*: the right answer expected for the current question;
- *coherent*: an answer that isn't expected but it is pertaining to the current question;
- *wrong*: an unexpected and not pertaining answer to the current question.

Moreover, to point out the differences between the LSAbot and Alice, the questions submitted to both the systems are, in particular, belonging to four categories:

- questions containing few words;
- ordinary questions (related to general knowledge);
- greeting questions;
- wrong questions, i.e. questions with grammatical mistakes.

In the following tables the percentage of correct, coherent and wrong answers obtained over a sample of 20 queries submitted to both systems is illustrated; a few example dialogs segments are also shown.

In table 4 and 5 some results obtained from the comparison between Alice and LSAbot are reported. Experimentals trials have been carried out by taking four sets (each composed of 35 queries) from the four aforementioned categories.

Dialogue examples. Numerical results show that in some specific cases the traditional pattern matching mechanism of Alice fails to sustain a fluent conversation, while LSAbot shows a better behaviour.

We point out that LSAbot and Alice share the same knowledge base. The only difference between the two systems is that the Alice traditional architecture is based solely on the pattern-matching mechanism, while LSAbot is based on the intuitive mechanism given by the sub-symbolic representation of the knowledge base into the automatically data driven conceptual space.

Alice tries to answer the user's query by using its pattern-matching based engine, that looks for a lexical correspondence between the user's query and the chat-bot categories. The Alice pattern matching module may fail in finding the right answer, even if its knowledge base contains categories with the right answer. LSAbot overcomes this drawback thanks to its association capability.

The cases in which Alice fails may be summed up as follows:

- when the user query is composed of only one single word, or when the query is composed of few words which don't match any pattern in the Alice knowledge base;
- when the query is grammatically incorrect and the pattern matching mechanism of Alice is not able to manage this particular mistake.

In the following a dialogue example with a query composed of one single word is reported:

Table 4. Percentage of correct, coherent and wrong answers on different 35 queries sets for the traditiona ALICE architecture

	ALICE		
	Correct	Coherent	Wrong
Queries of few words	11	0	89
Traditional queries	41	0	59
Greeting queries	100	0	0
Wrong queries	23	0	77

Table 5. Percentage of correct, coherent and wrong answers on different 35 queries sets for the LSAbot architecture

	LSAbot		
	Correct	Coherent	Wrong
Queries of few words	68	9	23
Traditional queries	63	11	26
Greeting queries	100	0	0
Wrong queries	100	0	0

Query: *Ada...*
Alice: *What is your favourite movie?*
LSAbot: *Ada is a trademark used for a structured computer programming language.*

Query: *Republic?*
Alice: *What is your real name?*
LSAbot: *Italy is a republic.*

Query: *World?*
Alice: *Can you tell me any gossip?*
LSAbot: *The world has been created by God*

Cleary, Alice is not able to answer since the question contains only few words and its form doesn't match any of its Aiml patterns. Hence, Alice tries to answer with default sentences, trying to switch the dialogue topic to another. On the contrary LSAbot can answer since it is based on a "conceptual" research within its knowledge base.

Another case in which LSAbot works better occurs when question's formulation does not comply with query patterns stored in Alice. In fact, LSAbot finds the answer conceptually related to the question regardless of its grammatical expression. In this example the question formulation complies with an Alice's query pattern :

Query: *What do you know about the C plus plus programming language?*
Alice: *It is a low-level programming language*
LSAbot: *C plus plus is the object oriented extension of the C programming language.*

while in this example the same question is expressed with other words, such that it does not comply with any Alice's query pattern.

Query: *Do you know C plus plus language?*
Alice: *Can you speak any other languages?*
LSAbot: *C plus plus is the object oriented extension of the C programming language.*

Finally, the following dialogue segments are related to the same question (complying with an Alice's query pattern): in the first segment the question is correctly written, while in the second segment it is wrongly written. LSAbot clearly shows better robustness than Alice with respect to errors in the question.

Query: *What is the Earth?*
Alice: *Earth, third planet from the sun, is our home.*
LSAbot: *Earth is a planet going around a star. Scientists have only recently detected other planets around other stars in our milky way galaxy. Do you like astronomy?*

while the following dialogue reports the wrong expression of the same query with the correspondent answers:

Query: *What is tha Earth?*
Alice: *Interesting question.*
LSAbot: *Earth is a planet going around a star. Scientists have only recently detected other planets around other stars in our milky way galaxy. Do you like astronomy?*

4   Conclusions and Future Work

In this paper an ad-hoc implementation of the LSA framework is presented, along with a conceptual interpretation of the automatically built data-driven semantic space. This interpretation allows to better design a natural human-like conversational agent, which overcomes limitations of traditional rule-based conversational agents, like Alice. The approach presented in this workregards aone-step interation butfuture works will run onthe lsa application for the whole interaction, in order to take in account the dialogue history and so the precedent contexts.

References

1. G. Pilato, G. Vassallo, M. Gentile, A. Augello, S. Gaglio LSA for Intuitive Chat-Agents Tutoring System *Proc. of International Conference on Methods and Technologies for Learning (ICMTL 2005)*, Palermo 9-11 March 2005, in press
2. G. Pilato, G. Vassallo, A. Augello, M. Vasile, S. Gaglio Expert Chat-Bots for Cultural Heritage *IX Convegno della Associazione Italiana Intelligenza Artificiale Proc. of. Workshop Interazione e Comunicazione Visuale nei Beni Culturali*, 15 Sept. 2004, Perugia, Italy
3. Alice:Artificial linguistic computer entity. alice.sunlitsurf.com/alice/about.html.
4. Michael W. Berry, Susan T. Dumais, and Todd A. Letsche. Computational methods for intelligent information access. In *Proceedings of the 1995 ACM/IEEE conference on Supercomputing*, 1995.
5. J.K. Cullum and R.A. Willoughby. *Real rectangular matrices, in Lanczos Algorithms for Large Symmetric Eigenvalue Computations-Vol. 1, Theory*. Boston, MA: Brickhauser, 1985.

6. S. Peters D. Widdows. Word vectors and quantum logic experiments with negation and disjunction. In *Mathematics of Language, 8, Bloomington, Indiana, June 2003*, 2003.
7. Scott C. Deerwester, Susan T. Dumais, Thomas K. Landauer, George W. Furnas, and Richard A. Harshman. Indexing by latent semantic analysis. *Journal of the American Society of Information Science*, 41(6):391–407, 1990.
8. P. Gardenfors. *Conceptual Spaces*. MIT Press, Bradford Books, Cambridge, MA, 2000.
9. M. Raubal. Formalizing conceptual spaces. In *Proc. FOIS 2004*, 2004.
10. R. Rosenfeld. A maximum entropy approach to adaptive statistical language modeling. *Computer Speech and Language*, pages 10/187–228, New York 1996.
11. P.W. Foltz T.K. Landauer and D. Laham. An introduction to latent semantic analysis. *Discours Processes*, 25:259–284, 1998.
12. H. Zhu. Bayesian geometric theory of learning algorithms. *Proceedings of the International Conference on Neural Networks (ICNN'97)*, 2:1041–1044, 1997.
13. The Cyn Project. *http://www.daxtron.com/123start.htm?Cyn*
14. The OpenCyc Project, *http://www.opencyc.org*
15. O.Stock Language-based interfaces and their application for cultural tourism *AI Magazine*, March 22, pp 85-97, 2001
16. K.Mori, A.Jatowt, M.Ishizuka Enhancing conversational flexibility in multimodal interactions with embodied lifelike agents *Proc. of the 8th international conference on Intelligent user interfaces*, Miami, Florida, USA, pp.270-272, 2003
17. A.Koutamanis Azile: an intelligent verbal interface for the retrieval of pictorial architectural information *proc. of CIB W78 conference, Distributing Knowledge in Building.*, 2002
18. E.Mathews, G. Tanner Jackson, A.Graesser, N.Person and the Tutoring Research Group Discourse patterns in why/autotutor *proc. of Natural Language Generation in Spoken and Written Dialogue, AAAI Spring Symposium 2003*, March 24-26., 2003
19. M. Stede, D. Schlangen Dialogue Management by Topic Structure *Proceedings of Catalog '04 (The 8th Workshop on the Semantics and Pragmatics of Dialogue, SemDial04), Barcelona, Spain, July (ISBN 84-609-2205-7)*

Solving Italian Crosswords Using the Web

Giovanni Angelini, Marco Ernandes, and Marco Gori

Dipartimento di Ingegneria dell'Informazione,
Via Roma 56, 53100 Siena, Italy
{angelini, ernandes, marco}@dii.unisi.it
http://airgroup.dii.unisi.it

Abstract. We designed and implemented a software system, called WebCrow, that represents the first solver for Italian crosswords and the first system that tackles a language game using the Web as knowledge base. Its core feature is the Web Search Module that produces a special form of web-based question answering that we call clue-answering. This paper will focus its attention on this task.

The web-search approach has proved itself to be very consistent: using a limited set of documents the clue-answering process is able to retrieve over two thirds of the correct answers. In many cases the targeted word is given in output among the very first most probable candidates (15% of correct answers in first position).

To complete the crosswords solving problem the system has to fill the grid with the best set of word answers. Currently, WebCrow's performances are interesting: crosswords that are "easy" for expert humans (i.e. crosswords from the cover pages of *La Settimana Enigmistica*^{TM}) are solved, in a 15 minutes time limit, with 80% of correct words and over 90% of correct letters. With crosswords that are designed for experts, WebCrow places correctly two thirds of the words and around 80% of the letters.

1 Introduction

Motivations and Relevant Literature. Crosswords are puzzles that engage millions of people everyday in a very challenging game for human intelligence. This problem is reputed as AI-complete [4]. The complexity is due to its semantics and the large amount of encyclopedic knowledge required. AI developed an interest for crosswords solving only recently. The first experience reported in the literature is the Proverb system [2] that reached human-like performances on American crosswords using a great number of knowledge-specific expert modules and a crosswords database of great dimensions[1].

We believe that recent developments in computer technology, such as the Web, search engines, information retrieval and machine learning techniques, can enable computers to enfold with semantics real-life concepts. With this in mind we designed a software system, called WebCrow, whose major assumption is to attack crosswords making use of the Web as its primary source of knowledge, being this the most extremely rich and self-updating repository of human knowledge. With respect to Proverb WebCrow

---

[1] Before Proverb, AI limited its analysis to the *crossword puzzles generation* problem [5]. This makes a closed-world assumption by requiring a predefined dictionary of legal words and results to be an NP-complete task that can be solved now in a few seconds.

S. Bandini and S. Manzoni (Eds.): AI*IA 2005, LNAI 3673, pp. 393–405, 2005.
© Springer-Verlag Berlin Heidelberg 2005

does not possess any knowledge-specific expert module, but only a limited set of useful modules which includes a dictionary and a small database[2].

The web-based clue-answering paradigm aspires to stress the generality of We-bCrow's knowledge and its language-independence. We will show in this paper that web search can produce extremely effective results providing the most important source of knowledge for the clue-answering process.

Problem Setting and Results. Italian crosswords tend to be extremely difficult to handle because they contain a great quantity of word plays, neologisms, compound words, ambiguities and a deep involvement in socio-cultural and political topics, often treated with irony. Hence, the system requires the possession of a very broad and fresh knowledge that is also robust to volunteer language vagueness and ambiguity.

We have collected a dataset of 685 solved Italian crosswords. These examples were mainly obtained from two sources: the main Italian crosswords magazine *La Settimana Enigmistica* (this publisher sets, as matter of fact, a standard for Italian crosswords) and an important on-line newspaper's crosswords section, *La Repubblica*.

Given a test set of 60 crosswords, WebCrow's challenge was to answer all the clues and to subsequently fill the slots with the highest percentage of correct words. As in many human competitions a 15 minutes time limit was given for each example.

The version of WebCrow that is discussed here is basic but it has already given very promising results. In over two thirds of the clues the correct answer was found by the Web Search Module and in nearly 15% this answer was the top of the list. The addition of the other modules has raised the coverage to 99% and the probability of having the targeted word in first position to over 35%. Finally, filling the puzzle WebCrow averaged on the overall test set around 70% words correct and 80% letters correct.

2   The System Architecture

WebCrow is a modular-based system (fig. 1). Therefore, it is also possible to plug in additional *ad hoc* modules in order to increase the system's performances.

The WebCrow solving process can be divided in two phases. During the first one, all the clues of a puzzle are passed by the coordinator to all the "List Generator" modules. Each of them returns for each clue a list of possible solutions. Afterwards the candidate lists are merged into a unique list for each clue.

Finally, WebCrow has to face a constrain-satisfaction problem. From each clue list a candidate has to be chosen and inserted in the crossword-puzzle, trying to satisfy the intrinsic constrains. The aim of this phase is to find an admissible solution which maximize the number of correct words inserted.

3   Using the Web for Clue-Answering: The Web Search Module

The objective of the Web Search Module (WSM) is to find sensible answers to crossword clues, that are expressed in natural language, by exploiting the Web and search

---

[2] The database used by Proverb was about one order of magnitude greater than ours.

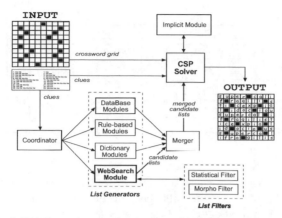

Fig. 1. WebCrow. A general overview of WebCrow's architecture.

engines (SE). This task recalls that of a Web-based Question Answering system. However, with crossword clues, the nature of the problem changes sensibly, often becoming more challenging than classic QA [9]. The main differences are:

– clues are mostly formulated in a non-interrogative form
– clues can be voluntarily ambiguous and misleading
– the topic of the questions are not limited to factoids.
– there is a unique and precise answer which is a word or a compound word. Instead, in QA the answer is sequence of words in which the target has to be recognizable by humans.

The only evident advantage in crosswords solving is that we priory know the exact length of the words that we are seeking. We believe that, thanks to this property, web search can be extremely effective and produce a strong clue-answering.

The inner architecture of the WSM is sketched in figure 2. There are four task that have to be accomplished by the WSM: the retrieval of useful web documents, the extraction of the answer candidates from these documents, the scoring/filtering of the candidate lists and, finally, the estimation of the list confidence. In this section all these components will be presented and analysed.

Although the WSM has been implemented only in a basic version, it is clear that this module, among the set of expert modules used by WebCrow, produces the most impressive answering performances, with the best coverage/precision balance. This is evident if we observe tab. 1 (first two columns). In over half of cases the correct answer is found within the first 100 candidates inside a list containing more than 10^5 words.

The contribution of the WSM can be appreciated in the last two rows of tab. 1 where we can observe the loss of performance of the whole system when the WSM is removed. The overall coverage of the system is mainly guaranteed by the dictionary module (sec. 4), but the introduction of the WSM is fundamental to increase sensibly the rank of the correct answer.

Also interesting is fig. 3 and fig. 4 where we take into consideration the length of the target. It can be observed that the WSM guarantees the system to well perform with long word targets, of great importance in the CSP phase.

Web Search Module

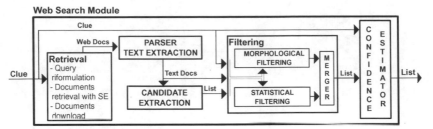

Fig. 2. Web Search Module. A sketch of the internal architecture of the Web Search Module.

Table 1. Modules Coverage. Cov reports the frequency with which the target word can be found within the candidate list. n-pos ($n = 1, 5, 100$) gives the frequency within the first n candidates. Len is the average list length. ALL(30 docs) was used in the final tests.

Module	Cov	1-pos	5-pos	100-pos	Len
WEB (30 docs)	68.1	13.5	23.7	53.2	499
CWDB-EXACT	19.8	19.6	19.8	19.8	1.1
CWDB-PARTIAL	29.0	10.6	20.1	28.4	45.5
CWDB-DICTIO	71.1	0.4	2.1	21.5	$>10^3$
RULE-BASED	10.1	6.9	8.3	10.1	12.4
DICTIONARY	97.5	0.3	1.6	21.3	$>10^4$
ALL BUT WEB	98.4	34.0	43.6	52.3	$>10^4$
ALL (30 docs)	99.3	36.5	50.4	72.1	$>10^4$

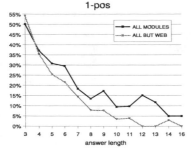

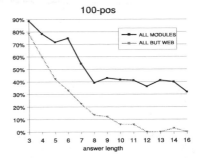

Fig. 3. Target in first position. The frequency of the target in first position in relation to its length with and without the WSM.

Fig. 4. Target in first 100 positions. The frequency of the target in the first 100 positions in relation to its length with and without the WSM.

3.1 Retrieving Useful Documents

The first goal of the answering process is to retrieve the documents that are better related to the clue. This can be done thanks to the fundamental contribution of search engine's technology (Google^{TM} was used in our testing). In order to increase the information retrieved through the search engine the clues go through a reformulation/expansion step. Each clue $C = \{t_1 t_2 ... t_n\}$ generates two queries: $Q^1 =< t_1 \wedge t_2 \wedge ... t_n >$ and $Q^2 =< t_1 \vee t_2 \vee ... t_n >$. Non informative words are removed from the queries.

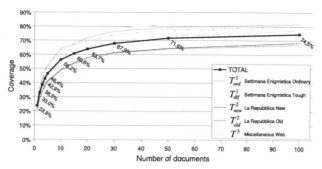

Fig. 5. WSM coverage. The coverage of the WSM in relation to the number of documents re-trieved for each clue. The coverage increases very rapidly until about 30 documents. After this limit, in order to increse the coverage we have to sensibly slow down the answering process.

A classic QA approach is to make use only of the document snippets in order to stress time efficiency. Unfortunately the properties of the clues make this approach use-less (the probability of finding the correct answer within a snippet has been experimen-tally observed below 10%) and we decided for a full-document approach.

The interrogation of the search engine and the download the documents represent two tasks that are extremely time consuming, absorbing easily over 90% of time in the entire clue-answering process. Therefore we have implemented it in a highly parallel manner: the WSM simultaneously downloads tens of documents adopting a strict time-out for each http request (20 secs.) and using SE's cached copies when necessary.

For each example of our test suite we have retrieved and downloaded a maximum of 200 docs per clue (max. 30 docs with Q^2). 615589 docs were downloaded in 44h 36m[3]. All the test sessions were subsequently made off-line using this *web image*.

3.2 Extracting and Ranking the Candidates

The process of generating a list of candidate answers given a collection of relevant documents goes through two important steps. First, the documents are analysed by a parser which produces as output plain ASCII text. Second, this text is passed to a list generator that extracts the words of the correct length, eliminates doubles and produces an unweighted candidate list. In order to increase the coverage, a list of compound words (i.e., a sequence of adjacent words fulfilling the length requirement) is generated from each document (compound words which occurs only once are omitted).

Both outputs are then passed to two submodules: a statistical filter, based on IR techniques, and a morphological filter, based on machine learning and NLP techniques. Both have been embedded in the WSM.

The candidates are ranked by merging together the information provided by the two list filters. The score-probability associated to each word candidate w is given by

$$p(w, C) = c\,(sf\text{-}score(w, C) \times mf\text{-}score(w, C)) \tag{1}$$

where $sf\text{-}score(w, C)$ is the score attributed to word w by the statistical filter,

---

[3] Bandwidth: 1Mb/s, effective $\approx$100KB/sec, avg. 230 docs/min, 167 docs/clue, 25.6KB/doc).

Table 2. Clue-Answering samples. The "easy" examples are usually those where the topic is directly addressed. Instead, the "tough" ones are usually very general or ambiguous.

"Easy" clues for the WSM	"Tough" clues for the WSM
≺*Confina con l'Abruzzo:* **molise**≻	≺*Documenti per minorenni:* **patentini**≻
1:*molise* 2:aquila 3:marche 4:umbria	1:necessari 2:richiesti 3:organismi
≺*Mal d'orecchi:* **otite**≻	≺*Il verbo di chi ha coraggio:* **lanciarsi**≻
1:*otite* 2:ictus 3:otiti 4:edemi 5:gocce	1:interiore 2:predicato 3:idealismo
≺*Un film di Nanni Moretti:* **carodiario**≻	≺*Larga e comoda:* **ampia**≻
1:palombella 2:portaborse 3:*carodiario*	1:bella 2:sella 3:barca 4:scala 5:valle
≺*Il Giuseppe pittore di Barletta:* **denittis**≻	≺*Una sciagura attraente:* **calamita**≻
1:leontine 2:molfetta 3:ritratto 4:*denittis*	1:passione 2:alcolico 3:fardello

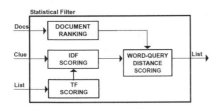

Fig. 6. Statistical Filter. A sketch of the internal architecture of the Statistical Filter.

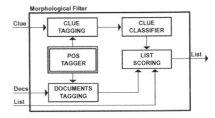

Fig. 7. Morphological Filter. A sketch of the internal architecture of the Morphological Filter.

$mf\text{-}score(w, C)$ is the score provided by the morphological filter, c is the normalizing factor that fulfills the probability requirement $\sum_{i=0}^{n} p(w_i, C) = 1$.

In QA systems it is important to produce very high precision only in the very first (3-5) answer candidates, since a human user will not look further down in the list. For this reason NLP techniques are typically used to remove those answers that are not likely correct. This answer selection policy is not well suited for clue-answering, a more conservative approach is required because the lack of the correct answer makes a greater damage than a low precision. The eq. 1 serves this goal: words that have low scores will appear at the bottom of the list but will not be dropped.

3.3   The Statistical Filtering

This submodule makes use of three types of information: the query given as input to the SE (Q^n: the n-th reformulation of clue C), the documents provided by the search engine (D_i is the i-th document of the SE's output) and a list of candidate answers w extracted from the documents. An additional element is used, $rank(D_i, Q^n)$: the document ranking, obtained using Google's output. Finally, we attribute a global score to each triple (w, Q^n, D_i) in the following way:

$$sf\text{-}score(w, Q^n) = \sum_{i=0}^{\#docs} \left(\frac{score(w, Q^n, D_i)}{length(D_i)} rank(D_i, Q^n) \right) \tag{2}$$

where $length(D_i)$ is the number of words in D_i. The score of a word within a single document is computed in a TF-IDF fashion. TF has been modified in order to take into account the inner-document distance between the word and the query. As shown in eq. 3, each occurrence of a word counts $1/dist(w_k, Q, D_i)$, whereas in normal TF each occurrence counts equally.

$$score(w, Q, D_i) = idf(w) \sum_{w_k \in occ(w, D_i)} \frac{1}{dist(w_k, Q, D_i)} \qquad (3)$$

$idf(w)$ is the classic inverse document frequency, which provides an immediate interpretation of term specificity. For compound words we take the highest idf value of the word components. $occ(w, D_i)$ represents all the occurrences of the word w in the document D_i. The distance between word w_k and query Q is computed as a modified version of the square-root-mean distance between w_k and each term w_{Q_t} of the query, suggested by [8]. The main bias of the original formula was to weight equally all the words of the query without taking into account that some words are more informative than others. As shown in eq. 4, we decided to overcome this problem by tuning the exponential factor of the square-root-mean distance using a normalized idf value of w_{Q_t}. This increases the relevance of those answer candidates that are close to the more informative terms in the query. This novel contribution has resulted experimentally more effective for our goals.

$$dist(w_k, Q, D_i) = \frac{\sqrt{\sum_{t=0}^{\#\text{terms} \in Q} (dist(w_k, w_{Q_t}, D_i))^{idf(w_{Q_t})}}}{\#\text{terms} \in Q} \qquad (4)$$

$dist(w_k, w_{Q_t}, D_i)$ denotes the minimum number of words that separate w_k and an occurance of the clue word w_{Q_t} in document D_i. After a preliminary testing we decided to limit to 150 words the maximum word-word distance. A default penalty distance of 300 is assigned to those words that exceed this limit, as we assume that the semantic link between two words is weaker.

This distance metric could be further improved (i.e. taking into account sentences, paragraphs, titles, punctuations, etc.) but it already provides a very informative tool.

Other improvements could be obtained using a crossword-focused idf function (the idf values used here were obtained through a non-focused crawling session) or making use of the context in which each candidate appears. Figure 8 shows the contribution of all the elements used within the statistical filter. In a non ranked list the probability of finding the correct answer increases linearly with the number of candidates taken into

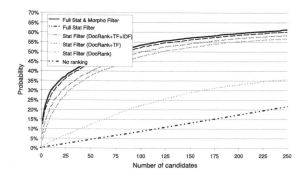

Fig. 8. Filtering Perfomaces. The graphic represents the probability of finding the correct answer in relation to the number of candidates that are taken into consideration.

consideration. It is easy to observe in figure 8 how the performances increase shifting from a basic filter to the full one which includes both the statistical and morphological information.

3.4   The Morphological Filtering

The aim of this filter is to rank the candidates according to the morphological class they belong to. For this reason we made use of a Part-of-Speech (PoS) tagger, which associates a morphological class to each word of a sentence. Figure 7 shows the information flow of the morphological filter.

The PoS tagger is used to tagged both the clue and each document related to it. Afterwards, the clue is processed by a multi-class classifier, which returns a weighted vector of the possible morphological classes the solution can belong to. Finally, for each word of the candidate list its morphological score is calculated by:

$$mf\text{-}score(w, C) = \sum_{i=0}^{\#\text{tags}} p(tag_i|w)score(tag_i, C) \tag{5}$$

$p(tag_i|w)$ is the information provided by the PoS-Tagger, $score(tag_i, C)$ is computed using the output of the classifier with the addition of a spread factor in order to enhance the impact of the classification.

With the attempt to maintain a strong language-independence we chose an automatic trainable PoS tagger, called TreeTagger [12], which is an extension of a basic Markov Model tagger. The TreeTager is based on two parts: a Lexicon and a Decision tree. Each word is first tagged using the Lexicon, which makes use also of a Prefix tree and a Suffix tree. This two trees are binary decision trees, generated by the training examples, which infer the possible tag of a word by examining, respectively, its beginning or ending. Finally, a binary decision tree is used. This takes into account the tags of the k preceding words and returns a vector of the probable tags, based on the examples seen in the training corpus. We used 23 different classes to distinguish: articles, nouns and adjectives, verbs, adverbs, particles, interlocutory words, numbers, punctuation marks, abbreviations and others. A detailed list is given in table 3. At first, the TreeTagger was trained using an automatically extracted corpus form TUT [13]. The tagger was then used to tag a new corpus based on some CWDB's clues and documents from the web. This new corpus was corrected and added to the first one. Finally, the TreeTagger was retrained, obtaining an accuracy of about 93% on a cross validation test set.

The clue classifier was built using multi-class Kernel-based Vector Machine [11] [10]. First, a training set was created by extracting about 7000 clue-target pairs from the CWDB. Each clue was tagged by the TreeTagger and a feature vector $\bar{x} \in \mathbb{R}^n$ was then automatically generated for each example. The features extracted from each clue-answer pair were: the length of the target, the number of words in the clue, the number of capital letters in the clue, a set of the 250 most frequent clue-words and the probability tag vector associated to each word of the clue. Finally, a target class $i \in \{1, \ldots, k\}$ was associated to each example. We made use of 21 different target classes: almost all the morphological ones with the addition of name initials (IP) and non-semantic words (NS). A detailed list is shown in table 5.

Table 3. Morphological classes. This is the full list of the morphological classes used in our PoS Tagger. The choice was to stress information relevant for finding the solution of a clue.

class	description
MS	Noun or Adj. or Pron., masc. sing.
FS	Noun or Adj. or Pron., fem. sing.
MP	Noun or Adj. or Pron., masc. pl.
FP	Noun or Adj. or Pron., fem. pl.
NP	Proper Noun
VS	Verb, cong. singular
VP	Verb, cong. plural
VI	Verb, base form
VOTHER	Verb, other
AMS	Article, masculine singular
AFS	Article, feminine singular
AMP	Article, masculine plural

class	description
AFP	Article, feminine plural
AV	Adverb
PART	Particle
NUM	Number
EP	Interlocutory words
ABBR	Abbreviation
PC	Compound Words
SCRIPT	Script words in html doc.
SENT	Punctuation a the end of a sentence
SENT2	Punctuation, all the others
OTHER	all the rest

Table 4. Coverage. Here is reported the probability of finding the correct answer in the first k positions.

Position	Coverage
1st pos	54.30%
2nd pos	73.01%
3rd pos	82.67%
4th pos	87.77%
5th pos	91.38%
6th pos	93.60%

Table 5. Class accuracy. For each class it is given the percentage of examples inside the training set and the accuracy of the classifier.

class	P ex.	acc.	class	P ex.	acc.	class	P ex.	acc.
MS	24.8%	50.2%	IP	2.9%	92.2%	NUM	0.8%	38.7%
NP	18.7%	68.2%	VI	2.6%	67.4%	AMS	0.4%	21.4%
FS	13.7%	32.4%	PC	2.3%	34.6%	VS	0.2%	0.0%
MP	11.2%	65.1%	PART	1.3%	25.5%	AMP	0.1%	20.0%
NS	9.0%	84.6%	AV	1.2%	16.3%	AFP	0.1%	33.3%
FP	5.2%	19.0%	EP	1.0%	5.0%	AFS	0.1%	33.3%
ABBR	3.7%	67.2%	OTHR	0.9%	12.5%	VP	0.1%	0.0%

The classifier learns a linear function $H : X \rightarrow Y$ of the type $H(\bar{x}, M) = \langle M, \Phi(\bar{x}) \rangle$, where

$$f(\bar{x}) = \operatorname*{argmax}_{i \in \{1,\dots,k\}} H_i(\bar{x}, M) \qquad (6)$$

is the predicted class and the i-th entry of the vector $\bar{y} = H(\bar{x}, M)$ corresponds to the score given to the class i. The goal is to minimize the empirical risk over all the training examples $\mathcal{R}(f) = \sum_t \Delta(y_t, f(\bar{x}_t))$ where $\Delta(y_t, \hat{y}_t)$ is the loss associated to the predicted class $\hat{y}_t = f(\bar{x}_t)$. $\Delta(y_t, \hat{y}_t) = 0$ if $y_t = \hat{y}_t$. Instead, $\Delta(y_t, \hat{y}_t) = pos\_loss + c \sum_{j:(y_j-y_t)>0} (y_j - y_t)$ if $y_t \neq \hat{y}_t$, where pos_loss is the distance in positions of y_t from the first value $\hat{y}_t$ and c is a normalization parameter.

Using a cross validation test over the training set described above, we obtain with a linear kernel an accuracy of 54.30% on the predicted class. The accuracy is not very high as there are many clues where it is hard, also for humans, to determine the exact class of the solution. This ambiguity occurs mainly between the classes of these two subset: {MS,FS,NP} and {MP,FP} [4]. For the latter reason and taking into account that

---

[4] For example, in some clues is not possible to determine the gender of the solution, such as ≺*Ricopre i vialetti:* **ghiaia, FS**≻ (≺*It can cover a drive:* **gravel**≻) or ≺*Si cambiano ad ogni portata:* **piatti, MP**≻ (≺*You use different ones at each course:* **plates**≻).

no candidate is pruned but just re-weighted, we considered as a more significant value the coverage of the classifier on the first n predicted classes. As shown in table 4, the coverage increases very rapidly and it is equivalent to 91.38% if we look over the first 5 predicted classes. Thus, as the number of different target classes is large, this can be considered a very good result. In fact, the use of the output of the clue classifier causes an increment in the WSM performance.

Table 5 shows the occurrence of each class in the data set, which should be similar to the one in the whole CWDB. No re-balancing has been made, as the learning algorithm, during each loop, process the "most violated" constraint using a cutting plane method. It can be seen also that there are several classes whose accuracy is high, such as IP, NS, VI, NP and MP.

In order to better exploit the morphological classifier, a submodule (NI) which generates name initials[5] was implemented.

3.5   Estimating a Confidence on the Lists

After generating a candidate, each module has to estimate the probability that this list contains the correct answer. This information is then processed by the merger, in order to correctly join the lists produced by the modules.

The confidence estimator of the Web Search Module has been implemented using a standard MLP neural network. This was trained on a set of 2000 candidate lists, using a cross validation set of 500 examples. The main features used for the description of a candidate list example include: the length of the query, the idf values of its words, the length of the list and the scores of the candidates. The output target was set to 1 when the list contained the correct answer, 0 when this was absent.

4   The Other Modules

Four different typologies of additional modules are present in WebCrow's design, namely the data-base, the rule-based, the implicit and the dictionary module.

The Data-Base Module. Three different DB-based modules have been implemented in order to exploit the 42973 clue-answer pairs provided by our crosswords database: CWDB-EXACT, that checks for exact clue correspondences in the clue-entries, CWDB-PARTIAL, that checks for partial matches by computing clue-similarity scores, CWDB-DICTIO, that simply returns the full list of words with the correct length.

The Rule-Based Module. Italian crosswords frequently contain answers that have no semantic relation with their clues, like ≺*Ai confini del mondo:* **mo**≻, but that are cryptically hidden inside the clue itself. This especially occurs in two-letter and three-letter-answers. With these clues the Web does not provide any help. Therefore we have implemented a rule-based module (RBM), containing eighteen rules for two-letter words and five rules for the three-letter case.

The Implicit Module. The implicit module attributes scores to sequences of letters. It is used in two ways. First, to help the grid-filling algorithm when there are no candidate

---

[5] E.g., ≺*Iniziali di Celentano:* **ac, IP**≻ (≺*Name initials of Celentano:* **ac**≻).

words left for a certain slot during the solving process and as most probable sequence of characters. Second, as a list filter to rank the terms present in the dictionaries. To do so we used tetra-grams probabilities that were computed from the CWDB.

The Dictionary Module. Dictionaries are used to increment the global coverage of the clue-answering. Two Italian dictionaries were used. The first one containing 127738 word lemmas, and the second one containing 296971 word forms. The output is given by the list of terms with the correct length, ranked by the implicit module.

5   Merging the Lists and Filling the Puzzle

The grid-filling phase requires to have unique lists for each slot. Hence, the first step is to merge all the lists produced by the different modules into one. The merger module attributes a probability $p(w)$ to all the words w that appear in the collection of candidate lists: $p(w) = c \sum_{i=0}^{m} (p_i(w) \times \text{conf}_i)$ where m is the number of modules used, conf_i is the confidence evaluation of module i, $p_i(w)$ is the probability score given by module i and c is a normalizing factor.

Crossword solving can be successfully formalized as a Probabilistic-CSP problem [3]. The slots of the puzzle represent the set of variables, the lists of candidates provide the domain of legal values for the variables. The goal is to assign a word to each slot in order to maximize the similarity between the final configuration and the target (defined by the crosswords designer). To compute this similarity we adopted the *maximum probability function*[6]. We search among the various solutions for the one that maximizes: $\prod_{i=1}^{n} p_{x_i}(v_i)$ where $p_{x_i}(v_i)$ is the probability that the value v_i is assigned to the variable x_i in the target configuration.

Finding the maximum probability solution is an NP-complete problem that can be faced using heuristic search techniques as A*. Due to the time restrictions and to the complexity of the problem we chose as a solving algorithm a CSP version of WA* [6] with cost function: $f(X) = \gamma(d)(g(X) + wh(X))$ where w is the weighting constant that makes A* more greedy, as in classic WA*, and $\gamma(d)$ represents an additional score, based on the number of assigned values d that makes the algorithm more depth-first, which is preferable in a CSP framework. This depth score speeds up the grid-filling but it also causes non-admissibility.

6   Experimental Results

The whole crosswords collection has been partitioned in five subsets. The first two belong to *La Settimana Enigmistica*, S_{ord}^1 containing examples of ordinary difficulty (mainly taken from the cover pages of the magazine) and S_{dif}^1 composed by crosswords especially designed for skilled cruciverbalists. An other couple belong to *La Repubblica*, S_{new}^2 and S_{old}^2 respectively containing crosswords that were published in 2004 and in 2001-2003. Finally, S^3 is a miscellaneous of examples from crossword-specialized web sites.

---

[6] A more efficient metric has been proposed in [3], the *maximum expected overlap* function. We will include this feature in our further work.

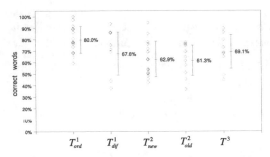

Fig. 9. WebCrow's performance on the five subsets. The performance over the full test set is of 68.8% correct words and 79.9% correct letters. Allowing an extended time limit of 45 minutes and using more documents, the system's performances increase by a 7% in average.

Sixty crosswords of the test set (3685 clues, avg. 61.4 each) were randomly extracted from these subsets in order to form the experimental test suite: T^1_{ord} (15 examples), T^1_{dif} (10 exs.), T^2_{new} (15 exs.), T^2_{old} (10 exs.) and T^3 (10 exs.).

The quality of the clue-answering provided by the Web Search Module can be observed in figure 5. By increasing the number of documents used, the coverage of the system can be augmented sensibly reaching 74,5% with 100 documents. The coverage is higher for the examples belonging to T^1_{ord} (up to 81,7%), T^1_{dif} (up to 77,4%) and T^3 (up to 80,6%). The clues from *La Repubblica* are objectively more difficult to answer, having a coverage of nearly 69%.

The coverage of the WSM's lists grows sensibly with the first increments in the number of retrieved documents. We found that an optimal balance in the trade off between precision, coverage and time cost is reached using 30 docs[7]. We took this as the standard quantity of sources to be used in the experiments because it allows WebCrow to fulfill the time limit of 15 minutes. If a complete solution is not found by the grid-filling algorithm within this time limit the best partial assignment is returned.

Figure 9 reports WebCrow's performance on each example. On T^1_{ord} the results were quite impressive: the average number of targets in first position was just above 40% and the CSP module raised this to 80.0% (90.1% correct letters). With T^1_{dif} WebCrow was able to fill correctly 67.6% of the slots (81.2% letters). On T^2_{new} WebCrow performs with less accuracy averaging 62.9% (72% letters). On T^2_{old}, due to the constant refreshing of Web's information, the average number of correct words goes down to 61.3% (72.9% letters). In T^3 WebCrow reached 69.1% words correct (82.1% letters).

7   Conclusions

The version of WebCrow that is discussed here is basic but it has already given very promising results. WebCrow's overall architecture allows to plug in several expert modules in order to increase the system's performances. The web-search approach has proved to be very consistent. We believe it could suite all those problems in which semantics and interpretation play an important role.

---

[7] In our testing it took an avg. of 8 minutes to answer all the clues of a crossword using 30 docs.

In our future work we believe that a robust NLP system could be of great impact in the answering of the clues. This can be done by adding several other list filters: stylistic, morpho-syntactical, lexical and logical. Moreover, we will improve the grid-filling algorithm. With these additions we are confident that WebCrow can become a strong Italian and multilingual crosswords solver.

References

1. Michael L. Littman, Greg A. Keim and Noam M. Shazeer: A probabilistic approach to solving crossword puzzles. Journal of Artificial Intelligence. **134** (2002) 23–55
2. Greg A. Keim, Noam M. Shazeer and Michael L. Littman: PROVERB: the probabilistic cruciverbalist. Proc. AAAI '99. (1999) 710–717
3. Noam M. Shazeer, Greg A. Keim and Michael L. Littman: Solving crosswords as probabilistic constraint satisfaction. Proc. AAAI '99. (1999) 156–152
4. Michael L. Littman: Review: computer language games. Journal of Computer and Games. **134** (2000) 396–404
5. M. L. Ginsberg, M. Frank, M. P. Halping and M.C. Torrance: Search lessons learned from crossword puzzles. Proc. AAAI '90. (1990) 210–215
6. I. Pohl: Heuristic search viewed as path finding in a graph. Journal of Artificial Intelligence. **1** (1970) 193–204
7. Matthew L. Ginsberg: Dynamic Backtracking. Journal of Artificial Intelligence Research. **1** (1993) 25–46
8. Cody Kwok, Oren Etzioni and Daniel S. Weld: Scaling question answering to the web. ACM Trans. Inf. Syst. **19,3** (2001) 242–262
9. Ellen M. Voorhees and Dawn M. Tice: Overview of the TREC–9 Question Answering Track. Proc. TREC-9. (2000)
10. Koby Crammer and Yoram Singer: On the algorithmic implementation of multiclass kernel–based vector machines. Journal of Machine Learning Res. **2** (2002) 265—-292
11. Ioannis Tsochantaridis et al.: Support vector machine learning for interdependent and structured output spaces. Proc. ICML 04. (2004)
12. H. Schmid: Improvements in Part-of-speech Tagging with an Application to German. Proc. EACL SIGDAT Workshop. (1995)
13. C. Bosco, V. Lombardo and D. Vassallo and L. Lesmo: Building a Treebank for Italian: a Data–driven Annotation Schema. Pro. LREC. (2002)

A Counterfactual-Based Learning Algorithm for $\mathcal{ALC}$ Description Logic

Floriana Esposito, Nicola Fanizzi, Luigi Iannone,
Ignazio Palmisano, and Giovanni Semeraro

Dipartimento di Informatica, Università degli Studi di Bari,
Via Orabona 4, 70125 Bari, Italy
lastname@di.uniba.it

Abstract. We tackle the problem of learning ontologies expressed in a rich representation like the $\mathcal{ALC}$ logic. This task can be cast as a supervised learning problem to be solved by means of operators for this representation which take into account the available metadata. The properties of such operators are discussed and their effectiveness is empirically tested in the experimentation reported in this paper.

1 Introduction

Ontologies play a key role for interoperability in the Semantic Web perspective. Nowadays, the standard ontology markup languages are supported by well-founded semantics of Description Logics (DLs) with a series of available automated reasoning services [1]. However, several tasks in an ontology life-cycle [12], such as their construction and/or integration, are still almost entirely delegated to knowledge engineers.

In the Semantic Web perspective, construction and maintenance of the knowledge bases should be supported by automated inductive inference services. Indeed, compiling a domain expertise in an ontology may be a difficult task depending on its extent and complexity. Moreover, it is also error-prone. With the growth of the size, it is likely that the knowledge base may turn out to be incorrect during its usage when confronted with the real-world. Moreover, time should also be taken into account: while some concepts tend to remain stable (especially top-level ones), those belonging to new domains may require incremental refinements.

So far, the automated induction and refinement of knowledge bases expressed in DL representations has not been investigated in depth. Classic approaches to learning DL concept definitions generally adopt heuristic search strategies to cope with inherent complexity of the problem and generally implement bottom-up algorithms (e.g. [8]). As a prototype, consider the *least common subsumer* (LCS) [5,4]. This operator tends to induce overly specific generalizations, which turn out to be poorly predictive (especially in case of noisy assertions). Moreover, the LCS may not yield a compact representation of the generalizations [2].

Besides, the LCS seems not to be a viable solution for rich DL languages, where the minimal generalization of concept descriptions simply amounts to their

S. Bandini and S. Manzoni (Eds.): AI*IA 2005, LNAI 3673, pp. 406–417, 2005.

disjunction. Indeed, when assertions become available that make the existing ontology inconsistent w.r.t. them, it is difficult to reconstruct correct concept definitions when only generalization can be performed (e.g. the LCS). Likely, the inductive process should be incremental, on the ground of the available metadata.

Other approaches propose a top-down search for correct concept definitions [3]. These methods are not completely operational: since refinement operators compute short moves in a vast space of candidate definitions, they become useless when disjoined from proper heuristics based on the available assertions. A more knowledge-intensive method is to be preferred.

In our approach, the overall learning problem is cast as a search problem in a space of $\mathcal{ALC}$ concept descriptions [11], a DL language that seems a good tradeoff between generality and expressiveness in a Semantic Web perspective. Imposing an order over this search space, operators are defined that can refine existing descriptions by dynamically traversing the space of candidate refinements guided by the assertions. The definition of complete refinement operators for $\mathcal{ALC}$ is not easy due to the absence of structural characterizations of the subsumption [1]. The proposed algorithm is founded on the notion of *multilevel counterfactuals* [14] adapted to an $\mathcal{ALC}$ representation. It consists of two mutually recursive loops of specialization and generalization with respect to the available assertions regarding the incorrect concepts. It can be shown that this method eventually converges to correct definitions (with respect to the intended model).

The presented experimentation will demonstrate that the method can effectively learn a target concept definition from instances which are artificially generated from an OWL ontology and the intended model (an *oracle*) with random perturbations. Generally, the method finds correct definitions and proves also able to detect relevant information coming from the instances, after being lifted to the concept level.

The paper is organized as follows. After the next section introducing the representation, in Sect. 3 the refinement operators and their properties are discussed. In Sect. 4 the experiment is reported proving the effectiveness of the approach. Finally, possible developments are reported in Sect. 5.

2   Background

Most of the ontology languages for the Semantic Web (e.g., OWL) are founded in Description Logics. In this section we recall syntax and semantics for the reference representation $\mathcal{ALC}$ [11] adopted in the rest of the paper, although some results may be extended to other DLs.

In a DL language, primitive *concepts* $N_C = \{A, B, \ldots\}$ are interpreted as subsets of a certain domain (of resources) and primitive *roles* $N_R = \{R, S, \ldots\}$ are interpreted as binary relations on such a domain (properties). Concept descriptions can be built using primitive concepts and roles by means of the constructors in Tab. 1. Their semantics is defined by an *interpretation* $\mathcal{I} = (\Delta^{\mathcal{I}}, \cdot^{\mathcal{I}})$, where $\Delta^{\mathcal{I}}$ is the *domain* of the interpretation and the functor $\cdot^{\mathcal{I}}$ stands for the *function*, mapping the intension of concepts and roles to their extension.

Table 1. $\mathcal{ALC}$ constructors and their meaning

Name	Syntax	Semantics
top concept	$\top$	$\Delta^{\mathcal{I}}$
bottom concept	$\bot$	$\emptyset$
concept negation	$\neg C$	$\Delta^{\mathcal{I}} \setminus C^{\mathcal{I}}$
concept conjunction	$C_1 \sqcap C_2$	$C_1^{\mathcal{I}} \cap C_2^{\mathcal{I}}$
concept disjunction	$C_1 \sqcup C_2$	$C_1^{\mathcal{I}} \cup C_2^{\mathcal{I}}$
existential restriction	$\exists R.C$	$\{x \in \Delta^{\mathcal{I}} \mid \exists y \ (x,y) \in R^{\mathcal{I}} \wedge y \in C^{\mathcal{I}}\}$
universal restriction	$\forall R.C$	$\{x \in \Delta^{\mathcal{I}} \mid \forall y \ (x,y) \in R^{\mathcal{I}} \rightarrow y \in C^{\mathcal{I}}\}$

A *knowledge base* $\mathcal{K} = \langle \mathcal{T}, \mathcal{A} \rangle$ contains two components: a *T-box* $\mathcal{T}$ and an *A-box* $\mathcal{A}$. $\mathcal{T}$ is a set of concept definitions $C \equiv D$, meaning $C^{\mathcal{I}} = D^{\mathcal{I}}$, where C is the concept name and D is a description given in terms of the language constructors. $\mathcal{A}$ contains extensional assertions on concepts and roles, e.g. $C(a)$ and $R(a,b)$, meaning, respectively, that $a^{\mathcal{I}} \in C^{\mathcal{I}}$ and $(a^{\mathcal{I}}, b^{\mathcal{I}}) \in R^{\mathcal{I}}$. A notion of *subsumption* between concepts is given in terms of the interpretations:

Definition 1 (subsumption). *Given two concept descriptions C and D in $\mathcal{T}$, C subsumes D, denoted by $C \sqsupseteq D$, iff for every interpretation $\mathcal{I}$ of $\mathcal{T}$ it holds that $C^{\mathcal{I}} \supseteq D^{\mathcal{I}}$.*

Axioms based on subsumption ($C \sqsupseteq D$) are generally also allowed in the T-boxes as partial definitions. Indeed, $C \equiv D$ amounts to $C \sqsupseteq D$ and $D \sqsupseteq C$.

Example 1. An instance of concept definition in the proposed language is:

$$Father \equiv Male \sqcap \exists hasChild.Person$$

which corresponds to the sentence:

"a father is a male (person) that has some persons as his children"
The following ones are instances of simple assertions:

$$Male(Tom), Male(Bill), hasChild(Tom, Bill)$$

Knowing that $Male \sqsubseteq Person$, one can deduce that:

$$Person(Tom), Person(Bill) \text{ and } Father(Tom)$$

Given these primitive concepts and roles, it is possible to define many other related concepts:

$$Parent \equiv Person \sqcap \exists hasChild.Person$$

and

$$FatherWithoutSons \equiv Male \sqcap \exists hasChild.Person \sqcap \forall hasChild.(\neg Male)$$

It is easy to see that the following relationships hold:

$$Parent \sqsupseteq Father \text{ and } Father \sqsupseteq FatherWithoutSons \qquad \square$$

Many semantically equivalent (yet syntactically different) descriptions can be given for the same concept. However, they can be reduced to a canonical form by means of rewriting rules that preserve their equivalence, e.g. $\forall R.C_1 \sqcap \forall R.C_2 \equiv \forall R.(C_1 \sqcap C_2)$ (see [1] for these issues). Preliminarily, some notation is needed to name the different parts of an $\mathcal{ALC}$ description: $\text{prim}(C)$ is the set of all the primitive and negated primitive concepts at the top-level conjunction of C; if there exists a universal restriction $\forall R.C'$ on the top-level of C then $\text{val}_R(C) = C'$ otherwise $\text{val}_R(C) = \top$ (a single one because of the equivalence mentioned above). Finally, $\text{ex}_R(C)$ is the set of the concept descriptions C' appearing in existential restrictions $\exists R.C'$ at the top-level conjunction of C.

Definition 2 ($\mathcal{ALC}$ normal form). *A concept description D is in $\mathcal{ALC}$ normal form iff $D \equiv \bot$ or $D \equiv \top$ or if $D = D_1 \sqcup \cdots \sqcup D_n$ with*

$$D_i = \bigsqcap_{A \in \text{prim}(D_i)} A \sqcap \bigsqcap_{R \in N_R} \left[\bigsqcap_{V \in \text{val}_R(D_i)} \forall R.V \sqcap \bigsqcap_{E \in \text{ex}_R(D_i)} \exists R.E \right]$$

where, for all $i = 1, \ldots, n$, $D_i \not\equiv \bot$ and for any R, every sub-description in $\text{ex}_R(D_i)$ and $\text{val}_R(D_i)$ is in normal form.

3   Learning Through Refinement Operators

Subsumption induces a partial order over the space of $\mathcal{ALC}$ descriptions, say $(\mathcal{ALC}, \sqsupseteq)$. In order to allow for an incremental treatment, differently from the standard approaches followed in the past, the problem of learning a concept definition can be formulated as a search in the mentioned space aiming at concept descriptions that are consistent with an intended model based on the available instances (henceforth called examples, where appropriate).

A general form of the problem may be the following:

Definition 3 (learning problem).
Given

- *a knowledge base $\mathcal{K} = \langle \mathcal{T}, \mathcal{A} \rangle$*
- *a set of positive and negative assertions $\mathcal{A}_C = \mathcal{A}_C^+ \cup \mathcal{A}_C^-$ about the membership of some individuals to a target concept C, and such that: $\mathcal{A} \cup \mathcal{T} \not\models \mathcal{A}_C$*

Find *a (new) definition $C \equiv D'$ so that $\mathcal{A} \cup \mathcal{T}' \models \mathcal{A}_C$,
where $\mathcal{T}' = (\mathcal{T} \setminus \{C \equiv D\}) \cup \{C \equiv D'\}$.*

Note that when the T-box $\mathcal{T}$ already contains a definition for the target concept $C \equiv D$, that is the case of a *refinement problem*.

As we said before, the solution to this problem is an algorithm that traverses the search space $(\mathcal{ALC}, \sqsupseteq)$ in order to find a new concept definition that is consistent with knowledge base augmented with the new assertions related to C.

The search is based on the notion of *refinement operator* [10] which is a function that, given the current description, computes a set of possible moves in the search space corresponding to the refinements of the current description. The interesting moves are those that, starting from an initial description, say D, lead to strictly more general ones w.r.t. the subsumption relationship, say D' such that $D' \sqsupset D$; or to a strictly more specific one D'' such that $D \sqsupset D''$.

Similarly to [3] for the $\mathcal{ALER}$ language, we can provide a starting definition of these operators for $(\mathcal{ALC}, \sqsupseteq)$.

Definition 4 (downward operator). $\rho = (\rho_\sqcup, \rho_\sqcap)$, *where:*
$[\rho_\sqcup]$ *given a description in normal form* $D = D_1 \sqcup \cdots \sqcup D_n$ *and* $1 \le i \le n$:

- $D' \in \rho_\sqcup(D)$ *if* $D' = \bigsqcup_{1 \le k \le n}^{k \ne i} D_k$
- $D' \in \rho_\sqcup(D)$ *if* $D' = D_i' \sqcup \bigsqcup_{1 \le k \le n}^{k \ne i} D_k$
  for some $D_i' \in \rho_\sqcap(D_i)$

$[\rho_\sqcap]$ *given a conjunctive description* $C = C_1 \sqcap \cdots \sqcap C_m$ *and* $1 \le i \le m$:

- $C' \in \rho_\sqcap(C)$ *if* $C' = C \sqcap C_{j+1}$ *for some* $C_{j+1} \not\sqsupseteq C$
- $C' \in \rho_\sqcap(C)$ *if* $C' = \bigsqcap_{1 \le j \le m}^{j \ne i} C_i \ \sqcap C_j'$ *where:*
    - $C_j' = \exists R.D_j',\ C_j = \exists R.D_j$ *and* $D_j' \in \rho_\sqcup(D_j)$ *or*
    - $C_j' = \forall R.D_j',\ C_j = \forall R.D_j$ *and* $D_j' \in \rho_\sqcup(D_j)$

It is straightforward to define the dual upward operator that seeks for more general hypotheses by adding or generalizing disjuncts.

Definition 5 (upward operator). $\delta = (\delta_\sqcup, \delta_\sqcap)$, *where:*
$[\delta_\sqcup]$ *given a description in normal form* $D = D_1 \sqcup \cdots \sqcup D_n$:

- $D' \in \delta_\sqcup(D)$ *if* $D' = D \sqcup D_{n+1}$
  for some new disjunct D_{n+1} *such that* $D_{n+1} \not\sqsubseteq D_i, 1 \le i \le n$
- $D' \in \delta_\sqcup(D)$ *if* $D' = D_i' \sqcup \bigsqcup_{1 \le i,k \le n}^{k \ne i} D_k$
  for some $D_i' \in \delta_\sqcap(D_i)$

$[\delta_\sqcap]$ *given a conjunctive description* $C = C_1 \sqcap \cdots \sqcap C_m$:

- $C' \in \delta_\sqcap(C)$ *if* $C' = \bigsqcap_{1 \le i,j \le n}^{j \ne i} C_i$
- $C' \in \delta_\sqcap(C)$ *if* $C' = \bigsqcap_{1 \le i,j \le n}^{j \ne i} C_i \ \sqcap C_j'$ *where:*
    - $C_j' = \exists R.D_j',\ C_j = \exists R.D_j$ *and* $D_j' \in \delta_\sqcup(D_j)$ *or*
    - $C_j' = \forall R.D_j',\ C_j = \forall R.D_j$ *and* $D_j' \in \delta_\sqcup(D_j)$

3.1   Properties

Various properties of refinement operators have been proposed [10]. For brevity, we just recall the most pertaining to this discussion.

Definition 6 (Properties). *Let* ρ *(resp.* δ*) be a downward (upward) operator for the* $(\mathcal{S}, \succeq)$ *space and* $C, D \in \mathcal{S}$

- ρ *(resp.* δ*) is* locally finite *iff* $\rho(C)$ *(resp.* $\delta(C)$*) is a finite set for any* C
- ρ *(resp.* δ*) is* proper *iff for all* $D \in \rho(C)$ *(resp.* $D \in \delta(C)$*) it holds that* $C \succ D$ *(resp.* $C \prec D$*)*
- ρ *(resp.* δ*) is* complete *iff for all* $C \succ D$ *(resp.* $D \succ C$*) it holds that* $D \in \rho^*(C)$ *(resp.* $D \in \delta^*(C)$*)*[1]

It can be shown that operators in Def. 4 and 5 are complete for $(\mathcal{ALC}, \sqsupseteq)$. We report just the proof for ρ as the one for δ is quite similar.

---

[1] Where $\rho^*(C)$ and $\delta^*(C)$ stand for the closures of the operators.

Proposition 1 (Completeness). *The operator ρ is complete.*

Proof. From Def. 6, if ρ were complete then for all D, C such that $D \sqsubset C$ we should have that there exists $E \equiv D$, $E \in \rho^*(C)$.

If by hypothesis $D \sqsubset C$ then (by the subsumption relationship) we have that $D \equiv C \sqcap D$. Let us take E as D put in $\mathcal{ALC}$-normal form then we have that

$$D \equiv E \sqcap C \tag{1}$$

with $E \equiv E_1 \sqcup E_2 \sqcup \cdots \sqcup E_m$. Let us suppose w.l.o.g. that C is in $\mathcal{ALC}$-normal form, therefore $C \equiv C_1 \sqcup C_2 \sqcup \cdots \sqcup C_n$.

Substituting the definitions of C and E in (1), we have: $D \equiv (C_1 \sqcap E_1 \sqcap E_2 \sqcap \cdots \sqcap E_m) \sqcup (C_2 \sqcap E_1 \sqcap E_2 \sqcap \cdots \sqcap E_m) \sqcup \cdots \sqcup (C_n \sqcap E_1 \sqcap E_2 \sqcap \cdots \sqcap E_m)$.

Now, let us build up D starting from C.

Let us consider $C^1 \in \rho_{\sqcap}(C)$ such that $C^1 \equiv (C_1 \sqcap E_1 \sqcap E_2 \sqcap \cdots \sqcap E_m) \sqcup C_2 \sqcup \cdots \sqcup C_m$ and then, iteratively for the length of C, let us apply $\rho_{\sqcap}$ to the other disjuncts C_i in order to have at the kth iteration $C^k = (C_1 \sqcap E_1 \sqcap E_2 \sqcap \cdots \sqcap E_m) \sqcup (C_2 \sqcap E_1 \sqcap E_2 \sqcap \cdots \sqcap E_m) \sqcup \cdots \sqcup (C_k \sqcap E_1 \sqcap E_2 \sqcap \cdots \sqcap E_m) \sqcup \cdots \sqcup C_m$. We finally obtain D. We have found a refinement chain such that $D \in \rho^*(C)$. Hence ρ is complete.

However, these operators are not locally finite owing to the freedom for the choice of the description C_{j+1}. Thus they are also extremely redundant, resulting useless for an actual efficient implementation, unless a further bias is imposed.

It can be shown that such operators are not proper either. It suffices to consider that in Def. 4 one can drop a disjunct that is already subsumed by the remaining ones obtaining, in this way, a concept equivalent to the starting one. As for Def. 5, one can still add a disjunct that, though not subsumed by each disjunct in the starting concept, is subsumed by the whole disjunction, obtaining again a non proper refinement.

3.2   Operators Depending on Examples

A possible solution is to take advantage of the knowledge present in the examples and counterexamples. Instead of using the examples in a mere *generate-and-test* strategy, based on these operators, they can be exploited more directly, in order to influence the choices made during the refinement process.

Therefore, we have consequently modified the operators of Def. 4 so that they exploit this information during the refinement generation: In the following we treat the examples as very specific descriptions at the concept language level (approximated *msc*'s; see [1] and the following section).

Definition 7 (new ρ). $\rho = (\rho_{\sqcup}, \rho_{\sqcap})$, *where:*
$[\rho_{\sqcup}]$ *given a description in normal form $D = D_1 \sqcup \cdots \sqcup D_n$:*

- $D' \in \rho_{\sqcup}(D)$ if $D' = \bigsqcup_{1 \leq i, j \leq n}^{j \neq i} D_i$
- $D' \in \rho_{\sqcup}(D)$ if $D' = D_i' \sqcup \bigsqcup_{1 \leq i, j \leq n}^{j \neq i} D_k$ for some $D_i' \in \rho_{\sqcap}(D_i)$

$[\rho_{\sqcap}]$ *given a conjunctive description $C = C_1 \sqcap \cdots \sqcap C_m$ and $E^- = \{E^{(n)} \mid n \geq 1\}$ a set of $\mathcal{ALC}$ concepts:*

- $C' \in \rho_\sqcap(C)$ if $C' = C \sqcap C_{j+1}$ for some $C_{j+1} \not\sqsupseteq C$ and $C_{j+1} \not\sqsupseteq E^{(i)}, E^{(i)} \in E^-$
- $C' \in \rho_\sqcap(C)$ if $C' = (C \sqcup \neg C_j) \sqcap C'_j$ for some $1 \leq j \leq m$, where:
  - $C'_j = \exists R.D'_j$, $C_j = \exists R.D_j$ and $D'_j \in \rho_\sqcup(D_j)$ or
  - $C'_j = \forall R.D'_j$, $C_j = \forall R.D_j$ and $D'_j \in \rho_\sqcup(D_j)$

Analogously, by modifying Def. 5, we obtain:

Definition 8 (new δ). $\delta = (\delta_\sqcup, \delta_\sqcap)$, *where:*
$[\delta_\sqcup]$ *given a description in normal form* $D = D_1 \sqcup \cdots \sqcup D_n$ *and* $E^+ = \{E^{(n)} \mid n \geq 1\}$ *a set of* $\mathcal{ALC}$ *concepts:*

- $D' \in \delta_\sqcup(D)$ if $D' = D \sqcup D_{n+1}$
  for some disjunct D_{n+1} such that $D_{n+1} \not\sqsubseteq D_i, 1 \leq i \leq n, D_{j+1} \sqsupseteq E^{(i)}, E^{(i)} \in E^+$
- $D' \in \delta_\sqcup(D)$ if $D' = D'_i \sqcup \bigsqcup_{1 \leq i, k \leq n}^{k \neq i} D_i$ for some $D'_i \in \delta_\sqcap(D_i)$

$[\delta_\sqcup]$ *given a conjunctive description* $C = C_1 \sqcap \cdots \sqcap C_m$:

- $C' \in \delta_\sqcap(C)$ if $C' = \bigsqcap_{1 \leq i, j \leq m}^{j \neq i} C_i$
- $C' \in \delta_\sqcap(C)$ if $C' = \bigsqcap_{1 \leq i, j \leq m}^{j \neq i} C_i \sqcap C'_j$, where:
  - $C'_j = \exists R.D'_j$, $C_j = \exists R.D_j$ and $D'_j \in \delta_\sqcup(D_j)$ or
  - $C'_j = \forall R.D'_j$, $C_j = \forall R.D_j$ and $D'_j \in \delta_\sqcup(D_j)$

The next step consists of embedding these operators in a learning algorithm that is capable to process the incoming examples incrementally.

3.3   The Algorithm: Implementing the Operators

These operators can be employed to solve the learning problem, as central points of the interleaving routines that, starting from a seed, compute (partial) generalizations as long as they do not cover any negative example. If this occurs, the specialization routine is invoked. This routine results to be an implementation of the counterfactuals approach [14] in the $\mathcal{ALC}$ language. Counterfactuals consist of downward refinement steps obtained by means of a difference operator that is particulary suitable for DLs that are endowed with disjunction such as $\mathcal{ALC}$. A sketch of the two interleaving routines mentioned above is reported in Fig. 1. A discussion on their correctness can be found in [6].

In order to compute specializations of a concept C, given a set of descriptions E^- as in Def. 7, one has to make sure of finding a conjunct that allows to discriminate the descriptions in E^-. For this purpose, we rely on the notion of concept difference proposed in [13]. In the following this difference between two descriptions C and D, also called *residual*, is defined as follows: $C - D = C \sqcup \neg D$.

Therefore, in the case of the downward operators, residuals between each element of E and the concept C to refine have to be computed. Then the negation of the conjunction of all the residuals, conjoined to C, will result in a specialized concept. Actually one could require this operation to be more *greedy* and, before conjoining the negation of all the residuals, it is more useful to generalize among

```
generalize(Positives, Negatives, Generalization)
input  Positives, Negatives: positive and negative msc approximations
output Generalization: generalized concept definition
begin
ResPositives ← Positives
Generalization ← ⊥
while ResPositives ≠ ∅ do
        ParGen ← select_seed(ResPositives)
        CoveredPos ← {Pos ∈ ResPositives | ParGen ⊒ Pos}
        CoveredNeg ← {Neg ∈ Negatives | ParGen ⊒ Neg}
        while CoveredPos ≠ ResPositives and CoveredNeg = ∅ do
            ParGen ← select(δ(ParGen), ResPositives)
            CoveredPos ← {Pos ∈ ResPositives | ParGen ⊒ Pos}
            CoveredNeg ← {Neg ∈ Negatives | ParGen ⊒ Neg}
        if CoveredNeg ≠ ∅ then
            K ← specialize(ParGen, CoveredPos, CoveredNeg)
            ParGen ← ParGen ⊓ ¬K
        Generalization ← Generalization ⊔ ParGen
        ResPositives ← ResPositives \ CoveredPos
return Generalization
end

specialize(ParGen, CoveredPos, CoveredNeg, K)
input   ParGen: inconsistent concept definition
        CoveredPos, CoveredNeg: covered positive and negative msc approx.
output K: counterfactual
begin
NewPositives ← ∅
NewNegatives ← ∅
for each N_i ∈ CoveredNeg do
        NewP_i ← residual(N_i, ParGen)
        NewPositives ← NewPositives ∪ {NewP_i}
for each P_j ∈ CoveredPos do
        NewN_j ← residual(P_j, ParGen)
        NewNegatives ← NewNegatives ∪ {NewN_j}
K ← generalize(NewPositives, NewNegatives)
return K
end
```

Fig. 1. The co-routines used in the method

the residuals themselves. Summarizing, given the description C to be specialized and the set of counterexample descriptions E^- not to be subsumed, the residuals $Res_i = E^{(i)} - C$ for each $E^{(i)} \in E^-$ can be computed and then one can look for a suitable generalization of each Res_i in order to have a unique Res_{ALL} that subsumes all the single residuals.

4   Experimentation

We present the empirical evaluation of the system called YINYANG, the Java implementation of the algorithm described in Fig. 1. The target of the evaluation will be the accuracy of the algorithm in finding a definition for a target $\mathcal{ALC}$ concept starting from a set of positive and a set of negative examples. Since it is difficult to find datasets and background ontologies suitable for $\mathcal{ALC}$, existing ILP datasets have to be properly transformed for being employed in DL settings (see [7]). In this experiment the background knowledge is a fixed hand-crafted ontology. It is an OWL-DL[2] ontology regarding people, their jobs and

---
[2] http://www.w3.org/2001/sw/WebOnt

T-Box concept axioms

$Woman \equiv \neg Male$	$Male \sqsubseteq Person$
$Indeterminate \sqsubseteq \neg Temporary$	$PartTime \sqsubseteq JobContract$
$Indeterminate \sqsubseteq \neg PartTime$	$Woman \sqsubseteq Person$
$Indeterminate \sqsubseteq JobContract$	$PhDStudent \sqsubseteq Person$
$Employee \sqsubseteq Person$	$Temporary \sqsubseteq JobContract$
$SelfEmpolyed \sqsubseteq Person$	$Role \sqsubseteq \top$

T-Box role domain axioms	T-Box role range axioms
$SelfEmpolyed \sqcup Employee \equiv \exists job.\top$	$\top \sqsubseteq \forall job.JobContract$
$Employee \equiv \exists contract.\top$	$\top \sqsubseteq \forall isMarriedWith.Person$

Fig. 2. Background ontology in the experiment

their marital status whose $\mathcal{ALC}$ representation is reported in Fig. 2. The target concept in the experiment represented the set of persons that are exempted from military service according to the (Italian) law. The $\mathcal{ALC}$ description of the target concept was: $MilitaryExempt \equiv Woman \sqcup PhDStudent \sqcup (Employee \sqcap \exists contract.(\neg Indeterminate))$.

In order to have a test set as independent as possible for each experimental session, an $\mathcal{A}$-box has been randomly generated as follows. Among the others, four concepts were chosen for the generation of individuals: *Woman, Man, PhDStudent* and *Indeterminate*. For each of these concepts 25 random instances per experimental session were created. The reason for explicitly determining the classes was to guarantee meaningful experimental sessions. Indeed, if the choice of these concepts were left to chance, it could have happened that instances could have been generated with no feature related to the target concept. The creation of an individual of a class consists in the generation of a random name for this individual and a random number of role assertions, depending on the roles whose domain is (or includes) the individual class. The choice whether to create a role assertion for an individual is random itself. The r-fillers for the assertions are, in their turn, individuals generated from the range class of the role. Actually, in order to further perturb and vary those role assertions, the r-filler class for the individuals to be created is the range class or one of its known subclasses in the taxonomy. In this way, for each experimental session, a test set was built up consisting of 100 individuals (25 per class), that appeared in a non fixed number of role assertions. The r-fillers of those assertions were created by means of the same method, as instances of one of the classes in the range class sub-taxonomy. The pseudo code procedure for the generation of an individual is sketched in Fig. 3.

Per each session a 10-fold cross validation was performed. In order to divide the individuals of the training set into positive and negative examples, the existence of an *oracle* was simulated by an OWL-DL reasoner with a knowledge base embedding the starting $\mathcal{T}$-Box (Figure 2) plus the correct model of the target concept (*MilitaryExempt*). Then, each example can be classified as positive (or

generateIndividual (c: Class)
```
name := chooseName()
add assertion c(name)
while c has more properties do
    p := next property
    if generateNextRandomBoolean()
        r := range of p
        crange := pickUpAClassFromSubTaxonomy(r)
        rfiller := generateIndividual (crange)
        add assertion p(name, rfiller)
```

Fig. 3. Algorithm employed to generate individuals

negative) if the reasoner states that it belongs (or does not belong) to the target concept. The same procedure has been applied to the validation set. After the training phase, the system induced the definition h as a result. Each example in the validation test could be classified as true/false positive or negative. Then we measured precision and recall both on positive and on negative examples. In order to combine precision and recall, the F-measure of the hypotheses was also computed, as follows:

$$F\text{-}Measure(h) = 2 \cdot Precision(h) \cdot Recall(h)/(Precision(h) + Recall(h))$$

For the sake of the significance, we repeated the 10-fold cross validation 30 times, generating a brand new dataset for each session. We report results in Table 2. From this Table it results an average F-measure of .923 over 30 cross validation sessions. We defined a trust interval with 95% confidence according to the following formula:

$$errors_S(h) \pm 1.96\sqrt{errors_S(1 - errors_S)/n}$$

where $errors_S(h)$ is the F-Measure value (representing a measure of the error made on a sample by the hypothesis h), n is the number of the experiment repetitions. The difference between the standard procedure (see [9]) and ours is that, instead of building and evaluating h on a fixed training and validation set, we tried to avoid exceptional values by averaging the results by means of the cross-validation procedure. Therefore the F-measure confidence interval has a lower bound of about .866 with a confidence of 95%. We claim the actual interval to be narrower: as a matter of fact we adopted an averaged 10-fold cross validation instead of a straight learn-and-validate method, therefore we should have smoothed outliers. The most common induced description for the target concept in the various sessions resulted the following:

$$Woman \sqcup PhDStudent \sqcup (Employee \sqcap \forall contract.Temporary) \sqcup$$
$$(Employee \sqcap \forall contract.PartTime)$$

It can be noticed that no reference is made to the Indeterminate contract of the generating definition. Indeed, this feature is actually non relevant. Computing the LCS of the examples generated from the mentioned description would save restrictions related to the *Indeterminate* contract because of the minimality

Table 2. Results of the 10-fold cross validation sessions

session	precision	recall	F-measure	session	precision	recall	F-measure
1	.924	.917	.921	16	.915	.930	.923
2	.926	.931	.929	17	.922	.933	.928
3	.913	.922	.917	18	.924	.924	.924
4	.929	.929	.929	19	.919	.931	.925
5	.891	.919	.905	20	.925	.932	.928
6	.927	.928	.927	21	.905	.930	.918
7	.924	.931	.928	22	.929	.920	.924
8	.917	.930	.924	23	.906	.928	.917
9	.918	.942	.929	24	.917	.930	.923
10	.887	.936	.910	25	.906	.933	.919
11	.919	.936	.928	26	.908	.933	.920
12	.910	.930	.920	27	.934	.937	.935
13	.922	.931	.927	28	.914	.942	.928
14	.913	.923	.918	29	.919	.907	.913
15	.927	.937	.932	30	.919	.936	.928
			precision		recall		F-measure
average			.917		.930		.923

of the operator. The induced concept and the target one differ in the type of the restriction. Indeed, in the former we found a universal restriction that is somewhat more specific than the existential one. This is due to the procedure for building the approximation of msc's that allows for an existential restriction just in case the r-filler of an assertion concerning the individual on which msc is being built (or estimated) is not known to belong to any concept (i.e. to $\top$). This results in very specific msc approximations but further developments can foresee more sophisticated mechanisms for this task. In fact, msc approximations are kept as specific as possible in order to comply to the msc definition but, for our purposes, we relax the need for specificity. Approximations can be exploited instead of actual msc's as long as those related to positive instances do not subsume the negative ones or viceversa. Therefore a lazy strategy could be devised which would compute approximations of msc's, up to a certain depth and specify only those that yield the problem mentioned above.

5   Conclusions and Further Developments

A methodology for learning and refining $\mathcal{ALC}$ knowledge bases has been proposed. It was based on the traversal by means of adequate refinement operators that exploit the target concept instances in the A-box for guiding the process. The solution has been experimentally evaluated is several domains: the presented experiment is exemplar for the outcomes obtained. Further developments can concern diverse directions. There is a need for the extension of the methodology to more complex DLs, namely those endowed with number constraints, like $\mathcal{ALCN}$. Another issue related to the reference language to be considered is the msc approximation. A more sophisticate strategy could be exploited in order to ease the burden of generalization. Though we are aware that these problems have been only partially solved, for the sake of brevity we preferred to defer their analysis and to keep the focus on learning and refinement.

Lastly, there are other empirical evaluations that it may be worth carrying out. Besides applying the algorithm to other domains, we plan to estimate empirically other aspects of the learning algorithm, such as the learning curve w.r.t. the number of examples or the dependance of the speed of learning w.r.t. the adopted abstraction methodologies (*msc* approximation). However our final purpose is the application of the implementation of the presented methodology in some ontology engineering toolkit such as the Protégé OWL Plug-in[3].

References

1. F. Baader, D. Calvanese, D. McGuinness, D. Nardi, and P. Patel-Schneider, editors. *The Description Logic Handbook.* Cambridge University Press, 2003.
2. F. Baader and A.-Y. Turhan. TBoxes do not yield a compact representation of least common subsumers. In *Working Notes of the 2001 International Description Logics Workshop*, volume 49 of *CEUR Workshop Proceedings*, Stanford, USA, 2001.
3. L. Badea and S.-H. Nienhuys-Cheng. A refinement operator for description logics. In J. Cussens and A. Frisch, editors, *Proceedings of the 10th International Conference on Inductive Logic Programming*, volume 1866 of *LNAI*, pages 40–59. Springer, 2000.
4. W.W. Cohen and H. Hirsh. The learnability of description logic with equality constraints. *Machine Learning*, 17(2-3):169–199, 1994.
5. W.W. Cohen and H. Hirsh. Learning the CLASSIC description logic. In P. Torasso, J. Doyle, and E. Sandewall, editors, *Proceedings of the 4th International Conference on the Principles of Knowledge Representation and Reasoning*, pages 121–133. Morgan Kaufmann, 1994.
6. F. Esposito, N. Fanizzi, L. Iannone, I. Palmisano, and G. Semeraro. Knowledge-intensive induction of terminologies from metadata. In S.A. McIlraith, D. Plexousakis, and F. van Harmelen, editors, *Proceedings of the 3rd International Semantic Web Conference*, volume 3298 of *LNCS*, pages 411–426. Springer, 2004.
7. J.-U. Kietz. Learnability of description logic programs. In S. Matwin and C. Sammut, editors, *Proceedings of the 12th International Conference on Inductive Logic Programming*, volume 2583 of *LNAI*, pages 117–132, Sydney, 2002. Springer.
8. J.-U. Kietz and K. Morik. A polynomial approach to the constructive induction of structural knowledge. *Machine Learning*, 14(2):193–218, 1994.
9. Tom M. Mitchell. *Machine Learning*, chapter 5 Evaluating Hypotheses, pages 128–153. McGraw-Hill, New York, 1997.
10. S.-H. Nienhuys-Cheng and R. de Wolf. *Foundations of Inductive Logic Programming*, volume 1228 of *LNAI*. Springer, 1997.
11. M. Schmidt-Schauß and G. Smolka. Attributive concept descriptions with complements. *Artificial Intelligence*, 48(1):1–26, 1991.
12. Steffen Staab and Rudi Studer, editors. *Handbook on Ontologies*. International Handbooks on Information Systems. Springer, 2004.
13. G. Teege. A subtraction operation for description logics. In P. Torasso, J. Doyle, and E. Sandewall, editors, *Proceedings of the 4th International Conference on Principles of Knowledge Representation and Reasoning*, pages 540–550. Morgan Kaufmann, 1994.
14. S.A. Vere. Multilevel counterfactuals for generalizations of relational concepts and productions. *Artificial Intelligence*, 14:139–164, 1980.

---

[3] http://protege.stanford.edu/plugins/owl

Relational Learning: Statistical Approach Versus Logical Approach in Document Image Understanding

Michelangelo Ceci, Margherita Berardi, and Donato Malerba

Dipartimento di Informatica, Università degli Studi di Bari,
Via Orabona 4, 70126 Bari
{ceci, berardi, malerba}@di.uniba.it

Abstract. Document image understanding denotes the recognition of semantically relevant components in the layout extracted from a document image. This recognition process is based on some visual models that can be automatically acquired by applying machine learning techniques. In particular, by properly encapsulating knowledge of the inherent spatial nature of the layout of a document image, spatial relations among logical components of interest can play a key role in the learned models. For this reason, we are investigating the application of (multi-)relational learning techniques, which successfully allows relations between components to be effectively and naturally represented. Goal of this paper is to evaluate and systematically compare two different approaches to relational learning, that is, a statistical approach and a logical approach in the task of document image understanding. For a fair comparison, both methods are tested on the same dataset consisting of multi-page articles published in an international journal. An analysis of pros and cons of both approaches is reported.

1 Introduction

The increasingly large amount of paper documents to be processed daily requires systems with abilities to catalog and organize these documents automatically on the basis of their contents. Functional capabilities like classifying, storing, retrieving, and reproducing documents, as well as extracting, browsing, retrieving and synthesizing information from a variety of documents are highly demanded. In this context, the use of document image understanding techniques to recognize semantically relevant layout components (e.g. title, abstract of a scientific paper or leading article, picture of a newspaper) in the layout extracted from a document image plays a key role.

This recognition process is based on some visual models, whose manual specification can be a highly demanding task. In order to automatically acquire these models, machine learning methods characterized by a high degree of adaptivity can be used. In the literature, several machine learning techniques have been applied for the document image understanding task. Aiello et al. [1] applied the classical decision tree learning system C4.5 [13] to learn classification rules for recognizing textual layout components. Palmero et al. [10] developed a neuro-fuzzy learning algorithm that ranks, for each new (unseen) block, candidate labels and selects the best. Le Bourgeois et al. [7] proposed to use the probabilistic relaxation [14] and Bayesian

S. Bandini and S. Manzoni (Eds.): AI*IA 2005, LNAI 3673, pp. 418–429, 2005.

Networks [11] for recognizing logical components. Walischewski [17] proposed to represent each document layout by a complete attributed directed graph (one vertex for each layout object) that represents frequency counts for different spatial relations. Incremental learning of the attributed directed graph is proposed. Akilende and Belaïd [2] proposed to infer a tree-based representation of the layout structure by means of a tree-grammar inference method from a set of training documents.

Although these methods often present interesting results, they are often based on learning algorithms that suffer from severe limitations due to the restrictive representation formalism known as single-table assumption [6]. More specifically, it is assumed that training data are represented in a single table of a relational database, such that each row (or tuple) represents an independent example and columns correspond to properties. This requires that non-spatial properties of neighboring objects be represented in aggregated form causing a consequent loss of information. On the contrary, the application of (multi-)relational learning techniques [6] allows spatial relations between layout components to be effectively and naturally represented, while, for example, decision trees and neural networks models are unsuitable to represent a variable number of spatial neighbours of a layout component together with their attributes.

Scope of this paper is to evaluate and systematically compare two different (multi-) relational learning approaches based on statistical approaches and logical approaches, respectively. In particular, we consider the statistical learner Mr-SBC [4], and the logical learner ATRE [8] and the comparison has been conducted in the document image understanding task. In order to test Mr-SBC and ATRE for the document image understanding task, both have been integrated in the Document Image Analysis system WISDOM++[1] [3] whose applicability has been investigated in the context of the IST-EU founded project COLLATE[2]. WISDOM++ permits the transformation of document images into XML format by means of several complex steps: preprocessing of the raster image of a scanned paper document, segmentation of the preprocessed raster image into basic layout components, classification of basic layout components according to the type of content (e.g., text, graphics, etc.), the identification of a more abstract representation of the document layout (layout analysis), the classification of the document on the ground of its layout and content, the identification of semantically relevant layout components (document image understanding), the application of OCR only to those textual components of interest, the storage in XML format. In the WISDOM++ context, the term document understanding denotes the process of mapping the layout structure of a document into the corresponding logical structure. The document understanding process is based on the assumption that documents can be understood by means of their layout structures alone. The mapping of the layout structure into the logical structure can be performed by means of a set of classification rules which can be automatically learned by properly describing a set of training documents or by applying a classification function estimating the probability that a layout component belongs to a determinate class (i.e. logical label).

The paper is organized as follows. In section 2 and 3, the application of the learning systems Mr-SBC and ATRE in the context of document image understanding is

---

[1] http://www.di.uniba.it/~malerba/wisdom++
[2] http://www.collate.de/

described. In section 4 experimental results on the same dataset consisting of multi-page articles published in an international journal are shown and conclusions are drawn.

2   Application of Mr-SBC

Mr-SBC (Multi-Relational Structural Bayesian Classifier) [4] is a (multi-)relational classifier that combines the induction of first order logic classification rules and the classical naive bayesian classifier [5]. In particular, it can be considered an extension of the naive Bayesian classifier in the case of the multi-relational setting.

Mr-SBC is particularly suited in the task in hand since it is tightly-coupled with a Relational DBMS and can directly interface, by means of SQL views, the database that WISDOM++ uses for storing intermediate data. Mr-SBC takes advantage of the database schema that provides useful knowledge of data model that can help to guide the learning process. This is an alternative to asking the users to specify background knowledge.

The problem solved by Mr-SBC can be formalized as follows:

Given:
- a training set represented by means of h relational tables $S=\{T_0, T_1, ..., T_{h-1}\}$ of a relational database D
- a set of primary key constraints on tables in S
- a set of foreign key constraints on tables in S
- a target relation $T \in S$
- a target discrete attribute y in T, different from the primary key of T.

Find
a naive Bayesian classifier which predicts the value of y for some individual represented as a tuple in T (with possibly UNKNOWN value for y) and related tuples in S according to foreign key constraints.

According to the Bayesian setting, given a new instance to be classified, the classifier estimates the probability that an instance belongs to a determinate class and returns the most probable class:

$$f(I)= arg\ max_i\ P(C_i|R) = arg\ max_i\ \frac{P(C_i)P(R|C_i)}{P(R)}$$

where $f(\cdot)$ is the classification function, I is the individual to be classified, C_i is the i-th possible class and R is the description of I in terms of first-order classification rules. In our domain, categories are logical labels that can be associated to layout components (individuals to be classified).

Although Mr-SBC can be used for Document Image Understanding tasks, some modifications are necessary. In particular, it is necessary to modify the search strategy in order to allow cyclic paths. As observed by Taskar et al. [16], the acyclicity constraint hinders representation of many important relational dependencies. This is particularly true in the task in hand, where a relation between two logical components is modelled by means of a relational table that expresses the existence of the topological relation. For example, suppose that we need to model the relation *on_top* between two layout components, from a database point of view, this is realized by means of the table "block" and a table "on_top" that contains two foreign keys to the table "block". The referenced blocks are considered one on top the other. In the original formulation of the problem solved by Mr-SBC, first-order classification rules do not consider the same table twice [4], therefore it is not possible to explore the search space by considering first the table "block", after the table "on_top" and finally, again, the table "block", thus it is not possible to take into account the topological relation. To avoid this problem, we modified Mr-SBC, allowing cyclic paths.

The second problem concerns with the classification of layout components. In document image understanding, it is possible that the same layout component is associated with two different logical labels. For example, suppose that the layout analysis is not able to separate the page number and the running head of a scientific paper. In this case we have a single layout component that contains two logical components: the page number and the running head. The classifier should associate that component with two labels. For this reason, it is necessary to resort to a multiple classification problem. In particular, we learn a binary classifier for each class. Each classifier is able to identify examples belonging to that class and examples that do not belong to it. This solution is usually adopted in Text Categorization when the problem is to establish if a document belongs to a particular class or not [15].

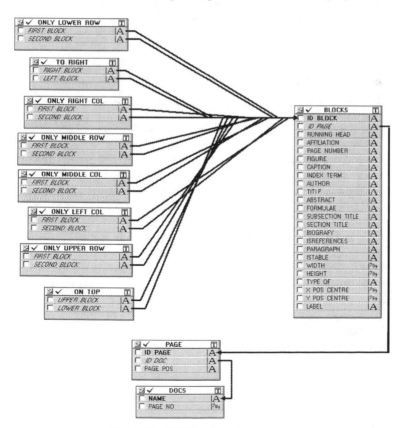

Fig. 1. Mr-SBC Database input schema

Table 1. Details of features used to describe logical components

Type	Name	Description	Values
Locational	x_pos_centre	The position of the component w.r.t. the x axis of a coordinate system	Numeric
	y_pos_centre	The position of the component w.r.t. the y axis of a coordinate system	Numeric
Topological	on_top	True if a block is above another block	Boolean
	to_right	True if a block is to the right of another block	Boolean
	only_right_col	True if a block is vertically aligned with another block on the right margin	Boolean
	only_left_col	True if a block is vertically aligned with another block on the left margin	Boolean
	only_middle_col	True if a block is vertically aligned with another block on the middle	Boolean
	only_middle_row	True if a block is horizontally aligned with another block on the middle	Boolean
	only_lower_row	True if a block is horizontally aligned with another block on the lower margin	Boolean
	only_upper_row	True if a block is horizontally aligned with another block on the upper margin	Boolean
Aspatial	type_of	The content type of a logical component	{image, text, horizontal line, vertical line, graphic, mixed}
Geometrical	height	The height of a logical component	Numeric
	width	The width of a logical component	Numeric

However, the use of multiple classification leads to the problem of "unbalanced datasets". In fact, data can be characterized by a predominant number of negative examples with respect to the number of positive examples (e.g. in the examples reported in section 4, the percentage of layout components classified as "*table*" is 1.4% of all layout components). Several approaches that face the problem of the unbalanced datasets have been proposed in the literature. Some of them are based on a sampling of examples in order to have a balanced dataset [9]. Other approaches are based on a different idea: given the class, a ranking of all the examples in the test set from the most probable member to the least probable member is computed and then, a correctly calibrated estimate of the true probability that each test example is a member of the class of interest is computed [18]. In other words, a probability threshold that delimitates the membership and the non-membership of a given test example to the class is computed. In our approach, we exploit the consideration that the naive Bayesian classifier for two-class problems tends to rank examples well (even if the classifier does not return a correct probability estimation)[18]. In our solution, the threshold is determined by maximizing the AUC (Area Under the ROC Curve) [12] according to a cost function:

$$cost = P(Ci) \cdot (1 - TP) \cdot c(\neg Ci;\ Ci) + P(\neg Ci) \cdot FP \cdot c(Ci;\ \neg Ci)$$

where $P(Ci)$ is the a-priori probability that an example belongs to the class Ci, $P(\neg Ci)$ is the a-priori probability that an example does not belong to the class Ci, $c(\neg Ci; Ci)$ is the cost of classifying a positive example as negative (for the class Ci) and $c(Ci; \neg Ci)$ is the cost of classifying a negative example as positive. TP is the true positive rate and FP is the false positive rate. We denote as *CostRatio* the value:

$CostRatio = c(Ci; \neg Ci)/c(\neg Ci; Ci)$.

The Mr-SBC database input schema (see figure 1) represents the logical structure of a document image. In particular, we represent locational features, geometrical features, topological relations and aspatial features (see Table 1).

3 Application of ATRE

ATRE [8] is a (multi-)relational ILP (Inductive Logic Programming) system that can learn logic theories from examples and which is able to handle symbolic as well as numerical descriptors. In this framework, ATRE learns first order rules that can be subsequently used in the classification step. Formally, ATRE solves the following learning problem:

Given:
- a set of concepts $C_1, C_2, \ldots, C_r$ to be learned,
- a set of observations O described in a language L_O,
- a background knowledge BK expressed in a language L_{BK},
- a language of hypotheses L_H,
- a generalization model G over the space of hypotheses,
- a user's preference criterion PC,

Find
a (possibly recursive) logical theory T for the concepts $C_1, C_2, \ldots, C_r$, such that T is complete and consistent with respect to O and satisfies the preference criterion PC.

The *completeness* property holds when the theory T explains all observations in O of the r concepts C_i, while the *consistency* property holds when the theory T explains no counter-example in O of any concept C_i. The satisfaction of these properties guarantees the correctness of the induced theory with respect to O.

In ATRE, observations are represented by means of ground multiple-head clauses, called *objects*. In this application, each object corresponds to a document page. All literals in the head of the clause are called *examples* of the concepts $C_1, C_2, \ldots, C_r$. They can be considered either positive or negative according to the learning goal. In this application domain, the concepts to be learned are logical labels (e.g. $title(X)=true$, $page\_number(X)=true$, etc.), since we are interested in finding rules which predict the logical label of a layout component. No rule is generated for the case $title(X)=false$.

The generalization model provides the basis for organizing the search space, since it establishes when a hypothesis explains a positive/negative example and when a hypothesis is more general/specific than another. The generalization model adopted by ATRE, called *generalized implication*, is explained in [8].

The preference criterion PC is a set of conditions used to discard/favour some solutions. In this work, short rules, which explain a high number of positive examples and a low number of negative examples, are preferred.

In ATRE, the application of a first-order logic language permits to represent both unary and binary function symbols. Unary function symbols, called *attributes*, used to describe properties of a single layout component (e.g. *height*), while binary predicate and function symbols, called *relations*, are used to express spatial relationships among layout components (e.g., *part-of* or *on_top*). Similarly to the case of Mr-SBC, for ATRE the following descriptors have been used to represent features reported in Table 1: *width(block)*, *height(block)*, *x_pos_centre(block)*, *y_pos_centre(block)*, *type_of(block)*, *on_top(block1, block2)*, *to_right(block1,block2)*, *only_left_col(block1, block2)*,.... Moreover, in ATRE the descriptor *part_of(page,block)* is necessary in order to describe that a layout component belongs to a document page.

An example of an object representation is reported in the following:

```
class(1)=tpami, affiliation(2)=false, …, paragraph(2)=false,
title(3)=true, ..., table(3)=false,
...
affiliation(15)=false, ..., references(15)=false, paragraph(15)=true
← page(1)=first, part_of(1,2)=true, ..., part_of(1,13)=true,
    width(2)=391, ..., width(13)=263,
    height(2)=9, ..., height(13)=58,
    type_of(2)=text, ..., type_of(13)=image,
    x_pos_centre(2)=354, ..., x_pos_centre(13)=411,
    y_pos_centre(2)=29, ..., y_pos_centre(13)=753,
    on_top(2,4)=true, ..., on_top(12,13)=true,
    to_right(11,12)=true, ..., to_right(3,6)=true,
    only_left_col(3,8)=true, ..., only_upper_row(8,10)=true.
```

where the constant 1 denotes the whole page, while the constants 2, 3, …,15 denote the layout components.

4   Experiments

For a fair comparison of the two learning methods, both Mr-SBC and ATRE are trained on the same dataset consisting of multi-page articles published in an international journal. In particular, we considered twenty-one papers, published as either regular or short, in the IEEE Transactions on Pattern Analysis and Machine Intelligence, in the January and February issues of 1996. Each paper is a multi-page document; therefore, we processed 197 document images in all and the user manually labeled 2436 layout components, that is, in average, 116 components per document, 12.37 per page. About 74% of the layout components have been labeled, the remaining components are "irrelevant" for the task in hand or are associated to "noise" blocks: they are automatically considered *undefined*. A description of the dataset is reported in Table 2.

The performance of the learning tasks is evaluated by means of a 5-fold cross-validation[3], that is, the set of twenty-one documents is first divided into five folds, and then, for every fold, Mr-SBC and ATRE are trained on the remaining folds and tested on the hold-out fold.

---

[3] Data in the first-order logic format are available on-line at the following url: http://www.di.uniba.it/~ceci/micFiles/5fold_cross_validation_Tpami.rar

Table 2. Dataset description: Distribution of pages and examples per document grouped by 5 folds

Fold No	Name of the multi-page document	No. of pages	No. of labeled components	Total No. of components
1	TPAMI_1	13	476	597
	TPAMI_13	3		
	TPAMI_14	10		
	TPAMI_16	14		
2	TPAMI_8	5	519	684
	TPAMI_15	15		
	TPAMI_18	10		
	TPAMI_24	6		
3	TPAMI_3	15	481	697
	TPAMI_7	6		
	TPAMI_12	6		
	TPAMI_20	14		
4	TPAMI_9	5	541	774
	TPAMI_11	6		
	TPAMI_19	20		
	TPAMI_21	11		
5	TPAMI_4	14	419	549
	TPAMI_6	1		
	TPAMI_10	3		
	TPAMI_17	13		
	TPAMI_23	7		
Total	21 documents	197	2436	3301

For each learning problem, the number of omission/commission errors is recorded. Omission errors occur when logical labelling of layout components are missed, while commission errors occur when wrong logical labelling are "recommended" by classifiers. In our study we do not consider the standard classification accuracy, because for each learning task, the number of positive and negative examples is strongly unbalanced and, in most cases, the trivial classifier that returns always "undefined" would be the classifier with the best accuracy. On the contrary, we are generally interested in reducing omission errs rather than maximizing accuracy.

In figure 2, results of Mr-SBC varying the *CostRatio* in {1,2,4,…,20} are reported. Increasing *CostRatio*, we give more importance to the cost $c(Ci; \neg Ci)$ rather than $c(\neg Ci; Ci)$. In fact, we note that, as we expected, increasing the *CostRatio*, the precision decreases and the recall increases.

In Table 3 results that permit to compare the two systems both in terms of efficiency and effectiveness of the learning task are reported (in this experiment, for Mr-SBC, we set *CostRatio*=10). We note that the statistical classifier is, in general, more efficient than the logical approach. In terms of omission errors, the two systems do not show great difference. However, looking at results on commission errors, we

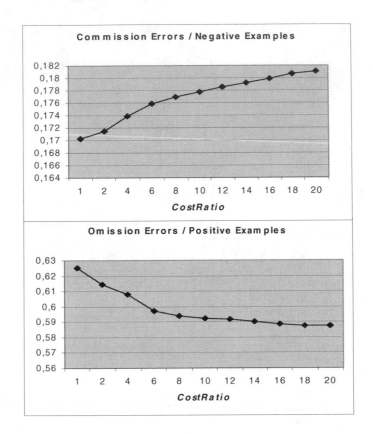

Fig.2. Avarage number of omission errors over positive examples and of commission errors over negative examples varying *CostRatio*

can conclude that ATRE outperforms Mr-SBC in terms of classification effectiveness. In a deeper analysis, we note that Mr-SBC outperforms ATRE, in terms of omission errors, when the size of the layout component does not show great variability (e.g. this is the case of *section title*, *subsection title*, *title* and is not the case of *table* and *figure*). This can be explained by considering that the discretization algorithm implemented in Mr-SBC does not take into account combination of features (e.g. the size of a layout component is computed independently from the page order) [4]. This aspect negatively affects the learned classification model. Concerning ATRE, we note that the results are characterized by a high percentage of omission errors and a low percentage of commission errors. This is due to a lower percentage of positive examples that generally leads to a specificity of learned rules with a low percentage of coverage of training examples. Specificity of learned rules is due to the fact that ATRE is asked to generate a complete theory, that is a set of rules that explain all positive examples. Moreover, ATRE was not able to learn the concept "*paragraph*" since the high number of positive examples significantly increases the complexity of the task.

Table 3 Mr SBC vs. ATRE: Average number of omission errors over positive examples, commission errors over negative examples and learning times (in secs)

	Omiss/Pos		Comm/Neg		Learning Times (s)	
	ATRE	Mr-SBC	ATRE	Mr-SBC	ATRE	Mr-SBC
Abstract	**0.55**	0.81	0.00	0.21	660	492
Affiliation	**0.50**	0.77	0.00	0.25	756	564
Author	0.46	**0.40**	0.00	0.26	732	504
Biography	0.63	**0.57**	0.00	0.26	636	444
Caption	**0.68**	0.74	0.03	0.23	12240	552
Figure	**0.13**	0.62	0.02	0.23	4440	960
Formulae	**0.45**	0.57	0.06	0.07	21120	624
Index Term	0.53	**0.27**	0.00	0.22	169.6	564
Reference	0.95	**0.60**	0.01	0.21	1884	480
Table	**0.69**	0.83	0.01	0.06	1668	528
Page No	**0.04**	0.26	0.00	0.01	490	660
Paragraph	----	**0.89**	----	0.03	----	1572
Running Head	**0.09**	0.55	0.00	0.01	485.4	504
Section Title	0.80	**0.48**	0.01	0.27	2052	516
Subsection Title	1.00	**0.72**	0.00	0.27	1068	468
Title	0.60	**0.39**	0.00	0.25	648	636

For a complete analysis, we have to consider that the statistical classifier is able to rank the layout components giving a "confidence" of the classification. Such information can help the user to manually correct and interpret classification results. On the other hand, ATRE returns a set of first order rules that can be easily interpreted by the user, thus allowing to understand the decisions taken. Some example of rule learned by ATRE are:

```
abstract(X1)=true        ←        alignment(X1,X2)=only_right_col,
height(X2) in [384...422], y_pos_centre(X1) in [169...197]

    figure(X1)=true ←- type_of(X1)=image, width(X1) in [12..227],
x_pos_centre(X1) in [335..570]

    references(X1)=true                ←                to_right(X1,X2)=true,
biography(X2)=true, width(X2) in [261..265]
```

They can be easily interpreted. For instance, the first rule states that a layout component with the baricentre at a point between 169 and 197 on the y-axis and vertically aligned with a layout component with height between 384 and 422 (e.g. the title) is an abstract. The last rule shows that ATRE can also automatically discover meaningful dependencies between concepts.

5 Conclusions

This work presents an application of (multi-)relational learning techniques to the problem of document image understanding. In particular, two learning methods, namely Mr-SBC and ATRE, based on a statistical approach and a logical approach, respectively, are compared. For the evaluation, both methods have been embedded in the DIA system WISDOM++.

While Mr-SBC directly interfaces the internal WISDOM++ database schema, ATRE needs some preprocessing in order to transform the internal representation of the layout structure in first-order logic representation. Results show that Mr-SBC is more efficient than ATRE in terms of running times. Concerning classification effectiveness, while ATRE outperforms Mr-SBC in terms of omission errors, in terms of commission errors the systems do not show great differences. Weaknesses for Mr-SBC and ATRE are respectively due to the discretization algorithm and to the strong assumptions of completeness and consistency of the learned theories. In terms of understandability of the learned model, although Mr-SBC provides a confidence of the classification result, ATRE provides a set of rules that are easily comprehensible to humans.

For future work, we intend to improve the Mr-SBC algorithm allowing contextual discretization and to explore the opportunity of weakening the conditions of applicability of rules in ATRE in order to significantly recover omission errors.

Acknowledgments

This work has been supported by the annual Scientific Research Project "Gestione dell'informazione non strutturata: modelli, metodi e architetture" Year 2005 funded by the University of Bari.

References

1. Aiello M., Monz C., Todoran L., Worring M.: Document Understanding for a Broad Class of Documents. International Journal of Document Analysis and Recognition IJDAR (2002) 5(1), 1-16.
2. Akindele O.T., Belaïd A.: Construction of generic models of document structures using inference of tree grammars. Proceedings of the 3rd ICDAR (1995) 206-209.
3. Altamura O., Esposito F., Malerba D.: Transforming paper documents into XML format with WISDOM++. International Journal on Document Analysis and Recognition IJDAR (2001) 4(1), 2-17.
4. Ceci M., Appice A., Malerba D.: Mr-SBC: a Multi-Relational Naive Bayes Classifier. Principles and Practice of Knowledge Discovery in Databases, 7th European Conference, PKDD (2003) volume 2838 of LNAI, pages 95–106. Springer-Verlag.
5. Domingos P., Pazzani M.: On the optimality of the simple bayesian classifier under zero-one loss. Machine Learning (1997) 29(2-3):103–130.
6. Dzeroski S., Lavrac N.: Relational Data Mining. Springer-Verlag, Berlin Germany (2001).
7. Le Bourgeois F., Souafi-Bensafi S., Duong J., Parizeau M., Coté M., Emptoz H: Using statistical models in document images understanding. Workshop on Document Layout Interpretation and its Applications, DLIA (2001).
8. Malerba D.: Learning recursive theories in the normal ilp setting. Fundamenta Informaticae (2003) 57(1):39–77.
9. Mladenic D., Grobelnik M.: Feature selection for unbalanced class distribution and naive bayes. Proc. of the 16th International Conference on Machine Learning ICML (1999) 258–267.

10. Palmero G.I.S., Dimitriadis Y.A.: Structured Document Labeling and Rule Extraction using a New Recurrent Fuzzy-neural System. International Journal of Document Analysis and Recognition IJDAR (1999) 181-184.
11. Pearl J.: Probabilistic reasoning in intelligent systems: networks of plausible inference. Morgan Kaufmann, 1988.
12. Provost F., Fawcett T.: Robust classification for imprecise environments. Machine Learning (2001) 42(3):203–231.
13. Quinlan J.R.: C4.5: programs for machine learning. Morgan Kaufmann Publishers Inc., 1993.
14. Rosenfeld A., Hummel R.A., Zucker S.W.: Scene labeling by relaxation operations, IEEE Transactions SMC 6(6), 1976.
15. Sebastiani F.: Machine learning in automated text categorization. ACM Computing Surveys (2002) 34(1):1-47.
16. Taskar B., Abbeel P., Koller D.: Discriminative probabilistic models for relational data. Proc. of Int. Conf. on Uncertainty in Artificial Intelligence (2002) 485-492.
17. Walischewski H.: Automatic knowledge acquisition for spatial document interpretation. Proc. of the 4th International Conference on Document Analysis and Recognition ICDAR (1997) 243-247.
18. Zadrozny B. Elkan C.: Obtaining calibrated probability estimates from decision trees and naive bayesian classifiers. Proc. of the 18th International Conference on Machine Learning ICML (2001) 609–616.

Handling Continuous-Valued Attributes in Incremental First-Order Rules Learning

Teresa M.A. Basile, Floriana Esposito, Nicola Di Mauro, and Stefano Ferilli

Department of Computer Science, University of Bari, Italy
{basile, esposito, ndm, ferilli}@di.uniba.it

Abstract. Machine Learning systems are often distinguished according to the kind of representation they use, which can be either propositional or first-order logic. The framework working with first-order logic as a representation language for both the learned theories and the observations is known as Inductive Logic Programming (ILP). It has been widely shown in the literature that ILP systems have limitations in dealing with large amounts of numerical information, that is however a peculiarity of most real-world application domains. In this work we present a strategy to handle such information in a relational learning incremental setting and its integration with classical symbolic approaches to theory revision. Experiments were carried out on a real-world domain and a comparison with a state-of-art system is reported.

1   Introduction

Traditional application of Machine Learning to intelligent systems development involves collecting a set of training examples, expressing them in a representation language such that the corresponding representation space facilitates learning, and using a learning algorithm to induce a set of concepts from the codified training examples. The induced concepts are subsequently validated, incorporated into an inferential system and deployed into an environment. It is well known that the choice of the proper representation for a learning problem has a significant impact on the performance of learning systems. In traditional learning problems, the training examples are typically represented as vectors of attribute-value (*attribute-value or propositional learners*). In most complex real-world domains, however, the exploitation of this kind of representation language could affect the learning efficiency. In such domains, the adoption of a more powerful representation language is required; for instance, the language of first-order logic, a natural extension to propositional representations, is able to describe any kind of relation between two or more objects. The systems that exploit such a representation are called *relational* or *Inductive Logic Programming* learning systems. Differently from the propositional representation, however, in which only a single mapping is possible between descriptions, this representation language allows a potentially large number of mappings between descriptions. Thus, it becomes more difficult to handle relationships among data and, in particular, numerical information due to the non-determinacy in relational learning, i.e. the possibility of associating more than one value to the numerical attributes for examples.

S. Bandini and S. Manzoni (Eds.): AI*IA 2005, LNAI 3673, pp. 430–441, 2005.

This is not true for the propositional case in which the correspondence between each attribute and its value is one-to-one for each example.

The problem is accentuated if we consider the approach exploited in the learning task. Classical approaches, using *batch* methodologies, assume/require that all the information needed is available at the beginning of the learning process. This is clearly not generally true for the knowledge assimilation process, in particular in those real-world applications that require the ability of incrementally revising a domain theory as new data is encountered. In these cases *incremental* learning, as opposed to batch learning, is needed. However, the management of numerical information in incremental approaches becomes more complex due to the fact that the induction of numerical attributes must take into account the non-determinacy in the relational learning and must be performed and revised each time a new observation is encountered.

In this paper, after a brief description of the works concerned with topic of handling numerical information in relational learning, we present a strategy to handle such information in an incremental relational learning setting and its integration with classical symbolic approaches to theory revision. Some experiments were carried out on a real-world domain and a comparison with a state-of-art system is reported.

2   Related Work

Inductive Logic Programming (ILP for short) algorithms have shown their inadequacy in dealing with the large amounts of numerical information that characterize most real-world application domains. This problem has been addressed by means of different approaches. In propositional learning, discretization has received a lot of attention [6, 8, 9] and it has proven to be a valuable technique with respect to efficiency and accuracy. The general idea of discretization [16, 13] consists in splitting a range of continuous values into intervals so as to provide useful information about classes. Moving towards relational learning, the first question in ILP is: *what to discretize?*. Indeed, in relational learning each attribute in the attribute-value representation is mapped in an *argument* of a predicate. So, instead of discretizing a numerical attribute, we have to discretize a numerical argument. The problem now is that each numerical argument has a corresponding query that generates all the values of the numerical argument that can have 0,1 or more values *per example*.

A number of methods have been devised to solve the problem: The first class of methods, as in LINUS [14], concerns the transformation of relational problems into equivalent propositional ones in order to handle real numbers by means of techniques already tested in decision tree induction systems. Different methods of propositionalization have been implemented in REPART [21] and in ICP [17]. In the former the propositionalization pattern is provided by the user, while in the latter it is built from the training set. More recently, a lazy propositionalization method that selectively propositionalizes the first-order logic training set by interleaving attribute-value reformulation and algebraic resolution has been proposed [1]. The other classes of methods born for handling numerical features in an ILP setting use *a priori* knowledge, either in a procedural form as in FOIL [5] or in a declarative form as in Progol [15]. FOIL automatically produces comparative literals by means of built-in relational predicates expressed on numerical variables already present in other non-comparative literals and compared with a threshold. The semantics of the built-in relational predicates, as well as the heuristics for the selection of the best threshold, are defined procedurally and embedded in the code of the system. On the contrary, Progol explicitly *codes* the capability of numerical reasoning in a declarative form as background knowledge.

Other techniques involved the classical statistical data analysis research area that was extended with new tools of formalization in order to deal with symbolic data. This kind of integration is more complex when using first-order computational learning models due to the practical and theoretical possibility of integrating different computational strategies, different knowledge representations and different processing methods in a common framework. In [12] the authors faced the problem of handling both numerical and symbolic data in first-order models, distinguishing the phase of *model generation* from examples, concerning the on-line discretization of numerical attributes and relations, and the phase of *model recognition* by means of a flexible probabilistic coverage test. Other hybrid approaches make cooperative techniques coming from ILP and Constraint Logic Programming by means of a transformation step of counter-examples into constraints [17]. The approach proceeds generating the equivalent Constraint Satisfaction Problem (CSP) of an ILP problem: all constrained clauses that cover positive examples and reject negative ones can be trivially derived from the solutions of the CSP corresponding to the original ILP problem. Successively, the CSP is solved by means of a constraint solver and this will allow to build the set of solutions in terms of hypotheses space.

Algorithms for mapping propositional Horn clauses to neural networks have been presented by several authors [19, 2, 20]. The basic idea underlying the proposed strategies in such context is that a propositional theory can be functionally described by an **and/or** graph having atomic expressions in leaves. Such a graph can be transformed into a neural network by replacing the boolean $\wedge$ and $\vee$ operators in the nodes with continuous, derivable functions and by adding weights on the links. This method was extended and adapted to first-order theories, First Order Neural Network (FONN), as in [4], where it is implemented a method to translate a first-order classification theory into a neural network of elementary computational units that are refined, by means of an error gradient descent, preserving the readability of the theory. The method works on a theory that is supposed to be already generated by a relational learner or manually given by a domain expert, and tries to refine exclusively the numerical information expressed on the arguments of the predicates. Finally, some works to face the problem of managing numerical data concern the combination of ILP strategies with Evolutionary Computation techniques. Examples of this kind of approaches are SMART+ [3] and the work by Divina et al. [7]. In the former case the system transforms the real numbers into discrete integers that can be encoded as binary numbers, and exploits genetic algorithms to handle such values. In the latter case, the Authors propose to handle numerical attributes by using the relational built-in constraints. During the execution of a genetic-algorithm-based inductive concept learner, a constraint for a numerical attribute is generated when that attribute is selected and, successively, it is modified during the evolutionary process by using genetic operators, that were defined by the Authors and that exploit information on the distribution of the values of attributes in order to update the interval boundaries of the constraints.

All the methods above mentioned are based on the assumption that batch approaches are applied to the learning task. Here we address the problem of handling numerical information in an incremental setting that exploits first-order logic as a representation language.

3   Handling Continuous-Valued Data in an Incremental FOL Learning System

In this section we present the extensions of the incremental ILP learning system INTHELEX [11] to make it able to handle numerical data. In such a system two entities are involved in the learning process, observations and hypotheses. Both are expressed by means of Datalog clauses (function-free Horn clauses - only constants or variables are allowed in the description), and are interpreted under the assumption of the Object Identity (OI) (*terms denoted in different way have to represent distinct objects in the description* [18]).

In the pure symbolic representation, both observations and hypotheses are represented using the same formalism, and differ in the kind of arguments on which their literals are built: constants in case of the observations, variables in case of the hypotheses. Now we need to extend the representation formalism to introduce numerical values in both observations and hypotheses. Trivially, in the observations we introduce the numerical constants and represent them in the same way of the symbolic ones; in the hypotheses, each numerical value is associated to a variable, that in the following we will call *numerical variable*, on which it is defined an interval properly determined on the grounds of the observations. Thus we can distinguish, in the observations: *numerical predicates* (iff at least one of its arguments is a numerical constant); *symbolic predicates* (iff its arguments are all symbolic constants); *numerical constants* (numeric strings); *symbolic constants* (alphanumeric strings that begin with a lower-case letter). As to the hypotheses, we firstly need to say that, in the following, a numerical constraint on a variable is so defined:

Definition 1 (Numerical Constraint). *A numerical Constraint C on a variable V is a disjunction of numerical intervals ($Range_1$; $Range_2$; ...; $Range_n$) where $Range_i = (Inf, Supp)$ for $i = 1 .. n$ and*
$Inf = (V \geq numerical\ value)\ OR\ Inf = (V > numerical\ value)$
$Supp = (V \leq numerical\ value)\ OR\ Supp = (V < numerical\ value)$

Thus, in the hypotheses we can distinguish: *numerical predicates* (iff at least one of its arguments is a numerical variable); *symbolic predicates* (iff its arguments are all symbolic variables); *symbolic variables* (variable - alphanumeric strings that begin with an upper-case letter); *numerical variables* (variable - alphanumeric string that begin with an upper-case letter) on which a numerical constraint is defined); *numerical constraints* reported above. It is worth noting that a numerical predicate always contains at least one symbolic term.

3.1   Modification to the Object Identity Framework

The extension of the representational language to make it able to describe numerical information in observations and hypotheses, highlighted a practical problem as regards the OI assumption that is used in the framework. Indeed, since the same numerical value could be associated as property of more than one object (e.g., same width for two blocks), we cannot impose the constraints derived from such assumption on numerical data. Thus, the transformation from a Datalog clause to its corresponding Datalog^{OI} (Datalog clause under the OI assumption) is reformulated in the following way:

Definition 2. *Any Datalog clause $C = \{L_1, L_2, \ldots, L_n\}$ has a corresponding Datalog^{OI} clause $C_{OI} = \{ core(C_{OI}) \bigcup constraints(C_{OI}) \}$, where:*
$core(C_{OI}) = \{ L_1, L_2, \ldots, L_n \} = C$
$constraints(C_{OI}) = \{\neq(t_1, t_2) | t_1, t_2 \in terms(C), t_1 \neq t_2 \; forall \; terms(C) \notin numeric\_terms(C)\}$
where numeric_terms(C) represents the set of constants that are numerical values or the set of variables that represent a numerical property.

Furthermore, the notion of substitution, regarded as a function mapping variables to terms, that under the OI assumption should be an injective mapping, has to be revised taking into account the above considerations. Thus, given a set of terms T, we say a substitution σ is an *OI-substitution with respect to T* if and only if for all couples of terms $t_1, t_2 \in T$ that are not number we have: $t_1 \neq t_2 \Rightarrow t_1\sigma \neq t_2\sigma$.

Let us now see how it is possible to formally define refinement operators, starting from the definitions given in [10], in order to take into account the numerical information on which the OI constraint is not valid.

Definition 3 (Downward Refinement Operator ρ_{OI}). *Let C be a Datalog^{OI} clause. Then, a clause D belongs to the set of the downward refinements of the clause C, i.e. $D \in \rho_{OI}(C)$, when either of these conditions hold:*

(i) *$D = C\theta$, where $\theta = \{X/a\}$, $X \in vars(C)$, $a \notin symbolic\_consts(C)$, that is, θ is a substitution replacing a symbolic variable of C with a new symbolic constant, i.e. not already present in C;*

(ii) *$D = C\theta$, where $\theta = \{X/a\}$, $X \in vars(C)$, $a \in numeric\_consts(Numerical\_Constraint)$, that is, θ is a substitution replacing a numerical variable of C with a numerical constant belongs to Numerical_Constraint that is the numerical constraint defined on the numerical variable that one is replacing;*

(iii) $D = C \cup \{\neg A\}$, *where* $\neg A$ *is a symbolic literal, such that:* $\neg A \notin C$;

(iv) $D = C \cup \{\{\neg A\}, \{Numeric\_Constraints\}\}$, *where* $\neg A$ *is a numerical literal, such that:* $\neg A \notin C$. $\{Numeric\_Constraints\} \notin C$ *is the set of numeric constraints defined on the numeric variables that are arguments of the literal A (note that if A does not contains variables, but only constants this set is empty).*

Definition 4 (Upward Refinement Operator δ_{OI}**).** *Let C be a Datalog^{OI} clause. Then, a clause D belongs to the set of the upward refinements of the clause C, i.e. $D \in \delta_{OI}(C)$ when either of these conditions hold:*

(i) $D = C\sigma$, *where* $\sigma = \{a/X\}$, $a \in symbolic\_consts(C)$, $X \notin vars(C)$, *that is,* σ *is an anti-substitution replacing a symbolic constant of C with a new variable;*

(ii) $D = C \setminus \{\neg A\}$, *where* $\neg A$ *is a symbolic literal, such that:* $\neg A \in C$;

(iii) $D = C \setminus \{\{\neg A\}, \{\neg Numeric\_Constraint\}\}$, *where* $\neg A$ *is a numerical literal, such that:* $\neg A \in C$ *and* $\{\neg Numeric\_Constraint\} \in C$ *is the set of numerical constraints that are defined on the set of numerical terms of the literal A.*

Note that: $C = H, \neg B_1, \ldots, \neg B_n \equiv (H : -B_1, \ldots, B_n)$ thus, adding/removing $\neg A$ from C is equivalent to add/remove a literal from the body clause. The operators above defined fulfill the same properties, that are deemed as desirable from a theoretical point of view, as the symbolic ones reported in [10].

3.2   Refinement Operators

Here we present a sketch of the procedure implemented by the refinement operators exploited in the system in order to handle the numerical information and their integration with the classical inductive refinement operators, that work on symbolic information, embedded in the system in consideration. When a new observation is taken into account three situations can happen: The observation (positive or negative) is correctly classified; The observation is positive and the system does not correctly classify it; The observation is negative and the system does not correctly classify it. In the first case the theory is correct and thus it does not need any revision. In the second (respectively, the third) case the theory is too specific (respectively, too general) and, thus, it needs to be revised: specifically, a generalization phase, or upward refinement, (respectively, a specialization phase or downward refinement) is required. The classical inductive refinement operators exploited in the framework operate in the following way:

- Generalization phase - Inductive Upward Refinement:
  1. eliminating one (or more) literal(s) from the clause that does not cover the positive observation;
  2. adding a new clause to the theory - the observation itself with constants properly turned into variables.
- Specialization phase - Inductive Downward Refinement:
  1. adding one (or more) literal(s), coming from the past positive observations to the clause that covers the negative observation;
  2. adding the negation of a literal, coming from the negative observation that caused the misclassification, to the clause that covers the negative observation.

A modification of these operators to handle numerical information is necessary. Firstly, we present the definition of inductive refinement operators able to handle numerical information. Then a framework for the integration of the operators that work on both numerical and symbolic information will be provided. As regards their definition, it is articulated in two phases, as reported in the following, one for the addition of a new numerical constraint and the other for the modification of an existing numerical constraint.

- **addition of a new numerical constraint.** Firstly, for each numerical constant c found in the observation it is replaced with a new variable V in the literal it is argument of. Then, to such a new variable V it is associated the proper numerical constraint based on the value of the numerical constant in the observation. In other words, given an observation, let $descr(c_1, c_2, c_3, \ldots, c_n)$ a numerical literal in such a observation. Now suppose that the **i-th** argument ($i = 1, \ldots, n$) is a numerical constant which value is k; then it will become: $descr(c_1, c_2, \ldots, V_i, \ldots, c_n), (V_i \geq k, V_i \leq k)$.

Example 1. Let C the following clause:
```
bicycle(a) ← part_of(a,b), part_of(a,c), wheel(b), large(b,10),
            wheel(c), large(c,15), distance(b,c,10).
```
The resulting clause is:
```
bicycle(a) ← part_of(a,b), part_of(a,c),
            wheel(b), large(b,Y), (Y >= 10, Y =< 10),
            wheel(c), large(c,Z), (Z >= 15, Z =<15),
            distance(b,c,W), (W >= 10, W =< 10).
```

- **modification of an existing numerical constraint.** This phase proceeds according to the situation at hand.
    i. *positive observation not covered - generalization of a numerical constraint.* Let $Constr$ be the numerical constraint that has to be modified, specifically generalized, due to a misclassification of a positive observation. This situation arises because at least one of the numerical values, that is a property of an object in the positive observation, does not fulfill the numerical constraint in the clause. Let v_i be such a numerical value. As we known, the numerical constraint $Constr$ is a disjunction of numerical intervals: $Constr = [Range_1; Range_2; \ldots; Range_m]$; the situations that can hold are the following:
        - v_i is included between two intervals
            if $(Range_j = (a_j, b_j)$ and $Range_{j+1} = (a_{j+1}, b_{j+1}))$ and $v_i \in [b_j, a_{j+1}]$ for some $j = 2, \ldots, m-1$ **then**
            $Range_j = (a_j, v_i)$ iff $|v_i - b_j| \leq |v_i - a_{j+1}|$ OR
            $Range_{j+1} = (v_i, b_{j+1})$ iff $|v_i - b_j| \geq |v_i - a_{j+1}|$
        - v_i is a value lower than the first value of the first interval
            if $Range_1 = (a_1, b_1)$ and $v_i \in]-\infty, a_1]$ **then** $Range_1 = (v_i, b_1)$
        - v_i is a value greater than the last value of the last interval
            if $Range_m = (a_m, b_m)$ and $v_i \in [b_m, +\infty[$ **then** $Range_m = (a_m, v_i)$

ii. *negative observation covered - specialization of a numerical constraint.* Let *Constr* be the numerical constraint to be modified, specifically specialized, due to a misclassification of a negative observation. This situation arises because at least one of the numerical values, that is a property of an object in the negative observation, fulfills the numerical constraint in the clause. Let v_i be such a numerical value. As we known, the numerical constraint *Constr* is a disjunction of numerical intervals: $Constr = [Range_1; Range_2; \ldots; Range_m]$; the situations that can hold are the following:
- v_i satisfies one of the intervals:

    if $Range_j = (a_j, b_j)$, $v_i \in (a_j, b_j)$ for some $j = 1, \ldots, m$ **then**
    $Range_j = (a_j, v_i[\ \lor \ ]v_i, b_j)$

The modification phases, generalization and specialization of numerical intervals, refer reciprocally. In this way, the resulting interval is not affected by the order of example sequence[1]. The addition phase could refer the modification phase that operates on the new numerical constraint just introduced in the clause. The stop criterion in these mutual references is the restoring of the theory correctness with respect to the previous examined observations. The schema reported in the following sketched the integration of the *numerical operators* above defined with the classical inductive operators.

- Inductive Upward Refinement (generalization phase) - Let be C the clause that does not cover the positive example, then:
  a) eliminate one (or more) symbolic literal(s) from C;
  b) eliminate one (or more) numerical literal(s), with the relative numerical constraints, from C;
  c) modify (generalization) the numerical constraints in C;
  d) add a new clause to the theory - the observation itself with symbolic constants properly turned into variables and with numerical constants properly associated to a variable on which a numerical constraint is imposed.

  The steps b) and c) concern the numerical refinement. The procedure described in b) is simultaneously activated with the procedure described in a) allowing the elimination of both symbolic and numerical literals. However, if a numerical literal is eliminated from the description of the clause, then the associated numerical constraints have to be eliminated too. If only symbolic literals are eliminated by the procedure and the correctness of the theory is not restored because of the presence of numerical constraints, then step c) is activated starting from the positive observation under examination and from all the previously negative observations seen. If it is not possible to modify the numerical constraints, they are removed from the description of the clause with their associated numerical literals.
- Inductive Downward Refinement (specialization phase) - Let be C the clause that covers the negative observation, then:

---

[1] However, the integration of these operators with the inductive symbolic ones, will suffer from the phenomenon of ordering effects – a phenomenon occurring when different orderings of the same training set give out different results.

a') add one (or more) symbolic literal(s), coming from the past positive observations to C;

b') add one (or more) numerical literal(s), coming from the past positive observations to C;

c') modify (specialization) the numerical constraints in C;

d') add the negation of a symbolic literal, coming from the negative observation that caused the misclassification, to C.

The specialization phase starts with the identification of the clause that erroneously covers the negative observation and analyzes the cause of the misclassification. Indeed, the misclassification of the observation can be due to the symbolic literals or to the numerical ones, i.e. to the violation of the numerical constraints. After this information is gained, the procedure continues with the proper step: if the numerical constraints are violated, step c') is activated with the specialization of the constraints, otherwise new (symbolic/numerical) literals are added to the clause (steps a') and b')). It is important to note that if a numerical literal is added then new numerical constraints, relative to the numerical variables of the literal, have to be created, modified and added to the clause as well.

4   Experiments

The numerical operators and their integration with the symbolic ones embedded in INTHELEX have been tested in the task concerning the extraction of rules for the automatic identification of logical components in scientific paper documents belonging to two different series (the Proceedings of the International Conference on Machine Learning, *ICML*, and the paper formatted according to the Springer Verlag Lectures Notes style, *SVLN*). The results were compared to those of the state-of-art ILP batch learning system Progol [15]. The first-order representation of the layout of such documents is made up of descriptions of the layout blocks that make up a paper document along with their size (height and width) and position (horizontal and vertical) in pixel, type (text, line, picture and mixed) and relative position (horizontal/vertical alignment, adjacency). All the experiments were performed according to a 10-fold cross validation methodology. For each class of documents, the layout blocks that are semantically significant for indexing/retrieval purposes were identified and annotated by expert users, and subsequently used as examples to learn rules for automatically recognizing them when new documents become available. Note that different document classes have different labels, as reported in the following (in square brackets the corresponding number of positive and negative instances is reported). The semantic labels of interest recognized by the domain experts for class *ICML* were: *abstract* [28+,340-], *author* [36+, 332-], *page_number* [27+, 341-] and *title* [29+, 339-]. As regards class *SVLN* the following labels characterizing the objects belonging to it were provided: *abstract* [32+,250-], *affiliation* [30+, 252-], *author* [30+, 252-] and *title* [30+,252-]. Each positive example for a label class to be learned was considered as negative for the others. Furthermore, any document block not labelled by the expert as significant was considered negative for all the components

Table 1. Understanding in scientific papers domain

	Clauses	Lgg's	Runtime (sec.)	Acc. %
ICML				
abstract	2.42	10.33	753.04	97.84
author	2.81	13.24	4055.14	97.66
page_number	2.48	12.24	1929.99	97.02
title	2.30	10.21	425.35	98.04
SVLN				
abstract	2.9	13	1800.61	94.93
affiliation	3.70	12.33	5285.94	94.52
author	4.48	13.96	7815.58	94.31
title	3.33	12.57	2119.14	94.14

to be learned. Table 1 reports the averaged results as regards number of clauses defining the concept (Cl), number of performed generalizations (Lgg), *Runtime* (in seconds) and Predictive Accuracy (Acc.). The overall outcomes reveal that the system was actually able to learn significant definitions for the layout blocks of interest in the documents. Indeed, the predictive accuracy is always very high reaching even 98.04% (never falls below 94.14%).

Figure 1 shows the definitions learned for the layout components of the *ICML* documents in one of the 10 folds. As shown, the learned rules have a high degree of understandability for human experts, thus it is possible to exactly recognize and map on a sample document the layout blocks referred to in the rules, e.g. the domain expert recognized block C, in the rule defining *logic_type_abstract*, as that containing the title (word) "Abstract" in a paper. The performance of the system were compared to that obtained by the Progol batch system (Table 2). For pairwise comparison a 10-fold cross validation paired t-test was used in order to evaluate the difference in effectiveness of the rules induced by the two systems according to the predictive accuracy metric. Requiring a significance level of $\alpha = 0.975$, the test revealed no statistically significant differences among them. Such a comparison turns out encouraging on the goodness of the proposed numerical operators. Indeed, Progol is an ILP system that exploits a batch strategy,

Table 2. Comparison with Progol

	Accuracy %		
ICML	INTHELEX	PROGOL	t VALUE
abstract	97.84	99.45	1.97
author	97.66	98.09	0.48
page_number	97.02	97.26	0.23
title	98.04	97.79	-0.27
SVLN			
abstract	94.93	95.02	0.05
affiliation	94.52	91.81	-1.53
author	94.31	91.13	-1.60
title	94.14	96.84	1.54

```
logic_type_abstract(A)  :-
    part_of(B,A),type_of_text(A),
    width(A,I),(I>=190,I=<210),
    part_of(B,C),type_of_text(C),
    width(C,D),(D>=79,D=<489),
    height(C,E),(E>=5,E=<15),
    x_pos_centre(C,F),(F>=7,F=<558),
    part_of(B,G),type_of_text(G),
    width(G,H),(H>=45,H=<54),
    on_top(G,A).
logic_type_author(A)  :-
    part_of(B,A),type_of_text(A),
    height(A,E),(E>=42,E=<71),
    width(A,F),(F>=109,F=<234),
    y_pos_centre(A,I),(I>=173,I=<272),
    part_of(B,C),type_of_text(C),
    on_top(D,A),
    alignment_center_col(G,D),
    width(G,H),(H>=502,H=<512).
```

```
logic_type_page_number(A):-
    type_of_text(A),part_of(B,A),
    part_of(B,C),type_of_hor_line(C),
    width(C,D),(D>=16,D=<512),
    height(C,E),(E>=1,E=<5),
    x_pos_centre(C,F),(F>=22,F=<343),
    width(A,G),(G>=9,G=<16),
    height(A,H),(H>=7,H=<8).

logic_type_title(A)  :-
    type_of_text(A),
    width(A,F),(F>=152,F=<505),
    part_of(B,A),part_of(B,C),
    type_of_text(C),part_of(B,D),
    on_top(A,D),
    x_pos_centre(D,E),(E>=291,E=<348).
```

Fig. 1. Learned definitions for ICML layout components

and hence it starts the learning process with all the observations available, which facilitates the operations on numerical data.

5   Conclusion and Future Works

In this paper we faced the problem of handling numerical information in an incremental setting exploiting first-order logic as a representation language. The limitations of relational learning systems in dealing with numerical data has been widely shown in the literature, the incremental nature of most real-world application domains further complicates the problem. We proposed a strategy to face these problems, and discussed its integration with classical inductive refinement operators. The strategy was embedded in the ILP system INTHELEX, and experiments carried out on a real-world domain showed good system performance, even compared to a state-of-art batch system. Future work will concern the optimization of such operators by exploiting statistical measures in the addition and modification phase of numerical constraints and extensive experimentation on different application domains.

References

[1] E. Alphonse and C. Rouveirol. Lazy propositionalisation for relational learning. In W. Horn, editor, *Proceedings of ECAI00*, pages 256–260. 2000.
[2] C. Baroglio, A. Giordana, M. Kaiser, M. Nuttin, and R. Piola. Learning controllers for industrial robots. *Machine Learning*, 23:221–250, 1996.

[3] M. Botta and A. Giordana. Smart+: A multi-strategy learning tool. In *Proceedings of IJCAI93*, pages 937–943, 1993.

[4] M. Botta and R. Piola. Refining numerical constants in first order logic theories. *Machine Learning*, 38:109–131, 2000.

[5] R.M. Cameron-Jones and J.R. Quinlan. Efficient top-down induction of logic programs, 1994.

[6] J. Catlett. On changing continuous attributes into ordered discrete attributes. In Y. Kodratoff, editor, *Proceedings of the Fifth European Working Conference on Learning*, volume 482 of *LNCS*, pages 164–178. Springer Verlag, 1991.

[7] F. Divina, M. Keijzer, and E. Marchiori. A method for handling numerical attributes in GA-based inductive concept learners. In *Genetic and Evolutionary Computation*, volume 2723 of *LNCS*, pages 898–908. Springer-Verlag, 2003.

[8] J. Doungherty, R. Kohavi, and M. Sahami. Supervised and unsupervised discretization of continuous features. In A. Prieditis and S. Russell, editors, *Proceedings of ICML95*, pages 194–202. Morgan Kaufmann, 1995.

[9] T. Elomaa. General and efficient multisplitting of numerical attributes. *Machine Learning*, 36:201–244, 1999.

[10] F. Esposito, N. Fanizzi, S. Ferilli, and G. Semeraro. Ideal theory refinement under object identity. In *Proceedings of ICML00*, pages 263–270, 2000.

[11] F. Esposito, S. Ferilli, N. Fanizzi, T.M.A. Basile, and N. Di Mauro. Incremental multistrategy learning for document processing. *Applied Artificial Intelligence*, 17(8/9):859–883, 2003.

[12] F. Esposito, D. Malerba, and V. Marengo. Inductive learning from numerical and symbolic data: An integrated framework. *Intelligent Data Analysis*, 5:445–461, 2001.

[13] U.M. Fayyad and K.B. Irani. Multi-interval discretization of continuous-valued attributes for classification learning. In *Proceedings of IJCAI93*, pages 1022–1027. Morgan Kaufmann, 1993.

[14] N. Lavrac and S. Dzeroski. *Inductive Logic Programming:Techniques and Applications*. Ellis Horwood, Chichester, 1994.

[15] S. Muggleton. Inverse entailment and Progol. *New Generation Computing, Special issue on Inductive Logic Programming*, 13(3-4):245–286, 1995.

[16] J.R. Quinlan. *C4.5: Programs for Machine Learning*. Morgan Kaufmann, San Mateo, CA, 1993.

[17] M. Sebag and C. Rouveirol. Constraint inductive logic programming. In L. De Raedt, editor, *Advances in Inductive Logic Programming*, pages 277–294. 1996.

[18] G. Semeraro, F. Esposito, D. Malerba, N. Fanizzi, and S. Ferilli. A logic framework for the incremental inductive synthesis of datalog theories. In N.E. Fuchs, editor, *Proceedings of LOPSTR98*, volume 1463 of *LNCS*, pages 300–321, 1998.

[19] V. Tresp, J. Hollatz, and S. Ahmad. Network structuring and training using rule-based knowledge. In S. Hanson, J. Cowan, and C. Giles, editors, *Advances in neural information processing systems 5*, pages 871–878. Morgan Kaufmann, 1993.

[20] L. A. Zadeh. Knowledge representation in fuzzy logic. In R. R. Yager and L. A. Zadeh, editors, *An Introduction to Fuzzy Logic Applications in Intelligent Systems*. Kluwer Academin, 1992.

[21] J.-D. Zucker and J.-G. Ganascia. Learning structurally indeterminate clauses. In D. Page, editor, *Proceedings of ILP98*, volume 1446 of *LNAI*, pages 235–244, 1998.

Prototypal Ambient Intelligence Framework for Assessment of Food Quality and Safety

M. Lettere, D. Guerri, and R. Fontanelli

Synapsis Srl, Livorno, Italy

Abstract. The holistic view of Ambient Intelligence proposed by the European IST Committee [1] suggests to start with the creation of an Ambient Intelligence (AmI) landscape for seamless delivery of services and applications [14][6]. In this paper we show the efforts that have been made to realize the AmI vision in a very challenging test bed such as the fine grained, continuous quality monitoring and traceability across entire food-chains. We employed our ideas in the framework of the GoodFood Integrate Project (FP6-IST-1-508774-IP)[3] which aims at developing a new generation of analytical methods based on Micro and Nano Technology solutions for safety and quality assurance along the food chain in the agrofood industry. The project proposes an AmI GRID vision that involves Remote Data Acquisition (RDA) for gathering information over a sensed environment, a communication infrastructure transporting data across the actors of the framework and a software component (AmI Core) represented by a set of systems involved in storage, monitoring, intelligent analysis and presentation of the data. We concentrated on both the infrastructure and the AmI Core. Regarding the infrastructure, we worked on the definition of a protocol for interconnecting the "Ambient hemisphere" of AmI (RDA) with the "Intelligence hemisphere" (AmI Core) and we developed a highly scalable, loosely coupled and bus-based interconnection scheme for the AmI Core. The AmI Core has been then populated with software entities (AmIDevices), in charge of the storage, monitoring, intelligent analysis and presentation of data. Fundamental results have been obtained in the definition and development of seamless integrating components designed for the abstraction, automatic composition, interaction between the Ambient and the Intelligence, user-friendly human interaction, computational efficiency, scalability and evolution. These results will guarantee the integration int the AmI framework of computer aided Decision Support Systems designed as a management tool to assist the domain experts in the different food-chains to achieve their target levels of efficiency, quality and risk management.

1   Introduction

The main application framework of the work described in this document is the GoodFood EC Integrated Project [3]. GoodFood aims at developing a new generation of analytical models based on Micro and Nanotechnology (MST and MNT) for safety and quality assurance along complete food production chains

S. Bandini and S. Manzoni (Eds.): AI*IA 2005, LNAI 3673, pp. 442–453, 2005.

of the agrofood industry. Nowadays, the technology used to assess food safety and quality relies on lab solutions that are bulky, costly, punctual and time consuming. The GoodFood multidisciplinary and universal approach will comply with the needs of ubiquity, fast response, simple use and full interconnection to the decisional bodies. The overall design of such systems relies on a Remote Data Acquisition (RDA) network, able to sense its physical environment gathering big amounts of observational data, and on Remote Actuators, able to respond to commands or events by concretely interacting with the outer world. This component match the concept of the Ambient hemisphere of AmI. The big amount of information produced, in terms of observational and management data, has to be filtered, stored, processed, analyzed and presented in order to support the typical scenarios of AmI, i.e. to provide the end-users with a complete framework of services exposed by intelligent and ergonomic user interfaces, accessible through local and remote, fixed and mobile, wired and wireless devices. All these activities closely match the concept of the Intelligence hemisphere of AmI.

In order to face all issues that arise in such a complex, wide and heterogeneous scenario, the GoodFood project proposes an innovative vision called *AmI GRID*. In this scenario, we concentrated on both the communication infrastructure and the remote data collection system, referred as AmI Core, by designing and developing a prototypal AmI framework for the assessment of food quality and safety. According to the ISTAG guidelines [1] for transforming the AmI vision in reality, we propose an innovative technological solution, based on the integration of distributed software agents, cooperating through a communication bus, according to peer-to-peer pattern. In particular, we developed a bus-based interconnection scheme (AmI Bus), integrating the software entities (AmI Devices) in charge of the storage, monitoring, intelligent analysis and presentation of data.

In the following sections we will explain the power of the solution in terms of seamless integration, automatic composition and abstraction: the adopted approach guarantees modularity, adaptiveness and scalability of the implemented system. Other key aspects of the solution are the robustness, guaranteed by the isolation of the AmI framework from possible failures occurring in the remote data acquisition level, and the portability, guaranteed by an implementation based on standard formalisms for data exchange (XML) and a portable programming enviroment (JAVA). This paper shows the technological and architectural choices made to design and implement the AmI GRID vision, and presents a preliminary prototype of the AmI framework for the assessment of quality and safety of the wine chain, the first case study addressed by the GoodFood Project.

2   State of the Art

In the agrofood industry there are clear requirements for the quality and safety controls across the entire manufacturing and supply chain. This assessment is a must, not only at the final market place, but for the whole chain, including food logistics during transport, storage and distribution [13]. Current solutions are based on time consuming laboratory analysis and expert human interventions. This approach is obviously costly, subjective and it's not massively applicable.

The evolution of ICT applications to agriculture in the last years, allowed the assessment of the "Precision Agriculture" approach. Precision agriculture is the practice of using remote sensing, soil sampling and information management tools to optimize agriculture production [5].

The GoodFood project has the objective to do a step forward, focusing on a multidisciplinary and universal approach based on the massive use of simple detection systems able to be used "near to the foodstuff". In particular, the GoodFood project aims at introducing Micro and Nano Technologies from the land to the market, providing two monitoring approaches: the continuous control, during life time, and the punctual monitoring [8], and to integrated them under an Ambient Intelligence umbrella, which allows fully interconnection and communication of multisensing systems. In particular, the introduction of the Ambient Intelligence paradigm aims at integrating the information acquired by sensors at each step of the food-chain, in a large-scale, distributed, heterogeneous and integrated platform for service provision [11]. The case-study selected for the demonstration of the AmI concept to the agro-food chain, is the wine chain due to its specific features and the economical sustainability of the AmI approach. In the first phase of the GoodFood project, the Ambient Intelligence paradigm has been studied from the user's perspective through a recognition of the potentialities, a description of the typical functionalities and an analysis of examples taken from the wine-chain. The technological perspective of the AmI vision should be analysed from two different points of view: a functional view, which distinguishes between the ambient side (the background, the environment) from the intelligent side (the foreground, the user); an architectural view, which distinguishes between the components and their integration.

During the first months of the GoodFood project, the AmI infrastructure has been designed and a first prototype has been developed, integrating the distributed network of sensors, the communication network and an intelligent software platform. The distributed network of sensors is based on a SensorWeb architecture [7], which represents the state-of-art approach to monitor and track physical process in a distributed environment, optimizing the energy consumption and maximizing the matching with the AmI paradigm requirements.

Concerning the software platform, critical issues are: system abstraction and automatic composition (to guarantee both the integration among heterogeneous systems and their interoperability and usability [12]), the computational efficiency, the interaction management between the ambient infrastructures and their intelligence, the dependability and the scalability.

In the following section we will describe the AmI GRID framework that we are developing to face this issues and we will present the results of a preliminary prototype of this framework.

3   The AmI Framework Technological Approach

In the framework of the EC GoodFood IP [3], the introduction of the Ambient Intelligence (AmI) paradigms aims to integrate the information acquired by sensors at each step of the food-chain in a large-scale distributed, heterogeneous and integrated platform for service provision and to improve the assessment of food quality and safety.

The overall design of such platform relies therefore on a Remote Data Acquisition (RDA) network which is able to sense its physical environment for big amounts of observational data and on Remote Actuators who are capable of responding to commands or events by concretely interacting with the outer world, on a communication infrastructure and on a remote data collection system, named *AmI Core*. The AmI Core has to filter, store, process, analyze and present the big amount of information produced by the RDA in terms of observational and management data, in order to support the end-users with a complete set of services through intelligent and ergonomic interfaces. All these activities closely match the concept of the *Intelligence hemisphere* of AmI.

In order to face all issues that arise in such a complex, wide and heterogeneous scenario, the GoodFood project proposes an innovative vision, called *AmI GRID*. In this context, we concentrated on both the communication infrastructure and, particularly, the AmI Core, designing and developing a prototypal AmI framework. In this section we briefly describe the GoodFood AmI GRID vision and then we propose the technological approach to realize the AmI framework.

The Figure 1 shows a Core Centric view of the AmI GRID vision, proposed by the GoodFood Project. In this representation the AmI Core is built up of a set of facilities operating on data. *Databases* are employed to store data. Techniques for *Knowledge Discovery in Databases (KDD)* are implemented to analyze data in order to find *"valid, new, potentially useful and understandable patterns in data"* [9]. *Decision Support Systems (DSS)* are software entities able to help out human technicians and operators, who access data through a set of *Intelligent and Intuitive Interfaces*, in understanding the domain and in taking decisions.

The AmI Core systems are wrapped by a complex shell representing the *Communication Infrastructure*. This shell groups the big variety of interconnection technologies involved in the process of integration among all the different systems across the Ambient Intelligence framework. At the periphery of this depiction reside the *Satellite Systems* that are needed to plug the AmI Core into the real world. The SensorWeb (keywords "Sensors", "Actuators" and "Mi-

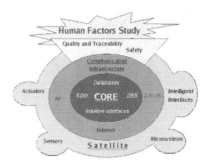

Fig. 1. A Core centric view of the AmI GRID vision

crosystems") is the interface between the AmI framework and the surrounding environment. The Intelligent Interfaces, instead, are meant to be interoperability gateways that provide connections of external systems or human operators to the AmI framework. Finally, the main outlet of the AmI Core aims at delivering all information in order to guarantee services like traceability, safety and quality of entire food chains. In the next section we propose the technological and architectural aspects of the AmI framework, focusing on the communication infrastructure and, in more detail, the AmI Core.

3.1   The AmI Framework General Architecture

The AmI framework is entirely developed using the Java platform. The AmI Core internal communication infrastructure is based on a scalable and open many-to-many communication scheme implemented by an entity called the *AmI Bus*. Entities, called *AmI Devices*, involved in implementing AmI framework functionality (i.e. storing, analyzing, monitoring and presenting data), are able to automatically connect to the AmI Bus and exchange information through messages according to the *AmI DOM* specification. *AmI Domain Object Model (AmI DOM)* is the open, extensible and scalable paradigm that enables a uniform, complete and object oriented mapping of the Ambient hemisphere of AmI. The AmI DOM specification results in a quite general way of mapping RDA structures at a very high level of abstraction. The Figure 2 shows a layered view of the AmI framework general architecture, used for implementing the AmI GRID vision. The RDA resides at the base of the layered view. RDAs typically contain heterogeneous subsets of sensing or actuator entities who communicate to the higher layers through proper *Gateway Nodes (GW)*. Each of the GWs has to connect to the AmI Core. The *Protocol Handler (PH)* is a particular AmI Device responsible for bridging the AmI Core to the RDA and vice versa. A PH has to be able to manage multiple connections from different GWs and to wrap and unwrap data to and from the common high level protocol based on the *AmI DOM* specification.

The following sections are focused on showing the choices, made to develop a first prototype of the AmI framework architecture. In particular, we will high-

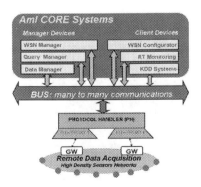

Fig. 2. A layered view of the AmI framework

light the power in terms of seamless integration, automatic composition and abstraction of a solution based on the combination of the main components of the AmI Core: AmI Devices, AmI Bus, AmI DOM and PH.

3.2   The AmI Core

This section describes the choices that have been made for implementing the AmI Core keeping some of the main criteria of the AmI GRID vision in mind and following the guidelines of the ISTAG to realize the AmI vision. Those criteria were seamless integration, automatic composition, abstraction, scalability and evolution. The use of a flexible communication infrastructure, based on a bus technology, the fine grained subdivision of responsibility among multiple software devices and the employment of an open object oriented domain description are the key ideas at the base of the proposed solutions. We're going then to describe the subsystems of the AmI Core.

AmI Bus
The AmI Bus is thought to be a sort of backbone at the center of the whole AmI Grid. As shown in Figure 2, every software entity (AmI Device) that in some ways participates to the overall AmI Grid application has to connect to the AmI Bus. The interface for establishing (and closing) a connection with the AmI Bus is well defined and simple. This makes it possible to easily create new AmI Devices that are automatically able to connect themselves to the AmI Bus. The developer of the AmI Device thus has to focus only on the device specific logic abstracting from the low level communication paradigm to be used. Another aspect that clearly emerges from Figure 3 is that there is no application level centralization point required for the communication. This means that much of the overhead related to typical request/response patterns (as in client-server approaches) can be avoided. The technology we chose for implementing the AmI Bus encapsulates into the bus logic a way for supporting multiple protocols. This means that on the same instance of the AmI Bus, different AmI devices could connect using different protocols conforming to different requirements in terms of performance, security, robustness 3. This feature enables the concept of ubiquitous computing and scalability because it actually enlarges in a considerable way the set of potential users. Supported patterns for communicating messages on the AmI Bus are *Named Queues* and *Publisher And Subscribers* [10]. These patterns can efficiently be used to implement point to point, multicast and broadcast communications. Another feature of the AmI Bus is persistence. Messages are kept stored across the lifetime of the AmI Bus enabling AmI Device that are not connected because of temporarily failure or maintenance to seamlessly access messages that would be lost. This techniques is very important for AmI Devices that are involved in vital tasks such the storage of data.

AmI Devices
A big step toward functional scalability and automatic composition is represented by the fine grained distribution of responsibilities across a set of AmI Devices. As shown in Figure 3 there are many AmI Devices with different

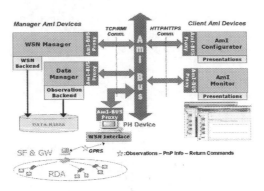

Fig. 3. AmI Bus with sample AmI Devices

functionality that loosely connect to each other through the AmI Bus. The fine grained distribution of responsibilities helps in reducing the overhead of code necessary to implement a certain AmI Device. It eases maintenance since the interfaces can be kept simple and each functionality is well isolated. In an evolving environment, where software designers are continuously cooperating with domain experts investigating new solutions to problems that arise during successive steps of iterative development processes, it is important that modules are loosely coupled in order to reduce the overall impact of changes on the application. This loosely coupling of AmI Devices through a bus based communication scheme and message exchange, facilitates the isolation of interfaces from implementations making it possible to update or even reimplement a single AmI Device without impacting on other AmI Devices that interact with it. A set of sample AmI Devices is shown in Figure 3. As a convenience, AmI Devices can be subdivided into *Client AmI Devices* and *Manager AmI Devices*. As said, there is no real client/server relation among the AmI Devices but the naming subdivision is useful to classify AmI Devices that perform strict AmI Core operations and AmI Devices that serve for interfacing human users to the AmI Core by performing presentation, configuration or visual monitoring.

There are two other differences between client and manager AmI Devices. Managers are single instance AmI Devices. This means that in a particular life cycle of the AmI Core, at most one instance of a particular manager can exist whereas clients can exist in multiple instances. Clients can run anywhere in the world and thus require particular protocols for connecting to the AmI Bus who ensure generality (for instance HTTP eases client execution in firewalled or proxied networks) and confidentiality (PKI and SSL might be required when authentication and encryption is required for sensible data). Managers, instead, generally run in protected areas such as business local area networks and thus could rely on less general or secure protocols.

AmI DOM
To enable AmI Devices for interaction and communication a common language has to be developed. The AmI DOM specification has been developed for this purpose and is designed to be general, open, extensible and object oriented. This

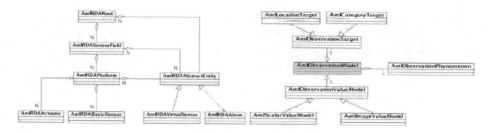

Fig. 4. UML diagrams of RDA structure and Observation Model Description (OMD)

requirements emerged because of the enormous range of applicability fields that AmI can be applied to and for facing the requirements of evolutionary design. The steps followed for the realization of the AmI DOM were to design a specification in XSD, an XML based formalism for specification of object oriented models, apply to it an automatic code generation tool and to include the generated code into the main project code tree. Moreover the serialization of the objects defined by the AmI DOM has been automated in order to make redefinitions of the AmI DOM transparent to the AmI Devices. This way of generating and keeping up to date the domain object model of the AmI Core makes it possible to easily change the AmI DOM impacting in a very light way on the design and implementation of the AmI Bus and the AmI Devices. In the AmI DOM specification there are two main "trees" of definition: the RDA description, that defines the structure of the RDA (shown in the left part of 4), and the OMD description, that describes the models of the observations that can be made by the RDA (shown in the right part of **??**). The RDA description is based on a hierarchical representation of the various entities that are comprised in a RDA. As shown there are a set of physical entities and a set of logical or virtual entities. Physical entities are *Basic Sensors*. Basic Sensors are involved in actually sensing the environment and producing *Observational Data*. Examples of Basic Sensors are temperature or humidity sensors but also the lens of a digital video monitoring device. Another class of physical entities are the *Platforms*. Platforms are *intelligent* nodes that encapsulate Basic Sensors and that communicate with other Platforms through any kind of communication infrastructure building up the actual WSN. Examples of Platforms are a videocam or the MICA Motes. Actuators are also physical entities. They are represented by the mechanical and electronical devices that interact with the environment of the RDA. Examples of Actuators are automatic irrigation devices or remotely steerable air conditioning systems. Virtual entities are added to the RDA by human operators through proper RDA manipulation client AmI Devices. Examples of virtual entities are *Virtual Sensors, Sensor Fields* and *Alarms*.

Virtual Sensors are entities that are associated to Basic Sensors or other Virtual Sensors. They are used to generate computed observational data. Transformation operators such as *average, min, max, var ...*, are applied to the data observed by the associated sensors producing new observations. In effect the applicability field of Virtual Sensors is much bigger. Virtual Sensors are employed to be placeholder for Basic Sensors that are not available on the market or are too expensive. Moreover Virtual Sensors can implement complete previsional models, by implementing very complex operators, to extract knowledge from a common RDA infrastructure. Sensor Fields are merely logical aggregations of physical and virtual entities. Examples of Sensor Fields are the vineyard, the cellar and the van transporting bottles in a wine chain monitoring application. Alarms are virtual entities that are associated to any collection of sensing entities (Virtual or Basic Sensors). An Alarm has Alarm Trigger Conditions and Alarm Actions associated to it. If an Alarm is triggered by some sensing entities then all the Alarm Action are executed. Alarm Actions can range from simply logging the event to automatic email and sms sending or activation of some Actuators.

The AmI Devices connected to the AmI Bus communicate by exchanging information wrapped in *AmI Messages* described by the *AmI Protocol Stack*. The AmI Messages define the uppermost layer of the stack. The second level of the protocol is based on the *gfTinyML* [4] representation of AmI DOM specific entities. gfTinyML is inspired by the work of OGC [2]. It is based on XML which has been chosen because of the openness and the existence of many tools for automatic generation, parsing and transformation of documents. The specification of the gfTinyML is delivered in the form of an XSD document. During the developing phase it emerged clearly that this specification has to remain open to accomplish all needs that could arise due to the evolving nature of the model.

Protocol Handler
A complex, heterogeneous and distributed application such as the AmI GRID presents noticeable challenges in terms of interconnection and communication infrastructure. In our AmI GRID vision one of the main issues related to communication is linking the Ambient hemisphere (the RDA) to the Intelligence hemisphere (the AmI Core). This communication represents a challenge in many ways: first there is the necessity to wrap up the many entities of the RDA that communicate in different ways according to heterogeneous protocols and medias. Then the RDA, an inherently *insecure place*, has to be isolated from the AmI Core to ensure that failures occurring inside it are not propagated to the AmI Core resulting in an overall failure of the framework.

To face these problems, the architectural proposal described in this paper suggests the introduction of a special AmI Device called AmI Protocol Handler (PH) that operates according to the *Mediator* and *Gateway* design patterns [10]. The PH is meant to be running in a *secure and efficient environment*, where secure is a term indicating a fixed machine, plugged to a stable power supply and communicating to the AmI Bus through a wired, secure networking infrastructure whereas efficient means able to support concurrency and parallelism. Functionally, the PH can be seen as multiplexer of connections to the RDA. Through a heavily multi-threaded implementation and a dynamic handling of code libraries, many different protocol parsers can be instantiated or removed in an *on demand* fashion enabling PH to talk to different RDA entities simultaneously and avoiding bottleneck situations typically occurring in a centralization point. All information flowing from the RDA to the AmI Core is gathered by the PH who wraps it into AmI Messages and sends it out on the AmI Bus. Vice-versa, all information addressed to any entity of the RDA coming from any AmI Device is translated into the proper protocol and sent out to the dedicated network link.

4   The Results

The ideas shown in this paper have contributed to the realization of an Ambient Intelligence framework that, following the suggestions of the ISTAG [1], aims at seamless integration and delivery of services and applications. We applied these ideas in the context of the GoodFood IP where the AmI concepts are exploited for the developing of a new generation MST and MNT based solutions for safety and quality assurance along the food chain in the agrofood industry.

The first test bed for the developed infrastructure will be the installation of a complete system for quality and safety assurance inside a wine production chain. In particular, a RDA in the form of Wireless SensorWebs will be installed across different locations of a wine producing farm, for example the Vineyard and the Cellar. A preliminary demonstration of this test bed has been presented in the GoodFood review, in Montreux, and it's now working. The RDA, located in Florence, communicates through wireless GPRS with a PH that resides in the secure area represented by a machine locate inside Synapsis Local Area Network. This PH is connected to the AmI Bus who also runs inside this secure area and to whom some Manager AmI Devices are connected for performing Core specific functionality. In particular, there is a RDA managing AmI Device for handling the dynamic changing of the RDA infrastructure (plug and play of new platforms of sensors, removal etc.) and a data management AmI Device responsible for making observational data persistent and for keeping the OMD up to date. Another manager AmI Device is the data query manager who is responsible for accepting queries on observational data and execute then in the most efficient way.

Many client AmI Devices are made available for performing different tasks ranging from configuration of RDA entities to real time monitoring and simple statistical analysis. The most up to date versions of those clients are available, according to specific user privileges policies over the WWW through a de facto standard for software version management as Java Web Start. A user can download the latest version of a client AmI Device by simply clicking on the right link of the HTML page. After performing its authentication procedure he will be prompted with the proper interface for performing the tasks the client was designed for. The client AmI Device is able to automatically and transparently connect back to the AmI Bus inside the AmI Core and data can be communicated over this channel according to the AmI DOM specification. As an option for clients running outside the secure area (LAN or VPN) the data can be encrypted to ensure confidentiality. As shown, this infrastructure makes it possible for end-user to seamlessly access data produced by a RDA from any place, through a set of cooperating and integrated technologies, using the latest versions of user interface software while this software is undergoing a continuous process of refinement toward ergonomics and user friendliness. Moreover the implemented AmI framework addresses the key architectural aspects for realizing the AmI vision:

- modularity, adaptiveness and scalability: the system is, in fact, based on software agents cooperating through a communication bus according to peer-to-peer pattern; moreover it is natively distributed and new agents machine can be added to the communication infrastructure;
- robustness and portability: the PH device isolates the AmI framework from possible failures occurring in the RDA and the framework, developed in Java, is based on standard technologies (XML, JMS) and open source tools (Open JMS, JFreeChart).

Finally, combining the virtual sensors and the alarms functionalities with computer aided Decision Support Systems, the AmI framework can provide the domain experts with intelligent tools for the assessment of the quality, the safety and the risk management in their agrofood-chains.

5   Conclusions and Future Work

This paper has shown a prototypal Ambient Intelligence (AmI) framework, realized in the context of the EC GoodFood Integrated Project. The project aims at developing a new generation of analytical models based on Micro and Nanotechnology for safety and quality assurance along complete food production chains of the agrofood industry and introducing the AmI paradigm to integrate the information acquired by the sensing systems at each step of the food-chain, in a large-scale, distributed, heterogeneous and integrated platform for service provision. In order to face all issues that arise in such a complex, wide and heterogeneous scenario, the GoodFood project proposes an innovative vision called *AmI GRID*. In this scenario, we concentrated on the software platform of the AmI GRID, that has to filter , store, process, analyse and present the big amount of information produced, in terms of observational and management data, by the RDA network. According to the guidelines of the ISTAG, to implement the AmI Core we have proposed an innovative technological solution, based on the integration of distributed software agents, cooperating through a communication bus, according to peer-to-peer pattern. In particular, we developed a bus-base interconnection scheme, integrating the software entities (AmI Devices) in charge of the storage, monitoring, intelligent analysis and presentation of data.

The first test bed for the developed AmI framework will be the installation of a complete system for quality and safety assurance inside a wine production chain. In particular, a RDA in the form of Wireless SensorWebs will be installed across different locations of a wine producing farm. A preliminary demonstration of this test bed has been just presented in the First Year GoodFood meeting, in Montreux, and it's now working. The first experiments have shown that fundamental results have been obtained in the definition and development of seamless integrating components designed for the abstraction, automatic composition, interaction between the Ambient and the Intelligence, user-friendly human interaction, computational efficiency, scalability and evolution.

In the next future we are going to introduce in the AmI Core new *data management* AmI devices. In particular, we will integrate a *KDD* AmI device, providing to the end-user advanced analysis tools to investigate data correlations, and a *DSS* AmI device, that will be designed as a management tool, assisting the domain experts in the different food-chains to achieve their target levels of efficiency, quality and risk management.

References

1. ISTAG Advisor Group. *Istag Report.* http://www.cordis.lu/ist/istag-reports.htm.
2. Open Geospatial Consortium. *OGC home site.* http://www.opengeospatial.org.
3. The GoodFood European Project (FP6-IST-508744-IP). *Food Safety and Quality Monitoring with MicroSystems.* http://www.goodfood-project.org.
4. TinyML. *TinyML home site.* http://kingkong.me.berkeley.edu/ nota/research/ TinyML.
5. Precision agriculture. *The International Journal on Advances in the Science of Precision Agriculture. Kluwer Academic Publisher*, 2001.
6. E. Aarts, H. Harwing, and M. Schuurmans. *Ambient Intelligence: The Invisible Future.* McGrawHill, 2001.
7. K. A. Delin and S. P. Jackson. Sensor Web for In Situ Exploration of Gaseous Biosignatures. In *IEEE Aerospace Conference, Big Sky, Montana-USA, 2000.*
8. I. Elmi, S. Zampolli, and C.G. Cardinali. An innovative e-nose approach for good quality Assessment: a mst solution exploting Gas-chromatographic selectivity. In *AISEM2005. 15-17 February, 2005, Florence, Italy.*
9. U. M. Fayyad and G. Piatetsky-Shapiro. *Advances in Knowledge Discovery and Data Mining.* AAAI/MIT Press, 1996.
10. E. Gamma, R. Helm, R. Johnson, and J. Vlissides. *Design Patterns, Elements of Reusable Object-Oriented Software.* Addison-Wesley, 2000.
11. G. Giorgetti and G. Manes. Ambient Intelligence in Agriculture: a Challenge for Wireless Sensor Network Technology. In *EWSN2005. 1-3 February 2005, Instabul, Turkey.*
12. D.S. Linthicum. *Next Generation Application Integration: From Simple Information to Web Services.* Addison-Wesley, Paperback, 2003.
13. B. Mazzolai, V. Raffa, V. Mattoli, and P. Dario. Enabling technologies for a flexible tag Gas sensing system in food logistics applications. In *AISEM2005. 15-17 February, 2005, Florence, Italy.*
14. P. Remagnino, G. Foresti, and T. Ellis. *Ambient Intelligence: A Novel Paradigm.* Springer, 1nd edition, 2004.

Managing Clinical Guidelines Contextualization in the GLARE System

Paolo Terenziani[1], Stefania Montani[1], Alessio Bottrighi[1], Mauro Torchio[2],
Gianpaolo Molino[2], and Gianluca Correndo[3]

[1] Dipartimento di Informatica, Univ. Piemonte Orientale "A. Avogadro",
Alessandria, Italy
{terenz, stefania, alessio}@mfn.unipmn.it
[2] Laboratorio di Informatica Clinica, Az. Ospedaliera S. G. Battista,
Torino, Italy
{gmolino, mtorchio}@molinette.piemonte.it
[3] Dipartimento di Informatica, Universita' di Torino, Torino, Italy
correndo@di.unito.it

Abstract. Computer-based tools to manage clinical guidelines are gaining an increasing relevance within the areas of Artificial Intelligence (AI) in Medicine and Medical Informatics. One of the most relevant obstacles to the application, use and dissemination of clinical guidelines is the gap between the generality of guidelines (as defined, e.g., by physicians' committees) and the peculiarities of the specific contexts of application. First, computer-based guideline managers must be integrated with the Hospital Information System (HIS), and usually different DBMS are adopted by different hospitals. Second, general guidelines do not take into account the fact that the tools needed for laboratory and instrumental investigations might be unavailable at a given hospital. Finally, a sort of "continuous adaptation" has to be supported, to manage the updates needed to cope with new clinical procedures. GLARE is a guideline manager which adopts advanced AI techniques to address the above contextualization issues.

1 Introduction

Clinical guidelines can be roughly defined as frameworks for specifying the "best" clinical procedures and for standardizing them. In recent years, the medical community has started to recognize that a computer-based treatment of guidelines provides relevant advantages, such as automatic connection to the patient databases and, more interestingly, decision making facilities. In the last decade, this observation has motivated the development of several domain-independent computer systems for guidelines management (consider, e.g., Asgaard [1], EON [2], GEM [3], GLARE [4], GLIF [5], GUIDE [6], PROforma [7], and [8], [9]).

Our contribution to this very active research area is represented by the system GLARE (Guidelines Acquisition, Representation and Execution) [4]. GLARE is being developed by a group of computer scientists from Universita' del Piemonte Orientale and Universita' di Torino, in collaboration with Azienda Ospedaliera S. Giovanni Battista in Torino, one of the largest hospitals in Italy. Despite the system is basically

S. Bandini and S. Manzoni (Eds.): AI*IA 2005, LNAI 3673, pp. 454–465, 2005.
© Springer-Verlag Berlin Heidelberg 2005

a research product, whose features are continuously refined and updated, the facilities it embeds have been formally tested or at least carefully examined by physicians. Moreover, physicians' opinions are referred to in every phase of the tool's upgrades, from design to implementation.

With respect to the other guideline managers described in the literature, GLARE embeds a set of unique and distinguishing functionalities, some of which are briefly summarized in section 2; in this paper, we concentrate on the description of the most recent one, i.e. guidelines *contextualization.*

Contextualization is an essential step to be taken before a guideline manager is really adopted in clinical practice. Actually, one of the most relevant obstacles to the exploitation and dissemination of clinical guidelines is the gap between the generality of guidelines themselves (as defined, e.g., by physicians' committees) and the peculiarities of the specific contexts of application. Contextualization involves several aspects. First, the guideline manager needs to be easily interfaced to the pre-existing software environment, namely to the locally available HIS, with its technological DBMS choice. Furthermore, it has to support the adaptation of general guidelines to the local setting, by (automatically) taking into account local resources (e.g. diagnostic instrumentation) unavailability, and locally applied procedures, which may require to discard some alternatives. Finally, it has to maintain guidelines up-to-date, allowing the introduction of new clinical procedures, but keeping the "history" of the previous versions and of their authors.

The GLARE's approach to contextualization is described in sections 3, 4 and 5, which represent the core contribution of this paper. Finally, section 6 is devoted to comparisons and conclusions.

2   Main Features of GLARE

2.1   Representation Formalism

GLARE relies on a limited but clear representation formalism [4], in which the basic primitives are *atomic* and *composite actions* (*plans*). Atomic actions are used to model elementary steps in a guideline, while composite actions represent more complex procedures, which can be defined in terms of their components via the *part-of* relation. A guideline itself is a composite action, which can be progressively refined by following the part-of chain, until atomic actions are reached. Three main types of atomic actions have been introduced in GLARE: *work actions, query actions,* and *decisions. Work actions* represent operative steps which must be executed at a given point of the guideline. *Query actions* are requests of information from the outside world (physicians, databases, knowledge bases). *Decision actions* are the means for selecting among alternative paths. Decision actions can be further subdivided into diagnostic decisions, used to make explicit the identification of the disease the patient is suffering from, and therapeutic decisions, used to represent the choice of a path, containing the implementation of a particular therapeutic process. Actions are described in terms of their attributes.

The order of execution of actions is established by means of a set of *control relations: sequence, controlled, alternative* and *repetition.* In particular, repetitions state that an action has to be repeated several times (maybe a number of times which is not known a priori, until a certain exit condition becomes true). On the other hand, controlled relations are used in order to represent temporally constrained actions, such as "start of A at least 1 hour after the beginning of B", and so on. (Possibly imprecise) action durations and temporal delays among actions can be specified.

2.2 Acquisition and Execution Tools

GLARE's architecture is composed by two main modules: an *acquisition tool*, meant to be adopted –e.g., by a committee of expert physicians- to introduce a new guideline in the system, and an *execution tool*, exploited by the user physician to apply a guideline to a specific patient. The tools strictly interact with a set of databases (see section 3).

In particular, the acquisition tool provides a user-friendly graphical interface to acquire guideline components. The overall guideline is depicted as a graph, where each action is represented by a node (different forms and colors are used to distinguish among different types of actions), while control relations are represented by arcs. By clicking on the nodes in the graph, the user can trigger other windows to acquire the internal descriptions (attributes) of the nodes. When clicking on composite actions, on the other hand, a new graph, showing the actions linked to the selected one by the part-of relation, is generated. The overall hierarchical structure of the guideline is also shown on the left of the interface window in the form of a tree, where plans can be seen as parents of their components (see figure 1).

The acquisition tool also provides physicians with different forms of consistency checking, such as *name* and *range checking, logical design criteria fulfillment* (for example, alternative arcs may only exit from a decision action), and *temporal consistency checking*. The latter issue has required the adoption and the extension of complex AI techniques, whose description is outside the scope of this paper, but that was extensively treated in [10].

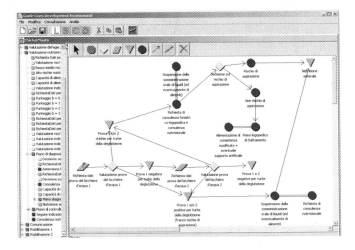

Fig. 1. A window of GLARE's acquisition tool graphical interface: on the left, the hierarchical structure of the guideline is displayed; on the right, the representation of control relations is shown in form of a graph

On the other hand, the execution tool is typically used when a user physician applies a guideline to a specific patient. This method is exploited for integrating guidelines into clinical practice [11]. It is possible to simulate the application of the guideline to a hypothetical patient as well, for education, critical review or evaluation purposes [11]. The execution tool also incorporates a decision support facility, which relies on decision theory concepts, and allows physicians to navigate through the guideline to see and compare alternative paths, stemming from decision actions (see next section) [12], [13].

2.3 Decision Making

Decision making is a central issue in clinical practice. In particular, supporting therapy selection is a critical objective to be achieved, especially in those situations in which several alternatives, which are basically clinically equivalent, are available for the given patient. To this hand, we have implemented a tool able to provide physicians with a complete scenario of the decision consequences, in terms of the utilities associated to the different health states, and the money, time and resources spent, by simulating the patient's evolution along the different paths stemming from the decision under examination, typically until the end of the guideline is reached.

The tool relies on decision theory, and its implementation has been preceded by a systematic analysis of the main guideline representation primitives (see section 2.1), and of how they could be related to decision theory concepts [13], [14].

In particular, in a well-formed guideline, a decision action is preceded by a query action, that is adopted to collect all the patient's parameters necessary (and sufficient) for taking the decision itself. Each decision is therefore based on a data collection completed at decision time, and does not depend on the previous history of the patient.

We can thus say that the guideline describes a discrete-time first-order Markov model, since each time a query action is implemented, the patient's situation is completely re-assessed. This observation allows us to represent a guideline as a Markov Decision Process [15]. The process is also completely observable, since in a guideline a decision can be taken only if all the required parameters have been collected: if some needed data are missing, the query action will wait for them and the decision will be delayed.In this context, the patient's state can be defined as the set of patient's parameters that are normally measured for taking decisions and for assessing therapy outcomes. Query actions are therefore the means for observing the state. State transitions are produced by all the work actions between two consecutive decisions.

Finally, the utility of a state can be evaluated in terms of life expectancy, corrected by Quality Adjusted Life Year (QALYs) [16]. Utility coefficients, as well as transition probabilities, could be typically extracted from the medical literature, or calculated by drawing statistics on the basis of locally available data.

In this setting, we are able to calculate the optimal policy, i.e. the sequence of decisions able to maximize the expected utility.

Moreover, our tool also gathers costs, resources and time spent to complete any path in the guideline, and couples this information with the calculation of the expected utility along the path itself. The optimal policy and the utility parameter are calculated relying on classical algorithms, such as value iteration [17], which have been adapted to the specific application domain. On the other hand, complex temporal constraint propagation techniques are necessary in order to deal with the temporal parameters (see [10] for details).

2.4 Testing

We have already tested our representation formalism and acquisition tool prototype. Several groups of expert physicians, following a few-hour training session, used GLARE to acquire algorithms concerning different clinical domains (e.g., bladder cancer, reflux esophagitis, and heart failure), with the help of a knowledge engineer. In all the tests, our representation formalism and acquisition tool proved to be expressive enough to cover the clinical algorithms, and the acquisition of a clinical guideline was reasonably fast (e.g., the acquisition of the guideline on heart failure – more than 100 nodes - starting from a non-structured textual representation, required only 3 days).

Moreover, physicians have been consulted both in the design phase and in the implementation phase of every other feature of the GLARE system.

Currently, both the vocabulary and the electronic patient record employed in GLARE are just prototypes (see section 3 for details). A formal testing of the overall system in the real clinical setting will therefore be completed as a future work.

3 Contextualization to the Software Environment: GLARE's Three-Layered Architecture

In order to face the need of making GLARE as independent as possible of the specific DBMS used to manage the HIS, we devised a three-layered architecture (see figure 2).

The highest layer (*system layer*) is composed by the execution and acquisition modules sketched in section 2. In particular, the acquisition tool manages the representation of clinical guidelines, which are physically stored into a dedicated database, called CG DB. Moreover, it interacts with four additional databases: the Clinical DB,

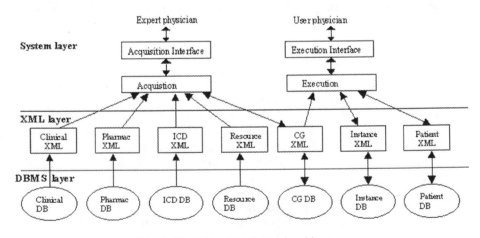

Fig. 2. GLARE's three-layered architecture

which provides a "standard" terminology to define the actions in the guideline; the Pharmacological DB, containing a list of drugs; the ICD (i.e. ICD9-CM) DB, providing an international coding of diseases, and the Resource DB, that gives information about the resources available at the specific hospital where the guideline is meant to be used.

On the other hand, the execution tool executes a guideline (which has been previously acquired and stored in the CG DB) on a given patient, strictly interacting with the user-physician through its interface, and retrieving data from the Patient DB (i.e. the electronic patient record). Different guidelines can be executed on the same patient (and, obviously, on different patients). The tool stores the state of each execution into the Instance DB.

Currently, GLARE is based on the prototype versions of the clinical terminology and of the electronic patient record which have been developed by the Azienda Ospedaliera S. Giovanni Battista in Torino. A commercial version of such prototypes is currently being built within DAISY, a joint project between Azienda Ospedaliera S. Giovanni Battista, and the Koinè Sistemi software house [18]. As soon as the running versions of the above prototypes will be available, GLARE will be integrated with them, in order to evaluate GLARE reliability in the real world and to develop clinical applications.The lowest layer of the architecture (*DBMS layer*) contains the DBMS, that physically stores the different databases described above, while the intermediate layer (*XML layer*) consists of a set of XML documents (one for each database). XML acts as an interlingua between the system layer and the DBMS layer: the acquisition and execution modules actually interact only with the XML layer, through which they obtain the knowledge stored into the DMBS. The use of XML as an interlingua allows us to express the guidelines in a format with characteristics of legibility, and to publish them on the Web, rendering easy their dissemination. On the other hand, the DBMS layer grants a homogenous management of the data, by integrating the guideline representation with the pre-existent HIS in the same physical DBMS.

The three-layered architecture makes GLARE mostly independent of the commercial DBMS adopted at the particular hospital. In fact, the interaction between the DBMS and the XML layer is devoted to a single software module (a Java package). Changing the DBMS only requires to modify such module and these changes are quite limited and well-localised. Thus, GLARE's three-layered architecture offers a useful support for adapting the tool to the software context.

4 Guidelines' Resource-Based Contextualization

In GLARE's representation formalism, the resources needed by each action of the guideline are explicitly declared among the attributes of the action itself. On the basis of such a description, we have devised a pre-compilation step, which can be used whenever a guideline has to be installed and adopted in a new context (hospital/department) in order to automatically adapt the guideline to the locally available resources.

The pre-compilation step provides the hospital/department administrators with the list of all the resources needed within the guidelines, considering all the alternative paths, to have from them the indication of which resources are locally available and which are not. Then, it automatically navigates the guideline in order to prune the branches that cannot be executed because of resources unavailability (of course, warnings are inserted, in order to advise user-physicians that alternative diagnostic/therapeutic paths could be "in principle" provided to patients – e.g., if moving to other more equipped hospitals). Pruning non-executable alternative paths brings out with a context-dependent guideline, that describes all and only those actions and paths that respect the original meaning of the general input guideline, and that can actually be implemented in the given context (since the required resources are available).

From the technical point of view, the algorithm performs a recursive navigation of the guideline, along the part-of hierarchy of graphs representing it, and considering the different types of actions. For instance, a decision action has to be pruned only in case all the alternative paths starting from it require locally unavailable resources, and a recursive call has to be raised whenever a composite action has to be taken into account (see [19] for more details).

5 Clinical Guidelines Local Adaptations and Updates

In GLARE, we provide a computer-assisted facility to modify guidelines, to cope both with the need to apply them to a new contexts of application (countries, hospitals and/or departments), and with the need to manage updates. In particular, while the contextualization when importing a guideline from different countries and/or institutions is usually performed by (or under the supervision of) a medical committee before the first exploitation of the guideline itself in a new context, periodical updates could be provided (at least in principle) by any physician; in this situation, a team of supervisors (i.e. the original guideline developers and/or a committee of local contextualization responsibles) will have to accept (i.e. validate) them before modifying the original version. Recording the identity of the author(s) of the proposals and of the acceptances might be required. Moreover, maintaining the "history" (i.e., the different versions) of the guidelines is very important. For instance, a physician might be called to justify her/his actions on a given patient P in the time span T on the basis of her institution's guidelines, but only considering the guidelines that were valid at time T. To fulfill this objective, multiple versions of the guidelines have to be maintained, together with the times at which each update has been performed.

In order to provide a general approach to the integrated treatment of contextualization and upgrades, we propose to implement the following functionalities:

(i)   management of authors (distinguishing between at least two levels: user physicians and supervisors);
(ii)   management of the status of any piece of knowledge in the guideline (distinguishing between proposed and accepted knowledge);
(iii) management of the history of knowledge (considering the time when each piece of knowledge has been proposed by users, and, possibly, accepted by supervisors);
(iv)   facilities for selecting the parts of a guideline to be changed/updated (possibly considering different levels of detail);
(v)   facilities for modifying (part of) a guideline;
(vi)   facilities for formulating queries and for visualising the updates.

In order to devise a modular, general, and system independent approach to face the above issues, we propose a three-layered architecture, consisting of:

(1) a data model layer, defining the data model and providing the basic operations;

(2) a query language layer, supporting an SQL-like high-level manipulation and query language, based on layer (1);

(3) an interface layer, which grounds on the previous layers, and provides users with the high-level functionalities above, accessed through a user-friendly graphical interface.

In the following, for the sake of brevity only the data layer is sketched, on the basis of a (simple) abstract example.

5.1 Managing Authors and Multiple Versions

We propose to enrich the guideline data model with the possibility of representing, for each unit of information (henceforth *IU;* in GLARE, the information units are the - atomic and composite- actions, the properties of actions, and their conditions):

(1) the time t_P when it has been proposed, and the author A_P who made the proposal;

(2) (if accepted) the time t_A when it has been accepted, and the author (supervisor) A_A who accepted it.

Therefore, in order to support the history of IU, in our proposal, two temporally ordered lists of pairs <t,A> are associated to each IU: the *TP* list for the proposals and the *TA* list for the acceptances. On the other hand, for the sake of efficiency, rejected proposals are physically deleted (even if, in principle, our approach can be trivially extended to maintain them).

Such an extended model is paired with the definition of two primitive functions, *insert* and *update* (we model *delete* operations as updates where no new value is substituted to the old one), which properly operate on the data model, by inserting/modifying the IU, and updating their TP and TA lists.

The treatment of *composite* IU (i.e., plans) deserves specific attention. Suppose, for instance, that an action A in a guideline G has been described (at the time t_0 when the guideline has been originally entered) as the sequence of two sub-actions A_1 and A_2, and that, at time t_1, an update has been made in the properties of A_2. In such a case, we would like to propagate along the part-of chain the update, stating that also the super-action A has been updated at time t_1. Of course, this bottom-up propagation needs to be applied recursively along the whole chain (i.e. we want to record that all the super-actions of A –if any- and, ultimately, the whole guideline G have been updated at time t_1). Therefore, in our approach, the insert and update operations also propagate the updates to the TP and TA lists of the upper IU in the part-of chain.

Moreover, also the set $S=\{S_1, ..., S_k\}$ of supervisors and the set $U=\{U_1, ..., U_h\}$ of user physicians must be maintained.

In the following, we exemplify our data model and insert/update operations via the abstract situation in figure 3, in which the history of the sample guideline records the changes below:

(0) The *initial* situation is modeled by the bold part of figure 3. We suppose we have a (part of a) guideline which, at the time of acquisition (denoted by t_0), is composed by an action A, which has a property P1 with value v1, and is composed by the actions A' (with property P1' with value v1' and property P2' with value v2') and A" (with property P1" having value v1"). Let S={S1} the set of supervisors, and U={U1,U2} the set of users. In particular, notice that, by default, in the initial situation, proposal and acceptance times exactly correspond (without any loss of generality, for the sake of simplicity we suppose that the initial acquisition is a supervised process).

(1) At time t_1, user U1 proposes to add to A the property P2, with value v2. This results in:

(i)   inserting the new IU P2=v2, with TP equal to $<t_1,U_1>$;

(ii)   adding the $<t_1,U_1>$ pair to the TP list of A;

(2) At time t_2, practitioner U2 proposes to change from v2' to v3' the value of the property P2' of A'. This results in

(i)   adding the IU P2'=v3' to A', with TP equal to $<t_2,U_2>$;

(ii)   appending $<t_2,U_2>$ at the end of the TP lists of A'

(iii)   appending $<t_2,U_2>$ at the end of the TP lists of A

(3) Finally, at time t_3, all of the proposals are accepted by S1. This results in adding the tag $<t_3,S_1>$ at the end of the TA lists of property P2' (with value v3') of A', property P2 of A, A', and A.

The final situation of the data is shown in figure 3.

A   {TP: **$<t_0,S1>$**,$<t_1,U1>$,$<t_2,U2>$ # TA: **$<t_0,S1>$**,$<t_3,S1>$}

P1=v1   {TP: **$<t_0,S1>$** # TA : **$<t_0,S1>$**}

P2=v2   {TP: $<t_1,U1>$ # TA : $<t_3,S1>$}

A'   {TP: **$<t_0,S1>$**,$<t_2,U_2>$ # TA: **$<t_0,S1>$**,$<t_3,S1>$}

P1'=v1' {TP: **$<t_0,S1>$** # TA: **$<t_0,S1>$**}

P2'=v2' {TP: **$<t_0,S1>$** # <TA : **$<t_0,S1>$**}

P2'=v3' {TP: $<t_2,U2>$ # <TA : $< t_3,S1>$}

A"   {TP: **$<t_0,S1>$** # TA: **$<t_0,S1>$**}

P1"=v2"{TP: **$<t_0,S1>$** # TA: **$<t_0,S1>$**}

Fig. 3. Internal representation of the history of a (simplified) guideline

For example, on the basis of the above data model the answer to the following types of queries can be easily provided.

Q1: Give me the (accepted) description of A' at time t_2.

A'.P1'=v1'

A'.P2'=v2'

Q2: Give me the update proposals regarding A made by U1 or U2 at time t_2

A' part-of A; A'.P2'=v2' ➔ A'.P2'=v3'

Notice that the updates to A' are taken into account since A' is part of A.

Q3: Give me the history (i.e., the different accepted versions) of A

At time t_0:	A.P1=v1
	A' part-of A; A'.P1'=v1', A'.P2'=v2'
	A" part-of A; A".P1"=v1"
At time t_3:	A.P1=v1, A.P2=v2
	A' part-of A; A'.P1'=v1', A'.P2'=v3'
	A" part-of A; A".P1"=v1"

6   Comparisons, Conclusions and Future Work

In the medical area there is an increasing consciousness that a proper management of the contextualization/update process is an essential step towards a widespread and systematic application of clinical guidelines in practice. For instance, [20] noticed that guidelines dissemination and integration into clinical practice should recognize the multiplicity of working settings and information systems environments within which the guidelines themselves are meant to be implemented.

In this paper, we have described how GLARE has been extended in order to face the below issues (i-iii) involved in the contextualization process, namely (i) the need to be easily interfaced to different locally available HIS, (ii) the need to cope with the local availability of resources, (iii) the need to adapt guidelines to cope with locally preferred/encouraged procedures, and how we plan to extended it to cope with (iv) the need to keep guidelines up-to-date, maintaining the history of the previous versions, and supporting the distinction between the proposal and validation steps.

Several approaches in the Medical Informatics literature have started to consider the problem of adapting clinical guidelines to the context of application.

As concerns the adaptation based on resources availability, one abstract solution is to have a high level description of the guideline's intentions, in order to ensure the adaptability of the procedure to different contexts still preserving the guideline's intentional objectives (see [21]). Such an approach has been followed in CAMINO (see [9]), a tool that provides users with a user-friendly interface to modify (e.g., by adding/removing/changing actions) a guideline, exploiting additional information about the hospital.

[22] proposes an approach in which the dependencies between actions in a guideline can be explicitly described, and where users' modifications of a general guideline must respect such dependencies.

The above solutions provide facilities to help physicians modify guidelines (consistently with guidelines' intentions and/or functional dependencies). On the other hand, GLARE's resource-based adaptation tool is a completely automatic facility: it takes as input a general guideline and the list of available resources, and prunes out non-executable alternative paths. Moreover, in GLARE, we also take into account the problem of adaptation to the software environment: the three-layered architecture makes easier the task of integrating our system with different commercial DBMS, thus providing a useful support to software contextualization.

Finally, to the best of our knowledge, none of the approaches in the literature take into account the distinction between different levels of authors (user physicians vs supervisors), and manages in a general an principled way the "history" of guideline updates, which are the core of our contribution. We believe that, besides being an advance within the area of clinical guideline management, our approach is also innovative with respect to the area of Temporal Databases (TDB). In particular, although our distinction between time of *proposal* and time of *acceptance* resemble TDB's distinction between *transaction* and *valid* time [23], there is no counterpart of our two-level treatment of authoring and of our management of the propagation of updates between composite IU in the TDB literature.

References

1. Shahar, Y., Miksch, S., Johnson, P.: The Asgaard Project: a Task-Specific Framework for the Application and Critiquing of Time-Oriented Clinical Guidelines, Artificial Intelligence in Medicine 14, (1998), 29-51
2. Musen, M.A., Tu, S.W., Das, A.K., Shahar, Y.: EON: a component-based approach to automation of protocol-directed therapy, JAMIA 3(6), (1996), 367-388
3. Shiffman, R.N., Karras, B.T., Agrawal, A., Chen, R., Menco, L., Nath, S.: GEM: a proposal for a more comprehensive guideline document model using XML, JAMIA 7(5), (2000), 488-498
4. Terenziani, P., Molino, G., Torchio, M.: A Modular Approach for Representing and Executing Clinical Guidelines, Artificial Intelligence in Medicine 23, (2001), 249-276
5. Peleg, M., Boxawala, A.A., et al.: GLIF3: The evolution of a Guideline Representation Format, Proc. AMIA 2000, 645-649
6. Quaglini, S., Stefanelli, M., Cavallini, A., Miceli, G., Fassino, C., Mossa, C.: Guideline-based careflow systems, Artificial Intelligence in Medicine 20(1), (2000), 5-22
7. Fox, J., Johns, N., Rahmanzadeh, A., Thomson, R.: Disseminating medical knowledge: the PROforma approach, Artificial Intelligence in Medicine, 14, 157-181, 1998
8. Gordon, C., Christensen, J.P.: Health Telematics for Clinical Guidelines and Protocols, IOS Press, (1995)
9. Fridsma, D.B. (Guest ed.), Special Issue on Workflow Management and Clinical Guidelines, JAMIA 22(1), (2001), 1-80
10. Terenziani P., Montani S., Bottrighi A., Torchio M., Molino G., Anselma L., Correndo G.: Applying Artificial Intelligence to clinical guidelines: the GLARE approach. In: Cappelli, A., Turini, F. (eds.), Lecture Notes in Artificial Intelligence Vol. 2829, Congresso Nazionale AI*IA 2003, Pisa, september 2003, Springer-Verlag, Berlin (2003), 536-547
11. Terenziani P., Mastromonaco F., Molino G., Torchio M.; Executing clinical guidelines: temporal issues, Proc. AMIA 2000, 848-852
12. Terenziani P., Montani S., Bottrighi A., Molino G., Torchio M.: Supporting physicians in taking decisions in Clinical Guidelines: the GLARE's "what if" facility. Proc. AMIA 2002, 772-776
13. Montani S., Terenziani P.: Decision theory issues for supporting therapy selection in computerized guidelines. In Bouchon-Meunier, B., Coletti, G., Yager, R.R. (eds.): Proc. Information Processing and Managing of Uncertainty in Knowledge-based Systems (IPMU), Casa Editrice Universita' la Sapienza, Roma, (2004), 591-598
14. Montani S., Terenziani P.: Mapping clinical guidelines representation primitives to decision theory concepts. In: Lopez de Mantaras, R., Saitta, L. (eds.): Proc. European Conference on Artificial Intelligence (ECAI) 2004, Valencia, August 2004, IOS Press, Amsterdam (2004), 1063-1064

15. Russel, S., Norvig, P. : Artificial Intelligence: a modern approach. Second edition, Prentice-Hall, (2003)
16. Gold, M.R., Siegel, J.E., Russell, L.B., Weinstein, M.C.: Cost-Effectiveness in Health and Medicine. Oxford University Press, New York, (1996)
17. Tijms, H.C.: Stochastic modelling and analysis: a computational approach, Wiley and Sons, (1986)
18. Molino G, Torchio M, Seidenari C, Giannella R, Olivero F – The key role of data structuring in EHR-supported patient care. In: Proc. STC Clinical data sets for continuity of care and evidence based medicine (J. Hofdijk et al, Eds), Rome, 2003: 26-29
19. Terenziani, P., Montani, S., Bottrighi, A., Torchio, M., Molino, G., Correndo, G.: A context-adaptable approach to clinical guidelines. Proc. MEDINFO'04, M. Fieschi et al. (eds), Amsterdam, IOS Press, (2004), 169-173
20. Boxwala, A.A., Tu, S.W., Peleg, M, Zeng, Q., Ogunyemi ,O., Greenes R.A., et al., Toward a representation format for sharable clinical guidelines, Journal of Biomedical Informatics, 34(3), (2001), 157-169,
21. Shahar Y., Miksch S., Johnson P.: An intention-based language for representing clinical guidelines, Proc AMIA 1996, 592-6
22. Boxwala A.A.: Applying axiomatic design methodology to create guidelines that are locally adaptable, Proc. AMIA 2002
23. Snodgrass R.T.: Ahn I., Temporal Databases, IEEE Computer 19(9), 35-42, (1986)

Water Management Policy Selection Using a Decision Support System Based on a Multi-agent System

Dominique Urbani and Marielle Delhom

SPE Laboratory, UMR CNRS 6134, University of Corsica, Quartier Grossetti,
BP 52 , 20250 Corté, France
durbani@laposte.net, delhom@univ-corse.fr

Abstract. In this paper, we present the framework of a decision support system for water management in the Mediterranean islands coupling a multi-agents system with a geographic information system. The platform developed makes it possible for users to better understand the current operation of the system, to apprehend the evolution of the situation, and to simulate different scenarios according to the selected water policies and the climatic changes hypothesis. We present the model and the simulations we ran to select the best rules to control the consumers during a period of water shortage.

1 Context and Motivation

Mediterranean region is one of the most sensitive areas in the EU regarding sustainable water use. Many islands are now subject to water restrictions during summer [1]. In some cases water has to be imported to the islands via tanker to satisfy the water demand. Since the major users of water are the agricultural and tourism sector, the maximum need for water occurs in the driest part of the year [2].To apprehend the evolution of the water problem [3] in these islands, and to simulate different scenarios according to the selected water policies [4] and the climatic changes hypothesis, we develop model based an the multi-agent systems approach. To study real case our simulator is coupled with a geographic information system that can be used as a decision support system.

2 A New MAS / GIS DSS Approach

The fresh water system concerns many actors from the national government to the simple citizen who have autonomous behavior, communicate, modify their environment and they are all moved by their own goals. Considering the autonomy of the parties, we choose the multi-agents system paradigm to build a model and run simulations. The multi agent approach, individual based model, makes the system global behavior emerge from the agent's individual actions and small decisions. This bottom up architecture permit to select elements related to water use and supply as well as some of the determining factors in a system characterized by the interaction of multiple processes. The MAS approach seems the right way to study the influence of individuals' attitudes on the system.

S. Bandini and S. Manzoni (Eds.): AI*IA 2005, LNAI 3673, pp. 466–469, 2005.
© Springer-Verlag Berlin Heidelberg 2005

The Mediterranean islands water systems, described in GIS, are characterized by their geography vegetation, topography, soil, hydrographic network, roads, and administrative areas. The rainfalls are linked with the topography of the island, the watershed behavior is determined by the soils nature and the land cover, and the human expansion areas are situated according to spatial criteria. Considering the extreme variety of Mediterranean islands and their complexity we cannot initialize our DSS using the common randomized virtual worlds usually used in the MAS but from real data. To describe and initialize the islands we use a geographic information system. This association facilitates the study of real cases initializing the agents and the environment with databases. The GIS data are used by the MAS to instance the agents.

3   DSS Architecture and Implementation

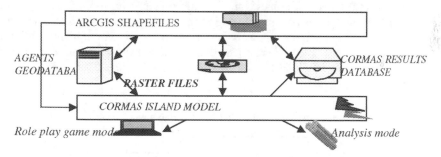

Fig. 1. DSS architecture and implementation

The developed decision support system [5] is based on the cooperation of two subsystems: a multi-agent system platform, a geographic information system. The GIS contain the data about the studied islands and information about the simulation. In addition of the data used during the MAS initialization the GIS stores the scenarios that should be explored and followed during automatic simulations. The geo database also records all data obtained by simulations to analysis. The MAS platform contains a model adapted to each type of agents considered in our study: from a soil model and underground waters to the company who distributes fresh water. The MAS provides interfaces to use the software as role play game or following scenarios simulator producing data for statistical analysis.

To implement the agents we chose the CORMAS [6] multi agent platform This Small Talk platform provides a framework for developing simulation models of coordination modes between individuals and groups who jointly exploit the resources [7]. The information about the agents and the geography are stored in the ARCGIS[8] database. From shapes map files the GIS software produces raster maps used by the MAS platform for the environment initialization: topography, land cover, hydrological characteristics and development sites status. The MAS platform uses an ODBC connection to read in the database the agents attributes and then instances them. The data about agents (new hotels, homes, dams ...) generated during the simulations are stored in the GIS database. The data concerning the land are stored in new raster maps. The attributes of agents (underground water levels, prices, water demand, economy, climatic conditions...) are stored in database provided by the CORMAS platform.

4 Experimentations

The environment is represented using a grid of cells. The model of the agent cell includes attributes about: land cover (transpiration), hydraulic conductivity, altitude, and underground water level and rules to compute: temperature, rain falls, evaporation, transpiration, underground water run-off, underground water level. We just consider the actors essential to model a real system taking into account the problematic of consumers' behaviors control with the following agents: drillings, tanks, water companies, consumers (hotels and homes), and a water police. During an alarm period a consumer will follow the restriction orders, dividing by two its amount of water, with a probability Pc if all his neighbors are civic, otherwise this probability equals Pu. If a consumer who does not respect the restriction instructions from the water company is controlled by the police, he and his 4 neighbors will all change behavior and will restrain their consumption.

Table 1. Score obtained with different strategies of control

Pc	Pu	Pp	R	Civic Consumers Rate %	Score
0,7	0,1	0,15	1	31	736
0,7	0,1	0,30	1	44	1025
0,7	0,1	0,45	1	51	1004
0,95	0,8	0	1	30	912
0,95	0,8	0,15	1	79	4601
0,95	0,8	0,30	1	86	4016

The selection of the best control policy is the aim of our experimentations; therefore we will completely expose the rules governing the consumers and the water authorities. Water police control consumers concerned by the alarm message with a probability Pp. When the authority finds an order offender, all according to the selected polices all the consumers located in cells around, in a range R, will be also controlled. The simulations use the same scenario established with data from the north peninsula of Corsica; a 16 km x 32 km area. This area is represented by a 32 x 64 grid where a cell represents a 500m x 500m area. In this area are located 33 drillings, 12 tanks, a water company, a water authority, 534 consumers and a very dry climate. A policy is considered as a good one if the consumers control rate is low and the rate civic consumers under restriction advises is low. Decision makers are looking for objectives data to support their decisions. To compare the efficiency of the different tested control policies we chose an indicator obtained using the average rate of civic consumer, between the steps 670-1035. SCORE = (AVERAGE_CIVIC_RATE)^2 x (1-Pp)/(1+Pp). The table 1 contains some policies' average scores (100 simulations per set of parameter values) and underlines that to make a good choice we must know the consumers' behaviors.

5 Conclusion

Once the software architecture validated, we are now focused on completing the current agents 'behaviors and add new actors in our island model. We show in this paper a how to use our software to select the best consumers' control policy. More results will be obtained by the next versions that will include more complex agents [9] after submission to experts for critics and validation. Moreover, in order to forecast weather, climatic conditions, river flow for example, we intend to use neural networks [10] [11]. Thus, our future work will concentrate on the definition of a hybrid framework integrated multi-agent system, neural networks and GIS.

References

1. P. Dugot "L'eau autour de la méditerranée". L'Harmatant 2001
2. Blue Plan : http://www.planbleu.org
3. "Management of water demand". Recommendations of the Mediterranean Commission on Sustainable Development adopted by the 10th meeting of the Contracting Parties to the Barcelona Convention, Tunis, 18-21 November 1997
4. J. MARGAT, "Mediterranean Basin Water Atlas", UNESCO, 2004.
5. D. Urbani, M. Delhom, " A Decision Support System for the Water Management in Mediterranean Islands based on a Multi-Agent System ", Proceedings of the AISTA, a conference of the IEEE Computer Society, Luxembourg, 2004
6. CORMAS description http://cormas.cirad.fr/indexeng.htm
7. Bousquet, F., Bakam, I., Proton, H. and Le Page, C. 1998. "Cormas: common-pool resources and multi-agent Systems". Lecture Notes in Artificial Intelligence 1416: 826-838.
8. Arc Info description http://www.esri.com/
9. D. Urbani, M. Delhom, J.F. Santucci "Definition of a Decision Support System to Control a Sheep Herd", Proceedings of the IEEE International Conference on Systems, Man, and Cybernetics, Washington, 2003
10. F. Chiari, M. Delhom, J.F. Santucci "Object Oriented and Neural Networks Simulation: an Application to the study of watersheds". Proceedings of the 4th Middle East Symposium on Simulation and Modelling, sponsored by the IEEE and SCS, Sharjah, UAE, Sept. 2002, pp 25-29.
11. F. Chiari, JB Filippi, M. Delhom, J.F. Santucci "Flow prediction using neural networks simulation and geographic information systems". Proceedings of the IEEE International Conference on Systems, Man, and Cybernetics, Nashville, 2000, pp. 382-386.

A CSP Approach for Modeling
the Hand Gestures of a Virtual Guitarist

Daniele Radicioni[1] and Vincenzo Lombardo[1,2]

[1] Centro di Scienza Cognitiva, Università e Politecnico di Torino,
Via Po 14, 10123 Torino, Italy
[2] Dipartimento di Informatica, Università di Torino,
Corso Svizzera 185, 10149 Torino, Italy
{radicion, vincenzo}@di.unito.it

Abstract. This work presents a model for computing hand gestures of
guitarists, within a broader system for the automatic performance of
music scores. The fingering model encapsulates the main physical and
bio-mechanical constraints that guitarists deal with in their daily practice, and is based on the CSP framework. It is interfaced with a physical
model of the classical guitar, which uses the fingering to compute some
sound synthesis parameters. We report on a preliminary test, where the
fingerings computed by the model are compared with those provided by
three human experts.

1   Introduction

In the last few decades there has been an increasing interest in exploiting AI
techniques for computer music tasks, such as music analysis, composition, im-
provisation and performance, see e.g., [1], [9] and [5]. In the present work we
tackle the task of *music performance*, that is the transformation of symbolic
representations of a *score* into *physical gestures*, needed to operate a music instrument. An environment of music performance consists of the interpretation
of the score, and the application of the gestures to some sound synthesis device
that represents the instrument; gesture modeling is favorably coupled with a
physical model of the instrument.

Within the broad area of the performer/instrument interaction, we emphasize the relevance of the *fingering problem*, which is an essential part of gesture
modeling, deeply affecting the technical and expressive qualities of the sounds
being produced. However, despite the salience of fingering in music performance,
scores often lack of fingering indications, considered unnecessary (being common
knowledge within a certain musical practice) or an execution choice. Namely, in
the context of guitar performance, fingering defines for each note in the score
both the *position* `<string, fret>` on the fingerboard, and the left hand finger
involved in playing (thus yielding the triples `<string, fret, finger>`, called
fingered positions), and sets the parameters that influence the final timbre of
the sound during performance: the succession of the positions individuated is

S. Bandini and S. Manzoni (Eds.): AI*IA 2005, LNAI 3673, pp. 470–473, 2005.

passed to a physical model of the classical guitar [2], which synthesizes the corresponding sounds. Provided that guitarists do use four fingers of the left hand (from the index to the little finger), n notes generate up to 4^n different fingerings in the worst case. Since the same note can be found on up to 4 positions, this number might grow up to 16^n. Thus, the case of guitar and of string instruments in general, is particularly challenging, and requires a considerable amount of experienced skills to human musicians, and automatic procedures aiming at an expressive performance outcome.

In this paper we illustrate a CSP approach for modeling the chord fingering process together with a preliminary experimental assessment of the result. CSP [3] is a well-known modeling technique for encoding problems expressed through constraints on variables; this approach is adequate for chord fingering, because the combination of fingered positions results from bio-mechanical and physical constraints over the hand and the instrument, respectively. This work is part of a larger project, that includes a bio-mechanical model for the hand gestures, estimating the major sources of difficulty in playing melodies [7], and adopts a *graph-based search approach*, that implements an overall motor behavior effort-saving strategy [8].

2   Chord Fingering Modeled Via CSP

Chord fingering is the counterpart in chronological terms of melody fingering, since while melodies are sets of notes to be played in sequence, chords are sets of notes to be played simultaneously. The fingering process takes in input chords described by a score in the traditional western music notation, and returns in output all the fingerings that satisfy a set of constraints coming from the instrument shape and the anatomy of the hand. The set of constraints is devised based on guitar handbooks from historical composers and contemporary teachers, and on a review of some of the didactic opuses of the early 19th Century guitar composers, so to express which combinations of fingered positions could actually be played by a human performer [8]. The fingering problem for chords can be cast in CSP terms as follows (Figure 1): we are given 1) a *set of variables*: the notes composing the chord; 2) a *finite and discrete domain* for each variable: from 1 up to 16 fingered positions per note; 3) *a set of constraints* defined over each pair of the original set of variables. The goal is to find one assignment to the variables such that the assignment satisfies all the constraints, thus being a viable fingering; yet, if more than a unique assignment arises, the goal is to rank them in order to predict which will be preferred by human performers.

The graph in Fig. 1 represents the chord fingering problem: each vertex represents a variable, so a note of the chord. The domain associated to that vertex includes all the fingered positions possible for that note. For example, the note F2, corresponding to the vertex x in the graph, could be played on <6,1,1>, i.e., on the 6th string, 1st fret, by index finger; on <6,1,2>, by middle finger; and so forth. When two variables influence each other's domain, they are connected with an edge: this explains why the graph in Fig. 1 is completely connected,

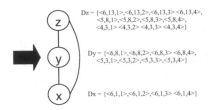

Fig. 1. A chord in input and the domains related to each note of the chord. Each triple in the note domains indicates `<string,fret,finger>`.

because all the fingered positions must be realized at the same time. The solution to the problem is computed by propagating the constraints to yield a simpler problem, and then performing a backtracking search to ground the variables.

Constraint propagation reduces the size of the variable domains while not affecting the final set of solutions. Since path-consistency has an exponential complexity, we adopt the *directional arc-consistency*, and *directional path-consistency* approaches [3], whose time and space complexity is $O(n^3 k^3)$, where n is the number of variables and k bounds the domain sizes, being up to 16. Recall that a graph is *directional-arc-consistent* relatively to *order* $d = (x_1, x_2, ..., x_n)$ iff every variable x_i is arc-consistent relative to every variable x_j s. t. $i \leq j$; and a graph is *directional-path-consistent* relatively to *order* $d = (x_1, x_2, ..., x_n)$ iff for every $k \geq i, j$ the pair $\{x_i, x_j\}$ is path-consistent relative to x_k [3]. Directionality limits consistency to apply only along a given order on variables: in the case of directional path-consistency that is adopted in this paper, given the order $< x_1, x_2, ..., x_n >$ coming from the increasing pitch, the requirement is that for all $i, j \leq k$ we have that $\{x_i, x_j\}$ is path-consistent relatively to x_k.

Once the graph has been made directional path-consistent, *depth-first* search with backtracking occurs. The search follows the natural order, and starts by combining pairs of fingered positions from higher strings (namely, the basses), lower frets and lower fingers. Underpinned by the didactic guitar literature, the search strategy implements a preference for comfortable fingerings, given the evidence that, in absence of higher cognitive constraints, e.g. phrasing or punctuation, performers choose the bio-mechanically easiest solutions [4]. This is immediately applicable to cases of chord fingering on spot (out of any musical context), like in pedagogical situations, which have been considered for the experimental validation.

3 Preliminary Experiment and Conclusions

To the ends of evaluating the model outlined, we compared its fingerings against those provided by three professional guitarists, to check *i*) whether the CSP approach, jointly with the set of physical and bio-mechanical constraints, allows computing the same hand gestures that actually guitarists adopt to play chords, and *ii*) whether the pruning strategy misses any solution given by the human performers. Both of these aspects are relevant, the former being concerned with the timbre reliability, and the latter with the system efficiency: the more predictive the system is, the more it can be pruningful, and then the more efficient. We selected 34 chords, all admitting at least two different fingerings; experts were requested to write on paper -when possible- three different fingerings for each chord, in the order of preference, with the triples <string, fret, finger>. They were also requested to indicate whether any fingering computed by the model was not practicable. The same chords were given in input to the model, and the output annotated.

All the fingerings computed by the model have been found viable (100% *precision*); the fingerings provided by human experts are a subset of the ones computed by the model, except for overall 6 cases (over 218 fingerings computed in total by the model, so 2.75% missing – 97.25% *recall*). Moreover, if we neglect the finger component of the triple, in the 92.1% of the cases the model correctly predicts the preferred fingering indicated by experts (which, disregarding the finger involved, agree in the 97% of the cases). Similarly, if we restrict the comparison between experts and model to the three cases where the experts exactly agreed on the triplets, the success ratio of the model is 75%.

Several complexity factors were disregarded, which may suggest a guideline for future work, such the fact that chords might also be part of musical patterns together with melodic fragments, and such patterns may be learned, stored and retrieved as a block [6]. Future work will attempt accounting for the fingering of whole blocks of notes, where the case-based reasoning methodology would seem to be profitable: such improvements will lead us to consider real pieces from the classical repertoire, and to explore the automatic expressive performance, where the modeling of instrument/performer interactions plays a central role.

References

1. Balaban, M., Ebcioglu, K., Laske, O. (Eds): *Understanding Music with AI – Perspectives on Music Cognition*, Menlo Park/CA: The AAAI Press, 1992.
2. Cuzzucoli, G., Lombardo, V.: *Physical model of the played classical guitar, including the player's touch*, Comput. Music J., **23**, 52–69, Summer 1999.
3. Dechter, R.: *Constraint processing*, Morgan Kaufmann, San Francisco/CA, 2003.
4. Heijink, H., Meulenbroek, R.G.J.: *On the Complexity of Classical Guitar Playing: Functional Adaptations to Task Constraints*, J. Motor Behav., **34**, 339–351, 2002.
5. Lopez de Mantaras, R., Arcos, J.L.: *AI and Music: From Composition to Expressive Performance*, AI Mag., **23**, 43–57, 2002.
6. Parncutt, R., Sloboda, J., Clarke, E., Raekallio, M., Desain, P.: *An ergonomic model of keyboard fingering for melodic fragments*, Music Percept., **14**, 341–382, 1997.
7. Radicioni, D., Anselma, L., Lombardo, V.: *A prototype to compute string instruments fingering*, Proceedings of the Conference on Interdisciplinary Musicology (CIM04), Graz/Austria, 2004, http://gewi.uni-graz.at/~cim04/.
8. Radicioni, D., Lombardo, V.: *Guitar fingering for music performance*, Proceedings of the International Computer Music Conference, Barcelona/Spain, 2005.
9. Widmer G.: *Discovering Simple Rules in Complex Data: A Meta-learning Algorithm and some surprising musical discoveries*, Artif. Intell., **146**, 129–148, 2001.

Experiences with CiceRobot, a Museum Guide Cognitive Robot

I. Macaluso[1], E. Ardizzone[1], A. Chella[1], M. Cossentino[2], A. Gentile[1], R. Gradino[1], I. Infantino[2], M. Liotta[1], R. Rizzo[2], and G. Scardino[1]

[1] Dipartimento Ingegneria Informatica, Università degli Studi di Palermo,
Viale delle Scienze Ed. 6, 90128 Palermo
[2] Istituto di Calcolo e Reti ad Alte Prestazioni, Consiglio Nazionale delle Ricerche,
Viale delle Scienze Ed. 11, 90128 Palermo

Abstract. The paper describes CiceRobot, a robot based on a cognitive architecture for robot vision and action. The aim of the architecture is to integrate visual perception and actions with knowledge representation, in order to let the robot to generate a deep inner understanding of its environment. The principled integration of perception, action and of symbolic knowledge is based on the introduction of an intermediate representation based on Gärdenfors conceptual spaces. The architecture has been tested on a RWI B21 autonomous robot on tasks related with guided tours in the Archaeological Museum of Agrigento. Experimental results are presented.

1 Introduction

The current generation of autonomous robots has showed impressive performances in mechanics and control of movements, see for instance the ASIMO robot by Honda or the QRIO by Sony. However, these state-of the-art robots are rigidly programmed and they present only limited capabilities to perceive, reason and act in a new and unstructured environment.

We claim that a new generation of cognitive autonomous robots, effectively able to perceive and act in unstructured environments and to interact with people, should be aware of their external and inner perceptions, should be able to pay attention to the relevant entities in their environment, to image, predict and to effectively plan their actions.

In the course of the years, we developed a cognitive architecture for robots ([3], [4]). The architecture is currently experimented on an autonomous robot platform based on a RWI B21 robot equipped with a pan-tilt stereo head, laser rangefinder and sonars (Fig. 1). The aim of the architecture is to integrate visual perception with knowledge representation to generate cognitive behaviors in the robot. One of the main features of our proposal is the principled integration of perception, action and of symbolic knowledge representation by means of an intermediate level of representation based on conceptual spaces [7].

We maintain that the proposed architecture is suitable to support robot perception, attention, imagination and planning; in other words, the claim of this paper is that our architecture is a good candidate to achieve an effective overall cognitive behavior.

S. Bandini and S. Manzoni (Eds.): AI*IA 2005, LNAI 3673, pp. 474–482, 2005.

Fig. 1. CiceRobot at work

In order to test our robot architecture in non trivial tasks, we employed it in the Ci-ceRobot project, a project aimed at developing a robotic tour guide in the Archaelogi-cal Museum of Agrigento. The task is considered a significant case study (see [2]) be-cause it involves perception, self perception, planning and human-robot interaction.

The paper is organized as follows. Sect. 2 presents some remarks of the adopted cognitive framework; Sect. 3 deals with the implemented cognitive architecture; Sect. 4 is devoted to describe the robot vision system and Sect. 5 describes the implemented human-robot interaction modalities. Finally, Sect. 6 is a detailed description of an example of the operations of the robot at work.

2   Remarks of the Adopted Theoretical Framework

The cognitive architecture of the robot is based on previous works ([3], [4]) and it is organized in three computational areas (Fig. 2). The Subconceptual Area is concerned with the processing of data coming from the robot sensors and in the considered case it is also a repository of behavior modules, as the localization and the obstacle avoid-ance module. This allows for standard reactive behaviors in order to face unpredict-able situations in real time.

In the Linguistic Area, representation and processing are based on a logic-oriented formalism. The Conceptual Area is intermediate between the Subconceptual and the Linguistic Areas. This area is based on the notion of conceptual spaces CS [7], a met-ric space whose dimensions are related to the quantities processed in the subconcep-tual area.

In the implemented robot system, in the case of static scenes, a knoxel corresponds to geometric 2D, 2D and ½ and 3D primitives according to the perceived data. It should be noted that the robot itself is a knoxel in its conceptual space. Therefore, the perceived objects, as the robot itself, other robots, the surrounding obstacles, all correspond to suitable sets of knoxels in the robot's CS. In order to account for the representation of dynamic scenes, the robot CS is generalized to represent moving and interacting entities [4]. The dynamic Conceptual Space lets the agent to imagine possible future interactions with the objects in the environment: the interaction between the agent and the environment is represented as a sequence of sets of knoxels that is imagined and simulated in the conceptual space before the interaction really happens in the real world. The robot can imagine itself going through the environment and refining the plan if necessary. Once a correct plan is generated, the ideal trajectory can be sent to the robot actuators.

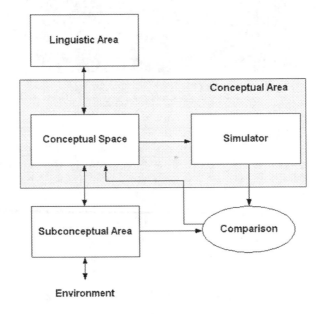

Fig. 2. The three computational areas

3   The Cognitive Architecture of the Robot

The described architecture has been implemented in the working robot and it is shown in Fig. 3. It should be noted that the three areas are concurrent computational components working together on different commitments.

The linguistic area acts as a central decision module: it allows for high level planning and contains a structured description of the agent environment. We adopted the Cyc ontology [6] extended with specific domain assertions and rules that allow common sense reasoning.

At this level, the Information Retrieval Module (IRM) allows to understand visitors queries and to find related information in an interactive way, as described in subsequent Sect.

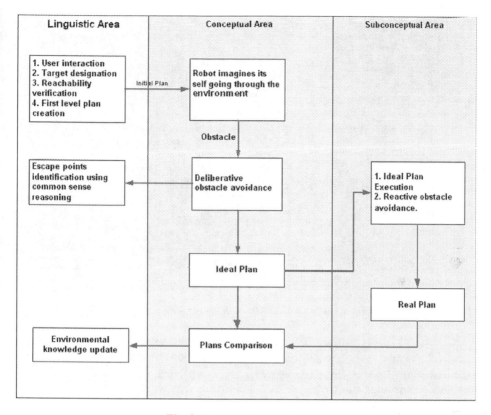

Fig. 3. The cognitive architecture

The linguistic planner receives the IRM results and converts them into knowledge base queries in order to obtain an initial plan which leads the robot to the selected targets, starting from the current configuration. This plan is the optimal solution to navigate the connectivity graph that describes the environment.

The planner, working on the conceptual area, verifies the applicability of the initial plan and, if necessary, modifies it. The planner operates on a 3D environment simulator (Fig. 4), based on VRML description of the robot environment in order to simulate and test the generated plans.

As previously stated, the dynamic conceptual space lets the agent to imagine possible future interactions with the objects. Therefore, by simulation it is possible to continually check the plan execution and, if it is not applicable (for instance because of the presence of some obstacles) a local re-planning task is started, asking the knowledge base a new optimal path to avoid the obstacle. An interesting feature of this approach is that it does not present local minima problems.

At this level, the robot imagines to go through the environment; when the robot finds an obstacle, then it refines the plan. The result is a plan that could be safely executed by the real robot in a static environment. Such a plane can be considered a sequence of expected situations.

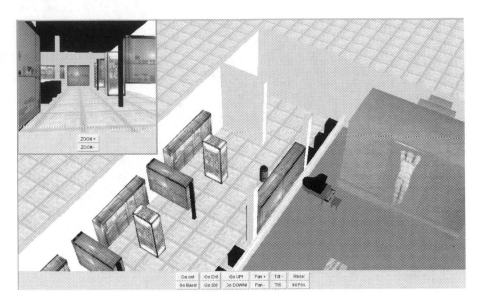

Fig. 4. Snapshot of the 3D simulator from the external and from the robot point of view

Of course the robot will not be able to exactly follow the geometrical path generated by the planner both because the environment is populated by unknown moving and interacting obstacle and also because of the sensory motor errors. In order to deal with such unexpected situations, the reactive modules are activated to control the robot at execution time.

Therefore, the effective trajectory followed by the robot could be different from the planned one. In our model, we propose a direct comparison between the expected results of the action as they were simulated during plan generation, and the effective results, according to the current perception.

The outcome of the comparison process is used to update the knowledge of the environment and to decide whether or not it is necessary to re-plan . This is quite useful when the robot, during the real trajectory, get trapped in a local minimum, for instance because of the collision avoidance module. In that case, the plan is interrupted, the current model of the world is revised and the system starts up the re-planning module.

4   The Vision System

The Vision System is responsible of the knowledge processing arising from vision sensors [9]. A calibrated stereo head and its pan-tilt allows the acquisition of the images of the museum environment during the execution of the robot task. The main task of the vision system is to perform the self-localization allowing to detect and correct the position of the robot in the scene. Preliminary stereo calibration is performed using the Calibration routine that processes the images of a grid.

Camera calibration. The pin-hole camera model requires the estimation of intrinsic parameters in order to allow three-dimensional reconstruction from stereo pairs. Given a world point X, the relation with its projection w on the image is

$$\lambda w = K[R \quad t]X \tag{1}$$

where K is the calibration matrix

$$K = \begin{bmatrix} f_x & 0 & c_x \\ 0 & f_y & c_y \\ 0 & 0 & 1 \end{bmatrix} \tag{2}$$

(c_x, c_y) are the coordinates of the central point, and (f_x, f_y) are focal lengths along image dimensions u and v. Moreover, the radial distortion introduced by lens is corrected estimating the coefficients k_1, k_2, p_1, and p_2 that are involves in the following model

$$u_D = u + u[k_1 r^2 + k_2 r^4] + [2p_1 uv + p_2(r^2 + 2u^2)]$$
$$v_D = v + v[k_1 r^2 + k_2 r^4] + [2p_2 uv + p_2(r^2 + 2v^2)] \tag{3}$$

where (u,v) are coordinates of the undistort image, (u_D, v_D) are coordinates of the distort image, and $r^2 = u^2 + v^2$. The calibration matrix is estimated by the standard algorithm described by Zhang [13] using a grid, and radial distortion coefficients by non-linear minimization algorithm [11] (see Fig. 5). Some filtering operations are performed on the acquired images in order to limit the influence of changing illumination during the robot movement.

Robot's self localization. Two critical issues are to be considered when the robot moves in the real world: the starting point and the initial orientation of the robotic platform are not exactly known, wheels friction and floor defects could be introduce great imprecision in the estimate of the current position of the robot taking in account the odometer. As consequence of that, the position of the robot needs to be updated during robot's movement using visual localization of known objects. The implemented vision system uses as landmark the same planar grid employed in the calibration phase: they are placed on the various walls of the museum and are visible to the robot also in presence of visitors.

When the self-localization is requested, the following operations are executed:

1. The coordinates of the nearest marker are obtained;
2. Camera pan-tilt movements are performed to view the marker by stereo head;
3. Additional corrections to pan-tilt position are computed to place the marker at the image centers;
4. 3D reconstruction of the marker points are performed by triangulation [8];
5. The new estimated position of the robot respect to the landmark is computed;
6. The robot position is updated.

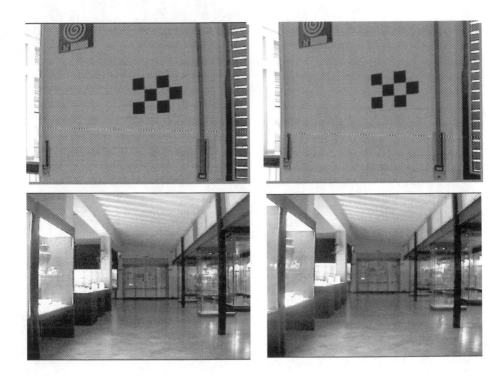

Fig. 5. In the first row, it is showed the calibration grid and the result of radial distortion removal. In the second row, a typical museum scene viewed by robot cameras. The light conditions and the structure of the scene are difficult to manage at the vision level.

Scene matching. The images acquired by the camera that represent the current perception of the robot are now matched with the corresponding expected scene generated by the planner and rendered by the 3D simulator previously described. Currently, this operation is simply performed by matching the corresponding landmarks in the acquired image and in the simulated one.

As previously stated, this comparison process has the role to synchronize the effective, external robot perception of the world with the inner robot expectations about the environment.

5 Human-Robot Interactions

Interaction between robot and visitors is a praiseworthy aspect of Cicerobot. The robot, not only explains to visitors the contents of windows but it also enables them to do queries to deepen topics related to objects that the windows themselves contain.
To this purpose, the robot is provided with an Information Retrieval Module (IRM) that finds information for an interactive presentation.

The main task of the IRM [1] is to provide the user with relevant information as a result of a request; at the same time, the quantity of less interesting information has to be minimized. Traditional search engines retrieve information through lexical criterions; so doing, all and only documents, containing the set of specified words in queries, or some logical combinations, are recovered. Then, information returned with this approaches is strongly dependent by the user request formulation.

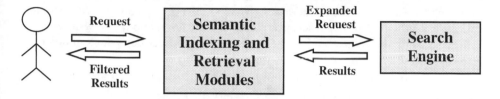

Fig. 6. The Information Retrieval Module

Well known problems of lexical information retrieval systems are the polysemy, i.e., a term that can have many meanings, and synonymy, a concept that can be expressed by different terms. Interposing semantic modules between user and traditional search engine may help to retrieve higher level of interesting information. In the current implementation, the interposed modules enable semantic indexing and search. Both of them are based on the Latent Semantic Analysis (LSA), a theory related to knowledge representation and induction [10] (see Fig 6). User Request is converted in an Expanded Request, so that the search engine is questioned not only on words contained in the user request but also on words semantically closed to those which build the initial query. The interposed semantic module is then used to semantically filter the Results.

The results of semantic analysis is a list of documents and a windows sequence semantically connected to the user query.

Another feature of the IR system is that afterwards the interaction with the user it can increase its own knowledge base, inserting in the local repository also new documents, obtained in research on Internet or in the offline research and coding them in the semantic space: in this way the system knowledge base is improved during time basing on the experience.

The robot speech generation is enabled by a Vocal User Interface (VUI) based on the VoiceXML standard [12]. The environment is based on the IBM™ WebSphere Voice Response Server, which runs on a laptop sitting on the robot and equipped with speakers.

6 CiceRobot at Work

The robot operates in the "Sala Giove" of the Archaeological Museum of Agrigento. The user of the robot inserts a query, and the IRM returns the corresponding list of documents shown by a web interface. Moreover, a sequence of related windows are returned. Starting from this information, the system generates the plan of the mission task.

Before the execution, the robot, as previously described, simulates the generated plan by using the 3D simulator, in order to check the plan itself and eventually to refine it.

After this step, the robot starts the visit. During the visit, the robot gives some general information about the museum. When the robot reaches one of the selected windows, it stops and it gives the related information previously retrieved by the IRM.

In the case that around one of the selected windows there are some visitors so that the robot is not able to reach it, CiceRobot will continue the visit and it will reschedule the skipped window. When, during the visit, CiceRobot perceives a visitor in its trajectory, the robot stops and it sends an alarm sound. During the whole visit, the images acquired by the camera are also sent via Internet to other computers in order to perform a sort of remote visit of the museum.

References

1. R. Baeza-Yates and B. Ribeiro-Neto. Modern Information Retrieval. Addison Wesley, 1999.
2. W. Burgard, A. B. Cremers, D. Fox, D. Hähnel, G. Lakemeyer, D. Schulz, W. Steiner, S. Thrun, Experiences with an interactive museum tour-guide robot, Artificial Intelligence 114 (1999) 3–55.
3. A. Chella, M. Frixione, and S. Gaglio, A cognitive architecture for artificial vision, Artificial Intelligence, pp. 89:73–111, 1997.
4. A. Chella, M. Frixione, S.Gaglio, Understanding dynamic scenes, Artificial Intelligence, Vol 123, pp. 89-132, 2000.
5. A. Chella, M.Cossentino, R. Pirrone, A. Ruisi, Modeling Ontologies for Robotic Environments, The Fourteenth International Conference on Software Engineering and Knowledge Engineering - July 15-19, 2002 - Ischia, Italy.
6. Cyc Home Page, Cycorp Inc., Austin, TX. http://www.cyc.com.
7. P. Gärdenfors, Conceptual Spaces, MIT Press, Bradford Books, Cambridge, MA, (2000).
8. R. Hartley and A. Zisserman, Multiple View Geometry in Computer Vision, Cambridge University Press, 2004.
9. I. Infantino, M. Cossentino, A. Chella, An agent based architecture for robotic vision systems, Agentcities iD3, Barcelona, Spain, 6-8 February 2003.
10. T. K. Landauer, P. W. Foltz, D. Laham, An introduction to Latent Semantic Analysis, Discourse Processes, pp. 259- 284, 1998.
11. G. Stein, Lens distortion calibration using point correspondences, in proc. Computer Vision and Pattern Recognition Conference, pages 602-608, 1997.
12. Voice Extensible Markup Language Home Page, http://www.w3.org/TR/2004/REC-voicexml20-20040316/
13. Z. Zhang, A Flexible New Technique for Camera Calibration, IEEE Transactions on Pattern Analysis and Machine Intelligence, vol. 22, n. 11, pp. 1330-1334, 2000.

Human-Robot Interaction Through Mixed-Initiative Planning for Rescue and Search Rovers

Alberto Finzi[1] and Andrea Orlandini[2]

[1] Dipartimento di Informatica e Sistemistica, Università degli Studi di Roma "La Sapienza",
[2] Dipartimento di Informatica e Automazione, Università degli Studi di Roma TRE

Abstract. We present an approach to human-robot interaction in Urban Search and Rescue (USAR) domains based on reactive mixed-initiative planning. A model-based executive monitoring system is used to coordinate the operator's interventions and the concurrent activities of a rescue rover. In this setting, the user's and the robot's activities are coordinated by a continuos reactive planning process. We show the advantages of this approach for both the operator situation awareness and human-robot interaction during rescue missions. We present the implementation of the control architecture on a robotic system (DORO) providing some experimental results obtained from testing in rescue arenas.

1 Introduction

Urban search and rescue (USAR) deals with response capabilities for facing urban emergencies, and it involves the location and rescue of people trapped because of a structural collapse. Starting in 2000, the National Institute of Standard Technology (NIST) together with the Japan National Special Project for Earthquake Disaster Mitigation in Urban Areas [26,27,13,10] has initiated the USAR robot competitions. NIST, in particular, features future standards of robotics infrastructures, pioneering robotics participation to rescue missions. RoboCup Rescue contests are a test-bed of the technology development of NIST project, and are becoming a central international event for rescue robots, and a real challenge for the robotics community. Rescue robots uphold human operators exploring dangerous and hazardous environments and searching for survivors. A crucial aspect of rescue environments, discussed in [4] and [16] concerns the operator situation awareness and human-robot interaction. In [16] the difficulties in forming a mental model of the "robot eye" are endorsed, pointing out the role of the team. Differently from real tests, like the one in Miami (see [4]), during rescue competitions the operator can follow the robot activities only through the robot perception of the environment, and its internal states. In this sense, the overall control framework has to capture the operator attention towards "what is important" so as to make the correct choices: follow a path, enter a covert way, turn around an unvisited corner, check whether a visible victim is really reachable, according to some specific knowledge acquired during the exploration. In this setting, a fully manual control over a robot rescue is not effective [3]: the operator attention has to be focused over a wide range of activities, losing concentration on the real rescue mission objective, i.e. locating victims. Moreover, a significant level of training is needed to teleoperate a rescue rover. On the

S. Bandini and S. Manzoni (Eds.): AI*IA 2005, LNAI 3673, pp. 483–494, 2005.

other hand, fully autonomous control systems are not feasible in a rescue domain where too many capabilities are needed. Therefore, the integration of autonomous and teleoperated activities is a central issue in rescue scenarios and has been widely investigated [11,30,7,15,30].

In this work we describe a mixed-initiative planning approach [1,19,2,5] to Human-Robot Interaction (HRI) in a rescue domain and illustrate the main functionalities of a rescue robot system[1]. We deploy a model-based executive monitoring system to interface the operators' activities and the concurrent functional processes in a rescue rover. In this setting, the user's and the robot's activities are coordinated by a continuos reactive planning process which has to (i) check the execution status with respect to a declarative model of the system; (ii) provide proactive activity while mediating among conflicting initiatives. In particular, we show that this approach can enhance both the operator situation awareness and human-robot interaction for the execution and control of the diverse activities needed during a complex mission such as the rescue one.

The advantage of this approach can be appreciated considering the HRI awareness discussed in [7]:

• robot-human interaction: given a declarative model of the robot activities, the monitoring system can be "self-aware" about the current situation, at different levels of abstraction; in this way, complex and not nominal interactions among activities can be detected and displayed to the operator;
• human-robot interaction: the operator can take advantage of basic functionalities like mapping, localization, learning vantage points for good observation, victim detection and localization; these functionalities purposely draw his attention toward the current state of exploration, while he interacts with a mixed initiative reactive planner [1].

Finally, the humans' overall mission can take advantage of the model, that keeps track of the robot/operator execution history, goals, and subgoals.

2   Rescue Scenario

The National Institute of Standard and Technology (NIST) has developed physical test scenarios for rescue competitions. There are three NIST arenas, denoted by yellow, orange, and red, of varying degrees of difficulty. A yellow arena represents an indoor flat environment with minor structural damage (e.g. overturned furniture), an orange arena is multilevel and has more rubble (e.g. bricks), a red one represents a very damaged unstructered environment: multilevel, large holes, rubber tubing etc. The arenas are accessible only by mobile robots controlled by one or more operators from a separated place. The main task is to locate as many victims as possible in the whole arena.

Urban search and rescue arena competitions are very hard test-beds for robots and their architectures. In fact, the operator-robot has to coordinate several activities: exploring and mapping the environment, avoiding obstacles (bumping is severely penalized), localizing itself, searching for victims, correctly locating them on the map, identifying them through a numbered tag, and finally describing their own status and conditions. For each mission there is a time limit of 20 minutes, to simulate the time pressure in a

---

[1] Doro is the third award winner in Lisbon contest (2004).

real rescue environment. In this contest human-robot interaction has a direct impact on the effectiveness of the rescue team performance.

We consider the NIST yellow arena as the test-bed for our control architecture mounted on our robotic platform (DORO). The main modules employed in DORO's control system are: *Map*, managing the algorithm of map construction and localization; *Navigation*, guiding the robot through the arena with exploration behaviour and obstacle's avoidance procedures; *Vision*, used in order to automatically locate victims around the arena.

The control sequence is based on a high level tasks cycle such as Localize, Observe general surroundings, look specially for Victims, Report (called LOVR in [16]). In our system, this cycle corresponds to these macro activities: map construction, visual observation, vision process execution and victim's presence report.

3   Human Robot Interaction and Mixed Initiative Planning in Rescue Arenas

There have been several efforts to establish the essential aspects of human-robot interaction, given the current findings and state of the art concerning robot autonomy and its modal-abilities towards humans and environments (see e.g.[6,11,4,25,12] and the already cited [16,15,30,7], specifically related to the rescue environment). It is therefore crucial to model the interaction in terms of a suitable interplay between supervised autonomy (the operator is part of the loop, and decides navigation strategies according to an autonomously drawn map, and autonomous localization, where obstacle avoidance is guaranteed by the robot sensory system) and full autonomy (e.g. visual information is not reliable because of darkness or smoke etc., and the operator has to lean upon the robot exploration choices).

In order to allow the tight interaction described above, we designed a control system where the HRI is fully based on a mixed-initiative planning activity. The planning process is to continuously coordinate, integrate, and monitor the operator interventions and decisions with respect to the ongoing functional activities, taking into account the overall mission goals and constraints. More precisely, we developed an interactive control system which combines the following features:

• **Model-based control.** The control system is endowed with declarative models of the controllable activities, where causal and temporal relations are explicitly represented [17,29,18]. In this way, hard and soft constraints can be directly encoded and monitored. Furthermore, formal methods and reasoning engines can be deployed either off-line and on-line, to check for consistency, monitor the executions, perform planning or diagnosis. In a mixed-initiative setting the aim of a model-based system is twofold: on the one hand the operator activities are explicitly modeled and supervised by the control system; on the other hand, the model-based monitoring activity exports a view of the system that is intuitive and readable by humans, hence the operator can further supervise the robot status in a suitable human robot interface.

• **Reactive executive monitoring.** Given this model, a reactive planning engine can monitor both the system's low-level status and the operator's interventions by continuously performing sense-plan-act cycles. At each cycle the reactive planner has to:

(i) monitor the consistency of the robot and operator activities (w.r.t. the model) managing failures; (ii) generate the robot's activities up to a planning horizon. The short-range planning activity can also balance reactivity and goal-oriented behaviour: short-term goals/tasks and external/internal events can be combined while the planner tries to solve conflicts. In this way, the human operator can interact with the control system through the planner in a mixed initiative manner.

• **Flexible interval planning.** At each execution cycle a flexible temporal plan is generated. Given the domain uncertainty and dynamics, time and resources cannot be rigidly scheduled. On the contrary, it is necessary to account for flexible behaviours, allowing one to manage dynamic change of time and resource allocation at execution time. For this reason the start and end time of each scheduled activity is not binded, but the values span a temporal interval.

• **High-level agent programming.** The high-level agent programming paradigm allows one to integrate procedural programming and reasoning mechanisms in a uniform way. In this approach, the domain's first principles are explicitly represented in a declarative relational model, while control knowledge is encoded by abstract and partial procedures. Both the system's and the operator's procedural operations can be expressed by high-level partial programs which can be completed and adapted to the execution context by a program interpreter endowed with inference engines.

4   Control Architecture

In this section, we describe the control system we have defined to incorporate the design principles introduced above. Following the approach in [17,29,28,8] we introduce a control system where decision processes (including declarative activities and operator's interventions) are tightly coupled with functional processes through a model-based executive engine. Figure 1 illustrates the overall control architecture designed for DORO. The physical layer devices are controlled by three functional modules associated to the main robots activities (mapping and localization, visual processing, and navigation). The *state manager* and *task dispatcher* in the figure are designed to manage communication between the executive and functional layers.

The *state manager* gets from each single module its current status so that any module can query the state manager about the status of any another module. The state manager updates its information every 200 msec., the task dispatcher sends tasks activation signals to the modules (e.g. *map_start*) upon receiving requests from the planner or the human operator. The overall computational cycle works as follows: the planner gets the modules status querying the state manager. Once the state manager provides the execution context, the planner produces a plan of actions (planning phase about 0.5 sec.) and yields the first set of commands to the task dispatcher. In the execution phase (about 0.5 sec.), each module reads the signals and starts its task modifying its state. At the next cycle start, the planner reads the updated status through the state manager and can check whether the tasks were correctly delivered. If the status is not updated as expected, a failure is detected, the current plan is aborted and a suitable recovery procedure is called.

The human operator can interact with the control loop both during the plan and the act phase. In the planning phase, the operator can interact with the control system by:

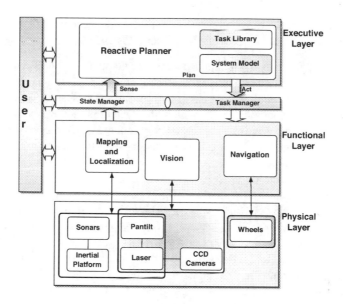

Fig. 1. Control architecture

(i) posting some goals which are to be integrated in the partial plan already generated; (ii) modifying the generated plan through the user interface; (iii) on-line changing some planning parameters, like the planning horizon, the lenght of the planning cycle, etc.

5 Model-Based Monitoring

A model-based monitoring system is to enhance both the system safeness and the operator situation awareness. Given a declarative representation of the system causal and temporal properties, the flexible executive control is provided by a reactive planning engine which harmonizes the operator activity (commands, tasks, etc.) with the mission goals and the reactive activity of the functional modules. Since the execution state of the robot is continuously compared with a declarative model of the system, all the main parallel activities are integrated into a global view and subtle resources and time constraints violations can be detected. In this case the planner can also start or suggest recovery procedures the operator can modify, neglect, or respect. Such features are implemented by deploying *high-level agent programming* in Temporal Concurrent Golog [23,21,9] which provides both a declarative language (i.e. Temporal Concurrent Situation Calculus [20,22,21]) to represent the system properties and the planning engine to generate control sequences.

Temporal Concurrent Situation Calculus. The Situation Calculus (SC) [14] is a sorted first-order language representing dynamic domains by means of *actions*, *situations*, i.e. sequences of actions, and *fluents*, i.e. situation dependent properties. Temporal Concurrent Situation Calculus (TCSC) extends the SC with time and concurrent actions. In this framework, concurrent durative processes [20,22,21] can be represented by fluent properties started and ended by durationless actions. For example, the process *going* (p_1, p_2) is started by the action $startGo(p_1, t)$ and it is ended by $endGo(p_2, t')$.

Declarative Model in TCSC. The main processes and states of DORO are explicitly represented by a declarative dynamic-temporal model specified in the Temporal Concurrent Situation Calculus (TCSC) . This model represents cause-effect relationships and temporal constraints among the activities: the system is modeled as a set of *components* whose state changes over time. Each component (including the operator's operations) is a concurrent thread, describing its history over time as a sequence of states and activities. For example, in the rescue domain some components are: *pant-tilt*, *slam*, *navigation*, *visualPerception*, etc.

Each of these is associated with a set of processes, for instance some of those are the following: *SLAM* can perform $slmMap$ to map the environment and $slmScan$ to acquire laser measures; *visualPerception* can use $visProcess(x)$ to process an image x. *navigation* can explore a new area ($nvWand$) or reach a target point x ($nvGoTo$); *pan-tilt* can deploy $ptPoint(x)$ (moving toward x) and $ptScan(x)$ (scanning x). The history of states for a component over a period of time is a *timeline*. Figure 2 illustrates a possible evolution of *navigation*, *slam*, and *pan-tilt* up to a planning horizon.

Hard time constraints among activities can be defined in the temporal model using Allen-like relations, e.g.: $ptPoint(x)$ *precedes* $ptScan(x)$, $ptScan(x)$ *during* $nvStop$.

Temporal Concurrent Golog. Golog is a situation calculus-based programming language which allows one to define procedural scripts composed of primitive actions explicitly represented in a SC action theory. This hybrid framework integrates procedural programming and reasoning about the domain properties. Golog programs are defined by means of standard (and not so-standard) Algol-like control constructs: (i) action sequence: $p_1; p_2$, (ii) test: ϕ?, (iii) nondeterministic action choice $p_1|p_2$, (iv) conditionals, while loops, and procedure calls. Temporal Concurrent Golog (TCGolog) is the Golog version suitable for durative and parallel actions, it is based on TCSC and allows parallel action execution: $a\|b$. An example of a TCGolog procedure is:

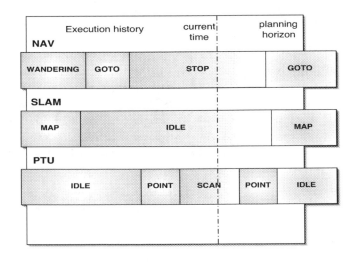

Fig. 2. Timelines evolution

$$\mathbf{proc}(observe(x),$$
$$\mathbf{while}\ (nvStop \wedge \neg obs(x))\ \mathbf{do}\ \pi(t_1, start(t_1))? :$$
$$[\mathbf{if}\ (ptIdle(0))\ \mathbf{do}\ \pi(t_2, startPoint(x, t_1)) : (t_2 - t_1 < 3)?)|$$
$$\mathbf{if}\ (ptIdle(x))\ \mathbf{do}\ \pi(t_3, startScan(x, t_3)) : (t_3 - t_1 < 5)?))).$$

Here the nondeterministic choice between $startPoint$ and $startScan$ is left to the Golog interpreter which has to decide depending on the execution context. Note that, time constraints can be encoded within the procedure itself. In this case the procedure definition leaves few nondetermistic choices to the interpreter. More generally, a Golog script can range from a completely defined procedural program to an abstract general purpose planning algorithm like the following:

$$\mathbf{proc}(plan(n),\ true?\ |\ \pi(a, (primitive\_action(a))?\ :\ a)\ :\ plan(n-1))$$

The semantics of a Golog program δ is a situation calculus formula $Do(\delta, s, s')$ meaning that s' is a possible situation reached by δ once executed from the situation s. For example, the meaning of the $a|b$ execution is captured by the logical definition $Do(a|b, s, s') \doteq Do(a, s, s') \vee Do(a, s, s')$.

Flexible Behaviours. Our monitoring system is based on a library of Temporal Concurrent Golog scripts representing a set of flexible behaviour fragments. Each of them is associated to a task and can be selected if it is compatible with the execution context. For example a possible behaviour fragment can be written as follows:

$$\mathbf{proc}(explore(d),\ [\pi(t_1, startMap(t_1)) \| \pi(t_2, startWand(t_2)) :$$
$$\pi(t_3, endWand(t_3)) : \pi(x, startGoto(x, t_3)) : (t_3 - t_2 < d)?))].$$

This Golog script is associated with the exploration task, it starts both mapping and wandering activities; the wandering phase has a timeout d, after this the rover has to go somewhere. The timeout d will be provided by the calling process that can be either another Golog procedure or a decision of the operator.

Reactive Planner/Interpreter. As illustrated before, for each execution cycle, once the status is updated (sensing phase), the Golog interpreter (planning phase) is called to extend the current control sequence up to the planning horizon. When some task ends or fails, new tasks are selected from the task library and compiled into flexible temporal plans filling the timelines. Under nominal control, the robot's activities are scheduled according to a closed-loop similar to the LOVR (*Localize, Observe general surroundings, look specially for Victims, Report*) sequence in [16]. Some of these activities can require the operator initiative that is always allowed.

Failure Detection and Management. Any system malfunctioning or bad behaviour can be detected by the reactive planner (i.e. the Golog interpreter) when world inconsistencies have to be handled. In this case, after an idle cycle a recovery task has to be selected and compiled w.r.t the new execution status. For each component we have classified a set of relevant failures and appropriate flexible recovery behaviours. For example, in the visual model, if the scanning processes fails because of a timeout, in the recovery task the pan-tilt unit must be reset taking into account the constraints imposed by the current system status. This can be defined by a very abstract Golog procedure, e.g.

$$\mathbf{proc}(planToPtuInit,$$
$$\pi(t, time(t))? : plan(2) : \pi(t_1, PtIdle(0) : time(t_1))? : (t_1 - t < 3)?))).$$

In this case, the Golog interpreter is to find a way to compile this procedure getting the pan-tilt idle in less than two steps and three seconds. The planner/Golog interpreter can fail in its plan generation task raising a *planner timeout*. This failure is critical. We identified three classes of recoveries depending on the priority level of the execution. If the priority is high, a safe mode has to be immediately reached by means of fast reactive procedures (e.g. $goToStandBy$). In medium priority, some extra time for planning can be obtained by interleaving planning and execution: a greedy action is executed so that the interpreter can use the next time-slot to end its work. In the case of low priority, the failure is handled by replanning: a new task is selected and compiled. In medium and low level priority the operator can be explicitly involved in the decision process in a synchronous way.

6   Mixed-Initiative Planning

The control architecture introduced before allows us to define some hybrid operative modalities lying between autonomous and teleoperated modes and presenting some capabilities that are crucial in a collaborative planning setting. In particular, following [2], our system permits *incremental planning*, *plan stability*, and it is also *open to innovation*. The high-level agent programming paradigm, associated with the short-range planning/interpretation activity, permits an *incremental* generation of plans. In this way, the user attention can be focused on small parts of the problem and the operator can assess local possible decisions, without losing the overall problem constraints. *Plan stability* is guaranteed by flexible behaviours and plan recovery procedures, which can harmonize the modification of plans, due to the operator's interventions or exogenous events. Minimal changes to plans lead to short replanning phases minimizing misalignments. Concerning the *open to innovation* issue, the model-based monitoring activity allows one to build novel plans, under human direction, and to validate and reason about them. Depending on the operator-system interaction these features are emphasized or obscured. We distinguish among three different mixed-initiative operational modalities.

- **Planning-based interaction.** In this setting, the planning system generates cyclic LOVR sequences and the operator follows this sequence with few modifications, e.g. extending or reducing process durations. Here task dispatching is handled in an automated way and the operator can supervise the decisions consistency minimizing the interventions. The human-operator can also act as an executor and manually control some functional activities scheduled by the planner. For example, he can decide to suspend automated navigations tools and take the control of mobile activities, in this way he can decide to explore an interesting location or escape from difficult environments. In this kind of interaction the operator initiative minimally interferes with the planning activity and *plan stability* is emphasized.
- **Cooperation-based interaction.** In this modality, the operator modifies the control sequence produced by the planner by skipping some tasks or inserting new actions. The operator's interventions can determine a misalignment between the monitoring system expectations (i.e. the control plan) and the state of the system; this is captured at beginning of the next execution cycle when the state monitor provides the current state of the modules. In order to recover the monitor-system adherence, the planner has to

start some recovery operations which are presented to the operator. Obviously, these activities are to be executed in real-time by verifying the satisfiability of the underlaying temporal and causal constraints. This modality enables maximal flexibility for the planner's and operator's initiatives. Indeed, they can dialogue and work in a concurrent way contributing to the mission completion (*incremental planning*): while the operator tries to modify the plan in order to make it more effective (i.e. the system is *open to innovation*), the monitoring system can validate the operator's choices an in the case of safety constraints violations, it warns the user and/or suggests suitable corrections.

• **Operator-based interaction.** This modality is similar to teleoperation, the system activities are directly managed by the operator (some minor autonomy can always be deployed when the operator attention is to be focused on some particular task, e.g. looking for victims). The operator-based interaction is reached when the operators' interventions are very frequent, hence the planner keeps replanning and cannot support the user with a meaningful proactive activity. In this operative scenario, the planner just follows the operators' choices playing in the role of a consistency checker. The monitoring system can notify the user only about safety problems and, in this case, recovery procedures can be suggested (*incremental planning* can be used only to generate non-critical planning procedures).

Each of these modalities is implicitly determined by the way the operator interacts with the system. Indeed, in a mixed-initiative setting, if the operator is idle, the monitor works in the planner-based mode. Instead, the operator's interventions can disturb such a status bringing the system toward the operator-based interaction. Note that for each mixed-initiative mode, the system continuously checks the activities performed, including human-operator actions, and when necessary it replans or provides suggestions to the operator.

7   Mixed-Initiative Approach at Work

The architecture discussed in this article is implemented on our robotic platform (DORO) and here we present some tests performed in a yellow rescue arenas.

The hardware platform for DORO is a two wheeled differential drive Pioneer from ActivMedia with an on-board laptop hosts navigation, map building, reactive planning routines and the on-board sensors control processing. An additional PC, for remote control, is also used for image processing. The two PCs are linked with an Ethernet wireless LAN (802.11a) to enable remote control and monitoring of the mobile robot. Two color cameras are mounted on top of the robot on a pant-tilt head. A laser range finder DISTO pro is mounted on the pan-tilt between the two cameras.

The robot motion control (speed and heading) and sonar readings are provided by a serial connection to the Pioneer controller using the Aria API facilities. Video streaming and single frames are acquired through the Image Acquisition Toolbox from Matlab (TM). Inertial data and laser measurements are acquired through dedicated C++ modules that manage the low level serial connections.

We tested the control architecture and the effectiveness of the mixed-initiative approach in our domestic arenas comparing three possible settings: (i) *fully teleoperated*: navigation, slam, and vision disabled; (ii) *mixed-initiative control*: the monitoring

Table 1. Experimental results for the three operational modalities

	Fully Teleop			Supervised			Autonomous		
Surface (m^2)	20	30	40	20	30	40	20	30	40
Explored (%)	85	78	82	85	82	79	49	80	75
Visited env.	5/6	7/9	7/9	6/6	8/9	7/9	3/6	7/9	6/9
Bumps (tot.)	11	7	9	3	2	2	2	1	2
Victims (x/4)	3.0	2.1	2.2	2.5	2.6	2.1	1.3	1.4	1.2
Operator (%)	100	100	100	10	15	15	0	0	0

system was enabled and the operator could supervise the rover status and take the control whenever this was needed; (iii) *autonomous control*. During mixed-initiative control tests, we considered also the percentage of time spent by the operator in *operator-based* mode (*operator* in Table 1). We deployed these three settings on yellow arenas considering increasing surface areas, namely, $20\ m^2$, $30\ m^2$, $40\ m^2$ (*surface* in Table 1), associated with increasingly complex topologies. For each test, there were 4 victims to be discovered. We limited the exploration time to 10 minutes. We performed 10 tests for each modality. Different operators were involved in the experiments in order to avoid an operator visiting the same arena configuration twice. For each test class we considered: (i) the percentage of the exlored arena surface; (ii) the number of visited and inspected topological environments (rooms, corridors, etc.) w.r.t. the total number; (iii) the overall number of encountered obstacles (i.e. arena bumps); (iv) the number of detected victims; (v) the operator activity (percentage w.r.t. the mission duration). The results are summarized in the Table 1 reporting the average values of each field.

Following the analysis schema in [24] here we discuss the following points: *global navigation*, *local navigation and obstacle encountered*, *vehicle state*, *victim identification*.

Concerning *global navigation*, the performance of the mixed-initiative setting are quite stable while the autonomous system performs poorly in small arenas because narrow environments challenge the navigation system which is to find how to escape from them. In greater and more complex arenas the functional navigation processes (path planner, nearest unexplored point system, etc.) start to be effective while the fully teleoperated behaviour degrades: the operator gets disoriented and often happens that already visited locations and victims are considered as new ones, while we never experienced this in the mixed-initiative and autonomous modes. The effectiveness of the control system for *local navigation* and *vehicle state* awareness can be read on the *bumps* row; indeed the bumps are significantly reduced enabling the monitoring system. In particular, we experienced the recovery procedures effectiveness in warning the operator about the vehicle attitude. E.g. a typical source of bumping in teleoperation is the following: the visual scanning process is interrupted (timeout) and the operator decides to go on in one direction forgetting the pan-tilt in a non-idle position. Enabling the monitor, a recovery procedure interacts with the operator suggesting to reset the pan-tilt position. The victim identification effectiveness can be assessed considering the founded victims in the autonomous mode; considering that visual processing was deployed without any supervision, these results seem quite good (we experienced some rare false-positive).

8   Conclusion

Human-robot interaction and situation awareness are crucial issues in a rescue environment. In this context a suitable interplay between supervised autonomy and full autonomy is needed. For this purpose, we designed a control system where the HRI is fully based on a mixed-initiative planning activity which is to continuously coordinate, integrate, and monitor the operator interventions and decisions with respect to the concurrent functional activities. Our approach integrates model-based executive control, flexible interval planning and high level agent programming. This control architecture allows us to define some hybrid operative modalities lying between *teleoperated mode* and *autonomous mode* and presenting some capabilities that are crucial in a collaborative planning setting. We implemented our architecture on our robotic platform (DORO) and tested it in a NIST yellow arena. The comparison between three possible settings (*fully teleoperated, mixed-initiative control, autonomous control*) produce encouraging results.

References

1. M. Ai-Chang, J. Bresina, L. Charest, A. Chase, J.C.-J. Hsu, A. Jonsson, B. Kanefsky, P. Morris, Kanna Rajan, J. Yglesias, B.G. Chafin, W.C. Dias, and P.F. Maldague. Mapgen: mixed-initiative planning and scheduling for the mars exploration rover mission. *Intelligent Systems, IEEE*, 19(1):8–12, 2004.
2. James Allen and George Ferguson. Human-machine collaborative planning. In *Proceedings of the 3rd international NASA Workshop on Planning and Scheduling for Space*, 2002.
3. David J. Bruemmer, Ronald L. Boring, Douglas A. Few, Julie L. Marble, and Miles C. Walton. "i call shotgun!": An evaluation of mixed-initiative control for novice users of a search and rescue robot. In *Proceedings of IEEE International Conference on Systems, Man and Cybernetics*, 2003.
4. J. Burke, R.R. Murphy, M. Coovert, , and D. Riddle. Moonlight in miami: A field study of human-robot interaction in the context of an urban search and rescue disaster response training exercise. *Special Issue of Human-Computer Interaction*, 19(1,2):21–38, 2004.
5. Mark Burstein and Drew McDermott. Issues in the development of human-computer mixed-initiative planning. *Cognitive Technology*, pages 285–303, 1996. Elsevier.
6. K. Dautenhahn and I. Werry. Issues of robot-human interaction dynamics in the rehabilitation of children with autism, 2000.
7. J. L. Drury, J. Scholtz, and H. A. Yanco. Awareness in human-robot interaction. In *Proceedings of the IEEE Conference on Systems, Man and Cybernetics*, October 2003.
8. A. Finzi, F. Ingrand, and N. Muscettola. Model-based executive control through reactive planning for autonomous rovers. In *Proceedings IROS-2004*, pages 879–884, 2004.
9. Alberto Finzi and Fiora Pirri. Flexible interval planning in concurrent temporal golog. In *Working notes of the 4th International Cognitive Robotics Workshop*, 2004.
10. Adam Jacoff, Elena Messina, and John Evans. A reference test course for urban search and rescue robots. In *FLAIRS Conference 2001*, pages 499–503, 2001.
11. Sara Kiesler and Pamela Hinds. Introduction to the special issue on human-robot interaction. *Special Issue of Human-Computer Interaction*, 19(1,2):1–8, 2004.
12. Sebastian Lang, Marcus Kleinehagenbrock, Sascha Hohenner, Jannik Fritsch, Gernot A. Fink, and Gerhard Sagerer. Providing the basis for human-robot-interaction: a multi-modal attention system for a mobile robot. In *Proceedings of the 5th international conference on Multimodal interfaces*, pages 28–35. ACM Press, 2003.

13. Bruce A. Maxwell, William D. Smart, Adam Jacoff, Jennifer Casper, Brian Weiss, Jean Scholtz, Holly A. Yanco, Mark Micire, Ashley W. Stroupe, Daniel P. Stormont, and Tom Lauwers. 2003 aaai robot competition and exhibition. *AI Magazine*, 25(2):68–80, 2004.

14. J. McCarthy. Situations, actions and causal laws. Technical report, Stanford University, 1963. Reprinted in Semantic Information Processing (M. Minsky ed.), MIT Press, Cambridge, Mass., 1968, pp. 410-417.

15. Brenden Keyes Michael Baker, Robert Casey and Holly A. Yanco. Improved interfaces for human-robot interaction in urban search and rescue. In *Proceedings of the IEEE Conference on Systems, Man and Cybernetics*, 2004. "To appear".

16. R.R. Murphy. Human-robot interaction in rescue robotics. *IEEE Transactions on Systems, Man and Cybernetics, Part C*, 34(2):138–153, 2004.

17. N. Muscettola, G. A. Dorais, C. Fry, R. Levinson, and C. Plaunt. Idea: Planning at the core of autonomous reactive agents. In *Proc. of NASA Workshop on Planning and Scheduling for Space*, 2002.

18. Nicola Muscettola, P. Pandurang Nayak, Barney Pell, and Brian C. Williams. Remote agent: To boldly go where no AI system has gone before. *Artificial Intelligence*, 103(1-2):5–47, 1998.

19. Karen L. Myers, Peter A. Jarvis, W. Mabry Tyson, and Michael J. Wolverton. A mixed-initiative framework for robust plan sketching. In *Proceedings of the 2003 International Conference on Automated Planning and Scheduling*, 2003.

20. J.A. Pinto and R. Reiter. Reasoning about time in the situation calculus. *Annals of Mathematics and Artificial Intelligence*, 14(2-4):251–268, September 1995.

21. Fiora Pirri and Raymond Reiter. Planning with natural actions in the situation calculus. *Logic-based artificial intelligence*, pages 213–231, 2000.

22. R. Reiter. Natural actions, concurrency and continuous time in the situation calculus. In *Proceedings of KR'96*, pages 2–13, 1996.

23. Raymond Reiter. *Knowledge in action : logical foundations for specifying and implementing dynamical systems*. MIT Press, 2001.

24. J.J. Scholtz, J. Young, J.L. Drury, and H.A. Yanco. Evaluation of human-robot interaction awareness in search and rescue. In *Proceedings of the 2004 International Conference on Robotics and Automation*, April 2004.

25. C. Sidner and M. Dzikovska. Human-robot interaction: Engagement between humans and robots for hosting activities. In *The Fourth IEEE International Conference on Multi-modal Interfaces*, pages 123–128, 2002.

26. S. Tadokoro, H. Kitano, T. Takahashi, I. Noda, H. Matsubara, A. Shinjoh, T. Koto, I. Takeuchi, H. Takahashi, F. Matsuno, M. Hatayama, J. Nobe, and S. Shimada. The robocup-rescue project: A robotic approach to the disaster mitigation problem. In *ICRA-2000*, pages 4089–95, 2000.

27. Satoshi Tadokoro. Robocuprescue robot league. In *RoboCup-2002*, pages 482–484, 2000.

28. R. Volpe, I.A.D. Nesnas, T. Estlin, D. Mutz, R. Petras, and H. Das. The claraty architecture for robotic autonomy. In *IEEE 2001 Aerospace Conference*, March 2001.

29. B. Williams, M. Ingham, S. Chung, P. Elliott, M. Hofbaur, and G. Sullivan. Model-based programming of fault-aware systems. *AI Magazine*, Winter 2003.

30. H. Yanco and J. Drury. A taxonomy for human-robot interaction. In *Proc. AAAI Fall Symposium on Human-Robot Interaction*, pages 111–119, 2002.

Anchoring by Imitation Learning in Conceptual Spaces

Antonio Chella[1], Haris Dindo[1], and Ignazio Infantino[2]

[1] Dipartimento Ingegneria Informatica, Università degli Studi di Palermo,
Viale delle Scienze Ed. 6, 90128 Palermo
[2] Istituto di Calcolo e Reti ad Alte Prestazioni , Consiglio Nazionale delle Ricerche,
Viale delle Scienze Ed. 11, 90128 Palermo

Abstract. In order to have a robotic system able to effectively learn by imitation, and not merely reproduce the movements of a human teacher, the system should have the capabilities of deeply understanding the perceived actions to be imitated. This paper deals with the development of a cognitive architecture for learning by imitation in which a rich conceptual representation of the observed actions is built. The purpose of the following discussion is to show how the *same* conceptual representation can be used both in a *bottom-up* approach, in order to learn sequences of actions by imitation learning paradigm, and in a *top-down* approach, in order to anchor the symbolical representations to the perceptual activities of the robotic system. The proposed architecture has been tested on the robotic system composed of a PUMA 200 industrial manipulator and an anthropomorphic robotic hand. The system demonstrated the ability to learn and imitate a set of movement primitives acquired through the vision system for simple manipulative purposes.

1 Introduction

Although the control of robotic systems has reached a high level of precision and accuracy, high complexity and task specificity are limiting factors for large scale uses. A promising approach towards simple robot programming is the "*learning by imitation*" paradigm (for reviews on different aspects on imitation see [15], [18]), which is usually seen in the context of "mapping of an observed movement of a teacher onto the movement apparatus of the robot". The development of a robotic architecture which can successfully benefit from the learning by imitation approach involves several difficult research problems as outlined in [10]. In the past years, different aspects of the problem were addressed in many working systems using various approaches ([4],[5],[6],[12],[13],[19]). However, the main emphasis is given to the problem of how to map the observed movement of a teacher onto the movement apparatus of the robot, and the imitation capabilities are limited to the so called "*indiscriminate imitation*" (i.e. mimicry) of the teacher's movements. We claim that in order to effectively learn by imitation, the system itself should have the capabilities to effectively understand the perceived actions to be imitated. Therefore, the system should be able to build an inner conceptual representation of the actions it observes.

In this paper we propose an architecture which tightly integrates visual perception with knowledge representation, with particular emphasis on the ability to transfer movement skills between a human teacher and a robot student. Our proposal is based

S. Bandini and S. Manzoni (Eds.): AI*IA 2005, LNAI 3673, pp. 495–506, 2005.

on the hypothesis that a principled integration of the approaches of artificial vision and of symbolic knowledge requires the introduction of an intermediate representation between these two levels. Such a role is played by *conceptual spaces*, according to the approach proposed by Gärdenfors [11]. The core of the architecture is a rich inner conceptual level where the perceptual data acquired by a real-time vision system are depicted.

The purpose of the following discussion is to show how the *same* conceptual representation can be used both in a *bottom-up* approach, in order to efficiently organize perceptual data and to learn movement primitives from human demonstration, and in a *top-down* approach, in order to anchor the symbolical representations to the perceptual activities of the robotic system and generate complex actions by combining and sequencing simpler ones.

To test our ideas we performed several experiments on an arm/hand robotic system equipped with a video camera. The robot learns simple manipulative capabilities shown by different human teachers. In order to allow cognitive processing of the perceived data, the system reconstructs and records all the relevant information in a scene, e.g. the teacher's internal coordinates (i.e. joint angles), the properties of the objects in the scene (i.e. position, shape, color), and anchors them, trough a series of conceptual spaces, to suitable linguistic representations [7] expressed using the logic of *situation calculus* [14]. Such representations may be employed to perform high-level inferences, e.g. those needed to generate complex long-range plans, or to perform reasoning about the acquired movements.

The paper is organized as follows: in the next section the cognitive architecture is summarized and detailed description of the conceptual representation is given. The third section explains how learning, anchoring and imitation is performed in our architecture, followed by a description of the experimentations done using the presented architecture.

2 The Cognitive Architecture

The proposed architecture is organized in three computational areas as shown in Fig. 1. The *Subconceptual Area* is concerned with the low-level processing of perceptual data coming from vision sensors through on a set of built-in visual mechanism (e.g. color segmentation, feature extraction, teacher's posture reconstruction). It is also responsible for directly controlling the robotic arm. We call this area subconceptual because a conceptual categorization of the information is not yet performed.

In the *Conceptual Area*, the information from the subconceptual area is organized into conceptual categories through a series of conceptual spaces with increasing level of representational complexity in which different properties of the perceived scene are captured: the *Perceptual Space* describes static properties of the perceived scene (e.g. human posture, geometrical properties of the objects, etc.), the *Situation Space* encodes the dynamicity of the scene (e.g. arm-approaching, ball-moving, etc.), while the *Action Space* encodes temporal sequences of Situations. However, representations in the conceptual area are purely quantitative and still independent from any linguistic characterization.

In the *Linguistic Area*, representation and processing are based on the well-known formalism of situation calculus. The symbols in this area are anchored to sensory data by mapping them on appropriate representations in the different layers of the conceptual area. In the following, a detailed description of each area is given.

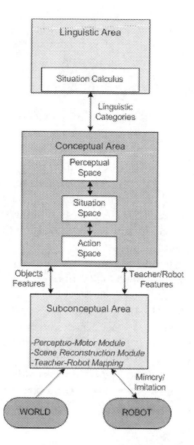

Fig. 1. The computational areas of the proposed architecture and their relation with the external world

2.1 The Subconceptual Area

The *Subconceptual Area* is concerned with the low-level processing of perceptual data coming from vision sensors and performs a set of hardwired visual mechanisms. It reacts to incoming visual stimulus, e.g. a particular color or shape, and performs a set of simple actions on that stimulus, e.g. color segmentation of the image or the extraction of particular features. For the sake of simplicity we further divide this area into two distinct processing modules.

The *Perceptuo-motor Module* processes the information about the human teacher and robot itself, (e.g. it reconstructs human joint angles or queries the robot for its current state). This module is also responsible of the issues related to the mapping of teacher's internal/external space (e.g. joint angles or Cartesian coordinates of the end-effector) to that of the robot (which is the classical *"correspondence problem"* in the imitation literature [1]). For the purposes of the present discussion we suppose that there exists an invertible function which performs the mapping from one space to another. Hence, the proprioceptive information about the robot's current state is directly related to that of the human and *vice versa*.

The *Scene Reconstruction Module* is concerned with processing perceptual properties about perceived objects in the scene (e.g. it computes spatial and shape properties of the objects).

2.2 The Conceptual Area

The conceptual spaces are based on geometric treatment of concepts and knowledge representations [11] in which concepts are not independent of each other but structured into domains (e.g. color, shape, kinematics and dynamic quantities and so on). Each domain is defined in terms of a set of quality dimensions (e.g. the color domain may be described in terms of hue/saturation/value quantities while the kinematics domain is described by joint angles). In a conceptual space objects and their temporal and spatial evolution are represented as points describing the quality dimensions of each domain. As a consequence, it is possible to measure the similarity between different individuals in the space by introducing suitable metrics. In the context of present architecture we propose three conceptual spaces capturing different temporal and spatial aspects of the scene as described in the following.

2.2.1 The Perceptual Space (PS)

The Perceptual Space PS is a metric space whose dimensions are strictly related with the quantities processed in the subconceptual area. By analogy with the term pixel, a point in the PS is called *knoxel* and it can be seen as an epistemologically primitive element at the considered level of analysis. Knoxels in the PS are usually geometric primitives describing the acquired static scene (e.g. object shape and position descriptors, joint angles, superquadrics parameters, etc.).

2.2.2 The Situation Space (SS)

In the Perceptual Space moving objects should be represented as a set of points corresponding to each time sample. However, such a representation does not capture the motion in its wholeness. In order to account for the dynamic aspects of actions, we propose a situation space SS in which each point represents a simple motion. In this sense, the dynamic space can be seen as an "explosion" of the static space in which each axis is split in a number of new axes, each one corresponding to suitable motion descriptors.

Formally, it is possible to choose a set of basis functions, in terms of which any simple motion can be expressed (e.g. by means of Discrete Fourier Transform or Principal Component Analysis). Such functions can be associated to the axes of the dynamic conceptual space as its dimensions. Therefore, from the mathematical point of view, the resulting SS is a *functional* space. A single knoxel in SS therefore describes a *simple motion*, i.e. the motion of a primitive shape. A *composite simple motion* is a motion of a composite object (i.e. an object approximated by more than one primitive shapes). A composite simple motion is represented in the SS by the set of knoxels corresponding to the motions of its components. However, the decision of which kind of motion can be considered simple and how to efficiently encode the motion is not straightforward and it is strictly related to the problems of motion segmentation and representation.

2.2.3 The Action Space (AS)

In a situation, the motion of all of the components in the scene occurs simultaneously, i.e. they correspond to a single configuration of knoxels in the conceptual space. To consider the composition of several simple motions arranged according to some temporal relation, we introduce the notion of *action* in the sense of Allen [2]. An action corresponds to a "scattering" of knoxels from one situation to another in the conceptual space. We assume that the situations within an action are separated by instantaneous events. In the transition between two subsequent configurations, a "scattering" of at least one knoxel occurs. This corresponds to a discontinuity in time that is associated to an instantaneous event.

The action can be represented by the ordered set of the two SS knoxels, before and after the scattering, and can be depicted as a vector in the Action Space. In this context, the movement primitives are seen as a sequence of actions that accomplish a goal-directed behaviour [17].

2.3 The Linguistic Area (LA)

Long term declarative knowledge is stored at the linguistic area. The more "abstract" forms of reasoning, that are less perceptually constrained, are likely to be performed mainly within this area. The elements of the linguistic area are terms that have the role of summarizing percepts, situations and actions represented in the conceptual spaces previously described, i.e., linguistic terms are anchored to the structures in the conceptual spaces.

In the linguistic area, the evolution of the conceptual space is represented in terms of logic assertions expressed in the situation calculus formalism. Indeed, the representation adopted by the situation calculus is in many respects homogeneous to the conceptual representation described in the previous section. The basic idea behind the situation calculus is that the evolution of a state of affairs is modeled in terms of a sequence of situations. The world changes when some *action* is performed. So, given a certain situation S_1, performing a certain action a will result in a new situation S_2. Actions are the sole sources of change of the world: if the situation of the world changes from, say, S_{i-1} to S_i, then some action has been performed. The initial situation S_0 models the initial state of the domain under consideration.

The situation calculus is based on the language of predicate logic. Situations and actions are denoted by first-order terms. The two place function *do* takes as its arguments an action and a situation: $S_i = do(a, S_{i-1})$ denotes the new situation S_i obtained by performing the action a in the situation S_{i-1}. Classes of actions can be represented as functions. For example, the one argument function symbol *pick_up(x)* could be assumed to denote the class of the actions consisting in picking up some object x.

3 Learning, Anchoring and Imitation in the Architecture

One of the most important abilities for an agent's cognitive development in social environments is the ability to *recognize* and *imitate* actions of other agents. In our model, the imitation facilitates skill transfer between agents through mapping (e.g. between a human teacher and a robot, or between two robots). However, imitation is not only a powerful learning mechanism, but it is also thought to be fundamental in the evolution of language and communication (e.g. the *mirror neurons* hypothesis, [3]) and it vertically links cognitive systems, from the lowest levels of perception and motor control, to the highest levels of cognition.

The learning phase in the architecture deals with a principled way to learning sequences of actions by imitation learning paradigm, and we will show how this task is more easily achieved using the above presented cognitive architecture. In addition, our architecture facilitates the anchoring problem as will be described later in this section.

We will focus on the problem of teaching the robotic system a simple task of *pushing-a-box*. This is done by observing a human teacher doing the task in a simplified bidimensional world. The same task may be shown several times and additional teachers may be involved. Our robotic setup composed of a conventional six degrees-of-freedom PUMA 200 manipulator and an anthropomorphic four-fingered robotic hand. However, the architecture has been tested only on the PUMA robotic arm, while the control of the robotic hand fingers is performed as a preprogrammed behavior and does not involve any particular learning strategy (for the learning approach for the robotic hand refer to our previous work [8]).

In the following, we first describe the bottom-up learning phase of the architecture in which perceptual information is organized and represented through a series of conceptual spaces. Then we explain how to perform top-down anchoring of symbolical terms to learnt entities in the conceptual spaces and how to perform imitation, once the system has learned a given task.

3.1 Processing in the Subconceptual Space

For the purposes of the present discussion we consider a simple bidimensional world populated with various objects of different shapes and colors in which learning takes place. The teacher shows her/his arm in front of a single calibrated camera while performing different instances of the same task. The perceptual processing is performed at the subconceptual level through the perceptuo-motor and scene reconstruction modules.

The system is driven by simple stimuli corresponding to the color and shape of the objects in the scene. For the learning to take place, the human arm must be visible in the scene. Machine vision techniques are used to perform color segmentation of the image in order to detect areas which contain the human arm, targets and eventual obstacles. Built-in functions associated with each stimulus perform human arm posture reconstruction and the object feature extraction.

Perceptuo-motor module in the Subconceptual Area is concerned with both human arm posture reconstruction and mapping between human and robot movements. We model the human arm as a simple 3 degrees-of-freedom planar manipulator. In order to easily reconstruct its posture we placed three color markers on the elbow, wrist and fingers respectively. The homography relationship between the image plane and the working plane of the human arm is computed during an offline calibration phase. The system tracks the image plane coordinates of the marker's centroids in each frame and uses this information to compute the world coordinates of the human arm joints. These are in turn used to calculate the corresponding arm joint angles, θ_{UA}, θ_{FA}, θ_H, related to upper arm, forearm and hand respectively. The human shoulder is supposed to be fixed during the experiment. This module is also responsible of the correspondence between the teacher's joint angles $[\theta_{UA}, \theta_{FA}, \theta_H]^T$ and that of the robot $[\theta_1, \theta_2,...,\theta_6]^T$.

This is performed by using relationships that guarantee a similar appearance between human and robotic arm in terms of smoothness and posture configuration.

The scene reconstruction module is concerned with the visual reconstruction of relevant objects in a scene (e.g. targets, obstacles, etc.). For each detected object we compute its centroid $[X_{obj}, Y_{obj}]^T$ and its principal direction θ_{obj} in human-centered co-ordinate system.

As a result, the perceptuo-motor module outputs the instantaneous stimulus $s_{PMM} = [\theta_{UA}, \theta_{FA}, \theta_H]^T$, which becomes the knoxel $k_{PS1}(s_{PMM}(t))$ in the related three-dimensional Perceptual Space, while the scene-reconstruction module's output is given by the stimulus $s_{SRM} = [X_{obj}, Y_{obj}, \theta_{obj}]^T$, which becomes the knoxel $k_{PS2}(s_{SRM}(t))$ in the related three-dimensional Perceptual Space.

3.2 Representation in Conceptual Spaces

We now turn to the problem of obtaining knoxels in the Situation and Action Spaces. As we have stated before, this is intimately related with the problems of motion seg-mentation and representation. To fix ideas, consider the temporal evolution of a knoxel in the Perceptual Space related to the motion of the human arm in the given task. Knoxels in the Situation Space are given by the dynamical parameters of the (composite) simple motion, while knoxels in the Action Space correspond to two sub-sequent situations generated by a scattering of the knoxels in the Situation Space. Therefore, it is sufficient to segment the overall motion into several simple motions.

We perform motion segmentation using a simple technique based on *zero-velocity crossing detection*. The zero-velocity occurs either when the direction of movement reverses or when no motion is present. It therefore may be associated to the scattering phenomenon in the dynamic conceptual space. In order to accurately detect the zero-crossings in the movement data, we first apply a low-pass filter to eliminate high-frequency noise components due to the inherently noisy visual reconstruction stage, and then seek for the zero velocities within an empirically-determined threshold. Data segments between two consecutive zero crossings correspond to simple motions in our architecture.

To efficiently encode the dynamical properties of the motion, we perform the Prin-cipal Component Analysis (PCA) on the simple motion data. PCA is a well-known statistical tool which performs projection of vectors on a linear space spanned by the eigenvectors of the covariance matrix of the data. The use of the PCA is motivated by the findings that human arm trajectories have very low dimension and that they con-verge toward a linear superposition of the first few principal components, thus allow-ing for efficient descriptions of a large class of human movements ([16]). In order to account for different temporal duration of simple motions, we first interpolate the data to a fixed length (in our experiment we choose 50), and then represent them as 50D vectors. Several simple motion from different teaching sequences are collected to-gether and PCA is performed on the data. We noted that generally the first five prin-cipal components account for the most of the data variance, which are used to encode the simple motions. Hence, these components becomes knoxels (i.e. points) in the five-dimensional Situation Space, and the compositions of subsequent situations be-comes knoxels (i.e. points) in the ten-dimensional Action Space. The whole process of obtaining points in the Conceptual Area is depicted in figure 2.

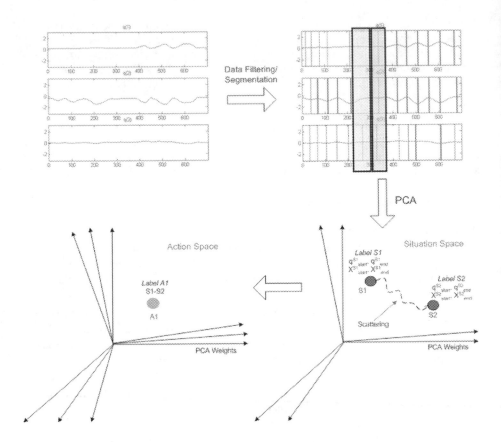

Fig. 2. Processing in the Situation and Action Spaces. Motion primitives, corresponding to the simple motion of the entities in the scene, are extracted through the zero-velocity crossing detection and encoded in the conceptual spaces by performing Principal Component Analysis.

3.3   Learning in the Architecture

Learning and recognition capabilities of our architecture are strictly related to the structure of the conceptual space. Its geometrical structure and the interpretation of the distance in terms of similarity, allows to geometrically treat the concepts, i.e. different geometric properties of regions correspond to different kinds of concepts. It is worthwhile noting that a special role in conceptual spaces is played by the so called *natural concepts*, which correspond to convex regions in the space. Hence, it is possible to account for prototypical effects: given a convex region representing a natural concept, the central points of the region correspond to "more typical" instances of the category, while the peripheral points correspond to "less typical" instances.

Learning capabilities are achieved by applying K-means clustering technique to obtain cluster centers in the Conceptual Area, and hence prototypical (natural) concepts. Cluster centers correspond to the manually labeled terms in the Linguistic Area. This also allows to rapidly recognize novel concepts and create additional clusters as well as associate an already learnt concept to an existing cluster.

3.4 Anchoring in the Architecture

Anchoring is the process of creating and maintaining the correspondence between symbols and percepts that refer to the same physical object ([9]). We will see how in our simple example of pushing-a-box, situation, actions and fluents may be anchored to the representations at the conceptual level, which are in turn connected to perceptions in the physical world (for a detailed description of the anchoring process in conceptual spaces refer to [7]).

3.4.1 Anchoring Situations and Actions

In order to anchor linguistic area expressions to structures in the conceptual area, an anchoring function Φ associates expressions of the situation calculus to their conceptual counterparts.

In terms of conceptual spaces, an action a is mapped on a suitable scattering of knoxels, corresponding to an ordered pair (SS_{i-1}, SS_i), where SS_{i-1} and SS_i are the configurations of the knoxels, respectively, before and after the scattering:

$$\Phi(a) = (SS_{i-1}, SS_i). \tag{1}$$

The initial situation S_0 corresponds to the initial configurations of knoxels SS_0 in the conceptual space:

$$\Phi(S_0) = (SS_0). \tag{2}$$

According to the situation calculus, a situation fully describes the state of affairs of the domain under consideration. Therefore, a generic situation S_i is individuated by the unique sequence of actions $(a_0, a_1, \ldots, a_{n-1}, a_n)$ that generates the corresponding sequence of situations starting form the initial situation S_0. As a consequence, S_i is anchored to the sequence of knoxel configurations generated by the sequence of scattering corresponding to the actions:

$$\Phi(S_i) = (SS_0, SS_1, \ldots, SS_{i-1}, SS_i). \tag{3}$$

In our example, suppose that the arm initially rests in the position p_1. The initial situation S_0 is anchored to the rest-state configuration $SS_0=\{\mathbf{k_a}, \mathbf{k_b}\}$, in which $\mathbf{k_a}$ is a knoxel representing the human arm in the SS and $\mathbf{k_b}$ is the knoxel representing the box. Now the arm begins to move from position p_1 towards position p_2. This is readily detected (sec. 3.2) by the motion segmentation on the data of the arm. A scattering occurs in the conceptual space, and the knoxel $\mathbf{k_a}$ changes its position. Therefore the new configuration of knoxels is $SS_1=\{\mathbf{k'_a}, \mathbf{k_b}\}$ and the new situation S_1 is anchored to the sequence (SS_0, SS_1). Such a scattering corresponds to an (instantaneous) action that is represented by the formula start_move_arm(p1, p2). During all the time in which the arm remains in the same motion state, the SS_1 remains unchanged (given that nothing else is happening in the considered scenario). When the motion of the arm ends in the position p_2, a further scattering occurs, $\mathbf{k'_a}$ disappears, and a new knoxel $\mathbf{k''_a}$ becomes active. Therefore, a new configuration $SS_2=\{\mathbf{k''_a}, \mathbf{k_b}\}$ is generated. This second scattering (SS_1, SS_2) corresponds to the instantaneous action end_move_arm(p_1, p_2). The knoxel $\mathbf{k''_a}$ corresponds again to a rest state of the hand, but now in the position p_2. The new situation S_2 is now anchored to the configuration (SS_0, SS_1, SS_2).

3.4.2 Anchoring Fluents

As a state of affairs evolves, it can happen that properties and relations change their values. In the situation calculus, properties and relations that can change their truth value from one situation to another are called (relational) fluents. An example of fluent could be the property of being in motion: it can happen that it is true that a certain object is in motion in a certain situation, and it becomes false in another. Fluents are denoted by predicate symbols that take a situation as their last argument. For example, the fluent corresponding to the property of being in motion can be represented as a two place relation $in\_motion(x, s)$, where $in\_motion(o, S_1)$ is true if the object o is in motion in the situation S_1. In the push-a-box example, a fluent $moving\_arm(p1, p2, s)$ is anchored to the knoxel in the SS which represents the human arm moving from a point p_1 to a point p_2.

In general, the anchoring function Φ for fluents behaves as follows:

$$\Phi(f(x^*, s)) = \{kt_1, kt_2, \ldots, kt_n\} \tag{4}$$

where f is a fluent, x^* are all the arguments of f except for the last, and $\mathbf{kt_i}$ are all the knoxels, or knoxel t-uples, that satisfy the fluent f in the situation s.

Fluents also permit to anchor actions with temporal duration. In the situation calculus, all actions in the strict sense are assumed to be instantaneous. Actions that have a duration may be represented as processes, that are initiated and are terminated by instantaneous actions and which correspond to relational fluents (e.g. the fluent $moving\_arm(p_1, p_2, s_i)$). The anchoring of processes immediately follows from the anchoring of actions and fluents without particular modifications of the Φ function.

3.4.3 Anchoring Concurrent Actions

Traditional situation calculus does not allow to account for concurrency. Actions are assumed to occur sequentially, and it is not possible to represent several instantaneous actions occurring at the same instant. However, when a scattering occurs in a SS it may happen that more knoxels are involved.

In the line of [7] we employ the function + in the language. Given two actions as its arguments, the function + produces an action as its result. In particular, if a_1 and a_2 are two actions, $a_1 + a_2$ denotes the action of performing a_1 and a_2 concurrently. According to this approach, an action is *primitive* if it is not the result of performing other actions concurrently. In our approach, primitive actions correspond to the scattering of a single knoxel in the SS; the contemporary scattering of several knoxels corresponds to a complex action resulting from concurrently performing different primitive actions. The anchoring function Φ does not need any modification; the main difference from the previous cases is that the scattering (SS_{i-1}, SS_i), corresponding to a complex action, involves a change in the position of more than one knoxel in the conceptual space.

In our example, the concurrence occurs when the human arm pushes the box and stops its motion. The complex action may be given by the following composition of primitive actions: $push\_box = end\_move\_arm + start\_move\_box$.

3.5 Imitating in the Architecture

Given a complex high-level plan, the imitation is performed by going backwards in the path of abstraction, starting from the highest AS level and generating goal-directed robot movements in the lowest PS level. An action is selected in the clustered Action Space and a set of corresponding situations is generated which are in turn processed to give the corresponding imaged knoxels in the Perceptual Space to be mapped on the robot actuators. During the task execution the system continuously compares the external perception of the world with its internal representation in the conceptual spaces. In this sense the conceptual space may be seen as geometrical *internal models* (slightly different from the Wolpert's internal models based on control theory formalism [20]). If there is a strong mismatch the system refines its hypothesis and generates a new set of movement primitives. In this way, the sequence of robot actions is modified in order to take into account of the inconsistencies between the expected and the real situation.

Fig. 3. Sequence of actions performed by the robot while executing the task of reaching and lifting an object. The control of the robotic hand fingers is performed as a reactive behavior and does not involve any learning or grasping strategy.

In order to test our architecture we perform preliminary experimentation in which three human teachers have shown 15 trials for each demonstrated task. The observed results showed that the system was able to learn demonstrated movement primitives and tasks, perform anchoring between perceptual and linguistic data and imitate complex movements based on those shown by human teachers. Fig. 3 depicts the obtained results in which the robot performs the learnt task of reaching and grasping a known object. At the moment, the evaluation of the experiment is qualitative, but we are working to obtain quantitative measurements of goodness and precision of the imitation.

Acknowledgments

This research is partially supported by MIUR (Italian Ministry of Education, University and Research) under project *RoboCare* ("A Multi-Agent System with Intelligent Fixed and Mobile Robotic Components").

References

[1] A. Alisssandrakis, C. L. Nehaniv, & K. Dautenhahn, "Solving the correspondence problem between dissimilarly embodied robotic arms using the ALICE imitation mechanism", in *Proceedings of the Second International Symposium on Imitation in Animals & Artifacts, The Society for the Study of Artificial Intelligence and Simulation of Behaviour*, pp. 79-92, 2003

[2] J.F. Allen, "Towards a general theory of action and time", *Artificial Intelligence*, vol. 23(2), pp. 123–154, 1984.

[3] M. Arbib, G. Rizzolati, "Neural expectations: A possible evolutionary path from manual skills to language", *Communication and Cognition*, 29(2-4):393-424, 1996.

[4] C. G. Atkeson, S. Schaal, "Learning Tasks From A Single Demonstration", in *proceedings of IEEE-ICRA*, pp. 1706-1712, Albuquerque, New Mexico, 1997.

[5] A. Billard, "Imitation: a means to enhance learning of a synthetic protolanguage in autonomous robots", *Imitation in Animals and Artifacts*, MIT Press, 2002.

[6] [6] A. Billard, M.J. Mataric, "Learning human arm movements by imitation: Evalutation of a biologically inspired connectionist architecture", *Robotics and Autonomous System*, no. 37, pp. 145-160, 2001.

[7] A. Chella, M. Frixione, S.Gaglio, "Anchoring symbols to conceptual spaces: the case of dynamic scenarios". *Robotics and Autonomous Systems, special issue on Perceptual Anchoring*, vol. 43, 2-3, pp. 175-188, 2003.

[8] [8] A. Chella, I. Infantino, H. Dindo, I. Macaluso, "A Posture Sequence Learning System for an Anthropomorphic Robotic Hand", *Robotics and Autonomous Systems*, 47, pp. 143-152, June 2004.

[9] S. Coradeschi, A. Saffiotti, "Perceptual anchoring of symbols for action", in *Proceedings of the 17th International Conference on Artificial Intelligence IJCAI-01*, Morgan Kaufmann, San Mateo, CA, 2001, pp. 407–412.

[10] K. Dautenhahn, C.L. Nehaniv, "The agent-based perspective on imitation", *Imitation in Animals and Artifacts*, MIT Press, 2002.

[11] P. Gärdenfors, *Conceptual Spaces*, MIT Press- Bradford Books, Cambridge, MA, 2000.

[12] J.A Ijspeert, J. Nakanishi, S. Schaal, "Movement imitation with nonlinear dynamical systems in humanoid robots", *in Proceedings of Intl. Conf. on Robotics and Automation (ICRA2002)*, Wahington, 2002.

[13] K. Ogawarw, J. Takamatsu, H. Kimura, K. Ikeuchi, "Generation of a task model by integrating multiple observations of human demonstrations", in *Proceedings of IEEE-ICRA*, Washington, DC, Usa, May 2002.

[14] R. Reiter, *Knowledge in Action: Logical Foundations for Describing and Implementing Dynamical Systems*. MIT Press/Bradford Books, Cambridge, MA, 2001.

[15] J. Rittscher, A. Blake, A. Hoogs, G. Stein, "Mathematical modelling of animate and intentional motion", Philosophical *Transactions: Biological Sciences (The Royal Society)*, no. 358, pp.475-490, 2003.

[16] T.D. Sanger, "Human arm movements described by a low dimensional superposition of principal components", *The Journal of Neuroscience*, 20(3): 1066-1072, 2000.

[17] S. Schaal, "Is imitation learning the route to humanoid robots?", *Trends in Cognitive Sciences* 3, 233-242, 1999.

[18] S. Schaal, A. J. Ijspeert, A. Billard, "Computational Approaches to Motor Learning by Imitation", *Philosophical Transactions: Biological Sciences (The Royal Society)*, no. 358, pp.537-547, 2003.

[19] A. Ude, T. Shibata, C.G. Atkeson, "Real time visual system for interaction with a humanoid robot", *Robotics and Autonomous System*, vol. 37, pp. 115-126, 2001.

[20] D. M. Wolpert, K. Doya, M. Kawato, "A unifying computational framework for motor control and social interaction", *Philosophical Transactions: Biological Sciences (The Royal Society)*, no. 358, pp. 593-602, 2003.

Bayesian Emotions: Developing an Interface for Robot/Human Communication*

F. Aznar, M. Sempere, M. Pujol, and R. Rizo

Department of Computer Science and Artificial Intelligence,
University of Alicante
{fidel, mireia, mar, rizo}@dccia.ua.es

Abstract. This paper presents a fusion model of robotic behaviour based on emotional psychology. The main purpose of this model is to provide a human interface that represents the present state of the robot. This interface has two main advantages, firstly it can easily be understood by non-computer experts, and secondly its use is independent of language. The use of emotional modules means that the emotional state of the robot can be obtained directly and, therefore, it is relatively simple to obtain a virtual face that represents these emotions. In addition, the model proposed here, is defined as a complement to the present robotic models. Some experimental data, to verify the correctness of this approach, is provided.

Keywords: Human Robot Interface, Autonomous Agents, Bayesian Units, Bayesian Programming.

1 Introduction

When people think about a robotic control interface they usually envisage a screen with different flashing lights and numerical indications from the sensors or robot devices that are meant to represent the condition of the robot. This kind of interface can mean that the use of the robot, the interaction and the diagnosis are limited to specialist users [1]. However, in some situations and certain fields it could be advantageous to have a simple interface, on which, people without any knowledge of computer science and robots, could interact effectively.

Nowadays, the development of new interfaces is an active field of investigation. The objectives of new designs are focused mainly on creating more intuitive interfaces to facilitate learning and adaptation [2] [3] [4]. Humanizing computer and robot interfaces has long been a major goal of both computer users and programmers [5]. Humanizing has at two main advantages, firstly that of making interfaces easier and more comfortable to use and secondly of giving interfaces a more human appearance [6]. The human face is one of the most compelling components of a human-like interface. Infants are born with instinctive information about facial structure; at birth infants exhibit preference for face-like patterns over others [6].

---

* This work has been financed by the Generalitat Valenciana project GV04B685

S. Bandini and S. Manzoni (Eds.): AI*IA 2005, LNAI 3673, pp. 507–517, 2005.
© Springer-Verlag Berlin Heidelberg 2005

Facial expressions are an important channel of nonverbal communication. Emotional expressions over time may make people's faces descriptive of their personalities and their state of mind. There are some papers that study the importance of the face in the interaction and communication between people [7] [8] [9]. When effective processes to humanize computer interfaces are developed, interfaces and methods able to imitate the bases of the human personality are required.

On the other hand, an autonomous agent must have a model of the environment to be able to interact with the real universe where it is working. Nevertheless, it is necessary to consider that any model of a real phenomenon will be incomplete due to the existence of uncertain, unknown variables that influence the phenomenon. The effect of these variables is to cause the model and the phenomenon to never have the same behaviour. Although reasoning with incomplete information continues to be a challenge for autonomous agents, learning and probabilistic inference tries to solve this problem using a formal base. Bayesian programming [10] [11] [12] is a formalism, based on the principle of the Bayesian theory of probability and is proposed as a solution when dealing with problems relating to uncertainty and incompleteness.

In this paper a model based on human behaviour for an autonomous agent is shown, this robotic model has plans and tasks to complete and is also able to imitate several human emotions such as fear or tiredness. A robot with emotional responses allows us to plan behaviour in a different way than present robotic architectures and provides us with a method of generating a new interface for human/robot interaction. The expression on the virtual face, included in the system, changes in response to the current emotions of the robot and its circumstances. In this way, the presented interface is more easily understood by a greater number of users than in traditional methods (the interface is independent of language and culture, because similar facial language and expression exists within different cultures). The interface and proposed model deal with uncertainty and incompleteness based on Bayesian programming. Several examples of execution are provided to determine the correctness of this approach.

2   Fusing with Bayesian Programming

As commented above, it is necessary to bear in mind that any model of a real phenomenon will always be incomplete due to the permanent existence of unknown, hidden variables that will influence the phenomenon. These variables cause the model and the phenomenon to adopt different behaviour. An artificial system must perceive, infer, decide and act using an incomplete model of the environment. Bayesian inference and learning try to solve this problem using a formal theory. Bayesian programming is a new formalism, and it is proposed as a solution when dealing with problems relating to uncertainty and incompleteness.

A Bayesian program is defined as a means of specifying a family of probability distributions. It is made up of different components (see figure 1).

The first is a declarative component where the user defines a description. The purpose of a description is to specify a method to compute a joint distrib-

$$\text{Program} \begin{cases} \text{Description} \begin{cases} \text{Spec} (\pi) \begin{cases} \text{Pertinent variables} \\ \text{Decomposition} \\ \text{Forms} \begin{cases} \text{Parametric} \\ \text{Programs} \end{cases} \\ \text{Identification based on Data}(\delta) \end{cases} \\ \text{Question} \end{cases}$$

Fig. 1. Structure of a Bayesian program

ution on a set of variables given a set of experimental data (δ) and preliminary knowledge (π). The second component is of a procedural nature and consists of using a previously defined description with a question. A question is obtained by partitioning the variables into three groups: *Searched*, *Known* and *Unknown*, computing a probability distribution of the form $P(Searched|Known)$. Answering this question consists in deciding a value for the variable *Searched* according to $P(Searched|Known)$ using the Bayesian inference rule:

$$P(Searched|Known \otimes \delta \otimes \pi) = \\ \frac{1}{\Sigma} \times \sum_{Unknown} P(Searched \otimes Unknown \otimes Known|\delta \otimes \pi) \qquad (1)$$

Considering both the system decomposition in modules and the fusion of information a definition of Bayesian processing Unit is proposed, based on the Bayesian programming formalism. A processing unit u is a description that defines this probabilistic distribution: $P(I \otimes S \otimes O \otimes |u)$, where I is an input variable that specifies the information to be processed, S is a state variable that represents the situation of the processing unit and O is an output variable that specifies the newly generated information.

The variables I, S and O are allowed to be atomic and can be made up of some random variables that will be assumed as discrete. The decomposition of this probabilistic distribution and its form is not limited. In this way, the decomposition of the variable or input variables can be defined using queries to other processing units. Specific learning is not specified in order to allow the system designer to use the method that he considers to be more appropriate. The variable state S represents the situation in a processing unit. For example, in reactive behaviours, where the input information directly provides the output information, the shape of the probability of this variable will tend to be uniform. In more complex behaviours S can take more complex shapes depending on the information to be processed and the desired output.

3   Architecture Proposed

An emotion is an affective state, a subjective reaction to the environment that shows internal feelings, motivations, wishes, needs and objectives. Emotions and the actions linked to them are an essential part of an organism's relation with its environment. They can be the means by which a person appraises the significance of stimuli and prepares the body for an appropriate response [13]. The core of an emotion is readiness to act in a certain way [14]. In this way, emotions can interrupt ongoing action; they also prioritise certain kinds of social interaction.

In the model proposed here an autonomous agent, which can have a traditional management system, is able to plan a set of objectives. With this system and using the principles of the emotional bases previously commented, a subconscious model that combines the emotions provided by the robot, is defined. These emotions depend on the condition of all variables (sensors, laser, batteries...) and the previous knowledge of the environment. An emotion can make the robot change its behaviour in a reactive or deliberate way.

In our case we have a previous navigation system that is able to deliver correspondence under petition [15]. This system will be expanded with four emotional modules to help achieve the tasks and provide an effective mechanism for building an interface with the characteristics outlined above.

3.1   Emotional Modules

An emotional module is a Bayesian processing unit that interacts with other emotional modules, with the traditional system for the resolution of objectives or with the robot using an interface connected directly to the robot. An emotional module usually has a corresponding human emotion. It is advisable to combine all the emotional modules using a Bayesian unit that we call subconscious. This unit is responsible for collecting all the *emotional charge* of the robot in a given moment.

As previously stated, an emotional module can act directly with the robot actuators. However, the conscious system must be connected to the robot to execute tasks. This conscious system refers to the traditional planning system of the robot. A Bayesian execution unit is proposed to be in charge of controlling the robot. This unit will carry out the tasks depending on the emotional values of the robot and the present piece of work to be completed.

Most emotional modules have a reactive base, this is the reason why they will not need a state variable, and so its use will be omitted in the rest of this paper. In our system (see figure 2) we use the following modules: a dissatisfaction module (defined to show the probability that the robot has a problem in the execution of its task), a tiredness module (defined as a protection system), a depression module that determines when work conditions are not suitable (for example, when sensor readings provide low reliability or tiredness levels are excessively high). It can produce a decrease in movement intensity or even halt the robot. And finally a fear module (to maintain the integrity of the robot and to take reactive action to avoid collisions and obstacles). This modules are grouped using a subconscious module (that determines the state of the robot and is used in the interface development). In order to execute an action we require an execution module. This is a system that determines which actions are more probable to execute. This probability depends on the outputs of the emotions that interact with the system as well as the actions proposed by the traditional system. We briefly will describe the emotional modules proposed:

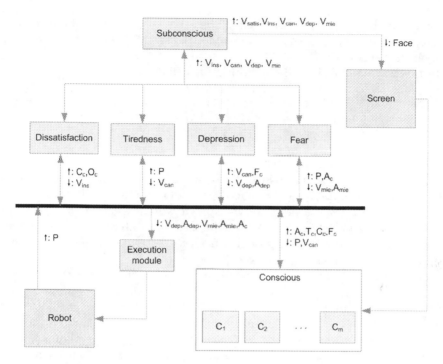

Fig. 2. Architecture example. Conscious module is a classic system for the interaction of the robot with the world. Subconscious module combines the emotional system modules determining the present state of the robot. A dissatisfaction module is defined to show the probability ($Vins$) that the robot has a problem in the execution of its task. There are two input variables that establish this probability: completed task rate (Cc) and task completion problems (Oc). Tiredness is defined as a protection system. In this way, the function of this unit is to calculate the condition of the robot from the time of continuous execution (Pt) and the state of the batteries ($Pbat$). The unit shows if the robot needs to return to the charge station in order to recharge its batteries or if the robot must restrict its movements ($Vcan$). The depression module determines when work conditions are not suitable, for example, when sensor readings provide low reliability or tiredness levels are excessively high. Knowing the system reliability (Fc) and tiredness level ($Vcan$) the robot will calculate the degree of depression ($Vdep$) and the action to be taken ($Adep$).A fear module is used to maintain the integrity of the robot and to take reactive action to avoid collisions and obstacles. Input variables are the action to be executed in this moment (Ac) and the readings from sensors (Ps). Starting from these variables, the module obtains an indication of the robot's degree of fear ($Vmie$) and the action to be executed ($Amie$) in order to avoid any actions that could damage the robot. Finally we use an execution module in order to determine which action are more probable to execute.

Dissatisfaction. A dissatisfaction module is defined to show the probability ($Vins$) that the robot has a problem in the execution of its task. There are two input variables that establish this probability: completed task rate (Cc) and problems rate to complete the task (Oc). These variables must be obtained from the conscious system (checking, for example, the state of the task manager or an equivalent module).

In this way, the following decomposition is defined:

$$P(Cc \otimes Oc \otimes Vins|\pi) =$$
$$P(Cc|\pi) \times P(Oc|Cc \otimes \pi) \times P(Vins|Oc \otimes Cc \otimes \pi) =$$
$$P(Cc|\pi) \times P(Oc|\pi) \times P(Vins|Oc \otimes Cc \otimes \pi)$$

Where π is the preliminary knowledge of the system that makes the decomposition possible. The next step is to identify the parametrical form of the previously defined joint distribution. $P(Cc|\pi)$ and $P(Oc|\pi)$ are uniform distributions (because we do not know if a problem will appear while executing the task). On the other hand, $P(Vins|Oc \otimes Cc \otimes \pi)$ is defined as a table, where the present degree of dissatisfaction will be specified from the rate of completed tasks and problems arising with the present task.

The specification of tables for some terms of the module decomposition provides some advantages. These advantages are obtained when we specify the problem to solve in an inverse way than usual. Given an output, any possible input that generated it, is reasoned. Inverse programming has two main advantages: it is robust in unexpected situations (an output will always be obtained even in not considered cases) and taking into account conditional independence the number of cases increases in a lineal way with the number of variables. More details can be found in [10].

Tiredness. Tiredness is defined as a protection system. This system tries to ensure that the robot never runs out of batteries and never works continuously in an excessive way. In this way, the function of this unit is to calculate the condition of the robot from the time of continuous execution (Pt) and the state of the batteries $(Pcan)$. The unit shows if the robot needs to return to the charge station in order to recharge its batteries or if the robot must restrict its movements $(Vcan)$.

Given these variables, the following joint distribution is defined:

$$P(Pt \otimes Pbat \otimes Vcan|\pi) =$$
$$P(Pt|\pi) \times P(Pbat|Pt \otimes \pi) \times P(Vcan|Pbat \otimes Pt \otimes \pi) =$$
$$P(Pt|\pi) \times P(Pbat|\pi) \times P(Vcan|Pbat \otimes Pt \otimes \pi)$$

The second equation is deduced from the fact that battery charge is independent of the execution time. Although it could seem unfounded, this is due to the fact that the robot has an automatic charge platform. The robot automatically disposes on the platform programmed by the conscious module. In this way, the execution time is not related to the charge level of the batteries.

On the other hand, $P(Pt|\pi)$ is specified as a uniform distribution (it is assumed that the user will not provide more tasks than the robot can support, therefore, the delay distribution of tasks caused by an excessive use of the robot, cannot be known a priori). $P(Pbat|\pi)$ distribution is known and it is given by the present level of battery charge. $P(Vcan|Pbat \otimes Pt \otimes \pi)$ is specified as a table where robot tiredness is defined given the execution time and the present state of batteries.

The tiredness probability $(Vcan)$ obtained by this unit can be used by the traditional planning system to propose alternative tasks, to put the robot charge forward or to plan another task different than that currently being undertaken (see figure 2). This module, therefore, does not interact directly with the robot although it is used by the depression module.

Depression. The depression module determines when work conditions are not suitable, for example, when sensor readings provide low reliability or tiredness levels are excessively high. When depression levels increase this module can produce a decrease in movement intensity or even halt the robot. Knowing the system reliability (Fc) and tiredness level $(Vcan)$ the robot will calculate the degree of depression $(Vdep)$ and the action to be taken $(Adep)$.

In this way, this joint distribution is defined with the following decomposition:

$$P(Vcan \otimes Fc \otimes Vdep \otimes Adep|\pi) =$$
$$P(Vcan|\pi) \times P(Fc|Vcan \otimes \pi) \times P(Vdep|Fc \otimes Vcan \otimes \pi) \times$$
$$P(Adep|Vdep \otimes Fc \otimes Vcan \otimes \pi)$$
$$= P(Vcan|\pi) \times P(Fc|\pi) \times P(Vdep|Vcan \otimes Fc \otimes \pi) \times$$
$$P(Adep|Vdep \otimes \pi)$$

A uniform distribution is supposed for $P(Vcan|\pi)$ and for the initial reliability of the system $P(Fc|\pi)$. On the other hand, $P(Vdep|Vcan \otimes Fc \otimes \pi)$ and $P(Adep|Vdep \otimes \pi)$ are defined as tables specified by the programmer. The first probability provides the degree of depression knowing levels of tiredness and system reliability. The second defines the action to be taken depending on the degree of depression calculated previously.

Fear. The main function of this module is to maintain the integrity of the robot and to take reactive action to avoid collisions and obstacles. Input variables are the action to be executed in this moment (Ac) (it must be provided by the conscious module, it is made up of variables that describe robot actuators, in this case $Vrot$ for rotational velocity and $Vtrans$ for transactional velocity) and the readings from sensors (Ps). Starting from these variables, the module obtains an indication of the robot's degree of fear $(Vmie)$ and the action to be executed $(Amie)$ in order to avoid any actions that could damage the robot.

In this way, the following decomposition is defined with these variables:

$$P(Ps \otimes Ac \otimes Vmie \otimes Amie|\pi) =$$
$$P(Ps|\pi) \times P(Ac|Ps \otimes \pi) \times P(Vmie|Ac \otimes Ps \otimes \pi) \times P(Amie|Vmie \otimes Ac \otimes Ps \otimes \pi) =$$
$$P(Ps|\pi) \times P(Ac|\pi) \times P(Vmie|Ac \otimes Ps \otimes \pi) \times P(Amie|Vmie \otimes \pi)$$

Initially the distribution of the sonar readings $P(Ps|\pi)$ and the distribution of the actions to be executed $P(Ac|\pi)$ are unknown. These terms are uniform distributions. $P(Vmie|Ac \otimes Ps \otimes \pi)$ is specified as a table that defines the fear degree of the robot from the sensor values and the action developed. Finally, $P(Amie|Vmie \otimes \pi)$ is a table that represents the action to be taken depending on the fear degree obtained.

Execution Module. As commented above, emotional modules and the traditional system can interact with the robot actuators. Therefore, it is necessary to define a system that determines which actions are more probable to execute. This probability depends on the outputs of the emotions that interact with the system $Vmie$, $Amie$ (for fear) and $Vdep$, $Adep$ (for depression) as well as the actions proposed by the traditional system A_c.

In this way, this joint distribution is defined with the following decomposition:

$$P(Vdep \otimes Adep \otimes Vmie \otimes Amie \otimes A_C) =$$
$$P(Vdep) \times P(Adep|Vdep) \times P(Vmie|Adep \otimes Vdep) \times$$
$$P(Amie|Vmie \otimes Adep \otimes Vdep) \times P(A_c|Amie \otimes Vmie \otimes Adep \otimes Vdep) \times$$
$$= P(Vdep) \times P(Adep|Vdep) \times P(Amie|Vmie) \times P(A_c) = \frac{1}{\Sigma} \prod_i P(A_i)$$

It is specified as the product of each term of the actions that form it. The distribution $P(Vdep)$ is supposed to be uniform for execution task and it is included in the normalization term $\frac{1}{\Sigma}$. $P(A_c)$ is defined starting from two terms. The first term is the actions to be executed by the conscious system obtained assigning probabilities to the set of actions to be executed. The second is the subconscious module that usually will have more execution priority than the conscious module. The rest of terms of the previous equation must be obtained from the remaining modules (tiredness and depression).

Subconscious. The subconscious module determines the state of the robot and is used in the interface development. This state is represented using a human face that expresses the emotions of the robot in a given moment. In this way, the input variables are the probability of the different emotions ($Vins, Vcan, Vdep, Vmie$). Starting from these variables the system will obtain the face ($Face$) that best represents these emotions. In this way, the following decomposition is defined:

$$P(V_i \otimes V_c \otimes V_d \otimes V_m \otimes Face) = \prod P(V|Face)$$

Conditional independence is therefore assumed for all emotions. This can seem a strong hypothesis, for example, in the emotions tiredness and depression, where both are related. Nevertheless, given a face it can be assumed that the probability that it represents an emotion is independent from the rest. This hypothesis provides some advantages [10]. On the other hand, it is defined:

$$P(V|Face) = G(\mu(V, Face), \sigma(V, Face))$$

Where G specifies a discrete Gaussian. The parameters of this Gaussian can be learned by asking the robot users. Everybody that interacts with the robot will, when given a face $Face$, evaluates how it represents an emotion V. In this module, a set of 17 representative faces have been designed.

4   Experimental Validation

The architecture proposed here has been designed for a correspondence delivery system presented in [15] and developed by the robot PeopleBot (`http://`

www.activmedia.com). This robot provides a good platform for the development of human/robot interfaces because of its upright shape and its touch screen. The emotional interface presented here has been implemented on this robot and shown on its screen. This interface is based on the probability distribution $P(V_i \otimes V_c \otimes V_d \otimes V_m \otimes Face)$ and concretely in one of the questions that can be asked to this unit applying equation 1: $P(Face|V_i \otimes V_c \otimes V_d \otimes V_m)$.

When a face is obtained from this distribution, this face is one of the 17 base faces designed for the system, where a base face represents a set of emotions. From this base face a transition to a neutral face is generated, a neutral face is a face devoid of emotion (see figure 4a). This process continuously provides

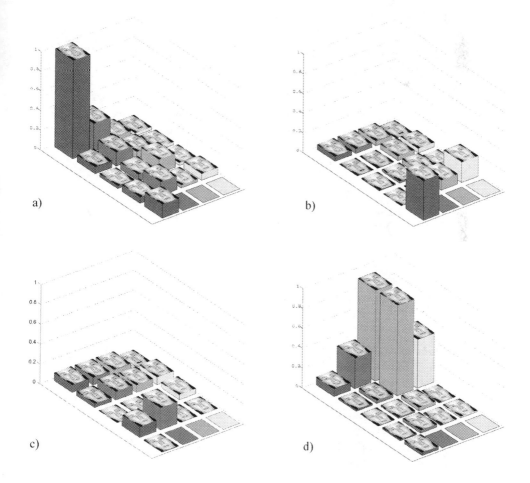

Fig. 3. Graphical representation of the probability $P(Face|V_i \otimes V_c \otimes V_d \otimes V_m)$. a) $(V_i, V_c, V_d, V_m) = (0,0,0,0)$ b) $(V_i, V_c, V_d, V_m) = (0.8, 0.9, 0, 0)$ c) $(V_i, V_c, V_d, V_m) = (0,0,1,0.9)$ d) $(V_i, V_c, V_d, V_m) = (0.2, 0.23, 0.21, 0.19)$.

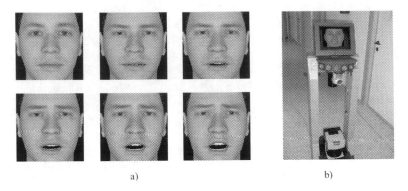

a)   b)

Fig. 4. a) Example of a fear sequence. The images show the transition from neutral face to the base face of fear. b) PeopleBot in its working environment.

uniformity and realism to the facial movements. In figure 3 the value of the distribution $P(Face|V_i \otimes V_c \otimes V_d \otimes V_m)$ in four specific moments is shown.

When the user wants to interact with the robot he has two options at his disposal. The first is to use a verbal command (using the speech recognition module integrated in PeopleBot) and the second is to use the touch screen where the face is shown. When the user clicks the screen, all the information needed for the management of the robot is shown. On the other hand, the use of emotions provides the same versatility and operation as traditional systems, with the difference that the separation between modules makes integration and reusability easier. The use of emotional modules provides the robot with an emotional state. This state can be used for planning, for the development of tasks and for building an interface like that proposed in this paper.

5   Conclusions

In this paper a model to imitate human emotional behaviour has been proposed. This model is based on Bayesian programming, and specifically Bayesian processing Units. The main purpose of this paper is to provide a communication interface that is visual, simple to use and whose interpretation is not restricted by language. In this way, a human face capable of showing different emotions has been integrated into a robot. An association between human emotions and the tasks to be executed by the robot has been produced. In this way the robot has been provided with emotional modules.

An emotional state of the robot is obtained from the information received from the emotional modules presented in this paper. Using this state, a representative face that defines this condition is obtained and shown as an indication of its present *feeling*.

Some experimental data, to verify the correctness of the model and the interface, have been provided.

In an uncertain world it is necessary to work taking this uncertainty into consideration. The model proposed here contains the uncertainty within itself because it is rigorously based on Bayes Theorem. Future studies will try to include a speech synthesizer that it is able to synchronize with the face of the interface and to show emotions.

References

1. Wagner, J., Van der Loos, H., Leifer, L.: Dual-character based user interface design for an assistive robot. Proc., 7th IEEE International Workshop on Robot and Human Communication (1998) 101–106
2. Sato, S., Sakane, S.: A human-robot interface using an interactive hand pointer that projects a mark in the real work space. Proc. of the 2000 IEEE ICRA (2000) 589–595
3. Adams, J.A.: Critical considerations for human-robot interface development. AAAI Fall Symposium: Human Robot Interaction. (2002) 1–8
4. Althaus, P., Ishiguro, H., Kanda, T., Miyashita, T., Christensen, H.I.: Navigation for human-robot interaction tasks. Proceedings of the 2004 IEEE International Conference on Robotics & Automation (2004) 1894–1900
5. Breazeal, C.: Affective Interaction between Humans and Robots. In: Advances in Artificial Life : 6th European Conference, ECAL 2001. Proceedings. Springer-Verlag GmbH (2001) 582
6. Walker, J.H., Sproull, L., Subramani, R.: Using a human face in an interface. In ACM Press New York, NY, U., ed.: Proceedings of the SIGCHI conference on Human factors in computing systems: celebrating interdependence ISBN:0-89791-650-6. (1994) 85 – 91
7. P., E., T., H., T., S., J., H.: Final report to nsf of the planning workshop on facial expression understanding. Technical report, National Science Foundation, Human Interaction Lab., UCSF, CA 94143 (1993)
8. Hager, J.C., Ekman, P.: 10. In: Social Psychophysiology: A Sourcebook. The Guilford Press (1993) 287–306
9. Schmidt, K. L., .C.J.F.: Human facial expressions as adaptations: Evolutionary questions in facial expression research. Yearbook of Physical Anthropology **44** (2001) 3–24
10. Lebeltel, O., Bessière, P., Diard, J., Mazer, E.: Bayesian robots programming. Autonomous Robots **16** (2004) 49–79
11. Bessière, P., Group, I.R.: Survei: Probabilistic methodology and tecniques for artefact conception and development. INRIA (2003)
12. Diard, J., Lebeltel, O.: Bayesian programming and hierarchical learning in robotics. SAB2000 Proceedings Supplement Book; Publication of the International Society for Adaptive Behavior, Honolulu (2000)
13. MIT Institute of Technology, M.: The MIT encyclopedia of the cognitive sciences. The MIT Press (1999)
14. Frijda, N.: The emotions. Cambridge University Press, UK (1986)
15. Aznar, F., Pujol, M., Rizo, R.: Obtaining a bayesian map for data fusion and failure detection under uncertainty. In Proceedings of the 18th International Conference on Industrial & Engineering Applications of Artificial Intelligence & Expert Systems (2005)

Robot Security and Failure Detection Using Bayesian Fusion*

F. Aznar, M. Pujol, and R. Rizo

Department of Computer Science and Artificial Intelligence,
University of Alicante
{fidel, mar, rizo}@dccia.ua.es

Abstract. This paper shows a Bayesian framework for fuse information. Using this framework we present a robotic system, based on two processing units. The system is used for the development of a task, done by an autonomous agent, arranged in an environment with uncertainty. This agent interacts with the world and is able to detect, only using its sensor readings, any failure of its sensorial system. Even it can continue working properly while discarding the readings obtained by the erroneous sensor/s. A security unit is also provided to make the system even more robust. The Bayesian Units brings up a formalism where implicitly, using probabilities, we work with uncertainly. Some experimental data are provided to validate the correctness of this approach.

Keywords: Bayesian Fusion, Failure Detection, Reasoning Under Uncertainty, Autonomous Agents, Robotics.

1 Introduction

When an autonomous agent is launched into the real world there are several problems it has to face. The agent could have a model of the environment representing the real universe where it will interact. Nevertheless, it is necessary to bear in mind that any model of a real phenomenon will always be incomplete due to the permanent existence of unknown, hidden variables that will influence the phenomenon. The effect of these variables is malicious since they will cause the model and the phenomenon to have different behavioural patterns.

In this paper a new fusion model, the Bayesian units, is shown. This model is used to specify the system architecture and determine how the information is fused. The proposed system is composed by two units. The first is used to model the environment for an autonomous agent as the Bayesian Maps [4] formalism. The second is used to send the commands to the robot while verifying its security. The autonomous agent will develop a generic task working with uncertainly. Also, a method of obtaining sensor reliability in real time using an abstraction of various Bayesians maps will be defined. Next, the described models will be applied to a real robot. Finally, conclusions and future lines of investigation to be followed will be highlighted.

---

* This work has been financed by the Generalitat Valenciana project GV04B685.

S. Bandini and S. Manzoni (Eds.): AI*IA 2005, LNAI 3673, pp. 518–521, 2005.
© Springer-Verlag Berlin Heidelberg 2005

2   Adapting the Agent to Uncertainty

The Bayesian maps [4],[5],[6] are developed as a method for representing the space. For a robotic system we need to fuse a wide variety of information, not only spatial one. A model to fuse any kind of information is proposed using the same Bayesian paradigm. We define a Bayesian processing unit (BU) u, as a description that define a joint distribution $P(I \otimes S \otimes O|u)$, where I is the input variable which specify the information to be processed, S is a state variable that represents the processing unit situation, finally O is an output variable that specify the information to be generated.

The I, S and O variables are not constrained to be atomic and could be designed with multiple random variables. For simplicity we will assume these variables as discrete. The decomposition of this joint distribution is not constrained too and could be defined using other questions to any system unit.

The Bayesian Units are a general formalism, for example it's easy to verify that the Bayesian Maps are indeed a special case of the Bayesian Units.

We propose to use the following system architecture composed by two Bayesian units. The first, the abstract map, is used for represent the space and for generate useful behaviour. It's based on the combination of four submaps using the abstract operator provided by [4]. This Bayesian Map is extended to provide more reliability, detecting incoherence in the robot's sensors. The executive unit obtains sensorial data and the output of the Bayesian map to return an action to the physical robot layer.

3   Data Fusion and Incoherence Detection

The combination or abstraction of maps is a method defined in [6] that is able to combine information (included in the sub map distributions) and generate a new map. This map is not only the combination of the individual sub maps but also provides a uniform model for the entire environment (even for places where the model is not specified).

We will assume independent sensorial elements (knowing the cause the consequences are independent). This is, indeed, a very strong hypothesis although it will be assumed because it provides a more robust system for malfunctions, improved signal quality and more efficient computation. Even so another question remains to be solved: How can the reliability distribution of one sensor be obtained? When the fusion process is defined as a product of a simpler terms related to each sensor we could obtain the sensor reliability in an easy way (for a given sub map):

$$P\left(Px_1^t \middle| Px_2^t \otimes Px_3^t \otimes ... \otimes Px_7^t\right) = 1 - \tfrac{1}{\Sigma} \sum_L \prod_i P\left(Px_i^t \middle| L\right) \tag{1}$$

It would be known if Px_1 (the reading of sensor 1) is emitting incorrect readings if a reading in time t persists in being inconsistent with the readings of other sensors in a predetermined period and for all locations L. This inconsistency may be detected by a very low probability for Px_1^t. Combining maps using abstraction operators provides some advantages, one of them being an emergence of robustness. In this way a method to combine the sensorial relia-bility of the submaps is provided. In equation 1 we define how to calculate the reliability of a sensor in a Bayesian submap. This reliability only depends on the term $P(Px|L)$. According to the definition of the abstract operator we can obtain this term for the abstraction of maps:

$$P(Px|L) = \sum_{A\,L'} P(L) \prod_i P\left(\Gamma^i \otimes L^i \otimes L^{i'} \otimes A^i \,\middle|\, I_i\right) \times P(L') \times P(A|L \otimes L') =$$

$$= P(L) \times \prod_i P\left(P^i \otimes L^i \otimes L^{i'} \otimes A^i \,\middle|\, L\right) \times \sum_{L'} P(L') \times \sum_A P(A|L \otimes L') =$$

$$= \tfrac{1}{\Sigma} \prod_i P\left(P^i \otimes L^i \otimes L^{i'} \otimes A^i \,\middle|\, L\right)$$

In the global map (the map obtained through the application of the abstrac-tion operator) the localization at time t (L) depends not only on the submaps localization L and localization at $t+1$ (L') but also on the sensorial readings (Px) and the actions (A) developed by the map. In this way the probability of sensor failure for the global map has been defined as:

$$PSF_1^t = P\left(Px_1^t \,\middle|\, Px_2^t \otimes Px_3^t \otimes \dots \otimes Px_7^t \otimes c_{abstract}\right) =$$

$$1 - \tfrac{1}{\Sigma} \prod_n \left(\begin{array}{c} P\left(P \otimes L \otimes L' \otimes A \,\middle|\, [L=c_1]\right) \times \tfrac{1}{\Sigma^7} \sum_{L_{c1}} \prod_i P(P_i|L) \times \\ \vdots \\ P\left(P \otimes L \otimes L' \otimes A \,\middle|\, [L=c_n]\right) \times \tfrac{1}{\Sigma^7} \sum_{L_{cn}} \prod_i P(P_i|L) \end{array} \right)$$

(2)

This computation can thus be interpreted as a Bayesian comparison of the relevance models with respect to the probability of the sensors failure. To de-termine if a sensor is working correctly, a threshold is needed (provided by the programmer) and also a normalization term. This term is required in environ-ments with high uncertainty (for example in environments where the agent is not prepared) because without this normalization the agent could think that all sensors are erroneous.

Using the provided units we have obtained the desired agent behaviour. In the next figure 1a, the path followed by the robot is shown for a complete route.

Developing the same route, an impulsive noise is introduced in the further-most left sensor. A table summarizing the data collected by the experiment is pro-vided where the following can be seen : the sensor readings, the value of $P(L|Px)$ for the global map and the sensor reliability for some selected landmarks.

4   Conclusions

In this paper a new model, the Bayesian units, has been presented as a method to perform multisensor data fusion. Using this model a physical agent develops a generic task working under uncertainty. The system contains the possibility of detecting any failures in the sensorial system, thereby detecting if any sen-sor is returning erroneous readings. Two units are provided, a Bayesian map for space representation and robot behaviour, and a reactive unit, in order to protect the robot from crashing into obstacles. Examples of both navigation and failure tolerance systems have been provided, which determine the correction of the models presented here. In an uncertain world it is necessary to work taking

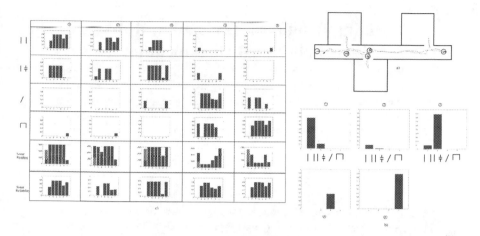

Fig. 1. a) Landmarks and route developed by the robot. The landmarks show the angle and the position where the tests are performed. b) $P(L|Px \otimes c_i)$ for each landmark and each map i (a map is represented by a symbol: corridor, door, wall and end of corridor). c) For each sonar (1...7) the reliability $P\left(Px_1^t \mid Px_2^t \otimes Px_3^t \otimes ... \otimes Px_7^t\right)$ is obtained for each submap and each landmark. The global reliability in the final row is also shown. The tests are done contaminating the first sensor readings with impulsive noise. The red bar (the brightest) shows the noise value used, the blue bar is the real value detected by the sensor.

this uncertainty into consideration. The models proposed here contain the uncertainty inside itself because they are rigorously based on the Bayes Theorem. Future studies will try to apply this data fusion method with different sensors sources and deliberative behaviours.

References

1. Lebeltel, O., Bessière, P., Diard, J., Mazer, E.: Bayesian robots programming. Autonomous Robots **16** (2004) 49–79
2. Bessière, P., Group, I.R.: Survei:probabilistic methodology and tecniques for artefact conception and development. INRIA (2003)
3. Diard, J., Lebeltel, O.: Bayesian programming and hierarchical learning in robotics. SAB2000 Proceedings Supplement Book; Publication of the International Society for Adaptive Behavior, Honolulu (2000)
4. Julien Diard, P.B., Mazer, E.: Hierarchies of probabilistic models of navigation: the bayesian map and the abstraction operator. Proceedings of the 2004 IEEE, Internationa Conference on Robotics & Automation. New Orleans, LA (April 2004)
5. J. Diard, P. Bessière, E.M.: Combining probabilistic models of space for mobile robots: the bayesian map and the superposition operator. Proc. of the Int. Advanced Robotics Programme. Int. Workshop on Service, Assistive and Personal Robots. Technical Challenges and Real World Application Perspectives p. 65-72, Madrid (ES) (October, 2003)
6. Julien Diard, P.B., Mazer, E.: A theorical comparison of probabilistic and biomimetic models of mobile robot navigation. Proceedings of the 2004 IEEE, Internationa Conference on Robotics & Automation. New Orleans, LA (April 2004)

Mining Relational Association Rules
for Propositional Classification

Annalisa Appice, Michelangelo Ceci, and Donato Malerba

Dipartimento di Informatica, Università degli Studi,
via Orabona, 4, 70126 Bari, Italy
{appice, ceci, malerba}@di.uniba.it

Abstract. In traditional classification setting, training data are represented as a single table, where each row corresponds to an example and each column to a predictor variable or the target variable. However, this propositional (feature-based) representation is quite restrictive when data are organized into several tables of a database. In principle, relational data can be transformed into propositional one by constructing propositional features and performing classification according to some robust and well-known propositional classification methods. Since propositional features should capture relational properties of examples, multi-relational association rules can be adopted in feature construction. Propositionalisation based on relational association rules discovery is implemented in a relational classification framework, named MSRC, tightly integrated with a relational database. It performs the classification at different granularity levels and takes advantage from domain specific knowledge in form of hierarchies and rules. In addition, a feature reduction algorithm is integrated to remove redundant features. An application in classification of real-world geo-referenced census data analysis is reported.

1 Introduction

Classification is one of the fundamental tasks in data mining and in the traditional data mining classification setting [16] data are generated independently and with an identical unknown distribution P on some domain $\mathbf{X}$ and are labeled according to an unknown function g. The domain of g is spanned by m independent (or predictor) random variables X_i (both numerical and categorical), that is $\mathbf{X}=X_1\times X_2\times\ldots\times X_m$, while the range of g is a finite set $Y=\{C_1, C_2, \ldots, C_L\}$, where each C_i is a distinct class. A data mining algorithm takes a training sample $S=\{(\mathbf{x}, y) \in \mathbf{X} \times Y \mid y=g(\mathbf{x})\ \}$ as input and returns a function f which is hopefully close to g on the domain $\mathbf{X}$. In practice, the goal is to learn the target concept associated with each class by finding regularities in examples of a class that characterize the class in question and discriminate it from the other classes. This formalization of the classification problem well faces with the *single-table assumption* [18] underlying most of classification methods proposed in the literature. Data are represented as a single table, where each row corresponds to an example and each column to a predictor variable or to the *target* variable Y. However, the growing importance of knowledge discovery and data mining in practical real world requires increasingly sophisticated solutions for classification problems when

S. Bandini and S. Manzoni (Eds.): AI*IA 2005, LNAI 3673, pp. 522–534, 2005.

data consists of a large amount of records that may be stored in *several tables* of a relational database. In this context, single table assumption appears too restrictive since both the predictor variables and the target variable are represented as attributes of distinct tables (relations).

(Multi-) relational data mining [18] is the branch of data mining research that overcomes limitations imposed by single table assumption and investigates methods able to extract knowledge from data stored in multiple relational tables. (Multi-) relational data mining methods are typically based on two alternative approaches: a structural approach and a propositional approach. While in the first case the whole hypothesis space is directly explored by the mining method, in the second case, known as *propositionalisation*, a transformation of relational learning problems into attribute-value representations amenable for conventional data mining methods is performed. In principle, methods implementing structural approaches are more powerful than methods implementing propositional approaches since information about how data were originally structured is not lost. Nevertheless, approaches to (multi-)relational data mining based on propositionalisation have gained significant interest in the last few years. This is mainly due to the fact that in many practical cases propositionalisation allows the reduction of the search space to a minimal subset including features obtained as transformation of the original (multi-)relational feature space. Another reason is given by the observation that the transformation of an original (multi-)relational problem into a single table format allows one to directly apply conventional propositional data mining methods, thus making a wider choice of robust and well-known algorithms available [10].

Several multi-relational data mining methods based on propositionalisation have been proposed in literature for classification tasks. Generally, they assume an individual-centered data transformation such that there is a one-to-one correspondence between each tuple in the original target table (table containing the target attribute) and each tuple in the single table obtained after the propositionalisation process. At now, multi-relational classification through propositionalization problems has been extensively investigated by resorting to the field of Inductive Logic Programming (ILP). For instance, LINUS [11] as well as its successor SINUS [10] and ST [9] are able to construct a set of boolean features defined in terms of conjunctions of literals starting from relational data expressed in some first-order formalism. Nevertheless, a different approach to propositionalisation is supported by systems that directly work with relational databases. Indeed, they generally construct a single central relation by simply summarizing and/or aggregating information found in other tables and performing join operations according to foreign key constraints [8]. In both cases, propositional features are constructed by considering the structure imposed on data by relationships (e.g. foreign key constrains) between tuples in the target table and tuples in related tables, while ignoring the structure eventually imposed by hierarchical relationships on tuples of the same table. This means that these methods are not able to derive a propositional description of the same individual exploiting different levels of granularity. This turns to be an interesting aspect in many applications that would benefit from concept hierarchies [7]. Another limitation in the existing approaches is the huge number of new features they produce. In particular, propositionalisation tends to produce large numbers of features, many of which are highly correlated or even logically redundant.

A simple example of a redundant feature is one that is never (or always) satisfied: e.g., 'a molecule having an atom which has a bond with itself'. While some forms of redundancy can be recognised at feature generation time, others can only come to light by examining the data [2].

In this paper we propose a multi-relational propositionalisation-based classification framework that makes use of discovered multi-level association rules in the propositionalisation step. Similarly to [3], association rules are extracted by means of a (multi-) relational association rule discovery system embedded in the framework that is able to generate association rules at multiple levels of granularity according to some domain knowledge. This allows the classification at different levels of granularity by taking advantage from a qualitative reasoning on a domain specific knowledge expressed in form of rules. Discovered rules are subsequently used to create a relational table for each granularity level where each column represent a boolean feature. Moreover, a feature reduction algorithm has been integrated to remove redundant features and improve efficiency of classification step without affecting accuracy of classifier. Finally, four well-known data mining algorithms are applied to the resulting table for classification purposes.

The paper is organized as follows. In the next section we present the architecture of the proposed framework. In section 3 we briefly present the process of mining of multi-level relational association rules while the propositionalization approach is described in Section 4. Finally, an application to in real-world geo-referenced census data analysis is reported in Section 5 and some conclusions are drawn.

2   System Architecture

The framework we present in this paper has been implemented in the system MSRC (Multi-Step Relational Classifier).

The problem solved by MSRC can be formalized as follows: *Given*: A training set represented by means of h relational tables $S=\{T_0,T_1,...,T_{h-1}\}$ of a relational database D; A set of primary and foreign key constraints on tables in S; a target relation (table) $T \in S$; A target discrete attribute y in T, different from the primary key of T; A background knowledge BK including some *hierarchies* H_k, $k \in \{j \in \aleph \mid 0 \leq j \leq h-1 \wedge T_j \neq T\}$ (one for each table $T_k \in S-\{T\}$) on tuples in $S-\{T\}$. Hierarchies H_k define *is-a* (i.e., taxonomical) relationship of objects represented as tuples in the table T_k; M *granularity levels* in the descriptions (1 is the highest while M is the lowest); A set of *granularity assignments* ψ_k which associate each object in H_k with a granularity level; a couple of thresholds *minsup[l]* and *minconf[l]* for each granularity level. *Find* multi-level classifiers that predict y for some individual represented as a tuple in T (with possibly UNKNOWN value for y) and related tuples in S according to foreign key constraints.

In Figure 1, the architecture of the multi-relational propositionalization-based classifier MSRC is presented. The *MRSC Engine* manages the system by allowing user interaction and by coordinating the activity of all other components. It interfaces the system with the database module in order to store intermediate information.

The *Association rules discovery module* is in charge of the extraction of association rules from data. In particular, given a database schema, a background knowledge and a Language Bias, the system is able to extract association rules and store them in an appropriate repository for subsequent use. The system embeds, for this task, SPADA [1] that mines association rules at multiple levels of granularity. The expressive power of the language bias of SPADA allows us to filter out rules that are not useful for classification purposes (see section 3).

The *Propositionalization Module* is in charge of the transformation of the tables in *S* in a single relational table. In the resulting table, columns represent the extracted rules, rows represent instances of the target table *T* and values are obtained by means of the propositionalization step (see section 4).

The *Feature Reduction Module* reduces the number of columns in order to remove redundant features that would uselessly increase the complexity of the learning task and negatively affect the classification effectiveness (see section 4).

Finally, the *Classification Module* is in charge of executing both the learning process and the classification process. The learning process takes as input the reduced relational table and returns a classification model. The classification process, takes in input the classification model and a tuple in *T* (with possibly UNKNOWN value for *y*) and returns the value of *y*. The classification model can be computed by means of four different learning algorithms, namely the JRIP[4], C4.5 [17], 1-NN and the Naive Bayesian classifier (NBC) [5].

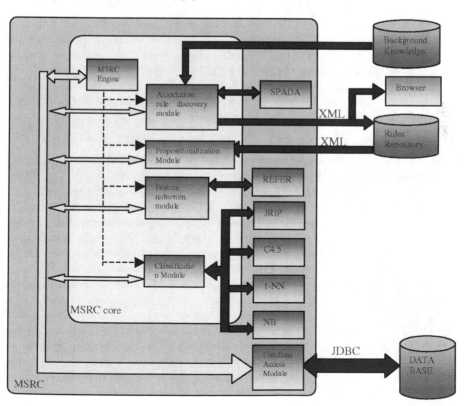

Fig. 1. MSRC architecture

In the following Sections, we first introduce the problem of discovering multi-level relational association rules and then we describe how these rules can be used to construct boolean features to be used in the classification step.

3   Relational Association Rules Mining

The discovery of relational association rules is a descriptive mining task that aims at detecting associations between *target objects* (represented as tuples of the target table *T*) and some *target-relevant objects* (represented as tuples in $S-\{T\}$). The former are the main subject of the description, while the latter are objects that are relevant for the task in hand and are related (by means of foreign key constraints) to the former.

In general, association rules are a class of regularities that can be expressed by the implication: $P \Rightarrow Q$ (*s*, *c*), where *P* (body) and *Q* (head) are a set of literals, called *items*, such that $P \cap Q = \varnothing$, the support *s* estimates the probability $p(P \cup Q)$, and the confidence *c*, estimates the probability $p(Q \mid P)$. The conjunction $P \wedge Q$ is called *pattern*. An example of relational association rule is:

$$is\_a(X, molecule), contains(X,Y), is\_a(Y, atom), charge\_of(Y,[0.7... 0.88]) \Rightarrow$$
$$contains(X, Z), is\_a(Z, atom), charge\_of(Z,[0.2 ... 0.3]), Z \neq Y (91\%, 100\%)$$

to be read as "If a molecule X contains an atom with charge between 0.7 and 0.88, then X contains another atom Z distinct from Y with charge between 0.2 and 0.3 with 91% support and 100% confidence." By taking into account some kind of taxonomic knowledge on target-relevant objects (e.g. atom is specialized as atom_A and atom_B) it is possible to obtain descriptions at different granularity levels (*multiple-level association rules*). For instance, a finer-grained association rules can be:

$$is\_a(X, molecule), contains(X,Y), is\_a(Y, atom\_A), charge\_of(Y,[0.7... 0.88])$$
$$\Rightarrow contains(X, Z), is\_a(Z, atom\_B), charge\_of(Z,[0.2 ... 0.3]), Z \neq Y (65\%, 85\%)$$

In this context, the process of discovery multi-level relational association rules correspondes to mine strong multi-level relational association rules, that is, relational association rules involving target-relevant objects at different granularity levels.

Hierarchies H_k define *is-a* (i.e., taxonomical) relationship of objects in the same table (e.g. atom-A *is-a* atom). Objects of each hierarchy are mapped to one or more of the *M* user-defined description granularity levels in order to deal uniformly with several hierarchies at once. Both frequency of patterns and strength of rules depend on the granularity level *l* at which patterns/rules describe data. Therefore, a pattern *P* (*s*%) at level *l* is *frequent* if $s \geq minsup[l]$ and all ancestors of *P* with respect to H_k are frequent at their corresponding levels. An association rule $Q \rightarrow R$ (*s*%, *c*%) at level *l* is *strong* if the pattern $Q \cup R$ (*s*%) is frequent and $c \geq minconf[l]$.

In MSRC, rules are extracted by means of the algorithm SPADA [13] that operates in three steps for each granularity level: i) pattern generation; ii) pattern evaluation; iii) rule generation and evaluation. SPADA takes advantage of statistics computed at granularity level *l* when computing the supports of patterns at granularity level *l+1*. In particular, SPADA exploits the expressive power of first-order logic to specify both the background knowledge BK, such as hierarchies and domain specific knowledge, and the language bias LB. Hierarchies allow to represent and manage objects at different levels of granularity, while the domain specific knowledge stored as a set of rules supports qualitative reasoning. On the other hand, the *LB* is relevant to allow data miners to specify his/her bias for interesting solutions, and then to exploit this bias to improve both the efficiency of the mining process and the quality of the discovered rules. In SPADA, the language bias is expressed as a set of constraint specifications for either patterns or association rules. Pattern constraints allow specifying a literal or a set of literals that should occur one or more times in discovered patterns. During the rule generation phase, patterns that do not satisfy a pattern constraint are filtered out. Similarly, rule constraints are used do specify literals that should occur in the head or body of discovered rules. In a more recent release of SPADA (3.1) [1] new pattern (rule) constraints have been introduced in order to specify exactly both the minimum and maximum number of occurrences for a literal in a pattern (head or body of a rule). An additional rule constraint has been introduced to eventually specify the maximum number of literals to be included in the head of a rule. In this way we are able to constraint the head structure of a rule requiring the presence of only the literal representing the class label and obtain patterns useful for classification purposes.

4 Transforming Association Rules in Boolean Features

Once relational association rules having only the class label in the head have been extracted for each level, they are converted in a set of boolean features such that the result can be used as input for attribute-value classification algorithms. More precisely, for each granularity level l, boolean features construction is performed by transforming the original set of tables S in a single relational table B whose columns correspond to each body of association rules discovered at level l. Before describing how B is obtained, we introduce: *i)* R': a set of relational association rules whose head contains a literal representing the class label; *ii)* $I_i \in T$: a target object instance (tuple of T); *iii)* B: the output table with $|R'|+1$ attributes. Tuples in B correspond to tuples in T.

The instance I_i can be logically represented as a set of ground facts describing both the target tuple in T and all target-relevant tuples that are related (e.g. foreign key associated) to the target table (see Figure 2). The body of a rule $R_j \in R'$ *covers* $I_i \in T$ if there exists a substitution θ, such that $body(R_j)\theta \subseteq I$.

In the case that the body of the rule R_j covers I_i, the j-th value of the tuple in B associated to the i-th instance of T is *true*, otherwise it is *false*. The $(|R'|+1)$-th column in B represents the target attribute y.

It is noteworthy that the number of attributes of B depends on the number of discovered association rules in R'. Since, the number of discovered association rules is usually high and many rules are strongly correlated, this may lead to generate boolean features which are highly correlated or even logically redundant.

The definition of feature redundancy we adopt in this work properly follows from reducts in rough sets theory [15], in which boolean features are redundant if their removal does not change the set of example-pairs having the same value for each feature. Hence, a feature f can be identified as *redundant* with respect to another feature g for distinguishing *positive* from *negative* examples of a class c if f is true for at least the same positive examples as g, and false for at least the same negative examples as g. Coherently with this definition, we may combine the association rule based propositionalisation with redundant feature elimination (feature reduction) in order to reduce the hypothesis space by excluding boolean features (or literals in ILP) which are redundant for learning. For this purpose, we integrate REFER [2], that is, a feature reduction method for multi-class problems that operates in an ILP setting.

Central to REFER is the notion of a *neighborhood* that is a subset of examples belonging to the same class such that the number of different features between examples is relatively small. Each neighbourhood is uniquely identified by two examples. The first example is where the neighbourhood construction starts and the second one is the termination point. Let e_s be a random starting example for the construction of a neighbourhood, the corresponding termination point is the closest example in e_t tagged with a different class label, referred to here as the *point* (or *example*) *of class change*. The neighbourhood $E(e_s, e_t)$ contains the set of training examples $e_{s_1}, e_{s_2}, ..., e_{s_k}$ such that:

$$class(e_s) = class(e_{s_1}) = ... = class(e_{s_k}), distance(e_s, e_{s_h}) \leq distance(e_s, e_t), \forall h=1,...,k$$

where the distance between two examples is computed as the *Hamming distance*, that is, the number of features whose values differ between the two examples. The neighbourhood construction proceeds in $E \setminus E(e_s, e_t)$ by considering the last example of class change as the current starting point and the process is repeated until the entire set of training examples is partitioned in neighbourhoods.

Redundant features are then eliminated by applying a revised version of REDUCE [12] method to each pair of neighbourhoods of different class. In particular, let E_l and E_m be a pair of neighbourhoods in E of different classes ($C_l \neq C_m$), the goal is to detect which features $f \in B$ describing examples in $E_l \cup E_m$ are non-redundant for discriminating between the classes C_l and C_m. We thereby eliminate features estimated redundant according to properties and dependencies among the features. Formally, a feature $f \in F$ *covers* a feature $g \in F$ with respect to $E_l \cup E_m$ if $T(g) \subseteq T(f)$ and $F(g) \subseteq F(f)$, where $T(f)$ ($T(g)$) is the set of all examples $e_i \in E_l$ such that f (g) has the value *true* for e_i and $F(f)$ ($F(g)$) is the set of all example $e_j \in E_m$ such that f (g) has the value *false* for e_j. The intuition is that a feature f is better than another feature g for distinguishing C_l from C_m if f is true for at least the same C_l examples as g, and false for at least the same C_m examples as g. The implicit assumption is that class C_l is the positive class we are trying to describe. This suggests the notion of useless features,

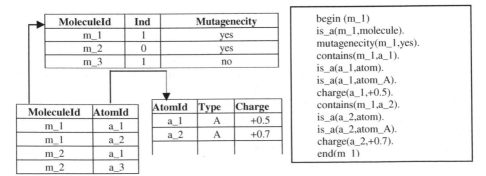

Fig. 2. Set of ground atoms representing relational data concerning molecules (target objects) and atoms (target-relevant objects). In this case a two level hierarchy is defined on atom, that is, atom is specialized as atom_A and atom_B.

those for which $T(f) = \varnothing$ or $F(g) = \varnothing$. Such features can be immediately removed from the set of features F regardless of the properties of other features. Furthermore, a feature $g \in F$ is considered as a redundant feature to be removed if there exists another feature $f \in F$ ($f \neq g$) such that f covers g.

Since, it is proved that REFER preserves the existence of a complete and consistent theory for each class label when eliminating redundant features [2], this method appears well-suited to reduce the set of features describing data at each granularity level, thus improving efficiency of classification step without comprising the existence of some classification model discriminating between examples tagged with different class label.

5 Experimental Results

In this section we present a real-world application MSRC in geo-referenced census data interpretation. For this study we consider both census and digital map data provided in the context of the European project SPIN! (Spatial Mining for Data of Public Interest). These data concern Greater Manchester, one of the five counties of North West England (NWE). Greater Manchester is divided into ten metropolitan districts, each of which is decomposed into censual sections or wards, for a total of two hundreds and fourteen wards. Census data are available at ward level and provide socio-economic statistics (e.g. mortality rate, that is, the percentage of deaths with respect to the number of inhabitants) as well as some measures describing the deprivation level of each ward according to information provided by Census combined into single index scores. We consider Jarman Underprivileged Area Score that is designed to measure the need for primary care, the indices developed by Townsend and Carstairs that is used in health-related analyses, and the Department of the Environment's Index (DoE) that is used in targeting urban regeneration funds. The higher the index value the more deprived a ward is. Both deprivation indices values as well as mortality rate are all numeric, but discrete values are here obtained by applying the Relative Unsupervised DiscrEtization RUDE algorithm [14] that discretizes each continuous variable in the context defined by remaining continuous variables. More precisely, Jarman index, Townsend index, DoE index and Mortality rate have been automatically discretized in (*low, high*), while Carstairs index has been discretized in (*low, medium, high*).

By considering Greater Manchester wards as target objects, we focus our attention on mining a classification model to predict discrete value of DoE index by exploiting not only socio-economic factors represented in census data but also geographical factors represented in some linked topographic maps. Spatial analysis is then enabled by the availability of vectorized boundaries of the 1998 census wards as well as by other Ordnance Survey digital maps of NWE, where several interesting layers (road net, rail net, water net, urban area and green area) forming target-relevant objects are found (see Table 1). Both ward-referenced census data and map data are stored in an Object-Relational spatial database, i.e., Oracle Spatial 9i database, as a set of spatial tables, one for each layer. Each spatial table includes a geometry attribute that allows storing the geometrical representation (e.g. point, line, and region in a 2D context) and the positioning of a spatial object with respect to some reference system in a single geometry field within a spatial table.

Table 1. Geographic layers

Layer name		Geometry	Number of objects
Road net	A-road; B-road; Motorway; Primary road	Line	2798
Rail net	Railway	Line	1054
Urban area	Large urban area; Small urban area	Line	381
Green area	Wood; Park:	Line	13
Water net	Water; River; Canal	Line	1067
Ward	Ward	Region	241

It is noteworthy that the spatial nature of both target objects and target-relevant objects poses two main degree of complexity that is the granularity of the spatial objects and the implicit definition of spatial relations. The former is due to the fact that non-target objects can be described at multiple levels of granularity. In this case, five different hierarchies can be defined to describe target-relevant layers (see Fig. 3). The hierarchies have depth three and are straightforwardly mapped into three granularity levels. The second source of complexity refers to the fact that both geometrical representation and relative positioning define implicitly spatial relations of different nature (e.g. topological) which can be explicitly modeled as many relational tables as the number of objects type and spatial relations. Modeling these spatial relations has a key role in this classification problem, since both the attribute values of the object to be classified and the attribute values of spatially related objects may be relevant for assigning an object to a class from the given set of classes.

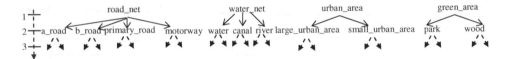

Fig. 3. Spatial hierarchies defined for road net, water net, urban area and green area

We adopt here some geometrical and topological algorithm based on the 9-intersection model [6] to extract topological relationships between target objects and target-relevant objects. For instance the relationship *crosses(ward_135, urbareaL_151)* denotes that *ward_135*, that is a specific Greater Manchester ward, is crossed by *urbanareaL_151* that is a large urban area. The number of computed relationships is 784,107. To support a spatial qualitative reasoning, a domain specific knowledge (BK) is expressed in form of a set of rules. Some of these rules are:

ward_urbanarea(X,Y) :- is_a(X,ward), connects(X,Y), is_a(Y, urban_area). ...
ward_urbanarea(X,Y) :- is_a(X,ward), inside(X,Y), is_a(Y, urban_area).

The use of the predicate *is_a* hides the fact that a hierarchy is defined for spatial objects which belong to the urban area layer. According to spatial relations introduced with BK, we easily obtain a relational representation of classification problem in question (see Figure 4).

Performances of MSRC are evaluated by means of a 10-fold cross validation. The first step consists in the extraction of association rules at different levels of granularity according to hierarchies defined on target-relevant objects. Rules contain useful information about relational patterns frequently occurring in data. For instance, by analyzing spatial association rules extracted with parameters *minsup* = 0.1, *minconf* = 0.6 we discover the following rule:

doe (A, low) ← is_a(A, ward), ward_urbanarea(A, B),
*   is_a(B, urban_area), jarman (A, low)*   (52.6%, 100%)

which states that a low DoE index value is observed in a ward *A* that includes an urban area *B* and has a low value of Jarman index. The support (52.6%) and the high confidence (100%) confirm a meaningful association between a geographical factor, such as living in urban areas where primary care are well satisfied, and low level of derivation when considering targeting urban regeneration funds. In the feature construction step, this rule defines the boolean feature "*is_a(A, ward)*∧ *ward_urbanarea(A, B)* ∧ *is_a(B, urban_area)* ∧ *jarman (A, low)*" that is true for each Greater Manchester ward with a low value of Jarman index such that there is at least an urban area that is topologically related (e.g. connects or inside) to the ward in question. At a granularity level 2, SPADA specializes the target-relevant object B by generating the following rule that preserves both support and confidence:

doe (A, low) ← is_a(A, ward), ward_urbanarea(A, B),
*   is_a(B, large_urban_area), jarman (A, low)*   (52.6%, 100%)

This rule clarifies that the urban area B is large. By varying granularity level as well as the value of *minsup, minconf* and the number of refinement steps *K* (pattern length) in association rule discovery, we obtain several experimental settings. For each setting, the set of discovered rules is transformed in a set of boolean features that is the conjuctions of literals derived from the body of each rule, and redundant features are removed to reduce feature space without affecting the existence of a complete and consistent theory for each class label. Finally, we apply the four classification learners embedded in MSRC and compare the percentage of correct classification averaged over 10-folds of cross-validation Results on average reduction percentage and average accuracy are reported in both Table 2. Results confirm that high number of association rules typically lead to redundant features. Percentage of feature reduction increases when the refinement step increases. This is due to the high number of similar rules (thus

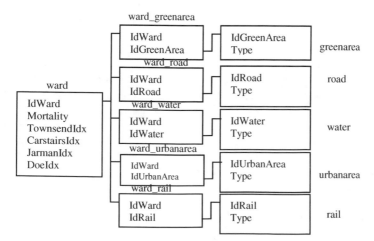

Fig. 4. Relational data describing ward-referenced census data and map data

producing redundant features). Another consideration is that the average predictive accuracies of classification models discovered at higher granularity levels (i.e. level=2) are sometimes better than the corresponding accuracies at lowest levels. This means that the classification model takes advantage of the use of the hierarchies defined on spatial objects. In this case, results at different abstraction levels provide insights on what are the non-target objects that affect the classification. For instance, when $K=7$, $minsup = 0.1$ and $minconf = 0.6$, naïve-bayes classification is strongly improved when considering the size of the urban area, the type of road, and so on. Moreover, results show that by decreasing the number of extracted rules (higher support and confidence) we have lower accuracy. This means that there are boolean features that strongly influence classification results and often these features correspond to rules which are not characterized by high values of support and confidence. Finally, we observe that, in this specific task, the higher the number of refinement steps (boolean features involving more literals) not necessarily means the better the model. This is mainly due to the fact that rules become very specific.

Table 2. DoE Index average accuracy

min sup	min conf	Granularity level	K	Avg. number of original features	Avg. perc. of feature reduction	Avg. Accuracy			
						NBC	1-NN	C4.5	JRIP
0.2	0.8		5	27.5	37%	81.64	80.73	**83.01**	**83.01**
0.2	0.8	1	6	221.1	44%	80.28	80.73	**83.01**	**83.01**
0.2	0.8		7	982.3	73%	75.56	80.28	**83.01**	**83.01**
0.2	0.8		5	492.8	29%	**82.55**	**82.55**	81.64	81.93
0.2	0.8	2	6	278.3	11%	82.10	**82.55**	82.10	**83.01**
0.2	0.8		7	1860.1	66%	80.28	**82.55**	81.19	81.02
0.1	0.6		5	233.2	48%	**83.01**	80.73	**83.01**	**83.01**
0.1	0.6	1	6	374	57%	80.28	80.73	**83.01**	**83.01**
0.1	0.6		7	904.2	74%	80.73	80.73	**83.01**	**83.01**
0.1	0.6		5	442.2	28%	**83.01**	81.30	82.10	81.02
0.1	0.6	2	6	635.8	27%	**82.55**	79.65	80.28	81.64
0.1	0.6		7	3051.4	68%	80.73	79.31	**81.19**	81.02

6 Conclusions

In this paper we have presented a novel relational classification framework named MSRC (Multi-Step Relational Classifier) that exploits relational multi-level association rules discovery to perform relational classifications at multiple level of granularity. Multi-level relational association rules are mined by taking advantage from a qualitative reasoning supported by domain specific knowledge in form of rules. For each level, relational rules are then transformed in boolean features making MSRC able to perform multi-level classification according to some robust and well-known propositional classification methods. Due to the high number of boolean redundant features constructed from association rules, MSRC integrates a feature reduction method that reduces feature space by removing redundant features without compromising classification effectiveness. The application in geo-referenced census data interpretation has confirmed that multi-level classification provides insights on what target-relevant objects really affect the classification and confirms benefits in considering concept hierarchies for classification purposes. Moreover, results show that support and confidence are not a valid criterion to filter rules, since rules characterized by low values of support and confidence positively affect classification results. As future work we intend to extend experimental evaluation by comparing MSRC with a (multi-)relational structural approach to multi-level classification.

Acknowledgments

We thank Simon Rawles and Peter Flach for working together in defining and developing the REFER algorithm. The work presented in this paper is partial fulfilment of the research objective set by the ATENEO-2005 project on "Gestione dell'informazione non strutturata: modelli, metodi e architetture".

References

[1] Appice, A., Berardi, M., Ceci, M., Lapi, M., Malerba, D., Turi, A: Mining interesting spatial association rules: two case studies. 86-97 (2004).

[2] Appice, A., Ceci, M. Rawles, S., Flach, P.: Redundant Feature Elimination for Multi-Class Problems. *Proc. of International Conference on Machine Learning*, 33-40, (2004).

[3] Ceci, M., Appice, A., Malerba, D.: Spatial Associative Classification at Different Levels of Granularity: A Probabilistic Approach. *Proc* of European Conference on Principles and Practice of Knowledge Discovery in Databases, LNAI 3202, 99-111, (2004).

[4] Cohen, W. W.. Fast Effective Rule Induction. *Proc. of the International Conference on Machine Learning,* 115-123, Morgan Kaufmann (1995).

[5] Domingos, P. & Pazzani, M.: On the optimality of the simple Bayesian classifier under zero-one loss, *29*, 103-130. (1997).

[6] Egenhofer, M.J.: Reasoning about Binary Topological Relations. *Proc. of the Symposium on Large Spatial Databases*, 143-160, (1991).

[7] Han J., Fu Y.: Discovery of multiple-level association rules from large databases., *In 21st International Conference on Very Large Data Bases, VLDB'95*, 420-431, (1995).

[8] Knobbe A.J., Haas M. & Siebes A: Propositionalisation and aggregates. In *5th European Conf. on Principles of Data Mining and Knowledge Discovery*, Springer-Verlag, (2001).

[9] Kramer S., Pfahringer B., and Helma C.: Stochastic Propositionalization of Non-Determinate Background Knowledge, *Proc. of the International Conference on Inductive Logic Programming*, LNCS 1446, 80-94, (1998).

[10] Krogel, M., Rawles, S., Zelezny, F., Flach, P., Lavrac, N., Wrobel S.: Comparative evaluation of approaches to propositionalization. *Proc. of the International. Conference. on Inductive Logic Programming,.* Springer-Verlag,197-214, (2003).

[11] Lavrac N. and Dzeroski S.: Inductive Logic Programming: Techniques and Applications. Ellis Horwood, (1994).

[12] Lavrač, N., Gamberger, D., Jovanoski V.. A study of relevance for learning in deductive databases. The Journal of Logic Programming, 16, 215-249. (1999)

[13] Lisi, F.A., Malerba, D.: Inducing Multi-Level Association Rules from Multiple Relations. Machine Learning, 55, 175-210, (2004).

[14] Ludl, M.C., Widmer, G.: Relative Unsupervised Discretization for Association Rule Mining. PKDD'00, LNCS 1910, 148-158, (2000).

[15] Modrzejewski, M.: Feature selection using roughsets theory. *Proceedings of the European Conference on Machine Learning*. Springer-Verlag,213-226, (1993).

[16] Mitchell, T. Machine Learning. McGraw Hill (1997)

[17] Quinlan, J.: *C4.5: Programs for machine learning*. Morgan Kaufmann (1993)

[18] Wrobel, S. Inductive logic programming for knowledge discovery in databases. In: Džeroski, S., N. Lavrač(eds.): Relational Data Mining, Springer: Berlin, 74-101, (2001).

Entity Recognizer in Hungarian Question Processing[*]

Domonkos Tikk[1], P. Ferenc Szidarovszky[2],
Zsolt T. Kardkovács[1], and Gábor Magyar[1]

[1] Dept. of Telecom. & Media Informatics,
Budapest University of Technology and Economics,
H-1117 Budapest, Magyar Tudósok krt 2, Hungary
{tikk, kardkovacs, magyar}@tmit.bme.hu
[2] Szidarovszky Ltd., H-1392 Budapest, POB 283, Hungary
ferenc.szidarovszky@szidarovszky.com

Abstract. In our ongoing research and development project, called "In the Web of Words" (WoW), funded by the National R+D Program in Hungary, we aim to create a complex search interface that incorporates—beside the usual keyword-based search functionality—(1) deep web search, (2) Hungarian natural language question processing, (3) image search support by visual thesaurus. This paper focuses on a particular and crucial part of the question processing problem (2): recognition of entities. Entities are expressions that have fixed form, and that are assigned context specific information in the dictionary. Due to the agglutinative feature of Hungarian language they often appear in the text differently as in the dictionary, therefore their detection requires special algorithms at processing.

1 Introduction

In WoW project our purpose is to create a complex search interface with the following features: search in the deep web content of contracted partners' databases, processing Hungarian natural language (NL) questions and transforming them to SQL queries for database access, image search supported by a visual thesaurus that describes in a structural form the visual content of images (also in Hungarian). This paper primarily focuses on a particular problem of question processing task: the entity recognition. Before going into details we give a short overview about the project's aims.

1.1 The Deep Web

The deep web (DW) is content that resides in searchable and online accessible databases, whose results can only be discovered by a direct query[1]. Without the directed query, the database does not publish the result. Result pages are

---

[*] This research was supported by NKFP 0019/2002.
[1] http://www.brightplanet.com

S. Bandini and S. Manzoni (Eds.): AI*IA 2005, LNAI 3673, pp. 535–546, 2005.

posted as dynamic web pages as answer to direct queries. Incorporating DW access in the internet search engines is a very important issue. Studies about the internet [1] show among other facts that: (1) the size of DW is about 400 times larger than that of the surface web that is accessible to traditional keyword-based search engines; (2) the size of DW is growing much faster than the surface web; (3) DW is the category where new information appears the fastest on the web; (4) DW sites tend to be narrower and deeper than conventional surface web sites; (5) DW sites typically reside topic specific databases, therefore the quality of the information stored on these sites are usually more adequate in the given topic than the one accessible through conventional pages.

Traditional search engines create their catalogs based on crawling web pages that have to be static and linked to other pages. Therefore dynamic web pages, even though they have unique URLs, are not searchable by such engines [2]. However, based on the above listed reasons, it would be highly desirable to make the content of the DW accessible to search engines, which can be normally accessed only through querying the search surface of the deep web sites. Hence, the user can retrieve his/her information need from the deep web, if s/he knows the appropriate deep web site that stores the sought information and is familiar with the search surface offered by the site. Deep web searchers aim at bridging this gap between the user and deep web sites. The information that resides on deep web site can be efficiently accessed if the structure of the databases is known by the searcher.

Initially, we intend to restrict the search space of our deep web searcher (DWS) to the following topics: books, movies, restaurants, and football. DWS accesses information in these topics of contracted databases. It communicates with databases by SQL queries through a mediator layer, which enables database owners to provide the necessary and only the necessary information about their database. Beside that the mediator layer insures feasibility of querying, controls

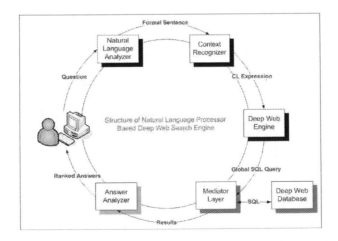

Fig. 1. Structure of our DWS enabling NL querying

authority rights, and assures authenticity and answering facilities. The structure of the system is depicted on Figure 1.

1.2   Natural Language Querying

One of the bottlenecks of traditional search engines is that they keep keyword-based catalogued information about web pages; therefore they retrieve only the keywords from users' queries and display pages with matched ones. This matching method neglects important information granules of a natural language query, such as the focus of the query, the semantic information and linguistic connections between various terms, etc. Traditional searchers retrieve the same pages for *"When does the president of the United States visit Russia"* and *"Why does the president of Russia visit the United States"*, though the requested information is quite different. Solutions that do not deal with the given morphosyntax of the sentence, e.g. Askjeeves [3], AnswerBus [4], Ionaut [5], also suffer from this problem.[2] These pieces of information could be very important when DW search is concerned, because e.g. the interrogative is not a keyword-like information (the ideal result does not contain it), but it specifies the focus of the query. DWSs communicate with the DW sites by accessing the residing database using a querying language (e.g. SQL). In the retrieval of the proper answer for the question, hence, the focus of the query should be encoded in the translated SQL query.

There has been a lot of work in recent years on both natural language processing and web-based queries. A non-exhaustive list of projects: Practice[6], START[7,8], NL for Cindi[9], Masque/SQL[10], Chat-80[11] or Team[12] provide solutions for English, Spanish NLQ[13], Sylvia-NLQ[14] for Spanish, Phoenix[15] for Swedish, Edite[16], LIL/SQL[17] for Portuguese, NChiql[18] for Chinese and KID[19] for Korean languages. A bilingual (Danish and Italian) question answering system with ontology harmonization is reported about in [20]. Although several ideas and techniques has been adapted from these systems to WoW, none of them can be applied directly to our purpose, both because of the peculiarity of DW search and that of the language.

In order to alleviate the shortcomings of keyword based search, in our DWS we enable the user to formulate his/her information need by NL question. Processing of arbitrary NL question is generally an extremely complicated problem for all languages and Hungarian is not an exception. In fact, due to the agglutinative nature of the language even dictionary based search algorithms have to be equipped with intelligent functionality because, e.g.,

1. the stem of words can change;
2. additional suffixes can modify the form of previous suffixes.

In this paper we deal with the natural language module of our DWS with a special focus on the particular important issue of entity recognition. First, a brief

---

[2] To test whether the solution is keyword based or not (even if the input is a NL question) try: "Who is the present King of France?" or "When did the president of Russia visit the United States?"

description is given about the NL module, then the entity recognition problem is treated in details.

Here we remark that, though, NL processing is always language-dependent but the non-language specific part of the operation, e.g. the structure of our system can directly be adapted for question processing in other languages.

1.3   Description of NL Module

We apply several restrictions on input questions of the system, which are originated from different reasons. First, DWS attempts to answer user queries on the basis of the content of a collection of topic-specific DW sites. The information stored at DW sites are typically factual ones, therefore we do not allow questions focusing on casuality (*"Why did the Allies win WW2?"*), intension (*"Would you like a cup of coffee?"*), subjective (*"How am I?"*) or other type of non-factual information. Second, there are grammatical limitations on input question in order to make NL question processing feasible: the system accepts only simple (only one tensed verb is allowed), well-formulated and -spelled interrogative sentences starting with a question word from a given list.

A basic tool that helps the operation of the module is the HunMorph morphological parser (MP) [21].

1.4   Definition of Entity

The knowledge base of the NL module contains various dictionaries storing the lexical information of special tokens (proper names, interrogatives, lists of some significant words, dates, URLs etc.). These tokens are called together *entities*. Our approach is not a (supervised) learning method that is trained to recognize unknown entities in free text. Its purpose is to recognize *known entities* from a collected data base in free text even if they are in inflected form. These entities are stored in a local data base and are extracted from databases of our contracted content providers.

Entities can be single or multi-word expressions and are of two basic types:

1. dictionary based: the entity has a fixed form that is stored in the dictionary (e.g. proper names, interrogatives, special words). Such entities are inserted to the dictionary on the basis of the content of partner DW sites. At insertion context information can also be linked to entities.
2. pattern based: only the possible patterns of the entity is given (e.g. URL, date, e-mail address). A candidate text is matched against the pattern when checking identity. A pattern consists of a set of simple rules, which is given for each pattern manually.

1.5   Operation of NL Module

NL module consists of two submodules: the tokenizer and the bracketing module. The input question is first passed to the *tokenizer*. Its first task is to identify tokens (syntactically relevant units) of the sentence. Tokens are one-word or multi-word expressions whose internal structures are irrelevant for the syntactic parsing of the sentence. Multi-word tokens are entities, such as personal names, institution, proprietary and company names, titles, addresses, etc. As Hungarian is a highly agglutinative language where major semantic/syntactic relations are signalled by a series of "stackable" suffixes, the identification of entities is a more complex task than simple pattern recognition and requires the support of a morphological parser [21]. It is described in detail in Section 2. MP assigns *part of speech* labels to tokens and provides their morphological analysis. This information is the basis of the subsequent bracketing phase. One of the characteristics of the morphological system of the Hungarian language is that many morphologically complex word forms are ambiguous in terms of their morphological structure. Such ambiguous tokens are disambiguated in parsed alternatives.

The bracketing module groups related tokens in brackets. The module has several submodules for recognizing: (1) adverbs and participles; (2) adjective groups; (3) conjunctions (logical operators); (4) genitive and; (5) postposition structures. Submodules use the morphological annotation of tokens: stem, part of speech, suffixes (entities are labelled by their type as "part of speech"). The operation of bracketing is not detailed in this paper, for further details see [22].

2   The Entity Recognizer

The entire algorithm of tokenizer relies on entity recognition. The entity recognizer (ER) has two main tasks:

- *searching*: determining the entities in the sentence;
- *annotating*: specifying the morphological characters of the entity.

The searching and annotating tasks are usually connected and cannot be performed separately.

In what follows we describe the algorithm of ER for fixed form *dictionary based* entities (see Subsection 1.4). The recognition of the pattern based entities is performed by Smart Tag Detector (STD), and is not detailed here.

Because an entity can consist of several words, theoretically all segment of an input question is a possible candidate. The number of segments in a sentence of size n is $n(n + 1)/2$. The average size of an input sentence is 7–10 words, while the size of the dictionary containing entities can be of order 10^6. Therefore it is much more efficient to search on the basis of sentence segments than on the basis of dictionary entries. The search of an expression in the dictionary can be optimized by organizing dictionary entries into hash table. Segments of a sentence are checked against the dictionary entries by decreasing size.

Another problem of entity recognition is that an entity can be a part of another one (see e.g. *The New York Times* is a newspaper). While in [23], the Blitz NL processor selects a unique entity among the recognized ones based on confidence values, we intend to recognize all entities of a sentence, and generate different parsed sentence alternatives. Consequently, regardless from the success of a search each subsegment is checked again for shorter entities.

The order of segment checks are the following:

1. We start with the entire sentence: $[1, \ldots, n]$.
2. Each subsegment of the sentence is examined by decreasing size: $[1, \ldots, j]$, where $j = n - 1, \ldots, 1$.
3. Segments starting with the second word are examined: $[2, \ldots, j]$, where $j = n, \ldots, 2$.
4. Systematically all segments are examined first ordered by the index of the first word and then by the length of the segment: $[i, \ldots, j]$, where $j = n, \ldots, i$, $i = 3, \ldots, n$.

Remark 1. It is obvious that not all the $n(n+1)/2$ segments are valid entity candidate. Considering that the first word of the sentence must be an interrogative, one may start from segment $[2, \ldots, n]$ and thus reducing the number of segments to $n(n-1)/2$.

In what follows we describe the entity recognition of a particular segment of the input question, called *candidate*. In Hungarian, the stem of a word can be modified when adding certain suffixes to it. In most cases only the last two letters of the word stem may change (*tűz* → *tüzet*[3]; *álom* → *álmot*[4]). Also, the previous suffix can be changed when an additional suffix is put at the end of a word (this case only happens when the entity itself is of inflected form that is further declined in the sentence: *Vissza a jövőbe* → *Vissza a jövőbét*[5]). In this case only the last letter may change. These considerations are reflected in the searching phase of ER.

A significant part of the entities are not Hungarian expression, and hence MP is not able to parse them. Nevertheless, when processing such an entity, the ER has to annotate them with morphological characters. We assume that for each entity a substitution word is given that is a morphologically parsable word having the same inflection as the last word of the entity. It is often the last word of the entity (if it is a nominative Hungarian word), or is generated algorithmically when inserting the entity entry into the dictionary. The substitution word plays role in the determination of the entity's suffixes.

We will use the following denotation:

- $\text{last}(x)$ denotes the last word of an expression x.
- $\text{length}(x)$ is the size of the word x in characters.
- $\text{trunc}(x, i)$ the word x truncated by i characters from the end.
- $\text{lchar}(x)$ the last character of x.

Further we use abbreviation C (candidate), S (substitution word) and E (entity). The flowchart of the algorithm is depicted on Figure 2.

1. If $\text{last}(E)$ is variable in form (i.e. can be inflected), nominative, Hungarian word (i.e. recognized by MP)

---

[3] fire [NOM] → fire [ACC]
[4] dream [NOM] → dream [ACC]
[5] Back to the future [NOM] → [ACC]

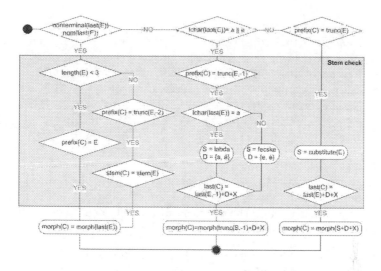

Fig. 2. Flowchart of the algorithm of entity recognizer

1.1 searching
    1.1.a If length(last(E)) $\geq$ 3 then it is checked whether trunc(E, 2) is a prefix of C.
    1.1.b If length(last(E)) $<$ 3 then it is checked whether E is a prefix of C.
1.2 stem check: If 1.1.a is successful, that is trunc(E, 2) is a prefix of C, then it should be examined whether the stem of last(C) and last(E) are identical. The reason of this is that after truncation there may be several words that match the prefix of last(E). This step can be skipped when 1.1.b is valid.
1.3 annotation: If the stems in 1.2 are identical then C is the entity E that is annotated with morphological characters of last(C). If both E and C have some non-terminal morpheme, that is discarded at annotation (see also Example 4).
2. If last(E) does not meet the condition of (1), i.e. it is either not recognized by MP, or invariable in form (i.e. cannot be inflected), or can be inflected but not nominative word.
    2.1 searching
        2.1.a If lchar(last(E)) $= a$ or $= e$ then the prefix matching is performed with trunc(E, 1).
        2.1.b If lchar(last(E)) $\neq a$ or $\neq e$ then the prefix matching is performed with E.
    2.2 determination of substitution word
        2.2.a If 2.1.a is successful and lchar(last(E)) $= a$ then $S = labda$; and when lchar(last(E)) $= e$ then $S = fecske$.
        2.2.b If 2.1.b is successful then we take the provided S of the E.
    2.3 annotation
        2.3.a The last word of the C has the following form: [trunc($last(E, 1)$)\{a,e\} rest], where rest is the remaining characters (if any) at the end of

last(c). The following strings are created and passed to MP: [trunc $(last(S,1))\{$a,á$\}$rest] ([trunc($last(S,1))\{$e,é$\}$rest]) if lchar(E) = a (lchar(E) = e), resp. Only one of the strings is a valid word, and hence will be recognized by the MP. The annotation of C will be the morphological characters of the valid words.

2.3.b The last word of the C has the following form: [Erest]. The following string is created and passed to MP: [Srest]. The annotation of C will be the morphological characters of the compounded word [Srest].

Remark 2. One can observe that the first case of the algorithm is more complicated at searching, because the matching is more complex when word of variable form are concerned. In contrast, the second case of the algorithm is more complicated at annotating because the suffixes of the entity can be determined only by a proper substitution word.

Remark 3. The search form of each entity can be stored in the dictionary and generated at the insertion of the entity entry by means of MP. It can save considerable time in the searching phase.

Remark 4. At 2.3 if length($rest$) = 0 then one can omit calling MP, because it means that there are no suffixes on the entity, so it can be considered a nominative noun.

Remark 5. We apply a semi-heuristic algorithm when assigning the substitution word S to each entity of case 2.2.b. S is selected from a table based on the last consonant and the vowels in the last of word of the entity. It is not 100% perfect but assigns good words in the vast majority of case (over 98%).

Remark 6. At 2.3 if length($rest$) = 0 then one can omit calling MP, because it means that there are no suffixes on the entity, so it can be considered a nominative noun.

2.1 Examples

Here we present some example to illustrate the algorithm of ER. The questions are taken from the sample inputs used for testing NL module.

Example 1. See also Figure 3.

Milyen költők vannak Arany Jánostól József Attiláig?[6]

E = *József Attila*, last(E) is recognized by MP as

`Attila[noun_prs]+[NOM]`

therefore 1) is the actual case. The matching is performed with search form "*József Atti*", and is successful when matched against segment C = *József Attiláig*

---

[6] What poets are between János Arany and Attila József? (e.g. concerning alphabetical order).

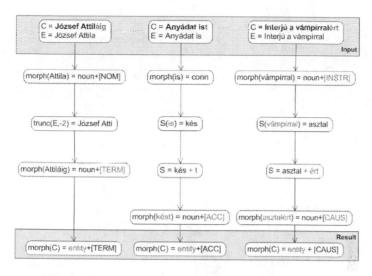

Fig. 3. Illustration of ER's algorithm on examples 1–3

(because the right choice of C is trivial in these examples, we will not specify it explicitly in the next). The result of MP for last(C) is

`Attila[noun_prs]+[TERM]`

It means that the entity E is found in C and it is annotated as [TERM].

Example 2. See also Figure 3.

Ki rendezte az Anyádat ist?[7]

$E = Anyádat \ is$. This is the case 2 (b), because the part of speech of *is* conjunction that cannot be inflected. Let S be *kés*[8], hence *kést* is passed to MP. The result is `kés[noun]+[ACC]` so the recognized entity is: *Anyádat is*$_{entity}$+[ACC].

Example 3. See also Figure 3.

Mennyit kell fizetnem az Interjú a vámpírralért?[9]

$E = Interjú \ a \ vámpírral$. This is also case 2, because last(E) is an inflected word: `vámpír[noun]+[INSTR]`. Let S be *asztal*[10], and so *asztalért* is passed to MP that returns: `asztal[noun]+[CAUS/FIN]`. The final result of ER will be *Interjú a vámpírral*$_{entity}$+[CAUS/FIN].

Example 4. See also Figure 4.

Ki rendezte Az én kis mosodámat?[11]

---

[7] Who directed And Your Mother Too?
[8] knife.
[9] How much I should pay for the Interview with the Vampire?
[10] table.
[11] Who directed My beautiful launderette?

544   D. Tikk et al.

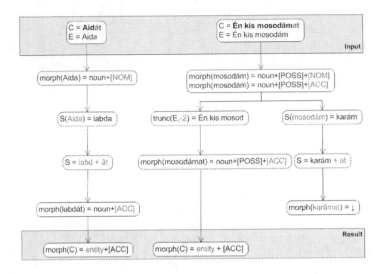

Fig. 4. Illustration of ER's algorithm on examples 4–5

The title of the movie in Hungarian is $E = Az$ *én kis mosodám*, where the stem of the last word (*mosoda*[12]) has a possessive suffix (-m). This word (mosodám) is further receives the accusative suffix (-(a)t). Observe that the entity has to be annotated only with accusative suffix. This entity activates both cases because the result of MP is:

```
mosoda[noun]+[POSS_SG_1]+[ACC]
mosoda[noun]+[POSS_SG_1]+[NOM]
```

The first row infers case 2. Let S be *karám*[13]; we create the string *karámat* based on the algorithm that is an invalid word, so this branch does not find any entity. The second row calls case 1. The stem of last$(E) = $ *mosodám* and last$(C) = $ *mosodámat* are identical, thus E is a prefix of C. Finally, the morphological characters are obtained as the difference of the morhposyntax of last(C) and last(E): as *Én kis mosodám*$_\text{entity}$+[ACC].

Example 5. See also Figure 4.

$$Hol\ játsszák\ az\ Aidát?^{14}$$

$E = Aida$. This is case 2 (a), because last(E) is not recognized by MP. Let S be *labda*[15], and so *labdát* is passed to MP that returns: `labda[noun]+[ACC]`. The final result of ER will be *Aida*$_\text{entity}$+[ACC].

---

[12] laundry.
[13] hurdle.
[14] Where Aida is played?
[15] ball.

2.2   Algorithm of the Tokenizer

The algorithm of the tokenizer is straightforward based on ER. It processes each segment of the question in the order specified above. If there are no entities starting with a given word W of the question, then a token is created from W itself and annotated with the respective output of MP. Whenever a single word is not recognized by MP, it is treated as a nominative noun.

3   Conclusions

In this paper we presented some results of the "In the web of words" (WoW) project that aimed to create a complex search interface that incorporates deep web search, Hungarian natural language question processing, image search support by visual thesaurus. The paper was focused on the processing of Hungarian questions and with special focus on the entity recognizer algorithm. Its goal is to recognized known entities (based on dictionary) in all possible inflected form. By means of a morphological parser we also determine morphological characteristics of recognized entities.

References

1. Bergman, M.K.: The deep web: surfacing hidden value. Journal of Electronic Publishing **7** (2001) http://www.press.umich.edu/jep/07-01/bergman.html.
2. Winkler, H.: Suchmaschinen. metamedien im internet? In Becker, B., Paetau, M., eds.: Virtualisierung des Sozialen, Frankfurt/NY (1997) 185–202 (In German; English translation: http://www.uni-paderborn.de/~timwinkler/suchm_e.html).
3. http://www.askjeeves.com/.
4. http://www.answerbus.com/.
5. http://www.ionaut.com:8400/.
6. Popescu, A.M., Armanasu, A., Etzioni, O., Ko, D., Yates, A.: Modern natural language interfaces to databases: Composing statistical parsing with semantic tractability. In: Proc. of Int. Conf. on Computational Linguistics (COLING04), Geneva, Switzerland (2004)
7. http://www.ai.mit.edu/projects/infolab/.
8. Katz, B., Lin, J.L.: Start and beyond. In: Proc. of World Multiconference on Systemics, Cybernetics and Informatics (SCI02). Volume XVI. (2002)
9. Stratica, N., Kosseim, L., Desai, B.C.: A natural language processor for querying Cindi. In: Proc. of SSGRR 2002, L'Aquila, Italy (2002)
10. Androutsopoulos, I., Ritchie, G.D., Thanisch, P.: Masque/SQL – an efficient and portable natural language query interface for relational databases. In: Proc. of IEA/AIE 93 Conference, Edinburgh (1993) 327–330
11. Warren, D., Pereira, F.: An efficient easily adaptable system for interpreting natural language queries. Computational Linguistics **8** (1982) 110–122
12. Grosz, B.J., Appelt, D.E., Martin, P.A., Pereira, F.C.: Team: An experiment in the design of transportable natural-language interfaces. Artifical Intelligence **32** (1987) 173–243

13. Rangel, R.A.P., Gelbukh, A.F., Barbosa, J.J.G., Ruiz, E.A., Mejía, A.M., Sánchez, A.P.D.: Spanish natural language interface for a relational database querying system. In Sojka, P., Kopecek, I., Pala, K., eds.: Proc. of TSD 2002. Volume 2448 of Lecture Notes in Computer Science. Springer-Verlag, Brno, Czech Republic (2002) 123–130

14. http://www.lllf.uam.es/proyectos/sylvia.html.

15. Cedermark, P.: Swedish noun and adjective morphology in a natural language interface to databases. Master thesis, Uppsala University, Department of Linguistics (2003)

16. Reis, P., Matias, J., Mamede, N.: Edite: A natural language interface to databases – a new perspective for an old approach. In: Proc. of ENTER'97. Information and Communication Technologies in Tourism, Edinburgh (1997) 317–326

17. Filipe, P.P., Mamede, N.J.: Databases and natural language interfaces. In: Proc. of 5th Jornada de Engenharia de Software e Bases de Dados (JISBD), Valladolid (2000) 321–332

18. Meng, X., Wang, S.: Overview of a chinese natural language interface to databases: Nchiql. International Journal of Computer Processing of Oriental Languages **14** (2001) 213–232

19. Lee, H., Park, J.C.: Interpretation of natural language queries for relational database access with combinatory categorial grammar. International Journal of Computer Processing of Oriental Languages **15** (2002) 281–303

20. Pazienza, M.T., Stellato, A., Henriksen, L., Paggio, P., Zanzotto, F.M.: Ontology mapping to support ontology-based question answering (2005)

21. Hunmorph: (2004) http://www.szoszablya.hu/termekek/hunmorph/.

22. Tikk, D., Kardkovács, Z.T., Andriska, Z., Magyar, G., Babarczy, A., Szakadát, I.: Natural language question processing for hungarian deep web searcher. In: Proc. of IEEE Int. Conf. on Computational Cybernetics (ICCC04), Wien, Austria (2004) 303–309

23. Katz, B., Yuret, D., Lin, J., Felshin, S., Schulman, R., Ilik, A.: Blitz: A preprocessor for detecting context-independent linguistic structures. In: Proc. of the 5th Pacific Rim Conference on Artificial Intelligence (PRICAI '98), Singapore (1998)

Recognition Algorithm for Korean Postpositions by Detecting Prosody Boundaries

Ki Young Lee[1], Jong Kuk Kim[2], and Myung Jin Bae[2]

[1] Department of Information Communication Engineering, Kwandong University,
7 San Imcheon-ri, Yangyang-eup, Yangyang-gun, Gangwon-do, Korea
`kylee@kd.ac.kr`
[2] Department of Information & Telecommunication Engineering, Soongsil University,
Sangdo 5-dong, Dongjak-gu, Seoul, Korea
`{Kokjk91, mjbae}@ssu.ac.kr`

Abstract. In this paper we proposes the algorithm of recognizing postpositions and suffixes in Korean spoken language, using prosodic information. At first, we detect grammatical boundaries automatically by using prosodic information of the accentual phrase, and then we recognize grammatical function words by backward tracking from the boundaries. The experiment employs 300 sentential speech data of 10 men's and 5 women's voice spoken in standard Korean, in which 1080 APs and eleven postpositions and suffixes are included. The result shows the recognition rate of postpositions in two cases. In one case that includes just correctly detected boundaries, the recognition rate is 97.5%, and in the other case that includes all detected boundaries, the recognition rate is 74.8%.

1 Introduction

In the field of speech recognition, the current main issue is to recognize continuous speech. For the system of recognizing independent words, the techniques showing the excellent recognition rate have been developed. But for the system of recognizing continuous speech, no suitable technique has been developed yet, especially for Korean. The main reason for this is that, in Korean spoken language processing, we do not have the method of using syntactic information about sentence structures such as subjects, objects, etc, although this information is necessarily required for understanding spoken language.

In English, this information can be obtained from the word order of a sentence and the word itself[1-3]. In Korean, this information is carried by the grammatical function words such as postpositions, inflectional suffixes, etc., not by the word order. Therefore, in order to parse Korean sentences, we must first find these grammatical function words. However, this approach has never yet been tried in spoken language processing for Korean, so far as we know.

The purpose of this study is to try to first recognize grammatical function words in Korean continuous speech. For doing this, we detect grammatical boundaries automatically at first, by using prosodic information, and then we recognize grammatical function words by backward-tracking from the boundaries.

S. Bandini and S. Manzoni (Eds.): AI*IA 2005, LNAI 3673, pp. 547–552, 2005.
© Springer-Verlag Berlin Heidelberg 2005

2 Characteristics of Korean Grammatical Function Words

In Korean, grammatical function words are postpositions and inflectional suffixes which follow main lexical category items such as nouns, verbs, etc. And along with these main lexical category items, they compose grammatical phrases. In written language, these phrases are separated by a space. So in the field of natural language processing based on texts, to parse a sentence, people first detect spaces and then find the grammatical function words by backward-tracking from the spaces.

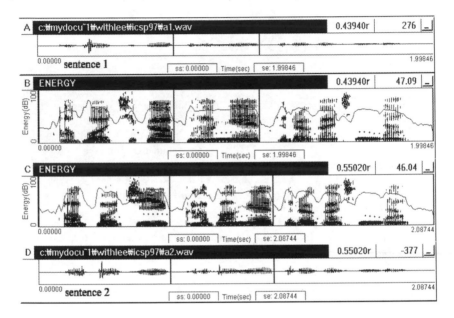

Fig. 1. The difference of prosodic features between "Father goes into the room(sentence 1)" and "Father goes into the bag(sentence 2)"

In spoken language processing, we also need this process in order to parse a sentence. That is, we must first detect phrasal boundaries and then recognize grammatical function words[4,5]. But unlike in written language, we are faced with the difficulty in detecting phrasal boundaries in spoken language, because the information on phrasal boundaries is carried by prosodic features.

We, the authors of this paper, proposed a technique of detecting prosodic phrases such as accentual phrases, etc. automatically by using prosodic information[6,7]. In Korean, prosodic units are almost similar to grammatical units which are separated by a space. Thus, if we detect prosodic units by using prosodic information, we can recognize grammatical function words by backtracking from the boundaries. Figure 1 shows the difference of prosodic features between the following two sentences:

Sentence 1:
[[abʌ ɟ i] ga]$_{SUBJ}$ [[paŋ] e]$_{LOC}$ [di ɾ ʌ gaʃ inda]
"Father goes into the room."

Sentence 2:
[abʌ ɟ i]ₛᵤBⱼ [[gapaŋ]e]_LOC [di ɾ ʌ gaʃ inda]
"Father goes into the bag."

In figure 1, we can see that the pitch contour of each prosodic unit (except the final one) is LH or LHLH pattern, and that the final syllable of each prosodic unit is longer than the intermediate syllable(Compare the third syllable [ɟi] of each sentence).

In sum, if using prosodic information, we can detect phrasal boundaries in Korean spoken language, and it enables us to recognize grammatical function words.

3 Recognition Algorithm for Korean Postpositions

In order to recognize Korean postpositions, we must first detect phrasal bounda-ries. For doing this, we employ the accentual phrase as prosodic unit, and segment a sentence(continuous speech data) into accentual phrases by using the pitch contour of L(HL)H pattern[8]. As the pattern matching method, we use DTW, because we use small data in this study(when the study started, we regarded this study as just a test to verify the possibility of our approach), and for small data the DTW method is conven-ient. After segmenting continuous speech into accentual phrases, we recognize gram-matical function words by backtracking from the end of the phrases, because Korean grammatical function words are postpositions and suffixes and so they appear in the final position of the phrases, as mentioned in the previous section. Our system of recognizing Korean postpositions are shown in the following figure 2.

3.1 Automatic Detection of Korean Accentual Phrase Boundaries

As the automatic detection algorithm of accentual phrases(APs), we employ the one-stage DP[9] and the standard patterns made by normalization[7]. The first step is to extract pitch contours from residual signals using autocorrelation. And then, pitch contours are normalized so that we can make standard patterns and test patterns for detecting the boundaries of APs by using one-stage DP.

There is a strong correlation(but no 100% agreement) between syntactic and prosodic phrases. In Korean, syntactic phrases are divided in orthography by a space, and are in accordance with accentual phrases although there are some exceptions(e.g., defec-tive nouns). Because the pitch contour marks the AP, we segment the speech signal of a sentence into APs by hand labelling, as follows, and then use the pitch contours of the segmented units as the standard patterns:

[i nɟ u-ni n]_TOPIC / [mai m-i]_SUBJECT / [aɾ imdaun]_ADJECTIVE / [yʌ in-imnida]_NOUN PREDICATE

"Eunju is a woman whose heart is beautiful."

The pitch contour of the signal appears as the form of LH. The normalized pitch contour extracted by the proposed method in the paper[8] has the leveled slope of the down-step effect, and its form of LH is more evident. We employ the comparison of pattern in the algorithm of segmenting APs. The method of pattern comparison is one stage DP which is able to compare continuous patterns, and the standard pattern is made of the normalized pitch and derivative pitch pattern extracted from the real speech signal and marked manually. The equation of the distance measure used in one stage DP is as follows:

$$d_{AB}(n, m) = (1-a)\{p_A(n) - p_B(m)\} + a\{\triangle p_A(n) - \triangle p_B(m)\}, \quad 0 \leq a \leq 1 \quad (1)$$

$$\triangle p(n) = d\{p(n)\}/dn \quad (2)$$

The equation (2), the time derivative of the normalized pitch sequence, shows the degree of pitch variation according to time series.

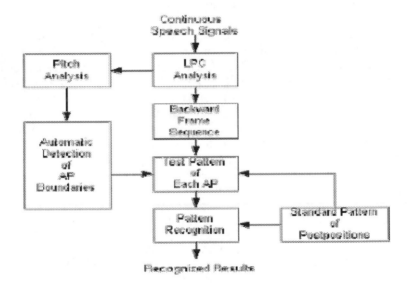

Fig. 2. The system of postposition recognition

3.2 Recognition of Postpositions

In the process of recognizing postpositions, we make test patterns aligned backward from the AP boundaries, and then execute the pattern recognition by comparing them with the pre-made standard pattern aligned backward. This study employs as the method of pattern recognition the DTW method using log likelihood.

4 Experimental Results

4.1 Experiment

We use speech signals of 10 kHz sampling rate, and 25.6 msec per frame, 12.8 msec for scanning interval. The script for data collection is composed of 20 sentences (all sentences are declarative), of which 4 sentences consists of 4 APs, 4 sentences of 5 APs, and 12 sentences of 3 APs. The total number of APs is 72. Ten male speakers and five female speakers of standard Korean read the script without any guideline, and record with their own equipment in order to keep the quality of data as natural as they can be. This experiment employs 300 sentential speech data of 10 men's and 5 women's voice spoken in standard Korean, in which 1080 APs are included.

For automatic detection of AP's boundaries, the multi-patterns of one sentence pronounced by three speakers are used as the standard pattern. To recognize postpositions, the speaker-dependent pattern of each postposition is used as the standard pattern. The number of postpositions which are the targets of recognition is eleven, including adjectival and declarative suffixes. They are the topic markers '-in, -nin,' the subjective markers '-i, -ga,' the directional marker '-ro,' the locative marker '-e,' the adjectival suffix '-n,' the declarative suffixes '-da, -yo, -dƷo,' and the final syllable '-li' of the adverb "p'alli".

4.2 Results

Figure 3 and 4 shows the correct detection rate of AP boundaries according to each speaker using the one stage DP and the equation of (1). The average correct detection rate of female speakers is 80.8%, and that of male speakers is 88.3%. The total average rate is 85.8%. Table 1 shows the recognition rate of postpositions in two cases. The first is the recognition rate of 97.5% for correctly detected boundaries (RRCDB), and the second is the rate of 74.8% for all detected boundaries(RRADB) which include wrongly detected boundaries.

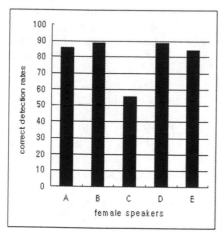
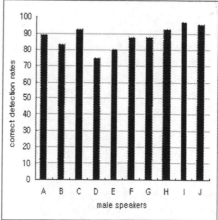
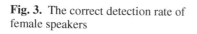

Fig. 3. The correct detection rate of female speakers

Fig. 4. The correct detection rate of male speakers

5 Conclusions

This study proposes the algorithm of recognizing postpositions and suffixes in Korean spoken language, using prosodic information. This method enables us to parse spoken sentences grammatically by extracting postpositions and suffixes which are grammatical function words. In addition, this method makes it possible for us to use the current recognition technique of independent words in recognizing spoken sentences. The experiment employs 300 sentential speech data of 10 men's and 5 women's voice spoken in standard Korean, in which 1080 APs and eleven postpositions and suffixes are included.

The result shows the recognition rate of postpositions in two cases. In one case that includes just correctly detected boundaries, the recognition rate is 97.5%, and in the other case that includes all detected boundaries, the recognition rate is 74.8%.

Acknowledgement. This work was supported by the Korean Science and Engineering Foundation, grant no. R01-2002-000-00278-0.

References

1. E. O. Selkirk, Phonology and Syntax, The MIT Press, Cambridge, Massachusetts, 1984.
2. M. Nespor and I. Vogel, Prosodic Pho-nol-ogy, Foris Publications, Dordrecht, 1986.
3. M. Beckman and J. Pierrehumbert, "Intonational structure in Japanese and English," Phonology Yearbook 3, ed. J. Ohala, pp. 255-309, 1986.
4. Minsuck Song, et al., "A theoretical model of spoken language processing," in Proc. of the 1994 Conference of HCI(Human and Computer Interface), Korea Information Science Society, pp. 1-9, 1994.
5. Kook Chung, et al., A Study of Korean Prosody and Discourse for the Development of Speech Synthesis/Recognition System, Annual Report of Korea Telecom Research and Development Group, 1996.
6. Jong Kuk Kim, Ki Young Lee, and Myung Jin Bae, "On a detection of Korean Prosody Phrase Boundaries," in Proc. of 5th International Conference (IDEAL 2004), pp.241-246, 2004.
7. Ki Young Lee, Jong Kuk Kim, and Myung Jin Bae,"Statistical Pitch Conversion Approaches Based on Korean Accentual Phrases," in Proc. of 8th Pacific Rim International Conference on Artificial Intelligence(PRICAI 2004), pp.919-927, 2004.
8. Sun-Ah Jun, The Phonetics and Phonology of Korean Prosody, Doctoral Dissertation, The Ohio State University, 1993.
9. Hermann Ney, "The use of a one-stage dynamic programming algorithm for connected word recognition," IEEE Trans. Acoustics, Speech and Signal Processing, Vol. ASSP-32, No.2, pp.263-271, 1984.

Fuzzy Multinomial Control Charts

Hassen Taleb and Mohamed Limam

LARODEC, Institut Suprieur de Gestion,
University of Tunis, 2000 Bardo, Tunisia

Abstract. Two approaches for constructing control charts to monitor multivariate attribute processes when data is presented in linguistic form are suggested. Two monitoring statistics T_f^2 and W^2 are developed based on fuzzy and probability theories. The first is similar to the Hotteling's T^2 statistic and is based on representative values of fuzzy sets. The W^2 statistic, being a linear combination of dependent chi-square variables, its distribution is derived by Satterthwaite's approximation. Resulting multivariate control charts are compared based on the average run length (ARL). A numerical example is given to illustrate the application of the proposed multivariate control charts and the interpretation of out-of-control signals.

1 Introduction

In the case of monitoring $p, p = 1, 2, ..$, multinomial QCs, the multivariate control chart proposed by [3] cannot be applied. The ambiguity of linguistic variables can be analyzed with fuzzy set theory. In the case of $p = 1$, a univariate control chart is used to control a multinomial process. [4], [7], [9] have introduced and discussed the construction of such control charts using both probability and fuzzy theory. In this article the case of monitoring more than one multinomial QCs is introduced. Construction of control chart for such multivariate attribute processes is analyzed using fuzzy sets and probability theories.

Industrial processes to be monitored in this paper depend on p correlated attribute quality characteristics $L_1, L_2, ..., L_p$. Each attribute, $L_j, \ j = 1, 2, ...p$, is a linguistic variable which describe quality of the product unit by a set of linguistic terms $L_{jk}, \ k = 1, ..., c_j$, where c_j is the size of the term set of L_j, such as high, meduim, bad,etc. Each term L_{jk} is associated with a fuzzy subset F_{jk} described by a membership function μ_{jk}. Each fuzzy subset can be converted into a representative value using one of the four existing transforming methods: fuzzy mode, fuzzy median, α level fuzzy midrange and fuzzy average, see [11],[12], [1] for more details. Using fuzzy arithmetic, it is possible to combine fuzzy subsets of one or all attributes. [7] have proposed two methods of combination. In the first method, fuzzy subsets F_{jk} are converted into their representative values r_{jk}. The weighted sum of r_{jk} in sample of size is the representative value of the attribute j. In the second method fuzzy subsets in term set j are combined using fuzzy arithmetic. The resulting fuzzy subset F_j is then converted into a representative value R_j. It is possible to retain fuzziness of obseravations one additional step. In

S. Bandini and S. Manzoni (Eds.): AI*IA 2005, LNAI 3673, pp. 553–563, 2005.

this third method, necessary in multivariate case, fuzzy subsets F_j corresponding to quality attributes are added using fuzzy operations. The obtained fuzzy subset F is associated with the sample of observations with respect to all quality characteristics. F is then converted into a representative value R. In these three methods, each sample is characterized by a numerical value. Next an overiew of the the first and the third methods, named respectively fuzzy probability and fuzzy membership approaches, is presented. The second method is similar to the third. The framework for the proposed multivariate fuzzy chart is presented in section 2. Multivariate probability control chart is discussed in section 3. A numerical example is given in section 4 to illustrate and compare the proposed approaches.

2 Multivariate Fuzzy Approach

2.1 Overview of the Two Fuzzy Approaches

Let A be a sample of n observations taken from a multivariate process in which quality depends on p correlated multinomial characteristics L_j. Product units are classified by each characteristic L_j into c_j categories. Categories L_{jk}, $k = 1, ...c_j$, are associated with fuzzy subsets F_{jk} described by membership functions μ_{jk}. A sample A of n observations can be expressed as follow:

$$A = \{\{(F_{11}, n_{11}), ..., (F_{1c_1}, n_{1c_1})\}; ...; \{(F_{p1}, n_{p1}), ..., (F_{1c_p}, n_{pc_p})\}\}, \qquad (1)$$

where n_{jk} is the number of observations classified by category L_{jk} such as $\sum_{k=1}^{c_j} n_{jk} = n$ for $j = 1, ..., p$. The goal is to determine a statistic, depending on all characteristics, using two methods of combination of fuzzy subsets F_{jk}: fuzzy membership and fuzzy probabilistic.

Fuzzy Probability Approach. A new statistic noted by T_f^2, similar to Hotelling's T^2, is proposed to control the multivariate multinomial process.

$$T_f^2 = (M_i - \bar{M})' \Sigma^{-1} (M_i - \bar{M}), \qquad (2)$$

where M is the mean vector corresponding to sample i of n observations and S is the covariance matrix, see [10]. The distribution of the T_f^2 statistic is given by:

$$T_f^2 \sim \frac{(m+n)(m-1)}{mn(m-p)} F_{p,m-p}, \qquad (3)$$

where $F_{p,m-p}$ represents an F distribution with p and $m-p$ degrees of freedom. Upper control limit (UCL)is chosen to be a precise percentile of $F_{p,m-p}$ distribution. If T_f^2 value corresponding to a given sample is greater than UCL, then the process is out-of-control. If not the process is in-control.

Fuzzy Membership Approach. Fuzziness is retained here one additional step. A sample i of n observations can be represented with only one fuzzy subset F_i with respect of all quality characteristics. It's expression is given by

$$F_i = \sum_{j=1}^{p} F_{ij} \tag{4}$$

F_i is then converted into a representative value R_i. R_i is the value, associated to sample i, to be plotted in-control chart. In this method multivariate multinomial control chart is transformed to a univariate control chart. This approach is similar to that proposed by [7] for monitoring univariate processes. Control limits are calculated as follow:

Step 1: Fuzzy subsets associated with sample $i, i = 1, ..., m$ are combined to give a fuzzy subset MF which describe the mean of all samples.

$$MF = \frac{1}{m} \sum_{i=1}^{m} F_i \tag{5}$$

The center line is obtained by transforming MF into its representative value
Step 2: The mean deviation of fuzzy subset MF denoted by $\sigma(MF)$ is calculated using fuzzy operations in tiangular fuzzy numbers in Kaufmann and Gupta (1985). If MF is represented by a triangular fuzzy number (MF_1, MF_2, MF_3) then

$$\sigma(MF) = \frac{MF_3 - MF_1}{2} \tag{6}$$

Step 3: Control limits should be located at $\pm k\sigma(MF)$ from the center line. The multiplier k will be detrmined using Monte carlo simulation such that the probability of Type I error will be equal to predetermined value.

3 Multivariate Probability Approach

Construction of multivariate control chart for multinomial processes can be conducted using the above approximation,[8]. Let $Z_{ij}^2 = \sum_{h=1}^{q_j} \frac{(n_{ijh} - n_{0jh})^2}{n_{ijh} + n_{0jh}}$, be a statistic to test the homogeneity of proportions between the base period 0 when the process is assumed to be in-control and each period i, $i = 1, 2, ..., m$. n_{ijh} and n_{0jh} are the number of units classified by QC j into category h in the period i and the base period 0 respectively.
Then, let

$$M_j = \sum_{i=1}^{m} Z_{ij}^2, \quad and \quad M = \sum_{j=1}^{p} M_j, \tag{7}$$

The number of degree of freedom of each M_j is $q_j - 1$. Then using Satterthwaite's approximation, the degree of freedom of M is given by

$$v = \frac{M^2}{\sum_{j=1}^{p} (M_j)^2 / (q_j - 1)} \tag{8}$$

The upper control limit of the multivariate attribute control chart is taken to be a percentile of the $\chi^2(v)$ distribution.

3.1   The Multivariate Attribute Control Chart

An alternative approach to fuzzy multivariate control charts will be based on the probability distribution. In the multivariate process for multinomial attribute data, described in section 2, let W_i^2 be a statistic for the sample i such that:

$$W_i^2 = \sum_{j=1}^{p} Z_{ij}^2. \tag{9}$$

The W_i^2 statistic has a chi-square distribution with an approximated degrees of freedom equal to v. Then, for each sample, W_i^2 is computed and then plotted on the control charts. The process is declared to be out-of-control if the statistic W_i^2 plot outside the control limit, if not the process remains in-control.

3.2   Interpretation of Out-of-Control Signals

Similar to other multivariate control charts, the most important step is the interpretation of out-of-control signals. Several techniques were suggested to help in this interpretation such as discriminant analysis, principal components, ...etc, [6]. The proposed approach is based on the Satterthwaite's approximation and univariate control charts. When the control chart declares an out-of-control signal, the following steps are needed to identify which attribute is more responsible:
Step 1: Compute M and v using Satterthwaite's approximation for the combination of all QC but the jth one. Then, for a certain QC, c_t, M and v values are respectively:

$$M_t = \begin{cases} \sum_{j=1}^{p} M_j, j \neq t \\ v_t = \frac{M_t^2}{\sum_{j=1}^{p}(M_j)^2/(q_j-1)}, j \neq t \end{cases} \tag{10}$$

Step 2: Let W_{it}^2 be the computed value of W_i^2 without considering the jth QC. Then, the statistic $W_{it}^2 = \sum_{j=1}^{p} Z_{ij}^2$, for $j \neq t$ has a $\chi^2(v_t)$ distribution.
Step 3: The upper control limit for each statistic W_{it}^2, UCL_t, is taken to be a percentile of the $\chi^2(v_t)$ distribution, $t = 1, 2, ..., p$
Step 4: Compute $d_t = W_{it}^2 - UCL_t$, for $t = 1, 2, ..., p$. For example, if d_t is negative for $t = 1$ and positive for $t = 2, 3, ..., p$, then the QC, c_1 is responsible for the out-of-control signal.
Step 5: Plot univariate control charts for each QC.

4   Numerical Example

In food process industry, appearance, colour and taste of a frozen food are three important QCs that have to be jointly monitored. The product unit's appearance could be classified by an expert as either good, medium or poor, and its colour as standard, acceptable or rejected. In addition the taste of a product unit is classified as either perfect, good, medium or poor. Then, we have three term sets of linguistic variables:

Term set 1 relative to the appearance, is
$T(c_1) = \{c_{11}, c_{12}, c_{13}\} = \{good, medium, poor\}$.
Term set 2 relative to the colour, is
$T(c_2) = \{c_{21}, c_{22}, c_{23}\} = \{Standard, acceptable, rejected\}$.
Term set 3 relative to the taste, is
$T(c_3) = \{c_{31}, c_{32}, c_{33}, c_{34}\} = \{perfect, good, medium, poor\}$.

4.1   Multivariate Fuzzy Quality Control Chart: MFQCC

Using fuzzy set theory, linguistic terms, $c_{jh}, j = 1, 2, 3, h = 1, .., q_j$ can be characterized by membership functions μ_{jh}. Membership functions associated with these three term sets are shown in figure 1. As introduced by [2], membership functions associated with F_j are calculated using fuzzy arithmetic. For the case of collected data given in table 1, quality manager decides to use $m = 20$ preliminary samples, of size $n = 220$ product units, for monitoring the multivariate process. Representative values R_j, and the values of the statistic T_f^2, are calculated for each sample and summarized in table 2. Using bootstrap resampling method, 10000 new samples are drawn with replacement. Using a computer program, the statistic given by equation (3) is calculated for each replication. Then, the upper control limit is calculated as a percentile of the T_f^2 distribution. The result obtained is $UCL = 7.626$, and the new T_f^2 control chart, used to monitor future observations, is shown in figure 2. For testing purposes additional data is taken from the frozen food process and is given in table 3. Statistic T_f^2 is

Table 1. Food process data

k	C_{11}	C_{12}	C_{13}	C_{21}	C_{22}	C_{23}	C_{31}	C_{32}	C_{33}	C_{34}
1	210	7	3	206	9	5	167	48	3	2
2	211	6	3	207	8	5	176	42	2	0
3	206	9	5	202	12	6	163	55	2	0
4	211	5	4	207	8	5	163	51	5	1
5	203	16	1	194	18	8	175	45	0	0
6	210	6	4	206	9	5	174	44	1	1
7	208	7	5	204	9	7	174	40	5	1
8	207	7	6	204	9	7	169	46	3	2
9	206	7	7	202	9	9	169	48	2	1
10	186	25	9	200	12	8	169	48	3	0
11	196	13	11	196	13	11	163	46	10	1
12	203	12	5	200	13	7	167	44	9	0
13	203	9	8	198	11	11	174	42	3	1
14	202	9	9	198	11	11	174	40	6	0
15	209	6	5	207	9	4	172	42	5	1
16	210	3	7	205	5	10	172	44	4	0
17	205	11	4	201	13	6	172	45	2	1
18	210	6	4	206	8	6	169	48	2	1
19	206	10	4	203	13	4	172	46	0	2
20	206	12	2	202	14	4	169	46	5	0

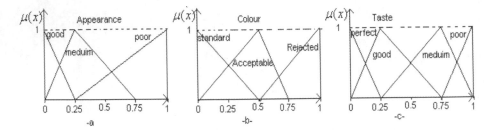

Fig. 1. Sets of Membership functions with a)-Fuzzy set relative to Appearance, b)-Fuzzy set relative to Colour and c)- Fuzzy set relative to Taste

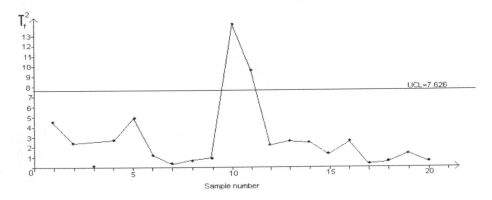

Fig. 2. Fuzzy multivariate control charts

Table 2. Sample's representative values

Sample	1	2	3	4	5	6	7	8	9	10
R_{j1}	0,090	0,089	0,098	0,091	0,093	0,092	0,096	0,099	0,102	0,128
R_{j2}	0,172	0,213	0,229	0,213	0,259	0,214	0,238	0,238	0,263	0,253
R_{j3}	0,252	0,241	0,246	0,254	0,238	0,243	0,249	0,251	0,246	0,245
T_f^2	4,716	2,363	0,182	2,838	4,789	1,356	0,396	0,407	0,753	14,666
Sample	11	12	13	14	15	16	17	18	19	20
R_{j1}	0,121	0,101	0,107	0,110	0,095	0,098	0,097	0,092	0,096	0,092
R_{j2}	0,293	0,242	0,291	0,291	0,202	0,272	0,230	0,224	0,206	0,207
R_{j3}	0,261	0,255	0,246	0,248	0,250	0,246	0,245	0,246	0,245	0,248
T_f^2	9,510	2,361	2,934	2,631	1,441	2,520	0,299	0,575	1,552	0,896

calculated and plotted in the control chart as shown in figure 3. If the computed statistic is smaller than $UCL = 7.626$, then the process is in-control, if not the process is out-of-control. In the latter case, the process will be stopped, and the responsible attribute variable for this shift should be identified. Hence, associated assignable causes are detected and eliminated.

Interpretation of Out-of-Control Signals. Figure 3 shows that process is out-of-control in periods represented by samples 22 and 25. To determine which

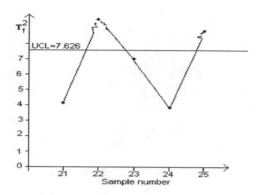

Fig. 3. Fuzzy multivariate control charts for additional data

Table 3. Additional data of the food process

k	C_{11}	C_{12}	C_{13}	C_{21}	C_{22}	C_{23}	C_{31}	C_{32}	C_{33}	C_{34}
21	202	10	8	204	11	5	169	44	5	2
22	184	25	11	206	12	2	174	44	1	1
23	208	7	5	196	13	11	174	44	1	1
24	206	6	8	196	13	11	174	40	5	1
25	210	2	8	198	12	10	165	44	1	10

Table 4. Representative values for additional samples

Sample	R_{j1}	R_{j2}	R_{j3}	T_f^2
21	0,108	0.216	0,254	4.137
22	0.134	0.182	0.243	50.415
23	0.096	0.293	0.243	7.003
24	0.104	0.293	0.249	3.854
25	0.100	0.279	0.271	29.344

Table 5. Out-of-control signal's interpretation

Sample	T_f^2	T_{1f}^2	T_{2f}^2	T_{3f}^2
22	50.415	7.19	28.696	45.108
25	29.344	29.6	23.456	2.856

variable is responsible for both cases, T_{jf}^2 is calculated and given in table 4. In addition, a univariate control chart is constructed for each variable as shown in figure 4. From table 5, T_{1f}^2 is 7.19, and by comparing it to the global value of T_f^2 and the other decomposed values T_{2f}^2 and T_{3f}^2, we notice, that the variable

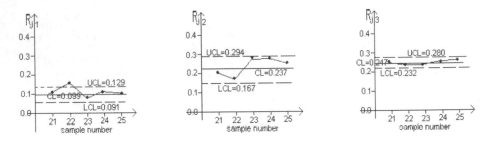

Fig. 4. Univariate control charts

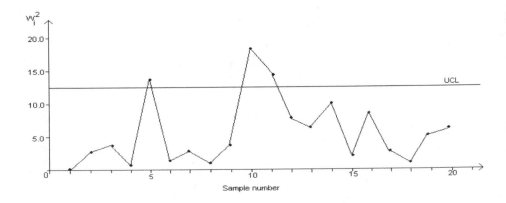

Fig. 5. Multivariate attribute control chart

responsible of the out-of-control signal in sample 22 is the QC c_1: appearance. This result is proved by the use of univariate control charts. In fact only the univariate control chart for appearance shows an out-of-control signals when sample 22 is taken.

Values of T_{1f}^2, T_{2f}^2 and T_{3f}^2, associated with sample 25 are 29.6, 23.456 and 2.856, respectively. This result indicates that variable 3 is more responsible for the shift causing the out-of-control signal. The univariate control charts indicate a stable process for the three quality characteristics. Then, the correlation between the three variables has an effect on the out-of-control signal detected by the multivariate fuzzy control chart when sample 25 is taken.

4.2   Multivariate Attribute Quality Control Charts: MAQCC

Control Limit. Using the same data of the food process, Z_{ij}^2 and W_i^2 values are summarized in table 6. Using equation (16) the associated degrees of freedom are $v = 5.9675$. The upper control limit, taken to be the 95th percentile of the $\chi^2(5.9675)$ distribution, is $UCL = 12.59$. For each sample i, if $W_i^2 < 12.59$, the process is in-control, if not the process is out-of-control. From table 6 it is clear that process is out-of-control when in periods of samples 5, 10 and 11. The MAQCC shown in figure 5, could be used to control future samples.

Table 6. Analysis of preliminary data

Sample	Z_{i1}^2	Z_{i2}^2	Z_{i3}^2	W_i^2
1	0,000	0,000	0,000	0,000
2	0,079	0,061	2,836	2,977
3	0,788	0,559	2,724	4,071
4	0,479	0,061	0,973	1,513
5	4,640	4,052	5,284	13,977
6	0,220	0,000	1,651	1,871
7	0,510	0,343	1,704	2,557
8	1,022	0,343	0,054	1,419
9	1,638	1,182	0,545	3,366
10	14,580	1,210	2,012	17,801
11	6,854	3,226	4,194	14,274
12	1,934	1,149	5,174	8,258
13	2,641	2,608	0,877	6,127
14	3,405	2,608	3,871	9,885
15	0,579	0,114	1,307	2,000
16	3,200	2,812	2,391	8,402
17	1,092	0,880	0,704	2,675
18	0,220	0,150	0,545	0,915
19	0,711	0,860	3,116	4,687
20	1,554	1,237	2,554	5,346

Table 7. W^2 statistic for additional data

Sample	Z_{i1}^2	Z_{i2}^2	Z_{i3}^2	W_i^2
21	2,957	0,210	0,686	3,853
22	16,412	1,714	1,651	19,777
23	0,510	3,226	1,651	5,387
24	2,388	3,226	1,704	7,318
25	5,051	2,254	6,519	13,823

Table 8. Out-of-control signal's interpretation

Sample	W^2	W_{i1}^2	W_{i2}^2	W_{i3}^2	UCL_1	UCL_2	UCL_3	d_1	d_2	d_3
22	19.777	3.4	18	18	11	9.8	8.9	-7.6	8.3	9.3
25	13.823	8.8	12	7.3	11	9.8	8.9	-2.2	1.8	-2.2

Interpretation of Out-of-Control Signal. The additional data in table 3 are used again and the statistic W_i^2 is calculated and compared to the UCL is illustrated in table 7. It is clear to note, as in the case of MFQCC, that samples 22 and 25 show that process is out-of-control. To find which variable is responsible of these two shifts, statistics W_{it}^2, d_t and the degrees of freedom v_t are computed and given in table 8. Univariate control charts can be used to give an additional information about out-of-control signal. The UCL of control charts for the first and second QC are equal to $\chi_{0.95}^2(2) = 5.991$, and for the third QC, UCL is equal to $\chi^2_{0.95}(3) = 7.815$. Using results in table 8, QC c_1 is found to be responsible for the out-of-control signal detected by sample 22. In sample 25, both $d_1$and d_3 are negative.Then we conclude that both QC, c_1 and QC, c_3 are responsible for the out-of-control signal. Using univariate control charts, table 7 shows that control chart for QC, c_1 detect an out-of-control situation when sample 22 is taken but no shift is detected by any of univariate control charts when sample 25 is taken. Then, for sample 25, the shift detected by the MAQCC can be the result of a change in the correlation between the process variables. The variables responsible are the first and the third QC.

4.3   Comparison of the Two Approaches

The multivariate control chart, based on binomial distribution, proposed by [3] deals with multivariate attribute processes where many quality characteristics are controlled simultaneously. Although this is a solution to the problem of controlling multivariate attribute process, it is limited to the case of binary classification of attribute quality characteristics. The proposed MFQCC and MAQCC, based on fuzzy and probability theory, can be applied to multivariate attribute processes for monitoring multinomial quality characteristics. The proposed control chart can not be compared to the traditional Hotelling T^2 control chart since the latter is not applicable to such processes. The Hotelling T^2 control chart is based on the normal distribution and the MFQCC is based on the distribution of representative values. Once the normality does not hold for the last distribution. Then, the T_f^2 statistic distribution is unknown, and a simulation study is needed to obtain the control limit for the proposed chart. However, the proposed MFQCC can be compared only to charts dealing with multivariate attribute processes for multinomial data. Hence, it is possible to compare MFQCC and MAQCC by applying then to the same process. The two multivariate charts are compared based on average run length (ARL) for a certain shift and their efficiency for detecting out-of-control shifts.

It is shown that samples 22 and 25 are out-of-control with respect to the two approaches. The interpretation of these two out-of-control signals give the same result. For the MAQCC, ARL can easily be calculated using chi-square distribution. For the MFQCC, ARL is calculated using simulation and bootstrap. For example, If the process shifts from the in-control signal, as in sample 1, to an out-of-control signal, as in sample 25, then for a sample of size 220, the ARL is 2.874 for the MFQCC, and 2.751 for the MAQCC. This shows that the two proposed charts have similar efficiency.

5   Conclusion

Two approaches are proposed to deal with a multivariate process when more than one multinomial quality characteristics is monitored. The first is based on fuzzy theory and the other is based on probability theory. The plotted statistic in the fuzzy approach is obtained after transforming fuzzy observations into their representative values. It's distribution is derived using Bootstrap resampling method. The alternative approach, the probability approach, use a statistic which is a combination of a chi-square statistics. Its distribution is derived from Satterthwaite approximation. Two methods are introduced for the interpretation of out-of-control signals. The resulted charts can be applied to multivariate processes when product units are classified by each attribute quality characteristic into more than two categories. The frozen food example is given to illustrate the construction of the MFQCC and MAQCC.

Although the proposed control charts are concluded to have similar results for the frozen food example, they denote some disadvantages. The MFQCC is based on fuzzy theory, and then it is strongly related to the choice of membership function and the degree of fuzziness. This choice is usually with no theoretical foundation. In addition, the distribution of the statistic used by MAQCC can not be determined directly and it is approximated by Satterthwaite method. Some other existing multivariate control charts, such as EWMA and CUSUM charts, can be generalized and developed to monitor multivariate process for multinomial categorical data and compared to the proposed charts.

References

1. Kanagawa, A., Tamaki, F., and Ohta, H.: Fuzzy Control Charts for Linguistic Data. Proc. of International Fuzzy Engineering Symposium'91, **2**(1991), 644-654.
2. Kaufmann, A.,and Gupta, M. M.: Introduction of Fuzzy Arithmetic Theory and Applications. (New York: Van Nostrand Reinhold).(1985).
3. Lu, S. X.: Control chart for multivariate attribute processes. International Journal of Production Research, **36** (1998), 3477 - 3489.
4. Marcucci, M.: Monitoring multinomial processes. Journal of Quality Technology, **17** (1985), 86-91.
5. Mason, R. L., Tracy, N. D., and Young, J. C.: A Practical Approach for Interpreting Multivariate T^2 Control Chart Signals. Journal of Quality Technology, **29** (1997),396406.
6. Mason, R. L., Tracy, N. D., and Young, J. C.: Decomposition of T^2 for Multivariate Control Chart Interpretation. Journal of Quality Technology, **27** (1995), 99108.
7. Raz, T., and Wang, J.,1990, Probabilistic and Membership Approaches in the Construction of Control Charts for Linguistic Data. Production Planning and Control, **1** (1990), 147-157.
8. Satterthwaite, F.W.: An Approximate Distribution of Estimates of Variance Components, Biometrics Bulletin, **2** (1946), 110 -114.
9. Taleb, H., and Limam, M.: On Fuzzy and Probabilistic Control Charts. International Journal of Production Research, **40** (2002), 2849-2863.
10. Taleb, H., and Limam, M.: Fuzzy Multivariate Control Charts for Multinomial Attribute Processes,. JT-CSIT04, (2004), 96-104.
11. Woodall, W. H.: Control Charts Based on Attribute Data: Bibliography and Review. Journal of Quality technology, **29** (1997), 172-183.
12. Woodall, W. H., Tsui, K-L., and Tucker, G. R. 1997, A Review of Statistical and Fuzzy Control Charts Based on Categorical Data. Frontiers in Statistical Quality Control **5**, Heidelberg, Germany: Physica-Verlag, (1997), 83-89.

Fuzzy Logic Resource Manager:
Fuzzy Rules and Experiments

James F. Smith III

Naval Research Laboratory, Code 5741,
Washington, D.C., 20375-5000,
Telephone: 202.767.5358
jfsmith@drsews.nrl.navy.mil

Abstract. A fuzzy logic expert system has been developed that automatically allocates electronic attack resources on different platforms in real time. This resource manager is made up of four trees, the isolated platform tree, the multi-platform tree, the fuzzy parameter selection tree and the fuzzy strategy tree. The isolated platform tree provides a fuzzy decision tree that allows an individual platform to respond to a threat. The tree's self-morphing property that increases its ability to adapt to changing events is discussed. The multi-platform tree allows a group of platforms to respond to a threat in a collaborative fashion. A genetic algorithm is used to optimize the resource manager. Experiments designed to test various concepts in the expert system are discussed, including its ability to: allow multiple platforms to self-organize without the benefit of a commander; to tolerate errors made by other systems; and to deal with multiple distinct enemy strategies.

1 Introduction

Modern naval battleforces generally include many different platforms, e.g., ships, planes, helicopters, etc. Each platform has its own sensors, e.g., radar, electronic support measures (ESM), and communications. The sharing of information measured by local sensors via communication links across the battlegroup should allow for optimal or near optimal decisions. The survival of the battlegroup or members of the group depends on the automatic real-time allocation of various resources, such as those related to electronic attack (EA) [1].

In this paper EA refers to the active use of electronic techniques to neutralize enemy equipment such as radar. An example of an EA resource is a machine that obscures a radar return using noise, i.e., a jammer.

A fuzzy logic algorithm has been developed that automatically allocates electronic attack resources in real-time. This paper describes the algorithm and how it was tested in digital simulation. The particular approach to fuzzy logic that will be used is the fuzzy decision tree, a generalization of the standard artificial intelligence technique of decision trees [2].

The system must be able to make decisions based on rules provided by experts. The fuzzy logic approach allows the direct codification of expertise forming a fuzzy linguistic description [3], i.e., a formal representation of the system in terms of fuzzy

S. Bandini and S. Manzoni (Eds.): AI*IA 2005, LNAI 3673, pp. 564–575, 2005.

if-then rules. This will prove to be a flexible structure that can be extended or otherwise altered as doctrine sets, i.e., the expert rule sets change.

The fuzzy linguistic description will build composite concepts from simple logical building blocks known as root concepts through various logical connectives: "OR", "AND", etc. Optimization has been conducted to determine the form of the membership functions for the fuzzy root concepts.

The algorithm is designed so that when the scenario databases change as a function of time, then the algorithm can be automatically re-optimized allowing the discovery of new relationships in the data. Alternatively, the resource manager (RM) can be embedded in a computer game that EA experts can play. The game records the result of the RM and expert's battle, automatically assembling a database of scenarios. After the end of the battle, the game makes a determination of whether or not to re-optimize the RM using a genetic algorithm (GA) and the newly extended database.

The game allows the simulation of various heterogeneous platforms such as ships, planes, helicopters, land based facilities, foot soldiers, missiles, etc. Various kinds of sensors, such as radars, communication systems, and so on can be modeled. The game also allows many different battlespaces including ocean, jungle, forest, dessert, urban areas or combinations of these. Finally all this information about heterogeneous systems and environments is incorporated into the data base and through GA based data mining into the parameters used by the RM. Ultimately, it is found experimentally that this approach results in a very robust real-time decision algorithm.

To be consistent with terminology used in artificial intelligence and complexity theory [4], the term "agent" will sometimes be used to mean platform, also a group of allied platforms will be referred to as a "meta-agent." Finally, the terms "blue" and "red" will refer to "agents" or "meta-agents" on opposite sides of a conflict, i.e., the blue side and the red side.

Section 2 briefly introduces the ideas of fuzzy logic including four significant membership functions and discusses optimization with genetic algorithms. Section 3 discusses the RM, emphasizing the isolated platform decision tree (IPDT), the IPDT's self-morphing property, and the multi-platform decision tree (MPDT). Section 4 describes five significant experiments that illustrate the RM's ability to allow multiple agents to self-organize without the benefit of a central commander, tolerate corrupted input data and to determine platform intent in the face of multiple distinct enemy strategies. Finally, section five provides a summary.

2 Fuzzy Sets and Logic

This section provides a basic introduction to the ideas of fuzzy set theory and fuzzy logic. Fuzzy set theory allows an object to have partial membership in more than one set. It does this through the introduction of a function known as the membership function, which maps from the complete set of objects X into a set known as membership space. More formally, the definition of a fuzzy set [5] is

If X is a collection of objects denoted generically by x then a fuzzy set A in X is a set of ordered pairs:

$$A = \{(x, \mu_A(x)) | x \in X\}$$

$\mu_A(x)$ is called the membership function or grade of membership (also degree of compatibility or degree of truth) of x in A which maps X to the membership space M.

The particular approach to fuzzy logic used here is the fuzzy decision tree. The fuzzy decision tree is an extension of the classical artificial intelligence concept of decision trees. The nodes of the tree of degree one, the leaf nodes, are labeled with what are referred to as root concepts. Nodes of degree greater than unity are labeled with composite concepts, i.e., concepts constructed from the root concepts [6] using "AND", "OR", and "NOT". Each root concept has a fuzzy membership function assigned to it. The membership functions for composite concepts are constructed from those assigned to the root concepts using fuzzy logic connectives and modifiers. Each root concept membership function has parameters that are determined by optimization using genetic algorithm (GA) based data mining [6,7].

For each root concept, a fuzzy membership function must be specified. There is not an a priori best membership function so a reasonable mathematical form is selected. This subjective membership function will be given in terms of one or more parameters that must be determined. The parameters may be set initially by an expert or they may be the result of the application of an optimization algorithm. The use of a genetic algorithm to determine the unknown parameters in root concept membership functions is discussed in the literature [6]. The RM has many root and composite concepts associated with it. Four such concepts are discussed below. They are "close," "heading-in," "ranging" and "banking."

As an example of a membership function definition consider the root concept "close." The concept "close" refers to how close the target/emitter on track i is to the ship, or more generally platform of interest. The universe of discourse will be the set of all possible tracks. Each track i has membership in the fuzzy set "close" based on its range R (nmi) and range rate dR/dt (ft/sec). The membership function is

$$\mu_{close}(i) = \frac{1}{1 + \alpha \cdot \dfrac{\max(R_i - R_{min}, 0)}{\max(-\dot{R}_i, \dot{R}_{min})}}.$$

The parameters to be determined by data mining are

$$\alpha, \quad R_{min}, \quad \text{and} \quad \dot{R}_{min}.$$

A concept analogous to "close" is the fuzzy concept "heading-in." Its membership function is a function of the heading angle, Θ_H, and its first time derivative of the heading angle with respect to time, $d\Theta_H/dt$,

$$\mu_{heading-in} = \frac{1}{1 + \beta |\Theta_{H,i} - \Theta_{HIN}| / \max(|\dot{\Theta}_{H,i}|, \dot{\Theta}_{HIN})}$$

The parameters to be determined by data mining are

$$\beta, \Theta_{HIN}, \quad \text{and} \quad \dot{\Theta}_{HIN}.$$

Ranging is a root concept that has a strong relationship to "close." The membership function for the concept "ranging" is a function of the second time derivative of the range as given below

$$\mu_{ranging} = \frac{1}{1 + \delta \Big/ \max\left(\left|\ddot{R}_i\right|, a_{\min}\right)}.$$

The two parameters to determine through data mining for ranging are

$$\delta \quad \text{and} \quad a_{\min}.$$

The root concept "banking" has a strong relationship to "heading-in" analogous to the ranging's relationship to "close." The membership function of the concept "banking" is a function of the second time derivative of the heading angle

$$\mu_{banking} = \frac{1}{1 + \chi \Big/ \max\left(\left|\ddot{\Theta}_{H,i}\right|, \ddot{\Theta}_{HIN}\right)}.$$

The two parameters to determine through data mining for "banking" are

$$\chi \quad \text{and} \quad \ddot{\Theta}_{HIN}.$$

3 Subtrees of the RM

The resource manager is made up of four decision trees, the isolated platform decision tree, the multi-platform decision tree, the fuzzy parameter selection tree and the fuzzy strategy tree. The EA decision algorithm, which can be called by the IPDT or the MPDT, is an expert system for assigning electronic attack techniques. The IPDT provides a fuzzy decision tree that allows an individual platform to respond to a threat [6], while the MPDT allows a group of platforms connected by communication links to respond to a threat in a collaborative fashion [8]. The fuzzy parameter selection tree is designed to make optimal or near optimal selections of root concept parameters from the parameter database assembled during previous optimization with the genetic algorithm. Finally, the strategy tree is a fuzzy tree that an agent uses to try to predict the behavior of an enemy. The EA decision algorithm, fuzzy parameter selection tree, strategy tree and communications model are discussed elsewhere [6, 8-13].

This section discusses the IPDT and the MPDT and how they make efficient use of the Network-Centric paradigm. The Network-Centric paradigm refers to strategies that make optimal use of multiple allied platforms linked by communication systems, resources distributed over different platforms, and decentralized command.

The IPDT allows a blue platform that is alone or isolated to determine the intent of a detected platform. It does this by processing data measured by the sensors, e.g., ESM, radar, etc. Even when an incoming platform's ID is very uncertain, the IPDT can still establish intent based on kinematics. When faced with multiple incoming platforms the IPDT can establish a priority queue of attacking platforms based on intent and threat to the agent.

In Figure 1, a significant subtree of the IPDT is given. The root concepts are those nodes of the tree of degree one. The other notes or boxes are composite concepts. The logical connective "AND" is represented by a vertex with a line on it; the logical connective "OR", by a vertex without a line; and the logical modifier, "NOT" by an edge with a circle on it.

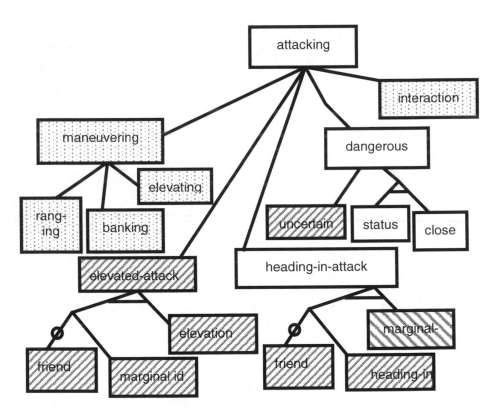

Fig. 1. A significant subtree of the IPDT that was evolved by the genetic program. The highest priority concepts have boxes with a white background; intermediate priority concepts, boxes with lines in background; and lowest priority concepts, boxes with dotted backgrounds.

The IPDT was originally written down based on human expertise. The same tree has been evolved automatically using a genetic program (GP), a computer program that uses the theory of evolution to automatically create other computer programs [14]. The GP can reproduce the IPDT obtained from expertise, but in some experiments it produces slightly altered trees. Experimental results related to one such variation are discussed in section 4.

A box with a white background represents a concept with the highest priority. A box with slanted lines in the background represents concepts of intermediate priority. A box with a "dotted" background represents lowest priority concepts. Lowest priority concepts are not evaluated in time-critical situations to save time, whereas depending on the time-criticality intermediate priority concepts may be evaluated and high priority concepts are always evaluated.

Based on input the RM can determine whether or not to evaluate low and intermediate priority concepts. When concepts are not evaluated the fuzzy decision tree is effectively altered, its shape changes or "morphs". Since the RM can decide to do this itself, these trees are said to have the *self-morphing property* [14].

There are three types of root concepts on the tree. All are dependent on measured information. The three types of root concepts are those that make direct use of physics and geometry, those related to uncertainty in ID, and those related to information that is a function of ID and stored in databases. Most of the functions of ID considered are information-theoretic in origin. The root and composite concepts of the sub-tree of the IPDT depicted in Figure 1 are similar to those found in the sensor management literature [2]. They differ in fuzzy membership functions, interpretation and application. Additional concepts on the IPDT not found in the literature will be the subject of a future publication.

The root concepts "close", "bearing-in", "ranging", and "banking," are directly related to physics. All four concepts are discussed in section 2.

Each root concept membership function is dependent on a physical observable O and frequently, its first derivative in time, dO/dt. The two dimensional space resulting from plotting dO/dt vs. O is a phase space. An action by the RM may be triggered if a membership function value exceeds threshold. The inequality between the root concept membership function and its threshold, upon inversion will give inequalities in O and dO/dt, typically. The resulting system of inequalities defines a region of phase space referred to as the admissible region where red can engage in activities without signaling its intent to blue. The membership function parameters that are found through data mining determine the boundaries of the admissible region of phase space. The admissible region can not in general be brought to zero area otherwise blue will carry out an action against everything not protected by some other concept.

Just as quantities related to geometry and kinematics such as range, bearing, elevation, and heading are all inputs to the IPDT, it is assumed that an ID classification is also an input. The ID classification is provided by an ID system separate from the RM. The ID is represented as a classification vector. The three ID subclasses making up the ID classification vector are *friend_type*, *neutral_type*, and *foe_type*. Ideally these would be non-fuzzy or crisp concepts, i.e, the ID of an incoming platform would be certain as to if it is a friend, neutral or foe. However, the RM has the ability to deal with uncertain ID, so each of the ID subclasses corresponds to a fuzzy set of the same name and each incoming platform has a fuzzy degree of membership in each of these fuzzy sets. This proves to be a very valuable approach and even in the case of very good ID information, this formalism is still very effective since relevent grades of membership can be assigned values of unity or zero.

At each time, when new input data is provided to the RM by sensors, the ID information is provided in the following format. The RM at input update time t, is provided with the ID uncertainty vector, $\vec{U}(i,t)$, whose elements are the grade of membership of the ith emitter in the fuzzy subsets for *friend_type*, *neutral_type*, and *foe_type*, i.e.,

$$\vec{U}(i,t) = (\mu_{friend}(i,t), \mu_{neutral}(i,t),$$
$$\mu_{foe-type(1)}(i,t), \mu_{foe-type(2)}(i,t),..., \mu_{foe-type(n)}(i,t))$$

where the subscripts *foe-type(1)*, *foe-type(2)*, ..., *foe-type(n)*, indicates there can be n foe types that can threaten a blue platform. The elements of the ID uncertainty vector are defined such that their sum is less than or equal to unity. The fuzzy membership function for the root concept lethal is a sum of the membership functions for each foe type. The RM can also deal with input relating to more than one friend-type and neutral-type, but that is beyond the scope of this discussion.

The IPDT made limited use of the Network-Centric paradigm, using the other networked platforms for surveillance and electronic intelligence. However, it is the purpose of the Network-Centric paradigm to use the multiple platforms to gain geometric, physical and tactical advantage by employing multi-platform techniques that are more effective than standard techniques. Such techniques require coordination and communication from platform to platform, as well as some command and control structure.

The IPDT allowed an isolated platform to respond to an incoming emitter. The RM running on the isolated platform based its decisions and hence response on standard sensor output, e.g., range, range-rate, heading, heading-rate, etc. The isolated platform's response can range from simply continuing to monitor the environment, to deciding to engage in EA. If a decision to engage in EA is made by the RM, a call is made to the fuzzy EA decision algorithm, which is discussed below.

As it stands, the IPDT can not take full advantage of the Network-Centric paradigm. To do this another decision tree, the MPDT is required. Using sensor output, the MPDT allows a group of platforms, connected by a communications network to work together in an optimal fashion to take advantage of the full potential of the Network-Centric paradigm.

Figure 2 depicts a significant subtree of the MPDT. The MPDT required many new rules, some analogous to rules found on the IPDT, but most quite distinct. The following will examine, at a coarse level some of these rules and their related fuzzy concepts.

The first rule to be defined is the fuzzy concept of a platform's "need". If the RM aboard a blue platform determines a threat is "attacking" by using the IPDT, then the detector should alert other platform's to its "need" for assistance.

A platform's "need" is a function of its ability to respond to a threat, and how destructive the threat is perceived to be. The composite concept "need" is constructed using the membership functions for the root concepts "self-help-effective" and "destructive", as shown in Figure 2. The membership function for "self-help-effective" is a function of the EA resources aboard the platform, where "need" is being determined.

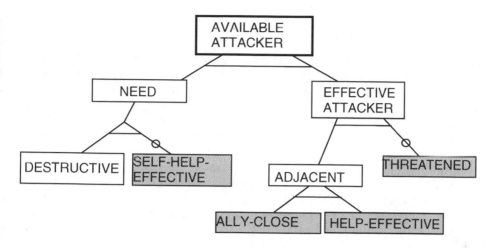

Fig. 2. A significant subtree of the multi-platform decision tree

The composite concept, "destructive" is constructed from the root concepts "potentially-destructive" and "kinetic-energy destructive" (not pictured). The fuzzy membership function for "potentially-destructive" is actually an index between zero and one, assigned by experts detailing how threatening the emitter is perceived to be in terms of its onboard hardware. The fuzzy membership function for "kinetic-energy-destructive" is a function of the emitter's estimated translational and rotational kinetic energy. In actual application there are other root concepts contributing to "destructive", the concept has been simplified here due to space limitations.

The composite concept of "need" reduces the amount of data that has to be sent over the network. It does this by sending processed information over the network, as opposed to raw data.

The composite concept "adjacent" checks platform/threat disposition, along with resources onboard the potential "helper" platform. A helper platform is one that is not threatened, but has received a communication message that another platform is threatened, i.e., the threatened platform is communicating to the helper that it has significant "need." The fuzzy root concept "ally-close" relates to how close the threatened ally is to the platform that is evaluating its ability to help in terms of the concept "adjacent." The root concept "help-effective" relates to how effective the helping platform might be if it should come to the assistance of the threatened platform that has "need."

The composite concepts "effective attacker" and "need" are combined through an "AND" connective to construct the composite concept "available attacker". If the membership function for "available attacker" exceeds a certain threshold the helping platform comes to the assistance of the platform with need. Note that the parts of the tree leading up to "need" are calculated on the threatened platform. The subtree for "effective attacker" and the final "AND" operation between "need" and "effective attacker" are calculated on the helping platform. This allows the RM to take advantage of multiple computers within the blue platform group and to reduce strain on the communication network.

4 Experiments

This section describes experiments that have been conducted to test various concepts on the fuzzy decision trees. The tests were first conducted in full digital simulation with the idea of eventually conducting the same tests using a combination of hardware and digital simulation, and finally field tests. The results reported here are from full digital simulation experiments. Similar hardware experiments using real radar, ESM, EA systems, multiple computers representing different agents, etc., have been conducted. The RM was very successful in both digital and hardware test.

The different platforms participating in experiment one are depicted in Figure 3. Platforms A and B are blue platforms with electronic support measures, electronic attack and communications resources. Neither A nor B has an onboard radar. Platform C is a blue land-based radar. Platforms A, B and C are allied blue platforms: each one runs its own copy of the RM.

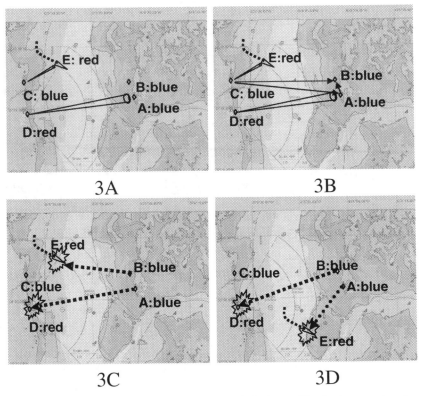

Fig. 3. Three blue platforms in conflict with two red platforms. The basic scenario of experiments one through five.

Platform D is a red land based radar hostile to the blue platforms. Finally, platform E is a fast moving red platform, that is known to be hostile to the blue forces based on its ID determined by the blue ID system.

In Figure 3A, red platform D scans blue platform A, radar emissions are denoted by cones for both red and blue platforms. At the same time blue radar C has detected red platform E. Red platform E is a missile with a missile radar onboard. Platform E's trajectory is selected to produce a high grade of membership in the root concept "close" on platform C's IPDT. This is done by selecting red platform E's trajectory so it has a large radially inbound component of velocity directed toward blue platform C. In Figure 3B, blue platform A determines it is threatened by red platform D's radar scan. Blue platform A communicates this information to blue platform B. Communications are denoted by black arrows. Simultaneously, blue platform C communicates its detection of red platform E to blue platforms A and B.

For blue platforms A and B jamming is represented by a "dashed" arrow with its arrowhead surrounded by a "burst" pattern. As depicted in Figure 3C, the resource manager onboard blue platform B jams red platform E. Likewise platform A's RM determines red platform C should be jammed.

In Figure 3D, red platform E has moved. The RM's onboard blue platforms A and B exchange EA-targets, that is, blue platform A jams red platform E and blue platform B jams red platform D. This is reasonable since as platform E moves, the blue platform that can most efficiently attack it changes.

The environment, platforms and resources in experiment two are identical to those of experiment one with the exception that in two, the blue ID system has incorrectly identified red platform E as a neutral.

Once the RM's on the blue platforms determine platform E is an enemy based on kinematics, the decisions of the RM's are the same as for experiment one when there was strong ID information. Experiments one and two, although simple, point out the RM's ability to determine a platform's intent using the output of an ID system or make such a determination based purely on kinematics.

On the IPDT, the concept "status" for these experiments has been allowed to take the value "not a friend." This is a concept suggested by the GP. The original concept in this box was "lethal." The concept "lethal" would have required that the ID system determine that platform E is an enemy before the concept "close" could be effective. Thus valuable kinematic information about red's hostile intent would never have been acted on. By using the GP's suggestion that "not a friend" be used in the "status," box, blue was able to act early against a particularly stealthy enemy. So experiment two supports the value of the GP evolved structure for the RM.

The RM requires no commanding platform for either experiment. Based on communications, in both experiments the roles of blue platforms A and B automatically switch at a reasonable time. This points up the RM's ability to allow a group of agents to self-organize. The RM's self-organizational properties arise from the MPDT. The MPDT must determine if the blue platform is "self-help-effective" and also if the red threat is in its queue of threats. The red platform may not be in its queue of threats if its is too far away, being dealt with by another blue platform, etc.

Experiment three differs only from experiment two in that at times red platform E is allowed to have a large absolute second time derivative of range so as to produce a high grade of membership in the root concept "ranging" on platform C's IPDT. As in the previous cases the RM gives the expected decisions and the various concept membership functions yield their anticipated values.

Once again experiment four is similar to experiment two. The only thing that is different is red platform E's trajectory. In this experiment red platform E is kept at a sufficient distance from blue platforms A, B, and C so as not to activate the blue RM based on range. Likewise, the absolute value of the first and second time derivatives of range are kept sufficiently small so as to not result in high grades of membership in the concepts "close" and "ranging." Instead, red platform E's trajectory was selected to emphasize values of the heading and heading-rate that would result in high values of the membership function for the concept "heading-in." The absolute value of the second time derivative of the heading angle was kept small so as to not result in a high value of the membership function for banking. As in previous experiments the simulation yielded the predicted results.

Finally, experiment five differs from experiments two through four only in that red platform E's trajectory is selected to give a high grade of membership in the concept "banking" and low grades of membership in the concepts "close," "ranging," and "heading-in. As in all previous cases the RM rapidly determined the hostile intent of the red platforms.

The five experiments of this section are in no sense the only experiments conducted to validate the RM. There have been many more, most of greater sophistication [6, 8-12]. The simple experiments provided here were conducted to point of up various properties such as the ability of the RM to self-organize without a central commanding platform. Also the experiments show the RM's ability to make the best decision when good ID information is available from an ID system and to make good decisions based on various kinematic properties of an incoming threat when information from an ID system is incorrect.

5 Summary

A fuzzy logic based algorithm for optimal allocation and scheduling of electronic attack resources distributed over many platforms is under development. Optimization of the resource manager is conducted by using a genetic algorithm as a component of a data mining process. The four decision trees making up the resource manager are discussed. These trees include the isolated and multi-platform decision trees that allow a lone platform and a collection of platforms to respond to a threat, respectively. Evolution of the IPDT using a GP, the non-uniqueness of the GP evolved IPDT, and the IPDT's self-morphing property are discussed. The self-morphng property makes the IPDT more adaptive. Five experiments are discussed that exhibit the RM's self-organizing properties and its ability to make good decisions with or without good ID system information. The RM is shown to make good decisions based on the kinematic behavior of an enemy even when the output of an ID system is in error. Finally, the RM is shown to make good decisions even though the enemy uses significantly different strategies in each experiment.

References

[1] Schleher, D. C.: Electronic Warfare in the Information Age. Artech House, Boston (1999) Chapter 1

[2] Blackman, S., Popoli, R.: Design and Analysis of Modern Tracking Systems. Artech House, Boston (1999) Chapter 11

[3] Tsoukalas, L.H., Uhrig, R.E.: Fuzzy and Neural Approaches in Engineering. John Wiley and Sons, New York (1997) Chapter 5

[4] Holland, J. H.: Hidden Order How Adaptation Builds Complexity. Perseus Books, Reading (1995) 1-15

[5] Zimmerman, H. J.: Fuzzy Set Theory and its Applications. Kluwer Academic Publishers Group, Boston (1991) Chapter 1

[6] Smith III, J.F., Rhyne II, R.: A Resource Manager for Distributed Resources: Fuzzy Decision Trees and Genetic Optimization. In: Arabnia, H. (ed.): Proceedings of the International Conference on Artificial Intelligence, IC-AI'99, Vol. II. CSREA Press, Las Vegas, (1999) 669-675

[7] Goldberg, D.E.: Genetic Algorithms in Search, Optimization and Machine Learning. Addison-Wesley, Reading (1989)

[8] Smith III, J.F., Rhyne II, R.: Genetic Algorithm Based Optimization of a Fuzzy Logic Resource Manager: Data Mining and Co-evolution. In: Arabnia, H. (ed.): Proceeding of the International Conference on Artificial Intelligence, IC-AI'2000, Vol. I, CSREA Press, Las Vegas (2000) 421-428

[9] Smith III, J.F., Rhyne II, R.: A Fuzzy Logic Algorithm for Optimal Allocation of Distributed Resources. In: Bar Shalom, Y. (ed.): Fusion 99: Proceedings of the Second International Conference on Information Fusion, International Society of Information Fusion, San Jose, (1999) 402-409

[10] Smith III, J.F., Rhyne II, R.: Fuzzy logic based resource allocation for isolated and multiple platforms. In: Kadar, I. (ed.): Signal Processing, Sensor Fusion, and Target Recognition IX, Vol. 4052, SPIE Proceedings, Orlando (2000) 36-47

[11] Smith III, J.F., Rhyne II, R.: Genetic algorithm based optimization of a fuzzy logic resource manager for electronic attack. In: Dasarathy, B. (ed.): Data Mining and Knowledge Discovery II, Vol. 4057, SPIE Proceedings, Orlando, (2000) 62-73

[12] Smith III, J.F., Rhyne II, R.: A Fuzzy Logic Resource Manager and Underlying Data Mining Techniques. In: Bar Shalom, Y. (ed.): Fusion 2000 Proceedings of the 3rd International Conference on Information Fusion, Vol. II, International Society of Information Fusion, Paris, (2000) WEB1-3 – WEB1-9

[13] Smith III, J.F.: Co-evolutionary Data Mining to Discover Rules for Fuzzy Resource Management. In: Allison, N. (ed.): Proceedings of the International Conference for Intelligent Data Engineering and Automated Learning. Springer-Verlag, Manchester, (2002) 19-24

[14] Smith III, J.F.: Fuzzy Logic Resource Manager: Evolving Fuzzy Decision Tree Structure that Adapts in Real-Time. In: Li, X. (ed.): Proceedings of the International Society of Information Fusion 2003, International Society of Information Fusion Press, Cairns, Australia, (2003) 838-845

Application of PGA on Optimization of Distribution of Shopping Centers

Bin Yu[1], Chun-Tian Cheng[1], Zhong-Zheng Yang[2], and Kwokwing Chau[3]

[1] Institute of Hydroinformatics, Department of Civil Engineering,
Dalian University of Technology, Dalian,116024, P.R. China
[2] Department of Architecture, Dalian University of Technology, Dalian, 116024, P.R. China
[3] Department of Civil and Structural Engineering, Hong Kong Polytechnic University,
Hunghom, Kowloon, Hong Kong, P.R. China
cekwchau@polyu.edu.hk

Abstract. In this study, the distribution of shopping centers is optimized in terms of realizing the shortest car-based shopping trips in an urban area. Modal split is performed between road and public traffic networks is calculated, and then the interaction between land-use and transportation in the context of choice of shopping destinations is modeled to build the optimal function. Parallel genetic algorithm (PGA) is applied to solve the optimal problem on distribution of the area of shopping centers. Several problems in application of PGA are discussed. A case study is undertaken in order to examine the effectiveness of this method.

1 Introduction

Before the popularity of motorization, mass transit, bikes and walking were the main traffic modes and urban center had the best mass transit facilities and densest residences. Therefore, shopping centers (SC) were mainly constructed in the centers. With extension of the mass transit network, SCs also extended to terminals or interchanges of railways or buses. This location pattern can be seen even now. However, with the advance of the motorization, merits of central business district (CBD) or main stations for SCs' location decreased [1]. Now households can enjoy the door-to-door transportation service offered by private cars, which is much more attractive than mass transit. However when they drive to SCs near CBD or large terminals, they will suffer from heave congestion and expensive parking cost. In order to satisfy the demand, large-scale shopping centers tend to appear in the suburb along artery roads where land price is cheaper and traffic flow is less. Today large scale SC with huge parking facilities in developed countries' suburbs is common and popular [2]. Locally, it increased citizen's quality of life in terms of shopping convenience. However, it made the city to sprawl and induced more car traffic. It even caused some deterioration of CBD.

Even though spatial distribution of SCs affects the behaviors of household location and shopping destination, this study does not tackle the location behavior of SCs but analyzes the behavior of selection of shopping destination with land-use and transportation model. Factors such as business spaces and transportation convenience between SCs and houses are used to model the behavior in selecting shopping

S. Bandini and S. Manzoni (Eds.): AI*IA 2005, LNAI 3673, pp. 576–586, 2005.
© Springer-Verlag Berlin Heidelberg 2005

destination. An optimal function, which minimizes total length of car-based shopping trips, is put forth, where business spaces of SCs in zones are set as dependent variables and total business space of SCs is the constraint. Through solving the optimal problem with GA, the optimal spatial distribution of SCs in an urban area can be determined.

2 Land-Use and Transportation Model

In general, during a time period, the total purchasing ability of a city can be considered as unchanged. It is reasonable to say that the total business space of SCs in a city is nearly a constant. However, spatial distribution of SCs changes according to geographical characteristics, house location and transportation network. This spatial distribution affects distribution and modal split of shopping trips seriously. In a city if other aspects are kept the same, the total length of car-based shopping trip changes according to the distribution.

The analysis of the distribution of the business space is based on the following two hypotheses: along with the perfect shape of the earth's surface, the business space around the center of a city will be distributed like a circle; the distribution and evolvement of the business space of the city will tend to the biggest entropy.

The known data are the business space in a certain area, and the aim is to simulate detail space distribution model. The steps are as follows: (1) Divide the researched space into grid with certain accuracy; (2) Set a center in each space and link its business area to the center; (3) With an interpolation method, insert the business space density to the gridding surface.

There are a lot of interpolation methods in common use, and the kernel estimation method is selected here. If s is used as a random point of the space R, s_i as the ith observation point and y_i as the ith observation value, then the definition of $\lambda_\tau(s)$ is as follows:

$$\lambda_\tau(s) = \frac{1}{\sigma_\tau(s)} \sum_{i=1}^{n} \frac{1}{\tau^2} k(\frac{(s - s_i)}{\tau}) y_i \qquad (1)$$

Herein, $k(\ )$ is a double-variable probability density function, which is named Kernel function; the parameter $\tau(\tau>0)$ is used to define the size of smoothing, which is named bandwidth, and in fact, τ is the radius of a circle whose center is s, so each s_i will affect $\lambda_\tau(s)$. If a bandwidth is given, a typical Kernel function is obtained as follows:

$$k(u) = \begin{cases} \dfrac{3}{\Pi}(1 - u^T u)^2, u^T u \le 1 \\ 0, \qquad\qquad \text{otherwise} \end{cases} \qquad (2)$$

So the following can be obtained:

$$\lambda_\tau(s) = \sum_{h_i \le \tau} \frac{3}{\Pi \tau^2}(1 - \frac{h_i^2}{\tau^2})^2 y_i \qquad (3)$$

Herein, h_i is the distance between the point s and the observation point s_i. The range of the points affecting $\lambda_\tau(s)$ is just the circle whose center is the point s and the radius is τ. No matter what kernel function is selected, if the bandwidth is added, the area around s point will be leveled. For bigger bandwidth, $\lambda_\tau(s)$ will tend to be flat and the local character will be blurred.

Different τ is generally adopted to simulate $\lambda_\tau(s)$ of different surfaces. If a τ is set which fits for a sparse area, it will also blur dense area. So, in order to optimize the kernel estimation to different points, its bandwidth should be adjusted. The more observation values will lead to more information. Based on this information, the smaller bandwidth can be adopted. Adaptive kernel function is the method that can rectify τ with different areas at any moment.

Based on a certain distribution of SCs, a land-use and transportation model can be employed to analyze the origin-destination (OD) traffic distribution and modal split of car in the context of shopping traffic.

In order to apply traffic demand model to analyze the selection behavior of shopping destination and traffic mode, it is supposed that a city is divided into a certain number of zones, in each of which there are certain SCs and households. First, the modal split model between car and railway is estimated for each zone in terms of shopping trips. A traditional method, namely stochastic utility function method, is applied to estimate the probability of each mode as follows:

$$P_{c,ij} = \frac{GT_{c,ij}^\alpha}{GT_{c,ij}^\alpha + GT_{b,ij}^\alpha} \tag{4}$$

where $GT_{c,ij}$ and $GT_{b,ij}$ represent generalized travel cost between zones i, j by car and railway, respectively.

The behavior of selection of shopping destination can also be analyzed in this way. Here shopping utility is defined by the accessibility of households to SCs, with its definition described in eq. (5). The probability of household in zone i shop in SC in zone j can be estimated with eq. (6). The total car-based shopping trip length from zone i to other zones can be estimated with eq. (7).

$$U_{ij} = q_j^\beta \left[P_{c,ij} \times f(GT_{c,ij}) + (1 - P_{c,ij}) \times f(GT_{b,ij}) \right] + \xi \tag{5}$$

$$P_{ij} = \frac{q_j^\beta \left[P_{c,ij} \times f(GT_{c,ij}) + (1 - P_{c,ij}) \times f(GT_{b,ij}) \right]}{\sum_{k=1}^{m} q_k^\beta \left[P_{c,ik} \times f(GT_{c,ik}) + (1 - P_{c,ik}) \times f(GT_{b,ik}) \right]} \tag{6}$$

where U_{ij} : Utility of household living in zone i shopping in zone j ; q_j : Business space of SC in zone j ; and, m : Number of traffic analysis zone.

$$\sum_{j}^{m} h_i P_{ij} P_{c,ij} d_{ij} \tag{7}$$

where h_i : Households in zone i ; and, d_{ij} : Distance between zones i, j along the road network.

3   Optimal Model and Its Algorithm

In term of environmental sustainability, the optimal distribution of SCs should help to realize the smallest length of car-based shopping trip in the city, since an effective method to reduce car emission is to decrease car mileages. Therefore, the optimal location model of SCs can be described with eq. (8).

$$Min \quad \sum_{i=1}^{m}\sum_{j=1}^{m} h_i P_{c,ij} \frac{q_j^{\beta}\left[P_{c,ij} \times f(GT_{c,ij}) + (1-P_{c,ij}) \times f(GT_{b,ij})\right]}{\sum_{k=1}^{m} q_k^{\beta}\left[P_{c,ik} \times f(GT_{c,ik}) + (1-P_{c,ik}) \times f(GT_{b,ik})\right]} d_{ij} \qquad (8)$$

$$S.T. \quad \sum_{j}^{m} q_j = Q$$

$$q_j \geq q_{j,min}$$

$$q_j \geq q_{ji,max}$$

where Q : total business space of SCs in the city; and, $q_{j,max}, q_{j,min}$: upper and lower limits of SCs' spaces in a zone, respectively.

This is a relatively complicated optimal problem which is difficult to be solved by conventional methods. In this paper, GA is used to solve the problem.

In recent years, GA has been shown to have advantages over classical optimization methods [3-9]. It has become one of the most widely used techniques for solving optimal problems in land-use planning. GA are heuristic iterative search techniques that attempt to find the best solution in a given decision space based on a search algorithm that mimics Darwinian evolution and survival of the fittest in a natural environment. The standard GA may not be good enough to solve this problem. A coarse-grained parallel GA, which not only accelerates search speed of GA, but also enlarges the population size and insulates child populations from one another, is employed here. It keeps the variety and decrease the probability of the premature convergence, and thereby it can improve the solution's quality and operation speed.

4   Genetic Algorithm Design

4.1   Parametric Study

There are four GA parameters, namely p_c, p_m, P_{size} and T_{max}. p_c means the crossover probability parameter that is typically set so that crossover is performed on most, but not all, of the population. It varies from 0.3 to 0.9. p_m is the mutation probability parameter that controls the probability of selecting a gene for mutation, which varies usually from 0.01 to 0.1. P_{size} is the population size parameter that provides sufficient sampling of the decision space while limiting the computational burden, which varies from 500 to 1000. T_{max} is the maximum number of generation, which varies from 1000 to 2000.

4.2 Coding

Population or business spaces of SCs are relatively large figures. So, decimal system (real value) is used to code the population of chromosomes. It means the located SCs' business spaces are used as the genes in chromosomes directly so that each chromosome will directly come into as decimal vector in the solution space. In other words, chromosome is the problem variable and genetic space is the problem space.

The total number of chromosomes is controlled by P_{size}. Each chromosome is a finite-length string of numbers that represents the values of the decision variables for that chromosome. Here the decision variables are the business spaces of SCs in zones. Even though it is tried to locate SCs to decrease the car-based shopping trips length, it is reasonable to think that business space in a zone has an upper and lower limits, $q_i \in [q_{i,min}, q_{i,max}]$, and they can be estimated based on current SCs' location pattern as shown in eqs. (9), (10) and (11).

$$q_{i,max} = q_{max} \times (h_i / h_{q_{max}})$$
$$where \quad q_{max} = \max(q_1,...,q_i,...,q_m) \tag{9}$$
$$where \quad h_{max} = \max(h_1,...,h_i,...,h_m)$$

$$q_{i,0}^0 = Random[q_{i,min}, q_{i,max}]$$
$$where \quad i = 1,...,M, p = 1,...,P_{size}, q_{i,min} = 0 \tag{10}$$

$$q_{i,0} = Q \times \frac{q_{i,0}^0}{\sum_k q_{k,0}^0} \tag{11}$$

4.3 Fitness Function

Here the variable penalty method is used to build fitness function. The fitness function F is an inverse of the original function f, with the deduction of the penalty function, and hence is to be maximized. The penalty coefficient M will become larger with the increment of the generation t, and its formation is shown in eq. (12), with coefficients β_1 and β_2 as constants.

$$F(q) = 1.0/(f(q) - M(t)(Q - \sum_{i=1} q_i)) \tag{12}$$

$$M(t) = \beta_1 t^{\beta_2}$$

4.4 Genetic Operators

Chromosomes are selected from the parent generation: The chromosomes are ranked according to the fitness and then based on the predetermined selected probability p_s, $p_s \times P_{size}$ are selected from the parent generation, whose fitness are relatively high. while the sifted out ones $(1 - p_s) \times P_{size}$ are replaced by chromosomes with higher fitness.

Genes are crossed over between two parent chromosomes: Parent chromosomes are paired. Even random selection method is adopted to select the crossing parent chromosomes and to generate child generation by linear crossover method. The genetic operation of crossover is performed on each mated pair based on the crossover probability.

Mutation operation is applied with a mutation rate to avoid being trapped in local optimal: A non-uniform mutation to the mutation operation is designed. If $\overline{Q} = (q_1, q_2, \cdots, q_n)$ is a chromosome and the gene q_k is selected for the mutation, the result of mutation of q_k is shown in eq. (13).

$$\overline{Q}' = (q_1^{t-1}, q_2^{t-1}, ..., q_{k-1}^{t-1}, q_k^t, q_{k+1}^{t-1}, ..., q_m^{t-1})$$

$$q_k^t = \begin{cases} q_k^{t-1} + \Delta(t, q_{k\,max} - q_k^{t-1}) & if & random(0,1) = 0 \\ q_k^{t-1} + \Delta(t, q_k^{t-1} - q_{k\,min}) & if & random(0,1) = 1 \end{cases} \qquad (13)$$

The function $\Delta(t, y)$ returns a value in between $[0,y]$ such that the value for the probability of $\Delta(t, y)$, which is given with (14).

$$\Delta(t, y) = y \times (1 - r^{(1-t/T_{max})^{\lambda}}) \qquad (14)$$

Here r is a random number between $[0,1]$. T_{max} and t are maximum number of generations and current generation, respectively. λ ($\lambda = 2 \rightarrow 5$) is a parameter, which determines the degree of dependency with the number of iterations. This property causes this operator to make a uniform search in the initial space when t is small, and a very local one in later stages. The stopping criterion is defined as follows: if iteration reaches maximum times, then the calculation is terminated and the maximum fitness is output; otherwise the algorithm returns to step 2 to continue the calculation.

5 Parallel Genetic Algorithm Design

The coarse-grained parallel genetic algorithm (PGA) is the fittest and the most widely used PGA which divides the initial population into several child populations by the number of processor [10-13]. Each child population operates independently and subsequently in different processor, while through certain evolution generations, each child population exchanges several excellent chromosomes from others.

5.1 Link Topology

The link among child populations adopts double tuning round and each one exchanges chromosome with both sides.

5.2 Migration Strategy

In coarse-grained parallel genetic algorithm, the most popular migration strategy is the fittest replace the worst. This strategy is adopted here, with the exchange number (n_m) being one. Some previous researches showed that it would destroy the child population variety and disturb solution quality if the migration epoch was too short. However, based on simulation results and the objective in this problem, the least migration epoch adopted is 4. Under this condition, the precondition of the solution quality can be ensured and the fastest convergence speed can be obtained.

6 Case Study

In order to examine the effectiveness of the method, a case study is carried out with the data of Dalian city in China (business space is over 1000m^2). There are 34 SCs and the total business space is about 2,238,417m^2. Zones, public transit and road networks are obtained from 2001 PT survey as Fig 1.

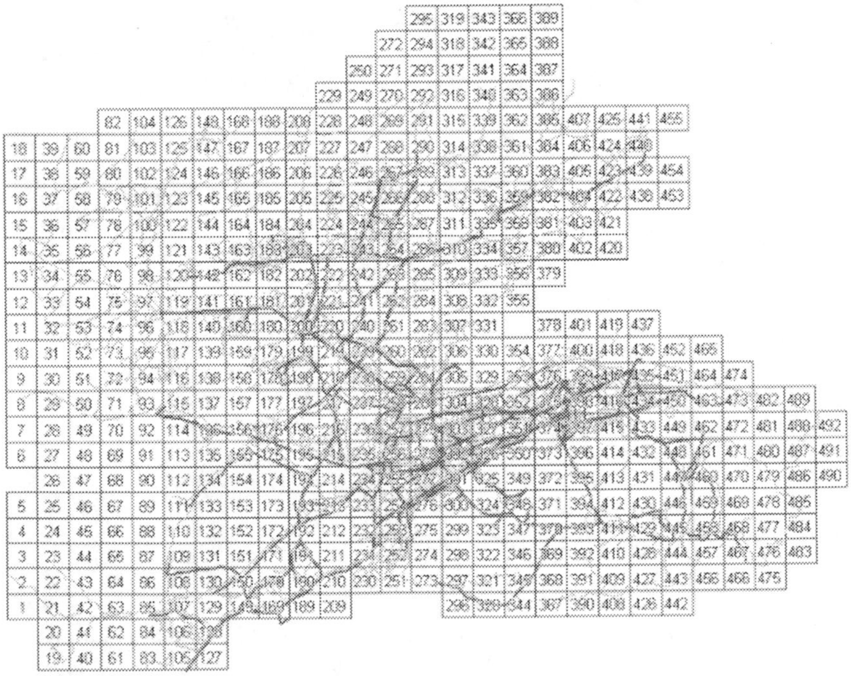

Fig. 1. Gridding Distribution of the city

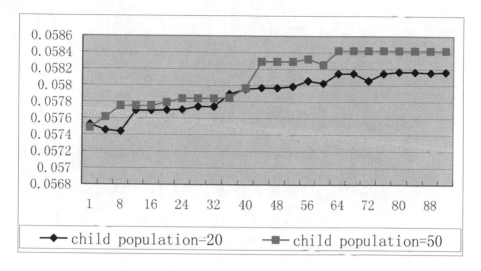

Fig. 2. Performances of PGA under different sizes of child population

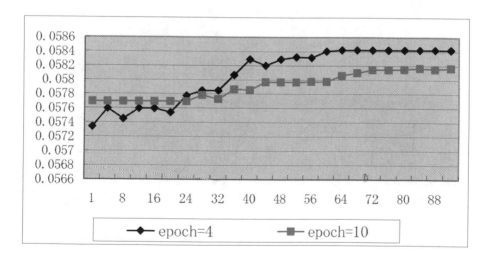

Fig. 3. Performances of PGA under different migration rates

The study area is divided into 492 grids (1km*1km), and 34 observation values. Owing to the relatively small size of observation values, a bigger bandwidth ($\tau=7$) is adopted. In the computation of the affected area of observation points, a similar area is adopted. When the distance between each grid to observation point is calculated, the road networks distance between two points, rather than the beeline, is adopted. It is found to be suitable for this practice. The SCs distribution can be obtained from eq. (1).

In order to estimate the modal split for each zone, the car OD traffic time is computed using the Dijstra algorithm. The railway OD traffic time is obtained from

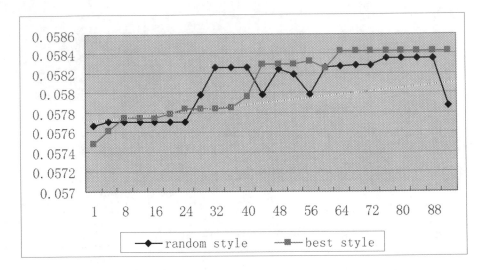

Fig. 4. Performances of PGA under different migration styles

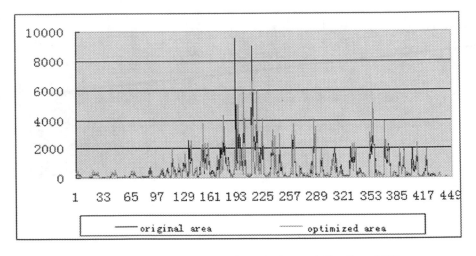

Fig. 5. Comparison between the solution and distributed SCs

former study [14]. Taking $\alpha = 2$, the modal split is calculated with eq. (4). It is set that $\beta = 1.0$ when calculating with eq. (6). It is further supposed that the transportation impedance function follows eq. (15).

$$f(GT) = 1/GT^2 \qquad (15)$$

PGA is then used to solve the optimal model. It can be observed from Fig 2 and Fig 3 that, if the size of population is maintained steady, the quality of optimization can be improved by adding the size of child population or migration rate. Fig 4 depicts PGA's capability in different migration styles. In general, random style overmatches the best style. However, the best style is adopted here, due to its better result and convergence speed. Fig 5 depicts comparison between the solution and distributed SCs. It can be seen that the solution results accord with practice. Compared to the existing situation, SCs distribution tends to be consistent with population density distribution and is more concentrated along public transit lines.

7 Conclusions

Through analyzing the behavior of selection of shopping destination based on traffic zone and transportation network, an optimal model is established in terms of environmental sustainability. The objective function in the model is to minimize the total length of car-based shopping trips subject to satisfying the purchasing ability of the households. The modal split model for railway and road modes is integrated into the optimal model. Parallel Genetic algorithm is used to solve this optimal problem. Some techniques, such as generation of initial population, methods of crossover and mutation, and coding chromosomes with real values, are suggested. These suggestions might be useful for further application of PGA in land-use and transportation model.

References

1. Hayashi, Y.: Proposing a Methodology for Planning 3-Dimensional Future of Cities with Higher Quality of Life under Sustainability Constrains. Proceeding of Civil Planning of JSCE **22(1)** (1999) 659-660
2. Ikoo S.: Problems, Goals and Policy of Nagoya, International Symposium - Sustainability in Urban Space and Transport in Nagoya (2001) 9-14
3. Goldberg, D.E., Kuo, C.H.: Genetic Algorithms in Pipeline Optimization. Journal of Computing in Civil Engineering ASCE **1(2)** (1987) 128-141
4. Holland, J.H.: Adaptation in Natural and Artificial Systems. University of Michigan Press, Ann Arbor (1975)
5. Chau, K.W.: Calibration of Flow and Water Quality Modeling using Genetic Algorithm. Lecture Notes in Artificial Intelligence **2557** (2002) 720-720
6. Chau, K.W.: A Two-Stage Dynamic Model on Allocation of Construction Facilities with Genetic Algorithm. Automation in Construction **13(4)** (2004) 481-490
7. Chau, K.W., Albermani, F.: Genetic Algorithms for Design of Liquid Retaining Structure. Lecture Notes in Artificial Intelligence **2358** (2002) 119-128
8. Chau, K.W., Albermani, F.: Knowledge-Based System on Optimum Design of Liquid Retaining Structures with Genetic Algorithms. Journal of Structural Engineering ASCE **129(10)** (2003) 1312-1321
9. Cheng, C.T., Ou, C.P., Chau, K.W.: Combining a Fuzzy Optimal Model with a Genetic Algorithm to solve Multiobjective Rainfall-Runoff Model Calibration. Journal of Hydrology **268(1-4)** (2002) 72-86
10. Zeng, G., Ding, C.: An Analysis on Parallel Genetic Algorithm, Computer Engineering. **27(9)** (2001) 53-55
11. Dai, X., Xu, C., Gong, X., Shao, H.: Convergence Analysis of Parallel Genetic Algorithm and Its Application to Optimization, Computer Engineering. **28(6)** (2002) 92-95

12. Han, B., Gao, J.: Application of Parallel Genetic Algorithm to Software Reliability Optimization, Computer Engineering **29(7)** (2003) 54-55
13. Lin, L, Feng, T., Zhou, W., Zheng, H.: Research and Application on Multigroup Parallel Evolutionary Neural Network. Journal of Ocean University of Qingdao **32(2)** (2002) 312-318
14. Yang, Z.: Obtaining an Optimal Employment Distribution with Mathematic Method to Control Commuting Transportation Demand China Civil Engineering Journal-Traffic Engineering Fascicule (2002)

BIOPACMAS: A Personalized, Adaptive, and Cooperative MultiAgent System for Predicting Protein Secondary Structure

Giuliano Armano[1], Gianmaria Mancosu[2], Alessandro Orro[1], Massimiliano Saba[1], and Eloisa Vargiu[1]

[1] University of Cagliari, Piazza d'Armi,
I-09123, Cagliari, Italy
{armano, orro, saba, vargiu}@diee.unica.it
http://iasc.diee.unica.it/
[2] Shardna Life Sciences, Piazza Deffenu 4,
I-09121 Cagliari, Italy
mancosu@shardna.it

Abstract. In this paper, we illustrate an application aimed at predicting protein secondary structure. The proposed system has been devised using PACMAS, a generic architecture designed to support the implementation of applications explicitly tailored for information retrieval tasks. PACMAS agents are autonomous and flexible, and can be personalized, adaptive and cooperative depending on the given application. To investigate the performance of the proposed approach, preliminary experiments have been performed on sequences taken from well-known protein databases.

1 Introduction

A common problem among computer scientists, biologists, and physicians is how to share massive amounts of raw data, which are typically unstructured, dynamic, heterogenous, and distributed over the web. In particular, accessing the widespread amount of distributed information resources entails relevant problems (e.g. "information overload" [26]). Moreover, different users are generally interested in different parts of the available information, so that personalized and effective information filtering procedures are needed. From a computer scientist perspective, the large number of heterogeneous and dynamically changing databases deemed biologically relevant have drawn the attention on suitable technologies able to tackle the intuitive complexity of the related problems. In our view, multiagent systems may improve the state-of-the-art in this research field. In fact, software agents have been widely proposed for dealing with information retrieval and filtering problems [14].

From our perspective, assuming that information sources are a primary operational context for software agents, the following categories can be identified focusing on their specific role: (i) "information agents", able to access to information sources and to collect and manipulate such information [26], (ii) "filter

S. Bandini and S. Manzoni (Eds.): AI*IA 2005, LNAI 3673, pp. 587–598, 2005.

Table 1. Capabilities of software agents

Capability	Focus on the ability of ...
Autonomy	Operating without the intervention of users.
Reactivity	Reacting to a stimulus of the underlying environment according to a stimulus/response behaviour.
Proactiveness	Exhibiting goal-directed behavior in order to satisfy a design objective.
Social ability	Interacting with other agents according to the syntax and semantics of some selected communication language.
Flexibility	Exhibiting reactivity, proactiveness, and social ability simultaneously [33].
Personalization	Personalizing the behavior to fulfill user's interests and preferences.
Adaptation	Adapting to the underlying environment by learning how to react and/or interact with it.
Cooperation	Interacting with other agents in order to achieve a common goal.
Deliberative capability	Reasoning about the world model and of engaging planning and negotiation, possibly in coordination with other agents.
Mobility	Migrating from node to node in a local- or wide-area network.

agents", able to transform information according to user preferences [25], (iii) "task agents", able to help users to perform tasks by solving problems and exchanging information with other agents [16], (iv) "interface agents", in charge of interacting with the user such that she/he interacts with other agents throughout them [24], and (v) "middle agents', devised to establish communication among requesters and providers [11]. Although this taxonomy is focused on a quite general perspective, alternative taxonomies could be defined focusing on different features. In particular, one may focus on capabilities rather than roles, a software agent being able to embed any subset of the capabilities briefly depicted in Table 1 (together with the corresponding focus).

In this paper, we concentrate on the problem of predicting secondary structures using a Personalized, Adaptive, and Cooperative MultiAgent System. In Section 2 relevant related work is briefly discussed. In Section 3 the Personalized, Adaptive, and Cooperative architecture, called PACMAS, is briefly depicted. In Section 4, all customizations devised for explicitly dealing with protein secondary structure prediction are illustrated. In Section 5, preliminary experimental results are briefly discussed. Section 6 draws conclusions and future work.

2   Related Work

In this section, some related work is briefly recalled, according to both an applicative and a technological perspective. The former is mainly focused on the task of secondary structure prediction, whereas the latter concerns the field of software agents, which the proposed system stems from.

2.1   Secondary Protein Structure Prediction

Difficulties in predicting protein structure are mainly due to the complex interactions between different parts of the same protein, on the one hand, and between the protein and the surrounding environment, on the other hand. Actually, some conformational structures are mainly determined by local interactions between near residues, whereas others are due to distant interactions in the same protein. Moreover, notwithstanding the fact that primary sequences are believed to contain all information necessary to determine the corresponding structure [3], recent studies demostrate that many proteins fold into their proper three-dimensional structure with the help of molecular chaperones that act as catalysts [15], [20]. The problem of identifying protein structures can be simplified by considering only their secondary structure; i.e. a linear labeling representing the conformation to which each residue belongs to. Thus, secondary structure is an abstract view of amino acid chains, in which each residue is mapped into a secondary alphabet usually composed by three symbols: alpha-helix (α), beta-sheet (β), and random-coil (c).

A variety of secondary structure methods have been proposed in the literature. Early prediction methods were based on a combination of statistical theory and empirical rules, applied to each amino acid of the protein to be predicted [9]. Artificial neural networks (ANNs) have been widely applied to this task [22] and represent the core of many successful secondary structure prediction methods, thanks to their ability of finding patterns without the need for predetermined models or known mechanisms.

The most significant innovation introduced in prediction systems was the exploitation of long-range and evolutionary information contained in multiple alignments. It is well known, in fact, that even a single variation in a sequence may dramatically compromise its functionality. To figure out which substitutions can possibly affect functionality, sequences that belong to the same family can be aligned, with the goal of highlighting regions that preserve a given functionality. PHD [31] is one of the first ANN-based methods that make use of evolutionary information to perform secondary structure prediction. In particular, PHD generates a profile using a BLASTP [1] search; then, the result is filtered using ClustalW [21]. Furter improvement have been obtained with both more accurate multiple alignment strategies and more powerful neural network structures. For instance, PSI-PRED [2] exploits the position-specific scoring matrix built during a preprocessing performed by PSI-BLAST [23]. This approach outperforms PHD thanks to the PSI-BLAST ability of detecting distant homologies. In a more recent work [5], Recurrent ANNs (RANNs) are exploited to capture long-range interactions. The actual system that embodies such capabilities is SSPRO [30].

2.2   Agents in Bioinformatics

Many of the algorithms (pattern matching, statistical, and/or heuristic/knowledge-based) able to deal with bioinformatics issues are available to biologists in various implementations, and many are available over the web. Multiagent systems have a lot to contribute to these efforts. In this section, we briefly introduce two multiagent systems that have been proposed in the literature.

BIOMAS [13] is a multiagent system for automated annotation and database storage of sequencing data for herpesviruses. It is based on DECAF [18], a multiagent system toolkit based on RETSINA [12] and TAEMS [10]. The resulting system eliminates tedious and always out-of-date hand analyses, makes the data and annotations available for other researchers (or agent systems), and provides a level of query processing beyond even some high-profile web sites. BIOMAS uses the distributed, open nature of its multiagent solution to expand the system in several ways that will make it useful for biologists studying more organisms, and in different ways.

Hermes [27] is a layered middleware system to design and execute activity-based applications in distributed environments. In particular, Hermes provides an integrated environment where application domain experts can focus on designing activity workflow and ignore the topological structure of the distributed environment. Hermes is structured as an agent-oriented system with a 3-layer architecture: run-time, system, and user. The layered middleware has been adopted in a bioinformatics domain, where mobile agents are used to support data collection and service discovery, and to simulate biological system through autonomous components interactions.

3   The PACMAS Architecture

PACMAS is a generic multiagent architecture, aimed at retrieving, filtering and reorganizing information according to users' interests. PACMAS agents are always autonomous and flexible; moreover, they can be personalized, adaptive, and cooperative depending on the specific application. The overall architecture (depicted in Figure 1) encompasses four main levels (i.e., information, filter, task, and interface), each of them being associated to a specific agent role. Communication occurs both horizontally and vertically. The former supports cooperation among agents belonging to a specific level. The latter supports the flow of information and/or control between adjacent levels through suitable middle-agents (which form a corresponding mid-span level).

Each level of the architecture is composed by a population of agents that can be combined together in accordance with the following modes: pipeline, parallel, and composition. In particular, (i) pipelines can be used to distribute information at different levels of abstraction, so that data can be increasingly refined and adapted to the user's needs, (ii) parallel connections can be used to model a cooperation among the involved components aimed at processing interlaced information, whereas (iii) compositions can be used for integrating different capabilities, so that the resulting behavior actually depends on the combination activity.

At the information level, a population of information agents is devoted to process data flowing from the information sources. Information agents play the role of wrappers, each of them is associated to one information source, and

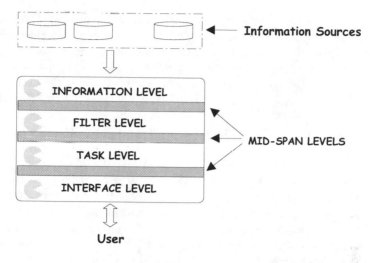

Fig. 1. The PACMAS Architecture

cooperates with other information agents to avoid information overload and redundancy. The information extracted from the information level is then made available for the underlying filter level.

At the filter level, a population of filter agents is aimed at selecting information deemed relevant to the users. Two filtering strategies can be adopted: generic and personal. The former applies the same rules for all users; whereas the latter is customised for a specific user. Each strategy can be implemented through a set of filters linked together with a pipeline connection, since data undergo an incremental refinement process. The information filtered so far is available to the task level.

At the task level, a population of task agents arranges the data according to users personal needs and preferences. Task agents are devoted to achieve users' goals by cooperating together and adapting themselves to the changes of the underlying environment. In general, they can be combined together according to different combination modes, depending on the specific application.

At the interface level, a suitable interface agent is associated with each different user interface. In fact, a user can generally interact with an application through several interfaces and devices (e.g., pc, pda, mobile phones, etc.). Interface agents usually act individually without cooperation. On the other hand, they can be personalized to display only the information deemed relevant to a specific user. Moreover, in complex applications, they can adapt themselves to progressively improve its ability in supplying information to the user.

At the mid-span level, a population of middle agents is aimed at dealing with the issue of establishing communication among requesters and providers. In the literature, several solutions have been proposed: e.g., blackboard agents, matchmaker or yellow page agents, and broker agents (see [11] for further details). In the PACMAS architecture, agents at the mid-span level can be implemented as matchmakers or brokers, depending on the specific application.

Keeping in mind that agents may be classified along several ideal and primary capabilities that they should embed, we propose a taxonomy that identifies three primary capabilities: Personalization, Adaptation, and Cooperation.

As for personalization, an initial user profile is provided in form of a list of keywords, representing users' interests. The information about the user profile is stored by the agents belonging to the interface level. It is worth noting that, to exhibit personalization, filter and task agents may need information about the user profile. This flows up from the interface level to the other levels through the middle-span levels. In particular, agents belonging to mid-span levels (i.e., middle agents) take care of handling synchronization and avoiding potential inconsistencies. Moreover, the user behavior is tracked during the execution of the application to support explicit feedback, in order to improve her/his profile.

As for adaptation, a model centered on the concept of "mixtures of experts" has been employed. Each expert is implemented by an agent able to select relevant information according to an embedded string of feature-value pairs, features being selectable from an overall set of relevant features defined for the given application (the decision of adopting a subset of the available features has been taken for efficiency reasons, being conceptually equivalent to the one usually adopted in a typical GA-based environment [17], which handles also dont-care symbols).

As for cooperation, agents at the same level exchange messages and/or data to achieve common goals, according to the requests made by the user. Cooperation is implemented depending on the guidelines imposed by the combination modes defined above (i.e., pipeline, parallel, and composition). The most important form of cooperation concerns the "horizontal" control flow that occurs between peer agents. For instance, filter agents can interact in order to reduce the information overload and redundancy, whereas task agents can work together to solve problems that require social interactions to be solved.

4   BIOPACMAS: PACMAS for Protein Secondary Structure Prediction

This section describes an application concerned with the problem of predicting protein secondary structure discussed using PACMAS. The resulting application has been called BIOPACMAS to put into evidence that the PACMAS architecture has been used in a typical bioinformatics problem.

A prototype of the system has been implemented using Jade [6] as underlying environment.

4.1   Agents for Predicting Protein Secondary Structures

Keeping in mind that the PACMAS architecture encompasses several levels, each one hosting a set of agents, in the following, we illustrate how each level supports the implementation of the proposed application.

At the information level, agents play the role of wrappers, which –in our view– can be considered a particular kind of filters, devised to process information sources. Each wrapper is associated to one information source. In the current implementation, information agents are not personalized, not adaptive, and not cooperative (shortly $\overline{PAC}$). Personalization is not supported at this level, since information agents are only devoted to wrap the datasets containing proteins. Adaptation is also not supported, since information sources are invariant for the system and are not user-dependent. Cooperation is also not supported by the information agents, since each agent retrieves information from different sources, and each information source has a specific role in the chosen application.

At the filter level, agents embody encoding methods. Let us briefly recall that encoding methods play an important role in the prediction of protein secondary structures. In fact, they describe the chemical-physics properties of aminoacid deemed more interesting for the prediction. Several populations of filter agents have been implemented, each of them performing a different encoding techiques: one-shot, substitution matrices, multiple alignment algorithms, and a techique that combines the specificity of the multiple alignment technique with the generality of the substitution matrices. Personalization is not supported by filter agents, since they always embody the same encoding methods for all users. Adaptation is also not supported either, since encoding methods do not change during the application. Cooperation is supported by filter agents, as some implemented encoding methods brings together several algorithms (e.g., the encoding method that combines multiple alignment with substitution matrices).

At the task level, a population of task agents, which are the core of this case study, perform the protein secondary structure prediction. The "internals" of each task agent is based on the micro-architecture proposed for the NXCS-Experts [4]. In its basic form, each NXCS expert E can be represented by a triple $< g, h, w >$, where: (i) g is a "guard" devised to check whether an input x can be processed or not, (ii) h is an embedded predictor whose activation depends on $g(x)$, and (iii) w is a weighting function used to perform output combination.

Hence, the output of E coincides with $h(x)$ for any input x "acknowledged" (i.e., matched) by g, otherwise it is not defined.

Typically, the guard g of a generic NXCS classifier is implemented by an XCS-like classifier, able to match inputs according to a set of selected features deemed relevant for the given application, whereas the embedded predictor h consists of a feed forward ANN, trained and activated on the inputs acknowledged by the corresponding guard. In the case E contributes to the final prediction (together with other experts), its output is modulated by the value $w(x)$, which represents the expert strength in the voting mechanism. It may depend on several features, including $g(x)$, the overall fitness of the corresponding expert, and the reliability of the prediction made by the embedded predictor. It is worth noting that matching can be "flexible", meaning that the matching activity returns a value in [0,1] rather than "true" or "false". In this case, only inputs such that $g(x) \geq \sigma$ will be processed by the corresponding embedded predictor (σ being a system parameter).

Task agents are not personalized, adaptive, and cooperative (shortly $\overline{P}AC$). Personalization is not required, since task agents exhibit the same behaviors for all the users. Adaptation is required, since each expert is suitably trained through a typical evolutionary behavior (as will be illustrate in the next Section). Cooperation is required, since they usually need other task agents to successfully achieve their own goals.

At the interface level, agents are aimed at interacting with the user. In the current implementation, this kind of agents has not been developed. Neverthenless, we are investigating how to implement a flexible behavior at the user side. In particular, a suitable web interface is under study. We envision an interface personalized for each user, in which the user can input a protein be predicted also being given the possibility of selecting the encoding technique be applied. The resulting information agents will be personalized, adaptive, and not cooperative (shortly $PA\overline{C}$). Personalization will be required in order to allow each user to customize the user interface. Adaptation will be required, since agents could adapt themselves to the changes that occur in the user preferences. Cooperation will not be required by the agents belonging to this architectural level.

As for the mid-span levels, the corresponding middle agents exhibit a different behavior depending on the mid-span level that they belonging to. In particular, let us recall that, in the PACMAS architecture, there are three mid-span levels, one between information and filter levels (in the following, IF level), one between filter and task levels (in the following, FT level), and one between task and interface levels (in the following, TI level). In this specific application personalization and adaptation are not supported by middle agents, since they are only devoted to connect together agents belonging to adjacent levels. Cooperation is supported by agents belonging to the IF and the FT levels, since in the training phase they are used to verify the prediction.

Table 2 summarizes involved agents together with the corresponding roles and capabilities.

Table 2. Agents Roles and Capabilities

Agents	The ability of ...	Capabilities
information agents	wrapping databases containing the test set, the training set, and the domain knowledge	PAC
IF middle agents	verifying the prediction during the training phase, together wiht the FT middle agents	PAC
filter agents	encoding proteins	PAC
FT middle agents	verifying the prediction during the training phase, together wiht the IF middle agents	PAC
task agents	predicting protein secondary structure	$\overline{P}AC$
TI middle agents	controlling the interactions among task and interface agents	$\overline{P}AC$
interface agents	interacting with the user	$PA\overline{C}$

4.2 Training Task Agents

The phase aimed at learning the underlying model is characterized by a typical, GA-like, evolutionary behavior.

In particular, the underlying model is learnt through an iterative process that take care of creating, training, and deleting task agents. Once selected a set of suitable task agents, according to the constraints imposed by the embedded guards, each task agent receives from the filter agents, through the mid-span level, the protein to be predicted. After the prediction, through the cooperation of middle-agents, the predicted secondary structures arc compared with the "true" ones while evaluating the reward used for updating the fitness of the corresponding task agent. Moreover, through a cooperative mechanism, task agents exhibit an evolutionary behavior. In particular, task agents can be deleted according to a policy that allow to perform agent's deletion in the case their fitness goes under a given threshold. Furthermore, agents could generate two offspring using the standard recombination and mutation operators.

5 Preliminary Experimental Results

To assess the performance of the system, and to facilitate comparison with other systems, preliminary experiments has been carried out. Since, the interface level is currently under study, to perform experiments an ad-hoc interface has been devised.

In this specific application, as information agent we have implemented: (i) an agent wraps the selected training set (the TRAIN database), (ii) an agent wraps

Table 3. Information sources

Dataset	Description
TRAIN	It has been derived from a PDB selection obtained by removing short proteins (less than 30 aminoacids), and with a resolution of at least 2.5 Å. This dataset underwent a homology reduction, aimed at excluding sequences with more than 50% of similarity. The resulting training set consists of 1180 sequences, corresponding to 282,303 amino acids.
R126	It has been derived from the historical Rost and Sander's protein dataset (RS126) [31], and corresponds to a total of 23,363 amino acids (the overall number has slightly varied over the years, due to changes and corrections in the PDB.)
AAindex	It contains information about hydrophobicity, dimension, charge and other features required for evaluating the given metrics. In the current application eight domain-specific metrics have been devised and implemented. A sample metrics is: Check whether hydrophobic amino acids occur in a window of predefined length according to a clear periodicity, whose underlying rationale is that sometimes hydrophobic amino acids are regularly distributed along alpha-helices.

Table 4. Experimental results, obtained from the R126 dataset

System	Q3
PREDATOR	70.3
DSC	71.1
NNSSP	72.7
PHD	73.5
CONSENSUS	74.8
BIOPACMAS	**74.9**
SSPRO	76.6

the test set (the R126 database), and (iii) an agent wraps a database containing information about the domain knowledge (the AAindex database). Datasets are briefly recalled in Table 3.

The performance of BIOPACMAS has been compared with NNSSP, PHD, DSC, PREDATOR, CONSENSUS, and SSPRO. The corresponding experimental results are summarized in Table 4.

Also considering that the proposed application is in a preliminary phase, results are encouranging, and we are investigating how to improve the results to perform better.

6   Conclusions and Future Work

In this paper an application devoted to deal with the issue of predicting protein secondary structures has been presented. The application has been devised using PACMAS, a generic architecture designed to support the implementation of applications explicitly tailored for information retrieval tasks. PACMAS stands for Personalized, Adaptive, and Cooperative MultiAgent Systems, since PACMAS agents are autonomous and flexible, and can be personalized, adaptive, and cooperative depending on the implemented application. Preliminary experimental results, performed on sequences taken from well-known protein databases, are encouranging, and point to the validity of the approach. As for the future work, we are investigating how to improve the behavior of information agents, to facilitate the task of implementing several encoding and multiple aligment algorithms (including PSI-BLAST services).

References

1. Altschul, S.F., Gish, W., Miller, W., Myers, E.W., Lipman, D.J.: Basic local alignment search tool. J. Mol. Biol. (1990) 215:403–10
2. Altschul, S.F., Madden, T.L., Schaeffer, A.A., Zhang, J., Zhang, Z., Miller, W., Lipman, D.J.: Gapped BLAST and PSI-BLAST: a new generation of protein database search programs. Nucleic Acids Res. (1997) 25:3389–3402
3. Anfinsen, C.B.: Principles that govern the folding of protein chains. Science. (1973) 181:223–230

4. Armano, G., Murru, A. and Roli, F., "Stock Market Prediction by a Mixture of Genetic-Neural Experts", Int. Journal of Pattern Recognition and Artificial Intelligence, 16(5), (2002) 501–526.

5. Baldi, P., Brunak, S., Frasconi, P., Soda, G., Pollastri, G.: Exploiting the Past and the Future in Protein Secondary Structure Prediction. Bioinformatics. (1999) 15:937–946.

6. Bellifemine, F., Poggi, A., and Rimassa, G.: Developing multi-agent systems with JADE Eventh International Workshop on Agent Theories, Architectures, and Languages (ATAL-2000), (2000).

7. Blundell, T.L., Johnson, M.S.: Catching a common fold. Prot. Sci. (1993) 2(6):877–883

8. Chotia, C.: One thousand families for the molecular biologist. Nature (1992) 357:543–544

9. Chou, P.Y., Fasman, U.D.: Prediction of protein conformation. Biochem. (1974) 13:211–215

10. Decker, K.S., and Lesser, V.R.: Quantitative modeling of complex computational task environments. Proceedings of the Eleventh National Conference on Artificial Intelligence, Washington, (1993) 217-224.

11. Decker, K., Sycara, K., and Williamson, M.: Middle-agents for the Internet. Proceedings of the 15th International Joint Conference on Artificial Intelligence (IJCAI'97), 578–583.

12. Decker, K.S., and Sycara, K.: Intelligent adaptive information agents. Journal of Intelligent Information Systems, 9(3) (1997) 239-260.

13. Decker, K., Khan, S., Schmidt, C., Situ, G., Makkena, R., and Michaud, D.: Bio-MAS: A Multi-Agent System for Genomic Annotation. International Journal Cooperative Information Systems, 11(3) (2002) 265–292.

14. Etzioni, O., and Weld, D.: Intelligent Agents on the Internet: fact, fiction and forecast. IEEE Expert, 10(4) (1995) 44–49.

15. Gething, M.J., Sambrook, J.: Protein folding in the cell Nature (1992) 355:33–45

16. Giampapa, J.A., Sycara, K., Fath, A., Steinfeld, A., and Siewiorek, D.: A Multi-Agent System for Automatically Resolving Network Interoperability Problems. Proceedings of the Third International Joint Conference on Autonomous Agents and Multiagent Systems, (2004) 1462 – 1463.

17. Goldberg, D.E.: Genetic Algorithms in Search, Optimization and Machine Learning. Addison-Wesley (1989)

18. Graham, J., and Decker, K.S.: Towards a distributed, environment-centered agent framework. Intelligent Agents VI, N.R. Jennings and Y. Lesperance (Eds.), LNAI-1757, Springer Verlag (2000) 290-304.

19. Henikoff, S., Henikoff, J. G.: Amino acid substitution matrices from protein blocks. Proc. Nat. Acad. Sci. (1989), 10915–10919.

20. Hartl, F.U.: Secrets of a double-doughnut. Nature (1994) 371:557–559

21. Higgins, D., Thompson, J., Gibson T., Thompson, J.D., Higgins, D.G., Gibson, T.J.: CLUSTAL W: improving the sensitivity of progressive multiple sequence alignment through sequence weighting, position-specific gap penalties and weight matrix choice. Nucleic Acids Res. (1994) 22:4673–4680

22. Hirst, J.D., Sternberg, M.J.E.: Prediction of structural and functional features of protein and nucleic acid sequences by artificial neural networks. Biochemistry, 31 (1992) 7211-7218.

23. Jones, D.T.: Protein secondary structure prediction based on position-specific scoring matrices. J. Mol. Biol. (1999) 292:195–202.

24. Lieberman, H.: Autonomous Interface Agents. Proceedings of the ACM Conference on Computers and Human Interface (CHI-97), (1997) 67–74.
25. Lutz, E., Kleist-Retzow, H.V., Hoernig, K.: MAFIAan active mail-filter-agent for an intelligent document processing support. ACM SIGOIS Bulletin, 11(4) (1990) 16 – 32.
26. Maes, P.: Agents that Reduce Work and Information Overload. Communications of the ACM, 37(7) (1094) 31–40.
27. Corradini F., and Merelli, F.: Hermes: agent-based middleware for mobile computing. Tutorial Book of 5th International School on Formal Methods for the Design of Computer, Communication and Software Systems: Mobile Computing, LNCS Vol. 3465 (2005).
28. Merikoski, J.: On the submultiplicativity of norms of Hlder and Minkowski type. Linear and Multilinear Algebra 6 (1978) 51-54.
29. Nwana, H.: Software Agents: An Overview. Knowledge Engineering Review, 11(3) (1996) 205–244.
30. Pollastri, G., Przybylski, D., Rost, B., Baldi, P.: Improving the Prediction of Protein Secondary Structure in Three and Eight Classes Using Neural Networks and Profiles. Proteins (2002) 47:228–235
31. Rost, B., Sander, C.: Prediction of protein secondary structure at better than 70% accuracy. J Mol Biol (1993) 232:584-599
32. Altschul, S.F., Madden, T.L., Schffer1, A.A., Zhang,J., Zhang, Z., Miller, W., and Lipman, D.J.: Gapped BLAST and PSI-BLAST: a new generation of protein database search programs. Nuclic acid Research,1997 Vol.25 No.17 33893402
33. Wooldridge, M., and Jennings, N.R.: Agent Theories, Architectures, and Languages: a Survey. Wooldridge and Jennings (Eds.), Intelligent Agents, Berlin: Springer-Verlag, (1995) 1-22.

Improving Neural Classification with Markov Chain

Inhaúma Ferraz and Ana Cristina B. Garcia

Universidade Federal Fluminense,
Departamento de Ciência da Computação,
Rua Passo da Pátria 156, Bl E, Sl 326, Niteroi, RJ, Brazil 24210-240
{ferraz, bicharra}@ic.uff.br

Abstract. Neural classifiers have been successfully used to determine rock properties in offshore oil reservoirs. However, the precision of those classifiers must be improved given the great cost resulting from errors when defining the quality of an oil reservoir. This paper presents a post-processing method based on the Markov chain that improved the classifier precision rate in 6%.

1 Introduction

Oil fields are determined by the distribution of porosity and permeability in the field, which are, in turn, determined by the distribution of lithofacies. Lithofacies, such as dolomite and limestone, denote a stratigraphic unit that reflects major properties of a rock bed layer and its depositional environment, differentiating it from other rock units.

Laboratorial tests on rock samples are the most precise method to define the rock stratigraphy; however, collecting rock samples are very expensive, especially in offshore areas.

From a set of indirect measurements on rock properties, such as gamma-ray log data, geologists must infer the rock lithofacies distribution, i. e, geologists are faced with a classification task. They should map a set of indirect measurements into lithofacies' classifications. Inferring classes from well logs is a classifier's task and it is a typical kind of supervised learning.

We have developed a system called nFac [1] that offered a suite of methods, such as neural networks, fuzzy and neural fuzzy methods. The best results were achieved by using standard back propagation neural nets with one hidden layer considering five inputs well log data.

Due to confidentiality agreement, the name of the lithofacies where substituted by insignificant acronym such as, A, AC e NR. Inconclusive results were marked as "?". Current success rate has been around 70% and inconclusive results, around 6%. Since the domain requires precise methods, we have focused our effort in improving the classifier method by including post-processing methods to classify all inconclusive answers.

The post-processing of the lithofacies classifiers' output is required to counterbalance the indetermination of the chosen method. Manual post-processing is usually the standard procedure. Users feel very uncomfortable with indeterminations. Quite frequently, user confidence is severely eroded when an output list shows

S. Bandini and S. Manzoni (Eds.): AI*IA 2005, LNAI 3673, pp. 599–602, 2005.

indeterminations (the error theory is not well accepted by our chromosomes). However, manual post-processing is a long, subjective and extenuating task. A very tantalizing challenge is to beat the manual post-processing method by adopting algorithmic procedures with high effectiveness, lack of fatigue and impersonal bias.

Hence, we developed a neural classifier, nFac [1], which significantly increased the success rate of this classification task. Despite the acceptable results (average of 75% success rate), improvements were still necessary, specially related to scenarios for which the classifier offered inconclusive results. This paper presents ADDMK, a Markovian post-processor method for determining unclassified results in lithofacies' rock classification that significantly improves the success rate of any classification tool. Besides presenting our method, we include a case study in which the method was applied to define a Brazilian oil reservoir, emphasizing the results.

2   Rock Lithofacies' Neural Classifier

When result classes are linearly separable it is easy for human to do final adjustments on inconclusive results as shown in figure 1. However, it is not often the case, as illustrated in figure 2.

The challenge is to find a method that offers the same improvement as expert visual interpretation over the inconclusive results, but without the subjectivity of human analysis.

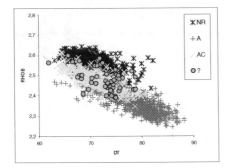 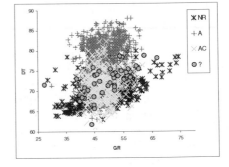

Fig. 1. Scatter plot obtained from a fortunate combination of physical properties (RHOB and DT) that indicates a clear distinction among the resulting classes

Fig. 2. Scatter plot obtained from an unfortunate combination of physical properties (DT and GR) that indicates a clear distinction among the resulting classes

3   MK: A Markovian Post-processing Method

Several models have been used to estimate lithology from lithology measurements and geophysical data. Neural networks or fuzzy neural networks use only geophysical data but ignore borehole lithology measurements. This work develops a model to incorporate geophysical data into lithology estimation by using spatial correlation of lithology, as well as a nonlinear cross-correlation between lithology and geophysical attributes. Lithology is represented as a sequence of lithofacies and we will use the sequence theory for its study.

The sequence of lithological classes is modeled as a discrete, finite, homogeneous, first order Markov chain of transitions between states. This state sequence can be unobserved or is generally hidden from the observer. The only necessary information about the hidden state sequence is an observed sequence of state-dependent outputs.

A sequence X1, X2 of random variables is called Markov (or Markoff) if, for any n, i.e., if the conditional distribution F of Xn assuming, Xn-1, Xn-2,..., X1 equals the conditional distribution F of Xn assuming only Xn-1.

If a matrix of transition probabilities is powered successively until a state is reached at which each row of the matrix is the same as every other row, forming a fixed probability vector, the resulting matrix is called a regular transition matrix. The matrix then gives the limit at which the probabilities of passing from one state to another are independent of the starting state, and the fixed probability vector expresses the equilibrium proportions of the various states. Regular matrices are also called steady-state probability matrices.

Given the Earth's subsurface origin, lithofacies' transition, i.e. the expectation of what should be the neighbor lithofacies, is clearly not a deterministic process. Predicting lithofacies' sequence is a stochastic process that can be Markovian modeled [2]. The underlying assumption of the statistical model is that the lithofacies' output vector can be characterized as a stochastic process, and that the parameters of the stochastic process can be estimated in a precise, well-defined manner.

Our Markov post-process method can be defined as the

Input Vector $= F (f_1, f_2, ..., f_n)$

where

n is the size of the output vector

fi ε {Valid lithofacies category $\cup$ {?}}, i.e., f_i is either a valid class or an inconclusive result.

We denote the results of application of Markov sequences with two indexes the first one indicating the order of the sequence and the second one indicating forward or backward application.

The algorithm used is

```
F = nFac (Eletrofacies Logs);
2. n = length (Input_Vector)
3. i = 1
4. While i <= n do
4.1. i = Get_Gap(F, i);
4.2. gs = Gap_size(F[i]);
4.3. Case gs
4.3.1. gs=1: F[i+1] = Max (M1f(i), M1b(i+2));
4.3.2. gs=2: F[i+1] = Max (M1f(i), M2b(i+3));
            F[i+2] = Max(M2f(i), M1b(i+3));
4.3.3. gs>2: For j = I+1 to i+gs-1 do
F[j] = Max (Mnf(i), Mnb(i+gs));
4.4. i = i + gs;
Return F
```

4 Case Study: Applying MK Post-processor to nFac Lithofacies' Classification Results

We compared the benefits of using Markov post-processor to those of using the data generated by a neural network classifier applied in six Brazilian oil wells. Five input data sources representing data from different oil wells were considered.

The average prediction success rate using no post-processor was 79,58%, using default post-processor it was 82,72% and using Markov chains post-processor it was 84,29%. The Markov chains method provides a better improvement in the classification success rate than the default probability method. Manual classifications, either through rules or through region discrimination, depend upon user's expertise.

The significant increase in the success rate and the geologists' (experts') positive evaluation upon applying our method have indicated the potential benefit of introducing it as part of the nFac Classifier.

5 Conclusions

The use of Markov chains to post-process classifier outputs led to promising good results, improving classification success rate.

We believe that the Markovian post-processing method leads to a significant improvement in the classifiers' success rate as the number of categories increase and the frequency distribution of each class gets more homogeneous.

References

1. Ferraz, I. N., Garcia, A. C. B., Sombra, C. L. Cooperative Filtering: The Role of Human Perception on Selecting Input Data to Supervised Learning Systems. In: IASTED International Conference Artificial Intelligence and Applications (AIA2002), Malaga (2002)
2. Bharucha-Reid, A Elements of the Theory of Markov Processes and Their Applications. Dover Publications, New York (1997)

Intelligent Neurofuzzy Model Based Control
of Electrically Heated Micro Heat Exchanger

F. Habibipour Roudsari, M. Khajepour, and M. Galily

Iran Telecommunication Research Center, Tehran, Iran
Ministry of Information and Communication Technology (ICT), Tehran, Iran
m.galily@gmail.com

Abstract. An intelligent neurofuzzy model based controller is proposed for temperature control in a electrically heated micro heat exchanger. The dynamics of the plant, which shows some highly nonlinear behaviors, will be identified using a locally linear neurofuzzy model and then the predictive control will be applied to govern the dynamics of the plant. Simulation results of the proposed controller demonstrate the effectiveness of that.

1 Introduction

Most of the existing predictive control algorithms use an explicit process model to predict the future behavior of a plant and because of this, the term model predictive control (MPC) is often utilized [1] for this control strategy. The goal for most of the applications is to maintain the system at a desired steady state, rather than moving rapidly between different operating points, so a precisely identified linear model is sufficiently accurate in the neighborhood of a single operating point. As linear models are reliable from this point of view, they will provide most of the benefits with MPC technology. Even so, if the process is highly nonlinear and subject to large frequent disturbances, a nonlinear model will be necessary to describe the behavior of the process [2]. Most of the nonlinear predictive control algorithms imply the minimization of a cost function, by using computational methods for obtaining the optimal command to be applied to the process. In this paper, we will apply a predictive controller to output temperature tracking problem in a electrically heated micro heat exchanger plant [3]. First, the nonlinear behavior of the process is identified using a Locally Linear Model Tree (LOLIMOT) network [4] and then predictive Controller is applied to the plant. Using the proposed strategy, the tracking problem of the temperature profile will be tackled.

2 Electrically Heated Micro Heat Exchanger

Electrically heated micro heat exchangers have been developed to accelerate the fluid and gas heating in a reduced space [3]. This system consists of a diffusion bonded metal foil stack with many grooves, the heating element are placed between the foils (Fig. 1). In a small volume, powers to 15 kW can be converted. The advantages of this heat exchanger are

S. Bandini and S. Manzoni (Eds.): AI*IA 2005, LNAI 3673, pp. 603–607, 2005.

- Fluids and gas heated by electrical power and not by additional flow cycle
- Efficient transformation of electrical energy in thermal energy
- Fast temperature change of the media and temperature good fit for sensitive media

Fig. 1. Electrically heated micro heat exchanger

3 Locally Linear Model Tree Identification of Nonlinear Systems

In the architecture of locally linear neurofuzzy network used in this work, each neuron realizes a local linear model (LLM) and an associated validity function that determines the region of validity of the LLM that are normalized as

$$\sum_{i=1}^{M} \varphi_i(\underline{z}) = 1 \tag{1}$$

for any model input $\underline{z}$ [4]. The output of the model is calculated as

$$\hat{y} = \sum_{i=1}^{M} (w_{i,o} + w_{i,1} x_1 + \dots + w_{i,n_x} x_{n_x}) \varphi_i(\underline{z}) \tag{2}$$

where the local linear models depend on $\underline{x} = [x_1, \dots, x_{n_x}]^T$ and the validity functions depend on $\underline{z} = [z_1, \dots, z_{n_z}]^T$. Thus, the network output is calculated as a weighted sum of the outputs of the local linear models where the $\varphi_i(.)$ are interpreted as the operating point dependent weighting factors. The network interpolates between different Locally Linear Models (LLMs) with the validity functions. The weights w_{ij} are linear network parameters. The validity functions are typically chosen as normalized Gaussians:

$$\varphi_i(\underline{z}) = \frac{\mu_i(\underline{z})}{\sum_{j=1}^{M} \mu_j(\underline{z})} \tag{3}$$

with

$$\mu_i(\underline{z}) = \exp(-\frac{1}{2}(\frac{(z_1 - c_{i,1})^2}{\sigma_{i,1}^2} + \dots + \frac{(z_1 - c_{i,n_z})^2}{\sigma_{i,n_z}^2})) \tag{4}$$

The centers and standard deviations are *nonlinear* network parameters. In the fuzzy system interpretation each neuron represents one rule. The validity functions represent the rule premise and the LLMs represent the rule consequents. One-dimensional Gaussian membership functions

$$\mu_{i,j}(z_j) = \exp(-\frac{1}{2}(\frac{(z_j - c_{i,j})^2}{\sigma^2_{i,j}}))$$ (5)

can be combined by a t-norm (conjunction) realized with the product operator to form the multidimensional membership functions in (3). One of the major strengths of local linear neuro-fuzzy models is that premises and consequents do not have to depend on identical variables, i.e. $\underline{z}$ and $\underline{x}$ can be chosen independently.

Using the above strategy, a locally linear model is adopted to the system for input data as shown in fig. 2. The identified and actual outputs can be seen in Fig. 3. As it can be seen, the error between these two values is not considerable and the identified model can match the system well. In the next section, we will use of this model in predictive control block.

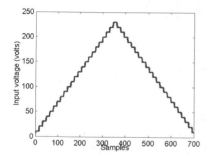

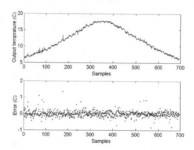

Fig. 2. Input voltage for system identification

Fig. 3. The identified and actual output temperature with error between theses two values

4 Predictive Controller Design

The objective of the proposed predictive control strategy is twofold: *(i)* to estimate the *future output* of the plant and *(ii)* to minimize a *cost function* based on the error between the predicted output of the processes and the reference trajectory. The cost function, which may be different from case to case, is minimized in order to obtain the optimum control input that is applied to the nonlinear plant:

$$J = \sum_{i=N_1}^{N_2} [y(k+i) - r(k+i)]^2 + \lambda \sum_{i=1}^{N_u} \Delta u^2(k+i-1); \quad \Delta u(k+i-1) = 0 \qquad 1 \le N_u < i \le N_2$$ (9)

where N_u is the control horizon, N_1 and N_2 are the minimum and maximum prediction horizons respectively, i is the order of the predictor, r is the reference trajectory, λ *is* the weight factor, and Δ is the differentiation operator. The command u may be subject to amplitude constraints:

$$u_{min} \leq u(k+i) \leq u_{max} \qquad i = 1,2,..., N_u \qquad (11)$$

The cost function is often used with the weight factor $\lambda=0$. A very important parameter in the predictive control strategy is the control horizon N_u, which specifies the instant time, since when the output of the controller should be kept at a constant value. The output sequence of the optimal controller is obtained over the prediction horizon by minimizing the cost function J with respect to the vector U. This can be achieved by setting

$$\frac{\partial J}{\partial U} = 0 \qquad U = \left[u(k-d),...,u(k-d+N_u-1) \right]^T \qquad (12)$$

The advantage of this nonlinear neural predictive controller consists in the implementation method that solves the key problems of the nonlinear MPC. The implementation is robust, easy to use and fulfills the requirements imposed for the minimization algorithm. The closed-loop system response using the predictive control algorithm based on LOLIMOT model is shown in Fig. 4.

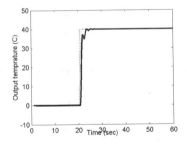

Fig. 4. Closed-loop system response using proposed predictive controller

5 Conclusion

In this paper, a predictive Controller was applied to electrically heated micro heat exchanger, which is a highly nonlinear plant. To this end, the dynamics of the system was identified using a locally linear algorithm. Then, a controller based on predictive strategy was applied to the system to tackle the output temperature tracking problem.

References

1. Camacho, E.F. Model predictive control, Springer Verlag, 1998
2. Badgwell, A.B., Qin, S.J. Review of nonlinear model predictive control applications, In Nonlinear predictive control theory and practice, Kouvaritakis, B, Cannon, M (Eds.), IEE Control Series, pp.3-32, 2001

3. Brander, J., Fichtner, M., Schygulla, U. and Schubert, K., Improving the efficiency of micro heat exchangers and reactors. In Irven, R. [Hrsg.] Micro reaction Technology: 4th International Conference; AIChE Spring Nat. Meeting, Atlanta, Ga., March 5-9, 2000
4. Nelles, O., Nonlinear system identification: From classical approaches to neural networks and fuzzy models. Springer, 2001

Managing Functional and Ontological Knowledge in the Design of Complex Mechanical Objects

Ettore Colombo, Gianluca Colombo, and Fabio Sartori

Department of Computer Science, Systems and Communication (DISCo),
University of Milan, Bicocca, via Bicocca degli Arcimboldi,
820126, Milan, Italy
Tel: +39 02 64487857; Fax: +39 02 64487839
{ettore, gianluca.colombo, sartori}@disco.unimib.it

Abstract. This paper presents a conceptual framework for the development of Knowledge Management (KM) systems to support experts in complex design activities. Designing a complex object is not simple, since it is concerned not only with problem solving issues, but also with the needs for capturing and managing the core knowledge involved in it. A complex object is typically made of a huge number of parts that are put together according to a first set of constraints (i.e. the *dynamic knowledge* or *functional knowledge*), dependable on the functional properties it must satisfy, and a second set of rules, dependable on what the expert thinks abut the problem and how he/she would represent it (i.e. the *static knowledge* or *ontological knowledge*). The paper introduces how to unify both types of knowledge, exploiting the SA–Nets formalism to capture the dynamic knowledge and an ontological approach to represent static knowledge.

1 Introduction

A growing number of studies, researches and information technology systems are focusing on the concept of *Community of Practice* (CoP) [9], combining the organizational aspects with the Knowledge Management (KM) topics. A CoP may be characterized as *a group of professionals informally bound to one another through exposure to a common class of problems, common pursuit of solutions, and thereby themselves embodying a store of knowledge* [5].

CoPs may deal with different kinds of problems, and some of them are focused on the Core Knowledge of a Company. We define the people involved in these communities Core Knowledge Practitioners (CKP). Generally, only a part of all knowledge used by a company to innovate its range of products is stored into documents or recorded in other kinds of repositories. Most of it constitutes an implicit asset (or tacit knowledge, see e.g. [6,8]) guiding the decision making processes, nourished and preserved as a personal practical competence by the *area experts*. From this point of view software instruments should not only be able to manage and share knowledge but also to support the analysis of knowledge repository of companies and to exploit it [3]. This shift of perspective is changing the KM approach that cannot only rely on document

S. Bandini and S. Manzoni (Eds.): AI*IA 2005, LNAI 3673, pp. 608–611, 2005.

management techniques but also on knowledge representation and management approaches developed in the Artificial Intelligence context (i.e. Knowledge Based Systems). In this framework we justify the adoption of the concept of CKP as the guideline to identification, acquisition and representation of Designers and Engineering Knowledge within companies deeply committed to product innovation as well as to the selection of the most suitable knowledge representation methods to manage Designers and Engineering Core Knowledge [2]. In the following, we'll refer to the specific Core Knowledge possessed by Mechanical Designers involved in configuration activity of complex objects as *Engineering Core Knowledge*, involved in the design and manufacturing of complex mechanical products. Section 2 briefly introduces the conceptual framework for the management of Engineering Core Knowledge, pointing out how the ontological representation of the considered domain and the adoption of SA–Nets could allow to overcome the difficulties in dealing with different knowledge subtypes Engineering Core Knowledge is made of. Finally, conclusions and future works are briefly exposed.

2   Framework Model

Engineering Design can be viewed as an articulate process composed of phases, where each phase represents a combinatory action on the parts the composite object is constituted of. To realize an object aligned with the desired market requirements, engineering designers have to deal at the same time with different kinds of knowledge coming from different epistemological sources: static (i.e. *ontological*) knowledge about objects and dynamic (i.e. *functional*) knowledge about processes (which is often expressed in a procedural form).

Designing a complex object can be thus divided into two subproblems from the KM point of view: how to represent dynamic knowledge and how to represent static knowledge. This is a general issue of the design problem, but we'll talk about a specific case in which the complex object to be configured is a mechanical component. From the static knowledge standpoint, a mechanical component can be considered as made of different parts that can be grouped on the basis of different levels of abstraction, as shown in Figure 1.

At the *Component Level* atomic components are placed, for which no design activity or knowledge are needed. Components are used to build more complex parts of the object, that are *aggregates*. An aggregate is a composition of one or more components and can include one or more other aggregates. Although aggregates have not specific meaning from the mechanical object point of view, they are useful to provide experts with a simpler way to deal with components. The last level of abstraction is constituted by *functional* units, that are built starting from aggregates and components, but different from them represent a functional property of the under construction object. The relationships among levels can be navigated according to a bottom–up or a top–down strategy: in the former case, it is necessary to start from the component level, in the latter the first level to consider is the functional one. While the bottom–up

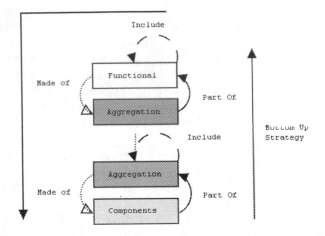

Fig. 1. *A mechanical object is made of three different kind of parts, bounded by three different types of relationships*

strategy is the most used when developing a KM system for supporting the design of complex objects (e.g. a case–based reasoning system calculates the similarity between two case according to the value associated to their attributes), the top–down strategy is closer to the real way of reasoning of an expert designer than the other one. The top–down strategy is implemented in our framework by the *include* and *made–of* relationships.

Dynamic knowledge is related to how taking care of design constraints in building the object: such constraints can be due to geometrical aspects (e.g. a component cannot be placed on an aggregate because of absence of space), customer requirements (e.g. don't use this type of component, use this one instead) or designer experience (e.g. the design of this functional unit influences the design of that one). This constraints can be captured by the adoption of a formalism like SA–Nets [7], that allows to manage the different steps in a synchronous or asynchronous fashion. More details about foundational issues behind our framework can be found in [1].

3   Conclusions and Future Works

This paper has introduced a conceptual framework for the representation of both functional and ontological knowledge involved in the design of complex mechanical objects. Static knowledge is captured by an ontological model of the object, while dynamic knowledge can be profitably managed through well known formal models, like e.g. SA–Nets.

The possibility to consider both knowledge types into a unique framework is very important step with respect to the development of KM systems in extremely dynamic domains, like ones in which CKP operate. The framework proposed can be considered as an initial step in the creation of a good design theory for the management of core and engineering knowledge involved in the building of complex mechanical objects.

This opinion has been partially confirmed by the participation to a research project in collaboration with Fontana–Pietro S.p.A, an Italian enterprise leader in dies manufacturing and in the construction of elite automobile bodies that works for some of the most important European car manufacturer (e.g. Mercedes–Benz, BMW, Ferrari, Renault, ...). A car die is a very complex mechanical product, that must be designed and manufactured in the shortest period of time and with the maximum level of accuracy to avoid loss of money and according to precise geometrical and customer constraints together with many rules inducted by designers on the basis of their own experience.

In that context, the ontological approach has allowed to build a die model shared by all the experts of the CKP community where it didn't exist before. Moreover, the developed KM system has been linked to sophisticated CAD tools used by Fontana–Pietro's experts, building an integrated environment able to completely support their creativity.

Anyway, a lot of work must be done in the future: in particular, the relationship between ontology and SA–Nets should be further investigated since it has been used superficially during the collaboration with Fontana–Pietro.

References

1. Bandini, S., Colombo, G. and Sartori F., *Towards the Integration of Ontologies and SA–Nets to Manage Design and Engineering Core Knowledge..* In Sicilia M. A. et al. (eds.), *Electronic Proceedings of ONTOSE 2005 – 1st International Workshop on Ontology, Coneptualization and Epistemology for Software and System Engineering,* Alacalá de Henares, June 2005 (to appear).
2. S. Bandini, C. Simone, E. Colombo, G. Colombo, F. Sartori, *The Role of Knowledge Artifact in Innovation Management: the Case of a Chemical Compound Designers' CoP,* Proc. C&T 2003 – International Conference on Communities and Technologies, Amsterdam, Kluwer Academic Publishers, pp 327-346, 2003.
3. Bandini, S., Manzoni S., *Modeling core knowledge and Pratices in a Computational Approach to Innovation Process,* in L. agnani, N. J. Nersessian (eds.), *Model-Based Reasoning: Science, Technology, Values,* Kluwer, New York, 2002, pp. 369-390.
4. Gero J. and Maher L.M., *A Framework for Research in Design Computing,* 15th ECAADE–Conference Proceedings, Vienna, 1997.
5. Hildreth P., Kimble C. and Wright P., *Communities of practice in the distributed international environment,* Journal of Knowledge Management, 4(1), pp. 27-38, 2000.
6. Liebowitz, J. 1999, *Knowledge Management Handbook,* Boca Raton, CRC Press, 1999.
7. Simone, C., *Computer-Supported Cooperative Work, Petri nets and related formalisms,* In Proceedings of Workshop on Petri Nets 1993, Chicago, June 22, 1993.
8. Takeuchi I., Nonaka H., *The Knowledge creating Company: How Japanese Companies Create the Dynamics of Innovation,* Oxford University Press, May 1995.
9. Wenger, E., Community of Practice: Learning, meaning and identity, Cambridge University Press, Cambridge, MA, 1998.

Author Index

Lecture Notes in Artificial Intelligence (LNAI)